Organizational Behavior
and Performance

Organizational Behavior and Performance

Second Edition

Andrew D. Szilagyi, Jr.

Associate Professor of Organizational Behavior
University of Houston

Marc J. Wallace, Jr.

Associate Professor of Business Administration
University of Kentucky

Goodyear Publishing Company, Inc.
Santa Monica, California

This book is dedicated to our wives,
Sandra Mary Szilagyi and Nancy Smith Wallace.

Current printing (last number):
10 9 8 7 6 5 4 3 2
ISBN: 0-87620-615-1
Y-6151-8

Printed in the United States of America

Book design: Francis Morgan, Educational Graphics
Production editor: Hal Humphrey

Library of Congress Cataloging in Publication Data
SZILAGYI, ANDREW D
    Organizational behavior and performance.

    First ed. (1977) by J. M. Ivancevich, A. D.
Szilagyi, Jr., and M. J. Wallace, Jr.
    Includes bibliographical references and indexes.
    1. Organizational behavior. I. Wallace,
Marc J., 1944-   joint author. II. Ivancevich,
John M. Organizational behavior and performance.
III. Title.
HD58.7.S97   1980   658.4   79-18711
ISBN 0-87620-615-1

CONTENTS

Part Five   Organizational Change and Development   521

Chapter 15   Organizational Change and Development:
A Framework   522

Chapter 16   Organizational Change and Development:
Selected Applications   559

Chapter 17   Organizational Behavior and Performance:
A Synopsis   607

PREFACE

Our approach to this second edition of *Organizational Behavior and Performance* had three goals: to streamline, to update, and to enhance applications. The streamlining efforts were directed at the chapters on intra-group behavior, where we have combined the two chapters in the first edition into one chapter. The result is a much smoother discussion without loss of content.

Our updating efforts represent a two-fold process. First, in each of the content sections of the book we have revised the material with studies that have been published since the publication of the first edition in 1977. To make this book as comprehensive and representative of the field of organizational behavior as possible, we have added a number of sections on current issues. Included in this second edition are discussions on group decision making, job satisfaction, behavioral modeling, work stress, career planning, socio-technical systems, assessment centers, and the quality of work life. We hope that the presentation of these new topics will continue to convey the exciting nature of the field of organizational behavior.

Finally, a comprehensive text in any field of study can be technically sound on one hand, but be boring exercise for the reader on the other hand. We strongly believe that to be a successful instructional mechanism for both the teacher and the student of organizational behavior, there *must* be a significant emphasis on the *application* of the presented material. To this end, we have made a concerted effort to stress managerial applications throughout each chapter with the use of examples, illustrations, and summary exhibits. Nine new cases and five new exercises have also been developed to strengthen this focus on application.

We are indebted to a number of colleagues who helped to improve this book in many different ways. We are especially grateful to the following, who shared with us their classroom teaching experiences with the first edition and a revised plan for the second edition:

W. Robert Sampson, Eastern Michigan University
Paul D. Miller, University of Miami
F. Joseph Thomas, University of Lowell (MA)
Tupper Cawsey, Wilfrid Laurier University, Canada
V. V. Baba, Concordia University, Canada

and

Susan Taylor, University of Wisconsin, Madison
James McFillen, The Ohio State University
Roger Lamm, University of California, Berkeley
Afzalur Rahim, Youngstown University

who reviewed in detail the revised manuscript for this edition. The students at the University of Houston and the University of Kentucky are also recognized for enduring the classroom testing of some of the book's new components. The typing responsibilities were in the capable hands of Joann Olivares, Janie Alexander, and Margaret Preuss, who are due a special thanks for meeting our sometimes unreasonable deadlines.

Also, we wish to acknowledge William W. Ecton, dean of the College of Business and Economics, University of Kentucky, and A. Benton Cocanougher, dean of the College of Business Administration, University of Houston, for their continued support of our efforts.

Finally, the book's strengths and weaknesses are the responsibility of the two authors. The effort and the exchange of ideas over a thousand-mile distance have blended our knowledge about organizational behavior and brought about the final product.

Of course, the individuals who suffered the most were our family members, who had only recently recovered from the writing of the first edition. The sound of a typewriter's noise from behind a closed door at all hours of the day and night has finally blended in nicely with the other noises of children, TV, dogs and cats, and so on. To our families, we can only express our love, for without their support, *Organizational Behavior and Performance,* Second Edition, would only be an idea.

ANDREW D. SZILAGYI, JR.
MARC J. WALLACE, JR.

STATEMENT OF PURPOSE

In this book, improved individual, group, and organizational performance are considered primary goals for organizations. Without satisfactory performance at these three levels, an organization cannot survive. Of course, performance is not the only goal of organizations in our society, but it certainly touches, in some way, every individual who must earn a living.

The subject area that focuses on performance within work settings is *organizational behavior*. This relatively new area of scientific inquiry deals with the way individuals and groups, as well as organizations themselves, act to create outputs, such as production and services. The field of organizational behavior is currently in a state of growth. Scholars and practitioners who associate themselves with this field have only just begun to synthesize principles, concepts, and processes that attempt to interpret different degrees of organizational behavior and performance. As a field, organizational behavior uses the *scientific method,* is *interdisciplinary,* studies *individuals, groups, organizations,* and the *environment,* borrows heavily on theories, models, and concepts from the *behavioral sciences,* is *contingency oriented,* and emphasizes *application.* In discussing performance throughout this book, these key characteristics will be highlighted.

This book is not intended to be a compendium on management, industrial and organizational psychology, personnel administration, and human relations. Instead, it focuses on the subject area of *organizational behavior* and how the practicing manager can utilize the theories and research of this field in dealing with problems involving people. It is our belief that managers can do a more effective job if they appreciate and practice careful *observation, diagnosis, analysis,* and *implementation.* It is the manager who must observe performance, diagnose potential problems, analyze information, and reach implementation decisions, which often involve some form of change. We believe that the required appreciation can evolve to some degree from the study of organizational behavior.

We have attempted to minimize the use of esoteric and extremely complex theories and studies. Those that we include are integrated, with examples and actual applications in organizational settings. Among the settings covered are industrial firms, banks, government agencies, hospitals, clinics, police departments, research laboratories, and educational institutions. It is in these organizations that theories and research must meet the test of reality.

Thirty realistic cases and experiential exercises are used so that the reader has an opportunity to apply the chapter materials and content in analyzing actual managerial problems involving organizational behavior. The cases are based primarily on the authors' research, consulting, and managing experiences. They are set in different types and sizes of organizations and include problems of all levels of management.

The book is divided into five interrelated parts. The first part focuses on *the field of organizational behavior*. The domain of the field and the performance framework for the book is spelled out in this part. The importance of diagnosis is developed in chapter 2, where the topic of how researchers study organizational behavior is discussed. Each of the dimensions presented in the performance model need to and can be studied. The model in chapter 2 (Exhibit 2–2) is the conceptual framework we use throughout the book. It, in essence, is the book in a graphical form.

The second part contains four chapters on *individual dimensions of organizational behavior*. The level of analysis in this part is the individual. Chapter 3 focuses on motives and personality. Chapter 4 investigates perception and learning. The motivation and performance of individuals within organizations is covered in chapter 5. The topic of job design as it involves individual task accomplishment is discussed in chapter 6.

Part three of the book concentrates on *groups and interpersonal influence*. Two chapters, 7 and 8, focus on groups and intergroup behavior. A major influence factor in organizations, leadership, is covered in chapter 9.

Organizational structure and processes are discussed in part four. Organizational dimensions and the environment are considered in chapter 10. The theme of chapter 11 is organizational design. Four important processes within any organization are decision making, communications, performance evaluation, and developing and implementing reward systems. These are covered in chapters 12, 13, and 14.

The final part of the book involves an analysis of *organizational change and development*. A framework for studying change and development is discussed in chapter 15. In chapter 16, selected applications of change and development are discussed in theoretical, research, and application terms. Finally, in chapter 17, the future and current directions of the field of organizational behavior are presented.

These seventeen chapters are written for readers interested in the field of organizational behavior and the teachers of this subject area. Both the reader and the instructor were considered in developing the many graphical models found throughout the book. We have found that learning about organizational behavior is enhanced by employing integrative tables, figures, and models that synthesize text material. The illustrations, cases, experiential exercises, glossary, and numerous examples were purposefully included so that reader interest is maintained throughout the book. We hope that students enrolled in courses dealing with organizational behavior and practical managers who appreciate an analytically based book focusing on performance are able to see this text as more than an academic exercise.

Organizational Behavior
and Performance

A Performance Oriented Framework to Study Organizational Behavior

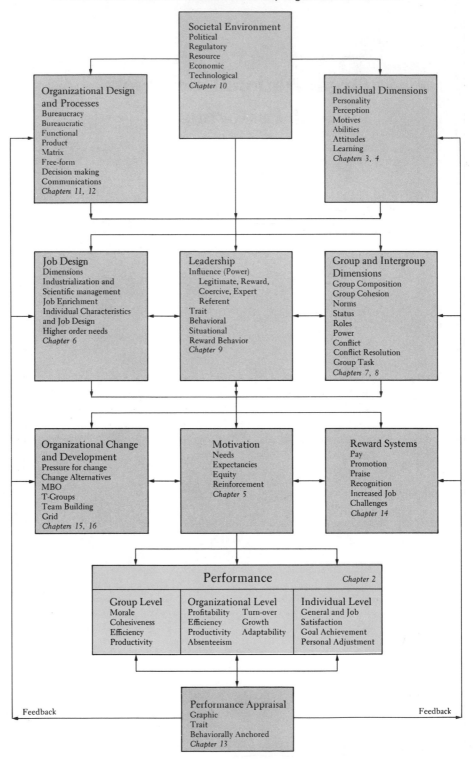

Societal Environment
Political
Regulatory
Resource
Economic
Technological
Chapter 10

Organizational Design and Processes
Bureaucracy
Bureaucratic
Functional
Product
Matrix
Free-form
Decision making
Communications
Chapters 11, 12

Individual Dimensions
Personality
Perception
Motives
Abilities
Attitudes
Learning
Chapters 3, 4

Job Design
Dimensions
Industrialization and
Scientific management
Job Enrichment
Individual Characteristics
and Job Design
Higher order needs
Chapter 6

Leadership
Influence (Power)
    Legitimate, Reward,
    Coercive, Expert
    Referent
Trait
Behavioral
Situational
Reward Behavior
Chapter 9

Group and Intergroup Dimensions
Group Composition
Group Cohesion
Norms
Status
Roles
Power
Conflict
Conflict Resolution
Group Task
Chapters 7, 8

Organizational Change and Development
Pressure for change
Change Alternatives
MBO
T-Groups
Team Building
Grid
Chapters 15, 16

Motivation
Needs
Expectancies
Equity
Reinforcement
Chapter 5

Reward Systems
Pay
Promotion
Praise
Recognition
Increased Job
Challenges
Chapter 14

Performance   *Chapter 2*

Group Level
Morale
Cohesiveness
Efficiency
Productivity

Organizational Level
Profitability   Turn-over
Efficiency   Growth
Productivity   Adaptability
Absenteeism

Individual Level
General and Job
Satisfaction
Goal Achievement
Personal Adjustment

Performance Appraisal
Graphic
Trait
Behaviorally Anchored
Chapter 13

Feedback

Feedback

PART ONE

The Field of Organizational Behavior

CHAPTER 1

An Overview of
Organizational Behavior
and Performance

A human being is not born with the ability to perform well in an organization, any more than he or she is born with the ability to invest money wisely or solve air-pollution problems. An adult's ability to perform is the product of individual attributes influenced by a long series of experiences, events, and circumstances, which occur within complex settings. In order to improve our understanding of performance, it is necessary to learn about human behavior within organizations. Our purpose in this book is to examine the field of organizational behavior, which offers a body of knowledge about human beings at work and information about their performance. Thus, it is our intent to improve your understanding about human behavior; this will require an examination of individuals, groups, and organizational structure, processes, change, and development. We hope our effort will show you that *organizational behavior* (1) concentrates on how people respond at work in organizations; (2) is becoming more scientifically based; (3) is not a panacea for all performance problems; and (4) is concerned primarily with description, not prescription.

The Field of Organizational Behavior

Any attempt to describe a field of inquiry often results in disagreements. This is especially true when attempting to express the meaning of the field of organizational behavior. Note that we refer to organizational behavior as a *field,* not a discipline or even an emerging discipline. A *discipline* is an accepted science with a theoretical foundation that serves as the basis for research and analysis. Organizational behavior, because of its broad base, recent emergence, and interdisciplinary orientation, is not accepted as a science. We are only just beginning to synthesize principles, concepts, and processes in this field of inquiry. Instead of adding to the controversy and disagreement, it seems more reasonable to describe, rather than to define, the field. Thus, we suggest:

> Organizational behavior is concerned with the study of the behavior, attitudes, and performance of workers in an organizational setting; the organization's and informal group's effect on the worker's perceptions, feelings, and actions; the environ-

ment's effect on the organization and its human resources and goals; and the effect of the workers on the organization and its effectiveness.

This description emphasizes a number of key points. First, formal organizations are only one of several concerns in organizational behavior. Individuals and groups as separate entities are also a part of this field of inquiry. Second, it is necessary to learn about individual and group behavior, attitudes, and performance. Third, organizations, informal groups, and environments play a role in how people behave and perform. The interrelatedness of the parts of an organization and the environment must be considered an important feature in unraveling issues that are typically discussed by managers and researchers. Fourth, individuals influence an organization's effectiveness or goal accomplishment. Finally, to comprehend organizational behavior it is necessary to delve into the behavioral sciences and employ the methods of science to study variables associated with this field.

Most managers welcome theories, research evidence, and conceptual explanations about organizational behavior phenomena. However, each of these scientific approaches rarely provides simple answers to behavior and performance matters. An important contribution of the organizational behavior field is the emphasis on moving beyond simple answers and discovering instead the relevant factors in a problem. A key to this discovery is a high regard for and interest in the scientific method. However, no attempt will be made here to urge the point of view that the scientific method is the only way a manager can or should analyze human behavior. Even John B. Watson, the father of the behavioral school of psychology, reminds us of the importance of common-sense knowledge of behavior.[1]

The type of methodology that we call "scientific" is a refinement of the procedures whereby we make our everyday observations—nothing more than a refinement, but a very important one. An appreciation of the need for controlled observation, the cornerstone upon which the scientific method rests, can help the manager discriminate between fact and fiction, opinion and prejudice, ideal and actual.

The scientific method is the basis of the disciplines and approaches that have contributed to the field of organizational behavior (see exhibit 1–1). Around 1913, but industrial psychologists were actively engaged in studies of individual differences in aptitude for and proficiency in work and the physical arrangement of the workplace. Munsterberg was applying the scientific method to these important issues in organizational settings.[2] His focus and level of analysis was the *individual*. The human relations approach, which was emphasized by many investigators in the 1930s and 1940s, also encouraged the use of the scientific method. Much of its philosophy and scientific orientation was captured in the writings of Mayo, McGregor, Argyris, and Likert. An important feature of this approach was the emphasis on creating a work force with high morale. The focus and level of analysis was the *group*.

An emphasis on individuals or groups only is incomplete, and from this incompleteness emerged the need for a more interdisciplinary and multileveled analysis, which in the 1960s and 1970s became known as *organizational behavior*. As exhibit 1–1 illustrates, this field is essentially an interdisciplinary conglomerate. It is distinct from industrial psychology, sociology, human relations, and history. It is not a behavioral science but can be viewed as an interdisciplinary application of behav-

Exhibit 1-1   The Evolution of Organizational Behavior

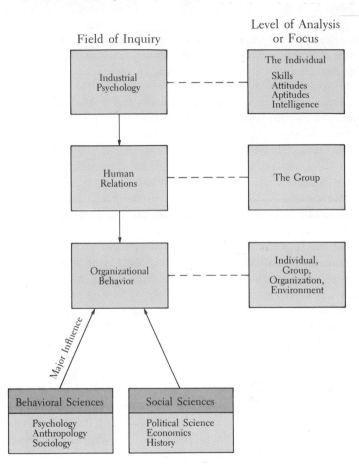

ioral science knowledge. Organizational behavior as a field of inquiry relies heavily on the principles of science and theory, but it also attempts to convey the importance of applying knowledge about behavior to actual organizational settings and problems.

The Behavioral Science Influence

The main contributor to the field of organizational behavior, as shown in exhibit 1-1, is the behavioral sciences. As a scientific grouping of disciplines, the behavioral sciences are less mature than the biological and physical sciences. It is difficult to isolate a date that represents when the term *behavioral science* began to be used. In the early 1950s, the term was used and associated with a Ford Foundation grant that supported a Behavioral Science Program. This program undoubtedly increased the attention afforded the research being done by behavioral scientists.

The core disciplines of the behavioral sciences are psychology, sociology, and anthropology. Although each of these disciplines is concerned with human behavior and nature, there are few commonly accepted theories among them. Not only is there theoretical disagreement, but there are also methodological controversies. In fact, there is widespread disagreement about the problems that need to be analyzed within organizations and society. Therefore, it seems reasonable to consider the behavioral science influence on organizational behavior as one of emphasis and approach. The behavioral scientist, like the organizational behavior practitioner and researcher, does not have a neatly defined theory of human behavior or a set of universally acceptable procedures for managing employees. The behavioral science emphasis and approach follow closely the fundamental steps of scientific inquiry: theory leads to research, which leads to application (i.e., theory → research → application).

Behavioral scientists work diligently at improving their ability to predict behavior. Because people and environments do change, this work focuses on *attempting* to predict how most people are *likely* to behave in a given set of circumstances and conditions. Each discipline applies its own methodology to the prediction problem, and each provides managers with insight into such important areas as individual differences, cultural influences, motivation, and organizational design. Note that the emphasis here is on the word *attempt*. There is to date no suggestion or the slightest hope that the predictions will be perfectly accurate under all circumstances and at all times.

Psychology

Psychology has had perhaps the greatest influence on the field of organizational behavior because it focuses directly on understanding and predicting individual behavior. In its development, the field of psychology has branched into a number of subdisciplines, each with a unique approach to understanding behavior. The variety of such approaches is evident in the following list of disciplines within psychology:

General Psychology

Experimental Psychology

Clinical Psychology

Consumer Behavior

Personality and Social Psychology

Industrial Psychology

Counseling Psychology

Educational Psychology

Consulting Psychology

Esthetics

Psychologists in all these areas definitely agree that motivation and learning are major determinants of behavior. *Motivation* usually refers to the mental processes that precipitate the behavior in question. Most psychologists study the process of motivation in seeking explanations for the force with which people act and the choices they make in their actions.

Equally important to psychologists is the process of *learning,* which has to do with relatively enduring changes and adaptations in behavior over time. The importance of learning is expressed as follows:

> Our entire way of life is predicated upon our ability to learn. Not only do we rely on learning to give us the basic skills with which we earn our daily bread, but also to educate our children for citizenship in a free society. . . . We believe that people learn their system of values, learn to love themselves and others, learn to channel their biological drives, even learn to be mentally ill. When we begin to analyze the learning process, therefore, we are probing the ultimate source of our humanity. . . .[3]

Learning is important in understanding organizational behavior because of the concepts and generalizations that have developed from it. Of special relevance to managers are the following:

Behavior is caused.

Behavior is purposive and goal directed.

Behavior results from the interaction of genetic and environmental factors.

Through the interaction of genetic and environmental factors, the individual develops a pattern of personality characteristics.

Individuals differ from one another in personal values, attitudes, personalities, and roles; yet, at the same time the members of a group must possess certain common values and characteristics.

Each of the social groups to which an individual belongs helps shape his or her behavior.

Each of these generalizations is associated with learning, which occurs throughout a person's life.

One of the most important attributes of psychology is the emphasis on the *scientific* study of behavior. Psychologists attempt to understand behavior on the basis of rational, demonstrable cause-effect relationships. Admittedly, this is a goal that is not always attained, and psychologists differ in how they pursue it.

Although learning and motivation are the main focus of psychology, the immediate applications to the field of organizational behavior are widespread. Basic knowledge of human behavior is important in work design, leadership, organizational design, communication, decision making, performance appraisal systems, and reward programs. These applied concerns are certainly within the domain of organizational behavior.

Sociology

Auguste Comte, a French philosopher of the nineteenth century, coined the term *sociology* as part of his work in proposing a reclassification and rearrangement of science.[4] He believed that the facts of human existence—social facts—were more important than philosophical speculation about these facts, and he felt that the use of scientific method in investigating these facts would show that society and social phenomena were subject to general laws.

Most sociologists today identify the discipline by using one of three statements. First, one might say that sociology has to do with human interaction, interaction being the influence of actors upon each other in social settings. Second, one might state that sociology is a study of plural behavior. Two or more interacting persons constitute a plurality pattern of behavior. A third concept is that sociology is the systematic study of social systems. A *social system* is a social unit that is structured to serve a purpose. It consists of two or more persons usually of different status, with different roles, playing a part in a pattern that is sustained by a physical and cultural base.

When analyzing organizations as social systems, it is pointed out that the following elements exist:

People or actors.

Acts or behavior.

Ends or goals.

Norms, rules, or regulations controlling conduct or behavior.

Beliefs held by people as actors.

Status and status relationships.

Authority or power to influence other actors.

Role expectations, role performances, and role relationships.

Therefore, organizations are viewed by sociologists as consisting of a variety of people with different roles, status, and degree of authority. The organization attempts to achieve certain generalized and specific objectives.

Because of the diverse interests of sociologists, one can find a variety of methods of inquiry, ranging from historical methods to highly developed, organized, and controlled experimental methods. Empirical data is used to test, illustrate, or extend theories. The discipline of sociology, like other behavioral sciences, has been associated with the following characteristics of a science:

1. It is *empirical;* it is based on observation and reasoning, not on supernatural revelation, and its results are not speculative.

2. It is *theoretical;* it attempts to summarize complex observations in abstract, logically related propositions that purport to explain causal relationships in the subject matter.

3. It is *cumulative;* theories and research build upon one another, new empirical evidence correcting, extending, and refining the older theories into newer ones.

4. It is *nonethical;* scientists do not ask whether particular social actions are good or bad; they seek merely to explain them.[5]

These characteristics illustrate that sociology is a discipline that applies the methods of science to the study of people in social systems. Sociological theories, research findings, and models have added, and will continue to add, to our understanding of organizations as social systems.

Anthropology

The aim of anthropology is to acquire a better understanding of the relationship between the human being and the environment. Adaptations to surroundings constitute culture. The manner in which people view their environment is a part of culture. Culture includes those ideas shared by groups of individuals and the languages by which these ideas are communicated. In essence, culture is a system of learned behavior. *Includes these ideas shared by groups of individuals*

To study the relationship between people and culture, it is necessary to collect and record data pertaining to both, and, like the other behavioral sciences, anthropology has borrowed its methods from older sciences. To achieve a thorough understanding, the study must be made of all human beings. The world is the laboratory of anthropologists, and human beings must be studied in their natural habitats. Understanding the importance of studying people in natural settings over time enables one to grasp the range of anthropology.

Perhaps more knowledge of our culture is now required to understand more clearly the behaviors that occur within organizations. Familiarity with some of the cultural differences of employees can lead to a greater managerial objectivity and depth in the interpretation of behavior and performance.

The behavioral sciences, when combined, have had a significant impact on the field of organizational behavior. They have provided a reference that encourages the use of the scientific method. That is, the spirit of inquiry pervades the field, and, despite growing pains, organizational behavior is coming into its own as a systematic area of study. Some of the more generally agreed upon influences of behavioral science on organizational behavior are:

The systematic use of theories and theory building to explain behavior, which provides a framework for studying phenomena.

An empirical base to study individuals, groups, and organizations.

The increased use of rigorous research methods.

Less use of armchair speculation in reaching managerial decisions.

An effort to communicate theories, research, and ideas to practicing managers as well as members of the field.

These characteristics are certainly noteworthy for a field that is actually only just beginning to accumulate its theories and research. The accumulation within the field appears to be proceeding along three levels of analysis—the individual, group, and organization (see exhibit 1–1).

The Contingency Orientation
of Organizational Behavior

One of the consequences of accepting the scientific method as the cornerstone of organizational behavior is a rejection of universal principles of managing emerging from the classical, behavioral, quantitative, or systems approaches to managing within organizations. Universal principles are usually quite prescriptive and definitive. For example, Weber, who is considered a classicist, recommended the use of a bureaucratic organizational structure; Likert, who is assumed to be a behavioralist, suggests developing a System 4 organization; another behavioralist, McGregor, implied that a Theory Y approach is best suited for an organization; and many classical scholars propose the use of a structured line-staff organization.

A more realistic approach for studying behavior and performance within organizations is called the *contingency approach.* This approach is directed toward developing managerial actions that are most appropriate for a specific situation and the people involved. By considering and weighing the relevant variables in a situation, the manager can proceed to develop the most appropriate action plan needed to accomplish important goals. Managers must be able to recognize, diagnose, and adapt to the given situation to use the contingency approach successfully.

The contingency approach is conceptually appealing but extremely difficult to follow. Attempting to pinpoint the important interrelationships among variables is extremely difficult. However, this is exactly what is needed; namely, to develop the most appropriate plan to solve a particular motivation, organizational design, performance appraisal, or training problem. The manager must analyze carefully each variable that is important and link the variables together to reach decisions, which makes the contingency approach much more than an enticing suggestion for managerial action. It requires management action in the form of decision making. Once the interrelationships are analyzed and the variables linked together, the manager must reach a decision. It is definitely not an "it all depends" philosophical position. After performing a careful analysis of a particular situation and conducting a thorough review of the variables and the theoretical and research literature, a manager must be satisfied that under the present circumstances a certain action is most appropriate, or he or she must decide on an alternative course.

Established contingency approaches will be covered in this book. It is the contingency orientation of organizational behavior that can be exciting for managers because it immediately notifies them that perfect or pat answers to organizational problems do not exist. If they did, all we would need to do is list them, one after the other, and refer to them at the appropriate time. Predicting behavior and performance is certainly much more elusive than this. Individuals, groups, and organizations need to be studied separately and then as interrelated parts before a manager can even hope to make some reasonably good predictions. Although the need to perform separate and interacting analyses is more difficult, it is the contingency approach that can improve the performance of managers. Simple answers for complex situations just do not exist, and this is why the field of organizational behavior is being recognized as a source of knowledge and a repository of information by theorists, researchers, and practitioners.

Levels of Organizational Behavior Analysis

Since the 1960s, the behavioral science influence on organizational behavior has highlighted three levels of analysis for the manager to consider: (1) the individual; (2) the group; and (3) the formal organization.

The Individual

When formal organizations are examined with the individual as the focal point, the research is often centered on understanding the interrelationships between psychological factors and work roles. What individual characteristics does a person bring into the organization? What are the organizational forces that affect the individual's attitudes, perception, state of motivation, or job satisfaction? Another area of individual interest is personality and the implications of personality for workplace behavior and performance. There is no way that a complete picture of organizational behavior can unfold unless the individual is studied and understood.

The Group

There is also a need to study the small group and such characteristics as group structure, process, development, and cohesion. The group's personality is called "syntality." Researchers have noted that work groups manifest characteristics apart from and beyond the sum of the personal attributes of the individuals making up the group. The group is certainly an entity that needs to be carefully studied independently. The group thinks. The group sets goals. The group behaves. The group acts. The sociologist expresses these activities as important enough to require careful study and analysis.

The Formal Organization

All organizations, regardless of their industry affiliation, size, and shape, are comprised of individuals and groups. However, organizations have unique characteristics in much the same sense as do individuals and groups. In fact, it is generally agreed that formal organizations can be compared on the basis of specific characteristics that are common to all of them. For example, one characteristic that provides some important insight about an organization is its size. We can count the number of managers or nonmanagers, or the number of patient beds, or the number of students, to acquire some indication of size. Other common characteristics that are of interest are the formalization policies, organizational climate, levels in the hierarchy, degree of centralization, and locus of decision making.

Organizations are also influenced by the environments in which they operate. A growing body of literature has concentrated on how environmental forces impinge upon the organization and influence its internal operations and employees. In addition, the organization affects individuals and vice versa. This phenomenon needs to be studied and better understood.

These three levels of analysis are not mutually exclusive. The field of organizational behavior embraces them as being complementary. In the past, the three levels were pursued with little coordination by behavioral scientists. Now, however, a major contribution of those interested in the organizational behavior field is the attempt to integrate these three levels of analyses, although this will require much more effort. The individual focus is no more important or valuable to the manager within an organization than is the group or formal organizational focus. There is no need to choose one level of analysis and exclude the others. The managers in businesses, health care, education, government, and religious organizations have problems in common that require an interdisciplinary approach. This can be provided by organizational behavior because it emphasizes all three levels of analysis—the individual, the group, and the formal organization.

Cummings has made an important position statement about organizational behavior that closely summarizes what we have said about the levels of analysis in the field.[6] He pictures the field as illustrated in exhibit 1–2. Three characteristics define organizational behavior:

1. *A body of constructs, models, and facts* drawn from observations about indi-

Exhibit 1–2 Dimensions and Themes of Organizational Behavior

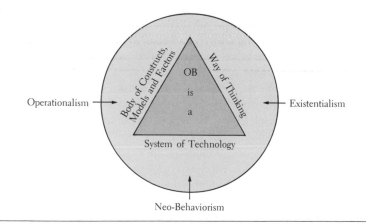

Reprinted from Larry L. Cummings, "Toward Organizational Behavior," *Academy of Management Review,* 1978, p. 93. Used with permission.

viduals, groups, and organizations and attempting to predict and explain performance.

2. *A way of thinking* that emphasizes the following: (a) an independent variable-dependent variable orientation; (b) change as a desirable outcome for organizations; (c) a humanistic tone with concern for the interests of organization members; and (d) a focus on performance effectiveness.

3. *A system of technology.* Out of basic research in the field, a set of specific tools have emerged for practitioners including training and development techniques, job-design techniques, methods for designing organizations, and personnel management techniques.

These three dimensions of organizational behavior are not static and in a vacuum, according to Cummings. On the contrary, they are constantly being altered and developed under the influence of three major themes that characterize the thinking of theorists and practitioners in the field:

1. *Existentialism* is a recognition that the phenomena studied in organizational behavior are very complex, and that there are few if any absolute laws that can be used to understand the phenomena.

2. *Operationalism* takes three basic forms: (a) an emphasis on mid-range models that focus on specific subareas of the field rather than an attempt at grand, global, all-encompassing models; (b) an emphasis on explicit operational definitions for each variable studied; and (c) great care and attention in insuring the technical qualities of measures used in research.

3. *Neo-Behavioralism* is a renewed interest in studying performance as a function of motivated behavior, with an emphasis on the cognitive decisions that influenced the behavior.

Organizational Behavior: A Recapitulation

Exhibit 1–3 should help in identifying and reviewing the key characteristics that make the field of organizational behavior unique.

First, it is interdisciplinary. Although not a formal discipline, organizational behavior draws heavily on knowledge about behavior generated in the behavioral sciences of psychology, sociology, and anthropology. Second, as an interdisciplinary approach, organizational behavior has its primary roots in the behavioral sciences. The social sciences of economics, political science, and history have had a secondary impact on the field.

Third, organizational behavior has inherited the tradition of scientific method in its investigations from its parent disciplines. Scientific method emphasizes the use of logic and theory in formulating research questions and the systematic use of objective data in answering such questions.

Exhibit 1–3 The Key Characteristics of the Field of Organizational Behavior

Characteristics	Brief Description of the Characteristics
Interdisciplinary Foundation	Organizational behavior has borrowed concepts, theories, models, and the orientation of the behavioral sciences in understanding behavior and performance.
Behavioral Science Foundation	The behavioral sciences—psychology, sociology, and anthropology—have provided the basic philosophy, characteristics of science, and principles that are so freely borrowed by the field of organizational behavior.
Scientific Method Foundation	Armchair speculation and common sense are not completely disregarded in the field of organizational behavior; the use of the scientific method takes precedence in attempting to predict and explain behavior and performance.
Analysis Level	Organizational behavior as a field is concerned with the in-depth analysis of individuals, groups, and formal organizations. Each level is of equal importance and needs to be scientifically studied.
Contingency Orientation	The organizational behavior field has no universally applicable set of prescriptions for managers. Instead, the contingency theme, which encourages the development of action plans that are based on the situation and the people involved, is considered the most relevant.
Concern for Application	Organizational behavior knowledge is suited for the practicing manager in an organization. Consequently, theories, research, and models need to be eventually communicated in language that is understood by the manager faced with individual, group, and organizational problems.

Fourth, organizational behavior is unique in its approach to behavior because it encompasses all three levels of analysis: individual, group, and formal organization. In addition, all three levels are treated with equal importance and attention.

Fifth, the field of organizational behavior realistically reflects the fact that behavior at all three levels of analysis is complex and problematic by refusing to deal in global, fixed, and immutable generalizations. The term *contingency orientation* reflects the need to consider the situation and individuals involved before drawing conclusions about behavior.

Finally, organizational behavior is marked by a concern for applications. The organizational behavior researcher must always be concerned with understanding real events in actual organizations and with communicating his or her results in a meaningful fashion to practicing managers.

The Plan of This Book

As stated previously, our purpose is to improve the reader's understanding of how people behave and perform within organizations. We will study the specific contributions of the behavioral sciences to applied organizational behavior. We will make no attempt to convert or teach you to be a "behavioral scientist"—this, of course, is impossible to accomplish by reading a book or taking a course. We attempt only to improve today's and tomorrow's managers' understanding of organizational behavior and performance. The manager needs to understand the three levels of analysis, and a conceptual framework to initiate this will be presented in chapter 2 and used throughout the book. Because of the diverse theories and increasing number of research studies in the behavioral sciences, a framework is needed to sort out the relevant from the irrelevant, the practical from the esoteric, and the common sense from the scientifically based findings and models. It is our objective to provide numerous realistic examples so that our readers can clearly see what is meant or implied by a theory or research finding. Through this procedure, we hope to convince our readers of the importance of theory, research, application, and scientific analyses for managers.

Many of the concepts presented in the model in chapter 2 may be unfamiliar at this early juncture in the book; the model will hopefully acquire more relevance and make more sense upon completion of the book. How the variables shown in the model can be studied is discussed in the second part of chapter 2.

The next four chapters, which compose the *individual* section of the book, have a distinct psychological flavor. We discuss individual characteristics, motivation, and work design. The vast majority of the theories and research in this section have emerged from the psychology discipline.

The third part consists of three chapters that are concerned with groups, intergroup behavior, and leadership. Although the leadership chapter is based largely on the theoretical and research findings of psychologists, there is a distinct sociological flavor to this part.

The organization and its structure and processes are the focus of the fourth section, which consists of five chapters. This section is largely interdisciplinary, with a strong psychological and sociological orientation throughout. Organizational design, decision making, communications, performance appraisal, and reward systems are analyzed in this section.

The fifth part emphasizes organizational change and development. Planning for and implementing change is a reality of managing within an organization. Thus, a systematic program is needed to cope with inevitable change within the organization.

At the end of each chapter, there is a section labeled "Applications and Implications for the Manager." This is a synopsis of the main points covered in the chapter, and they are assumed to be some of the major points of interest for understanding the tone and content of the chapter. In addition to this, many of the chapters include actual cases and experiential exercises that attempt to integrate many of the theories and research notions in an actual organizational setting. This real-world emphasis is intended to show the reader the practical value of the field of organizational behavior.

Notes

1. John B. Watson, *Behaviorism* (New York: Norton, 1924).
2. Hugo Munsterberg, *Psychology and Industrial Efficiency* (Boston: Houghton Mifflin, 1913).
3. George A. Miller, *Psychology: The Science of Mental Life* (New York: Harper & Row, 1962), p. 212.
4. Peter R. Senn, *Social Sciences and Its Methods* (Boston: Holbrook Press, 1971), p. 89.
5. Harry M. Johnson, *Sociology: A Systematic Introduction* (New York: Harcourt, Brace & World, 1960), p. 2.
6. Larry L. Cummings, "Towards Organizational Behavior," *Academy of Management Review,* January 1978, pp. 90–98.

Additional References

BERELSON, B., and STEINER, G. *Human Behavior: An Inventory of Scientific Inquiry.* New York: Harcourt, Brace & World, 1964.

DUNNETTE, M. D., ed. *Handbook of Industrial and Organizational Psychology.* Chicago: Rand McNally, 1976.

DUNNETTE, M. D., and KIRCHNER, W. K. *Psychology Applied to Industry.* New York: Appleton-Century-Crofts, 1965.

Faris, R. E. L., ed. *Handbook of Modern Sociology.* Chicago: Rand McNally, 1964.

HOEBEL, E. A. *Anthropology: The Study of Man.* New York: McGraw-Hill, 1972.

KOLASA, B. J. *Introduction to Behavioral Science for Business.* New York: Wiley, 1969.

NOTTERMAN, J. M. *Behavior: A Systematic Approach.* New York: Random House, 1970.

RUSH, H. M. *Behavioral Science Concepts and Management Applications.* New York: Conference Board, 1969.

SCHEIN, E. H. "Behavioral Sciences for Management." In *Contemporary Management,* edited by J. W. McGuire, pp. 15–32. Englewood Cliffs, N.J.: Prentice-Hall, 1974.

SCHULTZ, D. P. *A History of Modern Psychology.* New York: Academic Press, 1969.

WADIA, M. S. *Management and the Behavioral Sciences.* Boston: Allyn & Bacon, 1968.

YU, F. T. C. *Behavioral Sciences and the Mass Media.* New York: Russell Sage, 1968.

CHAPTER 2

The Study of Organizational Behavior: A Performance Model

In any applied field of inquiry, such as organizational behavior, an understanding of the research process is of great importance. This is true for a number of reasons. First, the theories and models developed must eventually have practical relevance for the manager. Unless they meet the test of reality, these theories not only have minimum value but their application in an organization may result in significant dysfunctional effects. Second, well-validated theories provide managers with an excellent basis for decision making or *problem solving*. For example, managers in retailing firms have recently been faced with increasing turnover rates among their hourly employees. Theories and models of turnover will assist these managers in diagnosing the causes of their problems by showing them that turnover is generally caused not only by internal organizational factors (such as the reward system, supervisory behavior, and/or the nature of the job) but also by uncontrollable external factors (such as the economy of the region and availability of comparable jobs).

Finally, understanding the research process can provide managers with a mechanism with which to *evaluate* research projects. It is a rare practitioner who does not frequently have research reports cross his or her desk. A vice president of manufacturing of a medium-sized oil-drilling company recently showed one of the authors a research report of an attitude survey conducted by an employee of the firm. The results of the survey pointed to a dramatic decline in employee morale (i.e., job satisfaction) at the main plant and recommended significant revisions in many company policies to overcome the apparent problem. The vice president was knowledgeable enough to note that: (1) less than 15 percent of the total employees were sampled; (2) the sampled employees were mostly from the late night shifts; and (3) the survey questions were poorly worded and lacked proven reliability. This ability to distinguish good research from bad research probably saved the company from investing valued resources into a problem than may not exist or may not be as severe as first reported.

The purpose of this chapter is twofold. First, a brief survey of the scientific process as applied to organizational behavior will be presented. (Some of these topics are covered in more depth in the Appendix.) Second, we will develop a conceptual model that will serve as a framework for the entire book. The model is a synthesis of our perspective of organizational behavior. The vast domain of the field should become evident when the model's dimensions are discussed.

Ways of Establishing Beliefs

In developing our knowledge about organizational behavior, it is important for us to consider the manner in which individuals establish, defend, or change their beliefs about various matters. This is an important issue because the confidence that can be placed in the validity of a belief is a function of the methods a person uses to establish and defend his or her position. For example, one individual may believe that "job performance causes job satisfaction," while a second proposes that "job satisfaction causes job performance." This may seem like a trivial issue, but it has tremendous implications for the performance of an organization: As a manager, should you try to facilitate the performance of your employees, resulting in high performance and high satisfaction; or should you try to facilitate employee satisfaction so that they can perform better?

We will consider four methods of establishing, defending, or changing beliefs about various phenomena. These four "ways of knowing" are tenacity, intuition, authority, and science.[1]

Tenacity, in its simplest form, is typified by the age-old rhetorical question, "Why should we change? We've always done it this way." In essence, it is a method of defending a belief through habit or inertia.[2] As many of us have experienced, tenacious beliefs are difficult to deal with because they frequently give rise to differences of opinion and allow no satisfactory method for resolution.

Some people appeal to a higher *authority* instead of simply holding on doggedly to a belief. In organizations, this process may refer to the use of outside consultants, lawyers, or skilled craftspeople. For example, as a young production engineer, one of the authors made repeated, futile attempts to restart a key piece of equipment that had malfunctioned. Finally, he appealed to an hourly employee, who had many years of experience in the plant, for help. In only a few minutes, the piece of equipment was functioning. Thirty years of experience had made the older employee a source of authority on the equipment in question. Continual use of authority, however, is less than an optimal strategy. Not only may different authority sources recommend vastly different solutions, but many of the recommendations may be plainly wrong. To solve a turnover problem, one consultant may recommend raising wage rates, and a second may advise the use of intensive supervisory training programs. Implementing either or both recommendations may be costly and ineffective when the real problem may be that the organization is hiring individuals who are overqualified for the particular jobs, resulting in employee boredom and dissatisfaction.

Intuition is a method for fixing beliefs that relies upon the appeal to obviously self-evident propositions. For example, the belief that "the whole is greater than any one of its parts" may lead to a dominant managerial strategy of using groups, rather than individuals, to make decisions. As we will discuss in later chapters, there are positive and negative features associated with group decision making. One of the problems associated with intuition is that such self-evident propositions may not be as true as first believed.

Finally, the research methods used to study organizational behavior are intimately entwined with the concept of *science* itself. In a general sense, science refers to the *pursuit of objective knowledge* gathered from careful observation and investigation. Thus, the term refers to a *method* (systematic acquisition and evaluation of information) and a *goal* (identifying the nature or principles of what is being studied) rather than to any specific phenomena.[3]

Tenacity, authority, and intuition are incapable of providing a sure knowledge base in *any* field, including organizational behavior. It is for this reason that the methods of *science* were developed.

The Nature of Science

Science is a badly misinterpreted word in our society. Many people use the word to describe the study of the inanimate physical universe, the tests being run in experimental laboratories, or the engineering knowledge needed to land astronauts on the moon. There are those who equate the word with a brilliant scientist who spins complex theories of magnetic polarity or thermodynamics. This interpretation places the scientist in an ivory tower at some distance from common people and everyday problems. An example would be the professor of organizational behavior who espouses a complex theory of motivation that is mathematically based but seems to have little value for the plant supervisor or the head nurse or the regional sales manager.

In the scientific world itself, there are two broad views of what constitutes science. First, the *static* view holds that science is an activity that contributes systematized information to the world. The scientist's task is to discover new facts and add them to an already existing body of knowledge.[4] This interpretation offers science as a way of explaining observed phenomena.

Second, the *dynamic* view regards science more as the activities performed by scientists. The present state of knowledge is considered important for the expansion of theory and research. This view has a problem-solving orientation rather than one of adding facts to an already existing body of knowledge.

The study of behavior within organizations utilizes both the static and dynamic approaches. It involves the pursuit of objective knowledge gleaned from careful observation, which heightens efficiency and helps cut out bias. Behavioral studies can involve controlled laboratory experimentation, of course without the test tubes. The development of systematic facts and knowledge is also needed by the practicing manager because the "seat of the pants" approach is so fraught with uncertainty that it hampers the development of theory and research. Finally, managers are problem solvers, and an appreciation of the dynamic view of science is congruent with their values, needs, and expectations. It is our contention that such factors as environmental uncertainty, individual differences, group dynamics, and organizational characteristics are so interrelated that a problem-solving style based on a thorough diagnosis of crucial variables is needed at all levels of management.

The Scientific Approach Applied to the Study of Organizational Behavior and Performance

The scientific approach is aptly presented by the view expressed by Braithwaite:

> The function of science . . . is to establish general laws covering the behaviors of the empirical events or objects with which the science in question is concerned, and

thereby to enable us to connect together our knowledge of the separately known events, and to make reliable predictions of events as yet unknown.[5]

The spirit of scientific investigation that emerges from this statement emphasizes characteristics of the scientific approach. The scientific approach actively seeks out information in a systematic and unbiased manner. The information generated usually involves keeping some records of the researcher's observations. The generation of information typically involves the use of questionnaires, interviews, visual observations, reviews of records, and other similar practices to create a data base. These data enable the researcher to conduct a relatively unbiased analysis that results in systematically connecting existing and discovered knowledge. By communicating the analysis to others, the researcher publicly displays his or her findings and/or predictions.

The scientific method applied to organizational behavior, as shown in exhibit 2–1, can be considered a process that consists of: (1) the *observation* of phenomena (facts) about individuals, groups, organizations, and environments; (2) the formulation of explanations for such phenomena using *induction* processes; (3) the *generation* of more specific predictions about phenomena in the real world, using *deduction* processes; and (4) the *verification* of these predictions through systematic, controlled study.[6] The behavioral scientist, for example, may have developed a belief that individual job performance causes job satisfaction (observation). The observation is considered factual because it has to be reproduced over time in scientific experiments. Going from specifics to generalizations, the scientist attempts to explain the facts (induction). He or she may explain the observed relationship by arguing that the performance levels are related to the increased motivation of the individuals observed. The tentative explanation is that "job performance causes job satisfaction" due to the relationship between motivation levels and performance. Going from generalizations to specifics, the scientist "predicts" what should happen in the real world if his or her explanation is a plausible one (deduction). Finally, the prediction that "job performance causes job satisfaction" would be tested by measuring performance levels and satisfaction over time (verification).

The scientific approach to studying organizational behavior and performance is different from the typically used managerial approach. First, the scientific approach emphasizes studying multiple events, whereas the practitioner approach focuses on a single example of behavior or performance. If conclusions about a person's performance are based solely on the individual's low output this past week, it may be erroneously concluded that the worker is a poor performer. The scientific approach, on the other hand, encourages a detailed and scientifically based study of the

Exhibit 2–1 The Scientific Method

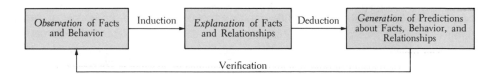

performance of the person over time, examination of the person's skill level, the group influences upon the individual, and other events that could possibly influence performance. The scientific approach advocates a thorough study and not just a "one shot" observation or even a study of a few isolated incidents.

Second, the scientific approach is more systematic than the practitioner approach. The researcher systematically tests theories, hypotheses, and models. The practitioner tests them in a more selective fashion. Evidence is often selected if it supports the hypothesis being considered. If managers believe that employees are primarily motivated by receiving a promotion, they can attempt to verify this belief. This selectivity often results in subjective conclusions about how people feel about promotion. The scientific approach carefully guards against personal biases or preconceptions in studying organizational behavior phenomena by requiring a scientific assessment of the problem or issue whenever possible.

Finally, the scientific approach attempts to control the variables that can influence organizational behavior and performance. The practitioner, because of the urgency of the situation, is often forced to disregard extraneous variables. The researcher attempts to control for confounding effects of extraneous variables so that reliable and valid inferences can be drawn from the analysis. The manager, pressed by time constraints, must react immediately and is often not able to even partially control extraneous variables. This difference is especially important when testing the applicability of a theory or model. Unless controls have been used in conducting the study of some phenomenon, little confidence can be placed in the interpretation of the observational data.

Theory as a Foundation

A theory is in essence an idea as to how something might be done or how certain variables interrelate; it is the foundation for a model of some aspect of the real world. The underlying motive for this resultant modeling is either that the real-world phenomena are so complex they need to be conceptually simplified in order to be understood, or that observation and theory by themselves do not reveal neatly ordered relationships among variables. A model is an attempt to make sense out of the observable world by ordering the relationships among the variables upon which the theorist is focusing.[7] For example, a manager may theorize that increased pay leads to increased performance. The manager would then focus upon the relationship of pay and performance that has been observed.

Any theory development in the field of organizational behavior can proceed through a number of steps. First, the elements or variables that will be studied are selected. In purely exploratory work, these variables are selected by the theorist, who has an idea and who selects variables assumed to be important in the refinement of the idea. Second, the theorist attempts to determine conceptually how these variables are related to each other. The interactions revealed by the model between variables help the theorist explain the relationships between and the impact of variables. That is, does pay lead to performance or does performance result in pay? Third, the boundary or scope of the theory needs to be specified. For example, the pay-performance theory may be applied to a specific occupation, organization, or individual. Whether there is a commonality among these three domains is another issue that need to be scientifically studied. The need to limit the boundaries of theories in organizational behavior is recognized by those giving attention to the contingency orientation. The sooner we recognize that settings, environments, individuals, and groups differ, the more enthusiastic and careful we become in specifying boundaries.

The Utilization of Theory

In the field of organizational behavior, theories provide the starting point for expressing propositions about behavior and performance. If the theorist can logically indicate how the propositions flow from the theory, they are generally accepted. After the propositions have been set forth, the theorist becomes concerned with whether they have any link with reality. Each proposition must be converted to a hypothesis by substituting for each named variable in the proposition an objective indicator. For example, the proposition that "increased pay leads to increased performance" must be converted to an empirically based hypothesis. It could be hypothesized as follows:

> If pay is increased by at least 10 percent from last year's figure, the number of generators examined by inspectors will increase by 15 percent during the next quarter.

Thus, the two variables "pay" and "performance" have been restated as a rather specific prediction that can be tested. The hypothesis provides a statement about the relations between two variables.

The hypotheses about relationships are what the researcher tests; this results in their being supported or not supported. Scientific testing allows the researcher to separate his or her values and opinions about the relationships from the relationships that actually exist.

One final thought about hypothesis testing concerns negative findings. Even when the variables are not related as hypothesized, knowledge is advanced. The rejection of a hypothesis based on empirical testing reduces the total universe of ignorance. Additional hypotheses may emerge from the negative findings. The researcher and practitioner cannot tell positive from negative evidence unless hypotheses are used as guides for research. It is possible to conduct research without hypotheses, but the advancement of our knowledge of human behavior in organizations appears to need the guidance provided by systematically formulated and tested hypotheses.

The Potential Value of Theory and Model Building

It is a generally accepted cliché that the use of scientific procedures such as theory formation and model building leads to *prediction*. This is basically why we work at developing logically deduced theories and testable models. A theory and model should, if thorough, result in reasonably accurate predictions. Models, like theories, are guidelines used to understand organizational behavior. A model can be graphically illustrated, which organizes one's thoughts and shows gaps in one's thinking about variable interactions.

Accurate prediction is the practical outcome of using scientifically based theory and models; the intellectual outcome is the understanding they provide of the characteristics within the domain being studied. The manager in most cases is more interested in prediction; the theorist is more concerned with understanding the theory and the model components more precisely. The practitioner often finds the understanding exercise too "theoretical." For example, "expectancy theory" of motivation is widely studied by theorists, but it is generally too complex for practitioners to spend time unraveling relationships, although they may unknowingly use the theory in various situations.

Research is needed to test organizational behavior theories. It is literally impossible to separate theory and research in the field of organizational behavior because the function of each is dependent upon the realization of the other. The practitioner is often interested in knowing if a theory or model has been tested to determine how much confidence to place on its predictions. Beyond this point, the manager of an organization has little interest in *testing* theories or models. The manager focuses on practice within the organization. This experience makes a significant contribution to theorist-researchers in the field of organizational behavior. For example, the manager may want to change the variables in a model put into practice because of experience. In addition, the manager may influence the choice of empirical indicators used in the model by researchers.

In order for a theorist-researcher to test theories, he or she needs to interact and communicate with practitioners. However, a real dilemma exists when a theorist-researcher needs to test a theory that is alien to the practitioner's way of doing things. Consequently, there is often a lag between the time a theoretical model becomes fashionable and when it is used by practitioners. As of today, there is no accepted model of organizational behavior. However, there are variables that are generally viewed as being within the domain of organizational behavior.

A Theoretical Model as a Framework

A theoretically based conceptual framework of organizational behavior and performance is provided in exhibit 2–2. At this point in the book, many of the dimensions and linkages between the variables presented may not be fully understood. We believe that by presenting our model early and by referring to it throughout the book the reader will gradually become more knowledgeable. This model does not attempt to predict behavior and performance, nor does it teach our readers to be behavioral scientists. Instead, it attempts to accomplish the following objectives:

Identify some of the key organizational, group, and individual variables studied in the field of organizational behavior.

Illustrate how these variables are related to each other.

Exhibit 2–2 A Performance Oriented Framework to Study Organizational Behavior

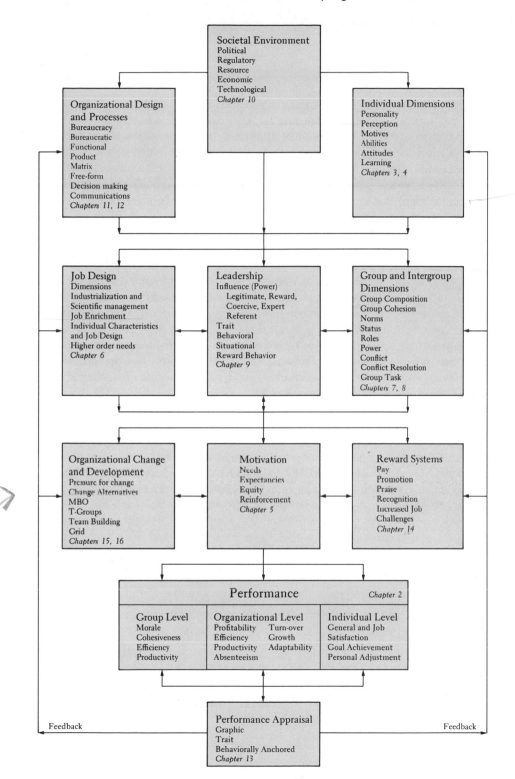

Chart out the domain of this book and indicate in what chapters each of the variables included in the model is found.

Emphasize the key characteristics of the field of organizational behavior: scientific method, interdisciplinary focus, three levels of analysis, behavioral science foundation, contingency orientation, and application bias.

Point out what variables influence *behavior* and *performance* in organizational settings. The emphasis in our model and throughout the book is on *performance* of the individual, group, and organization.

The best way to summarize and understand the model is to begin with the environmental factors at the top of the diagram and follow the chain of their impact through to the bottom.

Environmental Factors

One difficulty in studying organizations and people within them is that the organization must be distinguished from its environment. In essence, an organization's environment set is an arbitrary invention because the organization identifies its environment. There are environmental factors that are included and others that are excluded from consideration. We have identified some common environmental factors that influence individuals, groups, and leaders within most organizations as political, regulatory, resource, economic, and technological. Some factors are predictable and simple; others are complex and uncertain.

Individual Dimensions

An understanding of human attributes is essential in learning about behavior and performance. Personality, perception, motives, abilities, attitudes, and learning capacities are some of the crucial individual factors affecting performance within organizations. Managers who are planning and organizing work or leading subordinates must assess the fit between individuals and tasks. Making these judgments without some understanding of behavioral variables can result in irreversible reductions in performance and often leads to poor employee morale. Thus, individual behavior must be understood in order to elicit acceptable performance.

Organizational Design and Processes

The organization needs to have a design or structure that enables the employees to perform tasks that lead to satisfactory goal achievement. The type of design that is adopted—functional, product, matrix, or free-form—is influenced by such factors as: (1) the environment (simple or complex, stable or changing); (2) the technology of the organization; and (3) the major goals or objectives of the organization. Within the organization's design, the important processes of decision making and communication are performed.

Job Design

Within the larger organization, individual tasks are performed subject to the design of the jobs. The purpose of job design is to match the content and requirements of the task with the skills, abilities, and needs of the individual employee such that satisfactory levels of both organizational performance and employee morale are achieved. In some situations, tasks need to be modified because of changing technological, managerial, or individual requirements.

Group and Intergroup Dimensions

The coworkers with whom an individual interacts can affect how that person behaves and performs in an organization. Probably the most widely cited study of the impact of groups on individual members and nonmembers was performed at the Hawthorne plant of Western Electric in the 1920s.[8] Other studies and analyses of groups have focused on the composition, structure, norms, status, development, and cohesion. In addition, groups interact with other groups, which sometimes produces cooperation and sometimes conflict between groups. Whether the cooperation or conflict enhances performance is important information that a manager needs to examine on a regular basis.

Leadership

Each of the preceding dimensions—environment, individuals, organizational design, job design, and groups—are linked to and by leadership. The survival of any organization depends upon effective leadership in both the formal and informal settings. Of course, other variables affect survival, but leadership is perhaps the most important variable. For years, behavioral scientists and managers have searched for the formula for successful leadership. There have been trait, behavioral, situational, and path-goal approaches applied to the leadership puzzle. Each approach has an empirical base and group of advocates espousing the features and success of a theory or model. Undoubtedly, these preachings have led to some confusion in terminology, findings, and verification for the manager. Despite these problems, leadership serves as the link among individuals, groups, and the organization.

Motivation

The quality of an individual's performance involves his or her motivation. As shown in exhibit 2–2, motivation is influenced by the organization, the leader, the group, the reward system, the degree of change and development, and of course the individual's attitudes, skills, and effort expended. The state of motivation is described differently in various theories, some of which emphasize needs, expectancies, or perceived equity. It is our belief that there is no all-encompassing model of motivation that managers need to learn in order to encourage better job performance. Instead, the manager needs to understand the various motivation models and, more importantly, must consider the interaction of the variables that affect motivation.

Reward Systems

The motivation of employees is related to the organization's reward system. The distinction between intrinsic and extrinsic rewards is still somewhat controversial, but it provides some insight into the importance of rewarding individuals. *Intrinsic rewards* are rewards that satisfy higher order needs and are administered by the individual to himself or herself. *Extrinsic rewards* are administered by an external person, such as the individual's manager. Pay would be considered an extrinsic reward, and task accomplishment satisfaction would be viewed as an intrinsic reward.

Organizational Change and Development

Organizations and their members eventually need to change and develop or suffer the consequences of stagnation. The ultimate result of stagnation is an inability to survive in the environment. It is suggested later in the book that planned change and development is more effective than no planning or haphazard attempts at adaptation. The manager must be able to diagnose the individual's, group's, environment's, and organization's macro and micro domains in order to adapt properly. There are numerous strategies and techniques available that can be applied once a thorough diagnosis is performed. Among them are management by objectives (MBO) or goal setting, T-groups, team building, managerial grid, and life and career planning. A careful diagnosis is needed so that the problem-strategy-technique match is the best for the particular time and situation.

Performance

The performance factor is shown as the dependent or predicted measure in our framework. It serves as the vehicle for judging the effectiveness of individuals, groups, and organizations. At each of these levels, there are numerous criteria to evaluate effectiveness. There is definitely no single measure that can depict performance success at these three levels. Thus, we show a sample of the criteria used to assess performance—such as productivity, morale, absenteeism, goal achievement, and personal adjustment. Each of the criteria has a number of attributes, such as the time period covered, specificity, and ease of evaluation. For example, absenteeism can be judged daily, but growth assessments may cover a longer period of time. Absenteeism is specific, and growth is rather abstract and ill-defined. Thus, absenteeism can be measured fairly easily, but growth, because of its abstractness, may be difficult to evaluate.

The core notion in this book is *performance*. It is this variable that is the key to evaluating the effectiveness of individuals, groups, organizations, and leaders.

When performance is satisfactory, the organization is judged to be successful. Thus, all the variables in our framework are linked to the performance segment of the model. This is what applied organizational behavior is, from a managerial perspective.

Performance Appraisal

Performance appraisal is the more accepted term for criterion measurement. It is used to pinpoint strengths and weaknesses of individuals, groups, and organizations. In addition, performance appraisals serve as information sources for reward and punishment, change and development, structural modification, and job-design interventions. This type of invaluable information is important for planning, organizing, controlling, and directing work performed by the manager. Like most topics covered in our framework, there is no one best performance appraisal system. Some are better than others for a particular individual, group, or organization.

The theme of our model is that managing organizational behavior is a challenging task. It requires a broad knowledge of individual, group, and organizational properties. The reason this knowledge is required is that performance is the ultimate goal of organizations. It is more difficult to achieve adequate performance if knowledge is suppressed, not tapped, or misinterpreted. Therefore, the manager must know how to study or observe the properties shown in exhibit 2–2. That is, the manager must be a diagnostician. The behavioral scientist recommends the incorporation of the scientific approach in the study of the dimensions represented in the world. To rely solely on experience or common sense is assumed by the behavioral scientist to be inviting disaster. The behavioral scientist's style of studying organizational behavior dimensions emphasizes the importance of science, research design, and data collection. This style basically places a premium on what we call scientific diagnosis.

The Scientific Approach as a Process

The scientific approach to studying organizational behavior and performance can be considered a systematized form of inquiry. Interest in human beings dates back virtually to the dawn of the species. Descriptions and analyses of human behavior in organizations such as the military, the church, and government pervade our earliest writings on management and administration. Despite this pervasive interest, it is only in very recent history, the past eighty years, that we begin to find significant efforts to study behavior systematically, empirically, and by use of a specific process referred to as the scientific approach. The study of behavior therefore may be said to have a long past for a relatively short history.[9]

The scientific approach as a process involves a number of steps. These are shown in exhibit 2–3. The researcher usually proceeds through the six steps shown in the exhibit to study organizational behavior. This systematic flow of events distinguishes once again the scientific approach from the practitioner approach. The researchers,

Exhibit 2–3 Steps in the Research Process

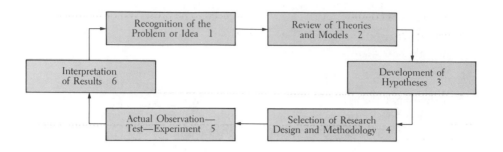

after completing the process and using a theoretical and/or empirical data base, develop a statement or explanation about some organizational phenomenon, such as job design, group process, leadership, or personnel development.

The Researcher-Manager Bridge

After each of the six scientific approach steps is completed and when the experimental test has been conducted, the researcher attempts to explain the findings. The researcher must communicate in comprehensible language the theories, models, and hypotheses supported by the findings. The word *comprehensible* must not be underestimated because the application of research findings in banks, hospitals, foundries, food-processing plants, or any organizational setting depends upon the practicing manager's ability to understand the explanation. If organizational researchers are to have an impact on managerial practices, they must offer managers a set of clear explanations for each study that is applicable to work settings.

Some researchers assume that it is the manager's responsibility to work hard at interpreting and applying research findings. We disagree with this thinking for a number of reasons. First, if behavioral scientists are to continue performing research in actual organizations, they must provide managers with something of value. The more lucid the explanation about a research study, the higher the probability that something of value will be discovered by the manager. Second, the behavioral scientist is trained to communicate findings; the manager is trained to operate the organization. Third, the bulk of the behavioral scientist's workday revolves around the particular research he or she is currently conducting. Managers, on the other hand, are only able to scan over research projects because other duties, such as motivating, evaluating, planning, and goal setting, consume most of their workday. Finally, behavioral scientists are devoted to the practice of increasing knowledge. A fundamental characteristic of this worthy pursuit is the requirement to communicate findings and provide explanations to fellow researchers, future researchers, and society in general. These requirements can be accomplished only through the effective explanation of what the scientist believes he or she has found in the data.

Again, we emphasize that the manager is concerned with applying worthwhile knowledge. The emphasis upon doing something to enhance performance has important implications for pointing out the distinction between behavioral scientists and managers. The manager is concerned with:

1. The present conditions that exist and that need to be preserved or modified.

2. The clarity of the mission, goals, and objectives and how the present conditions fit with these factors.

3. Whether change is needed and when it should be implemented.

4. Whether changes that are implemented achieve the goals set for them.

Both the behavioral scientist and manager agree that the present conditions need to be described accurately. The manager requires this for action; the scientist needs this information to create theories and models. Beyond this common interest, their interests diverge. The behavioral scientist wants to test and improve models, and the manager wants to improve performance. When the theory or model meets the test of application, we have the highest level of fruitful interaction between behavioral scientists and managers. It is this level of interaction that is a challenge for those who consider themselves applied organizational behavioralists.

Taxonomy of Organizational Research Strategies

Results of organizational research using the scientific approach just discussed are being supplied at an increasing rate through journals, monographs, internal documents, survey summaries, and professional conferences. These results vary with respect to methodology, measurement, range of application, and degree of control exercised on variables. A useful taxonomy that helps organize the various research factors and outlines the critical dimensions of research is illustrated in exhibit 2–4.

Breadth of Application

Pure research is done primarily for the sake of advancing knowledge. The behavioral scientist is concerned with understanding some phenomenon and is not particularly concerned with whether it can be used in practice.

Applied research has potential value in practice because it is concerned with explaining observations and using the findings to improve a situation. Performing usable research in organizational settings is an example.

Service research is the type that emerges when a behavioral scientist is hired as a consultant by a manager to study a problem. The practitioner has supposedly diagnosed the problem and, for a fee, engages a researcher to scientifically investigate this problem.

Action research involves the research investigation of a situation, identification of problems, and the introduction of strategies that will result in the minimization or elimination of the problems. The emphasis of this type of research is on change. The change may occur in structure, people, technology, or the environment, or some

Exhibit 2–4   Taxonomy of Potential Organizational Research Strategies

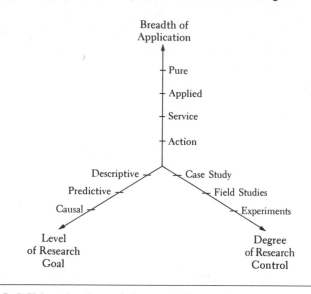

Adapted from G. C. Helmstadter, *Research Concepts in Human Behavior* (New York: Appleton-Century-Crofts, 1970), p. 28.

combination of these factors. The researcher is expected to bring about effective change that will be documented and displayed to managers.

Each of these research applications is worthwhile and needed to advance our knowledge of organizational behavior. The judgment as to which application is most suitable for a particular situation rests largely with the researchers and managers involved. They have goals that they want to accomplish, and these serve as bench marks for choosing a particular application from among the four possibilities.

Level of Research Goal

The level of research goal depends on what the expected result of the research is. If a researcher is interested in describing how people interact within a leaderless problem-solving group, the goal is *descriptive*. The span of control model developed by Graicunas is a well-known example of a descriptive measure of a structural feature.[10] It does little more than describe the potential number of interactions a manager will have with various spans of control.

Another goal of research, which is given a high priority by practicing managers, is referred to as *predictive*. The manager is interested in predicting individual behaviors, performance, and overall organizational goal accomplishments. If managers could find techniques, such as tests or performance appraisal interviews, that predict accurately the eventual performance of an employee, they could perform their jobs more easily. There are no tests or performance appraisal interviews that result in perfect predictions, but the predictive goal is still sought after and is important in organizational research.

In some situations, managers and researchers are not concerned about description or prediction but want to understand the direction of the relationship between variables. This type of research goal is referred to as *causal*. For example, one such area involves the notions of satisfaction and performance presented earlier. Three possible directional relationships for these two variables are proposed by various theorists, researchers, and practicing managers. These are:

1. Performance $\longrightarrow$ Satisfaction

2. Satisfaction $\longrightarrow$ Performance

3. Performance $\longleftrightarrow$ Satisfaction

Sophisticated statistical procedures and methodologies are used to determine directional relationships. To date, the causality between these two variables has resulted in some interesting yet contradictory results.[11]

Degree of Research Control ie., Research strategies

The type of research strategy selected influences the degree of *control* exercised when studying human behavior in organizations. *Case-study* research involves the use of data or information over which the researcher has no control. The experiment or situation has already occurred (i.e., the research is done ex post facto), so in this case the role of the researcher is to describe what happened during the occurrence. In *field* studies, the researcher has some control over the selection of subjects (people) being studied, the methodology being used (e.g., questionnaires, observations, interviews), the hypothesis being tested, and the length of time in which the study is conducted. The researcher generally has little or no control over the actual behavior of the subjects. Finally, *experiments* allow the researcher to control more closely some of the crucial variables under study. Experiments can occur in laboratory or actual field settings. For example, in a study of motivation the researcher may want to carefully examine how age is linked to this variable. Thus, four age groups of employees could be studied: (1) twenty–thirty year olds; (2) thirty-one–forty year olds; (3) forty-one–fifty year olds; and (4) fifty-one–sixty year olds. Currently, there is increased interest in studying female executives, their attitudes about their jobs, their positions in organizations, and their career growth. If a researcher wanted only to examine female attitudes in an experiment, the sex variable would be controlled.

Additional Factors to Consider in Selecting a Strategy

In selecting one of the four main behavioral research strategies—case study, field study, laboratory experiment, or field experiment—the researcher should be familiar with the similarities and differences of the strategies. The researcher must usually select the one strategy that will do the best job in attaining his or her research objectives. The strategies differ, of course, on such issues as:

1. The kinds of information or data they provide.

2. How "pure" or "unconfounded" the information is—that is, how confident the researcher can be about inferences made about the findings.

3. The degree to which the study results can be generalized beyond the specific research setting.

4. The amount of time and resources required to perform the research.

Instead of scientifically considering these and other similar issues, many researchers often select a favorite strategy, become comfortable with it, and use it in spite of its weaknesses. Prior habits, experiences, and prejudices, unfortunately play a significant role in the researcher's choice of strategy in some cases.

In order to evaluate the strengths and weaknesses of the four main strategies, the researcher should consider four factors in addition to the criterion of research control. These additional criteria are (1) manipulation; (2) realism; (3) scope; and (4) precision (see exhibit 2–5).

Manipulation.   Control and manipulation are similar in that they both deal with the power of the researcher over the variables under study. The former generally concerns shielding the research from unwanted external factors; manipulation deals with the ability of the researcher to actually alter the value of a variable in anticipation of a change in a second variable. A manager may feel that employee morale can be improved by updating the interpersonal skills of the supervisors. In order to test this assumption, one-half the supervisors are given a supervisory training program; the rest are not. Measures of employee morale are taken before and after the training program for both groups. The variable being manipulated is the attendance at the training program. Field and laboratory experiments are rated high on the manipulation criterion because the researcher can set them up scientifically.

Realism.   Realism is a major strength of case studies, field experiments, and field

Exhibit 2–5 Factors to Consider in Selecting a Research Strategy

Strategy	Control	Manipulation	Realism	Scope	Precision
Case Study	Low	Low	High	Moderate	Low
Field Study	Moderate	Low	High	High	Moderate
Laboratory Experiment	High	High	Low	Low	High
Field Experiment	High	High	High	Low	Moderate–High

Note: This evaluation rates strategies as *low, moderate,* or *high* on each factor.

studies because the researcher has some confidence that the behavior of the subjects is natural and representative of actual, ongoing human behavior. Taking subjects out of real-life situations and placing them in a laboratory, thereby reducing realism, is a weakness of the laboratory experiment strategy.

Scope.   Scope refers to the breadth of the study—namely, the number of variables and their relationships. This is a strength of field studies that primarily use questionnaires because multiple variables can be measured by this instrumentation. The researcher, for example, can study job satisfaction, leader behavior, job characteristics, and organizational policies with a simple questionnaire. This researcher should be aware that the longer the questionnaire, the greater the fatigue of the subject, possibly resulting in biased or invalid responses. By their nature, lab and field experiments are narrow in scope because the researcher is generally interested in the relationships between a limited number of variables.

Precision.   Research in the laboratory is usually more precise than the typical questionnaire-type field study. The use of multiple measures, such as observation by a panel of judges or recording the experiment on video tape for later playback, under controlled conditions permits the researcher to obtain more accurate information. For this reason, many researchers involved in field studies are beginning to use questionnaires coupled with interviews and/or observations to improve the precision of the measurement of their variables.

A More Basic Consideration in Selecting a Strategy

Field experiments and laboratory experiments emphasize the manipulation of variables, but field studies rarely involve this type of treatment. The reason for this distinction is more clearly understood when we classify treatment approaches as ﹥classified correlational or experimental. In *correlational studies*, researchers and managers do not typically infer causality between variables. The correlational approach is used to describe studies of organizational properties that are assumed to vary directly or inversely. In a field study, the researcher may attempt to discover the relationship between group cohesiveness and anxiety. Findings may show that an inverse relationship between these variables exists. That is, groups with high cohesiveness may have low anxiety; or it is just as plausible that low anxiety caused high cohesiveness.

On the other hand, *experimental approaches* rely on manipulation. Suppose you believe that goal-setting training can influence both the performance and satisfaction of a trained manager's subordinates. An organization agrees to allow you to train one group of randomly selected managers in a participation goal-setting approach and one group in an assigned goal-setting approach. The managers are geographically separated, and there are enough to randomly select thirty managers for each training program.

The training program in the experimental approach is considered the independent variable. The researcher is suggesting that the variable caused the changes in the dependent variables, performance and satisfaction. In a scientific approach using the experimental method, the hypotheses could be stated in a null format or an experimental format. The null format for our example would be:

> There will be no differences in performance or satisfaction between the two groups of subordinates with managers trained in participation goal setting and managers trained in assigned goal setting.

The experimental format of a hypothesis might be the following:

> The subordinates of managers trained in participation goal setting will have higher levels of performance and job satisfaction than will the other group supervised by managers trained in assigned goal setting.

The hypotheses, no matter how they are stated, are tested by the researcher. The differences found, if any, in the dependent variables are analyzed by the researcher. The conclusions reached, the degree of confidence associated with the findings and the hypothesis testing, and the use of the findings depend largely on the research design used to examine the properties.

Before the training program begins, the performance and job satisfaction of the subordinates of the participants are measured. If there are differences, they can be standardized by statistical techniques. Assume that little initial difference in the performance and satisfaction factors or in various characteristics of the participants is found. In this field experiment, the groups are said to be well matched. The major differences between the groups involve the manipulated variable, the training program.

The participants, after completing the training, return to their jobs. The performance and satisfaction of the subordinates are measured at various times after the training. Differences discovered in these could be attributed to the training program utilized. The researcher might suggest that the differences in the training programs caused the discovered differences in subordinate performance and satisfaction.

Applications and Implications for the Manager

The Study of Organizational Behavior

1. Four "ways" of establishing beliefs about phenomena are tenacity, authority, intuition, and science. Because science involves the pursuit of objective knowledge, it intimately entwines with the concept of organizational behavior.

2. Science is viewed as a method involving observation, induction, deduction, and verification.

3. Theories are the foundation for attempting to organize our thinking about the variables that are important in understanding organizational behavior. In reality, a theory is an attempt to model some aspect of the real world.

4. Theories are not only used in building conceptual models of behavior and

performance, but they are also used to improve prediction, understanding, and the diagnosis of organizational behavior properties.

5. A theoretical model is a vehicle for examining the linkage between variables. Our model shows the linkage between environment, individuals, groups, leadership, the organization, motivation, reward systems, organizational change and development, performance appraisal, and performance.

6. The behavioral science researcher is trained to acquire knowledge about organizational behavior by relying on scientific principles of inquiry. It is the role of the researcher to describe rather than prescribe to a manager.

7. Managers as problem-solvers need scientifically based information as well as common sense and experience to cope with the complex mix of variables that exist within an organization.

8. The difference in orientation of the behavioral science researcher and manager requires open and clear communication between them. The field of organizational behavior cannot develop further unless the dialogue and understanding between the behavioral scientist and manager improve. It is our contention that the behavioral scientist needs to begin the steps needed to make these improvements.

9. Research on organizational behavior phenomena can be descriptive, predictive, or causal. Each of these are goals of research.

10. The focus of scientific research in this book will be on field and laboratory research strategies. Field studies and experiments are conducted in ongoing organizations. Studies dealing with settings created to study some behavioral property are classified as laboratory experiments.

11. The various research strategies have inherent strengths and weaknesses. The factors to consider in selecting a particular strategy include control, manipulation, realism, scope, and precision.

12. The study of organizational behavioral properties shown in exhibit 2–2 is a continuous process. It is not a one-shot effort that can be stopped after some problem is resolved. Consequently, using various strategies, designs, and models generates important knowledge about human behavior that managers need to filter and interpret before applying this knowledge to individual, group, and organizationally based problems.

Review of Theories, Research, and Application

1. If job performance criteria are unclear to employees, what problems could result?

2. Select from the list below one job and attempt to develop performance criteria that take into consideration preciseness, time, and evaluation factors.
   a. Police officer
   b. Major league baseball manager
   c. Neurosurgeon
   d. Computer programmer

3. What are some dangers a contemporary manager in a dynamic industry would face by relying solely on "common sense and experience" in attempting to improve subordinate performance?

4. Discuss how hypotheses are related to theory.

5. Who (manager or researcher) is responsible for explaining the results of a field experiment? Why?

6. Why are managers often concerned about the disruptions created by performing field studies?

7. What are the advantages of performing a laboratory experiment versus a field experiment?

8. It is our assumption that the dialogue between researchers and practicing managers must be improved if knowledge about behavior within organizations is to scientifically mature. Do you agree with this philosophical position? Why?

Notes

1. McCohen and E. Nagel, *An Introduction to Logic and Scientific Method* (New York: Harcourt, Brace, 1934).

2. Eugene F. Stone, *Research Methods in Organizational Behavior* (Santa Monica, Calif.: Goodyear, 1978), p. 6.

3. John M. Neale and Robert M. Liebert, *Science and Behavior* (Englewood Cliffs, N.J.: Prentice-Hall, 1973), p. 2.

4. Fred N. Kerlinger, *Foundations of Behavioral Research* (New York: Holt, Rinehart & Winston, 1973), p. 7.

5. Robert Braithwaite, *Scientific Explanation* (Cambridge: Cambridge University Press, 1955), p. 1.

6. Stone, *Research Methods*, p. 8.

7. Robert Dubin, *Theory Building* (New York: Free Press, 1969), p. 24.

8. Fritz J. Roethlisberger and W. J. Dickson, *Management and the Worker* (Boston: Harvard Business School, Division of Research, 1939).

9. E. G. Boring, *A History of Experimental Psychology* (New York: Appleton-Century-Crofts, 1950), p. 8.

10. A. V. Graicunas, "Relationships in Organizations," in *Papers on the Science of Administration,* ed. Luther Gulick and Lyndall F. Urwick (New York: Columbia University, 1947), pp. 183–87.

11. For a more detailed discussion of directional relationships, see Charles N. Green, "The Satisfaction-Performance Controversy: New Developments and Their Implications," *Business Horizons,* October 1972, pp. 31–41.

Additional References

ATKINSON, J. W., and CARTWRIGHT, D. "Some Neglected Variables in Contemporary Conceptions of Decision and Performance." *Psychological Reports,* 1964, pp. 575–90.

BAILEY, K. E. *Methods of Social Research.* New York: Free Press, 1978.

BRANDT, R. M. *Studying Behavior in Natural Settings.* New York: Holt, Rinehart & Winston, 1972.

CHILD, J. "Managerial and Organizational Factors Associated with Company Performance, Part I. A Contingency Analysis." *Journal of Management Studies,* 1974, pp. 175–89.

DUBIN, R. "Theory Building in Applied Areas." In *Handbook of Industrial and Organizational Psychology,* edited by M. D. Dunnette, pp. 17–39. Chicago: Rand McNally, 1976.

DUNNETTE, M. D. *Personnel Selection and Placement.* Belmont, Calif.: Wadsworth, 1966.

GHORPADE, J. "Study of Organizational Effectiveness: Two Prevailing Viewpoints." *Pacific Sociological Review,* 1970, pp. 21–40.

GOODMAN, P. S.; PENNINGS, J. M.; and Associates. *New Perspectives on Organizational Effectiveness.* San Francisco: Jossey-Bass, 1977.

LIEBERMAN, S., and O'CONNOR, J. F. "Leadership and Organizational Performance: A Study of Large Organizations." *American Sociological Review,* 1972, pp. 117–30.

MAHONEY, R., and FROST, P. "The Role of Technology in Models of Organizational Effectiveness." *Organizational Behavior and Human Performance,* 1974, pp. 127–38.

MINER, J. *The Challenge of Managing.* Philadelphia: Saunders, 1975.

MOTT, P. E. *The Characteristics of Effectiveness.* New York: Harper & Row, 1972.

PRICE, J. L. "The Study of Organizational Effectiveness." *Sociological Quarterly,* 1972, pp. 3–15.

RIDGWAY, V. F. "Dysfunctional Consequences of Performance Measurements." *Administrative Science Quarterly,* 1955, pp. 240–47.

RUNKEL, P. J., and MCGRATH, J. E. *Research on Human Behavior.* New York: Holt, Rinehart & Winston, 1972.

STEERS, R. M. *Organizational Effectiveness: A Behavioral View.* Santa Monica, Calif.: Goodyear, 1977.

SUTTERMEISTER, R. A. *People and Productivity.* 3rd ed. New York: McGraw-Hill, 1976.

A Case of Performance

The Rose Gust Dilemma

Rose Gust, an attractive twenty-nine year old, was the first woman sales trainee hired by Mosby Electronics of Denver, Colorado. Rose was interviewed in Philadelphia, where she worked as a claims adjuster for a large insurance company. She grew tired, after five years, with the work of an adjuster and wanted to move into a sales position. A reference check with her supervisor in the insurance company revealed that she had been doing an excellent job. Thus, Mosby recruiters, after interviewing her and talking to her present employer, invited her to visit the company headquarters, and she accepted. Three days after her visit, she was given a competitive salary offer, which she accepted ten days later.

Mosby requires all sales trainees to attend a four-week product-familiarization and sales-technique training program. This is followed by the trainee being assigned a small sales territory for one year under the close tutelage of a sales-development manager.

The trainer and development director both felt that Rose was learning her job well and displayed high potential for a more responsible job after a minimum of field experience. The director, Ted Rogers, was so excited by Rose's progress six months after the training that he recommended that she be given the normal-size territory nine months before the scheduled time. A new territory in central Tennessee had recently become available due to the retirement of a sixty-two-year-old salesperson. The territory had been a major producer of sales revenues in the central sales region for the past eight years.

Rose received the promotion and took over her new assignment. After six months on the job, her immediate supervisor, Ray Cantrell, began to seriously question Rose's ability, motivation, training, and experience to adequately perform the job. She had not met sales quantity, new-order generation, or cost goals since she started the job. Ray talked with her four times in the past month to try to find some answer to the problem.

Ray then assigned an assistant to make calls with Rose and observe her techniques of selling first hand. Jim Stram, the assistant, after making thirty calls with Rose over a two-week period, reported back to Ray. Jim concluded that Rose was not well trained and became emotionally flustered when she had to handle technical questions about Mosby products. Because of the press of business, Ray did not have time to talk to Rose for three months. During the three months, her sales performance continued to deteriorate, and customer complaints on her tardiness in making calls, inability to answer questions, arrogance, and poor attitude had increased at an alarming rate.

Ray visited with Rose and discussed what he believed were performance problems. She became very upset about his assessment that her performance was below par and was angered to find out that Jim Stram had reported back to Ray. Rose believed that Jim was sent to counsel her and provide on-the-job training.

Case Primer Questions

1. What individual variables are extremely important in analyzing this case?

2. What environmental factors must be considered in reaching a solution to this case?

3. If you were Ray, what would you do to improve Rose's performance?

4. Do you believe that a male salesperson would have been handled differently by the organization? Why? Should he be?

A Case of the Scientific
Study of Organizational Behavior

The Baily-Jenkins Clinic

The Bailey-Jenkins Diagnostic Clinic is a specialized outpatient health-care organization located in Columbus, Ohio. The clinic specializes in diagnostic and preventive-medicine care for citizens of the Central Ohio community. The typical patient is given a complete diagnostic examination by highly specialized staff physicians using the latest computerized analysis equipment. If the examination reveals a physical disorder, the patient is then transferred to one of the nearby hospitals. The facilities of the clinic are open to the general public; however, approximately 40 percent of the patients are from area organizations that have contracts with the clinic for periodic examinations of their employees.

The clinic, founded in 1970 by Drs. J. T. Bailey and L. H. Sims, employs twelve specialized physicians and over two hundred technical and support personnel. Of the technical and support staff, nearly 70 percent are women, and approximately 20 percent are part-time employees (usually students from the nearby university medical school who worked late afternoons and evenings after classes).

During the first quarter in 1977, the clinic's director, Mr. Steve Mann, instituted a new staff-scheduling system; he changed the existing five-day/forty-hour workweek to a four-day/forty-hour week. Mr. Mann became acquainted with this new "modified workweek" concept through his reading of the managerial literature, his contacts in various local and national personnel associations, and his observations of other organizations in the Columbus area. Mr. Mann strongly believed that the clinic should be innovative not only in its medical practice but also in its personnel policies.

The "4/40" scheduling system would apply only to full-time technical and support personnel. Participating employees would be given either Friday or Monday off so they would have a three-day weekend. Mr. Mann also indicated that the new system would be evaluated after a six-month trial period.

As the end of the six-month trial period approached, Mr. Mann appointed a five-person task force to evaluate the "4/40" workweek and report back to him within thirty days. Of those on the task force, it was known that the assistant clinic director was positive toward the program, and the nursing and pathology supervisors were openly negative toward it. The opinions of the remaining two members were not known.

The task force completed its charge and submitted the final report to Mr. Mann. The report recommended that: (1) the new "4/40" personnel scheduling system not be continued; and (2) a return to the previous "5/40" workweek be instituted immediately. Excerpts of the report are as follows:

Report of the Personnel-Scheduling Task Force,
September 10, 1977

Recommendation

The task force appointed to evaluate the new four-day/forty-hour workweek recommends that the new scheduling program be terminated with a return to the previous five-day/forty-hour workweek. The task force believes that the disadvantages far outweigh the advantages of the new scheduling system.

Process

A two-step evaluation process, which included a survey questionnaire and informal interviews, was used.

1. A survey questionnaire was developed and sent to all full-time staff employees for completion. The employees were instructed to complete the survey while at work and to deposit it at Personnel Office on their way home. The results of the survey are attached [see exhibit 2–6]. The data show that: (1) less than 30 percent of the sampled employees favor continuation of the new program; and (2) the severity ratings of problems were higher than were the advantage ratings of the positive features.

Exhibit 2–6 Personnel-Scheduling Survey

Name: _____

Department: _____

1. Do you favor continuing the new "4/40" workweek?

   _*12*_ Yes   _*31*_ No

2. *Scheduling Problems:*
   On a scale from 1 (no real problem) to 5 (very severe problem), please *rate* the *severity* of the potential problems listed below for the new "4/40" system:

Problem	Rating	
1. Fatigue from longer work day	*3.72*	
2. Disruptions in personnel scheduling	*4.58*	
3. Increases in workload	*4.14*	Average Values
4. Increased communications problems	*3.90*	
5. Family problems due to later arrivals at home	*3.87*	

3. *Scheduling Advantages:*
   On a scale from 1 (no real advantage) to 5 (a significant positive feature), please *rate* the *advantages* of the new "4/40" system over the previous "5/40" system as noted below:

Potential Advantage	Rating	
1. Improved morale of employees	*2.81*	
2. Decreased absenteeism	*3.95*	
3. Increased leisure time	*4.11*	Average Values
4. Lower transportation costs	*4.15*	
5. Less wasted time	*2.70*	

2. Informal interviews were conducted with eighteen employees who did not participate in the survey. Of the eighteen employees, thirteen were not in favor of the new program. The most frequently mentioned problems concerned disruption at work and home. Decreased absenteeism and lower transportation costs were the most frequently mentioned positive features.

Case Primer Questions

1. What were the objectives in changing to the new "4/40" workweek?

2. Evaluate the work of the task force from a managerial perspective.

3. Evaluate the work of the task force as a field research study.

4. What should Mr. Mann do next?

A Performance Oriented Framework to Study Organizational Behavior

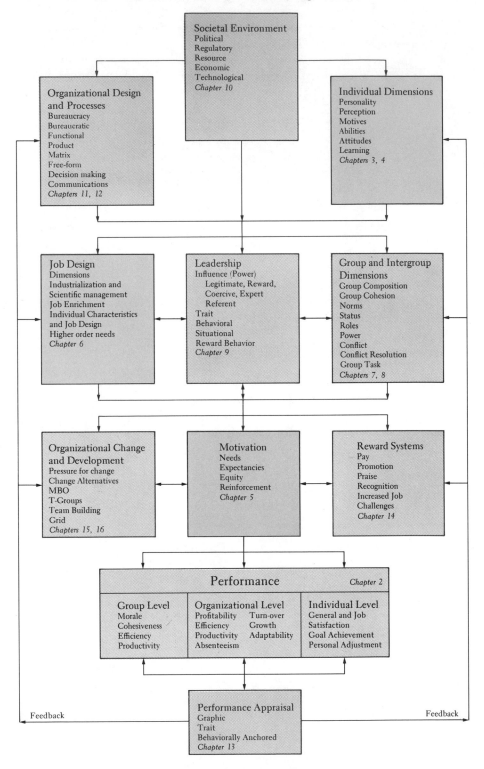

PART TWO

Individual Dimensions of Organizational Behavior

CHAPTER 3

Motives
and
Personality

A construction supervisor was planning the work to be carried out on three buildings his company had under construction. Specifically, he was concerned with the assignment of ten electricians to various tasks. The problem was not easy because of a number of important differences among the ten: differences in their job performances, in the kind of work demanded on each of the tasks, and in working conditions at each of the three building sites. One of the electricians, for example, was clearly the most careful worker, turning out wiring jobs that not only were safe but were of the highest technical quality. Another electrician was a very rapid worker and could be counted on to complete all tasks on schedule. A third electrician was an acceptable worker but could not get along with other people on the job. A fourth worker did an acceptable job, but was often absent from the job. To complicate matters, the supervisor had observed that each of the electrician's work output depended to a degree on the type of work he or she was doing and the conditions under which the job was to be done.

Confusing and complex decisions about people are not uncommon to practicing managers. Indeed, most managers face situations like that just described on a daily basis. The model we presented in chapter 2 (exhibit 2–2) reflects the fact that employees can vary a great deal in their performance within organizations. Individual variation in behavior and performance is a fact of life in organizations and one that practicing managers as well as students of organizational behavior attempt to explain and understand.

Performance is not the only characteristic on which people vary. Employees differ in absenteeism rates, sickness, length of time spent with the organization (tenure), their choice of workplaces, and their choice of careers. Unfortunately, there are no simple rules to follow in predicting, understanding, and dealing with these behavioral differences. The study of motives and motivation attempts to explain behavior. An important review of the topic of work motivation concluded, however, that many theories of work motivation have failed to result in useful rules for practicing managers to follow because the process of motivation itself is extremely complex.[1] Behind an employee's behavior lies a multitude of factors, each interacting with others to make a unique impact upon a given choice. The very act of studying this process may oversimplify our conception of motives and personality and thereby limit our understanding of it.

Any model of behavior and performance, therefore, must satisfy two competing demands. First, it must be sufficiently simple to allow us to organize facts about behavior and to make sense of what we observe. Second, the model must be complete enough to be an accurate predictor of effort, behavior, and performance in actual organizational settings. The model presented in chapter 2 is a schema that suggests that differences in performance are primarily a function of numerous variables—physical, mental, structural, environmental, and technological.

In chapters 3, 4, 5, and 6, we will be directing our attention to one source of influence on job performance—the individual employee. We will hold off consideration of factors beyond the individual (i.e., informal groups, leadership, the formal organization and its processes, reward systems, and the environment) until later in this book. In effect, we will be unable to discuss the impact of these larger factors on performance until we gain an understanding of individual employee behavior and performance.

These four chapters then, focus directly on the individual dimensions outlined in exhibit 2–2. These dimensions include the psychological factors of motives and personality (chapter 3), the psychological processes of learning and perception (chapter 4), the psychological process of motivation (chapter 5), and job design (chapter 6).   =>providing micro perspective of behavior of individual employee

These chapters will be a foundation for the rest of the topics presented in this book. We have taken the position that an understanding of group behavior, organizational structure, and organizational processes depends upon a thorough knowledge of individual dimensions of behavior and performance. The terms *micro* and *macro* are useful in placing the topics of individual behavior, organizational behavior, and performance into perspective. The micro perspective of chapters 3, 4, 5, and 6 focuses upon the behavior of the individual employee in an organization and addresses itself to decisions and choices people make about themselves, others, and employing organizations. A macro perspective focuses on informal groups and formal organizations that constitute a work environment in which individual behavior and performance occurs. A macro approach directs the investigator's attention to the processes and structures under which decisions are made by informal groups and formal organizations. When individuals and organizations interact with each other, the result can be described as performance. *Performance, then, is an outcome that occurs as a function of individual organizational behavior*. There is no need, however, to draw a sharp distinction between micro and macro approaches to understanding organizational behavior and performance; they are complementary perspectives on the same set of issues. However, the distinction is useful for presenting two facets of the same topic.

A Model of Individual Performance

Exhibit 3–1 presents a model of individual behavioral influences on performance. Ultimately, the manager is concerned with an employee's performance (e.g., the number of patients attended to by a nurse or the quality of a pipe fitting by a plumber). Exhibit 3–1 indicates that performance is a function of an employee's

Exhibit 3–1 Individual Behavioral Influences on Performance

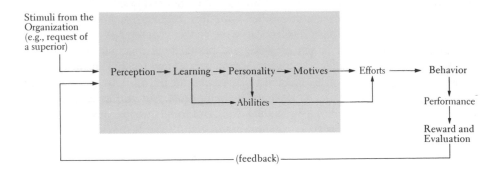

behavior and that behavior is jointly determined by an employee's level of effort and his or her abilities.

Most managers attempt to influence behavior and performance through some form of direction and guidance. Before an employee begins a new task, for example, a supervisor might request that the employee complete a trial set of tasks under observation. At the outset, he or she might give the employee some practice and instruction in the desired behavior on the job. In addition, after the tasks are completed the manager will probably review the completed work, suggest improvements where necessary, and reward the employee with a compliment for those tasks successfully completed. The instructions and initial training are stimuli from the organization that precede the individual's effort, behavior, and performance (as illustrated in exhibit 3–1). Another set of stimuli follow the performance and have a feedback effect on subsequent effort, behavior, and performance in similar circumstances (also as illustrated in the exhibit). Thus, exhibit 3–1 shows that individual effort, behavior, and performance occurs in response to environmental stimuli or events.

What is important in this chapter and in chapter 4, however, are those factors within the individual that *intervene* between environmental events and observable behavior. Behavior is external to the individual, and, as such, is readily observed empirically. Similarly, environmental events (e.g., the manager's order) are external and can be empirically observed. As shown in exhibit 3–1, there are five internal, psychological factors that intervene between observable events and observable behavior: (1) perception; (2) learning; (3) personality; (4) motives; and (5) abilities.

Personality helps to explain why specific behavior occurs. It deals with the content of behavior and affords a rather static view of the individual. Most behavioral scientists recognize two major aspects or parts of personality: (1) motives, which instigate and direct behavior; and (2) abilities, which give the person the necessary capacities to successfully act. Motives and abilities are both necessary for an act to occur. Perception and learning, in contrast, afford a dynamic or process view of behavior and explain how behavior changes or remains constant over time as employees grow and change in organizations.

The topics of perception, learning, personality, motives, and abilities are extremely difficult to separate and treat individually. Indeed, the factors are closely linked, as illustrated in exhibit 3–1, and share the following characteristics:

All five influence behavior and performance.

All five exist within what psychologists would call the human mind. As such, they are neither tangible nor amenable to direct observation. Managers can make only guesses about these factors. Some behavioral scientists have expressed their frustration about being required to make guesses or inferences about the mind by referring to the shaded area of exhibit 3–1 as a "black box."

Perception and learning are dynamic processes that can lead to changes in personality, motives, and abilities.

Managers daily explain behavior by referring to the four behavioral processes of perception, learning, personality, and motives. To give a concrete example, suppose a manager attempts to boost a subordinate's job output by complimenting the employee continually. The manager does this because he or she believes the employee is the "type" of person who needs constant complimenting and hopes the employee will respond by increasing performance. Instead, the employee reacts negatively, lowers his or her performance, and complains about being hassled. The employee does so because he or she has learned from experience that a compliment will be the only reward for above-average performance and really does not desire mere compliments. Elements of all four behavioral processes are evident in this scenario. Perception enters in—the manager and employee read two different messages into the same compliment. Motives enter in—the compliment as a stimulus sparked a behavior unexpected by the manager. Learning enters in—the employee is basing current behavior on experience. Finally, personality is involved—the manager misread the type of need the employee sought to satisfy.

Motives and Behavior

We have just established that motives operate as intervening psychological factors that influence behavior in response to environmental events. Exhibit 3–2 is derived from exhibit 3–1 and amplifies the role of motives in the behavioral process.

Behavioral scientists have traditionally grouped motives into the two categories indicated in exhibit 3–2. The first group includes drives, urges, feelings, forces, instincts, needs, desires, wants, emotions, impulses, and striving. All these terms refer to something internal that impels or pushes the individual to action or into a certain behavior. The second group of motives, on the other hand, refers to factors or events in the individual's environment. An incentive, purpose, interest, or aspiration, for example, is expressed with reference to an event an individual hopes will occur as a result of his or her behavior. In a sense, these factors attract behavior.

In summary to this point, we can say that motives are internal factors that influence observable acts and behavior. In addition, motives may be physiological in

Exhibit 3–2 Motivational Determinants of Behavior

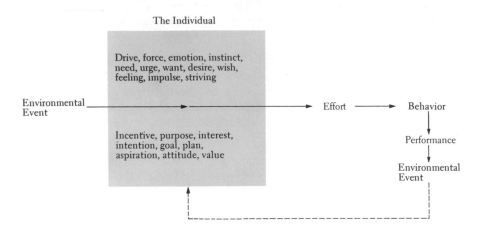

nature, such as a need for food, or psychological, such as desires, wishes, and aspirations. Finally, behavioral scientists distinguish between motive factors that emerge from within the individual and impel behavior, and those that involve individual concern with environmental events, which attract behavior.

The Role of Motives in Behavior

Before studying models of the process of motivation in chapter 5, it is important to understand the major questions these theories should answer about the role of motives in behavior. The explanation of a given act or series of acts is not as simple as the beginning of this section may have indicated. An employee may perform well, or be absent from work, or not get along well with others for a variety of reasons. Hunt has summarized seven fundamental influences motives have on behavior.[2] Any theory of motivation must address itself to the role of motives in each of these areas:

Motives serve to instigate as well as stop the actions of individuals.

Motives energize actions and control their vigor.

Motives determine those elements in the environment that attract the individual and those that repel.

Motives influence the choices a person makes among the alternative actions available.

Motives influence a person's choice of goals to pursue in a sequence of actions.

Motives influence changes in behavior over time and provide a basis for learning.

Motives cause a person to persist in using the same behavior or seeking the same goal when conditions have changed.

These seven areas of influence can be summarized by proposing four major roles of motives that must be examined in the study of behavior: (1) the role of motives in *instigating, maintaining,* and *stopping* a sequence of actions; (2) the role of motives in *evaluating* environmental events in terms of the individual's own goals; (3) the role of motives in determining *choice* and *direction* in behavior; and (4) the role of motives in *learning.* This last topic will be given a separate treatment in chapter 4.

Motive Process

At various times in the study of behavior, behavioral scientists have made different assumptions about the processes by which motives influence behavior. For a number of years, the process was thought of as simple and mechanical. Boulding, for example, characterized such formulations as assuming that behavior is generated by a process resembling a "clockwork."[3] According to this conception, an employee is like a machine that has been programmed to respond to its environment in predictable ways. This depicts the motive process as a simple reflex arc connecting an environmental event (such as an order from a supervisor) to a specific behavior (such as carrying out a work task).

According to this simple model, the environmental event leads to the arousal of a motive (perhaps a desire to please the supervisor), which in turn leads to an act (carrying out the work task). Upon completion of the task, an environmental event occurs (perhaps a reward of praise from the supervisor or payment of money) that satisfies or reduces the need originally motivating the behavior.

The simplistic conception of the motive process just presented, however, has a number of severe limitations. First, it presumes that the individual employee is a passive party in the process. All energy leading eventually to the behavior comes from outside the individual. Second, the individual has no say in interpreting events leading to behavior. He or she responds directly and mechanically to incoming stimuli. Third, all levels of need (that is, the experience of motives) are always uncomfortable to the individual. In other words, the employee is happiest when all needs have been satisfied and there are no environmental events instigating motives. Such a conception may be helpful in explaining the process of such elementary motives as sex, hunger, and pain but has been found lacking in explaining the way in which more complex motives influence behavior.

The notion of a simple reflex arc has largely been replaced by a more sophisticated and (hopefully) more realistic assumption about motive processes. The term *cybernetic* has been used to describe these more advanced models of motives. Cybernetic comes from the Greek term meaning something that steers itself or controls its own behavior. The need for cybernetic models arose with a number of empirical findings about behavior that conflicted with the reflex-arc notion:[4]

Deprivation from *all* incoming stimuli is aversive to people; individuals actually seek variety and stimulation from their environments.

Most motives are not aroused directly from signals from the individual's environment. The individual plays an active role in the process and compares incoming information to an internal standard. Discrepancy from that standard constitutes a motive and influences behavior.

The opportunity to seek change and variety in and of itself has been found to be rewarding to individuals.

The major implication of a cybernetic view of motives is that individuals actively respond to inputs from their environments by comparing such inputs to internal standards. A discrepancy between incoming information and the standard leads to a state of arousal that becomes a motive for subsequent adaptive behavior. This process is illustrated in exhibit 3–3. An employee, for example, will have certain expectations concerning the kind of work his or her supervisor expects. In effect, these expectations are internal standards. Work evaluations from the supervisor that vary a great deal from the employee's expectations will lead to a perceived discrepancy, and this discrepancy, in turn, will serve as a motive for the employee to change his or her behavior.

The notion that discrepancy between internal standards and incoming information can serve as motive for behavior is a major premise of the theory of *cognitive dissonance*.[5] According to this model, the nature of incoming stimuli from the environment is informational rather than energic. That is, individual employees are information processors who employ information standards when evaluating their interactions with work environments. *Cognitive dissonance* occurs when a person receives information that is unexpected or varies from internal standards. This discerned discrepancy in turn serves as a motive because it energizes and maintains behavior. Reduction of dissonance stops behavior and leads to the learning of actions that have resulted in dissonance reduction. Hence, dissonance reduction influences the direction and choice of behavior.

Behavioral research over the past fifteen years suggests that individuals react to a

Exhibit 3–3 Cybernetic Motive Process

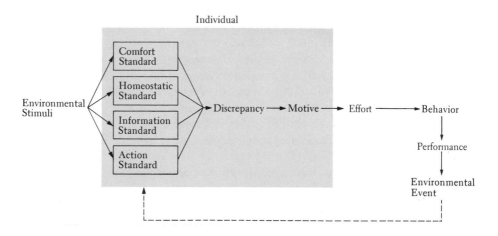

number of standards in their activities (including work behaviors). These standards can be summarized as follows:[6]

Introd Standards include

1. *Comfort standards* are physiological in nature and are based on the experience of pain or discomfort. Reaction to a blow on the head or a bee sting, for example, result in an automatic reaction to avoid the pain. All levels of discrepancy from this standard are aversive to the individual, and reaction to them is inborn and automatic.

2. *Homeostatic standards* are also automatic and physiological in nature. The need to satisfy hunger, for example, is a motive arising from a discrepancy from a homeostatic standard. Such standards serve to maintain balance in the various physiological processes of the body.

3. *Information standards* are fundamentally different from the two standards just described because they are cognitive. The individual makes a comparison between perceived information from the environment and consciously recognized expectations he or she has. Repeated experiences with people and objects on the job lead to a set of internal expectations about what to expect when interacting with them. Unexpected events with respect to people, objects, or places on the job cause dissonance and serve as a motive for behavior. A supervisor, for example, may take special care to seek out a subordinate and find out if there are any work or family problems troubling him. When asked what led her to suspect problems, she might note that after ten years of experience with this employee she has come to know the types of actions on his part that indicate that a problem exists. In other words, a discrepancy between what she expects to observe if everything is all right and what she actually observed served as a motive for her behavior.

4. *Action standards* are also informational in nature and are really a subtype of the standard just defined. Action standards are really values (moral and ethical) that employees have on the job. In other words, action standards involve expectations about the way things *should* be. Action standards often take the form of goals, intentions, plans, or moral values. For example, employees often compare their pay with others to determine if there is a fair or equitable distribution of rewards for actual work accomplished. The basis for the equity judgment is an action standard.

Informational and action standards are fundamentally different from comfort and homeostatic standards and deserve additional attention in our discussion of motives for at least several reasons. First, they are more important in understanding individual behavior in organizations because they provide the basis for the vast majority of employee motives. Second, they involve the perception of information rather than physical energy. Third, they do not assume that all levels of stimulation (discrepancy) are aversive to individuals. Fourth, they are not tied to basic physiological processes. Rather, they are learned over time through interaction with the environment. This is a critical point because it implies that the standard itself can be changed over time and can be adapted to different circumstances, which explains how employee attitudes towards management can change over time or lead to different reactions to the same management policies. Finally, the individual employee plays a very conscious and active role in the process of motivation under these two standards. In fact, the individual has some degree of personal control over the standards themselves.

Types of Motives

So far in our discussion of motives, we have concentrated on the role motives play in behavior and have examined the process by which motives are aroused. Social scientists have also studied the content of motives, namely, the specific needs or motives that are common among people in organizations. Behavioral scientists have developed many different and often confusing ways of classifying motives. Some have degenerated into extremely lengthy laundry lists of specific needs that extend to several hundred entries.

In order to avoid confusion, it is necessary to consider the motives of people in organizations at two levels of analysis. At a very general level, we can discuss basic types of motives (e.g., learned versus unlearned). In addition, we must also consider the specific kinds of motives that are typically found among people on their jobs.

Primary versus Secondary Motives

Several years ago, a large commercial jet aircraft with 150 passengers and crew crashed into a mountainside fifteen miles short of the runway, killing all on board. Subsequent investigation of the disaster found that absolutely nothing mechanical had malfunctioned. The accident was attributed to pilot error. Investigators pieced together the following scenario from the flight recorder: The approach was made during stormy weather and visibility was almost zero. The airport tower assigned the aircraft a glide path and advised an instrument landing. On-board computers can monitor altitude and direction and bring the plane to the edge of the landing strip. In this case, the pilot apparently did not trust the instruments and was convinced on the basis of his senses that the plane was much higher than the instruments indicated. He took manual control, reduced altitude, and crashed.

Those who train pilots often refer to the problem they experience of getting pilots to trust their instruments rather than relying on their own instincts. This illustrates a conflict between what behavioral scientists refer to as primary and secondary motives. A *primary motive* is one that is unlearned and is extremely resistant to change. All people, for example, are born with safety needs and do not have to learn to desire an escape from danger. In this instance, the pilot in question was responding to an almost instinctive need to avoid a crash by moving the aircraft to what he *believed* to be the proper altitude.

Secondary motives are not inborn but acquired over time through experience; secondary motives are learned. In this instance, the need to trust instruments is not inborn, but must be learned through experience with the aircraft. Similarly, most individuals are not born with a need for many of the rewards offered by organizations in our society, such as money, power, influence, or status. These motives are slowly acquired over time as people grow into adulthood and receive various educational experiences. In this particular incident, a primary motive (seeking safety through one's own senses) conflicted with a secondary need (trusting the instruments).

Instinctive versus Learned Behavior

Closely related to the distinction between primary and secondary motives is the distinction between instinctive (or unlearned) and learned behavior. A continuing controversy among behavioral scientists is the degree to which motives and subsequent work behavior are a function of unlearned factors (such as heredity and instinct) versus environmental experiences, which can shape and change motives and behavior.

There are those who argue that employees' motives and behavior patterns are primarily a function of inborn factors and thus relatively fixed and resistant to change throughout their lives. There are others who believe that the great majority of motives and behavior patterns are learned and can be changed throughout childhood and adulthood. An important corollary to this view is that motives and behavior are readily adapted and changed through interaction with one's environment over time.

A number of practical concerns rest on the resolution of this controversy. If we were to accept the instinct position, there would be little necessity for establishing institutions to change behavior. If criminal behavior patterns, for example, are primarily inborn, there would be little a prison could do to rehabilitate or change behavior. The same would be true for educational institutions set up to develop specific professional skills, such as those required in managerial or engineering occupations. If we accept the learning position, however, then prisons would be a primary method for rehabilitating prisoners, and educational institutions would be appropriate for training people to become managers and engineers.

Empirical research evidence has been presented in support of both sides of this issue. Studies conducted in the field of ethology (the study of instinctive behavior patterns) suggest that many complex activities are inborn and unfold naturally as the individual develops.[7] Popular extrapolations from this research have inferred that many patterns of work behavior are primarily instinctual. Thus, aggressive behavior among individuals or predispositions to acquire and protect possessions and territory cannot easily be changed within a single generation of people.

In contrast to the work of ethologists, the behaviorist position is that all behavior is learned through experience; that is, all people are born with identical potentials and what they become is a matter of environmental conditioning or training.[8] The reinforcement models to be presented in chapter 5 are very much influenced by the thinking of behaviorists. Perhaps the most dramatic and popular representation of behaviorist thinking is the work of B. F. Skinner.[9] According to him, all behavior patterns and actions are determined by reinforcement contingencies, that is, the way in which some actions are rewarded (or reinforced) and others are not. Behaviors that are rewarded will be acquired by the individual and repeated under similar circumstances. Actions that are not reinforced will not be repeated under similar circumstances in the future. Skinner's reinforcement model leads to a prescription for shaping and controlling an individual's behavior through systematically controlling the environment. Control of reward contingencies (e.g., designing and administering a pay incentive program) will lead to control over work behavior.

In reality, there are very few motives or behaviors that are either solely a function of instinct or solely a matter of learning. Rather, in most organizations managers are faced with a variety of motives and behaviors that are jointly influenced by a person's genetic inheritance and unique learning experience, as illustrated in exhibit 3−4.

Complex behavior in organizations, therefore, is seen as the result of an *interaction* between hereditary influences and environmental experiences. However, work habits do not result from simply adding hereditary and environmental factors together. Instead, an interaction model implies that at least some hereditary and some environmental factors are present in all motives and behaviors. Probably the best way to consider the interaction between heredity and environment as determinants of motives and behavior is to view heredity as providing the basic aptitudes that act as preconditions or potentials for a variety of specific behavioral patterns. The translation of these propensities into specific actions is the result of unique experiences a person has with the work environment.

Finally, the schema in exhibit 3−4 suggests that various motives and behaviors differ in the degree to which they are influenced by heredity and environment and therefore differ in how readily they can be changed and adapted to different circumstances. Intelligence, for example, is relatively fixed throughout adult life and remains fairly constant. Achievement needs or managerial skills, on the other hand, are far more fluid and can be changed through learning experiences.

Specific Work-Related Motives

So far, we have been considering types of motives in a very general fashion, considering the difference between learned and unlearned motives. On a much more specific level, we could consider the specific needs that employees seek to satisfy

Exhibit 3−4 Relative Flexibility of Common Motives and Behaviors

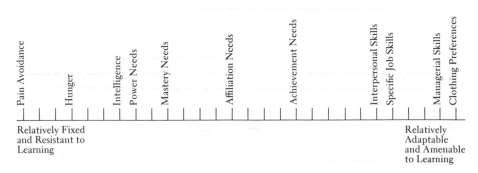

through their work. The list of specific work-related needs or motives that psychologists have identified is almost endless. Although we will consider a number of models or classification systems for work motives in chapter 5, several basic groups of needs have been consistently cited in organizational behavior research as important to employees on their jobs at various levels within organizations.[10]

Competence and Curiosity.   Earlier, we cited research in which subjects placed in a stimulus-free environment (nothing to touch, no sounds, odors, light, heat or cold, etc.) reacted very negatively. They found the experience to be extremely uncomfortable. Conversely, research on humans both in laboratory settings and within organizations leads to the conclusion that people find variety and challenge rewarding. This has led psychologists to propose that people have a basic need to become competent in interacting with their environments.[11] Thus, most employees experience a basic desire to have jobs that are not dull and repetitive. In addition, they strive to master the skills and techniques that are required by their jobs. This need is apparently strong enough that even on dull and repetitive jobs, people find ways to make the job more interesting.[12]

Achievement.   This is perhaps one of the most frequently investigated work-related motives. The scientists most closely connected with research on this motive are J. W. Atkinson and David C. McClelland. Atkinson defines the *motive* as a desire to accomplish objectives, and says its incentive value lies in the satisfaction a person experiences from accomplishment, a feeling of pride.[13] McClelland believes that the need for achievement varies among individuals and across cultures. A person's level of need for achievement can be measured, according to him, by examining what a person writes, says, or does. He has developed a technique known as the Thematic Apperception Test that presents the subject with an ambiguous picture. The individual's written description of what is going on in the picture is used to measure his or her level of need for achievement.[14]

High-need achievers tend to behave in characteristic fashion, according to McClelland's research. For example, they tend to avoid both high and low risk, preferring tasks that involve a moderate amount of risk. For example, they do not like gambling. In addition, high-need achievers like immediate feedback on how well they are accomplishing their tasks. They tend to gravitate, therefore, toward jobs that have clear task cycles and highly measurable and concrete results. They prefer to have money incentives associated with their work but value money as a symbol of accomplishment rather than for the things it can buy.

McClelland and his associates believe that need for achievement is learned, and where it is prevalent, business development will flourish. They have engaged in extensive training efforts in underdeveloped areas of the world, for example, to increase the need among entrepreneurs and workers because they argue that a major factor limiting economic development is a lack of need for achievement in the culture.

Affiliation.   A great deal of anecdotal evidence suggests that in addition to achievement motives people also experience a need for warmth and friendship in work relationships. In some cases, for example, industrial engineers have tried to improve work productivity by rearranging people and equipment more efficiently. Where opportunities for communication and interaction have been reduced by such arrangements, however, productivity has actually decreased. The development of friendships and mutual support among workers is almost a universal phenomenon in organizations and suggests that affiliation is a basic work-related need.

Equity.   In chapter 5, we will investigate a major motivation model called equity theory. The model's premise is the idea that employees share a need for a fair distribution of rewards within the organization. The notion is based upon Homan's concept of distributive justice,[15] which is that every employee should receive rewards from the organization that are proportionate to his or her contribution. Thus, an employee's need for equity would be violated if someone else were receiving a higher salary for exactly the same kind of work. Equity has been proposed as a major need motivating behavior within organizations.

A list of specific work-related motives could extend to many pages, but it is not our purpose to generate such a listing in this book. Rather, it is important for students of organizational behavior and practicing managers to develop an understanding of the processes by which a variety of motives influence individual behavior and performance.

Link between Motives and Learning

We have presented secondary motives as learned motives in this chapter. This raises the question of the relationships between motives (discussed here) and learning (to be presented in chapter 4). In a very real sense, motives and learning are two sides of the same coin and cannot, therefore, be easily separated into different discussions. The dependent variable of concern in both topics is behavior. Earlier, we defined *motives* as psychological factors that lead to specific forms of behavior within given work environments. Defined in this fashion, the examination of employees' motives takes a *static* look at behavior. In a sense, we try to explain a person's behavior at one point in time when we examine his or her motives. Learning, on the other hand, examines changes in behavior that occur over time as a result of an individual's experience on and off the job. The study of learning takes a *dynamic* view of behavior and is defined as the study of relatively permanent changes in behavior that occur as a result of experience or practice. A total view of employee behavior and performance must take both motives and learning into account.

Personality

So far, we have discussed how motives influence effort, behavior, and performance, and we have proposed that in addition to this process the manager should also consider the *specific kinds* of motives that lead to a specific act. In part, the study of personality is concerned with just this question: What motives influence behavior?

When a manager explains an employee's actions by noting that individual's specific motives, interests, abilities, skills, and so on, he or she is referring to the employee's personality.

Personality Defined

Whenever we type or classify a person according to a trait or set of traits, we are defining that individual's *personality*. In daily practice, managers use the concept of personality in predicting and explaining how their subordinates will react. For example, one might hear the following comments on subordinate performance from a manager: "Don't worry about Sam, he's the anxious type," or, "I know you're an aggressive type, so I'm assigning you to the sales force," or, "Don't read disapproval into her silence, she's just the silent type," or, "You can't expect much work out of Fred, he's just not the ambitious type." Indeed, many of the judgments we make about people (either in explaining or in predicting their behavior) are based upon beliefs we have concerning the *type* of person with whom we are dealing.[16]

Behavioral scientists use the term *personality* when they examine types of people. The hope is that once one has defined an individual's personality he or she will better be able to predict that person's behavior. Unfortunately, the term *personality* is very vague, and interpretation of the concept varies widely from person to person. In popular usage within organizations, the term *personality* often implies social or interpersonal skills. A leader "with personality" is attractive to colleagues and subordinates and is able to influence their thinking and actions. In other cases, "personality" refers to the impressions others in the organization have of an individual. Some may see that individual as lazy, but others may note that she or he is generous. Note that in all these usages one is trying to predict and/or explain behavior by classifying an employee into a single category of one or more human characteristics (anxious, silent, influential, lazy, generous). This is an extremely important point. The dependent variable of concern when one studies personality is behavior. When we type or classify a person, we are making an attempt to understand behavior.

Personality can be defined for our purposes as the combination of human characteristics or variables we employ to define or type an individual. If a manager defines a subordinate as "aggressive," for example, personality consists of only one variable. If the manager defines the subordinate as "aggressive and intelligent," personality consists of a combination of two characteristics. In practice, behavioral scientists have examined combinations of thousands of different characteristics in an attempt to define personality. In addition, they tend to agree that personality is relatively enduring. Personality, therefore, consists of human characteristics that are not quickly changed and lead to predictable patterns of behavior in the short run.

The number and variety of human characteristics that could be included in a definition of personality are limitless. Standard textbooks in the field of personality demonstrate that various theories of personality can be compared by contrasting the different variables or characteristics examined in them.[17] Some theories stress variables that are biological in nature, such as Freud's ideas concerning the id as a source of energy seeking release. Other theories have focused on social learning variables, such as the type and degree of various experiences that influence the development of personality. Still other theories cite a variety of emotions, aptitudes, skills, beliefs, values, and goals as all constituents of personality. It is not the purpose of this book to present a detailed survey of modern personality theory. Instead, the remainder of this chapter will focus on specific issues about personality that must be answered in understanding human behavior and performance in organizations and on two influential applications of personality theory to the study of organizational behavior.

Major Personality Issues

Personality has been defined as the combination of human characteristics that we would employ to type or classify a person. There still remains the question of the uses to be made of personality theories or models in the study and practice of management. Specifically, what questions about human behavior can be answered by a study of personality?

Byrne has provided a useful set of issues to define the substantive area of personality research:[18]

1. *Personality Development.* We have said earlier that employees vary widely in all personality characteristics. The concern in personality development is to understand how such differences come about. Research has demonstrated that, although a few personality characteristics are almost purely hereditary and some others are almost purely a matter of learning, most personality characteristics of concern in organizational behavior come about under the joint influence of these factors. At the very least, the following factors and experiences influence the development of individual personalities:

    (a) *Physiological determinants.* Hereditary endowment influences behavior through the provision of body type, musculature, nervous system, and other constitutional features. It is also believed that heredity plays a role in the determination of intelligence. In effect, physiological factors act as preconditions or potentials for a variety of different personality characteristics.

    (b) *Family and groups.* Substantial research evidence suggests that specific personality characteristics are influenced through social learning. In other words, early in life the values and beliefs of the parents have a direct influence on those developed in the child. Later, affiliative groups, that is, groups of people with whom we associate, influence our attitudes and values. In a very real sense, many aspects of adult personality are a function of learning within groups. This phenomenon can be observed on an everyday basis in organizations, when we see that a person in a given occupation, such as a medical doctor or airline pilot, demonstrates attitudes or styles that are unique to his or her profession.

    (c) *Culture.* In addition to having an overall influence on the family and other groups, cultures place demands and expectations on various occupations and organizations. These, in turn, influence the personalities of people in such jobs.

For example, American culture places certain broad expectations concerning behavior on the roles of ministers, judges, politicians, and entrepreneurs that have characteristic influences on the actions of such people. Ministers, for example, are expected to behave in a way that demonstrates strong value principles, empathy for other people, and selflessness in helping others.

2. *Personality Measurement.* A major concern of the organizational researcher as well as the practitioner is to accurately assess personality characteristics of employees and prospective job candidates. This can be done only by careful attention to dependent variables, such as behavior and performance, and the kinds of personality characteristics most likely to influence them. This area of concern also involves the development, pretesting, and use of reliable and valid measures of each characteristic.

In practice, many attempts have been made to measure personality. In some cases, paper-and-pencil measures have been developed to measure personality by an individual's self-report. The Minnesota Multiphasic Personality Inventory (MMPI) and the California Personality Inventory (CPI) are examples of paper-and-pencil psychological tests that allow the analyst to classify personality types on the basis of answers to a series of standardized questions.[19] In addition, interest measures have been developed to aid in matching a person's interest patterns with appropriate jobs.[20]

An alternative to self-reporting is the use of ratings made by another individual to assess personality. A supervisor, for example, may be asked to rate a subordinate on four personality dimensions, such as dependability, perseverance, moral integrity, and intelligence, when considering that subordinate for a job change or promotion.

A third approach to personality measurement is use of projective tests. These are measures that attempt to assess a person through his or her fantasies and interpretation. A widely used projective technique is McClelland's Thematic Apperception Test (TAT). The validity of TAT lies in its ability to measure levels of the achievement need through a subject's stories and interpretations.

Finally, a fourth approach to personality measurement is a direct observation of an individual's behavior in structured situations. Some organizations have employed trained observers to watch employee interactions in group task and discussion situations. Judgments are derived from the observations concerning such characteristics as facilitating the work of others, eliciting criticisms, guiding the work of others, providing resources to the group, and a variety of other interpersonal skills.

Each of the four assessment techniques discussed has unique strengths and weaknesses. None is superior in all settings and for all assessment purposes. Great care must be taken to insure the reliability and validity with which such techniques are used in actual organizational settings. This is particularly true in light of federal law and subsequent Supreme Court interpretation that makes organizations liable for civil damages if such methods are improperly used.

3. *Personality Structure.* Closely allied to the question of measurement is the issue of personality structure. Personality structure is very much like a snapshot

taken of an individual at one point in time. The picture catches a person at one instant and can be described in a static fashion on a number of characteristics, such as hair color, dress, and so on. The problem in the field of personality structure is to define what set of specific human characteristics constitutes a personality (note that the concern in structure is to identify the dimensions of personality, but the concern in measurement is to assess these dimensions). Two alternative approaches have been taken to this problem in applied behavioral research.

The first approach is deductive in nature and defines major dimensions in an a priori fashion based on a model or theory. One of the more successful and useful work personality models developed in this way is the Work Adjustment Model developed at the University of Minnesota.[21] (The second approach is inductive, and is discussed after our examination of the first model.)

deductive

The Work Adjustment Model proposes that behavior on the job, such as performance and turnover, as well as employee satisfaction with the job depends upon the degree of fit or correspondence between a work personality (characteristics of the employee) and the work environment (characteristics of the job and the employing organization). The model is illustrated in exhibit 3–5. High levels of correspondence between the employee's personality and the demands of the job will lead both

Exhibit 3–5 Work Adjustment

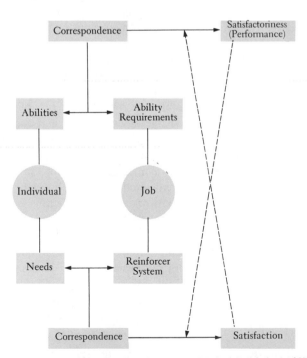

Adapted from Lloyd Lofquist and Rene Dawis, *Adjustment to Work: A Psychological View of Man's Problems in a Work-Oriented Society* (Englewood Cliffs, N.J.: Prentice-Hall, 1969), p. 54.

to favorable evaluations by management of job performance (labeled "satisfactori-ness" in exhibit 3–5) and high levels of job satisfaction on the part of the employee. The model led the researchers to deduce and empirically confirm a personality structure consisting of two major sets of characteristics: (1) nine specific job-related aptitudes and skills; and (2) twenty specific work-related needs. These dimensions are displayed in exhibit 3–6 and constitute the personality structure with which the theory is concerned. The ability dimensions should be self-explanatory; they repre-sent a variety of aptitudes that may or may not be important, depending upon the nature of the job to be carried out. Research has shown that people differ from each other on each of these ability variables. Hence, it is quite possible that two different individuals may have very different profiles across the nine specific job-related aptitudes and skills.

Each of the twenty need dimensions represents an independent need that a person may feel is not at all important to him or her. As in the case of abilities, it is quite likely for two different individuals to have entirely different profiles across the twenty need dimensions. According to the Work Adjustment Model, in order to adequately define an employee's personality one would have to assess him or her on measures of nine ability and twenty need dimensions.

The Work Adjustment Model emphasizes that the key to understanding perfor-mance and satisfaction in organizations is to examine the fit or degree of correspon-dence between employee personalities and the work environment. Focusing solely

Exhibit 3–6 Personality Structure Defined by the Theory of Work Adjustment

Ability Dimensions	Need Dimensions
1. Clerical ability	1. Ability utilization
2. Computational ability	2. Achievement
3. Spatial ability	3. Activity
4. Verbal ability	4. Advancement
5. Discriminative ability	5. Authority
6. Arithmetic ability	6. Company policies and practices
7. Perceptual ability	7. Compensation
8. Sensorimotor ability	8. Coworkers
9. Tool knowledge	9. Creativity
	10. Independence
	11. Moral values
	12. Recognition
	13. Responsibility
	14. Security
	15. Social service
	16. Social status
	17. Supervision—human relations
	18. Supervision—technical
	19. Variety
	20. Working conditions

David Weiss, Rene Dawis, Lloyd Lofquist, and George England, *Instrumentation for the Theory of Work Adjustment* (Minneapolis: Industrial Relations Center, University of Minnesota, 1966), pp. 134–35.

on personality or solely on the work environment will not be sufficient to explain performance and satisfaction. A great deal of research on employee effort, behavior, and performance during the past decade has proceeded from this premise. The models of employee motivation presented in chapter 5, for example, view employee behavior and performance as an adjustment process to jobs, informal groups, and formal organizational procedures. Chapter 6 presents the topic of job design, a process that focuses directly on the issue of employee-personality/work-environment fit. Increasingly, the field of organizational behavior views employee performance as a function of both individual adjustments to the organization and organizational adjustment to the individual.

An alternative approach to the definition of personality structure is inductive rather than deductive. In the absence of a theory or model, researchers measure individuals on a variety of possible dimensions. Data collected in this way is subjected to sophisticated mathematical techniques, such as factor analysis, to determine subject responses (answers to specific test items) that group or cluster together. Such groupings of closely related items are then proposed to measure a single underlying dimension of personality. Note that in contrast to the deductive approach (which depends upon a theory to define personality characteristics) the inductive approach allows the data itself to define various personality characteristics. Typical of this latter approach is the research of Guilford and his associates.[22] Their research yielded a proposed personality structure of ten dimensions illustrated in exhibit 3–7. A specific personality structure is measured by the use of a psychological inventory test that yields separate scores on each of the ten traits shown. Each trait score is based on answers to thirty items in the inventory.

Exhibit 3–7 Guilford-Zimmerman Personality Dimensions

General Activity—hurrying, liking for speed, liveliness, vitality, production efficiency versus slowness and deliberateness

Restraint—serious minded, deliberate, persistent versus carefree

Ascendance—self-defense, leadership, speaking in public, bluffing versus submissiveness

Sociability—having many friends, seeking social contacts and limelight versus shyness and having few friends

Emotional Stability—evenness of moods, optimism, composure versus fluctuation of moods

Objectivity—thick-skinned versus hypersensitive or self-centered

Friendliness—toleration of hostile action, acceptance of domination, respect for others versus belligerence, hostility, resentment, and contempt for others

Thoughtfulness—reflective, observing of self and others, mental poise versus interest in overt activities and mental disconcertedness

Personal Relations—tolerance of people, faith in social institutions versus faultfinding, critical of institutions

Masculinity—interest in masculine activities and other emotional responses characteristic of men versus interest in feminine activities and other emotional responses typical among women

Personality and Organizational Behavior and Performance

The practical utility of any model or measure of personality to an organization will depend on its ability to explain, predict, and control the behavior and performance of individual employees. Porter, Lawler, and Hackman aptly point out that personality *moderates* an employee's response to the organization.[23] Whether a person responds negatively or positively to a pay system, a particular style of supervision, a given form of communication, some level of cohesiveness within an informal group, or some change in technology will depend upon such personality characteristics as needs, expectations, interests, values, and abilities. In fact, it is important for managers to recognize that at any point in time, there is likely to be significant individual variation among employees with respect to critical personality dimensions. An effective organization will attempt to accommodate such differences in order to maximize adjustment between individuals and the organization for a majority of its employees.

A good illustration of organizational attempts to adjust to variation in employee personalities is the creation of "cafeteria" compensation plans in the past decade. Under these programs, instead of forcing each employee to accept the same mix of direct salary and indirect benefits, such as deferred compensation, insurance protection, vacation time, and retirement benefits, the employer presents each employee with a total amount of compensation to be paid for a year or a month. The employee can choose how much he or she wants to allocate to the various compensation-plan elements, thus maximizing individual preferences.[24]

The field of organizational behavior is still in its infancy with regard to the specific personality dimensions or characteristics that influence employee behavior and performance within specific organizational settings. Some of the more important personality dimensions that have been researched are summarized as follows:[25]

Authoritarianism is an attitude that is characterized by beliefs that there should be status and power differences among people in organizations and that the use of power is proper and important to effective organizational functioning.[26] Research on this construct suggests that people who score high on measures of authoritarianism are more inclined to conform to rules and tend to emerge as leaders in situations requiring an autocratic and demanding style.

Locus of control is a personality dimension described and researched by Rotter.[27] Locus of control can vary from high internal control to high external control. People who have high external-control perceptions believe that the events that occur to them are mostly a product of factors beyond their control. Conversely, people who have high internal-control perceptions believe that they can personally influence much of what happens to them. A major review of research on the concept summarized that internals (high internal-control types) are more satisfied on their jobs when they are working under a participative management system. Externals, in contrast, prefer a more directive style of management.[28]

Risk propensity is a personality characteristic involving likes and dislikes for taking chances in one's activities. Empirical research suggests that risk propensity is related to the kinds of decisions people make on their jobs. One study found, for example, that high-risk propensity types among managers take a shorter time to make choices and use fewer pieces of information in making choices.[29]

Dogmatism is a frequently studied personality characteristic consisting of a person's tendency to be closed versus open minded about issues. Research suggests that highly dogmatic managers tend to take a shorter time to make decisions, but are highly confident of their correctness.

In addition to research on these dimensions, a large body of research has developed regarding personality correlates of medical problems, including heart disease, ulcers, alcoholism, and drug abuse, that is important to managers. This research is attempting to provide management with the kinds of tools that would aid in diagnosing such problems among employees and would help employees in making the changes necessary to resolve such problems.[30]

In summary, an increasing body of research on people within organizations suggests that systematic variation among employees on a number of personality characteristics is associated with variation in behavior and performance. Such research, however, is still far from yielding a set of comprehensive principles for managers to follow in directing and controlling job performance.

Applications and Implications for the Manager

Motives and Personality

1. It is important to recall that the topics of individual motives and personality have a great deal in common. Both are employed in an attempt to understand and predict the behavior of individual employees in carrying out their jobs.

2. It is important for practicing managers to recognize that motives are factors that influence behavior in at least the following ways:

   (a) They serve to energize and arouse action.
   (b) They serve a directing function and influence choices people make.
   (c) They can serve as goals or intentions people make in carrying out their jobs.
   (d) They influence the learning of new behaviors.

3. Our knowledge about behavior in organizations suggests that most motives and subsequent behaviors of concern to managers have a heavy learning component and are, therefore, amenable to change through experience with the work environment. Hence, individuals can and do adapt their motives and behaviors to special demands within organizations.

4. The process by which motives influence behavior is more complex than a simple mechanical model would indicate. We have used the term *cybernetic* (referring to a system that "steers" or controls itself) to describe recently developed models of motive processes. These models point out that employees develop and respond to internal standards that are used to evaluate events that occur around them. Discrepancy between incoming stimuli and such standards gives rise to motives that in turn influence behavior.

5. Personality should be considered as an individual's unique profile of characteristics

relevant to the researcher or manager. Any number of human characteristics have been proposed over the years as being part of an individual's personality. They have included various motives; general intelligence; specific, task-related aptitudes, such as spatial skills, arithmetic skills, and mechanical skills; and a variety of characteristics including risk aversion, locus of control, dogmatism, authoritarianism, values, and beliefs.

6. In sorting through and considering the variety of human characteristics to be considered as part of personality, the manager should evaluate each proposed personality characteristic or dimension in terms of how well it predicts behavior and performance in specific organizational settings.

Review of Theories, Research, and Applications

1. Why is it that many theories of work motivation have failed in adequately predicting actual work behavior in real organizations?

2. What should a model of individual behavior in organizations contain if it is to be useful in the practice of management?

3. Characterize the differences between a micro and macro approach to the study of organizational behavior and performance.

4. Define *motives*. In your definition, discuss and contrast three major groups or classes of behavioral determinants. Why is it important to distinguish among them?

5. Cite four basic questions that should be asked with respect to motives. Why are these questions important to an understanding of motives?

6. Describe the difference between instinctive and learned behavior. Why is this difference important?

7. Compare and contrast the focuses of motive and personality models on behavior. Is it possible to integrate these approaches? If so, how?

8. How would you define *personality*?

9. What relevance does the concept of personality have for understanding and predicting employee performance?

Notes

1. Lyman W. Porter and Raymond E. Miles, "Motivation and Management," in *Contemporary Management: Issues and Viewpoints,* ed. Joseph McGuire (Englewood Cliffs, N.J.: Prentice-Hall, 1974), p. 545.
2. James McV. Hunt, "Intrinsic Motivation and Its Role in Psychological Development," in *Nebraska Symposium on Motivation,* ed. David Levine (Lincoln, Neb.: University of Nebraska, 1965), pp. 189–282.
3. Kenneth E. Boulding, "General Systems Theory—The Skeleton of Science," *Management Science,* April 1965, pp. 197–208.
4. See, for example, W. Bexton, W. Heron, and T. Scott, "Effects of Increased Variation in the Sensory Environment," *Canadian Journal of Psychology,* 1954,

pp. 70–76; Bexton, B. Doane, and T. Scott, "Visual Disturbances after Prolonged Perceptual Isolation," *Canadian Journal of Psychology,* 1956, pp. 13–18; D. E. Berlyne, *Conflict, Arousal, and Curiosity* (New York: McGraw-Hill, 1960); K. Montgomery, "The Role of Exploratory Drive in Learning," *Journal of Comparative Psychology,* 1954, pp. 60–64.

5. Leon Festinger, *A Theory of Cognitive Dissonance* (New York: Harper, 1957).

6. Hunt, "Intrinsic Motivation"; Richard deCharms, *Personal Causation* (New York: Academic Press, 1968).

7. K. Lorenz, "The Conception of Instinctive Behavior," in *Instinctive Behavior,* ed. C. Schiller (New York: International Universities Press, 1957), pp. 129–75; N. Tinbergen, *The Study of Instinct* (London: Oxford University Press, 1951); Tinbergen, *Social Behavior in Animals* (New York: Wiley, 1953); Tinbergen, *Animal Behavior* (New York: Wiley, 1965); R. Hinde, "Ethological Models and the Concept of Drive," *British Journal of the Philosophy of Science,* 1956, pp. 321–31.

8. John B. Watson, *Behaviorism* (New York: Norton, 1924).

9. B. F. Skinner, *Beyond Freedom and Dignity* (New York: Knopf, 1971).

10. Richard M. Steers and Lyman W. Porter, *Motivation and Work Behavior* (New York: McGraw-Hill, 1975).

11. R. White, "Motivation Reconsidered: The Concept of Competence." *Psychological Review,* 1959, pp. 297–333.

12. W. E. Scott, "The Behavioral Consequences of Repetitive Task Design: Research and Theory," in *Readings in Organizational Behavior and Human Performance,* ed. L. L. Cummings and W. E. Scott (Homewood, Ill.: Irwin, 1969).

13. J. W. Atkinson and N. T. Feather, *A Theory of Achievement Motivation* (New York: Wiley, 1966).

14. David C. McClelland, *The Achieving Society* (New York: Van Nostrand, 1961).

15. George C. Homans, *Social Behavior in Its Elementary Forms* (New York: Harcourt, 1961).

16. J. Wallace, "An Abilities Conception of Personality: Some Implications For Personality Measurement," *American Psychologist,* 1966, pp. 132–38.

17. See, for example, Donn Byrne, *An Introduction to Personality* (Englewood Cliffs, N.J.: Prentice-Hall, 1966); Calvin Hall and Gardiner Lindzey, *Theories of Personality* (New York: Wiley, 1970); Walter Mischel, *Introduction to Personality* (New York: Holt, Rinehart & Winston, 1971).

18. Byrne, *Introduction to Personality,* pp. 15–16.

19. *Minnesota Multiphasic Personality Inventory* (New York: Psychological Corporation, 1945); H. Gough, *California Personality Inventory* (Palo Alto, Calif.: Consulting Psychologists Press, 1957).

20. Edward K. Strong, Jr., *Vocational Interests Eighteen Years after College* (Minneapolis: University of Minnesota Press, 1955); G. F. Kuder, *Kuder Preference Record* (Chicago: Science Research Associates, 1953).

21. Lloyd Lofquist and Rene Dawis, *Adjustment to Work: A Psychological View of Man's Problems in a Work-Oriented Society* (Englewood Cliffs, N.J.: Prentice-Hall, 1969).

22. J. P. Guilford and W. S. Zimmerman, *The Guilford-Zimmerman Temperament Survey* (Beverly Hills, Calif.: Sheridan Supply Company, 1949).

23. Lyman W. Porter, Edward E. Lawler, III, and J. Richard Hackman, *Behavior In Organizations* (New York: McGraw-Hill, 1975).

24. G. T. Milkovich and M. J. Delaney, "A Note On Cafeteria Pay Plans," *Industrial Relations,* 1975, pp. 112–16; S. M. Nealy and J. G. Goodale, "Determining Worker Preferences Among Employee Benefits and Pay," *Journal of Applied Psychology,* 1967, pp. 357–61; and T. A. Mahoney, "Compensation Preferences of Managers" *Industrial Relations,* 1964, pp. 135–44.

25. William G. Scott and Terence R. Mitchell, *Organization Theory: A Structural and Behavioral Analysis* (Homewood, Ill.: Irwin, 1972), p. 219.

26. T. Adorno et al., *The Authoritarian*

Personality (New York: Harper & Brothers, 1950).

27. J. B. Rotter, "Generalized Expectancies for Internal vs. External Control of Reinforcement," *Psychological Monographs* 80, no. 609 (1966).

28. T. Mitchell, C. Smyser, and S. Weed, "Locus of Control: Supervision and Work Satisfaction," *Academy of Management Journal,* 1975, pp. 623–30. See also B. E. Collins, "Four Components of the Rotter Internal-External Scale: Belief in a Difficult World, a Just World, a Predictable World, and a Politically Responsive World." *Journal of Personality and Social Psychology,* 1974, pp. 381–91; V. C. Joe, "Review of the Internal-External Control Construct as a Personality Variable," *Psychological Reports,* 1971, pp. 619–40; E. J. Phares, *Locus of Control: A Personality Determinant of Behavior* (Morristown, N.J.: General Learning Press, 1973).

29. R. Taylor and Marvin D. Dunnette, "Influence of Dogmatism and Risk Taking Propensity and Intelligence on Decision Making Strategies for a Sample of Industrial Managers," *Journal of Applied Psychology,* 1974, pp. 420–23.

30. M. Bonami and B. Rimie, "Personality Correlates of Heart Disease," *Bulletin de Psychologie,* 1975, pp. 803–12; D. G. Kilpatrick, P. B. Sutker, and A. R. Smith, "Deviant Drug and Alcohol Use: The Role of Anxiety, Sensation Seeking, and Other Personality Variables," in *Emotions and Anxiety: New Concepts, Methods, and Applications,* ed. M. Zuckerman and C. D. Spielberger (Hillsdale, N.J.: Lawrence Erlbaum, 1976); and T. Akerstedt and T. Theorell, "Exposure to Night Work: Serum Gastrin Reactions, Psychosomatic Complaints, and Personality Variables," *Journal of Psychosomatic Research,* 1976, pp. 479–84.

A Case of Motives and Behavior

A Refusal to Accept an Attractive Job Change

Jack Dixon is the district sales manager for the eastern division of Culinary Stove, Inc., a medium-sized manufacturer of kitchen appliances, including electric and gas ranges, refrigerators, microwave ovens, dishwashers, trash compactors, and disposals. His district covers the New England states, New Jersey, New York, Pennsylvania, Ohio, Delaware, and Maryland. Job assignments of sales representatives reporting to him tend to fall into two distinct categories: (1) assignment to a large metropolitan area where traveling is at a minimum and there are many established accounts that bring in a great deal of repeat orders; and (2) assignment to broad geographical areas outside of the metropolitan areas, where the company presently does not have many established accounts and desires to expand aggressively.

The company has established a policy to attract their sales representatives into the second type of job assignment. The policy essentially establishes a bonus commission for new sales in the nonmetropolitan areas. All sales representatives are paid a straight 5 percent commission on sales credited to them. Sales in the expansion areas, however, will also receive an additional 3 percent commission. Thus, sales representatives will receive a total of an 8 percent commission on sales in the new areas. The company has estimated that, because of population growth and new industry moving into the area, an aggressive sales representative might be able to increase his or her annual income by as much as 30 percent.

Jack assumed that job assignments in the new areas would be extremely attractive to all the sales representatives. When a position became open last month, therefore, he presumed that he would have no trouble finding a person who wanted the job. He decided to offer the job first to the individual who had a combination of experience representing the firm and a high rate of performance measured by the annual sales he or she generated. Bob Jordan seemed to be a natural choice for the opening. He had fifteen years experience with the company and had recorded the highest level of sales in the district three out of the past five years.

Jack called Bob into his office in the morning and offered the position to him after explaining it and pointing out its advantages. He fully expected Bob to jump at the offer. Instead, he was shocked at Bob's reply:

"I appreciate your offer, Jack, but I'm really going to have to think about it. My answer will probably be no. You know, the kids are all in high school now and pretty used to their surroundings. Doris and I have a good circle of friends we would hate to leave. We like our house and would not like to leave our neighborhood. In addition, I've got a good shot at running for a position on our town council. I'd like to start devoting more of my time to township matters. I'm not sure what I'd do with the extra money. Sure, I can always use more money, but what the heck do I really need? Another car? A vacation? All in all, I'm pretty satisfied right where I am."

Case Primer Questions

1. What kinds of motives would you attribute to Bob in his reaction to the job offer?

2. What kinds of motives do you think Jack Dixon *assumed* Bob would have in reacting to the offer?

3. What are the differences in these motives, and how might such differences explain what happened?

4. Do you think Bob might have been operating under a different set of motives ten years ago, and would he have reacted differently to such an offer?

Experiential Exercise

Personality and Job Fit

Purpose

This exercise applies some of the principles about personality presented earlier in this chapter. To carry out this exercise, you will need to consider the kinds of personality characteristics that would be appropriate for a given type of job and the design measures of these characteristics.

The objectives of this exercise are to:

1. Give you experience in considering the personality characteristics that might be important to success in a given job.

2. Give you some insights into the possible

influences of personality on job performance.

3. Emphasize the central role of personality in work behavior.

How to set up the exercise

1. Break the class into groups of two or three students.

2. Have all students read the following statement:

You are a behavioral research team employed in the personnel division of a chain of ready-to-wear retail clothing stores. This business is extremely competitive and dynamic. In the past, you have been told that the salesperson who first greets a prospective customer is in an extremely critical position. If the customer does not like this individual, important sales will be lost to competing stores. In addition, styles and tastes are extremely volatile, changing from one season to the next and varying among customers.

Recently, your superior, Fred Marris, Vice President of Personnel, has received reports that an unusually high number of retail salespeople have been receiving poor performance evaluations and have been generally unacceptable to the firm. He called you into his office yesterday and said, "We have a real problem with the salespeople at the store level. I've received the annual performance review summaries from the retail outlets. In sixty of our seventy stores, at least several salespeople have been reported to have personality problems. Specific instances have involved not liking customers, not being able to relate to customers, and being surly with them. We've got to put a stop to this, and I want to devise some method for weeding those types out when we are considering them for that job. Perhaps you can devise a

personality measure that will give us the information we need."

In order to give you some background for the job, Marris made a copy of the position description for the job:

JOB TITLE: Retail Sales Clerk I
REPORTS TO: Retail Sales Manager

Description of Tasks:
Represents the store to customers; greets customers as they enter the store and attempts to interest them in various clothing lines; determines the customers' needs and shows them appropriate apparel; provides fashion advice when requested; provides expert judgment about the appearance of a given piece of clothing when being worn by a customer; prepares customer orders; writes up tickets and makes sales; maintains inventory and keeps clothing in proper condition when being displayed in the store.

3. Each team will consider the problem posed by the Vice President of Personnel and make a recommendation for action.

Instructions for the exercise

1. Each team must consider the problem together with the job description provided and identify the personality characteristics that are critical for success on this job.

2. Each personality characteristic identified must be described in *detail* and justified in a logical fashion as an important factor to success in the job.

3. A measuring device should be designed to assess each of the critical personality characteristics.

4. Regroup the class and have each team report their recommendations to the rest of the class for comments and discussion.

CHAPTER 4

Perception
and
Learning

It should be evident from chapter 3 that motives and personality, when used to explain an employee's behavior, make reference to the *content* of behavior and afford a rather static view of the individual. In this chapter, we take a more dynamic view by looking at two psychological processes that allow an individual to *adjust* his or her behavior to environments such as organizations. We have reproduced the essence of exhibit 3–1 in this chapter as exhibit 4–1 to restate the critical linkages between perception, learning, personality, motives, and abilities in determining behavior and performance.

Essentially, perception and learning are processes that allow a person to make changes in behavior over time; they facilitate adjustment. Thus, the process of feedback illustrated in exhibit 4–1 is critical. Most behavioral scientists today agree that the individual employee is a very conscious, active participant in the behavioral processes we are examining. Hence, as shown in exhibit 4–1, the individual uses feedback from the environment (for example, a supervisor's comment after completing a task, the results of a rating in a merit review, comments from coworkers) to make adjustments in his or her behavior.

If we accept that an employee is a conscious and active participant in the behavioral process, then the incoming arrows in exhibit 4–1 (both stimuli preceding the behavior and feedback following performance) are paths that carry stimulation that

Exhibit 4–1 Individual Behavioral Influences on Performance

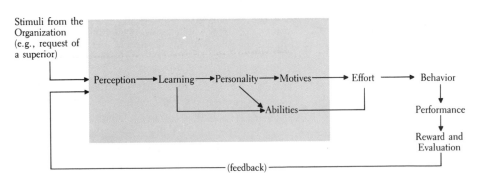

influences one or a combination of our senses. In fact, people working in organizations are constantly bombarded with incoming stimuli. Some are physical in nature, such as lighting, noise levels, temperature, humidity, or odors. Some are more complex stimuli that carry highly sophisticated information, such as blips on a radar screen, statistics presented in tabular form, or memoranda. Still other informational stimuli may be extremely complex. Social perception offers an interesting example of complex stimuli. A superior's tone of voice may carry information quite different from the actual words spoken. A lawyer's dress, hair color, physical bearing, sex, or race may all influence other people's reactions to him or her.

Perception is defined as the process by which individuals attend to incoming stimuli and organize or interpret such stimuli into a message that in turn indicates an appropriate action or behavior.[1] The study of perception, which we examine in detail later in this chapter, attempts to understand and explain the ways in which the process of interpreting stimuli influences behavior. So long as a person is conscious (and, some would argue, even unconscious), perception occurs. The capacity to perceive allows people to make a continuing adjustment to all environments (including work organizations) through changes or alterations in behavior. Hence, perception is an individual process that facilitates short-run changes in behavior as a result of interaction with organizational environments, *also* ~~as a result of feedback~~

In addition to short-run changes, individuals adapt their behavior in rather stable ways over the long run. This process is known as *learning,* and is indicated by the feedback loop in exhibit 4–1. The following example illustrates the ways in which an employee uses perception and learning on the job. A new manager is learning how to plan and assign tasks in her division as part of a formal job-rotation program. She is supervised by a senior manager in the department. At any given moment in this process, she is sensitive to a variety of cues or stimuli indicating how well she is doing: coaching comments from her supervisor, informal comments from coworkers and subordinates, summary comments coming across her desk from the operations under her control, phone calls, and so forth. Her perceptual capacities allow her to (1) be aware of these sources of information; and (2) translate them into meaningful information that will indicate any changes she might make in her own actions. This continual process is labeled *perception.*

At certain points in this process, some of the information she is perceiving comes in the form of feedback resulting from previous actions. Her supervisor, for example, might sit down at the end of the first day with her and say, "You did a great job in assigning John to the telex machine the way you did. First, he needed the experience; second, you provided for appropriate backup in case anything went wrong; and third, your manner was not at all threatening. If you keep up that kind of good work, you will move up very rapidly in this place!" Note that the superior's remarks carry at least two kinds of messages for the trainee: (1) The compliment is rewarding. At the very least, it satisfies a need for recognition and appreciation and holds out the prospect of a rapid career progression. (2) The feedback indicates that the trainee's actions were the *correct* ones in this situation. This knowledge, together with the satisfaction she has achieved, *increases the likelihood* that she will act or behave in the same fashion the next time a similar situation arises. Whenever a person makes a relatively stable change in his or her behavior as a result of feedback, *learning* has occurred. In the remainder of this chapter, we discuss the processes of perception and learning as major influences on employee behavior and performance.

Perception

Individuals in organizations are constantly showered by a complex variety of sensory stimulation: verbal orders, written messages, colors, odors, shapes, things to touch, mathematical expressions, public address system announcements, bells, and lights. In fact, it would be impossible to list all the sensory signals that employees receive during a normal work day. If we studied a typical employee's reaction more closely, we would probably be surprised at the number of signals he or she *ignores*.

Somehow, people attend to a subset of these signals and respond appropriately to them. This process is defined as *perception* and is illustrated in exhibit 4–2. The process of perception consists of the following sequence of steps: (1) awareness, or attention to the incoming stimulus; (2) translating incoming stimuli into some message (stimulus interpretation); and (3) deciding on the appropriate action or behavior in response to the message. Perception, then, is a form of behavior that allows individuals to interact with and adjust to the varying demands of the job and the organization. In studying perception, we have three primary concerns. First, we need to describe and define the nature of perception as behavior. Second, we must examine the influences of a number of factors such as motives, learning, and personality on perception. Third, we will discuss an illustration of applied perceptual research in organizations.

Perception Defined

When one responds to a telephone or a warning light, one is actually doing two things. First, one is attending to and receiving the sensory stimulation. Most people in their work filter out most stimuli. For example, we all have had the experience of becoming accustomed to the sound of a fan or the background music of a radio. Indeed, if the noise were to stop, our attention would be aroused. Thus, the first major activity in a perceptual process is *selectively attending* to specific incoming stimuli. Second, when one responds to a telephone or a warning light, one must organize the incoming information, translate it into a message (give it meaning), and respond appropriately. Thus, we can say that perception is a two-phase activity:[2]

1. Receiving inputs (both energy and information).

Exhibit 4–2 Process of Perception

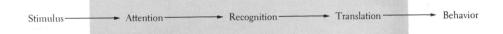

Stimulus ⟶ Attention ⟶ Recognition ⟶ Translation ⟶ Behavior

2. Translating inputs into messages that, in turn, modify behavior.

In various studies of these two phases, perception researchers have formulated a number of specific questions:

In what ways do individuals combine senses to (1) reinforce each other (as when a truck driver combines sight and hearing in maneuvering a vehicle); and (2) compensate for the loss or impairment of a sense (as when a blinded person's hearing becomes more acute)?

What are the *thresholds* for recognizing and responding to *changes* in sensory inputs (as when a doctor responds to a change in a measured heart rate or a machine operator recognizes a malfunction from a change in the sound of the equipment)?

What are the *thresholds* for recognizing and identifying the *source* of a change in sensory inputs (as when a machine operator recognizes the specific part of the machine that is malfunctioning) or the *direction* of the change in sensory inputs (as when the doctor recognizes that the heart rate has increased or decreased?)

Factors Influencing Perception

Note that the three perception questions above concern behavior. As such, perception is influenced by a variety of individual and situational factors.

Attributes of the object.   A major factor influencing a person's initial attention to an object is the *intensity* of the stimulus. Thus, a strong or shrill sound will be more effective than a soft one in a warning alarm. Managers will use voice modulation to get attention and convey meaning. *Motion* is another stimulus characteristic that can attract attention and indicate processes in tasks. Design engineers are very careful, for example, to insure that machine operators see only those motions that are critical to the proper operation of the equipment. *Physical size* is an additional attribute of objects that influence perception. Early research on what makes a good leader, for example, states that height enhances a person's ability to influence others.

Clearly, an important area of application concerning the effects of the object's attributes is in the area of interpersonal perception. A substantial amount of behavioral research suggests that physical features, such as sex, race, dress, facial expression, and body posture, influence both the attention we give to others and the judgments we form about them. Indeed, many broad classifications about the behavior and performance of others are based (for better or worse) on broad groupings of people according to their physical characteristics.[3]

Sometimes, attributes of the object can lead to barriers that distort perception. Two such barriers are the errors of *stereotyping* and the *halo* effect. When we stereotype, we form a judgment about people based on an "ideal" or "type" of impression we have formed about their group. Technically, a stereotype is a belief that causes one to attribute a characteristic to a person based upon a belief concerning that individual's entire group. For example, the label "Democrat" or "Teamster" brings to mind a picture of an individual that may or may not be accurate for the specific individual we are meeting.

When we stereotype, we pick out what we believe to be common characteristics about groups. As soon as we discover that an individual is a member of that group, we attribute those same characteristics to him or her. It is a very convenient way of categorizing individuals. Stereotyping, by itself, is not bad; indeed, it is a major way in which people can deal with a confusing array of information. Stereotyping, however, can be a source of error in perception when either one of two mistakes are made: (1) ignoring variation on the characteristic within a group (e.g., believing that all women have lower quantitative skills than men); or (2) holding mistaken beliefs about the characteristic for an entire group (e.g., Texans are all rich).

Mistaken stereotypes lie at the root of a great deal of employment discrimination against women and minorities historically. The following example illustrates the way in which stereotyping about sex-based differences can lead to discrimination in employment. A manager of a warehousing operation believes that all women are physically weaker than men, and, on this belief, adopts a policy of not hiring or placing women on jobs involving lifting. The manager has focused only on overall differences in physical capacity between men and women, while ignoring the tremendous variation *among* women (as well as among men) in physical capacity. In so doing, he has (1) denied access to the job to those women who are in fact capable of carrying out the tasks; and (2) artificially restricted the supply of labor for the job, which also tends to inflate labor costs.

Behavioral scientists are just now turning their attention to the sources or causes of stereotyping behavior in employment. Their concern is to find ways of correcting the problem. One recent study, for example, investigated the sources of sex-based stereotypes for ninety-six of the most common occupations. A sex stereotype is a perception that a job is more appropriate for a male or a female. The investigators theorized that when people stereotype the job of a surgeon as more appropriate for males, for example, they do so because: (1) most surgeons they have seen are male (*base rate* of males already in the occupation); or (2) they believe that the skills needed to be a surgeon are greater among males than they are among females; or (3) the occupation of health care appears to be more appropriate for males. In fact, the researchers have found that base rate (the proportion of males already on the job) is the best predictor of sex-type perceptions attached to jobs. Thus, the proportion of males or females one is accustomed to seeing on a job is apparently the most important contributor to stereotyped perceptions about whether males or females are better suited for various jobs.[4]

A second common perceptual error is the halo effect. It often occurs in performance evaluation (to be discussed in chapter 13). In making this error, the rater does not correctly treat several different dimensions of an employee's performance as truly separate when making an evaluation. Instead, the rater presumes that if an employee is high on one dimension, he or she must be high on all other dimensions. Likewise, an employee judged low on one dimension is presumed low on all others.

Attributes of the situation. Elements in the surrounding environment or work situation also influence perception in predictable ways. The time at which a message is transmitted can influence attention and interpretation. For example, if an employee has become accustomed to receiving a given inventory report during the third week of every month, he or she may completely ignore the report should it be transmitted at some other time, such as the first week of the month. In addition, general levels of noise, light, heat, and other conditions can influence the attention paid to signals.

Attributes of the person.   Probably the most important source of influence on perception are characteristics of the person, including his or her motives, previous learning (or expectations from the job), and personality. Dan Rather and Gary Paul Gates describe an episode in their account of Richard Nixon's presidential administration that stands as a vivid illustration of how personal characteristics influence the perception and interpretation of an order:

> The president was working alone, very late at night in a hotel room while on a trip. He opened the door, beckoned to a waiting aide and ordered, "Get me coffee." The aide immediately responded to the request. Most of the activities of the hotel including the kitchen were not operating at such a late hour. Hotel personnel had to be called in and a fresh pot of coffee brewed. All of this took time and the president kept asking about coffee while waiting. Finally a tray was made up with a carafe of coffee, cream, sugar, and some sweet rolls and was rushed to the President's suite. It was only at this point that the aide learned that the President did not want coffee to drink, but rather wanted to talk to an assistant whose name was Coffee.[5]

Rather and Gates correctly use the incident to describe the tense and often confusing conditions faced by presidential assistants in carrying out their tasks. In addition, the incident can be analyzed to illustrate the personal characteristics of the aide that might have led to the misperception of Nixon's order. (Note that this analysis is the authors', intended to illustrate a phenomenon, and does not in any way represent an attempt to describe the actual motives or personal characteristics of the people involved in the incident). The perceptual sequence of an aide in this situation is diagrammed in exhibit 4–3. In this case, the aide's motives influencing his perception of the order could include a need to please the president and avoid his displeasure. In addition, a need for positive recognition and approval could be

Exhibit 4–3   A Case of Misperception Caused by Personal Characteristics

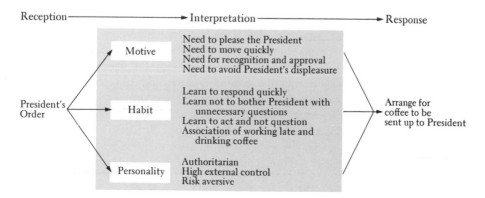

operating in a case of this type. Previous learning or habits also play a role in determining the aide's interpretation and choice of action. Aides to powerful figures such as the U.S. President are likely to learn to respond quickly to orders; to not bother the president with any unnecessary questions or clarifications; to learn to emphasize action and not question direct orders. The personality of an aide enters in influencing the perception of a presidential order. To the extent that the aide has authoritarian values, he may place a great deal of importance on responding quickly without question. In addition, an aversion to risk taking and a belief that there is not much he can do to influence events occurring around him on the job would lead predictably to the response made. Finally, the aide's previous learning influenced his actions in that he associated late-night work and coffee; therefore, he made this connection rather than the correct one.

It is important for managers as well as students of organizational behavior to reflect upon the joint influence of motives, personality, and previous learning when attempting to understand the work behaviors of individuals in specific organizational settings. What may appear to be "stupid" or "irrational" behavior to an outsider may indeed be perfectly understandable and predictable given an understanding of the people and situations involved.

An Illustration of Applied Perceptual Research

Much of what we know about perception is the product of basic laboratory research in the field of psychology. Increasingly, however, organizational behavior researchers are investigating perceptual phenomena among employees in actual work settings. This kind of effort is illustrated by a recent interest in employees' perceptual responses to the pay they receive for their work, about which management still knows very little. In order for money to influence behavior, the employee must have some perception of it. At the very least, he or she must be aware of money. Several of the questions raised earlier about perception are relevant in this regard. For example, what is the smallest increase in pay that will be noticed and perceived as meaningful by employees? Would a 2 percent pay increase be meaningful; or would a 10 percent increase be necessary? Is it possible that one type of employee would react to a 4 percent pay increase as meaningful, but another type of employee would not react favorably to an increase unless it were 8 percent? What kinds of variables would account for the difference in perceptual reactions?

Actually, such questions involve the issues of threshold phenomena. Specifically: (1) For a given type of information, what is the least amount required to activate the individual or capture his or her attention? (2) For a given type of information, what is the smallest difference the individual can react to? Studies of the smallest increase in pay that is perceived as meaningful have been carried out in recent years.[6] One study examined variation in the "smallest meaningful pay increase" (SMPI) among a broad sample of employees in a variety of occupations.[7] The researchers found that three major types of factors influence an employee's SMPI: (1) current level of pay; (2) what he or she considers to be a "usual" pay increase based on company practice in the past; and (3) future consumption plans, including cost-of-living increase expectations and plans to improve family living standards. All three factors were found to be positively associated with the amount of a pay increase perceived as meaningful by the employee. In addition, it was found that the relative importance of the first two factors versus the third factor varied systematically with the type of subject in their study. If the employee was the type who treated pay as a sign of recognition from the organization, the first two factors were more important as predictors of SMPI than was the third factor. Conversely, for employees who treated pay as instrumental for achieving additional outcomes (e.g., adding to their purchases), variation in consumption plans was the most important predictor.

So far, we have been considering the short-run adjustments individuals make in their behavior through the process of perception. In addition to short-run adjustments, individuals are also capable of making relatively stable, long-run adjustments in behavior through the process of learning, which will be our concern for the rest of this chapter.

Learning

Most people have been close to formal learning situations for a significant part of their lives. Children in most cultures grow up spending most of their days in elementary and secondary schools. Some extend this period to twenty or more years if they attend college and graduate schools. In addition, many organizations attempt to design a learning component into jobs in order to maintain necessary skills among employees. Outside of formal settings, we know that a vast amount of learning takes place informally from the time of birth as a matter of experience.

In spite of our familiarity with the process, many people are confused about the nature of learning. To what extent can we attribute a person's behavior to learning? Will people learn things in spite of their environments? What is the difference between learning a behavior and acquiring it "naturally"? Can a skill, such as impressing others or operating a lathe, be acquired, or must an individual be born with such a talent as part of their personality? These kinds of questions demand that managers have a thorough understanding of what learning is and in what ways learning influences behavior.

Learning Defined

An authoritative source defines *learning* as follows: "Learning is the process by which an activity originates or is changed through reacting to an encountered situation, provided that the characteristics of the change in activity cannot be explained on the basis of native response tendencies, maturation, or temporary states of the organism."[8] A more applied definition is: "Learning is a relatively permanent change in behavior which occurs as a result of experience."[9] Both these definitions contain implications that are important in determining what is and is not learning.

First, learning is an inferred process that is believed to influence behavior. We cannot directly observe learning, just as we cannot directly observe motivation or personality. When a person says, "Joe learned how to convince a customer he needed to buy that product," the implication is that the source of Joe's behavior or performance was an experience that resulted in learning.

Second, the definitions emphasize that learning results in a *relatively* permanent change in behavior. Behavior that is learned, therefore, is relatively constant over time. We rarely hear, for example, of a person having to learn how to ride a bike, type, recite the alphabet, or how to add and subtract all over again once they have learned how.

Third, and closely related to the second point, the definitions imply that learning is only one of several factors that influence behavior. The definitions draw a strong distinction between changes in behavior resulting from learning and changes that result from far more temporary conditions, such as fatigue, health, drugs, and the like. Thus, workers may slow down in performance towards the end of a shift not because they are learning to work more slowly but because they are tired. Indeed, learning researchers have documented hundreds of times that a "spontaneous recovery" to the original level of performance occurs after the employee has rested. Learning and fatigue have opposite effects on behavior or performance.[10] Fatigue causes a decrease in performance strength and effectiveness; learning leads to an increase in performance strength and effectiveness.

Fourth, the definitions imply that some behaviors may simply be a matter of instinct or genetic inheritance; that is, such behaviors were not learned, nor are they capable of change through learning. This is the issue of instinctive versus learned behavior raised in chapter 3. As a matter of practicality, in organizations most complex activities are a product of the joint influences of genetic and environmental factors. The work of a computer programmer is a good illustration of this point. A certain level of logic and language aptitude (influenced by inherited factors) is a necessary precondition for on-the-job success. However, the individual must learn specific skills, including at least one programming language and how to use it efficiently, before logic and language aptitudes can be transformed into specific job activities.

Finally, the definitions draw a distinction between changes in behavior that occur as a matter of learning and those that occur because of maturation or aging. Maturation (as well as aging) and learning have separate influences on behavior in at least two ways. First, some patterns of behavior change simply as a child or adult grows older as a result of normal socialization processes. These changes have little to do with conscious or formal learning and occur in almost any type of environment. Second, the potential to learn some skills is influenced by aging. Until proper muscular development is reached, for example, a child cannot be taught specific motor skills, such as walking, running, or throwing a ball. In addition, it is believed that changes caused by aging may limit an elderly person's capacity to learn certain skills. For example, an older person may have more difficulty than younger employees in learning computer programming skills.

What we have said about learning is summarized in exhibit 4–4. Specifically: learning is a source of change in behavior and performance that is distinct from three other sources of behavioral change: (1) maturation and aging; (2) native response tendencies, such as instinctive reflexes; and (3) temporary factors such as fatigue,

Exhibit 4–4 Learning and Performance

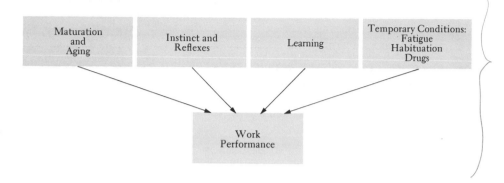

habituation, or drugs. Learning is unique as a source of behavioral change because it comes about as a result of a person's experience with an environment. This distinction is critical because it emphasizes the point that learning is a unique determinant of behavior; unique because the change in behavior comes about as a result of an individual's experience. We will note later that many learning scientists feel strongly enough about this point to claim that learning cannot take place unless the learner actually experiences what has to be learned.

Major Learning Questions

Before examining the two major models of the learning process, it is important to ask what questions they should answer for us concerning individual behavior in work settings. Such a list of questions will serve to outline what we need to know about the process of learning and will also be a yardstick for evaluating learning models. In addition, these questions will provide a means for integrating various learning theories.

We have adapted a series of questions about learning common in the field of psychology to serve these purposes:[11]

1. *What are the limits of learning?* This is a capacity question dealing with an individual's ability to learn specific work behaviors. We have already noted that inborn aptitudes may limit and/or enhance a person's ability to learn new skills.

2. *What is the role of practice in learning?* This question deals with the degree to which the learner must actually participate in the process. Some theories propose that the individual cannot learn without actually doing or practicing the behavior to be learned. Other theories allow an individual to play a much less active role and claim that some behaviors can be learned simply by watching others.

3. *How important are drives, incentives, rewards, and punishment in learning?* The question here is to what degree is motivation necessary for learning to take place? Can people learn if they don't want to learn?

4. *What is the role of understanding and insight in learning?* Some models take a very mechanistic view of learning, claiming that learning is nothing more than the establishment of stimulus-response (S-R) connections through experience. More cognitive learning theories say that understanding and insight play an important role in learning.

5. *Does learning one behavior help in learning another behavior?* This question deals with the phenomenon of earlier learning influencing later learning. We will see that previous learning can help or hinder learning something new, depending upon a variety of circumstances.

6. *What happens when people remember and forget?* How do these processes operate and how does learning influence them?

The answers to these questions not only will expand managers' knowledge about learning, but also have practical implications for managing the course of learning in organizations. The theories described in the next section should be contrasted and integrated by considering the way in which each addresses these questions.

Major Models of Learning

The topic of learning has received a great deal of attention within the field of psychology since the earliest work of Pavlov at the turn of the twentieth century. A great deal of empirical research has yielded reliable information about how people learn. We will examine two major models of learning: classical conditioning and operant or instrumental conditioning. Both models focus on a stimulus-response (S-R) connection as a basic unit of learning but consider two different processes by which such connections are thought to be established: stimulus association and reinforcement. The first model considered is that of Pavlov and is called *classical conditioning*. The second model, *instrumental* or *operant conditioning*, is that of Hull and Skinner. The school of thought surrounding the development of this model is often called the behavioral school.

Classical conditioning.   Pavlov is credited with the fundamental research leading to our understanding about a major way in which learning takes place, namely classical conditioning. In addition, Guthrie developed the model to its modern form.[12] Pavlov's research paradigm is illustrated in exhibit 4–5. Classical conditioning begins with an S-R connection that already exists. Pavlov focused on physiological S-R connections, such as reflexes, which he labeled unconditioned (or unlearned). A dog's salivation in the presence of meat is an example of such a connection. When presented with meat, the unconditioned stimulus, the dog's unlearned response is to salivate. Pavlov's finding was that new S-R connections can be conditioned or learned through the process of repeatedly pairing an unconditioned stimulus, such as meat, with a conditioned stimulus, perhaps a bell. Note that before being paired with the unconditioned stimulus, the conditioned stimulus (the bell) does not result in the salivation response. In other words, before the procedure, the S-R connection in the lower half of the box in exhibit 4–5 does not exist. After conditioning, however, the bell alone will lead to the salivation response.

Exhibit 4–5 Classical Conditioning

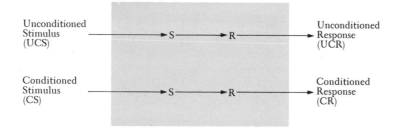

Thus, classical conditioning is defined as the formation of an S-R link (or habit) between a conditioned stimulus and a conditioned response through the repeated pairing of a conditioned stimulus with an unconditioned stimulus. Note that the unit of learning (what has been conditioned) is the S-R connection in the lower portion of exhibit 4–5. Evidence that learning has occurred would consist of the conditioned stimulus (CS) eliciting the conditioned response (CR) alone after the period of repeated pairings.

An illustration of classical conditioning in a work setting would be an airplane pilot learning how to use a newly installed warning system. In this case, the habit (or S-R connection) to be learned is to correct the plane's altitude (response) when a warning light indicates that the plane's altitude has dropped below some critical limit (stimulus). The pilot already knows how to respond appropriately to the trainer's warning to increase altitude (in this case, we would say that the trainer's warning is the unconditioned stimulus and the corrective action of increasing the plane's altitude is the unconditioned response). Using the paradigm shown in exhibit 4–5, the training session would consist of the trainer warning the pilot to increase altitude each time the warning light goes on. Through repeated pairings of the trainer's warning (unconditioned stimulus) and the warning light (conditioned stimulus), the pilot eventually learns to adjust the plane's altitude in response to the warning light alone, even though the trainer is not present. Again, as in exhibit 4–5, the unit of learning is the S-R connection or habit linking the conditioned stimulus with the conditioned response.

Closely associated with classical conditioning as a vehicle for learning new behaviors are the processes of *stimulus generalization* and *stimulus discrimination*. Learning research has demonstrated that individuals can respond to two separate stimuli in the same way on the basis of their similarities, or can behave differently in the presence of two separate stimuli on the basis of differences in their characteristics.

To illustrate the principle of stimulus generalization, suppose a new supervisor has learned what perfect job performance on the part of a subordinate should be. In effect, he or she has learned a criterion against which to evaluate or compare the actual work performance of subordinates. Exhibit 4–6 represents the actual performance of ten subordinates (S_1 through S_{10}) ordered in terms of each employ-

Exhibit 4–6 Stimulus Generalization and Discrimination

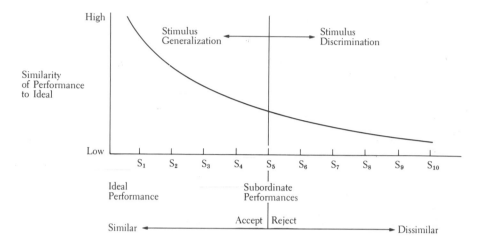

ee's performance effectiveness or similarity to the ideal performance criterion. The performances of subordinates 1 through 4, although not identical in terms of quality, are relatively close to the ideal in terms of stimulus similarity (that is, aspects of the performance being examined by the supervisor). On the basis of this similarity, the supervisor responds to these performances in a similar manner and judges them to be acceptable. This kind of judgment is an example of the process of stimulus generalization. The performances of subordinates 5 through 10, on the other hand, are sufficiently different from the ideal for the supervisor to reject them as unacceptable. The trained evaluator, on the basis of a dissimilarity between S_5 through S_{10} and the ideal performance criterion, rejects their performances as unacceptable. In this case, the supervisor has engaged in the process of stimulus discrimination.

Stimulus generalization and discrimination are highly important as facilitators of learning through classical conditioning. Because of our ability to recognize similarities, for example, we are able to transfer what we already know (already present S-R connections) to new situations through the process of stimulus association and generalization. Classical conditioning is a major avenue of learning among individuals in work organizations. As an applied concern, trainers in organizations take great care to make sure that conditions in the classroom or training facility are as similar as possible to actual work conditions in order to assure that what is learned can be transferred to the job.

Instrumental or operant conditioning.   Instrumental or operant conditioning is a second major process by which S-R connections (habits) are learned or acquired. The key process in instrumental conditioning is the reinforcement or reward of desired behaviors. Models of the influence of reinforcement on motivation and behavior are examined in detail in chapter 5; we will focus on the role of reward in learning or changing behavior here.

The study of learning through reinforcement dates to the work of Watson,[13] about the same time Pavlov was carrying out his studies. Watson believed that behavior was influenced by rewards from the environment. Put simply, people change their behavior by repeating acts that are rewarded and not repeating acts that the environment fails to reward. Behaviorists like to talk about "shaping" behavior by controlling rewards and selectively rewarding only desired behaviors.

Thorndike formalized Watson's notions about the influence of environmental rewards into a principle that has become known as the *Law of Effect*. As expressed by Thorndike, this principle states that an S-R connection will be strengthened if the response (R) is followed by a "satisfying state of affairs" (reward). Conversely, the S-R connection will be weakened if the response is not followed by a reward.[14]

Hull and his associates developed a formal learning model based on the Law of Effect that incorporates three important elements:[15]

1. *Drive* is an internal state of need. It can be started by a variety of conditions or events. A person under a state of increased drive is aroused, and his or her behavior is energized. Drives, then, act as motives as defined in chapter 3; that is, they instigate action. The presence of drive (or a motive) is necessary for a person to learn. In common language, we would say that a person must want to learn in order for training to have an effect.

2. *Habit,* as we have said earlier, is the S-R connection that is learned through conditioning. Strictly defined, it is a learned or conditioned connection between a condition or event (stimulus) in the individual's environment and a response or set of responses (behavior) to those events. Habits determine choice in behavior at any given point in time. In addition, S-R connections are the central units of learning in behaviorist theory.

3. *Reinforcement* is the presentation of an event following the desired behavior that serves to strengthen the habit.

Exhibit 4–7 illustrates the basic model for instrumental conditioning. A stimulus arouses a motive (or drive, to use Hull's term) that, when combined with a habit (S-R connection), leads to a given behavior. If the act or behavior is followed by a reward (or reinforcement) two things happen to the individual: (1) the need or motive leading to the behavior is satisfied (Law of Effect); and (2) the habit or S-R connection is strengthened, increasing the probability that the behavior will be repeated under similar circumstances when the need or motive arises. In addition, it

Exhibit 4–7 Instrumental Conditioning

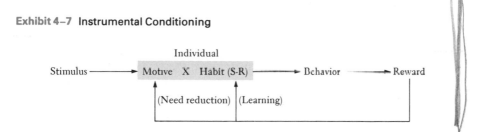

Individual

Stimulus ⟶ Motive X Habit (S-R) ⟶ Behavior ⟶ Reward

(Need reduction) (Learning)

is important to note that rewarding a single habit not only strengthens that habit but also *weakens* alternative habits that have not been rewarded. Reward strengthening a habit is technically what the instrumental conditioning model calls *learning*. Thus, we can define *instrumental conditioning* as the learning of a habit or S-R connection through reinforcement or reward.

Over the past thirty years, Hull's model has been tested extensively, especially with respect to reinforcement. Although the role of reinforcement or rewards in motivation is examined thoroughly in chapter 5, it is important to touch on the most important findings in this research here. Investigators have concluded that two major forms of reinforcers exist and that both of these are fundamentally different from punishment. *Positive reinforcement* is the presentation of something attractive following the desired behavior. *Negative reinforcement* or *avoidance* consists of allowing the person to *escape* from an aversive or disagreeable condition following the desired response or behavior (for example, relief from pain). Both positive and negative reinforcement strengthen the habit leading to the desired behavior and, therefore, contribute to learning. Punishment, in contrast, is fundamentally different from positive and negative reinforcement, and does not lead to learning the desired response. *Punishment* consists of *presenting* an unpleasant or aversive condition to a person following an *undesired* behavior. Note that the person is being presented with unpleasantness rather than being allowed to escape it, and that punishment focuses attention on the undesired behavior rather than the desired behavior.

Most behavioral scientists strictly believe that only through positive and negative reinforcement can learning the desired response occur. Punishment, strictly speaking, does not contribute to learning the desired response. Escape from punishment, however, can contribute to an employee's learning to avoid the undesired behavior.

In addition to reinforcement (positive and negative) and punishment, a fourth process can influence behavior—*extinction*. In the process of extinction, neither reward nor punishment follows an undesired behavior. Suppose an employee engages in temper tantrums to gain a supervisor's attention. One option for the supervisor in trying to change the subordinate's behavior is to *ignore* the tantrum. He neither reinforces the tantrum by responding and granting the employee's demand nor punishes the employee with a reprimand. He simply does not reply in any fashion. Every time the supervisor ignores the tantrum, the likelihood that the tantrum will be repeated decreases. In effect, ignoring the undesired behavior *extinguishes* the behavior.

Complex Learning

A great number of practical applications in directing the work behavior of employees have been drawn from the basic research that went into the development of learning theory. In an applied setting, such as a business organization, learning is extremely complex. We have already noted that Hull dealt with complex learning by proposing that entire structures of S-R connections, called habit family hierarchies, are learned. Research in complex learning has led to the discovery of several important phenomena that help us understand the higher-order learning that is evident when employees learn and adapt in carrying out work tasks: (1) a learning curve; (2) a plateau; (3) an asymptote; (4) a slope; and (5) spontaneous recovery.

A learning curve is a graph that describes the course of learning. It describes how work behavior changes during the time a new habit is being formed through practice and experience with the work environment. These practices are known technically as *learning trials*. Exhibit 4–8 displays a typical learning curve for a new employee. Several dependent variables or measures of behavioral change can be considered on this graph: (1) *behavior strength* (how much effort goes into work behavior); (2) *behavior probability* (the likelihood the behavior will be repeated under similar circumstances); (3) *behavior quality* (how well or accurately the behavior or work task is carried out); and (4) *resistance to extinction* (how many times the behavior would be repeated if not reinforced). Each of these qualities could be represented on the vertical axis in exhibit 4–8. Time and the number of trials are defined along the horizontal axis. During the time that elapses, the person responsible for training can have the employee repeat the desired work behavior and then reward him or her. These practices are the learning trials. Other periods of time can be blocked off as rest periods, during which nothing related to the training takes place.

The graph in exhibit 4–8, therefore, indicates the change in work behavior that occurs as a function of practice. Several factors of the learning curve warrant more attention.

First, the *slope* of the curve (Δy/Δx) represents the change in behavior that occurs per unit change in practice (or for every practice trial). As such, it is a measure of the speed with which learning has occurred. A practical concern of an organizational trainer is to maximize this slope because it is the first major criterion of how effective a training program has been in changing behavior.

Exhibit 4–8 Employee Learning Curve

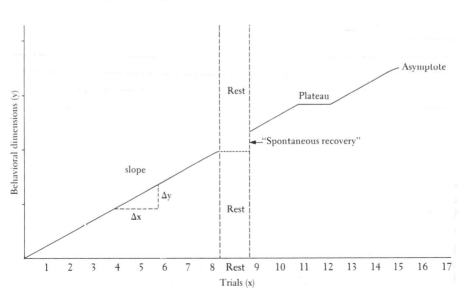

A second major characteristic of the learning curve is the *asymptote*, which represents the maximum amount work behavior has changed as a result of the learning experience. The difference between the response strength, response quality, response probability, or resistance to extinction before the first learning trial and the asymptote is a measure of just how much change has occurred in work behavior during the course of learning. As such, it is a major measure of training effectiveness, to be maximized in applied settings.

A third part of the learning curve, the *plateau,* can occur several times during the course of learning. A plateau can be very frustrating to the employee who is learning new tasks because it is a time during which practice is occurring but *no new learning* is apparent. A number of causes for plateaus have been found. First, and most important, is the fact that a series of separately learned habits (S-R's) are being integrated into a more efficient sequence. It takes some time for an individual to integrate this new behavior, and therefore these plateaus would be necessary before any further improvements in behavior or performance could occur. A second probable cause of plateaus is a temporary drop or lagging in motivation to learn as one becomes fatigued or bored by the learning process. Finally, plateaus can result in part because old learning is being extinguished. Whatever their cause, plateaus are virtually universal phenomena in employee learning within organizations. It is important as a practical matter that managers and others responsible for training do not mistake plateaus as evidence that no further learning is possible, and that they attempt to arrange practices in a way that minimizes the frequency and duration of plateaus.

Finally, exhibit 4–8 notes the occurrence of a rest period. Following this, job performance makes a *spontaneous recovery* to a level higher than it was before the rest period. At first, this may appear incongruous because presumably nothing related to the learning process has occurred during the rest period. What has happened, however, is that prior to the rest fatigue was interfering with the learning process and masking some of the influence learning was having on performance. The spontaneous recovery, therefore, represents changes in work performance that actually occurred before but were hidden until the rest period dispelled the inhibiting effects of fatigue.

Evaluation of Learning Models

We began our discussion of the classical and instrumental conditioning models with several questions that any model of learning should address in order to be useful. Research over the past twenty years leads to the following conclusions about the two models.

Capacity.   Most researchers agree that in organizational settings an individual's physical and mental capacities are important influences on work behavior, but only within very broad limits. Most tasks within organizations are sufficiently complex to demand specific skills that are, in large part, learned. Indeed, as we indicated in chapter 3, base levels of intellectual and physical abilities and learning *interact* to influence individual behavior and performance. Both are necessary although not sufficient conditions for behavior. Note, also, as illustrated in exhibit 4–1, that effort intervenes between abilities and performance. In other words, the capacity to act alone will not have any influence on behavior and performance. Both effort (the product of motivation) and capacity are required for behavior and performance.

Practice.   To what extent is actual practice on the part of the trainees necessary for learning to take place? Opinion is still mixed on this question. Clearly, research models demonstrate that without any practice neither classical nor instrumental conditioning will have an effect. Taken in their strictest sense, however, the classical and instrumental models imply that learning can occur *only* with repeated trials, in a time-consuming, trial-and-error fashion.

Understanding and insight.   Research on complex learning suggests that individuals have a number of capacities that can *supplement* physical practice and make the course of learning far more efficient. An employee, for example, has the capacity to *understand* an explanation or schema that lays out what is to be learned. In addition, behavioral scientists have documented the role of *modeling* in learning. In this process, the learner copies the behavior of an expert, quickly adopting the desired changes in behavior. Thus, the individual employee is not a passive partner in the learning process, dependent upon blindly following a path of trial and error. The capacities of understanding and modeling intervene in the process and make it more efficient.[16]

How important is reinforcement to learning? We know that in classical conditioning reinforcement does not play a role, so that some types of learning can take place without reward. However, reinforcement is central to instrumental conditioning and research clearly demonstrates its potent influence on behavior change. The process of reinforcement will be presented in detail in chapter 5, although it is important to note at this point that many learning theorists believe that rewarding through instrumental conditioning is a more readily managed and implemented form of training in organizations than is classical conditioning.[17] Hence, the process of reinforcement is a critical source of behavioral influence within organizations.

Does learning one behavior help in learning another behavior? Research on this question demonstrates that at least three phenomena are involved in the process by which previously learned behaviors influence new learning: (1) stimulus generalization; (2) the hierarchy of S-R connections (habits); and (3) the process of proactive inhibition. Recall that earlier in this chapter we defined *stimulus generalization* as an individual's ability to respond similarly to stimuli that are similar in their characteristics. Stimulus generalization allows us, then, to take behaviors or skills that we have already learned and use them in learning new, but similar, behaviors. Suppose an employee must learn to use a new pneumatic tool. If he or she is already experienced with other pneumatic tools, then the employee will probably learn more quickly and effectively than if he or she were inexperienced.

Very similar to stimulus generalization is the phenomenon known as the hierarchy of habit. According to this process, the sequence and coordination of a series of acts is as important as the learning of each act separately. Thus, when a person is learning a complex sequence of behaviors and tasks, in addition to learning each act as a unit, he or she must also learn to control and coordinate the entire sequence. In this sense, learning one act before another not only helps in learning the next act, but is *necessary* for being able to perform the new series of tasks efficiently and effectively.

Stimulus generalization and the hierarchy of habit facilitate the learning of new behaviors. Sometimes, previous learning can interfere with new learning. Behavioral scientists use the term *proactive inhibition* to describe the phenomenon in which behavior that has been previously learned interferes with or inhibits new behavior to be learned. Suppose, for example, that two people are learning how to type. One has never had any experience with a typewriter, while the other has adopted a haphazard, personal, and very inefficient style of typing. The individual with no experience will probably learn how to type correctly more efficiently and effectively than the one with previous experience. The one with previous experience has the additional burden of unlearning or *extinguishing* the poor typing style before the proper style can be learned.

In summary, the classical conditioning model and the instrumental model have clearly withstood the test of scientific research. It is safe to consider them as very accurate representations of two major ways in which learning occurs.

Attitude Formation— A Special Case of Learning

Traditionally, behavioral scientists have divided attitudes into two major groups: (1) those that are *cognitive* (for example, beliefs or expectations about cause-effect relationships between events); and (2) those that are *evaluative* (for example, liking or disliking an event). An example of a cognitive attitude would be an employee's belief that superior job performance would be rewarded by praise from a superior. An example of an evaluative attitude would be the degree to which he or she would like or value such praise.

Most behavioral scientists agree that we are born with very few attitudes; that is, attitudes of both types are primarily acquired through *learning*. Thus, an employee's belief that superior job performance will be rewarded or that being late for work will result in a loss of pay or that a certain supervisor's word cannot be trusted develop through the processes of classical and instrumental conditioning. In addition, attitudes that involve a liking or disliking for certain groups on the job or for certain superiors are also largely a product of conditioning. It is believed, for example, that a liking or desire for money as a reward is acquired through the process of operant conditioning.[18]

Although attitudes are primarily learned, we must also recognize that as components of personality they are relatively enduring and resistant to change in the short run. This proposition is borne out in practice by the reported difficulty such groups as the National Association for the Advancement of Colored People (NAACP), the Congress on Racial Equality (CORE), the National Organization of Women (NOW), and other interest organizations have in changing popular beliefs and preferences regarding racial minorities and women. The empirical research literature abounds with evidence regarding the way learned attitudes towards women result in systematic sex-biased decisions against them in employment.[19]

Job Satisfaction as an Attitude

A common feature of people working in organizations is that they soon develop a set of attitudes about the work, supervision, coworkers, pay, and so on. This set of attitudes is usually referred to under the term of *job satisfaction*. Like any other attitude, job satisfaction consists of cognitions (beliefs, knowledge, or expectations), emotions (feelings, sentiments, likes, or dislikes), and behavioral tendencies. Job satisfaction attitudes also vary in intensity and consistency. For example, a worker in a warehouse may initially hold a strong dislike for the new supervisor (intensity) because he or she was given the job instead of the worker. With constant day-to-day interactions, however, this dissatisfaction turns to satisfaction because of the quality of behavior and interactions the worker has with the new supervisor (consistency, or the aspect of change).

level in organization age of employee)

Because it is based on the concepts of learning and perception, job satisfaction is usually measured with the use of a standardized attitude survey or questionnaire. (See exhibit A–1 in the Appendix for an example of a job satisfaction questionnaire.) Many well-validated questionnaires have been developed over the years.[20] Although the questionnaires differ in terms of the number of questions and the response format (i.e., "strongly agree" to "strongly disagree," "very true" to "very false," and so on), the basic objective is to gather information about how the individual feels about his or her employment in the organization. The typical attitude dimensions that have been investigated include work, pay, supervision, promotion opportunities, coworkers, benefits, working conditions, company, and management.[21]

The Importance of Job Satisfaction to the Manager

If job satisfaction is an attitude, or internal state of the individual, why should the manager be concerned with it, given the dominant focus on more "objective" factors, such as performance, efficiency, and survival? The answer is that the manager should be *very* concerned with levels of employee job satisfaction because these attitudes have been shown to be strongly related to more objective measures, such as performance.

The exact relationship between job satisfaction and performance has been the subject of much research and controversy over the years.[22] Some managers and scholars believe that satisfaction causes performance; in other words, a happy worker is a productive worker. Others feel that performance causes satisfaction—a high performing worker will derive satisfaction from doing well on his or her job. Still others believe that satisfaction and performance cause each other—a satisfied worker is more productive, and a more productive worker becomes more satisfied. The true relationship may never be fully known. It may be the case that a different relationship may exist in each individual. The overriding fact, however, is that performance and job satisfaction are strongly interwoven.

More concrete results have been reported concerning other causes and outcomes of job satisfaction. For example, job dissatisfaction has been shown to strongly influence the rates of turnover and absenteeism.[23] The more dissatisfied the worker, the higher the absenteeism and the greater the propensity to leave the organization (see chapter 14 for more details). Concurrently, the type of job, the quality of supervision, the nature of the group, and the accuracy and adequacy of the reward system have been shown to impact the level of job satisfaction. The relationship between these factors and job satisfaction will be covered in more depth later in this book.

Job Satisfaction Trends and Differences Within Organizations

We have all at one time or other come across magazine or newspaper articles that have discussed the state of worker satisfaction in terms such as "blue-collar blues" or "white-collar woes."[24] These articles have attempted to show that a crisis in worker morale was developing that was reflected in decreased performance and productivity and increased turnover and absenteeism. The major claimed cause of this state of worker satisfaction was jobs that were routine, mundane, boring, and offered too few people the opportunity for personal growth and development. The only feasible solutions concerned massive job redesign programs that would create jobs that were meaningful, responsible, and challenging.

Interestingly, many national surveys of worker satisfaction have failed to detect such problems on a large scale. Exhibit 4–9 summarizes the results of selected national surveys conducted by the Survey Research Center of the University of Michigan and the National Opinion Research Center. As the exhibit reveals, job satisfaction has risen in the twenty years since the 1958 survey, but remained fairly stable during the last decade.

Results such as those presented in exhibit 4-9 might lead to the conclusion that a

Exhibit 4–9 Percentage of Satisfied Workers, 1958–1977

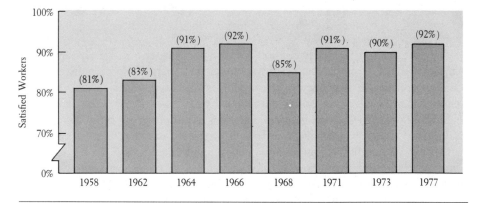

Source: U.S. Department of Labor, *Job Satisfaction: Is There a Trend?* Manpower Research Monograph no. 30, Manpower Administration, 1974, p. 4.

problem of worker dissatisfaction does not exist. A more detailed examination of job satisfaction attitudes, however, would suggest that this would be an erroneous conclusion. For example, exhibits 4–10 and 4–11 present variations in job satisfaction levels by occupational group and age. The results shown in exhibit 4–10 indicate that job satisfaction decreases as one moves from professional/managerial jobs to nonsupervisory/labor types of positions. As we will point out in chapter 6, jobs differ in terms of design characteristics, such as variety, autonomy, challenge, and significance, which would impact the level of job satisfaction.

Exhibit 4–11 suggests that job satisfaction increases with age. At least two possible reasons can be given to explain these results. First, it is the normal behavior of the individual to evaluate anything—be it a job, relationships with other persons, pay levels, and so on—in comparison with another object or thing that has been experienced.[25] When a person takes a first job early in adulthood, he or she probably has little or no prior full-time work experience with which to compare it. Comparisons are thus made with others around the person, or with some "ideal" state. It is not hard, then, to see why young workers tend to be less satisfied.

Second, closely aligned with the first, is the issue of "expectations." We all develop expectations about our future jobs from various sources, including from what we read and what others tell us. Frequently, our strongest expectations about work develop during the job search and placement process. We read company brochures, listen to company representatives during interviews, visit the organization for a tour and more intensive interviews, and become involved in general conversations with others familiar with the organization. In many cases, we may develop or acquire somewhat distorted opinions about the organization that may or

Exhibit 4–10 Mean Job Satisfaction Values by Occupational Group

Occupational Group	Mean Job Satisfaction*
Professional and technical (N = 323)	25
Managers, officials, and proprietors (N = 319)	19
Sales (N = 112)	11
Craftsmen and foremen (N = 270)	8
Service workers, except private household (N = 238)	−11
Clerical (N = 364)	−14
Operatives (N = 379)	−35
Nonfarm laborers (N = 72)	−42

*Mean values are based on a 28-question measure of overall job satisfaction. A higher numeric score indicates greater job satisfaction. The mean of this measure in 1973 was –2; its standard deviation was 84.

Source: Job Satisfaction: Is There a Trend? Manpower Research Monograph no. 30, U.S. Department of Labor, Manpower Administration, 1974, p. 10. Data taken from. R. P. Quinn and L. J. Shepard, The 1972–73 Quality of Employment Survey: Descriptive Statistics, with Comparison Data from the 1969–70 Survey of Working Conditions (Ann Arbor, Mich.: Survey Research Center, 1974).

Exhibit 4–11 Mean Job Satisfaction Values by Age

Age	Job Satisfaction*
16–20 (N = 175)	−41
21–29 (N = 584)	−27
30–44 (N = 657)	10
45–54 (N = 443)	9
55 or older (N = 292)	23

*A higher numeric score indicates greater job satisfaction. The mean of this measure was −2; its standard deviation was 84.

Source: Job Satisfaction: Is There a Trend? Manpower Research Monograph no. 30, U.S. Department of Labor, Manpower Administration, 1974, p. 12. *Data taken from:* R. P. Quinn and L. J. Shepard, *The 1972–73 Quality of Employment Survey: Descriptive Statistics, with Comparison Data from the 1969–70 Survey of Working Conditions* (Ann Arbor, Mich.: Survey Research Center, 1974).

may not be totally realistic. These opinions, attitudes, or expectations remain intact until we actually participate or experience situations in the organization. If our expectations are met, we are satisfied; if they go unmet, dissatisfaction may develop.

Throughout this book, we will refer to individual job satisfaction as an important outcome of organizational behavior. It is crucial for the reader to understand that satisfaction is an attitude that may vary in intensity, stability or consistency, level in the organization, and the age of the individual employee.

A Concluding Note

In summary, it is important to note how influential the process of learning is on virtually all forms of behavior within organizations. The capacity to learn both through instrumental and classical conditioning endows people with an almost limitless ability to adjust to a variety of work environments with relatively enduring patterns of behavior. In addition, we should recognize the fact that a great deal of learning takes place on an informal basis within organizations. Actual job experience, for example, is probably the single most important source of learning within organizations. Finally, we should note that the influence of learning is not limited to overt, physical forms of behavior. We have seen earlier that virtually all forms of behavior, including physical activities, beliefs, attitudes, and even perceptual behavior, are subject to the effects of learning.

As shown in exhibit 4–1, behavioral scientists agree that in addition to motives and personality, employee learning is influenced by interaction with environments. This employee-organization interaction is extremely critical to an understanding of behavior and performance. When we focus on this interaction itself, we are examining the *pathways* along which individuals interact with and respond to the organization. Behavioral scientists have correctly identified perception and learning as the two major processes allowing such interaction.

Applications and Implications for the Manager

Learning and Perception

1. Managers should note that the processes of learning and perception are the primary mechanisms by which employees interact with and adjust to their jobs, informal groups, and the formal organization.

2. Perception is a process through which short-run changes are made in behavior in response to inputs from the work environment. The process itself consists of two major actions: attention to incoming stimuli, and translation of such stimuli into a message that leads to a behavioral response.

3. Perception is a form of behavior and, therefore, influenced by at least the following factors: (1) characteristics of the object or source of incoming stimuli (such as a supervisor issuing a work request); (2) the situation or conditions under which the stimuli occur (such as the timing of a message); and (3) characteristics of the perceiving person. This last category is extremely important in determining the way incoming stimuli will be interpreted and the subsequent response. An individual's motives, previous learning, and personality all influence perception. Managers must take such considerations into account in predicting the way their actions and orders will be perceived by others.

4. Learning is a process through which relatively permanent changes occur in a person's behavior and subsequent performance because of experiences on the job, in the organization, and in training programs. It is important to distinguish learning from changes in behavior that occur as a result of factors other than learning. These include fatigue, maturation, aging, and drugs.

5. Learning occurs under two separate kinds of processes: classical conditioning and instrumental or operant conditioning. Classical conditioning consists of the establishment of a habit or stimulus-response (S-R) connection through the association of two stimuli. Instrumental conditioning is the establishment of an S-R connection through rewarding or reinforcing specific behaviors. An understanding of both stimulus association and reinforcement is necessary for managers who wish to direct and alter the work behavior of subordinates.

6. Managers who wish to reinforce desired work behaviors must consider the type of reinforcement (positive versus negative). Learning researchers recommend that managers actually reinforce desired behaviors and avoid punishment.

7. The learning curve is a graphical representation of the process of learning. The dependent variables of interest include response strength and response quality. As a person gains experience with work tasks, several characteristic events occur. The second characteristic of concern is a plateau where no new learning is evident. Finally, the learning curve measures the total amount that has been learned (total change in behavior).

Review of Theories, Research, and Applications

1. How do perception and learning as psychological processes differ from motives and personality in our understanding of individual behavior?

2. In what ways can characteristics of people influence their perception of the job? Give an organizational illustration for each of your points.

3. Define and explain the process of *perception*. How does perception influence behavior?

4. Incorporate the concepts of motive, personality, perception, and learning into a model of individual behavior in organizations. Explain how the four concepts fit together.

5. Define *learning* as a process. How is it unique as a source of change in behavior?

6. Develop and explain a practical illustration of learning through the process of classical conditioning. What are the important factors at work in this process?

7. Develop and explain a practical illustration of learning through instrumental or operant conditioning. What are the important factors at work in this process?

8. Explain the difference between positive reinforcement and punishment. Why is it that strict learning theorists maintain that learning can occur only under conditions of positive reinforcement?

9. What is stimulus generalization? In your definition, give a practical illustration of the concept.

Notes

1. See, for example, William Dember, *The Psychology of Perception* (New York: Holt, Rinehart & Winston, 1965).

2. Dember, *Psychology of Perception*, p. 6.

3. See, for example, R. Tagiuri and L. Petrullo, eds., *Person Perception and Interpersonal Behavior* (Stanford, Calif.: Stanford University, 1958); Paul Secord and Carl Backman, *Social Psychology* (New York: McGraw-Hill, 1964); M. Segall, D. Campbell, and J. Herskovits, *The Influence of Culture on Visual Perception* (Indianapolis: Bobbs-Merrill, 1966).

4. Linda A. Krefting, Philip K. Berger, and Marc J. Wallace, Jr., "The Contribution of Sex Distribution, Job Content, and Occupational Classification to Job Sextyping: Two Studies," *Journal of Vocational Behavior*, 1978, pp. 181–91.

5. Dan Rather and Gary Paul Gates, *The Palace Guard* (New York: Harper & Row, 1974), p. 109.

6. Sheldon Zedeck and Patricia Smith, "A Psychological Determination of Equitable Payment," *Journal of Applied Psychology*, 1968, pp. 343–47; John Hinrichs, "Correlates of Employee Evaluations of Pay Increases," *Journal of Applied Psychology*, 1968, pp. 481–89.

7. Linda A. Krefting and Thomas A. Mahoney, "Determining the Size of Meaningful Pay Increases," *Industrial Relations*, 1977, pp. 83–93.

8. Ernest R. Hilgard and Gordon Bower, *Theories of Learning* (Englewood Cliffs, N.J.: Prentice-Hall, 1966), p. 2.

9. Bernard Bass and James Vaughn, *Training in Industry: The Management of Learning* (Belmont, Calif.: Wadsworth, 1966), p. 8.

10. Hilgard and Bower, *Theories of Learning*, p. 4.

11. Ibid., pp. 7–10.

12. Ivan Pavlov, *Lectures on Conditioned Reflexes* (New York: International, 1927); Edwin Guthrie, *The Psychology of Learning* (New York: Harper & Row, 1952).

13. John B. Watson, *Behavior, An Introduction to Comparative Psychology* (New York: Holt, Rinehart & Winston, 1914).

14. Edwin L. Thorndike, *The Psychology of Learning* (New York: Teachers College, 1931), p. 2.

15. C. L. Hull, *Essentials of Behavior* (New Haven: Yale University, 1951); Hull, *A Behavior System: An Introduction to Behavior Theory Concerning the Individual Organism* (New Haven: Yale University, 1952).

16. F. Logan, *Fundamentals of Learning And Motivation* (Dubuque, Iowa: W. C. Brown, 1971).

17. H. J. Klausmeier, *Learning And Human Abilities* (New York: Harper & Row, 1975); S. A. Mednick, H. R. Pollio, and E. F. Loftus, *Learning*, 2 ed. (Englewood Cliffs, N.J.: Prentice Hall, 1973); and W. Wickelgren, *Learning and Memory* (Englewood Cliffs, N.J.: Prentice-Hall, 1977).

18. Robert L. Opsahl and Marvin D. Dunnette, "The Role of Financial Compensation in Industrial Motivation," *Psychological Bulletin,* August 1966, pp. 94–118; Edward E. Lawler III, *Pay and Organizational Effectiveness* (New York: McGraw-Hill, 1971).

19. S. Cohen and K. Bunker, "Subtle Effects of Sex Role Stereotypes in Recruiters' Hiring Decisions," *Journal of Applied Social Psychology*, 1975, pp. 566–73; S. Feldman and S. Kiesler, "Those Who Try Harder Are Number Two: The Effects of Sex on Attribution of Causality," *Journal of Personality and Social Psychology,* 1976, pp. 119–21; K. Deaux and T. Emswiller, "What Is Skill for the Male Is Luck for the Female," *Journal of Personality and Social Psychology,* 1974, pp. 80–85; W. Clay Hamner et al., "Race and Sex as Determinants of Ratings by Potential Employers in a Simulated Work Sampling Task," *Journal of Applied Psychology,* 1974, pp. 705–11; B. Rosen and T. Jerdee, "The Influence of Sex-Role Stereotypes on Personnel Decisions," *Journal of Applied Psychology,* 1974, pp. 9–14.

20. Patricia Smith, Lorne M. Kendall, and Charles L. Hulin, *The Measurement of Satisfaction in Work and Retirement* (Chicago: Rand McNally, 1969).

21. Edwin A. Locke, "The Nature and Causes of Job Satisfaction," in *Handbook of Industrial and Organizational Psychology,* ed. Marvin D. Dunnette, (Chicago: Rand McNally, 1976), pp. 1297–350.

22. Charles N. Greene, "The Satisfaction-Performance Controversy: New Developments and Their Implications," *Business Horizons,* October 1972, pp. 31–41.

23. Lyman W. Porter and Richard M. Steers, "Organizational, Work, and Personal Factors in Employee Turnover and Absenteeism," *Psychological Bulletin,* August 1973, pp. 151–76.

24. J. Richard Hackman and J. L. Suttle, *Improving Life at Work* (Santa Monica, Calif.: Goodyear, 1977).

25. R. P. Quinn and L. J. Shepard, *The 1972–73 Quality of Employment Survey: Descriptive Statistics, with Comparison Data from the 1969–70 Survey of Working Conditions* (Ann Arbor, Mich.: Survey Research Center, 1974).

Additional References

ADAMS, J. S. *Learning and Memory.* Homewood, Ill.: Dorsey, 1976.

BANDURA, A. *Social Learning Theory.* New York: General Learning Press, 1971.

BERLYNE, D. E. "Arousal and Reinforcement." *Nebraska Symposium on Motivation,* 1967, pp. 1–110.

BEYNON, H. *Perceptions of Work: Variations Within a Factory.* Cambridge: Cambridge University Press, 1972.

BIGGS, J. B. *Information and Human Learning.* Glenview, Ill.: Scott, Foresman, 1971.

BRUNNER, J. S., ed. *Beyond the Information Given: Studies in the Psychology of Knowing.* New York: Norton, 1973.

COUCH, W. T. *The Human Potential: An Essay on Its Cultivation.* Durham, N.C.: Duke University Press, 1974.

CRAIG, R. L. *Training and Development Handbook.* 2nd ed. New York: McGraw-Hill, 1976.

DUNNETTE, M. D., ed. *Handbook of Industrial and Organizational Psychology.* Chicago: Rand McNally, 1976.

EDWARDS, A. L., and ABBOTT, R. D. "Personality Traits: Theory and Technique." In *Annual Review of Psychology, 1973,* edited by P. Mussen and M. Rosenzweig, pp. 241–78. Palo Alto, Calif.: Annual Review, 1973.

HASLERUD, G. M. *Transfer, Memory and Creativity: After-learning as Perceptual*

Process. Minneapolis: University of Minnesota Press, 1972.

HILL, W. *Learning: A Survey of Psychological Interpretations.* Scranton, Pa.: Chandler, 1971.

HITT, W. D. "Two Models of Man." *American Psychologist,* 1969, pp. 651–58.

HOLZMAN, P. S. "Personality." In *Annual Review of Psychology, 1974,* edited by M. Rosenzweig and L. W. Porter, pp. 247–76. Palo Alto, Calif.: Annual Review, 1974.

KLEIN, G. S. *Perception, Motives, and Personality.* New York: Knopf, 1970.

LANDY, FRANK J. "An Opponent Process Theory of Job Satisfaction." *Journal of Applied Psychology,* 1978, pp. 533–47.

LEE, DENNIS M., and ALVARES, KENNETH M. "Effects of Sex on Descriptions and Evaluations of Supervisory Behavior in a Simulated Setting. *Journal of Applied Psychology,* 1977, pp. 405–10.

LOCKE, D. *Perception and Our Knowledge of the External World.* London: Allen & Unwin; New York: Humanities Press, 1967.

McCLELLAND, D. C. "Toward a Theory of Motive Acquisition." *American Psychologist,* 1965, pp. 321–33.

MacKINNON, NEIL J. "Role Strain: An Assessment of a Measure and Its Invariance of Factor Structure Across Studies." *Journal of Applied Psychology,* 1978, pp. 321–28.

MILNER, J., and DACHLER, H. P. "Personnel Attitudes and Motivations." In *Annual Review of Psychology, 1973,* edited by P. Mussen and M. Rosenzweig, pp. 379–402. Palo Alto, Calif.: Annual Review, 1973.

NEISSER, U. *Cognitive Psychology.* New York: McGraw-Hill, 1966.

ORPEN, CHRISTOPHER. "Work and Nonwork Satisfaction: A Causal-Correlational Analysis." *Journal of Applied Psychology,* 1978, pp. 530–35.

PORTER, L. W. "Turning Work into Nonwork: The Rewarding Environment." In *Work and Nonwork in the Year 2001,* edited by M. D. Dunnette. Monterey, Calif.: Brooks-Cole, 1973.

SCHEIN, E. H. "The Individual, the Organization, and the Career: A Conceptual Scheme." *Journal of Applied Behavioral Science,* 1971, pp. 401–26.

A Case of Conflict in Reinforcements

Problems in Altering Hazardous Work Habits

Petrie Construction Company is a large contractor specializing in the construction of large commercial buildings. The company does much of its own work, employing crews who excavate, lay foundations, erect structural steel, and do exterior masonry.

Jack Marsden is a project director for the company and in that position is the overseer of a given project. In this case, Marsden's group is working on a large sports arena that will be part of a major city's convention center.

He has just received an order from the local administrative office of the federal Occupational Safety and Health Administration (OSHA) closing the project down until the following list of hazardous practices are stopped:

1. Operating heavy equipment (bulldozers, forklifts, etc.) in reverse gear without a warning signal.

2. Sixteen ironworkers reported carrying out their tasks without hardhats.

3. Truck drivers delivering materials operating their vehicles at speeds greater than 20 mph on the work site.

4. Ironworkers working on structural steel without first setting out safety nets.

5. Carpenters operating saws with the safety guards removed.

Just after receipt of the order, the phone rang, and Bob Petrie, President of the firm, was at the other end of the line.

"Jack, what is this about your project getting shut down by OSHA! Are you nuts? We've been over this time and time again. The feds are serious about enforcing the law, and we can't afford to cross them. I've got a copy of their order, and they've got some very stupid things your people are doing down there. What are you going to do about it?"

Marsden replied, "I know all about that, sir, and am simply out of solutions to the problem! Before the project began, we had a very careful training program for each of the crews, just as the OSHA people had recommended. We ran each employee through the rules, tested them for their knowledge of the rules, and had each demonstrate proper work procedures to their foremen. I've talked to the crews as groups and spoken to individual employees about the necessity of following procedures. But I can't be down on each site all the time to police these people! I don't know why the training program didn't work. They've simply fallen back into old work habits."

Case Primer Questions

1. Why do you suppose the employees are reverting to old work habits? Why did the training program not have its intended effect?

2. Is there anything in the nature of reinforcements operating that might explain what happened in this case?

3. Do you think repeating the same training program would help?

4. If your answer to question 3 is no, what recommendations would you make to bring about a change in the workers' behavior?

Experiential Exercise

Evaluating the Source of a Message

Purpose

This exercise illustrates some of the principles of perception discussed and is intended to provide experience involving people's evaluation of the source of a message.

The objectives of this exercise are to:

1. Provide a realistic application of perceptual filtering by examining the influence of the source of a message on its reception and interpretation.

2. Give you some insight into the process by which people evaluate the source of a message.

How to set up the exercise

1. Break the class into three-member groups for a role-playing session. There will have to be at least two different groups for this exercise: (1) a "negative" group and (2) a "positive" group.

2. There will be three roles in each group: (1) a supervisor; (2) a neutral observer; and (3) a subordinate. Assign roles at this stage.

Instructions for the exercise

1. Group A—"Negative" group: The *subordinate* must read the following instructions: "Relationships with your boss are extremely bad. He (she) is always hassling you and coming up with last-minute things to do, usually at the end of the day. In addition, he (she) never bothers to thank you when you do a good job."

The *supervisor* must read the following instructions: "You will call your subordinate on the phone in a few minutes and make the following request (be sure to read the words *just* as they are written): '(name of subordinate), I'm sorry to be calling you so late in the day, but something slipped my mind. I've got a board meeting tonight, and I wonder if you could stay behind thirty minutes after work to help me calculate some figures I'm going to need. I'll let you come in a half hour late tomorrow morning if you will.' "

2. Group B—"Positive" group: The *subordinate* must read the following instructions: "Relationships with your boss are extremely good. He (she) has never hassled you and is very understanding and considerate in making job assignments to you. Very rarely has he (she) come up with a last minute request, and when he (she) does, you know it's really an emergency."

The *supervisor* must read the following instructions: "You will call your subordinate on the phone in a few minutes and make the following request (be sure to read the words *just* as they are written): '(name of subordinate), I'm sorry to be calling you so late in the day, but something slipped my mind. I've got a board meeting tonight and I wonder if you could stay behind thirty minutes after work to help me calculate some figures I'm going to need. I'll let you come in a half hour late tomorrow morning if you will.' "

3. Have each group role play the phone call with the neutral person observing.

4. Regroup the class and have the neutral observers report back what occurred. Have the class discuss and draw conclusions about any difference between the two role groups.

CHAPTER 5

Motivation

Managers in all types of organizations are continually faced with the fact that vast differences exist in the performance of a group of employees. Some employees always perform at high levels, need little or no direction, and appear to enjoy what they are doing. On the other hand, other employees perform only at marginal levels, require constant attention, and are often absent from their work stations.

The reasons for these differences in performance are varied and complex. In chapters 3 and 4, we saw that we could attribute some of these differences to certain individual characteristics, such as personality, intelligence, or ability. We could also focus on organizational influences such as the job, the supervisor's style, or the reward system used by the organization as contributing to these differences in performance. The core concept associated with each of these properties is *motivation*.

This chapter is divided into three major sections. First, an attempt will be made to define motivation and to stress its importance to managers in organizations. Second, we will present a review of some of the many motivational theories that have been developed, including both the early managerial approaches and the current contemporary theories. We will also provide a selected review of the many research studies on each theory. Finally, we will discuss some of the managerial applications suggested by these theorists. This theory-research-application progression is developed to illustrate two major points.

The first point is to make note of the complexity of the motivation process in organizations. As our discussion of the progression of theories from the early managerial approaches to the current contemporary theories will show, motivating employees involves not only individual characteristics, but also supervisory and organizational factors. Second, we hope to illustrate the need for managers not only to understand the various approaches to motivation but also to develop the necessary skills and abilities to diagnose motivational problems. This ability to diagnose is one of the most important elements of a manager's job, and one that is stressed throughout this book.

The Study of Motivation

The topic of motivation in organizations has received increased attention in recent years among practicing managers and organizational researchers. As a recent publication by General Electric, "Managing Motivation," states:

> When it comes to being highly productive on the job, to feeling a sense of success and achievement, to being a real contributor, what do you really believe about yourself and others? Does money count first—the desire to draw a bigger paycheck? Is it the competitive instinct—the urge to win over others? Is fear the principal factor or does motivation come from the promise of reward? Is it just ego—the desire for recognition, approval, status? Or is it the sheer enjoyment of being part of a busy, cooperative, professional team?
>
> These are questions to which behavioral scientists have been addressing themselves for years. Yet, oddly enough, few of their findings and theories have been effectively applied by managers who have learned their managing skills from bosses or from managerial courses that have tended to stress techniques—rather than a fundamental understanding of the managers' role in the human resource area.[1]

There are at least three major reasons that account for the emergence of motivation as a principal topic of interest. First, the ever-increasing external forces of national and international competition, economic, social, technological, and governmental conditions have forced management to develop and acquire new techniques and mechanisms to increase—or at least maintain—the levels of organizational efficiency and effectiveness. This requires the effective utilization of all of the resources of the organization—financial, physical, and human.[2]

Second, and closely related to the first, is the growing perspective of considering the human resources of the organization for long-term development and growth. Organizations had long considered their human resources in terms of an infinite labor pool in which frequent changes can occur because of the endless supply of qualified individuals. More concern is being placed by managers on developing, stimulating, and maintaining an effective work force at all skill levels through the use of such strategies as job design, management by objectives, and skills training.

Finally, the view of people in the workplace has undergone a significant change. Early managerial approaches considered the individual worker as only a "small cog in the wheel" who was motivated only by money. As we will point out, workers are motivated to perform by many different factors, including job challenge, achievement, advancement, and money.[3]

In summary, it is apparent why the topic of motivation remains one of the most important when considering organizational behavior and performance. The view of the individual worker as an unlimited resource who is solely motivated by economic means is far too simplistic. What managers need are approaches to acquire, motivate, and retain valuable human resources.

Definition of Motivation

The term *motivation* originates from the Latin word *movere,* which means "to move." This definition, however, is far too narrow to describe a very complex process. Given the obvious importance and complexity of motivation, it still remains an illusive concept to define and understand.

Motivation theorists have developed slightly different viewpoints of motivation that place emphasis on different concepts. In general, the differing views about motivation lead to a number of different conclusions: *regarding motivation*

focus

1. The analysis of motivation should concentrate on factors that *arouse* or *incite* a person's activities.[4]

2. Motivation is *process* oriented, and concerns choice, direction, and goals.[5]

3. Motivation also concerns how behavior is *started, sustained,* or *stopped* and what kind of subjective reaction is present in the person while this is going on.[6]

These conclusions will serve as the basis for our discussion of contemporary theories of motivation.

A Basic Motivation Model

Building upon these conclusions, we can now provide a basic model of motivation that incorporates the concepts of needs, drives, goals, and rewards. The initial step in developing the basic motivation model is to relate these variables in a sequential or process framework, as shown in exhibit 5–1, which will provide a foundation for the discussion of the different motivational approaches.

The model presents motivation as a multi-step process. First, the arousal of a *need* creates a state of disequilibrium (i.e., tension) within the individual that he or she will try to reduce through his or her behavior. Second, the individual will *search* for and *choose* strategies to satisfy these needs. Third, the individual will engage in

Exhibit 5–1 A Basic Motivational Model

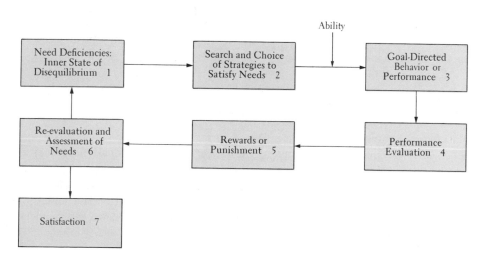

goal-directed behavior or performance to carry out the selected strategy. An important individual characteristic, ability, is seen as intervening between the choice of behavior and the actual behavior. This is to recognize that individuals may or may not have the necessary background (i.e., ability, skills, experience, or knowledge base) to attain a particular chosen goal (e.g., becoming president of AT&T at an early age). Fourth, an evaluation of the performance is conducted by the individual (or others) concerning the success of his or her performance in achieving the goal. Performance directed at satisfying a need for developing a sense of pride in one's work is usually evaluated by the individual. On the other hand, goal-directed behavior for satisfying a financial need (e.g., merit pay increase) is generally evaluated by another person (e.g., supervisor). Fifth, *rewards* or *punishment,* depending on the quality of the performance evaluation, are given. Finally, the individual *assesses* the degree to which the behavior and rewards have satisfied the original need. If this motivation cycle has satisfied the need, a state of equilibrium or *satisfaction* with respect to that *particular* need exists. If the need remains unsatisfied, the motivation cycle is repeated with possibly a different choice of behavior.

Consider, for example, a civil engineer recently assigned to the design and construction of a petroleum refinery. Because the engineer has been with the company for a number of years, he or she recognizes a desire or need to be promoted to the position of project manager (need deficiency or arousal). A number of ways to satisfy this need are available, including continued excellent performance, obtaining an advanced degree, asking for a promotion outright, or moving to another company (search for strategies). The engineer decides to excel on this project as the strategy to satisfy the need (choice of strategy). Recognizing that he or she has the necessary ability to excel in performance, the engineer works hard toward the successful completion of his or her assignment (ability and goal-directed performance). After the project has been completed, the engineer's performance is evaluated by his or her supervisor (performance evaluation), resulting in a promotion to project manager (reward). Because the original need for promotion has been satisfied, our engineer is in a state of equilibrium (satisfaction) with respect to this *particular* need. Other needs may arise later that may start the cycle all over again.

This model will serve as the framework for our initial discussion of motivation theories. At the end of the chapter, we will reevaluate and present a further development of the model.

Early Motivation Theories

Most theories of motivation—both early and current—are based on the principle of hedonism. The underlying principle of hedonism is that individuals behave in a manner to seek pleasure and to minimize displeasure. The concept dates back to the early Greek philosophers, and later emerged in the writings of Locke, Mill, and Bentham.[7] Although this philosophical approach provided some basis for identifying why individuals act the way they do, it did not provide a framework for understanding why people choose a particular behavior over another.

At the turn of the century, the major theme of motivation theory began moving from a philosophical to a more psychological, and a more managerial, approach. The theories that evolved attempted to explain the behavior of individuals through an investigation of variables that focused both on the individual and the situation in which the individual interacted.

The early managerial motivational theories (1910–1960) have been identified as prescriptive models because they purport to tell the manager how to motivate employees. Two approaches—the works of Taylor and McGregor—will be discussed.

Taylor: Scientific Management

The approach to managerial motivation developed from the works of Frederick W. Taylor has been termed *scientific management.*[8] Taylor's approach to motivation addressed the study and design of work that would maximize worker efficiency.

The framework of Taylor's approach was based on a number of premises about the individual in the workplace. These were: (1) the problem of inefficiency is a problem for management, not the worker; (2) workers have a false impression that if they work too rapidly, they will become unemployed; (3) workers have a natural tendency to work at less than their capacities; (4) it is management's responsibility to find suitable individuals for a particular job and then train them in the most efficient methods for their work; and (5) employee performance should be tied directly to the pay system, or an early incentive or piece-rate wage system. In other words, Taylor believed that employee efficiency would improve significantly by motivating employees through a piece-rate system and by designing the work such that a "single best method" could be utilized. The most fundamental problem with Taylor's approach from a motivational viewpoint concerned his rather simplistic assumptions about the nature of human motivation. In particular, the individual worker is motivated to work by more than money; more recent research suggests that workers seek to satisfy a variety of needs in the workplace—the need for security, social fulfillment, and a challenging job—and that they will respond to a variety of incentives, including pay, to increase productivity.

In an effort to overcome such problems, managers began to reexamine the assumptions and processes of motivation and to investigate and develop different methods to increase production and to provide an environment for secure jobs for their workers. Pay still remained a central aspect of motivational approaches in organizations; however, managers began looking at other aspects, such as the style of the leader, the nature of the job, and other benefit systems, as possible factors affecting human motivation.

Human Relations Movement

After the scientific management approach had been tried by many organizations, a growing number of managers recognized that this approach had many shortcomings in the workplace. In particular, two major shortcomings were salient: (1) It was incorrect to view all employees as lazy individuals who required constant close supervision and were motivated solely by money. Managers could point to a number of workers who not only were self-starters but could work very effectively without constant supervision. (2) Workers are motivated to perform their jobs by factors other than money, such as the challenging nature of the job, satisfying interactions with coworkers, recognition, achievement, and the possibilities of personal growth and development. Recognition of the individual, the group, and the job situation as influences in worker motivation developed into a movement we now term the human relations movement.[9]

The human relations movement was characterized by a number of prescriptions or techniques designed to assist managers in motivating employees. This set of techniques focused on three primary managerial activities: (1) encouraging workers to participate in managerial decisions; (2) redesigning jobs to allow for greater challenge and a broader range of participation in the organization's activities; and (3) improving the flow of communications between superior and subordinate employees.

One of the major contributors to the human relations movement was Douglas McGregor. In his principal work, McGregor advanced two beliefs about human behavior that could be held by different managers: Theory X and Theory Y.[10] Theory X represents the traditional approach to managing and is characterized by the following basic assumptions about human beings:

1. The average human being has an inherent dislike of work and will avoid it if possible.

2. Because of this human characteristic, most people must be coerced, controlled, directed, or threatened with punishment to get them to put forth adequate effort toward the achievement of organizational objectives.

3. The average human being prefers to be directed, wishes to avoid responsibility, has relatively little ambition, and wants security above all.[11]

Theory Y was based on a quite different set of assumptions:

1. The expenditure of physical and mental effort is as natural as play or rest.

2. External control and the threat of punishment are not the only means for bringing about effort toward organizational objectives. People will exercise self-direction and self-control in the services of objectives to which they are committed.

3. Commitment to objectives is a function of rewards associated with their achievement.

4. The average human being learns, under proper conditions, not only to accept but to seek responsibility.

5. The capacity to exercise a relatively high degree of imagination, ingenuity, and creativity in the solution of organizational problems is widely, not narrowly, distributed in the population.

6. Under the conditions of modern industrial life, the intellectual potentialities of the average human being are only partially utilized.[12]

Theory X was a widely accepted management practice prior to the human relations movement. Through the early behavioral studies and the growing acceptance of behaviorally oriented concepts, many practicing managers recognized that the total acceptance of the assumptions about human behavior in the workplace were questionable, and, in part, unacceptable. By contrast, the acceptance of the Theory Y approach, with its tenets of participation and concern for worker morale, encouraged managers to begin practicing such activities as: (1) delegating authority for many decisions; (2) enlarging and enriching jobs of workers by making them less repetitive; (3) increasing the variety of activities and responsibilities; and (4) improving the free flow of communication within the organization.

This particular approach to the motivation of individuals in organizations is not without its major limitations. For example, the human relations movement provided little understanding of the basic elements of human motivation—that is, how to motivate workers—nor did it take into account the fact that different individuals can be motivated by completely different aspects. In addition, it appears that too much emphasis was put on informal group processes without knowledge of the complexities of group dynamics. Still others pointed to the fact that what is successful in one organization may not be successful in other, quite differently designed organizations.

Even with its major limitations, the human relations approach to motivation proved to be of great value not only by creating a reorientation of thinking and managerial practice but also by influencing behavioral scientists and practicing managers alike to seek better ways of understanding the motivation process in organizations. The movement toward further inquiry provided the foundation for the development of the contemporary theories of motivation.

Contemporary Approaches to Motivation

In our earlier discussion of the definitional problems of motivation, we pointed out that there were a number of different ways people could interpret the concept of motivation. These different views provided the means for behavioral scientists to develop the three major categories of contemporary motivation theories: content, process, and reinforcement. These approaches are summarized in exhibit 5–2.

Content Theories

Content theories of individual motivation focus on the question of what it is that energizes, arouses, or starts behavior. The answers to this question have been provided by various motivational theorists in their discussion of the concepts of needs or motives that drive people and the incentives that cause them to behave in a particular manner. A need or motive is considered to be an internal quality to the individual. Hunger (the need for food), or a steady job (the need for security), are seen as motives that arouse people and may cause them to choose a specific behavioral act or pattern of acts. Incentives, on the other hand, are external aspects associated with the goal or end result the person hopes to achieve through his or her

Exhibit 5–2 Contemporary Approaches to Motivation

Type	Characteristics	Theories	Managerial Examples
Content	Concerned with factors that arouse, start, or initiate motivated behavior	1. Need hierarchy theory 2. Two-factor theory 3. ERG Theory	Motivation by satisfying individual needs for money, status, and achievement
Process	Concerned not only with factors that arouse behavior, but also the process, direction, or choice of behavioral patterns	1. Expectancy theory 2. Equity theory	Motivation through clarifying the individual's perception of work inputs, performance requirements, and rewards
Reinforcement	Concerned with the factors that will increase the likelihood that desired behavior will be repeated	1. Reinforcement theory (operant conditioning)	Motivation by rewarding desired behavior

actions. The income earned from a steady day of work (motivation by a need for security) is valued by the person. It is this value or attractiveness that we define as incentive.

The three most publicized and researched content theories of motivation are Maslow's need hierarchy, Herzberg's two-factor theory, and Alderfer's ERG theory. These theories have received considerable attention in both research studies and managerial application.

Maslow's need hierarchy.   Maslow's need hierarchy theory postulates that people in the workplace are motivated to perform by a desire to satisfy a set of internal needs (Step 1 in exhibit 5–1).[13] Maslow's framework is based on three fundamental assumptions:

1. People are wanting beings whose needs can influence their behavior. Only unsatisfied needs can influence behavior; satisfied needs do not act as motivators.

2. A person's needs are arranged in an order of importance, or hierarchy, from the basic (e.g., food and shelter) to the complex (e.g., ego and achievement).

3. The person advances to the next level of the hierarchy, or from basic to complex needs, only when the lower need is at least *minimally* satisfied. That is, the individual worker will first focus on satisfying a need for safe working conditions before motivated behavior is directed toward satisfying a need for achieving the successful accomplishment of a task.

Maslow proposed five classifications of needs, which represent the order of importance to the individual. These needs have been identified as: (1) physiological; (2) safety and security; (3) social and belonging; (4) ego, status, and esteem; and (5) self-actualization. A general representation of this hierarchy is shown in exhibit 5–3.

Physiological needs are the primary needs of individuals, such as the need for food, drink, shelter, and the relief from or avoidance of pain. In the workplace, such needs are represented by concern for salary and basic working conditions (e.g., heat, air conditioning, and eating facilities).

When the primary, or physiological, needs have been minimally satisfied, the next higher level of needs, the *safety and security needs,* assume importance as motivators. These are reflected in the need for freedom from threat, protection against danger and accidents, and the security of the surroundings. In the workplace, individuals would view these needs in terms of such aspects as safe working conditions; salary increases; job security; and an acceptable level of fringe benefits to provide for health, protection, and retirement needs.

When physiological and safety and security needs have been minimally satisfied, *social needs* become dominant. These needs concern such aspects as the need for friendship, affiliation, and satisfying interactions with other people. In organizations, such needs are operationalized by a concern for interacting frequently with fellow workers, employee-centered supervision, and an acceptance by others.

Ego, status, and esteem needs, the next level, focus on the need for self-respect, respect from others for one's accomplishments, and a need to develop a feeling of self-confidence and prestige. The successful attainment or accomplishment of a

Exhibit 5–3 Maslow's Need Hierarchy

General Factors	Need Levels	Organizational Specific Factors
1. Growth 2. Achievement 3. Advancement	Self-actualization	1. Challenging job 2. Creativity 3. Advancement in organization 4. Achievement in work
1. Recognition 2. Status 3. Self-esteem 4. Self-respect	Ego, Status, and Esteem	1. Job title 2. Merit pay increase 3. Peer/supervisory recognition 4. Work itself 5. Responsibility
1. Companionship 2. Affection 3. Friendship	Social	1. Quality of supervision 2. Compatible work group 3. Professional friendships
1. Safety 2. Security 3. Competence 4. Stability	Safety and Security	1. Safe working conditions 2. Fringe benefits 3. General salary increases 4. Job security
1. Air 2. Food 3. Shelter 4. Sex	Physiological	1. Heat and air conditioning 2. Base salary 3. Cafeteria 4. Working conditions

Ascending Order

Complex ← Basic

particular task, recognition by others of the person's skills and abilities to do effective work, and the use of organizational titles (e.g., Manager, Senior Accountant, Director of Nursing) are examples.

Self-actualization, the need to fulfill oneself by maximizing the use of abilities, skills, and potential, is the highest level of the need hierarchy. People with dominant self-actualization needs could be characterized as individuals who seek work assignments that challenge their skills and abilities, permit them to develop and to use creative or innovative approaches, and provide for general advancement and personal growth.

To illustrate Maslow's concept, consider a newly graduated marketing student from a well-respected university in Pennsylvania who takes a sales position with a food products company in California. The initial interview trip plus the follow-up visit to locate housing have removed his concerns about base salary and housing (physiological needs). Because our new salesperson has a wife and small son, he seeks out information about such aspects as medical insurance coverage, use of company car, and so on (safety and security needs). The collected information, coupled with a long discussion with his supervisor about job security, have satisfied his concerns about these factors. The frequent interactions the salesperson has with his supervisor, fellow workers, and clients have proven to be most satisfying (social needs).

As time passes, the salesperson concentrates more and more effort toward doing his job as effectively as he can. Within three years, he has received a promotion to Sr. Salesperson and awarded the yearly sales award the last two years in a row (ego, status, and esteem needs). With the passing of a few more years, our salesperson begins to feel somewhat uneasy in his position. He feels a sense of needing to learn new things, to work on different projects, and generally trying to exercise more innovativeness and creativity in his work (self-actualization needs). Subsequent years find our salesperson in the newly created position of General Manager of Product Development. Outside activities include active participation in local civic and charitable affairs, plus a revitalized interest in manufacturing stringed musical instruments in his garage workshop.

This example (which is an actual situation of an acquaintance of one of the authors) serves to illustrate Maslow's basic concepts. That is, needs are: (1) motivational; (2) ordered in an importance, or basic-to-complex, hierarchy; and (3) ascending the hierarchy is based on lower-need satisfaction.

An important point for managers to consider is that highly deficient needs, or needs that have gone unsatisfied for a long period of time, serve to cause such behavioral responses as frustration, conflict, and stress. Individual reaction to frustration, conflict, and stress differs from person to person depending upon environmental, organizational, and personal factors. These reactions to need deficiencies take the form of at least four different "defensive behaviors."

1. *Aggression* is a physical or verbal defensive behavior that can be directed toward a person, object, or the organization. Physical aggression can take the form of such things as stealing or equipment sabotage. Verbal aggression can be

the emotional outburst of an employee directed toward the supervisor concerning unsafe working conditions.

2. *Rationalization* is a defensive behavior that takes the form of such activities as placing the blame on others or having a "take it or leave it" attitude. An employee may rationalize a small pay increase by attributing it to poor supervision or inadequate resources, when in fact it was the particular individual's unsatisfactory performance that caused the small pay increase.

3. *Compensation* concerns the behavior of a person going overboard in one area to make up for problems or need deficiencies in another area. A person whose need for interaction with fellow employees goes unsatisfied during normal working hours may compensate by being extremely active in company-related social, recreational, or civic activities.

4. *Regression* is a defense that significantly alters the individual's behavior. After being turned down for promotion to the position of a loan officer, the head teller may change his or her behavior from being friendly and open to being terse, highly task oriented, or temperamental.

These defensive behaviors can result from the inability of an employee to satisfy a personally important need. These behaviors are realities in any organizational setting, and it is the responsibility of the manager to understand the causes.

Research on Maslow's need theory.   Since its development, a number of research studies have been conducted on the need hierarchy theory in organizations. From the standpoint of needs in motivation and satisfaction, a number of interesting results have been reported. For example, upper-level managers place less emphasis on safety and security needs and more importance on higher-order needs than do lower-level managers.[14] Some would explain this as involving the process of career change and advancement.[15] In addition, differences in need levels were found in comparing managers in small companies to larger firms, line managers to staff managers, and American managers working abroad to foreign managers.[16] A number of observations are necessary, however, to further clarify the need hierarchy approach. First, despite some interesting and supportive research, other findings have raised a number of issues and criticisms about the theory and the viability of the five need levels. For example, selected data from managers in two different companies found little support that a hierarchy of needs existed.[17] These studies identified two, not five, levels of needs: a biological level and a global need level encompassing the higher-order needs.

A second criticism is that an individual's needs should be viewed not in a static but in a dynamic context. Individual needs are constantly changing due to the various situations in which people become involved. For example, a manager striving to satisfy ego and esteem needs in his or her work may become concerned with job-security needs when adverse economic conditions have resulted in worker layoffs and terminations. Third, more than one level of need may be operational at the same time for an individual. The project engineer may be striving to satisfy a self-actualization need while simultaneously being concerned with safety needs.

Finally, the theory states that a satisfied need is not a motivator. Although in a general sense this may be true, it is also true that individual needs are never fully or permanently satisfied as a result of a single act or actions. As we already pointed out, it is the nature of needs that they must be continually and repeatedly fulfilled if the individual is to perform adequately.[18] If a number of needs are operating at one time, they would seem to contradict the idea of need satisfaction occurring in a fixed hierarchical order.

Although many of the current research results both fail to consistently support the need hierarchy approach and question its conceptual clarity, it still has a common-sense appeal to managers. The theory is simple and has relevance and importance to managers because individual needs, no matter how defined, are critical factors in understanding behavior.[19]

Herzberg's two-factor theory.   A second popular content theory of motivation, closely related to Maslow's need hierarchy, was proposed by Herzberg.[20] The theory, which has been called the two-factor theory or the motivation-hygiene theory, has been widely received and applied by managers concerned with the motivation of their employees.

The original research used in developing the theory was conducted with 200 accountants and engineers using the critical-incident method for data collection. Herzberg used interview responses to questions such as, "Can you describe, in detail, when you feel exceptionally good about your job?" "Can you describe, in detail, when you feel exceptionally bad about your job?" The results obtained from this research methodology were fairly consistent across the various subjects. Good feelings about the job were reflected in comments concerning the *content* and experiences of the job (e.g., doing good work or a feeling of accomplishment and challenge); bad feelings about the job were associated with *context* factors, that is, those surrounding but not directly involved in the work itself (e.g., salary and working conditions). This procedure revealed two distinct types of motivational factors: *satisfiers* and *dissatisfiers*. The Herzberg research resulted in two specific conclusions:

1. There is a set of extrinsic job conditions that, when not present, result in *dissatisfaction* among employees. If these conditions are present, this does not necessarily motivate employees. These conditions are the dissatisfiers or *hygiene* factors because they are needed to maintain at least a level of no dissatisfaction. These factors are related to the *context* of the job and are called dissatisfiers. These include:

   (a) Job security
   (b) Salary
   (c) Working conditions
   (d) Status
   (e) Company policies
   (f) Quality of technical supervision
   (g) Quality of interpersonal relations among peers, supervisors, and subordinates
   (h) Fringe benefits

2. A set of intrinsic job conditions exist that help to build levels of *motivation,* which can result in good job performance. If these conditions are not present,

they do not result in dissatisfaction. These set of aspects are related to the content of the job and are called satisfiers. These include:

(a) Achievement
(b) Recognition
(c) Work itself
(d) Responsibility
(e) Advancement
(f) Personal growth and development

As shown in exhibit 5–4, Herzberg has reduced Maslow's five need levels into two distinct levels of analysis. The hygiene factors or dissatisfiers are analogous to Maslow's lower-level needs (i.e., physiological, safety, and social needs). They are essentially preventive factors that serve to reduce dissatisfaction. Hygiene factors, if absent in the workplace, lead to high levels of dissatisfaction; if present, they create a state of "zero dissatisfaction" or neutrality. By themselves, hygiene factors (or job-context factors) do not motivate individuals to better performance.

The motivators, or satisfiers, are equivalent to Maslow's higher-level needs. These are the job-content factors that motivate people to perform. According to Herzberg, only such aspects as a challenging job, recognition for doing a good job, and opportunities for advancement, personal growth, and development function to provide a situation for motivated behavior.

As an example, consider the assembly-line workers in various manufacturing firms. For years, these firms have experienced severe worker motivational problems that have resulted in such negative outcomes as high levels of turnover, absenteeism, grievances, and low productivity. In response to these problems, many firms have reacted by instituting costly fringe-benefit plans, significant wage increases, and elaborate security and seniority programs. Even with such massive programs, motivational problems still remain.

In Herzberg's framework, these managerial reactions have focused primarily on the hygiene factors surrounding the job, which has resulted in bringing individuals

Exhibit 5–4 Herzberg's Motivator-Hygiene Theory

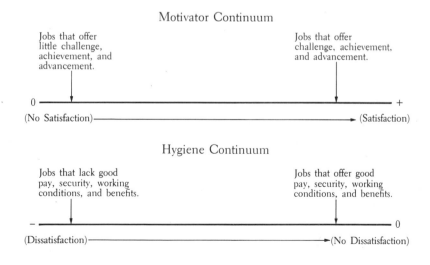

to the theoretical "zero point" of motivation. The two-factor theory would predict that improvements in motivation would only appear when managerial action focused not only on the factors surrounding the job but on the job itself. This can be done by partially removing the boredom and routineness inherent in most assembly-line jobs and developing jobs that can provide increased levels of challenge and opportunities for a sense of achievement, advancement, growth, and personal development. We will cover this topic more in depth in chapter 6.

Research on the two-factor theory.   Along with the other contemporary motivational theories, Herzberg's two-factor theory has received a great deal of attention from behavioral scientists. And as one might expect, both supportive[21] and non-supportive[22] findings have been reported. The research has variously shown that: (1) a given factor (such as pay) may cause satisfaction in one sample and dissatisfaction in another; (2) satisfaction or dissatisfaction of a factor may be a function of the age and organization level of the worker; and (3) individuals may confuse company policies and supervisory style with their own ability to perform as factors causing satisfaction or dissatisfaction.

Despite the important contributions made by Herzberg, the two-factor theory has been criticized for a number of reasons. First, the major criticism concerns the methodology used to develop the theory. The critical-incident method, while requiring people to look at themselves retrospectively, does not adequately provide a vehicle for the expression of other factors to be mentioned. There is a tendency for the most recent events of a person's work experience to be identified with such a methodology. This tends to ignore or diminish the impact of past and possibly equally important events. A second methodological point concerns the nature of the original sample used by Herzberg. Critics have questioned whether it is justified to generalize to other occupational groups from such a limited sample (i.e., accountants and engineers in Pittsburgh). The technology and environments of the two study groups may vary considerably from such groups as nurses, sales representatives, or secretaries in other areas of the country.

An additional criticism concerns that fact that little attention has been directed toward testing the motivation and performance implications of the model.[23] That is, the focus has been on "satisfaction," not on the actual motivation of the individual employee. As we know from exhibit 5–1 (and we will soon present in other motivational theories), satisfaction and motivation are two different aspects; motivation is usually associated with goal-directed behavior (box 3 in exhibit 5–1), and satisfaction is an attitude that *results from* goal-directed behavior.

Finally, and probably most importantly, the two-factor theory fails to account for differences in individuals. Herzberg's approach basically assumes individual employees will be similar in their responses to the work environment. A close examination of the people around each one of us, however, will generally reveal some people who will react, or be motivated, by jobs that involve challenge, achievement, advancement, and so on. On the other hand, there are some people who are equally motivated by money and job security. Trying to motivate employees through job-content factors is bound to result in only partial success.

Although the list of major criticisms continues to expand, the reader should not underestimate the value or the impact of the theory. As in the case of the need hierarchy approach, Herzberg's theory has a common-sense appeal to managers about the nature of the work environment. Managers appear to feel comfortable with the suggestions of the theory and the limited results of organizational applications. The serious student of organizational behavior, however, should be cautious of approaches that have a subjective appeal and about which significant questions have been developed from a scientific vantage point.

Alderfer's ERG theory.   Alderfer's ERG theory is a more recently proposed motivation approach that seeks to establish "human needs in organizational settings."[24] Alderfer condenses the Maslow hierarchy into three need categories: existence (E); relatedness (R); and growth (G).

Existence needs are all the various forms of physiological and material desires, such as hunger, thirst, and shelter. In organizational settings, the need for pay, benefits, and physical working conditions are also included in this category. This category is comparable to Maslow's physiological and certain safety needs.

Relatedness needs include all those that involve interpersonal relationships with others in the workplace. This type of need in individuals depends on the process of sharing and mutuality of feelings between others to attain satisfaction. This need category is similar to Maslow's safety, social, and certain ego-esteem needs.

Growth needs are all those needs that involve a person's efforts toward creative or personal growth on the job. Satisfaction of growth needs results from an individual engaging in tasks that not only require the person's full use of his or her capabilities, but also may require the development of new capabilities. Maslow's self-actualization and certain of his ego-esteem needs are comparable to these growth needs.

ERG theory is based upon three major propositions: (1) The less each level of need has been satisfied, the more it will be desired (i.e., *need satisfaction*). For example, the less existence needs (e.g., pay) have been satisfied on the job, the more they will be desired. (2) The more lower-level needs have been satisfied, the greater the desire for higher-level needs (i.e., *desire strength*). For example, the more existence needs have been satisfied for the individual worker (e.g., pay), the greater the desire for relatedness needs (e.g., satisfying interpersonal relationships). (3) The less the higher-level needs have been satisfied, the more the lower-level needs will be desired (i.e., *need frustration*). For example, the less growth needs have been satisfied (e.g., challenging work), the more relatedness needs will be desired (e.g., satisfying interpersonal relationships). This relationship is shown in exhibit 5–5.

Two important differences between ERG theory and the need hierarchy should be pointed out. First, the need hierarchy theory is based upon a satisfaction-progression approach; that is, an individual will progress to a higher-order need once a lower-order need has been satisfied. ERG theory, on the other hand, incorporates not only a satisfaction-progression approach but also a frustration-regression component. Frustration-regression describes the situation in which a higher-order need remains unsatisfied, or frustrated, and greater importance or desire is placed on the next lower need. As shown in exhibit 5–5, for example, frustration of growth needs results in greater desire for relatedness needs. The second major difference is closely related to the first. That is, unlike the need hierarchy approach, ERG theory

Exhibit 5-5 Satisfaction-Progression, Frustration-Regression Components of ERG Theory

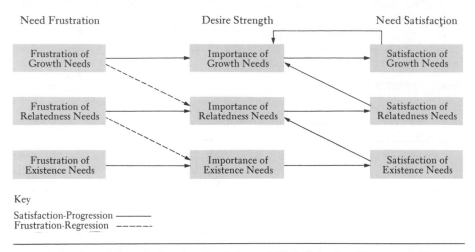

Frank J. Landy and Don A. Trumbo, *Psychology of Work Behavior,* (Homewood, Ill.: Dorsey Press, 1976), p. 301.

indicates that more than one need may be operative at any one time.

Consider a newly hired young accountant in a large accounting firm. On entry into the firm, our accountant was concerned with the level of pay, the security of the job, and the nature of the working conditions (existence needs). While on the job for a short time, however, the accountant feels satisfied with his or her pay, job security, and working conditions (need satisfaction). With existence needs satisfied, our accountant begins making an attempt at developing friendly relations with fellow employees (relatedness needs and desire strength). Some time later, after satisfactory interpersonal relationships have been developed (need satisfaction), the accountant asks for a promotion to a different, more challenging, and more responsible job (growth need). The supervisor indicates, however, that such a promotion is not available at this time, but will come later, after more job-related experience has been gained (need frustration). Given this situation, the accountant concentrates on performing his or her current job as best possible to indicate his or her capabilities to higher management (regression to relatedness needs).

Research on the ERG theory.   Because of its rather recent introduction, very few studies have been reported that have tested ERG theory. The reported studies using sample of students, managers, and bank employees have, in general, revealed stronger support for the ERG theory than for either the hypotheses of Maslow's need heirarchy or a simple need-frustration foundation (that any frustrated need will increase in strength, but no connection between different types of needs).[25]

Because ERG theory is relatively new motivational framework, major criticisms of its approach have not been great in number. Some recent studies, however, have questioned the theory's universality; that is, there is some evidence that the theory will work in some organizations but not in others.[26] The reasons for these results apparently relate to the general nature of the work in the studied companies (see chapter 6). Various behavioral scientists, however, view ERG theory as the most current, valid, and researchable theory of motivation based on the need concept.[27]

For managers, ERG theory provides a more workable or realistic approach to motivation than the theories of Maslow or Herzberg. Because of the dual components—satisfaction-progression and frustration-regression—it provides a clearer understanding of human behavior in organizations.

Summary of content theories.   The three content theories have emphasized the basic motivational concepts of needs, satisfiers-dissatisfiers, and desires. Exhibit 5–6 summarizes the relationship among the three content theories. Each of them has attempted to explain individual behavior from a slightly different perspective; none of the three theories should be accepted by the practicing manager as the sole framework for understanding behavior in organizations. As will be pointed out later in the chapter, critics are skeptical of attempting to explain behavior solely on the basis of needs, desires, and satisfaction because such approaches provide only a minimal understanding of what actions the individual will choose so that his or her needs will be satisfied. Even so, people have needs, various job factors result in differing degrees of satisfaction, and individual desires are real aspects in organizations. These theories provide an excellent comparison for the discussion of process and reinforcement theories of motivation.

Process Theories

The content theories of motivation provided managers with a better understanding of the particular work-related factors that arouse employees to motivated behavior. These theories, however, provide little understanding of why people *choose* a particular behavioral pattern to accomplish work goals. This choice aspect is the objective of what we have termed *process* theories. Expectancy theory and equity theory

Exhibit 5–6   Content Motivation Theories

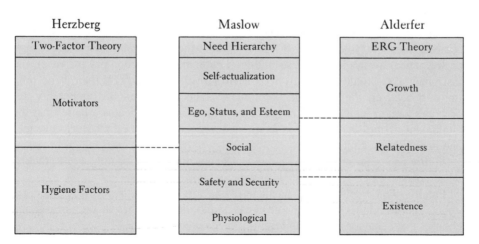

Herzberg	Maslow	Alderfer
Two-Factor Theory	Need Hierarchy	ERG Theory
Motivators	Self-actualization	Growth
	Ego, Status, and Esteem	
	Social	Relatedness
Hygiene Factors	Safety and Security	
	Physiological	Existence

are the two major process theories that concern this approach to motivation in organizations.

Expectancy theory.   In its basic form, expectancy theory relates to *choice behavior.* Specifically, the theory states that individuals will evaluate various strategies of behavior (e.g., working hard each day versus working hard three days out of five) and then choose the particular strategy that they believe will lead to those work-related rewards that they value (e.g., pay increase). If the individual worker believes that working hard each day will lead to a pay increase, expectancy theory would predict that this will be the behavior he or she will choose.

Building on the earlier work of Tolman,[28] Lewin,[29] and Atkinson,[30] Vroom presented a process theory of work motivation that he calls an instrumentality or expectancy theory.[31] The key variables in Vroom's formulation are expectancies, valences, outcomes, instrumentalities, and choice.

Expectancy is the perceived belief concerning the likelihood that a particular behavioral act will be followed by a particular outcome. The degree of belief can vary between 0 (complete lack of a relationship between the act and a given outcome) and 1 (complete certainty that an act will result in a given outcome).

Valence is the strength of an employee's preference for a particular outcome. Unlike expectancies, valences can be either positive or negative. In a work situation, we would expect such outcomes as pay, promotion, and recognition by superiors to have *positive* valences; such outcomes as conflict with coworkers, job pressure, or reprimands from the supervisor may have *negative* valences. Theoretically, an outcome has a valence because it is related to the needs of the individual. This variable (i.e., valence) provides a partial link to the content theories.

An *outcome* or *reward* is the end product of a particular behavior, and can be classified as a first- or second-level outcome. A means-end framework is used to show how first-level outcomes are linked to second-level outcomes. Generally speaking, first-level outcomes refer to some aspect of *performance,* such as work-goal accomplishment, and are thought to be the result of the individual's task performance effort. Second-level outcomes, on the other hand, are viewed as the consequences to which the first-level outcomes are expected to lead, such as pay increases or promotions.

Instrumentality refers to the relationship between first- and second-level outcomes and can vary between + 1.0 and − 1.0. If the first-level outcome (e.g., high performance) always leads to a second-level outcome (e.g., good pay increase), the instrumentality would be perceived as having a value of +1.0. If there is no relationship between the first- and second-level outcomes, then instrumentality approaches zero. Finally, an instrumentality value of −1.0 indicates a belief that the attainment of the second level outcome is certain without the first-level outcome, and impossible with it.

Ability generally refers to the individual's capacity for performing a task; that is, what a person can do rather than what they will do.

Finally, *choice* concerns the particular behavioral pattern the individual decides upon. The individual weighs the advantages and disadvantages of each action and chooses that behavior which will lead to valued outcomes.

To illustrate the three main components of expectancy theory, consider the case of an assistant administrator of a large urban hospital who has been given the responsibility and authority to coordinate a major physical expansion of the hospital. As shown in exhibit 5–7, the administrator believes that there are three possible first-level outcomes (completion of expansion ahead of schedule, completion on schedule, or completion behind schedule) that can lead to at least three second-level outcomes (pay raise, promotion, or recognition).

Component 1 ($V_j = f(V_k \times I)$) suggests that the value for each first-level outcome is a function of the valence of the second-level outcome times the instrumentality of the second-level outcome. As noted in exhibit 5–7, the valence associated with completion of expansion ahead of schedule is equal to 12.6 [i.e., $V_j = (8 \times .6) + (10 \times .5) + (4 \times .7)$].

Component 2 ($F = f(V_j \times E)$) states that the force or motivation to perform is equal to the valence of the first-level outcome times the expectancy that effect will lead to that particular outcome. For the administrator in our example, the force for *each* first-level outcome is 6.3 [$F_1 = (12.6 \times .5)$] for completion ahead of schedule, 3.4 [$F_2 = (5.6 \times .6)$] for completion on schedule, and -5.9 [$F_3 = (-7.4 \times .8)$] for completion behind schedule. According to expectancy theory, individuals will choose behaviors that lead to valued rewards; therefore, the administrator's *choice* of motivated behavior will be to attempt to complete the hospital expansion ahead of schedule. The astute reader will note that the two components formulated to determine force or motivation are *multiplicative* in nature. That is, as shown in exhibit 5–8, for motivation to be at a high level, valence, instrumentality and expectancy must *each* be high. Whenever one or more of these factors is low, the *resultant motivation* is also low.

For example, case 2 in exhibit 5–8 may be a situation for our hospital administrator where no matter how valued the rewards are, or how high performance

Exhibit 5–7 Expectancy Theory

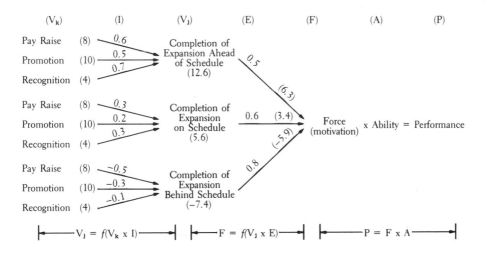

Exhibit 5–8 Example Combinations of Expectancy Theory Variables

Case	Valence (Value of outcome)	Instrumentality (Performance will lead to outcome)	Expectancy (Effort will lead to performance)	Force or Motivation
1.	High	High	High	High
2.	High	High	Low	Low
3.	High	Low	High	Low
4.	Moderate	Moderate	Moderate	Moderate
5.	Low	High	High	Low
6.	Low	Low	Low	Low

usually is rewarded in the organization, there is not enough time or resources available for him or her to perform at the high level (i.e., low expectancy). Case 3 could illustrate a situation in which the administrator can do the work and the rewards are valued, but from past experience it is known that this organization does not reward high performance. The result is a low instrumentality and, hence, lower motivation.

Component 3 ($P = F \times A$) indicates that actual performance is a multiplicative function of force to perform (motivation) and the individual's ability. In essence, this relates what a person *wants to do* (motivation) with what they *can do* (ability). For our administrator to actually complete the proposed expansion ahead of time, the motivation *and* ability (e.g., skills in project management and control) must be equally high in value.

Since Vroom's initial model, expectancy theory has undergone at least four developments.[32] First, the theory was extended by making the distinction between extrinsic outcomes (e.g., pay and promotion) and intrinsic outcomes (e.g., recognition, achievement, and personal development). Extrinsic valences refer to outcomes that come to the individual from others because of his or her performance; intrinsic valences are associated with the job itself. Second, a further distinction was made between two types of expectancies. Expectancy I is concerned with the perceived relationship between effort expended and first-order outcomes, such as performance or work-goal accomplishment. Expectancy II, similar to Vroom's concept of instrumentality, is concerned with the relationship between first-level outcomes (e.g., performance) and second-level outcomes or rewards (e.g., pay, recognition, or achievement). These expectancies have come to be known as EI (effort-to-performance) and EII (performance-to-reward) expectancies or probabilities.

The third development concerns the broadening of the theory to include the possible effects of other work-related variables on the major variables of the theory.[33] These revisions include: (1) the possible impact of personality variables (e.g., self-esteem and self-confidence) in the formation of expectancy perceptions; (2) the effect of past experiences on expectancy development; and (3) the inclusion of role perceptions and environmental conditions as possibly affecting the relationships with motivation and actual performance.[34]

Finally, the theory was extended to include the variable of work-related satisfaction.[35] According to the new model, satisfaction is viewed as being a function of actual performance and the real rewards gained from that performance. This introduces the topics of performance evaluation and organizational reward systems, which will be discussed later in this book.

The further developments and extensions to Vroom's original formulation have resulted in a fairly complex motivational model. This complexity should not be viewed by the practicing manager as another academic exercise in "muddying the waters." Instead, it should be viewed as an attempt to depict the true complexities inherent in the understanding of employee motivation in organizations. The new framework provides the manager with an understanding that motivation is not only affected by such variables as expectancies and valences but also can be affected by individual characteristics (e.g., personality and ability) and additional variables in the work situation at least under the partial influence of the manager (e.g., past experiences, role perceptions, and reward systems).

Research on the expectancy theory.   Since the introduction of Vroom's model, the number of research efforts that have investigated the expectancy theory has grown significantly.[36] The various published reviews of expectancy theory research have revealed that: (1) the dimensions of effort-to-performance and performance-to-reward expectancies have generally shown to be positively related to the individual outcomes of performance and satisfaction; (2) personality variables appear to have an effect on an individual's expectancy and valence perceptions; and (3) the predictive power of the expectancy model with respect to performance and satisfaction is not significantly improved when expectancies and valences are combined (multiplicatively or additively), as compared to the two variable relationships noted in (1) above.

Although this ongoing research appears to be encouraging in comparison with the research conducted on the content theories, a number of problems associated with expectancy theory have been highlighted. First is the problem noted by Lawler and Suttle when they state that expectancy theory "has become so complex that it has exceeded the measures which exist to test it."[37] The variables in expectancy theory have typically been measured using survey questionnaires, which are usually different from researcher to researcher and have not always been scientifically validated.[38] Comparisons from study to study are thus questionable.

Second, and closely related to the first, is that the complexity of the model makes it very difficult to test fully. Few studies have been reported that have tested all the variables within the expectancy theory framework. Finally, the research evidence does not support the notion that individuals mentally perform the complex multiplicative calculations required by the model before effort is exerted. Effort-to-performance expectancies, performance-to-reward expectancies, and valences apparently are valid components that relate to an individual's motivation and subsequent performance. Whether these component variables act independently to predict motivation, or are combined in some mathematical form, is a subject for future research efforts.[39]

Even though significant problems exist with expectancy theory, there are certain implications for managerial practice. First, individuals make conscious evaluations with respect to the result of their efforts (performance) and the outcomes of their performance (rewards). Second, a manager can clarify and increase a subordinate's effort-to-performance expectancy through the use of coaching, guidance, and participation in various skills training programs. Third, rewards must be closely and clearly related to those behaviors of individuals that are important to the organization. This has definite implications for the nature of the reward system in organizations and the necessity of having rewards be contingent on an individual's performance. Finally, individuals differ in the value (valence) they place on the rewards they can receive from their work. Managers, therefore, should place some emphasis on matching the desires of the employee with the particular organizational reward. Expectancy theory can provide the manager with a framework for explaining the direction of behavior of employees and for highlighting certain organizational influences that may have an effect on their motivated behavior.

Equity theory.   A second process approach to motivation is termed *equity theory.* Equity theory states that if individuals perceive a discrepancy between the amount of rewards they receive and their efforts, they are motivated to reduce it; furthermore, the greater the discrepancy, the more the individuals are motivated to reduce it. Discrepancy refers to the perceived difference that may exist between two or more individuals. The differences may be based on subjective perception or objective reality.

Adams has been associated with the initial development and testing of the theory.[40] He defines a discrepancy, or inequity, as existing whenever a person perceives that the ratio of his or her *job outcomes* to *job inputs,* in comparison with a reference person's outcomes to inputs, are unequal. The reference person may be someone in an individual's group, in another group, or outside the organization.

In equity theory, inputs are such aspects as effort, skills, education, and task performance that an individual employee brings to or puts into the job. Outcomes are those rewards that result from task accomplishment: pay, promotion, recognition, achievement, and status.

Adams postulates that individual employees compare inputs and outcomes with other workers of roughly equal status. If the two ratios are not in balance, the individual is motivated to reduce the inequity. Exhibit 5–9 illustrates the equity-inequity possibilities for an example employee. The figure presents a three-step process: (1) comparison of outcome/input ratios between focal person and reference person; (2) decision (equity = satisfaction, inequity = dissatisfaction); and (3) motivated behavior to reduce inequity.

There are a number of behavioral patterns that an individual can follow to reduce an inequitable situation. First, when inequity is caused by a lower outcome/input ratio for the focal person (underpayment), this person may attempt to improve outcomes as compared to the reference person. For example, an employee who believes that he or she is being paid less than another worker for comparable inputs could ask for an adjustment in income, such as a cost-of-living or pay-scale rate adjustment. Another mechanism may be to decrease an input by reducing productivity or increasing time off from the job. A third possible mechanism for adjusting inequity in an underpayment situation is for the focal person to change his or her

Exhibit 5-9 Equity Theory

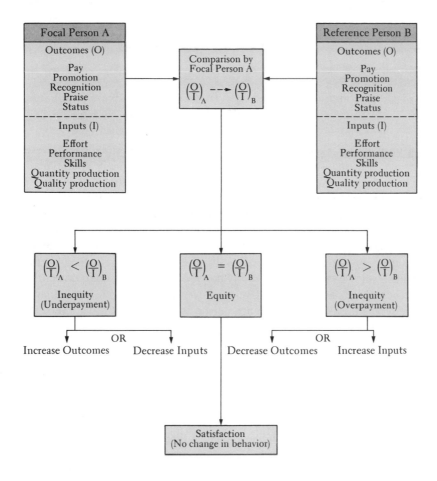

reference person to bring about a more realistic comparison. When inequity is caused by the focal person's ratio of outcomes/inputs being greater than the reference person's (overpayment), the individual will be motivated to remove this inequity by decreasing outcomes, or most probably, increasing inputs.

When outcomes concern hourly or piece-rate (incentive) monetary payments, equity theory predicts some interesting situations for the manager, as shown in Exhibit 5-10. In an underpayment situation where the individual is paid on an hourly basis, inequity is resolved by decreasing both the quantity and quality of production. Under a piece-rate, or incentive system, inequity is reduced by increasing production quantity, but also reducing the quality of production. A similar framework is shown for the overpayment condition.

Research on equity theory. The majority of the research studies on equity theory have focused on pay levels as the basic *outcome* and effort or performance level as the primary *input* factor.[41] In general, the underpayment situation has been sup-

Exhibit 5-10   Equity Theory Predictions in Hourly Rate and Piece-Rate Conditions

	Underpayment		Overpayment	
Quantity of Production	Piece Rate ↑	Hourly Rate ↓	Piece Rate ↓	Hourly Rate ↑
Quality of Production	Piece Rate ↓	Hourly Rate ↓	Piece Rate ↑	Hourly Rate ↑

ported in many of the reported studies; the overpayment situation, however, has been much less supported due to problems of trying to define or operationalize the exact meaning of "overpayment."[42] Other studies have shown that such demographic factors as sex and value systems have affected perceptions of equity.[43]

Research has also pointed out certain problems or criticisms of equity theory. First, in many of the reported studies the reference person has not always been classified. This is much less of a problem in laboratory experiments as opposed to field studies. In current studies, rather than specifying a reference *person,* the individual is allowed to use an *internally* derived standard of comparions (e.g., past experiences, beliefs and opinions developed over time).[44] This helps to alleviate not only the problem of who the reference person is, but also the situation of multiple reference persons for multiple outcomes.

Second is the problem of an over-reliance on laboratory studies to test the theory. Issues of generalizations to real-life organizations and managers become important. The few field studies have been quite supportive of inequity (i.e., underpayment) as being a key predictor of turnover and absenteeism.[45]

Third, the majority of research generally supports the notions concerning underpayment, but supportive overpayment research has not been forthcoming. In reality, this probably is not too surprising: how many individuals in organizations will admit to being overpaid?! If a person initially perceives an overpayment situation, the easiest way to reach equity is to change the reference standard or person. Finally, the theory has focused almost entirely on the outcome of pay. As we have shown, the general orientation of contemporary theories of motivation have shown that pay is not the only factor that motivates people.

Equity theory provides at least three guidelines for managers to consider. First is the emphasis on equitable rewards for employees. When individuals believe that they are not being rewarded in an equitable fashion, certain morale and productivity problems may arise. Second, the decision concerning equity (or inequity) is not made solely on a personal basis but can involve comparison with other workers, both *within* and *outside* the organization. In other words, it is not only important how much an employee is being paid, but how much he or she is being paid compared to other employees who have the same or similar jobs. Finally, individuals' reaction to inequity can take many different forms. Motivated behavior to reduce inequity can include changes in inputs and changes in outcomes, with the level or direction depending on whether the inequity was perceived to be underpayment or overpayment.

Even with the inherent criticisms and limitations, equity theory has a certain intuitive appeal to managers. Each of us has been in a situation in which we believed that the rewards for our efforts had not been adequate, particularly when we compared ourselves to others. Understanding the manner or process in which this inequity is reduced is an important skill for managers to develop.

Summary of process theories.   The two approaches that we have examined— expectancy and equity theory—have provided a process explanation of motivation. The two theories have similarities and differences. The tension created when inequity occurs is similar to the force construct in expectancy theory. However, expectancy theory is concerned with explaining motivation through an individual path-goal framework (i.e., effort → performance → reward) to maximize rewards; equity theory focuses on the motives and level of effort on the job and the comparison that is developed through a reference person. In other words, the major difference between the two process theories is that through an expectancy theory framework the employee would choose a level of work effort that would possibly maximize his or her outcomes or rewards; in an equity theory framework, however, this employee would choose a level of work effort that was equitable to some reference person or internal standard.

In our discussion thus far of contemporary theories of motivation, we have examined the principal factors of arousal (content theories) and choice or goal-directed behavior (process theories) as they related to individual motivation. One final perspective of motivation examines how motivated behavior on the part of the employee is *maintained* over time. This is the area of reinforcement theory and, in particular, operant conditioning.

Reinforcement Theory

As we discussed in chapter 4, operant conditioning, based largely on the works of Skinner,[46] is a reinforcement approach to the concept of learning. In this section, we will discuss how operant conditioning can also be viewed as a motivation model that is concerned with the arousal, direction, maintenance, and alteration of behavior in organizations. Stated differently, we will point out that, properly reinforced, the likelihood of desired behaviors can be increased and the likelihood of undesired behaviors can be reduced.

Operant conditioning in motivation.   Although there is no single accepted theory of operant conditioning, there is a set of fundamental ideas and principles. First, there is an emphasis on *objective, measurable behavior* (e.g., number of units produced, adherence to budget and time schedules) as opposed to difficult to measure and observe inner-person states (e.g., needs, motives, drives, and so on). The focus of attention is on the behavior itself, which can be observed and measured.

Second, a process known as *contingencies of reinforcement* is stressed.[47] As noted in chapter 4, this refers to the sequence between a stimulus, the response or actual employee behavior, and the consequences of that behavior (reinforcement). Stated simply, if, in a given work situation (i.e., stimulus), an individual acts in a way desired by the organization (i.e., response), then the reward (i.e., consequence of behavior) should match the behavior. From a motivational viewpoint, through the use of stimuli and consequences or rewards, the employee has been *motivated* to perform a desired behavior; in essence, the motivated behavior has been *learned.* For example, if a sales manager informs a sales representative that if the sales rep can reach 110 percent of sales quota by the end of the quarter (i.e., stimulus), he or she will receive a 10 percent bonus (i.e., consequence). If the goal is met and the bonus given, not only has motivated behavior developed, but a similar stimulus in the future will cause a similar response on the part of the sales rep; or, in other words, motivated behavior will be *maintained.* The types of reinforcement will be discussed in the next section.

Third, the shorter the *time interval,* or *reinforcement schedule,* between the employee's response (performance) and the administration of the reinforcer (reward or consequence), the greater the effect the reinforcer will have on behavior.[48] Consider, for example, the inventory manager in a large retail store who stayed late one night to insure that the store's goods were properly stocked and displayed for the next day's sale. Because the store manager had specifically asked for help for the sale, the inventory manager was somewhat confused that she had heard nothing about her performance. Finally, a week later, the store manager complimented her on her past performance. The inventory manager could only think to herself, "If it was so important, why did the store manager wait so long to say something?" Had the store manager praised her work the next day, for example, the connection between stimuli (store manager's request for help), response (overtime by the inventory manager), and consequence (recognition of good performance) would have been made stronger. How will she respond to similar requests in the future?

The fourth and final principle concerns the *value and size of the* reinforcer.[49] In formal terms, the greater the reinforcer's value and size to the individual, the greater the effect on subsequent behavior. The president of a small lumber company in Oregon may give each worker a large turkey for Thanksgiving and a $100 bonus for getting a rush order out on time. A mill operator may be quite pleased because the turkey will help feed eight children at the holiday dinner plus the bonus will come in handy for Christmas shopping. The mill superintendent, however, may say to himself, "I break my back to ship that big order and all I get are pennies and a dead bird!" This example indicates that individuals differ in their reaction to reinforcers.

The four fundamental principles of reinforcement theory—measurable behavior, contingencies of reinforcement, reinforcement schedules, and the value and size of the reinforcer—serve as the foundation of this approach to motivation. Because of their particular importance, the *contingencies of reinforcement* and *schedules of reinforcement* will be discussed in detail.

Contingencies or types of reinforcement.   As we noted in chapter 4, there are at least four types of reinforcement available to the manager for modifying an employees' motivation: (1) positive reinforcement; (2) punishment; (3) negative reinforcement or avoidance learning; and (4) extinction.[50]

1. *Positive Reinforcement.* The application of this type of reinforcement to a given response or behavior *increases* the likelihood that the particular behavior by the

individual will be repeated. For example, an engineer is given the task of designing a new piece of equipment (stimulus). The engineer exerts a high level of effort and completes the project in time (response). The supervisor reviews the work and not only praises the engineer for his or her work, but recommends, for example, a pay increase for the excellent work (positive reinforcement).

2. *Punishment.* The application of punishment is used to *decrease* the likelihood that the undesired behavior or response by the individual will be repeated. Just as positive reinforcement strengthens a particular behavior, punishment weakens it. For example, hourly workers in a plastics plant are given one hour for lunch (stimulus). When a particular worker continually takes an hour and thirty minutes for lunch (response), the supervisor will call the particular worker into his office and reprimand him for his behavior (punishment). The use of this punishment will hopefully change this worker's response back to acceptable behavior.

3. *Negative Reinforcement or Avoidance.* Just as with positive reinforcement, this type of reinforcement is a method used by managers to *strengthen* desired behavior. When a particular reinforcement can prevent the occurrence of an undesired stimulus, it is termed avoidance learning. Consider again the example of the worker who takes more than an hour for lunch. In order to avoid reprimand and criticism by the supervisor for taking more time for lunch than allotted, other workers make a special effort to take only an hour for lunch. The distinction between positive reinforcement and avoidance learning should be made carefully. With positive reinforcement, the individual works hard to gain the rewards from the organization that result from good work performance. With avoidance learning, however, the individual works hard to avoid the undesired consequences of the stimulus. The behavior is strengthened in both cases.

4. *Extinction.* Positive reinforcement and avoidance learning are used to strengthen desired responses or behavior on the part of the individual; punishment and extinction are reinforcement methods that can be used to reduce or eliminate undesirable behavior. Extinction is the withholding of positive reinforcement for a previously acceptable response or behavior. With continued nonreinforcement over time, the response or behavior will eventually disappear or be eliminated. In an organizational setting, for example, a company may offer their salespersons a bonus for every order from a new customer. This results in increased effort on the part of the salespersons to cultivate new sales outlets. After a period of time, the company evaluates this bonus system to be too costly to maintain, and therefore eliminates it. The sales force, not seeing any further reward (or reinforcement) for extra effort in developing new sales, reduces their effort to normal levels. The company, by removing the reinforcement, caused an extinction of the behavior on the part of their salespersons. A summary of the four reinforcement methods is shown in Exhibit 5–11.

The objective of each of the four reinforcement types is to modify an individual's behavior so that it will benefit the organization. Reinforcement will either increase

Exhibit 5–11   Types of Reinforcement

Type of Reinforcement	Stimulus	Response	Consequence or Reward
Positive Reinforcement Application increases the likelihood that a desired behavior will be repeated	High performance is rewarded in the organization	→ Individual performs at a high level (desired behavior)	→ Pay increase, recognition, praise
Punishment Application decreases the likelihood that an undesired behavior will be repeated	Only one hour is given for lunch each day	→ Individual continually takes more than one hour for lunch (undesired behavior)	→ Reprimand by supervisor
Avoidance Likelihood of desired behavior is increased by knowledge of consequences	Individuals who take more than one hour for lunch will be reprimanded by supervisor	→ Individuals take only one hour for lunch	→ No reprimand
Extinction Removal of positive reinforcement to eliminate an undesired behavior	1. Bonus given to salesperson for each new customer order	→ Salespersons *work hard* to get new orders	→ Bonus
	2. Bonus removed for each new customer order	→ Salespersons exert only nominal effort to get new orders	→ No bonus

the strength of desired behavior or decrease the strength of undesired behavior, depending on the organization's needs and the individual's current behavior.

Schedules of reinforcement.   The issues concerning the manner in which consequences or rewards are given contingent on employee behavior are known as *schedules of reinforcement*. Two broad classifications of reinforcement schedules have been identified: *continuous* and *intermittent*. The former involves a situation in which behavior is reinforced each time it occurs. The worker who assembles a pocket calculator knows his or her behavior is correct (i.e., reinforcement) when the unit passes a quality-control check.

Intermittent reinforcement occurs when a reinforcer is given after some instances of the employees' behavior, but *not* after each instance. Within intermittent reinforcement, two distinctions are made. First, reinforcers can be given after the passage of a certain amount of time—an *interval* schedule—or after a certain number of occurrences of the desired behavior—a *ratio* schedule. Second, reinforcers can be given in an unchanging format—*fixed* schedule—or constantly changing format—*variable* schedule. Thus, in combination, four general types of reinforcement schedules are possible: *fixed interval, fixed ratio, variable interval,* and *variable ratio* (see exhibit 5–12).

A *fixed interval* schedule involves a constant or fixed amount of time passing before the reinforcer is administered. The simplest example would be the weekly or monthly paycheck. The *fixed ratio schedule,* on the other hand, concerns a reinforcer that is given after the occurrence of a certain number of desired behaviors. The interior designer in a large furniture store, for example, knows that she will receive a 12 percent commission on each sale of furniture to customers. The ratio is fixed (12 percent), but the total amount of income is dependent on her performance.

In a *variable interval* schedule, the reinforcer is given dependent on the passage of time, but the amount of time varies around some average. For example, college graduates entering work in a retail store know that they will probably be promoted to the position of Assistant Department Manager after one year's continuous full-time employment. Some may be promoted after ten months, others twelve months, and still others fourteen months. The average for the group, however, is twelve months or one year.

Finally, in a *variable ratio* schedule, a certain number of desired behaviors must occur before the reinforcer is given, but the number of behaviors varies around some average. The use of verbal praise, recognition, or a bonus are typical examples. Not every behavior is praised; the number of behaviors that occur before praise is given varies from one time to the next. A summary of the schedules of reinforcement are shown in exhibit 5–13.

As an applied organizational example of reinforcement schedules, consider the program at Parsons Pine Products, Inc., of Ashland, Oregon.[51] This company uses six different incentives in their "positive reinforcement" plan:

1. *Hourly Wage Rate* (fixed interval)—Typical wage rates paid in weekly checks.

2. *"Well" Pay* (fixed interval)—Extra eight hours wages to workers who are neither absent nor late for a full month's work.

Exhibit 5–12 Intermittent Reinforcement Schedules

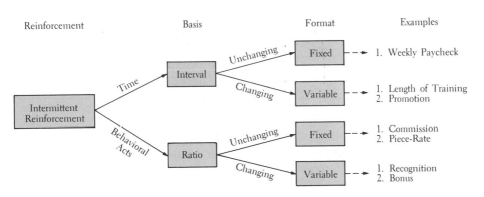

127

Exhibit 5–13 Schedules of Reinforcement

Schedule of Reinforcement	Reinforcer Applied	Reinforcer Removed	Example
1. Continuous Reinforcement	Quickest approach to establish a new motivated behavior.	Quickest approach to extinguish a new motivated behavior.	Reward after each unit is produced.
2. Intermittent Reinforcement	Slower approach to establish new motivated behavior.	Slower approach to extinguish new motivated behavior.	
a. Variable interval b. Variable ratio	Frequencies of motivated behavior is more consistent.	Slower extinction rate of motivated behavior.	a. Promotion b. Praise, recognition, and monetary bonus.
c. Fixed interval d. Fixed ratio	Frequencies of motivated behaviors are less consistent than variable schedules.	Faster extinction rate of motivated behavior than variable schedules.	c. Weekly or monthly paycheck d. Piece-rate or sales commission.

3. *"Retro" Pay* (fixed ratio)—Offers a bonus to workers based on any reduction in premiums received from the states' industrial accident insurance fund.

4. *Safety Pay* (fixed interval)—Two hours extra wages for remaining accident-free for a month.

5. *Profit-Sharing Bonus* (variable interval)—Distributing to all workers the amount of company income over 4 percent after taxes.

6. *Recognition Plan* (variable ratio)—Praising and recognizing good worker performance.

What has been the result of this plan? For the company, absenteeism and lateness have been reduced almost to zero, accident rate and costs have been reduced over 90 percent, and productivity has increased. For the employee, total income has risen between 25 percent and 35 percent. Under the Parson's Plan, an employee earning $10,000 a year can add as much as $3,500 to his or her income.

Research on reinforcement theory.   The application of operant conditioning techniques to organizations has been both limited and controversial. The major research efforts have been conducted primarily with the use of laboratory experiments in quasi-realistic settings. Thus, there is insufficient data available to allow for detailed application and generalization of this approach to individual behavior in organizations.

There are certain findings emerging from the limited research that deserve mention. First, the reinforcement of the relationship between behavior (performance) and rewards is very important for maintaining motivated behavior on the part of the individual. Employees react positively when they perceive that rewards are contingent on good performance, but react negatively when the rewards are not contingent on performance.[52] When individuals are continually not rewarded for good performance, decreased motivation and performance may result. Second, variable ratio schedules of reinforcement have been found to be the most powerful in sustaining motivated behavior in individual employees. The implications of these results have direct application to the reward systems used by organizations, and will be discussed fully in chapter 14.

Although there are positive implications of operant conditioning for managers, there have developed equally strong criticisms of this approach to motivation. First, operant conditioning techniques tend to ignore the individuality and complexity of a person's behavior. Critics point out that operant conditioning, with its programmed or rigid reinforcement methods, oversimplifies the behavior of individuals, particularly in formal organizations. In addition, operant conditioning does not take into account such individual characteristics as needs, desires, or the varying importance of different types of rewards.[53]

Second, with its heavy emphasis on external reward systems, operant conditioning ignores the fact that individuals can be reinforced or motivated by the job itself. This approach tends to place too much emphasis on controlling behavior through the manipulation of "lower-level needs" and does not consider that individuals might have other, "higher-level needs" as motivators.

Finally, critics claim that because the majority of the research on operant conditioning originates from laboratory efforts, generalization and application to real-life organizational settings remains relatively untested. Although laboratory experiments provide a high degree of control over extraneous variables that is not readily available in real organizations, we cannot make solid generalizations of its application to large, complex organizations.

Both the research and criticisms of operant conditioning will continue to develop in the coming years. For the manager, the most important factor in the application of operant conditioning is that employees should be rewarded contingent on their performance, not for factors that are nonperformance based. Managers must learn how to design and implement effective reinforcement programs that will enable employees to be productive and satisfied with their work.

An Integrative Motivational Model

Earlier in this chapter, we presented a basic motivational model that focused on the fundamental elements of needs, desires, and choice behavior. Now that we have reviewed the major contemporary theories of motivation, a more complete and integrative model can be developed. This integrative model, presented in exhibit 5–14, further develops the model by including a number of factors, such as effort, ability, satisfaction, and reinforcement, that have been found to be important for understanding the motivational process of individuals in organizations.

We have attempted to show that there is no universal theory of motivation that has been accepted by both behavioral scientists and practicing managers. The integra-

Exhibit 5–14 An Integrative Motivation Model

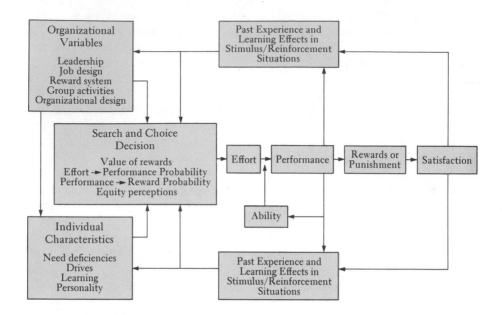

tive model in exhibit 5–14 is not intended to be a universal motivational approach, but should be viewed only as means of integrating the various concepts that have been discussed.

The focal point of the model is *effort,* or the amount of energy a person exerts while performing a job. Effort is shown as being influenced by *individual characteristics, organizational variables,* and the *search and choice* of particular behavioral patterns. Effort is transformed into actual performance through the moderating influence of the individual's *ability* to perform the desired work. *Rewards* are then administered based on the level of performance, leading to *satisfaction.* Satisfaction becomes an integral part of the motivational process because it entails the fulfillment of a need acquired by experiencing various job activities and rewards. Finally, the cyclical or dynamic nature of motivation is provided by *past experience and learning,* the feedback to the previously defined process variables.

An example may help to clarify the model. Consider the case of Jack, a young accountant recently hired by a major accounting firm. Jack is one of ten newly hired accountants who have been assigned to various auditing groups in the company. In analyzing this new situation, Jack comes to two conclusions: (1) he feels he has a high need to achieve and wants to eventually become a partner in the company; and (2) through previous investigations and conversations, he believes that the organization may provide the necessary opportunities for the satisfaction of these needs for achievement and advancement. Jack recognizes that one method to satisfy these needs is to choose to work hard and do as well as he can on all of his assignments. Jack has a willingness to learn and knows that he has the ability to do well because of his educational background and previous summer employment as a junior accountant.

During the next year, Jack concentrates on performing his job as well as he can and by trying to complete his work on time and in a professional manner. At the year-end review, Jack's supervisor rewards him with praise for a job well done, a good pay increase, and assurances that such continued good performance could lead only to further advancement in the company. Jack summed up his first year with the company as being a satisfying experience that has strengthened his belief about the nature of the organization and his abilities to do a good job. He decides to continue his present high level of motivated behavior because he knows that through effort and good work, he can satisfy his need for achievement and eventually be promoted to a partner in the company.

This example, although simplified, highlights the complexities involved in understanding the process of motivation in organizations. Managers cannot control all factors in this process; however, through increased knowledge and the ability to diagnose the various factors affecting an individual's behavior, a better understanding can be gained concerning the manager's role in determining and influencing the process of motivation in their organizations.

So far in this chapter, we have attempted to provide a basic understanding of the theoretical foundations of motivation in organizations. The value of this foundation lies not only in the possibilities for further theoretical development but also in its applicability to real organizations. In the next section, we will examine three selected applications of motivation in organizational settings.

Managerial Applications of Motivation

The number of practical applications of motivation theories is large, and each could be developed into a full volume. Some of the more important areas—leadership, job design, organizational design, and reward systems—will be covered in separate chapters in this book. Here we will examine specific applications of behavior modification, goal setting, and modified workweeks.

Behavior Modification

An approach to motivation in organizations that uses operant conditioning as its foundation is called *behavior modification*. [54] As we discussed earlier in this chapter, the premise of operant conditioning is that desired behavior by the employee will be repeated if it is reinforced. The administration of reinforcement or rewards is assumed to increase the likelihood that the behavior immediately preceding the reinforcement will reoccur.

The approach recommended by proponents of behavior modification is that of positive reinforcement. Generally, research findings suggest that positive reinforcers are more effective than are negative reinforcers in achieving lasting changes in behavior (although negative reinforcement can be effective in causing the short-term elimination of undesired behavior).

Whatever type of rewards the manager considers using, the important aspect to remember is that the closer desired behavior is followed by positive reinforcement, the more likely it is that the behavior will be repeated. This is probably one of the reasons why pay (salary or hourly wage) is considered a hygiene factor by Herzberg; pay is a reward the employee receives at some later time, often long after the occurrence of the desired behavior. Because of the time lag between the desired behavior and a reinforcer such as pay, behavioral scientists recommend the use of such reinforcers as recognition, praise, compliments, and other verbal approaches. These are easier to apply and can be administered soon after the desired behaviors are recognized and evaluated. Monetary payments in the form of incentive pay or bonuses can also be used as positive reinforcers.

A typical behavior modification program, shown in exhibit 5–15, usually follows a specific development format.

1. *Job analysis* involves the process of defining the requirements of the job, the areas of responsibility and authority, and so on.

2. *Defining performance measures* concerns an attempt to define the measures or

Exhibit 5–15 Behavior Modification Program

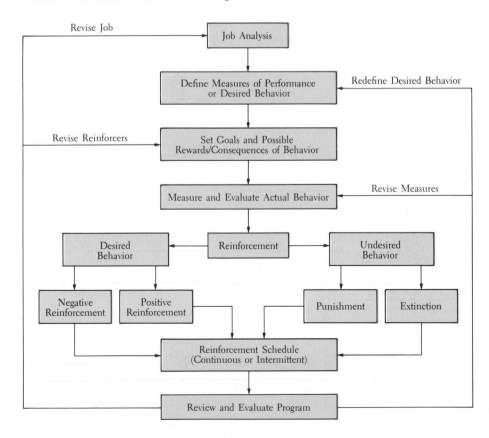

criteria of job performance (e.g., number of units produced, sales volume, time and cost objectives). This may be a difficult, but not impossible, step for firms that use non-job-related factors to measure performance (e.g., cooperativeness, ability to get along with others, and other subjective criteria), or that have no formal performance evaluation system at all.

3. _Setting goals_ involves the important step of stating what is (or what is not) desired behavior on the part of the employee. Goals may concern such aspects as productivity improvement, decreased absenteeism, and so on.

4. In _measurement of actual behavior,_ the superior or the employee himself or herself keeps a record of the individual's daily work. This can be done through observation or actual record keeping. Having the employee keep a performance record has the added effect of a self-feedback mechanism.

5. The _reinforcement_ stage involves the application of a reinforcer _dependent_ or _contingent_ upon the employee's behavior (i.e., desired or undesired behavior).

6. _Reinforcement schedules_ concern the timing of the reinforcer. As noted earlier, this can be continuous or intermittent depending on the specific behavior. For example, a continuous schedule may be applied for punishment (undesired behavior), while a fixed or variable schedule may be used with positive reinforcement (desired behavior).

7. Finally, the program is _reviewed and evaluated_ with respect to its success. If the program is successful, little or no change may be necessary. On the other hand, a review of the program results may require a revision of job definition, types of reinforcers, measures of performance, or a redefinition of what is desired behavior, or a combination of all four.

Since the initial applications, the list of organizations using positive reinforcement has grown steadily. A selected list of participating organizations and their success with the application of this theory is shown in exhibit 5–16.

Even though the results have been impressive, managers must interpret them cautiously. Tying the positive reinforcement directly to improved organizational effectiveness, as Emery Air Freight did, may stretch the realities of the situation.[55] During this period, Emery experienced a rapid growth because of changes in the marketplace. Positive reinforcement may certainly have had an effect, but it should not be considered as the sole cause of the improvements.

A second point of caution concerns the type of reinforcer that is used. Although feedback, praise, and recognition are certainly viable techniques, employees may eventually want to see the continual productivity increases reflected in their paycheck (see Michigan Bell example in exhibit 5–16). Over time, a backlash effect may develop so that employees consider positive reinforcement as just another management tool used to benefit the company, not to reward their contributions.

The jury is still out on the effects of positive reinforcement programs in organizations.[56] It is apparent, however, that its use will continue to expand, probably taking various forms in different organizations. Whatever the technique used, it should be made clear to managers that tying rewards to performance is a powerful approach to the motivation of employees.

Exhibit 5–16 Results of Behavior Modification Programs in Selected Organizations

Organization	Type of Employee	Specific Program Goals	Reinforcers	Results
Emery Air Freight (1969–76)	Cross-section of total workforce (500 out of 2,800)	1. Increase productivity 2. Improve service quality	Frequent use of praise and recognition	1. Estimated savings of $3 million over 3 years 2. Attainment of performance goals increased from 30 percent to 95 percent of the time
Michigan Bell: Maintenance Service (1974–76)	Supervisors, mechanics, and maintenance workers (220 out of 5,500)	1. Improve productivity 2. Improve quality 3. Improve safety 4. Improve customer relations	Daily, weekly, and quarterly self- and supervisory feedback	1. Improved costs efficiency 2. Improved service quality and safety 3. No change in absenteeism, but a decrease in pay satisfaction
General Electric (1973–76)	Employees at all levels (1,000)	1. Increase productivity 2. Decrease turnover and absenteeism 3. Approve training 4. Meet EEOC objectives	Frequent use of praise, feedback, and other reinforcers	1. Increased productivity 2. Decreased direct labor costs 3. Improved training of minority workers
B. F. Goodrich Chemicals (1972–76)	Manufacturing workers at all levels (100 out of 420)	1. Increase productivity 2. Improved meeting of scheduled deadlines	1. Weekly use of praise and recognition 2. Freedom to choose one's work activity	Production increased 300 percent

Adapted with permission of the publisher from W. C. Hamner and E. P. Hamner, "Behavior Modification on the Bottom Line," *Organizational Dynamics*, Spring 1976, pp. 12–14. © 1976 by AMACOM, a division of American Management Associations.

Goal Setting

A growing number of practicing managers and behavioral scientists believe that one of the most important elements in any motivation program are *goals* or *results expected* for the individual employee. A *goal* is defined simply as what the individual is consciously trying to do.

The basic framework was provided by Locke, who proposed a theory of goal setting that concerns the relationship between conscious goals and task performance.[57] The basic premise of the approach is that an employee's conscious goals influence his or her work behavior. Stated simply, concrete or hard goals result in a higher level of performance than do easy goals, and specific hard goals result in a higher level of performance than do no goals or a generalized goal of "do your best."[58] In practical terms, individual motivation and performance are improved if the employee knows *clearly,* and is *challenged* by, what needs to be done.

Goal setting is directly related to each of the three contemporary approaches to motivation. In content theories, goal setting concerns the needs of the employee. Relating goals to needs and providing the means to attain these goals can result in need satisfaction and improved motivation. In process theories, particularly expectancy theory, goal setting relates to worker outcomes, the valence associated with these outcomes, and the process of attaining these outcomes (expectancies and instrumentality). Finally, as we have discussed in the section on reinforcement theory, goal setting serves as the foundation for the use of reinforcement (see exhibit 5–15).

As depicted in exhibit 5–17, goal setting usually involves five steps. First, certain *incentives* for performance are provided by the *environment;* or, more specifically, some part or individual in the organization. This step generally involves the establishment of what the organization wants done (i.e., target results) and the clarification of rewards (pay increase, promotion, or recognition) that are associated with potential goal attainment. Second, the *goal-setting participative process* concerns the manner in which the goals are established. This usually involves the subordinate and his or her superior in either a two-way joint decision-making process (i.e., participative goal-setting), a one-way process from superior to subordinate (i.e., assigned goal-setting), or just a "do your best" approach. Third, the nature of the established goals determines the *goal-setting attributes* of clarity,

Exhibit 5–17 Goal-Setting Process

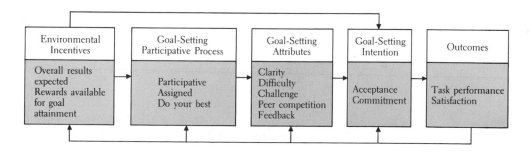

difficulty, challenge, peer competition, and feedback. Fourth, the acceptance and commitment to the established goals concerns the *intention* to work towards goal attainment by the employee.[59] Note the direct impact of incentives on intention in exhibit 5–17. From content and process motivation theories, this is an evaluation by the employee of the value of the reward and the degree of need satisfaction associated with goal attainment. Finally, the *outcomes* of goal setting include such aspects as task performance and satisfaction.

For example, consider the first-line packaging supervisor in a food products company. The company has embarked on a cost effectiveness program in an attempt to reduce production costs by 15 percent over the previous year *(environmental incentives)*. If this goal is met by responsible employees, a cash bonus will be awarded *(incentives* and *goal-setting participative process)*. In translating the overall company goal into his or her particular area of responsibility, the supervisor believes that cutting production costs by 15 percent will be a difficult, challenging but manageable task *(goal-setting attributes)*. The supervisor accepts the goal as one that will be good for the company, the department, and his or her personal development *(goal-setting intention),* and therefore works hard over the next year to attain the needed level of cost cutting *(outcomes)*.

A number of goal-setting research studies have been reported in an attempt to investigate the relationship between conscious work goals and employee behavior. In general, the results of these efforts have revealed the following:

1. Setting clear and specific goals has a greater positive effect on performance improvement than does "do the best you can" goal setting.[60]

2. Employee goals that are perceived to be difficult to achieve tend to lead to better performance than do easy goals, so long as the goals are accepted by the individual.[61]

3. Support has been reported for the superiority (in terms of performance improvement) of participative goal setting over the use of assigned goals.[62]

4. The use of frequent performance feedback in the goal-setting process results in higher performance by individuals than when performance feedback sessions were not used.[63]

5. There is growing evidence that individual characteristics, such as age, sex, race, education level, dominant needs (growth, achievement, and autonomy), and personality factors, act as important moderators between goal-setting and employee performance.[64]

The astute reader may conclude that goal setting and behavior modification are essentially the same approach because they both focus on the "if-then" component. Although this is currently a controversial topic among practicing managers and behavioral scientists, certain similarities and differences exist:[65]

1. In behavior modification, the focus of attention is on *three* behavioral actions: (a) behavioral events (actual day-to-day behavior); (b) the level of individual performance; and (c) the overall effectiveness of the behavior with respect to the

overall organization (the relationship between performance and performance standards). In general, goal setting has focused primarily on the third of these behavioral actions.

2. Because of the above, goal-setting programs generally take longer to implement and to show tangible results.

3. In practical applications, goal-setting programs have placed greater attention on the establishment of goals, but behavior modification focuses on reinforcers and the contingencies of reinforcement.

4. Goal setting emphasizes *self-control* on the part of the employee; behavior modification focuses on organizational, or *external* control.

5. Finally, the concept of individual needs (and other individual characteristics) plays an important role in goal setting. As we noted earlier, Skinner-based behavior modification programs do not recognize such concepts because they are not measureable behaviors.

The studies in organizations that have investigated goal setting as a means of improving worker motivation and performance have shown that goal-setting programs have been quite effective. This improved effectiveness has been reported over an extended period of time, in a number of different organizations, and on nonmanagerial levels.

Much work still needs to be done, however, before a comprehensive understanding of this motivational approach is achieved. In particular, further work is needed in such areas as: (1) determining the effects of individual characteristics (i.e., personality) in goal setting; (2) developing a clearer understanding of the advantages and disadvantages of participative versus assigned goal setting; and (3) understanding the specific determinants of goal acceptance and goal commitment. A further application of goal setting—management by objectives—will be discussed in a later chapter.

The Modified Workweek

In a number of organizations, an attempt has been made to improve motivation and performance of employees by implementing a shorter workweek. Interest in the modified workweek is part of the reexamination of work time patterns that is going on in most industrialized nations.

The implementation of this concept has taken a number of different forms. In European countries, the interest has centered on flexible work schedules that permit employees to start and finish work at their discretion so long as they complete a specified number of hours per week or month. In the United States, the emphasis has been placed on the four-day, forty-hour workweek, as opposed to the conventional five-day, forty-hour workweek.

It has been assumed that the modified workweek can be used as a mechanism by management to improve worker motivation and performance.[66] This belief is based on two propositions: (1) the newer arrangement allows for a concentrated ten-hour workday, eliminating some of the daily start-up costs; and (2) the modified workweek is appealing to employees as it permits them to redistribute their free time into other valued activities, and this may result in higher satisfaction and lower turnover and absenteeism.

Although the number of companies that have adopted the four/forty week is approaching 2,000, there are few studies that have evaluated it in terms of actual behavioral or performance outcomes.[67] A Department of Labor pilot study of 16 firms showed that, although productivity increased in some organizations, there was no change in others, and even a decrease in some. This study also revealed that although turnover is generally assumed to improve with the four/forty workweek, there was little confirmation of this assumption.[68]

A second study of the impact of the four/forty workweek was conducted in a nonunionized pharmaceutical company. It was found that over a period of time employees adjusted well to the modified workweek and that absenteeism decreased after its introduction. In addition, it was reported that such factors as age, plans for the use of nonwork time, and job pace were important influences in employees' attitudes toward the shorter workweek.[69]

Finally, a study in separate divisions of a manufacturing firm was conducted to investigate the effects of the four/forty workweek over one-year (short-run) and two-year (longer-run) periods. The results revealed that certain individual satisfaction and performance factors improved over the one-year, or short-term, period of time. After two years, however, no significant improvements were reported in either individual satisfaction or performance variables as compared to the starting period.[70] The long-run, or two-year, part of this study suggests that the conversion to a four/forty workweek may not be as beneficial as claimed. It could be that the initial innovation of the modified workweek may have worn off, and workers reverted back to existing or previous patterns of behavior. Through the first year of the introduction of the modified workweek, satisfaction and productivity measures increased. However, between the first and second years of operation, these same measures decreased until the previous plateau was reached.

Viewed from a motivational theory framework, these results are not as surprising as first thought. From a content theory view, the modified workweek could be considered a hygiene factor. According to Herzberg, hygiene factors help to reduce dissatisfaction, but do not act as motivation factors. Process theory would also predict these results. An interpretation through expectancy theory would point to the increase and then the decrease in valence once the modified workweek had been in effect for a period of time. Equity theory would indicate that there was an absence of inequity (i.e., underpayment or overpayment) because both the focal person and potential reference persons were operating under the same system. Finally, from reinforcement theory, the absence of continued reinforcers would help to explain the increase and then decrease in the behavioral outcomes.

Although some of the evidence being reported from the studies of the modified workweek have not been as supportive as expected, nevertheless the trend toward both further adaption and investigation will continue. Other factors must be investigated—such as task difficulty, physical fatigue, attitudes toward leisure time, age, sex, and geographic area—before the claims or disclaimers concerning the modified workweek can be supported.

Applications and Implications for the Manager

Motivation

1. An individual is motivated to perform a job by a number of factors. These factors include individual aspects (e.g., needs, drives, and goals) and job aspects (e.g., the work itself and the rewards).

2. Early approaches to motivation viewed the worker basically as a lazy human being who must be constantly supervised and who is motivated only by money. The contemporary approach views the worker as a self-starter who seeks responsibility and autonomy and who can be motivated by factors other than money. These points are brought out by comparing the works of Taylor and McGregor's Theory X and Theory Y.

3. Contemporary theories of motivation include three orientations: content (factors that arouse or start behavior), process (concerning choice, direction, and goals), and reinforcement (factors that increase the likelihood that desired behavior will be repeated, or increase the likelihood that undesired behavior will stop). Although each approach is comprehensive and emphasizes different components, no universally accepted theory of motivation has been developed. The manager should try to analyze the situation as best he or she can and apply the particular techniques or mechanisms that are believed to be most effective in improving motivation.

4. Maslow's need hierarchy approach focuses on an individual's needs as being the primary mechanism for motivation. If a need is active, it serves as a motivator; if the need has been minimally satisfied, it no longer acts as a motivator. Five levels of needs are identified—each of which can apply to the workplace. Although Maslow's approach has been criticized from many sources, it still remains a viable framework to interpret at least one component of motivation—human needs. Individuals have needs and act or behave in a manner to satisfy them. Understanding what needs are active in an employee can help the manager to explain the particular behavioral pattern that the employee is exhibiting.

5. Herzberg's two-factor theory, like Maslow's approach, focuses on needs as being the prime motivator of individuals. Although this approach has been severely criticized and deals primarily with satisfiers and dissatisfiers, it has made a significant impact on the managerial function. The value to the manager of two-factor theory is the knowledge that certain factors in the workplace motivate people, but others do not. These factors, however, may vary from company to company and from individual to individual, making the task of categorizing motivators and nonmotivators difficult.

6. Alderfer's ERG theory provides the most current approach to motivation based on a need framework. For the manager, it develops not only three realistic need classifications (existence, relatedness, and growth needs), but also identifies three process components of needs (need satisfaction, desire strength, and need frustration) that provide a framework for the knowledge of the level of individual motivated behavior.

7. Expectancy theory provides an approach to motivation from a directional or choice framework. The manager may view this theory as being too complex for understanding and application. In its simplest form, however, the knowledge that individuals place certain values on work-related rewards and make conscious estimates of effort-performance-reward relationships is of value for understanding individual motivation in organizations. The manager has many tools or mechanisms at his or her disposal that can influence these components and thus affect the level of motivation of the employee.

8. The basis of equity theory focuses on an everyday situation in organizations— namely, the comparison of inputs and outcomes by individuals with other individuals. Equity in these comparisons is satisfying to individuals; inequity, however, is dissatisfying and produces tension that motivates the employee to a particular behavior. Although the majority of the work in this approach has focused on pay, it is a

more straightforward and easily understood approach for the manager and provides some interesting findings with respect to underpayment and overpayment situations.

9. The final motivation theory that was discussed, operant conditioning, examines the application of one of the manager's primary mechanisms of authority—the power to reward and punish. The occurrence of desired behavior can be increased and the likelihood of undesired behavior in employees can be decreased with proper application of rewards and punishment. The principal feature of this approach to motivation is that individual behavior can be influenced through the connection between organizational stimuli, performance, and rewards or consequences. Strengthening or weakening this link through rewards or punishment can result in an employee

behavioral pattern that is desired by the manager.

10. The nature of goals serve to direct the motivated behavior of the employee. Specific goals increase performance, and difficult goals result in higher performance levels than do easy goals. Although many unanswered questions regarding the process of goal setting remain, the fact that goals provide direction to the individual and generally increase performance should not be overlooked.

11. The effects of the modified workweek on employee behavior remain questionable. The initial results of the implementation of the four/forty workweek revealed results that are advantageous for the short run, but negligible in the long run. Additional work and research on this subject needs to be done before the modified workweek is accepted as a viable motivational technique.

Review of Theories, Research, and Applications

1. Compare the need hierarchy, two-factor, and ERG theory approaches to motivation. What are their similarities and differences?

2. Under what conditions would monetary rewards be a motivational approach to employees?

3. Discuss the managerial implications of underpayment and overpayment from the viewpoint of equity theory.

4. How can a manager influence an individual's perceptions of valence, effort-to-performance, and performance-to-reward expectancies?

5. Should salaries, merit increases, and bonuses be made public or kept secret?

6. Discuss the advantages and disadvantages of operant conditioning as a motivational tool.

7. How would you present expectancy theory to a group of managers?

8. Why is Herzberg's two-factor theory so popular with managers even though the criticisms are significant?

9. Discuss how goal setting can be used to increase employee performance.

10. Why have the results of the modified workweek been less than satisfactory in terms of increasing employee performance and satisfaction?

Notes

1. "Managing Motivation," *General Electric Monogram,* November–December 1975, pp. 2–5.

2. Richard M. Steers and Lyman W. Porter, *Motivation and Work Behavior* (New York: McGraw-Hill, 1975), p. 4.

3. Charles Perrow, *Complex Organizations* (Glenview, Ill.: Scott, Foresman, 1972).

4. Joan W. Atkinson, *An Introduction to Motivation* (Princeton, N.J.: Van Nostrand, 1964).

5. James L. Gibson, John M. Ivancevich, and James H. Donnelly, Jr., *Organizations* (Dallas: Business Publications, 1976).

6. M. R. Jones, ed., *Nebraska Symposium on Motivation* (Lincoln: University of Nebraska, 1955).

7. The writings of these individuals are discussed in Steers and Porter, *Motivation and Work Behavior,* p. 5.

8. Frederick W. Taylor, *Scientific Management* (New York: Harper & Row, 1911).

9. James H. Donnelly, Jr., James L. Gibson, John M. Ivancevich, *Fundamentals of Management,* 3rd ed. (Dallas: Business Publications, 1979).

10. Douglas McGregor, *The Human Side of Enterprise* (New York: McGraw-Hill, 1960).

11. Ibid., pp. 33–34.

12. Ibid., pp. 47–48.

13. Abraham H. Maslow, *Motivation and Personality* (New York: Harper & Row, 1954).

14. Lyman W. Porter, *Organizational Patterns of Managerial Job Attitudes* (New York: American Foundation for Management Research, 1964).

15. Douglas T. Hall and K. E. Nougaim, "An Examination of Maslow's Need Hierarchy in an Organizational Setting" *Organizational Behavior and Human Performance,* 1968, pp. 12–35.

16. Lyman W. Porter, "Job Attitudes in Management: IV Perceived Deficiencies in Need Fulfillment as a Function of Size of the Company," *Journal of Applied Psychology,* December 1963, pp. 386–97; Lyman W. Porter, "Job Attitudes in Management: II Perceived Importance of Needs as a Function of Job Level," *Journal of Applied Psychology,* April 1963, pp. 141–48; and John M. Ivancevich, "Perceived Need Satisfactions of Domestic Versus Overseas Managers," *Journal of Applied Psychology,* August 1969, pp. 274–78.

17. Edward E. Lawler III, and J. L. Suttle, "A Causal Correlational Test of the Need Hierarchy Concept," *Organizational Behavior and Human Performance,* 1972, pp. 265–87.

18. Edwin A. Locke, "The Nature and Causes of Job Satisfaction," in *Handbook of Industrial and Organizational Psychology,* ed. Marvin D. Dunnette (Chicago: Rand McNally, 1976), p. 1309.

19. M. A. Wahba and L. G. Birdwell, "Maslow Reconsidered: A Review of Research on the Need Hierarchy Theory," *Organizational Behavior and Human Performance,* 1976, pp. 212–40; Gerald R. Salancik and Jeffrey Pfeffer, "An Examination of Need-Satisfaction Models of Job Attitudes," *Administrative Science Quarterly,* September 1977, pp. 427–56.

20. F. Herzberg, B. Mausner, and B. Snyderman, *The Motivation to Work,* 2nd ed. (New York: Wiley, 1959).

21. V. M. Backman, "The Herzberg Controversy," *Personnel Psychology,* 1971, pp. 155–89.

22. D. A. Whitsett and E. K. Winslow, "An Analysis of Studies Critical of the Motivation-Hygiene Theory," *Personnel Psychology,* 1967, pp. 391–416.

23. John P. Campbell et al., *Managerial Behavior, Performance, and Effectiveness* (New York: McGraw-Hill, 1970), p. 354.

24. Clayton P. Alderfer, *Existence, Relatedness, and Growth* (New York: Free Press, 1972).

25. C. P. Schneider and Clayton P. Alderfer, "Three Studies of Measures of Need Satisfaction in Organizations," *Administrative Science Quarterly,* December 1973, pp. 489–505.

26. John P. Wanous and A. Zwany, "A Cross-Sectional Test of Need Hierarchy Theory," *Organizational Behavior and Human Performance,* 1977, pp. 78–97.

27. Clayton P. Alderfer, "A Critique of Salancik and Pfeffer's Examination of Need Satisfaction Theories," *Administrative Science Quarterly,* December 1977, pp. 658–69.

28. E. C. Tolman, Purposive Behavior in Animals and Men (New York: Appleton-Century-Crofts, 1932).

29. Kurt Lewin, *The Conceptual Representation and the Measurement of Psychological Forces* (Durham, N.C.:

Duke University, 1938).

30. Atkinson, *Introduction to Motivation.*

31. Victor H. Vroom, *Work and Motivation* (New York: Wiley, 1964).

32. Campbell et al., *Managerial Behavior,* p. 345.

33. Robert J. House, H. J. Shapero, and M. A. Wahba, "Expectancy Theory as a Predictor of Work Behavior and Attitudes: A Re-evaluation of Empirical Evidence," *Decision Sciences,* July 1974, pp. 481–506.

34. L. H. Peters, "Cognitive Models of Motivation, Expectancy Theory and Effort: An Analysis and Empirical Test," *Organizational Behavior and Human Performance,* 1977, pp. 129–48.

35. Lyman W. Porter and Edward E. Lawler III, *Managerial Attitudes and Performance* (Homewood, Ill.: Irwin, 1968).

36. Terence R. Mitchell, "Expectancy Models of Job Satisfaction, Occupational Preference and Effort: A Theoretical, Methodological, and Empirical Appraisal," *Psychological Bulletin,* 1974, pp. 1053–75.

37. Edward E. Lawler III, and J. L. Suttle, "Expectancy Theory and Job Behavior," *Organizational Behavior and Human Performance,* 1973, p. 483.

38. F. Schmidt, "Implication of a Measurement Problem for Expectancy Theory Research," *Organizational Behavior and Human Performance,* 1973, pp. 243–51.

39. J. M. Feldman, H. J. Reitz, and R. J. Hilterman, "Alternatives to Optimization in Expectancy Theory," *Journal of Applied Psychology,* December 1976, pp. 712–20.

40. J. Stacy Adams, "Toward an Understanding of Inequity," *Journal of Abnormal and Social Psychology,* November 1963, pp. 422–36.

41. I. R. Andrews, "Wage Inequity and Job Performance," *Journal of Applied Psychology,* January 1967, pp. 39–45; Paul S. Goodman and A. Freedman, "An Examination of Adams' Theory of Inequity," *Administration Science Quarterly,* December 1971, pp. 271–88; and J. Stacy Adams and S. Freedman, "Equity Theory Revisited: Comments and Annotated Bibliography," in *Advances in Experimental and Social Psychology,* ed. L. Berkowitz (New York: Academic Press, 1976).

42. M. R. Carrell and J. E. Dettrich, "Equity Theory: The Recent Literature, Methodological Considerations, and New Directions," *Academy of Management Review,* April 1978, pp. 202–10.

43. Ibid., p. 206.

44. Paul S. Goodman, "An Examination of Referents Used in the Evaluation of Pay," *Organizational Behavior and Human Performance,* 1974, pp. 340–52.

45. M. R. Carrell and J. E. Dettrich, "Employee Perceptions of Fair Treatment," *Personnel Journal,* 1976, pp. 523–24.

46. See B. F. Skinner, *Contingencies of Reinforcement* (New York: Appleton-Century-Crofts, 1969); B. F. Skinner, *Beyond Freedom and Dignity* (New York: Knopf, 1971).

47. F. Luthans and R. Kreitner, *Organizational Behavior Modifications* (Glenview, Ill: Scott, Foresman, 1975).

48. L. K. Miller, *Principles of Everyday Behavior Analysis* (Monterey, Calif.: Brooks-Cole Publishing, 1975).

49. R. M. Tarpy, *Basic Principles of Learning* (Glenview, Ill: Scott, Foresman, 1974).

50. W. Clay Hamner, "Reinforcement Theory and Contingency Management in Organizational Settings," in *Organizational Behavior and Management: A Contingency Approach,* ed. Henry L. Tosi and W. Clay Hamner (Chicago: St. Clair Press, 1974), pp. 86–112.

51. "How to Earn Well-Pay," *Business Week,* 12 June, 1978, pp. 143–46.

52. D. J. Cherrington, H. J. Reitz, and W. E. Scott, "Effects of Contingent and Non-Contingent Rewards on the Relationship Between Satisfaction and Performance," *Journal of Applied Psychology,* 1971, pp. 531–36.

53. Hamner, "Reinforcement Theory," pp. 104–8.

54. W. Clay Hamner and Ellen P. Hamner, "Behavior Modification on the Bottom

Line," *Organizational Dynamics,*
Spring 1976, pp. 2–21.

55. "At Emery Air Freight: Positive
Reinforcement Boosts Performance,"
Organizational Dynamics, Winter 1973.

56. Edwin A. Locke, "The Myths of
Behavior Mood in Organizations,"
Academy of Management Review,
October 1977, pp. 543–553.

57. Edwin A. Locke, "Toward a Theory of
Task Motivation and Incentives,"
*Organizational Behavior and Human
Performance,* 1968, pp. 157–89.

58. Gary P. Latham and Gary A. Yukl, "A
Review of Research on the Application
of Goal Setting in Organizations,"
Academy of Management Journal,
December 1975, pp. 824–45.

59. D. W. Organ, "Intentional vs. Arousal
Effects of Goal Setting," *Organizational
Behavior and Human Performance,*
1977, pp. 378–89.

60. S. E. White, Terence R. Mitchell, and
C. H. Bull, "Goal-Setting, Evaluation
Apprehension and Social Cues as
Determinants of Job Performance and
Job Satisfaction in a Simulated
Organization," *Journal of Applied
Psychology,* December 1977, pp.
665–73.

61. Latham and Yukl, "A Review of
Research," p. 834.

62. John M. Ivancevich, "Effects of Goal
Setting on Performance and Job
Satisfaction," *Journal of Applied
Psychology,* October 1976, pp. 605–12.

63. J. S. Kim and W. Clay Hamner, "Effect
of Performance Feedback and Goal
Setting in Productivity and Satisfaction
in an Organizational Setting," *Journal
of Applied Psychology,* February 1976,
pp. 45–57.

64. John M. Ivancevich, "Individual
Differences and Organizational Goal
Setting Issues, Research, and New
Directions," *National Academy of
Management Meeting,* August 1978.

65. Luthans and Kreitner, *Organizational
Behavior Modification,* p. 64.

66. V. E. Schein, E. H. Maurer, and J. F.
Novak, "Impact of Flexible Working
Hours on Productivity," *Journal of
Applied Psychology,* August 1977, pp.
463–65.

67. W. R. Nord and R. Costigan, "Worker
Adjustment to the Four-Day Week: A
Longitudinal Study," *Journal of
Psychology,* August 1973, pp. 60–66.

68. U.S. Department of Labor, *The Revised
Workweek: Results of a Pilot Study of 16
Firms,* Bulletin 1846 (1975), pp. 1–31.

69. See John M. Ivancevich, "Effects of the
Shorter Workweek on Selected
Satisfaction and Performance
Measures," *Journal of Applied
Psychology,* December 1974, pp.
717–21.

70. John M. Ivancevich and H. C. Lyon,
"The Shortened Workweek: A Field
Experiment," *Journal of Applied
Psychology,* February 1977, pp. 34–37.

Additional References

BEHLING, O.; SCHRIESCHEIN, C.; and
TOLLIVER, J. "Alternatives to Expectancy
Theories of Motivation." *Decision
Sciences,* 1975, pp. 449–61.

DECI, E. L. "The Effects of Contingent and
Non-Contingent Rewards and Controls
in Intrinsic Motivation." *Organizational
Behavior and Human Performance,*
1972, pp. 217–29.

DUNNETTE, M. D. *Work and Non-Work in
the Year 2001.* Monterey, Calif.:
Brooks-Cole, 1973.

GRAEN, G. "Instrumentality Theory of Work
Motivation: Some Experimental Results
and Suggested Modifications." *Journal
of Applied Psychology Monograph* 53,
1969, pp. 1–25.

IVANCEVICH, JOHN M. "The Performance to
Satisfaction Relationship: A Causal
Analysis of Stimulating and
Non-Stimulating Jobs." *Organizational
Behavior and Human Performance,*
1978, pp. 350–65.

LAWLER, E. E., III. "Job Attitudes and
Employee Motivation: Theory, Research,
and Practice." *Personnel Psychology,*
1970, 223–37.

———. *Pay and Organizational
Effectiveness.* New York: McGraw-Hill,
1971.

MITCHELL, T. R., and BIGLAN, A. "Instrumentality Theories: Current Issues in Psychology." *Psychological Bulletin,* 1971, pp. 432–54.

McCLELLAND, D. C., and WINTER, D. G. *Motivating Economic Achievement.* New York: Free Press, 1969.

SCHWAB, DONALD P.; OLIAN-GOTTLIEB, JUDY D.; and HENEMAN, HERBERT G., II. "Between-Subjects Expectancy Theory Research: A Statistical Review of Studies Predicting Effort and Performance." *Psychological Bulletin,* 1979, pp. 139–47.

STEERS, R. M. "Task-Goal Attributes in Achievement and Supervisory Performance." *Organizational Behavior and Human Performance,* 1975, pp. 392–403.

A Case of Motivation

The Richardson Bros. Department Store

The Richardson Bros. department store is a large, full product line retail organization located in Los Angeles, California. The company had nine large branch stores located in various suburbs of the city. The downtown store not only reported more sales volume than any of the individual branches, but it also housed the offices of top management and the central functions of personnel, data processing, buying, operations and planning, and the office of controller.

The credit division, headed by the division vice president, Mr. Benjamin Hageman, was within the office of the controller and was responsible for all credit aspects of the retail sales. Two divisional managers were responsible for the main functions of the division: (1) *credit* (departments of approval, authorization, new accounts, and credit promotion); and (2) *accounts receivable* (billing and collections).

In April 1978, the credit division manager was promoted to the position of vice president of accounts payable. Mr. Hageman appointed Mr. Jim Davis, the department manager of authorization, as the new divisional manager of credit. Mr. Davis, age thirty-two, had been with Richardson Bros. for six years and had compiled an excellent record of performance as a supervisor and then department manager. He not only had a degree in accounting but had recently passed his CPA exam. Prior to his employment at Richardson, Mr. Davis worked as an auditor for a local accounting firm.

Shortly after Davis' appointment, the other credit department managers, Mr. Jeff Stillwater (approval), Ms. Karen Jefferson (new accounts), and Mr. Sam Silvermann (credit promotion), met with Mr. Hageman and expressed strong displeasure with Mr. Davis' appointment as their new supervisor. They pointed out that each of them was equally or more qualified. They were not only older than Mr. Davis, but their tenure with Richardson was longer and their performance and education was equal to Davis'. Mr. Hageman, who was known for his strict autocratic and authoritarian behavior, dismissed their complaints and basically told them that he was the boss and it was his right to make that decision! Mr. Davis knew of the negative feelings of the department managers, but he decided to put such issues behind him and to move forward.

In June, Mr. Stillwater left the company to take a job with another local retailer. He openly discussed his negative feelings about Mr. Davis' promotion and the way Mr. Hageman had handled the situation. Mr. Davis also noticed changes in the behavior of Ms. Jefferson and Mr. Silvermann. Ms. Jefferson's usual high performance was beginning to decline. Although the number of transactions handled by her department was only slightly below last year's standard, she was allowing too many errors to be made by her subordinates. Mr. Silvermann, whose wife recently gave birth to their fourth child, frequently discussed the need for a salary increase because of increasing inflation and the heavy department workload.

Although Mr. Davis was aware of these problems, he was more concerned with completing a project given to him by Mr. Hageman. Identified as the "integrated systems approach," it involved the complete conversion of credit transactions from a file system to computer terminals. Mr. Hageman had told Davis that he wanted the system operational before the big Christmas season.

By September, not only was work on the systems project a month behind schedule, but the general level of performance of the credit area declined markedly. As a result, Mr. Davis went directly to Mr. Hageman to discuss the situation. The following discussion took place.

Davis: As you are aware, we are behind schedule on the systems project. The only solution I can think of is to authorize overtime for all divisional employees. By working three extra hours each day and a half day on Saturday, I think we should be able to finish the project on time without hurting our normal activities.

Hageman: You know our budget situation—overtime is taboo this year. As for overtime for supervisors and managers, it's their responsibility to get the work done on time. If more time is needed, tell them to come in on their own time.

Davis: I can't do that! They've already asked for big salary increases because of the workload associated with the systems project and our normal everyday work.

Hageman: Salary discussions are more than four months away. What I'm interested in is performance *today!* It seems to me that your departmental employees are not putting out the level of effort that is required of them.

Davis: You're probably right about that, but what can I do about it?

Hageman: That's your job, not mine! I gave you the divisional managers' job because I thought you could do it. You'd better find a solution quick—fire the whole bunch if you have to! I want results, not a lot of overtime.

After the meeting with Hageman, Davis decided that firing people was not the answer. He already had a tough time hiring new people to offset the high hourly turnover rate. In past jobs, he could handle any problems that came up, but this one had him frustrated, puzzled, and personally worried.

Case Primer Questions

1. Evaluate the behavior of Mr. Davis and the three department managers in terms of: (1) ERG theory; (2) equity theory; and (3) expectancy theory.

2. Evaluate the goal-setting process between Mr. Hageman and Mr. Davis.

3. What should Mr. Davis do to motivate his employees?

Experiential Exercise

Motivation Factors in the Job

Purpose

1. To examine the application of motivation theories to job factors.

2. To understand the relationship between motivation and differences in individuals.

Required understanding

The student should understand the different approaches to motivation in organizations.

How to set up the exercise

Set up groups of four to eight students for the forty-five to sixty minute exercise. The groups should be separated from each other and asked to converse only with members of their own group.

Instructions for the exercise

Exhibit 5–18 presents a list of twelve factors that relate to most jobs in organizations. Two specific job levels are identified: (1) middle-level managers; and (2) first-line, nonsupervisory employees (e.g., blue-collar workers).

1. *Individually,* group members should rank in order the twelve factors on the basis of their influences on motivation from 1, (most influential) to 12, (least influential for motivation (*No* ties, please). The individual group members should provide *two* rank-orders: (1) as they believe middle-level managers would respond to these factors (if exercise is given to advanced classes, or evening working students, have them rank the factors as they themselves evaluate them); and (2) as they believe nonsupervisory, blue-collar (e.g., assembly line) workers would respond to these factors.

2. *As a group,* repeat the instructions presented in step 1 above.

3. The group ranking should be displayed and a spokesperson should discuss the rationale for the group decision and how much variation existed in *individual* ranks.

Exhibit 5–18 Motivation Factors

Factor Description	Ranking	
	Middle-level Manager	*Nonsupervisors (blue collar)*
1. *Recognition:* Receiving recognition from peers, supervisor, and/or subordinates for your good work performances.		
2. *Sense of Achievement:* The feelings associated with successful completion of a job, finding solutions to different problems, or seeing the results of one's work.		
3. *Advancement:* The opportunity for advancement or promotion based on one's ability.		
4. *Status:* Being accorded various position-based aspects as your own secretary, nicely appointed office, selected parking place, or other prestige elements.		
5. *Pay:* A wage that not only covers normal living expenses but provides additional funds for certain luxury items.		
6. *Supervision:* Working for a supervisor who is both competent in doing his or her job and looks out for the welfare of subordinates.		
7. *Job Itself:* Having a job that is interesting, challenging, and provides for substantial variety and autonomy.		
8. *Job Security:* Feeling good about your security within the company.		
9. *Coworkers:* Working with coworkers who are friendly and helpful.		
10. *Personal Development:* Given the opportunity in your job to develop and refine new skills and abilities.		
11. *Fringe Benefits:* A substantial fringe benefit package covering such aspects as personal protection.		
12. *Working Conditions:* Safe and attractive conditions for doing your work.		

CHAPTER 6

Job Design

One of the major objectives of this book is to stress the importance of the individual employee as one of the most valued resources of the organization. The design of the employee's job and the general nature of job assignments relates not only to how effectively this human resource is utilized, but also to the topic of job design.

Job design is important to managers because the way jobs are structured, designed, and coordinated has a direct and significant impact on the performance of the organization. Such factors as the number of employees required to accomplish a performance objective; the diversity of activities performed; the required skills, abilities, and training; and the authority, responsibility, and the level of supervision required are all related to the topic of job design.

Our discussion of job design will be examined in four parts. In the first section, an overall definition and discussion of the historical development of job design will be presented. The theoretical foundations of job design will constitute the second section. Third, we will present a selected discussion of current applications of job design in a variety of organizations. Finally, an integrative model of job design, which attempts to tie together the major issues in the chapter, will be presented.

Definition and Historical Development of Job Design

Job Design Defined

Because job design is concerned with the individual's job, we will initially define it in the following manner:

> Job design concerns the content, functions, and relationships of jobs that are directed toward the accomplishment of organizational purposes and the satisfaction of the personal needs of the individual job holder.

As this definition reveals, job design is concerned with a number of aspects of an individual's job. Among these are the job content, the requirements of the job, the required interpersonal relationships, and the performance outcomes. These job design factors are presented in exhibit 6–1.

The *job content* includes those aspects that define the general nature of the task. *+ iuclude*
Among these aspects are: (1) variety; (2) autonomy; (3) complexity or routineness;
(4) difficulty; and (5) the task identity (i.e., doing the whole job, or just part of it).

The *job functions* are the requirements and methods involved in each job. This
factor includes: (1) job responsibilities; (2) authority; (3) information flow; (4) work
methods; and (5) coordination requirements.

Relationships concern the interpersonal component of the individual's job, including: (1) the extent of interaction or dealing with other individuals that is required; (2) friendship opportunities; and (3) teamwork requirements. *+ iclude*

Performance outcomes concern the level of job performance. Two aspects are
identified: (1) criteria dealing with *task accomplishment* (e.g., productivity, effectiveness, efficiency); and (2) criteria concerning *employee responses* to the job
(e.g., satisfaction, absenteeism, and turnover).

The final factor involves the *feedback* from the outcomes of the job. Feedback
generally originates from two sources: (1) direct feedback from working on the task;
and (2) feedback from other individuals, including an individual's peers, superiors,
or subordinates.

The principal point of this exhibit is that any managerial effort directed toward
job design should consider all its dimensions. In the following section, we will
examine how managers and behavioral scientists have incorporated these dimensions in the major approaches to job design.

Historical Development of Job Design

The historical development of job design has progressed through three stages: (1) job
specialization; (2) employee-response approaches; and (3) the contemporary approaches. This historical development is shown in exhibit 6–2.

Exhibit 6–1 A Framework for Job Design

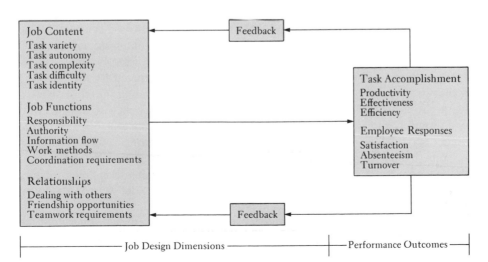

Exhibit 6–2 Historical Development of Job Design

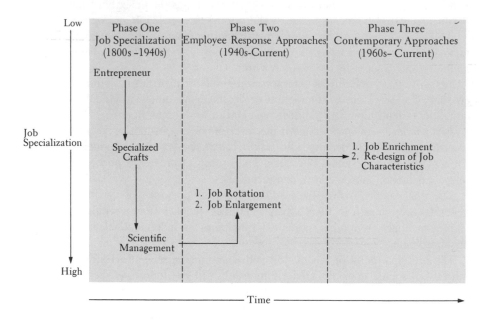

During phase one, the period of industrialization, the emphasis of job design was on the increasing specialization of jobs. Before industrialization, the industrial base of most countries focused on the independent shop owner, craftsman, or entrepreneur. In these operations, a few people (or even one person) were responsible for the design, manufacture, and sale of a product or service. The work proceeded generally at a casual pace, with fairly unstructured tasks and responsibilities.

As industrialization continued, although small firms were still the dominant type of organization, there was a shift toward division of labor and further job specialization.[1] Another development in the industrialization phase was the introduction of scientific management principles.[2] This development was characterized by the consolidation of smaller companies into larger firms and the increased emphasis on the division of labor, assembly-line processing, and a high level of job specialization.

During phase two, there was a growing awareness of negative employee responses to jobs. The high level of job specialization promoted by the scientific management approach created a number of problems centering on the individual worker's morale and behavior. Such problems as low satisfaction, high absenteeism, and turnover were partially attributed to the boredom and monotony created by the highly specialized, routine nature of the individual employee's work. The early response by management to this situation were the techniques of "job rotation" and "job enlargement."[3] These techniques, which generally focused on either rotating individuals between different jobs or giving workers more to do, were only stopgap measures to solving the worker reaction problem.

Phase three involves the contemporary approaches to job design. In each of the various methods within this phase, there is an acknowledgement that improvement in the jobs of workers could come only at the expense of job specialization and through changes in the content, functions, relationships, and feedback of the work. Two contemporary approaches have been identified: (1) job enrichment; and (2) the redesign of job characteristics. *Job enrichment* emphasizes Herzberg's "motivators" of job challenge, achievement, responsibility, and recognition.[4] The *redesign of job characteristics* not only focuses on the key job characteristic dimensions of content, functions, and relationships but also considers the importance of *individual differences* in reactions to job-design efforts.

The distinguishing characteristics of each of these approaches to job design are summarized in exhibit 6–3. Each of these topics, beginning with scientific management, will be discussed in this chapter.

Job Specialization: Scientific Management

The scientific management approach was initiated and encouraged by the work of Taylor and his associates and was formulated in response to the problems and needs of organizations that were in the midst of industrialization. It became, and to some extent still is, the traditional approach to the design of work in many organizations.

Exhibit 6–3 Characteristics of Approaches to Job Design

Approach	Characteristics
Specialization Scientific management	Emphasis on efficiency of work through specialization, standardization, and repetitiveness. Employee concerns focused primarily on monetary incentive payments.
Employee-Response Approaches Job rotation	Workers rotated between similar jobs in order to reduce monotony, boredom, and alienation. Actual jobs remained relatively unchanged.
Job enlargement	Jobs horizontally expanded, giving the worker more to do in order to alleviate the same problems identified by job rotation.
Contemporary Approaches Job enrichment	Founded on Herzberg's two-factor theory; emphasizes the concepts of increased job challenge, responsibility, and autonomy.
Redesign of job characteristics	Focused on the redesign of such job dimensions as variety, autonomy, task identity, and feedback, with an increased emphasis on the effects of individual differences between employees and their different reactions to redesigned jobs.

Job Design

Job design is one of the most important components of scientific management. In its basic format, it assumes that jobs should be simplified, standardized, and specialized for each component of the required work. In general, organizations operationalized this basic job design format by breaking each job down into very small but workable units, standardizing the necessary procedures for performing the work units, and teaching and motivating workers to perform their jobs under conditions of *high efficiency.* As Taylor suggested:

> Perhaps the most prominent single element in modern scientific management is the task idea. The work of every workman is fully planned out by the management at least one day in advance, and each man receives in most cases complete written instructions describing in detail the task which he is to accomplish. . . . The task specifies not only what is to be done but how it should be done and the exact time allowed for doing it. And whenever the workman succeeds in doing his task right, and within the time unit specified, he receives an addition of from 30 percent to 100 percent to his ordinary wages.[5]

For example, consider a forklift operator on a railroad loading dock. The operator's task is specified and designed such that the location of the units to be loaded, the manner of lifting and transporting the units, the loading pattern to be used in the boxcar, and the number of units to be loaded per day are spelled out well in advance. The driver is not only trained to do his or her job but may receive a bonus if more than the required units are loaded per workday.

Perhaps the most extensive adaptation of Taylor's approach to job design has been in manufacturing firms, particularly those with assembly lines. A large-scale study in the 1950s of workers on assembly lines revealed the following characteristics of their jobs:[6]

1. *Mechanical pacing.* The speed at which employees work is determined by the speed of the conveyor line rather than by their natural rhythm or inclination.

2. *Repetitiveness.* Individual employees perform the same short-cycle operations over and over again during the work day.

3. *Low skill requirements.* The jobs are designed to be easily learned to minimize training costs and provide maximum flexibility in assigning individuals to positions.

4. *Concentration on only a fraction of the product.* Each job consists of only a few of the hundreds or thousands of operations necessary to complete the product.

5. *Limited social interaction.* The workplace, noise level, and physical separation of workers spaced along a moving line make it difficult for workers to develop meaningful relationships with other employees.

6. *Predetermination of tools and techniques.* The manner in which an employee performs his job is determined by staff specialists. The worker may never influence these individuals.

Scientific management principles were widely implemented throughout the industrialized world. The assembly line was by far the most well-known adaptation; however, the principles were used in many other types of work, particularly where the job could be broken down into manageable units and specialized for efficiency.

Advantages and Disadvantages of Scientific Management

The job-design framework provided by scientific management was one of the most significant factors of modern management thought. As such, a number of advantages to managers were expected from adopting this approach. First, through scientific examination, jobs could be designed to incorporate the maximum use of specialization and simplification to afford maximum worker efficiency.

Second, if jobs could be broken down into highly specialized units, an economic advantage could be provided because such jobs could be filled with predominantly low-skill workers, who were a relatively inexpensive resource and readily available. Third, because of the skill requirements, only a minimum amount of training of workers was needed, which provided a further economic advantage. In addition, further cost savings could be realized because the low skill and minimal training requirements make the work force relatively interchangeable, and workers often could be replaced or shifted to different jobs with only a slight disruption in the production process.

Finally, scientific management provided managers with a high degree of control over the quantity and quality of the work for two reasons. First, with a high degree of mechanization workers have less opportunity to become physically tired while doing their work. A relatively stable level of quality and quantity of output should be predicted. Second, with standardization and specialization, supervisors would have a better control over workers. Deviation from standards would be easily recognized and corrected under such conditions. In summary, the principle benefit of this method is that many of the *uncertainties* of the job have been identified and controlled, providing management with the opportunity to emphasize further improvements in production efficiency.

In some instances, however, implementation of these principles did not result in many of the expected benefits. This approach places a great deal of emphasis on the task accomplishment portion shown in exhibit 6–1, with only minimal concern for the employee responses to these jobs.[7] In some organizations, the expected gains in efficiency and productivity were more than offset by problems originating from the workers' reaction to the design of their jobs. The movement toward greater job specialization, while providing benefits to the planning and scheduling of the work, also created many jobs that were routine and boring, leading to many situations of worker dissatisfaction, turnover, and absenteeism.

This is not to imply that all assembly-line processes are inferior. There are many such production operations where the severity of these problems have not been encountered or have been diminished by certain management practices. The main point is that the effectiveness of any job-design effort should consider both the task accomplishment factor *and* employee responses to their jobs. Other approaches to job design that considered both task accomplishment and employee responses were needed. Two such job-design strategies are job rotation and job enlargement.

Approaches to Job Design that considered task accomplishment + employee responses include

Job Rotation and Job Enlargement

Soon after World War II, a growing movement among managers and behavioral scientists developed concerning the design of workers' jobs, a movement that we will call *employee response approaches*. The problems created by the scientific management approach to job design developed to such a stage that "blue-collar blues" became a common malady.[8] The initial response by managers concerned two job-design methods: job rotation and job enlargement.

1) Job Rotation

The premise of job rotation is that the various tasks performed by workers are interchangeable, and workers can be "rotated" from task to task without any major disruption in the work flow. Exhibit 6–4 depicts the basic process of job rotation. Consider an automobile assembly line where task I is installing the carpets, task II is installing the seats, and task III is installing the dashboard. During time 1, worker A performs task I, worker B task II, and worker C task III. During time 2, worker A now performs task II, worker B task III, and worker C performs task I.

With this approach, there is really no major change in the actual jobs of the workers. However, management assumes that by rotating employees between different jobs the boredom and routineness can be minimized by providing workers the opportunity to develop other skills and also a larger perspective of the total production process.

Exhibit 6–4 Job Rotation

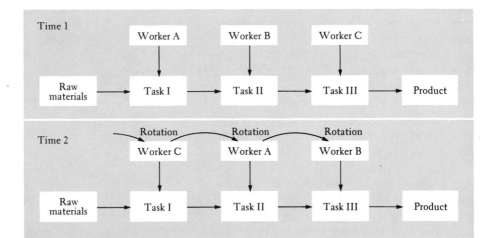

Nevertheless, job rotation is only a short-term solution to a much larger problem. Neither the jobs nor the expectations of the workers have been significantly altered. The monotony and boredom may be relieved for a short time, but the routineness may remain. Critics have pointed out that with job rotation individual workers have merely been exposed to a different series of monotonous and boring jobs.

2) Job Enlargement

Job enlargement represented the first attempt by managers to redesign jobs. The basic feature of this technique is the *horizontal* expansion of jobs to include a greater variety of tasks. Job enlargement advocates recognized that the boredom and dissatisfaction with many jobs can be traced to the short work cycle built into different tasks. For example, in an automobile assembly line, it only takes a few minutes for workers to install headlights, the steering wheel, or the radio.

Horizontal expansion involves increasing the number and variety of skills and activities performed by the individual worker. In most cases, the enlarged job includes certain activities originally held by other workers. In exhibit 6–5, suppose that tasks I through IV, respectively, involve installing the carpets, seats, dashboard, and radio in an automobile. After enlargement, worker A may be responsible for installing the carpets *plus* the seats, worker B installs both the seats *and* the dashboard, and worker C installs the dashboard *and* the radio.

By increasing the variety of skills required and expanding the number of operations, it was anticipated that the monotony and boredom would be reduced, resulting

Exhibit 6–5 Job Enlargement

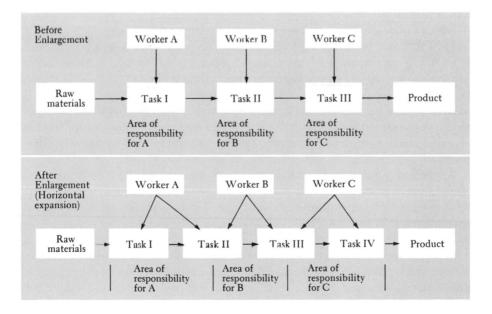

155

in a higher level of job satisfaction.[9] A number of critics, however, claim that job enlargement is merely a different tool used by management to increase productivity and to reduce the total workforce. They contend that the essential nature of jobs remained unchanged in that the jobs were still boring and dissatisfying. Job enlargement only gave workers more to do. If the same work could be accomplished by fewer workers, critics claim that managers would use this opportunity to eliminate unnecessary workers.[10]

Besides the problems caused by the essentially unchanged nature of the work, neither job rotation nor job enlargement was guided by any systematic conceptual or theoretical framework. In essence, these solutions were short-term "seat of the pants" strategies implemented by managers in an attempt to solve much larger problems. As we pointed out in chapter 2, any attempt to alter individual behavior should be based on a well-founded conceptual framework that explicitly identifies the key variables, relationships between variables, and anticipated performance outcomes.

Contemporary Approaches

Job rotation and enlargement, though only short-term strategies, provided at least some relief to the employee-response problems associated with scientific management. Longer-term solutions to these problems were needed by managers. Two such approaches have gained contemporary popularity: job enrichment and the redesign of job characteristics. As the reader will soon note, the experiences gained from the use of job rotation and enlargement were not totally lost. Each of these "employee-response approaches" serve as elements of the contemporary approaches.

Job Enrichment

Herzberg's two-factor theory serves as a framework for job redesign efforts aimed at increasing worker satisfaction and performance. As presented in chapter 5, the basis of Herzberg's approach to job enrichment focuses on two factors: hygiene factors and motivators. When hygiene factors are not present in the job, a state of dissatisfaction is created within the worker. When present, however, dissatisfaction is reduced to zero, but this does not create a state of satisfaction. Motivators (e.g., job challenge, autonomy, responsibility, and achievement) concern the intrinsic aspects of job content, which, when present, lead to satisfaction and motivated performance.[11]

Applied to job design, the two-factor theory focused on "vertical expansion" changes to the work itself—that is, the "motivators" of the theory.[12] To illustrate the application of job enrichment, consider the job of a press operator in an automobile plant. The operator's job consists of taking flat sheets of steel, aligning the sheets in the press, and operating the press, which converts the flat sheet to a contoured piece of metal in the form of an automobile door. Before job enrichment, the operator is responsible for the manufacture of a certain number of doors per day. Raw-material input and finished-product output are controlled by a conveyer belt system.

How could this press operator's job be enriched? The following changes, involving Herzberg's motivators, could be implemented:

1. *Responsibility.* Increase the worker's responsibility by making the operator responsible not only for production but also quality control and the scheduled maintenance on the press. These three aspects—production, quality control, and maintenance—serve to create a complete "natural unit of work" for the operator (i.e., task identity and variety).

2. *Decision making.* Increase the operator's authority and autonomy through such aspects as setting production standards, controlling the pace or speed of the conveyor line, and removing some supervisory controls (i.e., task autonomy).

3. *Feedback.* Provide direct feedback to the operator by making performance data directly available. In some cases, permit the operator to actually collect and maintain such data (i.e., task feedback).

4. *Accountability.* Reward the operator (e.g., praise, recognition) on the basis of the degree to which performance goals are obtained.

5. *Personal growth and development.* The above four points provide new learning experiences for the operator (i.e., becoming acquainted with quality control and maintenance procedures). Also, permit the operator to offer suggestions as to improvements to the present system. In addition, structure possible career growth beyond the present job.

6. *Achievement.* By increasing such aspects as responsibility, autonomy, and accountability, a sense of achievement, or accomplishing something worthwhile, could develop for the operator.

There are a number of advantages and disadvantages to Herzberg's approach to job enrichment. On the plus side, enriched jobs should provide greater motivation and opportunities for satisfaction than are provided by routine or simplified tasks. It was hoped that this higher level of motivation and satisfaction would produce increased productivity, a higher-quality product, and decreased turnover and absenteeism.

The basic disadvantages of job enrichment generally concern the costs associated with implementing such a program. Enriched jobs may involve added training costs, revamping or expansion of physical facilities, and higher pay because skilled workers are generally required for most jobs. Some consideration should also be given to the fact that some workers, particularly older workers, may resist changes because they have become quite "set in their ways." It was argued, however, that the advantages of increased satisfaction, motivation, and performance more than offset the disadvantages associated with job enrichment efforts. Since its introduction, job enrichment programs have been implemented in a number of organizations, including AT&T, Texas Instruments, General Food, IBM, and Polaroid.[13]

Problems with job enrichment.   Like many approaches from the behavioral sciences that propose to solve some worker-related problems, job enrichment has a number of drawbacks. Two of the most significant problems concern the *theoretical*

ie van drages to jobs simultained

framework and the specific job enrichment *implementation strategies* used by managers.

As we pointed out in chapter 5, there is considerable controversy concerning the
validity of the Herzberg model.[14] The theoretical framework does not specify which
of the crucial job dimensions satisfy which motivation needs, and the model does
not include how the individual worker's characteristics relate to the job enrichment
conditions.

There are a number of specific problems with the implementation of job enrichment programs. Many job enrichment applications have involved a number of simultaneous changes in the variety of work, the amount of responsibility and autonomy
required, the amount of feedback to the worker, and the degree of teamwork required.[15] When job enrichment programs produce positive effects, is this due to
one, two, or all these job-design changes? The problem is that there have been few
studies that have identified which of these particular job-design changes are more
important than others. There is also a lack of evidence regarding which job-design
dimensions are crucial and what specific effects a change in any one of these
dimensions will have. The result is that many managers have opted for a "shotgun"
approach, making many changes to jobs simultaneously in the hope that results will
be positive.

There are six major factors that can go wrong when organizations redesign work
through a job enrichment framework:[16]

1. *Absence of diagnosis before jobs are redesigned.* Rarely does management
   insist that a systematic study of jobs and the people affected be carried out
   before a job enrichment project begins. A diagnosis would possibly reveal that:
   (1) some jobs are as good as they will ever be; (2) some jobs are already too
   complex—additional "enrichment" will only further complicate the problem;
   (3) employees may differ markedly in their readiness or ability to handle enriched jobs; and (4) management has failed to assess its own commitment (in
   terms of time and resources) to the job enrichment program. The belief that job
   enrichment will "cure all" is never fulfilled.

2. *The work itself remains unchanged.* When faced with the time and resource
   problems associated with a major change effort, such as job enrichment, managers change jobs only slightly by adding minor tasks. Efforts to actually change
   what people do on their jobs are not made.

3. *Failure to consider unexpected effects.* Even when significant job redesign
   programs have been instituted, unexpected "spinoff effects" may occur. Possible effects on other "nonenriched" jobs and disruption or elimination of already
   efficient, effective, and motivating procedures may occur and thereby diminish
   the positive impact of the overall program. For example, allowing a group of
   machine operators greater autonomy in setting their work pace may disrupt the
   raw-material flow and finished-stock inventory procedures.

4. *Programs are rarely evaluated.* Any proposal to alter organizational behavior
   should be scientifically evaluated. Few job enrichment programs have been so
   evaluated. Generally, verbal descriptions, observations, or one-shot case

studies have been the prevalent mode for evaluation. A few of the reasons for this inadequacy are: (1) the inability to translate human behavioral gains into dollars and cents; (2) the inability to determine cause and effect relationships; (3) a lack of expertise in evaluation procedures; and (4) an overemphasis on successful accomplishment (wanting to look good) and a disinclination to admit failure.

5. *Lack of training in job enrichment.* As in many organizational change efforts, managers either are not given complete and up-to-date information or learn just enough about the method to feel comfortable. As a result, incorrect procedures are used, or wide variations in methods are found within the same company.

6. *Creeping bureaucracy.* Many times, job enrichment efforts are just "tacked on" to the management process and are never fully integrated into the organization; the organization will tend to revert to the old established methods when job enrichment does not fully live up to its advantages.

Additional criticism of job enrichment programs was provided by Fein, who pointed out that when examined closely the prominent job enrichment studies reveal some significant, but hidden, findings.[17] These include the following:

1. What actually occurred was often quite different from what was reported to have occurred.

2. Most of the studies were conducted with hand-picked employees who did not represent a cross section of the total working population.

3. Only a handful of job enrichment cases have been reported in the past ten years, despite the impression that it has widespread usage.

4. In all instances, the experiments were initiated by management, never by workers or unions.

It is Fein's contention that in some cases positive effects were due more to common-sense management than to job enrichment. He also believes that job enrichment works primarily for those who seek fulfillment from their work and that contrary to popular belief most people seek fulfillment outside, not on, their jobs.[18] In addition, it seems that the majority of job enrichment programs have been directed toward medium- to high-skill level employees, whose jobs are inherently enriching.

Fein believes that if managers want to improve the quality of working life, they should ask the workers what is desired. Satisfaction can come from pay, job security, and a workable climate, not only from involvement, responsibility, and greater job variety.[19]

Whether job enrichment is a powerful motivator and mechanism for increased satisfaction and performance remains an unresolved problem. In our evaluation framework, job enrichment, at least theoretically, is directed at both the task accomplishment and the worker-reaction criteria. In actual practice, the results have been less than predicted. Despite these many problems, job enrichment as a job redesign strategy should continue to be accepted as a possible approach because of its common-sense appeal to managers. It is incumbent on managers, however, to understand not only the questions concerning the theoretical foundation of job enrichment, but also the problems associated with implementing this job redesign strategy. This requires both a careful diagnosis before the job enrichment program begins and a detailed evaluation during and after its implementation.

Redesign of Job Characteristics: Need Satisfaction and Individual Differences

For a given job or similar jobs in an organization, most managers would agree that there is a wide variation in the reactions to the job within a group of workers. Depending on how the work is designed, jobs can provide various opportunities for employees to satisfy important individual needs or accomplish certain specific goals for the organization. Maslow's need hierarchy suggests that some jobs offer workers the opportunity to satisfy material and security needs (e.g., adequate pay, benefits, and safe working conditions), social needs (e.g., satisfying interactions and friendly relations with coworkers, supervisors, or clients), and higher-order needs (e.g., growth, advancement, achievement, autonomy, and challenge).[20]

The outcomes of any job are a function of the type of job *and* the individual. That is, the individual's *performance* on the job and the need *satisfaction* experienced with the work are a joint function of the way the work is designed and kinds of needs or goals that are of major importance to the individuals. For a sales representative, high performance and need satisfaction will result—if the individual is well suited for the work—because achievement and autonomy are requirements of the job. For a maintenance superintendent, a successful match between the job and the individual may focus on the aspects of technical expertise, cooperativeness, achievement, and control of tension and anxiety. For a bank teller, performance and need satisfaction will be outcomes when the aspects of attention to detail and an orientation toward interpersonal relationships match the individual to the job. As has been stated:

> What we need, then, are ways of running organizations that recognize the importance of treating people differently and placing them in environments and work situations that fit their unique needs, skills, and abilities.[21]

This points out the necessity for an organization to design jobs to fit the important differences that exist among individual employees. Motivation and performance will be enhanced if the work can be designed so that employees believe they can satisfy individual needs and organizational goals by working hard. However, managers would be faced with an insurmountable task if they had to design a job for each individual worker. The middle ground is to consider two broad need categories: lower-level needs (safety, security, and social) and higher-level needs (ego, status, and self-actualization).

In most organizations, many lower-level needs are often well satisfied with the existing design of jobs. There are many workers who are happy and well satisfied working on routine and repetitive jobs.[22] A self-selection process may occur when certain workers seek out routine jobs because they want only the satisfaction of lower-level needs (e.g., pay, fringe benefits, safe working conditions) from their jobs. They seek fulfillment of higher-order needs outside work activities through hobbies, participation in civic activities, and so on. An attempt to "enrich" jobs for these workers would probably be met with resistance and possible failure. As Fein points out:

> Some [workers] prefer to remain in highly repetitive, low-skill jobs even when they have an opportunity to advance to higher skill jobs through job bidding. A minority of workers strive to move into skilled jobs such as machinists, mechanics, set-up men, group leaders, utility men, and other such jobs where there is considerable autonomy in the work performed. . . .
>
> Apparently what happens is that a worker begins a new job—decides whether the work suits his needs and desires. Impressions about a job are a composite of many factors: pay, proximity to home, the nature of the work, working conditions, the attitude of supervision, congeniality of fellow workers, past employment history of the company, job security, physical demands, opportunities for advancement, and many other related factors. A worker's choice of a job is made in a combination of ways, through evaluating various trade offs. Working conditions may be bad, but if the pay and job security are high, the job may be tolerable. . . .
>
> A year or two after entering a plant, most workers are in jobs or job progressions which suit them or which they find tolerable. Those who are no longer on the job have been "selected" out, either by themselves or by management.[23]

It may be erroneous to consider that the majority of employees will either react favorably to routine, highly specialized jobs (scientific management) or to jobs that have been expanded vertically (job enrichment). At least two groups of employees may exist: one group may desire the satisfaction of lower-level needs and actively seek routine jobs; another group of employees may be characterized by a need for jobs that are challenging and offer opportunities for personal growth and advancement. Because many organizations offer jobs in which lower-level needs can be easily satisfied, it could be suggested that major job redesign efforts should be directed toward employees with higher-order needs.[24]

Behavioral scientists have suggested for some time that individuals may experience higher-order need satisfaction when they learn that as a result of their own efforts they have accomplished something that they believe is personally worthwhile or meaningful. In more specific terms, higher-order satisfaction should be obtained when an employee's job has the following dimensions, or psychological states.[25]

1. *The job should allow a worker to feel personally responsible for a meaningful portion of his or her work.* A job is meaningful to an individual when he or she feels that work accomplishment is the result of personal effort and control so that he or she feels personally responsible for whatever successes or failures that may result. A way of operationalizing this dimension is through *job autonomy.* The autonomy dimension may be a key factor in an individual's choice of a given occupation.

2. *The job should involve doing something that is intrinsically meaningful or*

otherwise experienced as worthwhile to the individual. There are three ways that jobs can be made more meaningful or worthwhile. First, individual's jobs can focus on an entire unit as opposed to just a portion of it. For example, a bank teller may be responsible for satisfying all the customers' needs, including transactions involving checking, savings, loan payments, and utility bills, rather than specializing only in savings account deposits and withdrawals. Behavioral scientists term this dimension *task identity.* A second way is to require the individual to develop and use a variety of skills and abilities in order to accomplish a goal. In the case of the maintenance superintendent, the technical knowledge of the plant's machinery, the skill to supervise and interact with workers and peers, and the ability to plan and implement a successful plant shutdown and repair without lost sales provides a significant level of *task variety.* Finally, jobs should have a substantial and perceivable impact (i.e., *task significance)* on the lives of other people, whether in the immediate organization or in society at large. By selling products, the sales representative not only satisfies the customer, but also provides workers jobs and a livelihood at the manufacturing plant. A degree of task significance is thus attached to the salesperson's job.

3. *The job should provide feedback about what is accomplished.* Knowledge of one's task performance is a requirement for higher-order need satisfaction. If an employee is working on a job that is meaningful and worthwhile, for which he or she is held personally responsible, satisfaction of higher-order needs will not be obtained unless some form of *task feedback* is provided. Feedback may originate from either doing the task itself or from other individuals, such as the supervisor, coworkers, or customers. The sales representative receives feedback from the volume of sales orders and evaluations from the sales manager. The maintenance superintendent obtains feedback from the successful functioning of the machinery, from the plant manager, and other workers. Finally, a bank teller can receive feedback on task accomplishment from satisfied (or dissatisfied) customers or from the branch manager and fellow tellers.

Task variety, identity, significance, autonomy, and feedback have been termed "core" dimensions because they relate directly to the attainment of personal satisfaction.[26] A theoretical model for considering individual differences in job design is shown in exhibit 6–6.[27] The model depicts the relationship between the core job characteristic dimensions, the critical psychological states, the personal work outcomes, and the level of employee growth need strength.

Following from the model, a job highest in motivating potential must be high in all three psychological states. If one or more of the psychological states of the job is low, then a lower level of personal and work outcomes can be expected. For example, if the maintenance superintendent feels personally responsible for what he believes is a meaningful job, but receives feedback on his performance only infrequently, it is doubtful that the highest outcomes can be realized.

Exhibit 6–6 also suggests some implementation concepts for increasing the core job characteristic dimensions.

Exhibit 6–6 Relationship Between Job-Design Dimensions and Employee Need Strength

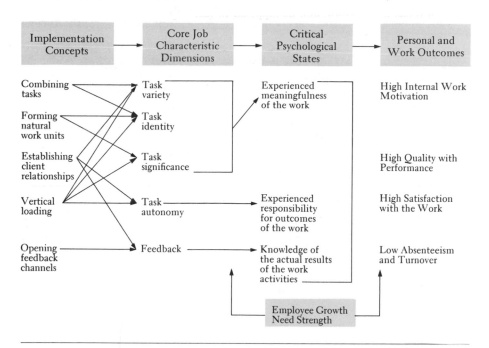

Adapted from J. R. Hackman, G. Oldham, R. Janson, and K. Purdy, "A New Strategy for Job Enrichment," *California Management Review,* Summer 1975, p. 62. © 1975 by the Regents of the University of California. Reprinted from *California Management Review* 27, no. 4, p. 62, by permission of the Regents.

1. *Combining tasks.* This implementation strategy reflects a movement away from the high task specialization dictated by the scientific management approach by combining highly specialized tasks into one larger work module. For the bank teller, this can be done again by having the teller be responsible for many customer transactions, rather than one. A combination of tasks affects both the *task variety* and the *task identity.*

2. *Forming natural work units.* This implementation effort focuses on the "ownership" of a job by giving the worker continuing responsibility for an identifiable body of work. For example, rather than specializing in the sale of only one product line, the sales representative may be held responsible for the sales of *all* the company's products to particular customers. A sense of *task identity* and *task significance* is thus provided to the individual.

3. *Establishing client relationships.* The individual worker can gain a new perspective on his or her work by establishing direct relationships with clients. For example, the shipping supervisor in a manufacturing firm may be concerned about the condition of the product when it arrives at the customer's location. Giving this individual the opportunity to talk directly with the client or

to visit the customer's plant provides the opportunity to increase the *variety, autonomy,* and *feedback* associated with the job. In addition, something such as new loading procedures to reduce damage in shipping may result, further enhancing the job's meaningfulness and the organization's performance.

4. *Vertical loading*. As does job enrichment, this aspect concerns providing the employee greater latitude and responsibility for conducting tasks. For the bank teller, vertical loading could include such aspects as having greater discretion in setting schedules, deciding on work methods, checking quality, training less experienced workers, setting the work pace, and developing new solutions to problems. The implementation strategy directly impacts on the *autonomy, variety, task identity,* and *significance* of the job.

5. *Opening feedback channels*. Providing employees with the opportunity for greater *feedback* helps them learn whether their performance is improving, decreasing, or remaining at a stable level. Most feedback channels focus on the information given to the employee by the supervisor. Another method is learning about performance directly from the job. For the bank teller, additional feedback can be provided by maintaining personal records, calculating the number of transactions and errors, and the use of an on-line computer system to provide the individual with additional performance data.

Finally, the model suggests that higher-order psychological needs, particularly *employee growth need strength,* are important considerations for implementing job-design changes. Some employees have strong growth needs for personal development, for increasing their knowledge and abilities, and for learning new skills. For example, the young accountant working in an auditing group may need to develop new diagnostic and analytical skills. The development of these new skills may then enable this individual to transfer, or be promoted, to the administrative services department, where the focus is on consulting with clients on a variety of managerial problems beyond auditing. Individuals such as this accountant are high in growth need strength.

On the other hand, not everyone is able to become motivated by his or her work, even when the critical psychological states are operative. For example, the assistant manager of a small savings and loan association may be quite satisfied in his position. He may believe that he is using his skills and abilities to the fullest extent and may resist the promotion to a branch-manager position at the main downtown office because he has low growth need strength at this time.

Exhibit 6–7 shows how an employee's growth need strength may have a significant moderating effect on the relationship between the dimension of a job and the work outcomes.[28] This figure suggests that workers with high growth need strength will be positively motivated when they have jobs that are high in the core job dimensions, resulting in higher satisfaction and performance and lower absenteeism and turnover. Individuals whose growth needs are not so strong may react adversely to jobs that are high in the core job dimensions. The variety, task identity, and autonomy may create a feeling of overstretching one's ability and skills to effectively do the job. This may be one of the reasons for certain reported results of job

Exhibit 6-7   Moderating Effect of Employee Growth Need Strength

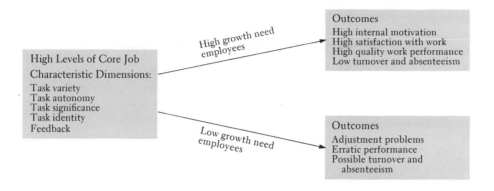

Adapted from J. R. Hackman, G. Oldham, R. Janson, and K. Purdy, "A New Strategy for Job Enrichment," *California Management Review,* Summer 1975, p. 60. © 1975 by the Regents of the University of California. Reprinted from *California Management Review* 27, no. 4, p. 60, by permission of the Regents.

enrichment programs. Attempting to enrich the jobs of a large group of workers could have a variety of outcomes because high growth need employees will react favorably to this job redesign effort, but those with lower growth needs will react negatively.

A word of caution about individual differences is required at this point. Managers should avoid categorizing their employees into rigid, inflexible categories for any particular length of time. As we pointed out in our discussion of motivation, individual needs are *dynamic* characteristics that may change over time. At one point in time, managers can identify employees who are likely to react favorably to jobs with high core dimensions and those who would probably react negatively. However, at some later time, individual employees may develop higher growth needs that had been dormant for a number of years, thus making them candidates for job-design changes. It would be unfair to these individuals to block their chances for satisfaction of growth needs by locking them in their present positions because of a low growth need at some time in the past. If the organization cannot provide a new, challenging position, this individual would leave the organization.

Research on the job characteristics model.   Although the job characteristics model is fairly recent, a number of studies have been reported that have tested the effects of individual differences on the relationship between job characteristics and employee behavior. The results of these studies have revealed the following:

1. The studies investigating growth need strength have generally supported the notion that employees with high growth needs will react more favorably (e.g., job satisfaction) in jobs that have high levels of variety, autonomy, feedback, and task identity.[29] Along this line, researchers have recently adopted a conven-

tion to simplify the core job dimensions. In essence, the individual job dimensions are combined (additively) to form a new global variable, termed job scope.

2. In both field and laboratory studies, the nature of the worker's value system has been shown to be an important individual characteristic affecting the reaction to job dimensions. In a study involving approximately five hundred workers in forty-seven jobs from eleven different organizations, it was found that the cultural values of urban and rural workers had a significant impact on worker responses.[30] Rural workers responded more favorably to complex jobs; urban workers were more satisfied with more specialized jobs. In a laboratory study, subjects were classified as having either intrinsic work values (i.e., oriented toward job-content factors such as achievement, challenge, and development of new skills) or extrinsic values (i.e., oriented toward job-context factors such as group affiliation, friendship, and employment policies). It was found that subjects with intrinsic work values were more satisfied with a complex task, and subjects with extrinsic work values responded more favorably to the more specialized task.[31]

3. In one study involving telephone workers, the impact of worker values and growth need strength were related to the reaction of workers to different job characteristics.[32] The results revealed that high growth need strength of employees had a stronger impact on job satisfaction than did worker value orientation.

The limited findings to date strongly suggest that individual differences have a significant impact on the effectiveness of any job redesign effort. Even with these rather consistent results, certain problems exist that managers should consider. First, the list of possible individual characteristics is almost endless. Though higher-order need strength is certainly an important characteristic, it may not hold for some workers in some organizations or settings. Which individual characteristics are important for a particular situation remains an unanswered question. Second, as has been discussed earlier, most individual characteristics, such as needs, desires, and motives, are relatively dynamic and changeable factors. A slight change in an individual worker's need structure may alter the worker's response to the job from one of satisfaction to one of dissatisfaction, or vice versa. Third, the exact meaning of or relationships between such constructs as "experienced meaningfulness of the job" (critical psychological state) or "internal work motivation" (outcomes) are not totally clear.[33] Current thinking is oriented toward a belief that job characteristics affect the "intrinsic" motivation of the employee. Recall that the discussion in chapter 5 on reinforcement theory pointed toward the "extrinsic" motivation potential of such rewards as pay, promotion, and recognition. By linking job design and reinforcement theory, the manager can possibly motivate employees through *extrinsic* reinforcers or through *intrinsic* job-design changes.

Finally, the measurement of individual characteristics is only in a crude state. Without such measures, it would be a questionable practice to attempt to classify individuals into different subgroups for job redesign programs. The behavioral sciences have not yet advanced to the point where techniques for accurate and reliable diagnosis and prediction are readily available to managers.

Even considering these issues, the job characteristics model has made significant advances in understanding the response of employees to job design programs. No longer should managers blindly attempt to enlarge or enrich the jobs of *all* employees. The job characteristics model not only provides clearer implementation concepts that help to alleviate the "shotgun" approach of job enrichment, but consideration must be given to the impact of *individual differences* to any changes in the design of an employee's job.

A Summary of Job-Design Strategies

In our discussion of job design, we have examined four approaches: (1) scientific management; (2) job rotation and job enlargement; (3) job enrichment; and (4) the redesign of job characteristics to better account for individual differences. A summary of these four approaches is presented in exhibit 6–8.

Exhibit 6–8 Summary of Job-Design Approaches

Approach	Characteristics	Results
Scientific Management	Emphasis on efficiency of work through job specialization, standardization, control, and repetitiveness.	Adverse worker response to the high degree of boredom and monotony in terms of morale and turnover. High costs for training, and wage and benefit plans.
Job Rotation and Job Enlargement	Workers are either rotated between similar jobs (rotation) or the job is expanded horizontally (enlargement) to include more things to do.	Only short-term strategies to alleviate worker morale problems. Jobs remain essentially unchanged. Criticism has focused on management's use of these techniques to increase productivity while reducing the number of employed workers.
Job Enrichment	Based on Herzberg's theory, this approach emphasizes vertical job expansion by increasing the worker's job challenge, responsibility, and autonomy.	Generally positive results have been reported. The problems focus on the inadequacy of the theory, difficulties in implementation, and failure to consider technological and individual characteristic differences.
Redesign of Job Characteristics	This approach emphasizes the redesign of the core job characteristic dimensions to recognize the different reactions to jobs by individuals. Growth need strength is identified as a key moderating variable.	Positive findings, but only from limited samples. Problems include the identification and measurement of an infinite number of individual characteristics, the dynamic nature of individual needs, and the ambiguity associated with the model's variables and relationships.

The table reveals three major points. First, only job enrichment and the job-redesign approaches were guided by *theoretical frameworks*. In the case of the former, Herzberg's two-factor theory was utilized; the need hierarchy approach generally served as the foundation for the latter. Even though Herzberg's theory is in question, the importance of a theoretical framework for understanding critical variables, their relationship with other variables, and possible outcomes should not be underestimated in guiding the work of both behavioral scientists and practicing managers.

Second, each of the job-design approaches differs in its focus. Scientific management emphasizes such aspects as job specialization, repetitiveness, and low-skill requirements as means towards the goal of organizational efficiency. Job rotation and enlargement are short-term strategies emphasizing horizontal expansion and are designed to counteract the human factor problem associated with the scientific management approach to job design. Outcome criteria include both an emphasis on task accomplishment *and* worker attitudes and morale. Job enrichment emphasizes improving worker productivity and morale through vertical expansion of jobs. Finally, the redesign of job characteristics approach focuses on both redesigning the core job characteristic dimensions and on the necessity for considering individual differences.

Third, different results and problems have been associated with each of the job-design approaches. Scientific management's emphasis on job specialization and efficiency helped to create problems of worker alienation. Job rotation and job enlargement were only "stopgap" methods that resulted in minimal changes to the jobs of workers. The generally positive results of job enrichment programs are somewhat overshadowed by the criticism of its theoretical framework, the problems associated with implementation, and the failure to consider individual differences in reactions to enriched jobs. Finally, the redesign of job characteristics approach has been supported in only a limited number of studies. The fact that individual differences make up an important component in its framework is a strong plus. However, the rather limitless list and the dynamic nature of individual needs and methods used to measure individual differences remain a significant problem.

As this summary suggests, the various approaches to job design have made significant advances during this century. However, we are not yet to the point at which a particular job-design theory or strategy has been universally accepted by both managers and behavioral scientists. In the following section, we will illustrate certain job-design applications to highlight both the successes and failures each has encountered.

Job-Design Applications

As might be expected from the importance of the topic to organizational performance, job-design approaches have received wide attention throughout the industrialized world. In fact, a recent study of the largest corporations in the list of *Fortune's* 1,000 companies revealed that a high percentage of the responding companies either had tried, or soon will try, to implement job-design programs.[34]

In surveying the literature, it can be determined that various organizations have attacked the problem of worker dissatisfaction and boredom in many different ways, depending on the particular problem they faced. In order to provide the reader with at least a brief summary of job design applications, three applications will be discussed. These include: (1) job enrichment at AT&T; (2) the General Foods experience; and (3) job design in Sweden.

In reviewing these three approaches to job redesign, the different strategies and methods that were used in the sample organizations should be considered. In some cases, the main strategy was job enrichment, in others it was a combination of job rotation and job enrichment, and in still others the emphasis was on teamwork and the redesign of job characteristics.

Job Design at AT&T

In the 1960s, AT&T was experiencing high turnover rates among clerical workers who were responsible for compiling telephone directories. This high turnover rate resulted in increased employment and training costs.[35] The job enrichment program developed by management involved the implementation of four concepts.

First, instead of twenty-one separate steps, including a lengthy verification procedure in which one clerk checked another clerk's work, the routine was decreased to fourteen steps. In addition, each clerk could do all fourteen steps, rather than a single, monotonous task.

Second, supervisors were encouraged to give the clerks some responsibility for handling the work control procedures. These responsibilities included such procedures as rejecting material because of poor quality and cutting off service for nonpayment by customers.

Third, direct feedback of a worker's performance was provided by having each clerk evaluate and monitor the quality and quantity of his or her own performance.

Finally, decision centers were established, which involved physical relocations. At each location within the unit's building, a particular set of customers to be worked with was identified.

This work-flow change involved changes in all five core job dimensions: variety, autonomy, task significance, task identity, and feedback. The results revealed not only cost savings but also improvements in efficiency and worker attitudes and turnover.

The second job-design program, however, was not as successful.[36] In this project, the focus was on two different telephone operator jobs: the "directory assistance" job and the "toll" job. The directory assistance job involved looking up telephone numbers at the request of customers. The job specified precise phraseology in dealing with customers. In addition, the operators were not allowed: (1) to leave their positions without checking with their supervisors; (2) to switch at their own initiative between the directory assistance job and the toll job; (3) to deal with a request to provide an unlisted number; or (4) to decide whether or not to serve a customer with a large number of requests. The toll job involved placing long-distance calls for customers and handling the timing and billing for the calls that were placed. Almost all the operators were trained for both jobs and spent some time on each during any given day.

In order to redesign the operator's jobs, the following changes were introduced:

1. Operators were given more freedom in choosing what phraseology to use in dealing with customers.

2. Operators were free to move from directory assistance to toll operations (and vice versa) at their own discretion if they observed an unequal load on the two services.

3. Operators were free to elect to service a customer with a large number of requests.

4. Operators were allowed to take and report their own counts of calls handled.

After six months using the new work-design procedure, training costs decreased and slight increases in the variety and autonomy of the job were noted. Even after the change, however, the core job dimensions were still relatively low in comparison with other company jobs. The findings also showed a *decrease* in satisfaction, particularly in the satisfaction with interpersonal relations for some of the older workers. In general, the findings revealed minimal effects of the job redesign program on the younger operators, and negative effects on the attitudes of the older workers.

The results of this study of telephone operators point to three factors discussed earlier in this chapter. First, in redesigning jobs, consideration should be given to important individual differences. In this study, the age and tenure on the job were important aspects of the effectiveness of the job-design project. Second, to some workers, the interpersonal dimensions of a job are equally or more important than the core job dimensions of variety, autonomy, and so on. Positive changes in the core dimension may result in negative effects on the interpersonal factors. Finally, managers should consider the fact that some jobs cannot be radically changed. In the case of the telephone operators, the redesigned jobs were still relatively low in the core job dimensions. Because of technological and efficiency considerations, some jobs may have to remain routine and specialized.

The General Foods Experience

In 1968, General Foods was considering the construction of a plant in Topeka, Kansas, to manufacture pet foods. Because of continuing problems at their existing plants—product waste, sabotage, frequent shutdowns and low worker morale—the management of General Foods wanted to try a set of innovative behavioral techniques at this new plant. The basic design of the new plant was oriented around the principles of skills development, challenging jobs, and teamwork.

The new design incorporated seven basic features:[37]

1. *Autonomous work groups*. The work force of seventy employees was divided into teams of between seven and fourteen employees. Two types of teams were

created: (a) *processing teams,* involved with the actual production process; and (b) *packaging teams,* whose responsibility included packaging, storage, and shipping. These teams were self-managed by the workers; they were involved in making work assignments, screening and selecting new members, and had added responsibility for the decision making for large segments of the plant's operations.

2. *Challenging job assignments.* The basic design of each job was developed to eliminate boring, routine jobs as much as possible. Each job—whether on the manufacturing line or in the warehouse—was designed to include a high degree of variety, autonomy, planning, liaison work with other teams, and the responsibility of diagnosing and correcting mechanical or process problems.

3. *Job mobility and rewards for learning.* Because each set of jobs was designed to be equally challenging, it was possible to have a single job classification for all operators. Employees could receive pay increases by developing new skills and mastering different jobs. Team members were, in essence, paid for learning more and more of the plant's operations.

4. *Information availability.* Unlike most manufacturing plants, the operators at this new plant were provided the necessary economic, quantity, and quality information normally reserved for supervisors or managers.

5. *Self-government.* Rather than working with a set of predetermined rules and procedures, such policies were developed as the need arose. This resulted in fewer unnecessary rules to guide the work. Only critical guidelines or rules were developed, and generally these were based on the collective experience of the team.

6. *Status symbols.* The typical physical and social status symbols of assigned parking spaces, wide variations in the decor of offices and rooms, and segregated entrance and eating facilities were eliminated. There existed an open parking lot, single entrance for both office and plant workers, and a common decor throughout the entire plant. This was instituted to reinforce the teamwork concept.

7. *Learning and evaluation.* The most basic feature of the plant was the commitment to continually evaluate both the plant's productivity and the state of worker attitudes and morale. Before any change was made in the plant, an evaluation of the impact on both productivity and worker morale was made.

As in any major redesign program, the management at the new plant were faced with a number of implementation problems. First, a source of tension among employees developed concerning pay rates. There were four basic pay rates in the plant: (1) starting rate; (2) single rate (mastery of one job); (3) team rate (mastery of all jobs within the team); and (4) plant rate (mastery of all operator jobs within the plant). Because the decision on pay rates was primarily the responsibility of the team leader, certain questions about the judgment of job mastery and whether workers had an equal opportunity to learn jobs developed.

Second, because the management philosophy at this particular plant was quite different from that at other plants, difficulties arose whenever employees of the new plant interacted with other General Foods personnel. Problems of resistance and a lack of acceptance and support developed.

Finally, the expectations of a small minority of workers did not coincide with the new teamwork philosophy of the plant. Certain employees resisted the movement toward greater responsibility and the teamwork concept. Again, individual differences among employees may have a significant impact on the effectiveness of any job redesign effort.

Was the new plant successful with its innovative work arrangement? A review after eighteen months of operation suggested positive results. For example, fixed overhead costs were 33 percent lower than in the older plants, quality rejects were reduced by 92 percent, and the safety record was one of the best in the company. Focusing on the human side, morale was very high, absenteeism was 9 percent below the industry norm, and turnover was far below average.

The initial success of the General Foods plant lends support to large-scale job redesign programs. However, managers should be aware of certain factors at the pet-foods plant that facilitated the success of the program.[38] First, the job redesign project was implemented in a new plant. It probably was much easier to change worker expectations in a new situation, rather than confront a deeply ingrained work culture in an older plant. Second, the new plant was not only isolated geographically from other parts of the company, but the work force was relatively small (70 employees) *and* nonunionized. This created a rather unique environment where internal and external pressures could be controlled, or at least minimized.

Third, the manufacturing technology was well suited for the job design change. In particular; (1) the manufacturing process was designed so that there was significant room for worker attitudes and performance to affect manufacturing costs and product quality; (2) it was technically and economically feasible to eliminate some of the inherently boring and routine jobs; and (3) because of the nature of the work flow, a high degree of communication and interaction between employees was a requirement for good performance. The concept of teamwork, therefore, fit well in this plant. Finally, there was a commitment on the part of the management to the new, innovative approach to job design. Without this commitment, particularly from top management, intense pressure from other groups would be expected to bring the new plant in line with existing company policies and practices.

How would one evaluate the General Foods experience in job design as of today? The word "mixed" would probably be most accurate.[39] On one hand, the company has applied a somewhat similar design system at a second dog-food plant in Topeka, at a coffee plant in New Jersey, and plans to do the same at two plants in Mexico and among white-collar workers at its White Plains headquarters. At the original Topeka plant, production costs, turnover, and accidents continue to be lower than the other company plants.

On the other hand, a number of significant changes to the job-design system have occurred at the original Topeka plant. The changes, which have included replacement of plant top management and removal of much of the autonomy, self-government and self-development of the team approach, have significantly altered the original job-design concept. Writers have attributed these changes to "creeping bureaucracy" and a weakened commitment by General Foods top management.[40] In essence, the original Topeka plan was never fully integrated or accepted into the total organizational system. Changes were required before acceptance into the total company system was attained.

What lessons can be learned by managers from the Topeka job-design experience? First, the facilitating factors discussed previously should be interpreted by managers as an indication that *situational* factors (e.g., location, technology, new plant) can affect the success of any job-design program. Second, job-design programs must be integrated and accepted by the total organizational system. Rarely can such a *radically* different system of work be kept in isolation from other sub-units of the company. In other words, managers should be prepared to alter their programs from the original plans. Overall, the Topeka experience points out that it is crucial for managers in organizations to carefully *diagnose* and analyze their particular situation in order to identify both facilitating and constraining factors for program success.

Job Design in Sweden

During the late 1960s and early 1970s, two of Sweden's most well-known automobile manufacturers—Saab and Volvo—were facing a perplexing problem.[41] In most of their manufacturing and assembly plants, turnover equaled or surpassed 50 percent annually, and absenteeism approached 20 percent. In addition, a national survey revealed that only 4 out of 100 students graduating from high school in Sweden indicated a willingness to take rank-and-file factory jobs. This resulted not only in the increased difficulty to fill jobs on the factory floors, but also an increased dependence on foreign workers (58 percent of the work force was foreign). Problems of placement, training, and an epidemic of wildcat strikes developed.

At Saab, management believed that something had to be done to revise this costly trend in personnel problems. Any response to these conditions, however, had to have as its number-one objective the *maintenance of high productivity levels*. That is, in any program to alleviate work-force problems (or as termed by Saab, the enhancement of *industrial democracy*), a satisfactory productivity level must be maintained. This is congruent with our earlier contention that any job redesign program should be concerned with a twofold outcome: task accomplishment *and* employee responses (see exhibit 6–1). Emphasizing one outcome over another will generally lead to possibly more serious problems.

Saab's redesign of work initially focused on the engine factory where four machine lines operated—the cylinder block, the cylinder head, the connecting rod, and the crankshaft. The traditional engine assembly line was replaced by small groups, generally from five to twelve workers. Team members divided the work among themselves. For example, they may decide to do one-half the assembly on each engine—a ten-minute task—or follow the engine around the bay and assemble the entire engine—a thirty-minute task. Under the old assembly-line method, the average operation per worker was less than two minutes. The team could also decide on their own work pace and the number and length of breaks, so long as they met the overall requirements of assembling 470 engines in each ten-day period.

The initial results of the job redesign program were positive, negative, and neutral. On the *positive side:* (1) the flexibility of the plant's production increased; (2) line balancing costs were reduced due to longer station time; (3) less money was invested in assembly tools; (4) quality of the product improved; (5) productivity increased; and (6) employee attitudes improved while turnover decreased from 45 percent to 20 percent. On the *negative side* was the reduced production speed due to group assembly, and the idling of some very expensive automatic equipment. Finally, the *neutral results* concerned the fact that absenteeism remained unchanged at around 15 percent.

Whether Saab will expand the group assembly concept to other manufacturing activities remains in doubt. A group assembly experiment with an entire truck diesel engine was abandoned because of the complexity of the assembly task (1,500 parts taking six hours). On the other hand, group assembly was applied successfully to the production of automobile doors. The direction that Saab will take with group assembly appears to be a function of the type of manufacturing technology involved in the assembly operation and productivity and employee satisfaction considerations.

At Volvo, management's response to the personnel problems was somewhat similar to Saab's.[42] In a truck assembly plant, production teams were established with workers who had common work assignments. The production teams elected their own supervisors, scheduled their own output within management requirements, distributed work among members, and were held responsible by management for their own quality control.

In the automobile assembly plant, a combination of job rotation and job enrichment was used. In job rotation, the employee changed jobs once or several times daily, depending on the nature of the work. Job enrichment was operationalized by having workers follow the same auto body for a number of work stations along the line for approximately twenty minutes—seven or eight times the average job cycle.

The results of these two job redesign projects were mixed. In the truck assembly plant, absenteeism and turnover decreased, and product quality increased. It was noted, however, that absenteeism and turnover were traditionally lower in this plant and that the normal jobs were inherently more complex and interesting than those in the auto plant. The workers were also more highly skilled and tended to regard themselves as above the typical rank-and-file auto worker. In the auto assembly plant, turnover decreased from 40 percent to 25 percent, but absenteeism nearly doubled. Management attributed these results to a combination of the effects of the job-design program and external forces, including a national economic slowdown and government legislation that enabled workers to stay off the job with little or no effect on salary.

Even with these mixed results, Volvo has stepped up its job-design efforts.[43] Their new auto plant at Kalmar is an example of the increased effort. The new plant is noted for the following characteristics.[44]

1. The plant consists of four six-sided structures, three of them two stories tall and the other single story, that fit together forming the general shape of a cross. This is shown in exhibit 6–9.

Exhibit 6–9 Diagram of Small Workshop at Volvo Assembly Plant at Kalmar

1. Stores.
2. Body buffers.
3. Material intake by electric trucks.
4. Preassembly.
5. Materials.
6. Bodies (on the left, stationary; on the right, moving).
7. Pause area.
8. Toilets, etc.
9. Changing rooms.

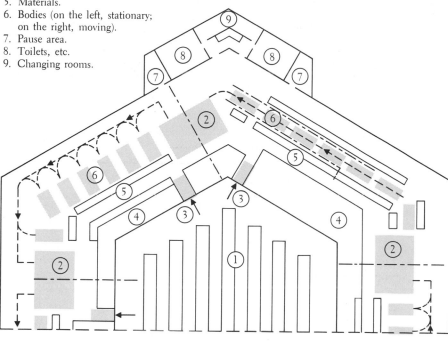

Source: William F. Dowling, "Job Redesign on the Assembly Line: Farewell to Blue-Collar Blues?" *Organizational Dynamics* 2 (1973).

2. The windows are big, and workshops are compartmentalized, so the workers located along the outer walls have natural light and a sensation of being in a small workshop.

3. Kalmar's employees are grouped into twenty-five teams of fifteen to twenty-five persons each. Each team handles a general area, such as door assembly, electrical wiring, or fitting upholstery. Team members can exchange jobs or change teams when they wish. They can also vary the work pace, keeping up with the general flow of production, but speeding up or pausing as they wish. As a result, the plant has fewer supervisors than a normal auto plant.

4. Computers flash hourly productive rates onto display screens, providing instant feedback to the employees.

5. Individual autos are mounted on flexible trolleys that track along a computer tape on the floor. If problems arise, an auto can be shuttled off into a parking

position while others glide by on the track. Because trolleys can roll an auto 90 degrees on its side, much of the physically fatiguing work of conventional assembly lines has been eliminated.

The Kalmar plant is not without criticism. Some of these criticisms include the following:[45]

1. The plant cost approximately $25 million, some 10 percent to 30 percent more than a conventional plant.

2. Production costs are expected to be higher than normal.

3. In addition, the Kalmar plant can assemble only 30,000 to 60,000 autos per year, depending on the number of shifts. Typical U.S. plants can assemble 200,000 to 400,000 per year. U.S. manufacturers contend that a plant with Kalmar's design and U.S. production rates would stretch for ten miles.

Volvo's management points out, however, that the Volvo is essentially a low-volume/high-cost product, so increased production costs can be absorbed. In addition, the lower absenteeism and turnover rates at Kalmar are very attractive to management.

The similarities and differences of the Saab and Volvo examples should be pointed out. Saab's efforts remained on a small scale and emphasized the redesign of work through the use of production teams. Volvo, on the other hand, implemented job redesign on a larger scale, utilizing job rotation, job enrichment, and production teams. Two aspects, however, were similar. First, technological considerations of the plant were weighed heavily before any redesign was implemented. Second, and most important, work-design changes aimed at improving worker behavior and attitudes were made with productivity goals also in mind.

Beyond the similarities and differences between Saab and Volvo, another issue for managers to consider is that the experiences of organizations in one country may have only limited applicability in other countries.[46] That is, it may not be possible to transfer a technique from one culture to another without careful consideration of the underlying reasons for the technique's success or failure. For example, in Sweden the nature of the educational background of workers, the impact of unions, the influence of legislative acts that practically guarantee employment, and the general attitudes toward worker participation and power sharing are significantly different from those in the United States, Japan, or England. In the United States, the emphasis on productivity creates a toleration for fluctuations in unemployment. A certain degree of insecurity is built into most jobs. Sweden, however, is committed to the notion of full employment, so the issue of job security is only of minimal importance. Thus, Swedish managers were faced with the problems of employee job dissatisfaction earlier than other countries.

The movement by workers toward more satisfying jobs, greater involvement and participation, coupled with the continuity of their economic well-being should continue in most industrialized nations. The methods by which managers approach the resolution of these issues must be tempered with a concern for both *internal factors* (e.g., technology and individual differences) and *external factors* (e.g., cultural, governmental, and legal differences).

An Integrative Model of Job Design

In reviewing the three job-design application examples, it appears that there has been a wide variation in organizationally based job-design programs. It is our belief that the reason for these wide application variations is twofold. First, at this time, there is no universally accepted conceptual or theoretical framework for job design to guide managers. It appears that most job-design programs utilize a combination of job rotation, job enlargement, job enrichment, revision of job characteristics, and teamwork methods. As researchers and practitioners, we have not advanced to the point in our theoretical development where we can predict the effectiveness of one technique (or a combination of techniques) over another.

Second, and possibly more important, job-design programs cannot be developed and implemented in *isolation* from the total organization or the cultural environment. The "situational" factors, such as the uniqueness of the General Foods plant and the cultural environment in the Swedish experience, can, and will, affect the effectiveness of any job-design effort.

The study of job design presented in this chapter has revealed and identified certain important situational factors that should be considered in the design of employee's jobs. An integrative model that attempts to identify these important situational factors and their impact on job design is presented in exhibit 6–10. This model is not intended to be an exhaustive approach to the study of job design. Rather, it is meant to be a tool to be used by managers to view the concept of job design in a much larger framework of the total organization. The model includes four basic factors:

1. *Core job-design factors*. This reproduces exhibit 6–1, which identified two key factors:
   (a) *Job-design factors,* including the aspects of job content, job functions, and the required relationships.
   (b) *Outcome factors,* which focus on the twofold criteria of job design: (1) task accomplishment; and (2) worker reactions.
2. *Environmental factors*. This aspect identifies the necessity of considering the larger external environment and its influence on job-design programs. Four factors have been included in this component:
   (a) *Social environment,* including the impact of broad-based cultural aspects, such as discussed in the job-design applications in Sweden. As has been noted in chapters 3 and 4, the cultural and social background of individuals have a significant effect on their subsequent organizational behavior.

(b) *Economic environment,* which focuses on the influence of such aspects as the growth or decline of the competitive marketplace and the seasonal or period fluctuations in the economic climate.

(c) *Political environment,* which recognizes that legislative acts (e.g., discrimination, full employment, equal opportunity), attitudes towards unionism, and so on, must all be considered in any organizational job redesign program.

(d) *Geographical environment,* which takes note, as in the case of the General Foods experience, that regional differences in culture and activities may have developed within a larger environmental unit (e.g., country).

3. *Internal organization factors.* This aspect acknowledges that certain internal factors may affect, or be affected by, a job-design program. Among these are the following:

(a) *Technology,* which generally focuses on the major process component of an organization. For example, it may be much easier to implement radical job-design changes in a service type of organization (e.g., bank, hospital, or governmental agency) than in an assembly-line oriented organization. In this latter type of organization, the heavy investment in capital equipment may make it impossible to introduce radical job design changes. The objectives of job design may be accomplished in these organizations with the use of work teams, processing units, or modular functions only when the basic characteristics of the manufacturing processes (i.e., assembly line) remain relatively unchanged.

(b) *Monetary compensation systems* may be affected by changes in the design of work. As noted in the General Foods experience, many workers see increases in responsibility, autonomy, variety, and involvement as also requiring increases in pay; their perceptions of equity must be maintained.[47] Traditional pay plans, however, have not always included such job-design changes in their evaluation framework. In some cases, then, job-design changes may also require significant alteration in the monetary compensation systems of organizations.

(c) *Unionism* may pose serious problems to job-design efforts. The basic framework of job design is directed toward the elimination of frustrating work, boredom, and alienation; these same factors, however, are some of the elements upon which unionism is founded. In some cases, therefore, union resistance to major job redesign programs can be expected. If job design is to have a chance for success, it is apparent that both unions and management must be involved in the development, implementation, and evaluation of job-design efforts.[48]

(d) *Bureaucratic pressure* concerns the impact of other units within the organization that have not been subjected to the redesign of their work. This develops into a situation of the "haves" and the "have nots," with the latter exerting pressure on the former to fall back in line with previously established rules and procedures. This aspect will be the first, and certainly not the last, test of management's commitment to the job-design program.

4. *Individual characteristics.* As we have discussed at length, individual differences among employees may have a significant effect on the success of any job-design program. Such salient characteristics of the employee include:

(a) *Need system,* with particular emphasis on the strength of the individual's higher-order or growth needs. Consideration should also be given to the fact that needs are *dynamic* in nature and can significantly change over time.

(b) *Value orientation,* which is an individual's predisposition toward *intrinsic* (e.g., responsibility, challenge, and autonomy), and *extrinsic* (e.g., pay, security, and stability) values.

(c) *Personality and learning* differences emphasize a worker's ability to learn and handle the increased responsibility, challenge, and involvement generally associated with the more prominent job-design methods.

Exhibit 6–10 An Integrative Model of Job Design

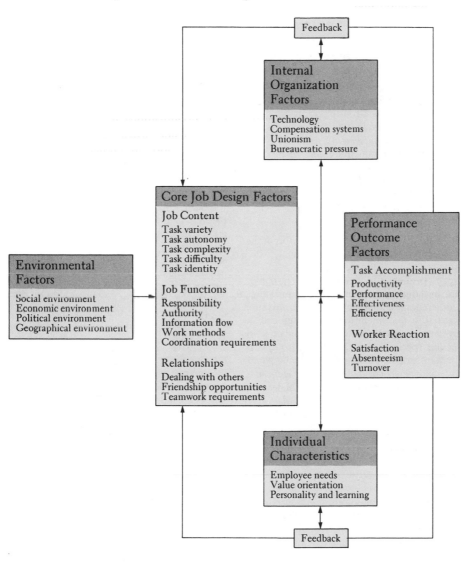

This integrative model attempts to synthesize some of the most important components and knowledge concerning managerial approaches to job design. Perhaps the most significant feature of the model focuses on the necessity for practicing managers to *identify, diagnose,* and *evaluate* the potential impact of the many situational variables surrounding the development and implementation of a job-design program. There must be an awareness and acknowledgement by managers that the redesign of work takes place within the total environment we call an organization, not in isolation. Influences from, and effects on, other organizational systems must be identified and weighed carefully before major implementation efforts are begun.

Applications and Implications for the Manager

Job Design

1. Job design concerns the content, functions, relationships, and expected outcomes of jobs. It is important for managers to consider that outcomes concern both *task accomplishment* (i.e., performance, productivity, and so on) and *human factors* (i.e., satisfaction, turnover, and absenteeism). Job-design programs should consider both these factors in the development, implementation, and evaluation phases.

2. The historical development of job design followed a three-phase advancement, which focused on: (1) the degree of job specialization; (2) management's response to the human factor problem; and (3) the contemporary approaches. Industrialization created a movement toward greater and greater job specialization. The higher levels of job specialization, however, also created human problems that were not anticipated by managers. The point for managers to consider is that these problems (at least partially) originated from a lack of congruence between the expectations of employees and of management.

3. The initial reaction by managers to the human factor problems associated with job specialization were the strategies of job rotation and job enlargement. These job-design strategies were considered only as short-term measures to alleviate worker alienation and dissatisfaction. In most cases, the work of employees was generally not changed to any great extent, and the basic causes of worker problems remained unaffected. Short-term, positive effects were noted in worker satisfaction, but these were overshadowed by negative comments from critics and labor groups claiming these methods were only another management tool to increase productivity at the expense of the workers.

4. Job enrichment was one of the first job-design strategies that was based on a theoretical foundation. The emphasis on achievement, job challenge, responsibility and autonomy proved to be moderately successful in certain applications. However, problems associated with the theory, the failure to consider individual differences in reactions to enriched jobs, and implementation and evaluation difficulties placed the universal application of job enrichment in question.

5. The current focus on the redesign of core job characteristic dimensions has emphasized not only implementation strategies but also the critical psychological states and individual differences, particularly growth needs. The manner in which individual differences are operationalized and measured remains a significant problem.

6. The selected applications of job-design programs emphasized that there does not yet exist a universally accepted approach to the redesign of work. The examples illustrated a variety of approaches used by different

organizations in differing environments. The major point for managers to consider is that when positive or negative results are obtained it is difficult to ascertain which of the implementation approaches had the main effect on the results. For example, whether teamwork is a more powerful job-design approach than job enlargement in improving task accomplishment and worker attitudes and behavior remains relatively untested.

7. The integrative model presented has drawn attention to the fact that managers must be able to diagnose and evaluate the environment for the implementation of a job-design program. Job-design efforts do not occur in isolation from the rest of the organization or the overall environment. Thus, consideration should be given not only to the particular job design strategy but also to the effects of (or effects on) the internal organization, individual worker differences, and the larger environment.

Review of Theories, Research, and Applications

1. Discuss the development of job design from the perspective of time, degree of job specialization, and awareness of the problems of worker alienation.

2. Why are the advantages of the scientific management approach to job design not fully realized?

3. Why are job rotation and job enlargement considered short-term job-design strategies developed to counter worker alienation?

4. Discuss how an assembly-line worker's job in an auto plant can be enlarged.

5. Discuss the theoretical problems associated with job enrichment.

6. How can managers overcome some of the implementation problems associated with job enrichment?

7. Discuss the differences between horizontal and vertical job expansion.

8. What individual characteristic differences besides growth need strength and value orientation could affect the impact of increasing the core job characteristic dimensions?

9. Why is feedback an important element in any job-design program?

10. Discuss the impact of cultural differences on job-design programs.

Notes

1. Alan C. Filley, Robert J. House, and Steven Kerr, *Managerial Process and Organizational Behavior,* 2nd ed. (Glenview, Ill.: Scott, Foresman, 1976).

2. Frederick W. Taylor, *The Principles of Scientific Management* (New York: Harper & Row, 1947).

3. Edward E. Lawler III, *Motivation in Work Organizations* (Monterey, Calif.: Brooks-Cole, 1973).

4. F. Herzberg, B. Mausner, and B. Snyderman, *The Motivation to Work,*

2nd ed. (New York: Wiley, 1959); F. Herzberg, "The Wise Old Turk," *Harvard Business Review,* September–October 1974, pp. 70–80.

5. Taylor, *Principles of Scientific Management,* p. 59.

6. C. R. Walker and Robert H. Guest, *The Man in the Assembly Line* (Cambridge, Mass.: Harvard University, 1952).

7. Lawler, *Motivation in Work Organizations,* p. 149.

8. D. N. Scobel, "Doing Away with the

Factory Blues," *Harvard Business Review,* November–December 1975, pp. 132–42.

9. Robert H. Guest, "Job Enlargement—A Revolution in Job Design," *Personnel Administration,* January 1957, pp. 9–16.

10. L. E. Lewis, "The Design of Jobs," *Industrial Relations,* January 1966, pp. 21–45.

11. Herzberg, "Wise Old Turk," p. 72.

12. B. Scanlon, *Principles of Management and Organizational Behavior* (New York: Wiley, 1973), p. 330.

13. "Job Design and Employee Motivation," *Personnel Psychology,* 1969, pp. 426–38; R. N. Ford, "Job Enrichment Lessons from AT&T," *Harvard Business Review,* January–February 1973, pp. 96–106; W. T. Paul, K. B. Robertson, and F. Herzberg, "Job Enrichment Pays Off," *Harvard Business Review,* March–April 1969, pp. 83–98.

14. Robert J. House and L. A. Wigdor, "Herzberg's Dual-Factor Theory of Job Satisfaction and Motivation: A Review of the Evidence and a Criticism," *Personnel Psychology,* Winter 1967, pp. 369–89.

15. Michael Beer, "The Technology of Organizational Development," in *Handbook of Industrial and Organizational Psychology,* ed. Marvin D. Dunnette (Chicago: Rand McNally, 1976), pp. 972–73.

16. Reprinted from "Is Job Enrichment Just a Fad?" by J. Richard Hackman, *Harvard Business Review,* September–October 1975, pp. 129–39. Copyright © 1975 by the President and Fellows of Harvard College; all rights reserved.

17. M. Fein, "Job Enrichment: A Re-evaluation," *Sloan Management Review,* Winter 1974, pp. 69–88.

18. M. Fein, "The Real Needs of Blue Collar Workers," *The Conference Board Record,* February 1973, pp. 26–33.

19. See Report of a Special Task Force to the Secretary of Health, Education, and Welfare, *Work in America* (Cambridge, Mass.: MIT, 1972).

20. Abraham H. Maslow, *Motivation and Personality* (New York: Harper & Row, 1954).

21. Edward E. Lawler III, "For a More Effective Organization, Match the Job to the Man," *Organizational Dynamics,* Summer 1974, pp. 19–29.

22. Ibid., p. 22.

23. Fein, "Job Enrichment," pp. 82–83.

24. C. L. Hulin and M. R. Blood, "Job Enlargement, Individual Differences, and Worker Responses," *Psychological Bulletin,* 1968, pp. 41–55.

25. Lawler, *Motivation in Work Organizations,* p. 158.

26. J. Richard Hackman and Edward E. Lawler III, "Employee Reactions to Job Characteristics," *Journal of Applied Psychology,* 1971, pp. 259–86.

27. J. Richard Hackman and Greg Oldham, "Development of the Job Diagnostic Survey," *Journal of Applied Psychology,* 1975, pp. 159–70.

28. J. Richard Hackman, Greg Oldham, R. Janson, and Ken Purdy, "A New Strategy for Job Enrichment," *California Management Review,* Summer 1975, pp. 57–71.

29. Henry P. Sims and Andrew D. Szilagyi, "Job Characteristic Relationships: Individual and Structural Moderators," *Organizational Behavior and Human Performance,* 1976, pp. 211–30.

30. A. N. Turner and Paul R. Lawrence, *Industrial Jobs and the Worker* (Boston: Harvard University, 1965).

31. D. Robey, "Task Design, Work Values, and Worker Response: An Experimental Test," *Organizational Behavior and Human Performance,* 1974, pp. 264–73.

32. John P. Wanous, "Individual Differences and Reactions to Job Characteristics," *Journal of Applied Psychology,* 1974, pp. 616–22.

33. Richard M. Steers and R. T. Mowday, "The Motivational Properties of Tasks," *Academy of Management Review,* October, 1977, pp. 645–58.

34. W. E. Reif, D. N. Ferrazzi, and R. J. Evans, "Job Enrichment: Who Uses It and Why," *Business Horizons,* February 1974, pp. 73–78.

35. Ford, "Job Enrichment Lessons from AT&T," pp. 96–106.

36. Edward E. Lawler III, J. Richard Hackman, and S. Kaufman, "Effects of Job Redesign: A Field Experiment,"

Journal of Applied Social Psychology, 1973, pp. 49–62.

37. R. E. Walton, "How to Counter Alienation in the Plant," *Harvard Business Review,* November–December 1972, pp. 70–81.

38. Ibid., p. 79.

39. *Business Week,* "Stonewalling Plant Democracy," March 28, 1977, pp. 79–82.

40. Ibid., p. 81.

41. W. F. Dowling, "Job Design in the Assembly-Line: Farewell to the Blue Collar Blues?" *Organizational Dynamics,* Spring 1973, pp. 51–67.

42. C. H. Gibson, "Volvo Increases Productivity Through Job Enrichment," *California Management Review* (Summer 1973), pp. 64–66.

43. P. G. Gyllenhammar, *People at Work* (Reading, Mass.: Addison-Wesley, 1977).

44. *Wall Street Journal,* "Auto Plant in Sweden Scores Some Success With Worker Teams," 1 March 1977.

45. Ibid., p. 1.

46. N. Foy and H. Gadon, "Worker Participation: Contrasts in Three Countries," *Harvard Business Review,* May–June 1976, pp. 71–83.

47. Michael Beer and Edgar F. Huse, "A Systems Approach to Organizational Development," *Journal of Applied Behavioral Science,* 1972, pp. 79–101.

48. M. S. Myers, "Overcoming Union Opposition to Job Enrichment," *Harvard Business Review,* May–June 1971, pp. 37–49.

Additional References

ANDERSON, J. W. "The Impact of Technology on Job Enrichment." *Personnel,* 1970, pp. 29–37.

BLOOD, M. R., and HULIN, C. L. "Alienation, Environmental Characteristics, and Worker Responses," *Journal of Applied Psychology,* 1967, pp. 284–90.

CONANT, E. H., and KILBRIDGE, M. D. "An Interdisciplinary Analysis of Job Enlargement: Technology, Costs, and Behavioral Implications." *Industrial and Labor Relations Review,* 1965, pp. 377–97.

DAVIS, L. E., and CHERNS, A. B., eds. *The Quality of Working Life.* New York: Free Press, 1975.

FORD, R. N. *Motivation through the Work Itself.* New York: American Management Association, 1969.

GOODING, J. "It Pays to Wake Up the Blue-Collar Worker." *Fortune,* July 1970, pp. 133–39.

HACKMAN, J. R. "Work Design." In *Improving Life at Work: Behavioral Science Approaches to Organizational Change,* edited by J. R. Hackman and J. L. Suttle. Santa Monica, Calif.: Goodyear, 1977.

JENKINS, D. *Job Power: Blue and White Collar Democracy.* New York: Doubleday, 1973.

MONCZKA, R. M., and REIF, W. E. "A Contingency Approach to Job Enrichment Design." *Human Resource Management,* Winter 1973, pp. 9–17.

O'TOOLE, J., ed. *Work and the Quality of Life: Resources Papers for Work in America.* Cambridge, Mass.: MIT, 1974.

PAUL, W. T., and ROBERTSON, K. B. *Job Enrichment and Employee Motivation.* London: Gower Press, 1970.

RUSH, H. M. *Job Design for Motivation.* New York: Conference Board, 1972.

SUOJANEN, W. W.; SWALLOW, G. L.; and McDONALD, M. J. *Perspectives on Job Enrichment and Productivity.* Atlanta: Georgia State University, 1975.

A Case of Job Design

The Lordstown Plant of General Motors

In December 1971, the management of the Lordstown Plant was very much concerned with an unusually high rate of defective Vegas coming off the assembly line. For the previous several weeks, the lot with a capacity of 2,000 cars had been filled with Vegas which were waiting for rework before they could be shipped out to the dealers around the country.

The management was particularly disturbed by the fact that many of the defects were not the kinds of quality deficiencies normally expected in an assembly production of automobiles. There was a countless number of Vegas with their windshields broken, upholstery slashed, ignition keys broken, signal levers bent, rear-view mirrors broken, or carburetors clogged with washers. There were cases in which, as the plant manager put it, "the whole engine blocks passed by 40 men without any work done on them."

Since then, the incident in the Lordstown Plant has been much publicized in the news media, drawing public interest. It has also been frequently discussed in the classroom and in academic circles. While some people viewed the event as "young worker revolt," others reacted to it as a simple "labor problem." Some viewed it as "worker sabotage," and others called it "industrial Woodstock."

This case describes some background and important incidents leading to this much publicized and discussed industrial event.

General Motors

The General Motors Corporation is the nation's largest manufacturer. The company is a leading example among many industrial organizations that have achieved organizational growth and success through decentralization. The philosophy of decentralization has been one of the most valued traditions in General Motors from the days of Alfred Sloan in the 1930's through Charles Wilson and Harlow Curtice in the 1950's and up to recent years.

Under decentralized management, each of the company's car divisions—Cadillac, Buick, Oldsmobile, Pontiac, and Chevrolet—was given a maximum autonomy in the management of its manufacturing and marketing operations. The assembly operations were no exception, each division managing its own assembly work. The car bodies built by Fisher Body were assembled in various locations under maximum control and coordination between Fisher Body and each car division.

In the mid-1960's, however, the decentralization in divisional assembly operations was subject to a critical review. At the divisional level, the company was experiencing serious problems of worker absenteeism and increasing cost with declines in quality and productivity. They were reflected in the overall profit margins which were declining from 10 percent to 7 percent in the late 1960's. The autonomy

By Professor Hak-Chong Lee, School of Business, State University of New York at Albany. Copyright 1974 by Hak-Chong Lee. Used with permission.

in the divided management in body manufacturing and assembly operations, in separate locations in many cases, became questionable under the declining profit situation.

In light of these developments, General Motors began to consolidate in some instances the divided management of body and chassis assembly operations into a single management under the already existing General Motors Assembly Division (GMAD) in order to better coordinate the two operations. GMAD was given an overall responsibility to integrate the two operations in these instances and see that the numerous parts and components going into car assembly got to the right places in the right amounts at the right times.[1]

The General Motors Assembly Division (GMAD)

GMAD was originally established in the mid 1930's, when the company needed an additional assembly plant to meet the increasing demands for Buick, Oldsmobile, and Pontiac automobiles. The demands for these cars were growing so much beyond the available capacity at the time that the company began, for the first time, to build an assembly plant on the west coast that could turn out all three lines of cars, rather than an individual line. As this novel approach became successful, similar plants turning out a multiple line of cars were built in seven other locations in the east, south, and midwest. In the 1960's the demand for Chevrolet production also increased, and some Buick-Oldsmobile-Pontiac plants began to assemble Chevrolet products. Accordingly, the name of the division was changed to GMAD in 1965.

In order to improve quality and productivity, GMAD increased its control over the operations of body manufacturing and assembly. It reorganized jobs, launched programs to improve efficiency, and reduced the causes of defects that required repairs and rework. With many positive results attained under GMAD management, the company extended the single management concept to six more assembly locations in 1968 that had been run by the Fisher Body and Chevrolet Divisions. In 1971, GM further extended the concept to four additional Chevrolet-Fisher Body assembly facilities, consolidating the separate management under which the body and chassis assembly had been operating. One of these plants was the Lordstown Plant.

The series of consolidation brought to eighteen the number of assembly plants operated by GMAD. In terms of total production, they were producing about 75 percent of all cars and 67 percent of trucks built by GM. Also in 1971, one of the plants under GMAD administration began building certain Cadillac models, thus involving GMAD in production of automobiles for each of GM's five domestic car divisions as well as trucks for both Chevrolet and GMC Truck and Coach Division.

The Lordstown complex

The Lordstown complex is located in Trumbull County in Ohio, about 15 miles west of Youngstown and 30 miles east of Akron. It consists of a Vega assembly plant, a van-truck assembly plant, and a Fisher Body metal fabricating plant, occupying about 1,000 acres of land. GMAD, which operates the Vega and van-truck assembly plants, is also located in the Lordstown complex. The three plants are in the heart of the heavy industrial triangle of Youngstown, Akron and Cleveland. With Youngstown as a center of steel production, Akron the home of rubber industries, and Cleveland as a major center for heavy manufacturing, the Lordstown complex commands a good strategic and logistic location for automobile assembly.

The original assembly plant was built in 1964–66 to assemble Impalas. But in 1970 it was converted to Vega assembly with extensive rearrangements. The van-truck assembly plant was constructed in 1969, and the Fisher Body metal fabricating plant was added in 1970 to carry out stamping operations to produce sheet metal components used in Vega and van assemblies. In October 1971, the Chevrolet Vega and van-assembly plants and Fisher Body assembly plant, which had been operating under separate management, were merged into a single jurisdiction of GMAD.

Work force at the Lordstown Plant

There are over 11,400 employees working in the Lordstown Plant (as of 1973). Approximately 6,000 people, of whom 5,500 are on hourly payroll, work in the Vega assembly plant. About 2,600 workers, 2,100 of them paid hourly, work in van-truck assembly. As members of the United Auto Workers Union, Local 1112, the workers command good wages and benefits. They start out on the line at about $5.00 an hour, get a 10 cents an hour increase within 30 days, and another 10 cents after 90 days. Benefits come to $2.50 an hour.[2] The supplemental unemployment benefits virtually guarantee the worker's wage throughout the year. If the worker is laid off, he gets more than 90 percent of his wage for 52 weeks. He is also eligible for up to six weeks for holidays, excused absence or bereavement, and up to four weeks vacation.

The work force at the plant is almost entirely made up of local people, with 92 percent coming from the immediate 20-mile radius. Lordstown itself is a small rural town of about 500 residents. The sizable city closest to the plant is Warren, 5 miles away, which together with Youngstown supplies about two-thirds of the work force. The majority of the workers (57.5 percent) are married, 7.6 percent are home owners, and 20.2 percent are buying their homes. Of those who do not own their own homes (72 percent), over one-half are still living with their parents. The rest live in rented houses or apartments.

The workers in the plant are generally young. Although various news media reported the average worker age as 24 years old, and in some parts of the plant as 22 years, the company records show that the overall average worker age was somewhat above 29 years as of 1971–72. The national average is 42. The work force at Lordstown is the second youngest among GM's 25 assembly plants around the country. The fact that the Lordstown Plant is GM's newest assembly plant may partly explain the relatively young work force.

The educational profile of the Lordstown workers indicates that only 22.2 percent have less than a high school education. Nearly two-thirds or 62 percent are high school graduates, and 16 percent are either college graduates or have attended college. Another 26 percent have attended trade school. The average education of 13.2 years makes the Lordstown workers among the best educated in GM's assembly plants.

The Vega assembly line

Conceived as a major competitive product against the increasing influx of foreign cars that were being produced at as low as one-fourth the labor rate in this country, the Vega was specifically designed with maximum production efficiency and economy in mind. From the initial stages of planning, the Vega was designed by a special task team with the most sophisticated techniques, using computers in designing the outer skin of the car and making the taps that form the dies. Computers were also used to match up parts, measure the stack tolerances, measure safety performance under head-on collision, and make all necessary corrections before the first 1971 model car was ever built. The 2300-cubic-centimeter, all-aluminum, 4-cylinder engine was designed to give gas economy comparable to the foreign imports.

The Vega was also designed with the plant and the people in mind. As GM's newest plant, the Vega assembly plant was known as the "super plant" with the most modern and sophisticated designs to maximize efficiency. It featured the newest engineering techniques and a variety of new power tools and automatic devices to eliminate much of the heavy lifting and physical labor. The line gave the workers an easier access to the car body, reducing the amount of bending and crawling in and out necessary in other plants around the country. The unitized body in large components like pre-fab housing made the assembly easier and lighter with greater body integrity. Most difficult and tedious tasks were eliminated or simplified, on-line variations of the job were minimized, and the most modern tooling and mechanization was used to the highest possible degree of reliability.

It was also the fastest moving assembly line in the industry. The average time per assembly job was 36 seconds, with a maximum of 100 cars rolling off the assembly line per hour for a daily production of 1,600 cars from two shift operations. The time cycle per job in other assembly plants averaged about 55 seconds. Although the high speed of the line did not necessarily imply greater work load or job requirement, it was a part of GM's attempt to maximize economy in Vega assembly. The fact that the Vega was designed to have 43 percent fewer parts than a full-size car also helped the high-speed line and economy.

Impact of GMAD and reorganization in the Lordstown Plant

As stated previously, the assembly operations at Lordstown had originally been run by Fisher Body and Chevrolet as two plants. There were two organizations, two plant managers, two unions, and two service organizations. The consolidation of the two organizations into a single operating system under GMAD in October 1971 required a difficult task of reorganization and dealing with the consequences of manpower reduction such as work slowdown, worker discipline, grievances, etc.

As duplicating units such as production, maintenance, inspection, and personnel were consolidated, there was a problem of selecting the personnel to manage the new organization. There were chief inspectors, personnel directors, and production superintendents as well as production and service workers to be displaced or reassigned. Unions that had been representing their respective plants also had to go through reorganization. Union elections were held to merge the separate union committees at Fisher Body and Chevrolet into a single-union bargaining committee. This eliminated one full local union shop committee.

At the same time, GMAD launched an effort to improve production efficiency more in line with that in other assembly plants. It included increasing job efficiency through reorganization and better coordination between the body and chassis assembly, and improving controls over product quality and worker absenteeism. This effort coincided with the plant's early operational stage, which required adjustments in the line balance and work methods. Like other assembly plants, the Vega assembly plant was going through an initial period of diseconomy caused by sub-optimal operations, imbalance in the assembly line, and somewhat redundant work force. According to management, line adjustments and work changes were a normal process in accelerating the assembly operation to the peak performance the plant had been designed for after the initial break-in and startup period.

As for job efficiency, GMAD initiated changes in those work sequences and work methods that were not well coordinated under the divided managements of body and chassis assembly. For example, previous to GMAD, Fisher Body had been delivering the car body complete with interior trim to the final assembly line, where often times the workers soiled the front seats as they did further assembly operations. GMAD changed this practice so that the seats were installed as one of the last operations in building the car. Fisher Body also had been delivering the car body with complete panel instrument frame, which made it extremely difficult for the assembly workers to reach behind the frame in installing the instrument panels. GMAD improved the job method so that the box containing the entire instrument panel was installed on the assembly line. Such improvements in job sequences and job methods resulted in savings in time and the number of workers required. Consequently, there were some jobs where the assembly time was cut down and/or the number of workers was reduced.

GMAD also put more strict control over worker absenteeism and the causes for defective work; the reduction in absenteeism was expected to require less relief men, and the improvement in quality and less repair work were to require less repairmen. In implementing these changes, GMAD instituted a strong policy of dealing with worker slowdowns via strict disciplinary measures including dismissal. It was rumored that the inspectors and foremen passing defective cars would be fired on the spot.

Many workers were laid off as a result of the reorganization and job changes. The union was claiming that as many as 700 workers were laid off. Management, on the other hand, put the layoff figure at 375, to which the union later conceded.[3] Although management claimed that the changes in job sequence and method in some assembly work did not bring a substantial change in the overall speed or pace of the assembly line, the workers perceived the job change as "tightening" the assembly line. The union charged that GMAD brought a return of an old-fashioned line speedup and a "sweatshop style" of management reminiscent of the 1930's, making the men do more work at the same pay. The workers were blaming the "tightened" assembly line for the drastic increase in quality defects. As one worker commented,

"That's the fastest line in the world. We have about 40 seconds to do our job. The company adds one more thing and it can kill us. We can't get the stuff done on time and a car goes by. The company then blames us for sabotage and shoddy work."

The number of worker grievances also increased drastically. Before GMAD took over, there were about 100 grievances in the plant. After, grievances increased to 5,000, 1,000 of which were related to the charge that too much work had been added to the job. The worker resentment was particularly great in "towveyor" assembly and seat sub-assembly areas. The "towveyor" is the area where engines and transmissions are assembled. Like seat sub-assembly, there is a great concentration of workers working together in close proximity. Also, these jobs are typically for beginning assemblers, who tend to make the work crew in these areas younger and better educated.

The workers in the plant were particularly resentful of the company's strict policy in implementing the changes. They stated that the tougher the company became, the more they would stiffen their resistance even though other jobs were scarce in the market. One worker said, "In some of the other plants where the GMAD did the same thing, the workers were older and they took this. But, I've got 25 years ahead of me in this plant." Another worker commented, "I saw a woman running to keep pace with the fast line. I'm not going to run for anybody. There ain't anyone in that plant that is going to tell me to run." One foreman said, "The problem with the workers here is not so much that they don't want to work, but that they just don't want to take orders. They don't believe in any kind of authority."

While the workers were resisting management orders, there were some indications that the first-line supervisors had not been adequately trained to perform satisfactory supervisory roles. The average supervisor at the time had less than 3 years of experience, and 20 percent of the supervisors had less than 1 year's experience. Typically, they were young, somewhat lacking in knowledge of the provisions of the union contract and other supervisory duties, and less than adequately trained to handle the workers in the threatening and hostile environment that was developing.

Another significant fact was that the strong reactions of the workers were not entirely from the organizational and job changes brought about by GMAD alone. Management noted that there was a significant amount of worker reactions in the areas where the company hadn't changed anything at all. Management felt that the intense resentment was particularly due to the nature of the work force in Lordstown. The plant was not only made up of young people, but also the work force reflected the characteristics of "tough labor" in steel, coal, and rubber industries in the surrounding communities. Many of the workers in fact came from families who made their living working in these industries. Management also noted that worker resistance had been much greater in the Lordstown Plant than in other plants where similar changes had been made.

A good part of the young workers' resentment also seemed to be related to the unskilled and repetitive nature of the assembly work. One management official admitted that the company was facing a difficult task in getting workers to "take pride" in the product they were assembling. Many of them were benefiting from the company's tuition assistance plan, which was supporting their college education in the evening. With this educated background, obviously assembly work was not fulfilling their high work expectations. Also, the job market was tight at the time, and they could neither find any meaningful jobs elsewhere nor, even if found, could they afford to give up the good money and fringe benefits they were earning on their assembly-line jobs. This made them frustrated, according to company officials.

Many industrial engineers were questioning whether the direction of management toward assembly line work could continue. As the jobs became easier, simpler, and repetitive, requiring less physical effort, there were less and less traces of skill and increased monotony. The worker unrest indicated that they not only wanted to go back to the work pace prior to the "speedup" (pre-October pace), but also wanted the company to do something about the boring and meaningless assembly work. One worker commented, "The company has got to do something to change the job so that a guy can take an interest in the job. A guy can't do the same thing eight hours a day year after year. And it's got to be more than the company just saying to a guy, 'Okay, instead of six spots on the weld, you'll do five spots.'"

Strike

As worker resentment mounted, UAW Local 1112 decided in early January 1972 to consider possible authorization for a strike against the Lordstown Plant in a fight against the job changes. In the meantime, the union and management bargaining teams worked hard on worker grievances; they reduced the number of grievances from 5,000 to a few hundred; management even indicated that it would restore some of the eliminated jobs. However, the bargaining failed to produce accord on the issues of seniority rights and shift preference, which were related to the wider issues of job changes and layoff.

A vote was held in early February 1972. Nearly 90 percent of the workers came out to vote—the heaviest turnout in the history of the local. With 97 percent of the votes supporting, the workers went out on strike in early March.

In March 1972, with the strike in effect, the management of the Lordstown Plant was assessing the impact of GMAD and the resultant strike. It was estimated that the work disruption because of the worker resentment and slowdown had already cost the company 12,000 Vegas and 4,000 trucks amounting to $45 million. There had been repeated closedowns of assembly lines since December 1971 because of the

Exhibit 6-11   Flowchart of Major Assembly Operations

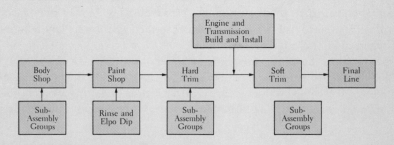

worker slowdowns and the cars passing down the line without all necessary operations performed on them. The car lot was full with 2,000 cars waiting for repair work.

There had also been an amazing number of complaints from Chevrolet dealers—6,000 complaints in November alone—about the quality of the Vegas shipped to them. This was more than the combined complaints from the other assembly plants.

The strike in the Lordstown Plant was expected to affect other plants. The plants at Tonawanda, New York and Buffalo, New York were supplying parts for Vega. Despite the costly impact of worker resistance and the strike, management felt that the job changes and cost reductions were essential if the Vega were to return a profit to the company. The plant had to be operating at about 90 percent capacity to break even. Not only had the plant with highly automated features cost twice as much as estimated, but also the Vega itself ended up weighing 10 percent more than had been planned.

While the company had to do something to increase production efficiency in the Lordstown Plant, management was wondering whether it couldn't have planned and implemented the organizational and job changes differently in view of the costly disruption of operations and the organizational stress the plant had been experiencing.

Case notes

1. A typical assembly plant has five major assembly lines—hard trim, soft trim, body, paint, and final—supported by sub-assembly lines that feed to the main lines such components as engines, transmissions, wheels and tires, radiators, gas tanks, front and sheet metal, and scores of other items. The average vehicle on assembly lines has more than 5,500 items with quality checks numbering 5 million in a typical GMAD assembly plant in a 16-hour a day operation.

2. In GM, the average worker on the line earns $12,500 a year with fringe benefits of $3,000.

3. All of the workers who had been laid off were later reinstated as the plant needed additional workers to perform assembly jobs for optional features to Vega, i.e., vinyl top, etc., which were later introduced. In addition, some workers were put to work at the van-assembly plant.

Case Primer Questions

1. What work related factors contributed to employee dissatisfaction?

2. What individual characteristics contributed to the state of employee dissatisfaction?

3. What impact did the employee dissatisfaction problems have on the plant's productivity and quality?

4. Would the technique of job rotation have helped to eliminate some of the employee dissatisfaction problems?

5. What do you think General Motors learned from the Lordstown experience?

Experiential Exercise

Job Characteristics Exercise

asked to converse only with members of their own group.

Purpose

1. To measure the actual and desired characteristics of jobs.

2. To understand the elements that constitute a job.

3. To compare job characteristics with comparison samples.

4. To discuss methods of improving jobs.

Required understanding

The student should be familiar with job-design concepts.

How to set up the exercise

Set up groups of four to eight people for the forty-five minute exercise. The groups should be separated from each other and

Instructions for the exercise

1. *Individually,* group members should:
   a. Complete the job characteristics instrument in exhibit 6–12 as it relates to their job. Note that *two* responses are required: (1) *actual* (column 1); and (2) *desired* (column 2) characteristics.
   b. Score the instrument for the eight job characteristics using the form in exhibit 6–13. The computed scores should be transferred to the *final scores column* where: (1) column 1 are the *actual* scores; (2) column 2 are the *desired* scores; and (3) column 3 are the *comparison* scores to be provided by your instructor.

2. As a *group,* discuss each individual's scores, particularly when differences exist between *actual* and *desired* scores. Compare these scores with the *comparison* scores in column 3. Discuss methods of improving these jobs (see exhibit 6–6).

Exhibit 6–12 Job Characteristics Instrument

The following questions are concerned with the characteristics of your job. Each of the questions should be evaluated according to the following responses:

Very Little	Little	A Moderate Amount	Much	A Great Deal
1	2	3	4	5

Two separate responses are required. In column 1, please mark your response according to how you evaluate the *actual* characteristic of your job. In column 2, please mark your response according to how you would like, or *desire,* that characteristic to be.

Question	Column 1	Column 2
1. To what extent does your job provide the opportunity to do a number of different duties each day?	_____	_____
2. How much are you left on your own to do your work?	_____	_____
3. To what extent can you tell how well you are doing on your job without being told by others?	_____	_____
4. To what extent do you feel like your job is just a small cog in a big machine?	_____	_____

Exhibit 6–12 (continued)

Question	Column 1	Column 2
5. To what extent do you start a job that is finished by another employee?	_____	_____
6. Does your job require a great deal of skill to perform it effectively?	_____	_____
7. How much of your job depends upon your ability to work with others?	_____	_____
8. To what extent does your job limit your opportunity to get to know other employees?	_____	_____
9. How much variety of tasks is there in your job?	_____	_____
10. To what extent are you able to act independently of supervisors in doing your work?	_____	_____
11. Does seeing the results of your work give you a good idea how well you are performing?	_____	_____
12. How significant is your work to the overall organization?	_____	_____
13. To what extent do you see projects or jobs through to completion?	_____	_____
14. To what extent is your job challenging?	_____	_____
15. To what extent do you work pretty much by yourself?	_____	_____
16. How much opportunity is there in your job to develop professional friendships?	_____	_____
17. To what extent does your job require you to do the same thing over and over again each day?	_____	_____
18. To what extent do you have the freedom to decide how to do your work?	_____	_____
19. To what extent does doing the job itself provide you with feedback about how well you are performing?	_____	_____
20. To what extent do you feel like you are contributing something significant to your organization?	_____	_____
21. To what extent do you complete work that has been started by another employee?	_____	_____
22. To what extent is your job so simple that virtually anyone could handle it with little or no training?	_____	_____
23. To what extent is dealing with other people a part of your job?	_____	_____
24. To what extent can you talk informally with other employees while at work?	_____	_____

Exhibit 6–13   Scoring Instructions

For each of the eight job characteristics (A through H), compute a total score by summing the responses to the appropriate questions. Note that some questions are *reversed* (e.g., #17), and that the response to these should be subtracted from 6 to get a response value. Transfer the scores to the *final scores,* where column 1 are *actual* scores, column 2 are *desired* scores, and column 3 are *comparative* scores to be provided by your instructor.

Variable	Column 1 Actual			Column 2 Desired			Final Scores 1 2 3
	Question		*Response*	*Question*		*Response*	
	(#1)	=	+ ___	(#1)	=	+ ___	
A	(#9)	=	+ ___	(#9)	=	+ ___	
	(6 – #17)	=	+ ___	(6 – #17)	=	+ ___	
	(Total ÷ 3) = A_1 =		+ ___	(Total ÷ 3) = A_2 =		+ ___	( ) ( ) ( ) A_1 A_2 A_3
	(#2)	=	+ ___	(#2)	=	+ ___	
B	(#10)	=	+ ___	(#10)	=	+ ___	
	(#18)	=	+ ___	(#18)	=	+ ___	
	(Total ÷ 3) = B_1 =		+ ___	(Total ÷ 3) = B_2 =		+ ___	( ) ( ) ( ) B_1 B_2 B_3
	(#3)	=	+ ___	(#3)	=	+ ___	
C	(#11)	=	+ ___	(#11)	=	+ ___	
	(#19)	=	+ ___	(#19)	=	+ ___	
	(Total ÷ 3) = C_1 =		+ ___	(Total ÷ 3) = C_2 =		+ ___	( ) ( ) ( ) C_1 C_2 C_3
	(6 – #4)	=	+ ___	(6 – #4)	=	+ ___	
D	(#12)	=	+ ___	(#12)	=	+ ___	
	(#20)	=	+ ___	(#20)	=	+ ___	
	(Total ÷ 3) = D_1 =		+ ___	(Total ÷ 3) = D_2 =		+ ___	( ) ( ) ( ) D_1 D_2 D_3
	(6 – #5)	=	+ ___	(6 – #5)	=	+ ___	
E	(#13)	=	+ ___	(#13)	=	+ ___	
	(6 – #21)	=	+ ___	(6 – #21)	=	+ ___	
	(Total ÷ 3) = E_1 =		+ ___	(Total ÷ 3) = E_2 =		+ ___	( ) ( ) ( ) E_1 E_2 E_3
	(#6)	=	+ ___	(#6)	=	+ ___	
F	(#14)	=	+ ___	(#14)	=	+ ___	
	(6 – #22)	=	+ ___	(6 – #22)	=	+ ___	
	(Total ÷ 3) = F_1 =		+ ___	(Total ÷ 3) = F_2 =		+ ___	( ) ( ) ( ) F_1 F_2 F_3

Exhibit 6–13 (continued)

Variable	Column 1 Actual			Column 2 Desired			Final Scores 1 2 3		
	Question		*Response*	*Question*		*Response*			
	(#7)	=	+ ____	(#7)	=	+ ____			
G	(6 – #15)	=	+ ____	(6 – #15)	=	+ ____			
	(#23)	=	+ ____	(#23)	=	+ ____			
	(Total ÷ 3) = G_1 = + ____			(Total ÷ 3) = G_2 = + ____			( ) G_1	( ) G_2	( ) G_3
	(6 – #8)	=	+ ____	(6 – #8)	=	+ ____			
H	(#16)	=	+ ____	(#16)	=	+ ____			
	(#24)	=	+ ____	(#24)	=	+ ____			
	(Total ÷ 3) = H_1 = + ____			(Total ÷ 3) = H_2 = + ____			( ) H_1	( ) H_2	( ) H_3

A Performance-Oriented Framework to Study Organizational Behavior

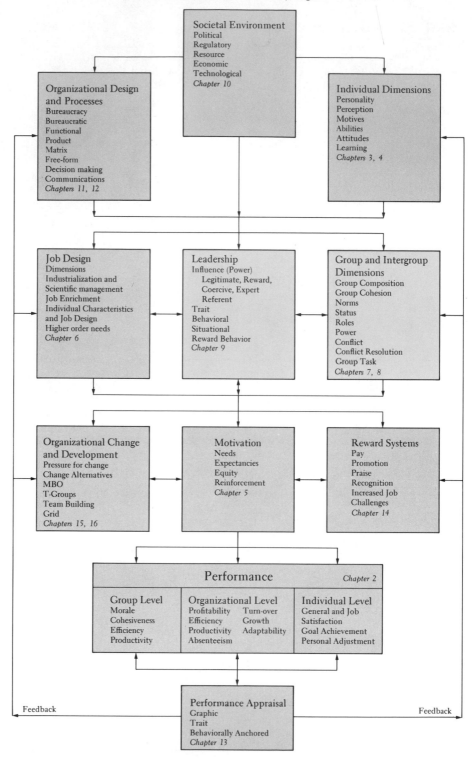

Societal Environment
Political
Regulatory
Resource
Economic
Technological
Chapter 10

Organizational Design and Processes
Bureaucracy
Bureaucratic
Functional
Product
Matrix
Free-form
Decision making
Communications
Chapters 11, 12

Individual Dimensions
Personality
Perception
Motives
Abilities
Attitudes
Learning
Chapters 3, 4

Job Design
Dimensions
Industrialization and
Scientific management
Job Enrichment
Individual Characteristics
and Job Design
Higher order needs
Chapter 6

Leadership
Influence (Power)
  Legitimate, Reward,
  Coercive, Expert
  Referent
Trait
Behavioral
Situational
Reward Behavior
Chapter 9

Group and Intergroup Dimensions
Group Composition
Group Cohesion
Norms
Status
Roles
Power
Conflict
Conflict Resolution
Group Task
Chapters 7, 8

Organizational Change and Development
Pressure for change
Change Alternatives
MBO
T-Groups
Team Building
Grid
Chapters 15, 16

Motivation
Needs
Expectancies
Equity
Reinforcement
Chapter 5

Reward Systems
Pay
Promotion
Praise
Recognition
Increased Job
Challenges
Chapter 14

Performance   *Chapter 2*

Group Level
Morale
Cohesiveness
Efficiency
Productivity

Organizational Level
Profitability   Turn-over
Efficiency   Growth
Productivity   Adaptability
Absenteeism

Individual Level
General and Job
Satisfaction
Goal Achievement
Personal Adjustment

Performance Appraisal
Graphic
Trait
Behaviorally Anchored
Chapter 13

Feedback   Feedback

PART THREE

Groups and Interpersonal Influence

CHAPTER 7

Intragroup
Behavior

The study and management of groups in organizations is a fundamental concept of organizational behavior. The primary reason for this importance is the fact that much of an organization's daily activity and decision making is conducted within groups. It is through the actions of groups that many of the manager's goals and objectives can be achieved.

In this chapter, we will discuss the elements of behavior *within* groups—intragroup behavior—from a threefold perspective. First, a framework for the study of behavior within groups will be presented. Second, the various types of groups in organizations will be examined. Finally, four important dimensions of groups will be discussed, including: (1) individual characteristics; (2) situational factors; (3) group development; and (4) the emergence of group structural dimensions.

Our discussion of groups will continue in later chapters. In the next chapter, the behavior between groups—intergroup behavior—will be discussed; and in chapter 9, we will discuss group management—leadership.

The Formation and Study of Groups

The study of groups is of importance to both the behavioral scientist and the manager. For the behavioral scientists, the study of groups has become a major area of current research in sociology, social psychology, and organizational behavior.[1] The study of groups has become an object of current research for at least three reasons. First, the group is a crucial element in social order in our culture. Groups serve not only as the focal point of social life, but provide an important source of direction to the individual for understanding social values and norms. Second, the group serves as an important mediating function between the individual and society in general. The individual may be able to satisfy economic, status, or friendship related needs through group membership. Finally, groups are less complex to study, examine, and experiment with than the larger organization.

For the manager in an organization, the behavior and performance of groups provide the primary mechanism for the attainment of organization goals. In order to provide for effective goal accomplishment, the manager must be familiar with:

1. The process of influencing group behavior toward goal attainment.

2. The climate for maximum interaction and minimal conflict between group members.

3. The means for the satisfaction of individual needs, which may be different from individual to individual within each group.

Each of these reasons for studying groups is related to performance—the central theme of this book. Lack of group direction, a tense and stressful climate, continual conflict, and a lack of individual need satisfaction all can contribute—together or individually—to the performance, or lack of performance, of the group. Thus, the pervasiveness of groups and their inherent link to performance are sufficient reasons why groups in organizations will remain a topic of learning and study to behavioral scientists and managers alike.

Theorists and researchers have provided numerous, varied, and overlapping definitions of *a group*.[2] This is because these individuals are each investigating different aspects relating to the same phenomena—namely, group behavior.

For our purposes in this book, *a group* will be defined as:

> A collection of two or more individuals who are interdependent and interact with one another for the purpose of performing to attain a common goal or objective.

The principal characteristics presented in this definition—goals, interaction, and performance—are crucial to the study of behavior in organizations. This definition should distinguish a group from a collection of individuals attending a football game or waiting at a bus stop because goals, interaction, and performance are not present in these situations.

Group Formation

"Why do groups form?" is a complex question that has been an issue with academicians and practicing managers for many years. Some of the more important reasons include: (1) task accomplishment; (2) formal problem solving; (3) proximity and attraction; and (4) socio-psychological purposes.

Task accomplishment is the primary reason for the existence of formal groups in organizations. For purposes of attaining a particular goal, the organization will formally bring individuals together into a group for the completion of the selected task or tasks. Such groups are designated by the structure of the organization and include such examples as engineering design, production, maintenance, sales promotion, and so on.

Problem-solving groups, like task accomplishment groups, are established by the organization for the attainment of some desired goal. The principal characteristic of problem-solving groups is that they may be temporal in nature—that is, they may be disbanded after the goal has been accomplished. Committees and task forces generally fall into this category.

Individuals join together for *proximity and attraction* purposes if they have similar characteristics, if they interact and communicate frequently with each other, and if they perceive this interaction to be rewarding. For example, secretaries within a large department may form an informal group because their desks are located near one another and because they perform similar tasks. Their group activity may be both informal, such as having lunch together, or formal, such as petitioning management for higher salaries.

Socio-psychological group formation generally comes about because individual *needs* can be more adequately satisfied in groups. Examples of such individual needs include: (1) *safety* (e.g., production workers banding together to protest to management about safety and health hazards on the job); (2) *security* (e.g., the formation of industry lobbying efforts to present or protect industry interests in legislative matters); (3) *social* (e.g., the formation of recreation associations within organizations for individuals with a need to affiliate with other workers); (4) *esteem* (e.g., the desire of an engineer to join a particular project because of the perceived power, prestige, and status of that group); and (5) *self-actualization* (e.g., the need of a research scientist to be transferred to a particular product research group because membership in that group will provide that person with the opportunity to be more creative and innovative).

These are only some of the many reasons why people join groups. This is not meant to be an exhaustive list, nor are the reasons mutually exclusive. The principal thrust of why groups form is twofold: (1) for organization purposes of *goal attainment;* or (2) for *satisfaction* of individual *needs.*

The Study of Groups

A framework for the study of behavior *within* groups is presented in exhibit 7–1. The variables in the exhibit do not represent all the possible dimensions, but only those that have been frequently studied by behavioral scientists.

Exhibit 7–1 A Framework for Group Behavior

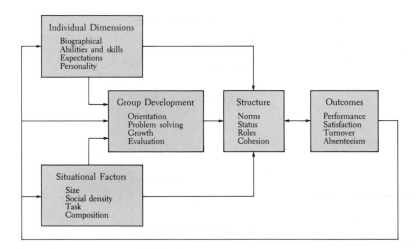

Some specific dimensions influencing group outcomes shown in exhibit 7–1 are: individual dimensions; situational factors; group development; and structural factors. Each will be discussed in separate sections in this chapter. The reader should conclude from the exhibit the rather complex nature of intragroup behavior. That is, there are many factors that can influence the level of group performance. *(handwritten annotations in right margin)*

Types of Groups

Various methods are used to classify the types of groups that exist in our society. These systems can include such designations as family, friendship, functional, task or project groups, and interest groups. In organizations, the predominant operating groups are the functional group, task or project groups, and interest groups.

An additional distinction can be made by classifying groups as either formal or informal. Formal groups are those whose primary purpose is facilitating, through member interaction, the attainment of the goals of the organization. Informal groups, on the other hand, are groups that generally emerge naturally from the interaction of the members, and that may or may not have purposes that are related to or congruent with the goals of the organization. The nature of the organization's structure often has a significant influence on facilitating the interaction process, and therefore on informal group formation. For example, the departmentalization, physical layout, type of production process, personnel practices, or supervisory climate all may facilitate the formation of informal groups within the typical organization. The various types of groups are summarized in exhibit 7–2.

Functional Groups

The functional group in an organization is a group generally specified by the structure of the organization. A salient element of the typical functional group is the relationship between the supervisor and his or her subordinates. For example, the head nurse of a hospital ward is designated by the administrator of the hospital to be responsible for the care of ward patients through the process of translating the directions of the physicians to subordinates. In order to facilitate the performance of this goal, the head nurse supervises a group of subordinates including registered nurses, licensed practical nurses, and nurses' aides. The goals, interactions, interdependencies, and performance levels are specified by the organization. Functional groups are usually classified as formal organizational groups.

Task or Project Groups

When a number of employees are formally brought together for the purpose of accomplishing a specific task—for a short-term or long-term period—such a collection of individuals is called a task or project group. For example, the plant manager of a chemical-processing plant may be interested in identifying potential safety problems in the plant. To provide a coordinated effort, he or she creates a four-person task force consisting of the production superintendent, maintenance superin-

Exhibit 7–2 Types of Groups in Organizations

Group Type	Characteristics	Examples
Functional Groups	1. Member relationships specified by the structure of the organization. 2. Involves a superior-subordinate relationship. 3. Involves the accomplishment of ongoing tasks. 4. Generally can be considered a formal group.	1. Head nurse supported by registered nurses, practical nurses, and nurses' aides. 2. Manager of accounting supported by staff accountants, financial analysts, computer operators, and secretaries.
Task or Project Groups	1. Member relationships established for the accomplishment of a specific task. 2. Can be short-term or long-term duration. 3. Can involve superior-subordinate relationship. 4. Generally can be considered a formal group.	1. Project-planning teams. 2. Committees. 3. Special task forces.
Interest and Friendship Groups	1. Member relationships formed because of some common characteristic, such as age, political beliefs, or interests. 2. Generally can be considered a formal or informal group. 3. Can have goals that are congruent or incongruent to the goals of the organization.	1. Trade unions (can also be a functional group). 2. Social groups. 3. Recreation clubs.

tendent, director of engineering, and the safety engineer. The manager appoints the production superintendent as the group leader and requests the group to report back within thirty days concerning any safety problems they have identified. If any problems are found, the plant manager may create other task forces to work toward the elimination of the potential problems.

The purpose of the group had been identified (locate potential safety problems), as had the particular task (report back to the plant manager within thirty days). These activities create a situation that encourages the members of the task force to communicate, interact, and to coordinate activities if the purpose of the group is to be accomplished. Most task or project groups are also considered to be formal organizational groups.

Interest and Friendship Groups

Because of common characteristics, such as age, political beliefs, or recreational interests, employees may form interest or friendship groups. Examples of such groups are the company recreation teams, groups developed to support local charities, or workers who are somewhat dissatisfied with company practices who band together to present a united front to management on such issues as pension plans, health insurance, or union formation and recognition. Such groups are formed in order to attain some common purpose, which may be consistent or inconsistent with the overall goals of the organization. Generally speaking, such groups are informal and exist until their purposes have been accomplished. On the other hand, when groups of individual employees develop long-term relationships (such as unions and other collective bargaining units) these informal groups may become formal groups within the organization's framework.

When looking at the typical individual's relationships within an organization, it becomes apparent that the managers and operating employees alike belong to many different and overlapping formal and informal groups. Membership in functional groups is designated by the formal organizational structure, which specifies roles and expected behavior, including who will be the superior and who will be the subordinate. In other words, the purpose and work flow are primary determinants of the composition of functional groups. Membership in task or project groups is generally specified by the purpose for which the group is formed.

The membership and composition patterns of interest and friendship groups are not closely controlled by the organization. However, managerial action (such as lack of attention to safety problems, layoffs, lack of satisfaction of individual social needs) may influence the communication and interaction patterns of employees, causing these individuals to informally affiliate with each other. Such groups— either formal or informal—can create problems for management when the goals of these groups are incongruent with the goals of the organization.

The various types of groups have been studied by behavioral scientists for a number of years. In the next section, we will examine some of the contemporary theories that have been developed to study group behavior and performance.

Individual Dimensions

Individual members of groups bring with them certain individual characteristics that may have an influence on group behavior. An individual's typical behavioral patterns, how he or she reacts to others, and his or her available skill and abilities all have an impact on how other group members will react to him or her, their subsequent interactions, and eventual performance as a group.

The study of the influence of individual characteristics on groups is important to the manager for at least three reasons: (1) individual characteristics can determine what the individual member is *able to contribute* to group activity; (2) individual characteristics can determine what the individual *wants to contribute* to group activities; and (3) individual characteristics can determine the extent to which the individual will *interact* with other group members toward goal accomplishment. The discussion of individual characteristics and group behavior includes four main components: (1) biographical and physical characteristics; (2) abilities and intelligence; (3) personality; and (4) expectations.

Biographical and Physical Characteristics

Biographical and physical characteristics, which include a wide range of characteristics such as age, sex, and physical size, were among the first to be investigated by researchers of group behavior. The research to date, however, has not determined any consistent pattern of relationships between these individual characteristics and group performance.[3]

Although there are no hard-and-fast rules regarding biographical and physical characteristics, certain tentative relationships have been found of which a manager should be aware. For example, increasing age has been shown to be related to increased social interaction, an increased tendency to be a leader, but decreased conformity to group norms.[4]

Overall, the results indicate that there are certain biographical and physical characteristics that may relate to group activity. There has been no evidence, however, that any of these individual characteristics are clearly and consistently related to group performance across different organizations.

Abilities and Intelligence

Individual members have abilities that can be used by the group for goal accomplishment. This is important to the manager because these abilities indicate what the individual is able to do, how well the individual will interact with other group members, and how effectively the individual will perform in the group. The research studies that have investigated the relationship between individual abilities and intelligence and subsequent group behavior and performance have shown more consistent patterns than those of biographical characteristics.

In general, studies have shown that the individual who has specific and crucial abilities that are related to the task of the group will: (1) be more active in group activity and generally contribute more; (2) be more influential in group decisions and have a tendency to become the group leader; and (3) be more satisfied with the group's behavior if his or her talents have been effectively utilized.[5]

Considering both task-related and intellectual abilities, it has been shown that such abilities are consistently related to overall group performance. However, the reported relationships have not been consistently strong, which may indicate that other factors—such as the nature of the task or the style of leadership—may be more influential in determining group performance.

Personality Traits

Biographical and physical characteristics and abilities and intelligence are factors that the individual brings to the group and determine, to some extent, the nature of the individual's *contribution* to group activity. Personality traits, on the other hand, are individual characteristics that may have a strong influence on how the individual will *behave* and *interact* with other group members.

Many studies have been reported that have attempted to link numerous personality traits to group behavior and performance. Traits that have been considered include: (1) authoritarianism and dominance; (2) acceptance of others; (3) anxiety; (4) extroversion or introversion; (5) self-reliance and dependability; and (6) sociability. These results reveal that personality traits have a significant impact on *group processes and interaction*. However, the general finding appears to be that personality traits have only a minor influence on group performance.[6]

but

4 Expectations

Stogdill has defined an *expectation* as the readiness for reinforcement. In other words, an individual's behavior is influenced by the way in which he or she anticipates that events will occur. In this regard, we must consider three different sets of expectations that operate in groups.

1. The expectation that individuals have for the ability to do a competent job and to perform well.

2. The expectation the individual has for his or her group, including the degree of participation by other members, interpersonal relationships, and rewards for good performance.

3. The expectation the group has for the individual's contribution to group activity and eventual goal accomplishment.[7]

For the manager, the research on expectations clearly indicates that unclear or ambiguous expectations in any of the three classifications can result in problems of morale, turnover, and lower group performance.

The first expectation concerns the individual's perception of his or her own ability to do a competent job. If the individual has the desire to perform, the proper blend of guidance, autonomy, and feedback can clarify the job so that the individual can move successfully toward goal accomplishment. For example, the recently hired college graduate accountant assigned to an auditing group of an accounting firm may feel confident about her knowledge of the theory of auditing, but she may be unsure of her ability to implement auditing practices in real-life situations. The leader of the auditing group can assist this individual in clarifying her expectations by: (1) structuring and guiding the individual through some initial auditing tasks; (2) allowing the individual some autonomy in performing a minor task; and (3) providing the individual with feedback on the level of performance attained. Throughout this exercise, the new accountant can clarify her expectations of job competence in a nonthreatening situation where learning and experiences are tied together.

The individual's and the group's expectations of one another can generally be clarified by the manager through the use of standard rules, procedures, and policies. An interesting study of individual expectations was conducted by one insurance company that used a new recruiting booklet that detailed the advantages, problems, and frustrations encountered by insurance agents on their jobs.[8]

The findings revealed that just as many applicants were recruited with the new "realistic" booklet as with the old "hard sell" booklet, but the percentage of new recruits exposed to the realistic booklet still on the job after six months was substantially higher. Although it cannot be stated that only the new recruiting booklet caused the increase in survival rate, it can be inferred that the clarification of job-related expectations possibly did have an effect.

Individual characteristics, then, are important aspects for the manager to consider in understanding the performance of individual group members and also the group as a whole. Research has shown, however, that the relationship between individual characteristics and group performance is not strong.

Situational Factors

Some of the factors that influence behavior within groups can to some extent be controlled by the organization. That is, the organization can create certain conditions under which the group functions. These conditions can include the size of the group, social density, the type of task, and the composition of the group.

Group Size

In setting up groups to carry out some function (e.g., the task force discussed earlier to examine safety problems in a chemical plant), managers are faced with the initial decision about the size of the group. In general, the research on group size has shown the following:

1. Very small groups (i.e., two to four members) show more tension, agreement, and asking of opinions, while larger groups show more tension release and giving of information. It is argued that in small groups it is more important that everyone get along with one another, whereas in larger groups, members can be more direct in their opinions.[9]

2. Groups with an even number of members have a greater difficulty in obtaining a majority, and therefore, create a state of more tension.

3. Members of smaller groups report greater satisfaction than those in larger groups. Apparently, in small groups members have more freedom from psychological restrictions.[10]

4. The relationship between group size and performance appears to be inconclusive and may depend more on the type of task being performed.

Although the studies on group size have proved interesting, it appears that other factors, such as the nature of the group task, can have a greater influence on member behavior and satisfaction. Managers must be aware of the potential negative aspects of increased group size (e.g., less interaction and satisfaction), but they should not attempt to build a group around some ideal number.

Social Density

The physical, or spacial, locations of members of a group is a significant factor in determining the degree of member interaction. This is particularly true for members of functional groups, who occupy specific locations in offices. With the current emphasis on the redesigned office layouts—from rectangular offices with few windows and solid doors, to the "open concept" with many cubicles, many windows, and few doors—managers need to be concerned about how group-member interaction can be improved.

To better understand the effects of spacial locations, the concept of social density is introduced. *Social density* is defined as the number of group members within a certain *walking distance* (e.g., fifty feet) of each group member. Walking distance, as opposed to a straight-line distance, is preferred because it gives a better measure of the effort needed for face-to-face interactions. As shown in exhibit 7–3, some members may share a wall and be *physically* only eight feet apart; if face-to-face interactions are required, one individual may need to walk thirty feet to the other's office. Exhibit 7–3 shows that two designs can be equal in *physical* space, but differ radically in *social density.*

Much of the research on social density has shown that increased density, or "crowding," may result in dysfunctional consequences.[11] That is, social-density increases are likely to be viewed by individuals as creating cramped or crowded conditions, which can disrupt behavior and arouse stress and tension. The majority of these studies, however, have been conducted in such nonorganizational settings as laboratory experiments, dormitories, or urban neighborhoods, which places a question mark on the generalizability of the findings.[12]

Exhibit 7–3 Physical Space and Social Density Space

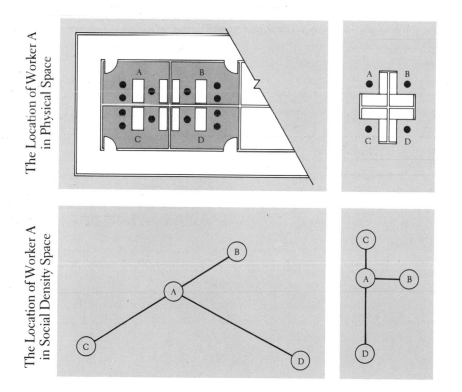

207

The studies of social density in organizations have generally found that density *increases* have resulted in more positive effects. In particular:

1. In an R&D organization, the frequency of flow of technical information increased when the distance between desks decreased.[13]

2. Also in a technical organization, engineers reported less stress and tension when authority figures and needed colleagues were located in close proximity.[14]

3. In a move to a new building, specialists in product planning and new business development of a petroleum company reported greater feedback, friendship opportunities, and work satisfaction with the increased social density in the new building.[15]

The important factor for managers to gain from these studies is that the *nature of the task* performed by the group members is a crucial consideration. That is, engineers, scientists, and planning specialists *require* frequent interaction with other individuals in order to effectively perform their work. A spacial arrangement that improves the frequency of interaction of group members would be viewed in a positive manner by group members and may help in improving overall performance.

Types of Tasks

A means of classifying group tasks concerns the *objective* or *purpose* of the task. Three basic objectives have been identified for task classification: (1) production tasks; (2) discussion tasks; and (3) problem-solving tasks.[16] *Production* tasks require group members to provide individual inputs and then to synthesize them into an integrative unit. Food preparation in the hospital or assembly-line production in an automobile manufacturing plant can be categorized as production tasks. *Discussion* tasks require the members of a group to discuss and resolve some issue, summarize their results, and present their results to some authority. A teaching excellence nominating committee is an example of a discussion task. *Problem-solving* tasks require group members to review the problem, generate potential solutions, and select one of the alternatives as the best solution. A group of managers investigating a possible financial merger with another company is an example.

Task type influences have been investigated using the production, discussion, and problem-solving scheme.[17] One study included 108 three-person groups that were analyzed according to six general behavior dimensions: (1) action orientation; (2) length of response; (3) originality; (4) optimism; (5) quality of presentation; and (6) issue involvement. The results revealed that:

1. Groups involved in production tasks were characterized by an emphasis on accomplishing their task on time with a minimum of error.

2. Discussion tasks were characterized by high involvement in the issues and on the process of providing group members the opportunity for clarifying, explaining, and defending their positions.

3. Groups involved with problem-solving tasks were characterized by their high action orientation; there was an emphasis on both accomplishing the task cor-

rectly and providing a forum for individual members to present, clarify, and defend their views.

4. Group leaders involved with problem-solving tasks were far more active and influenced group behavior to a greater extent than did leaders of production and discussion task groups.

Task difficulty and group performance studies have demonstrated that the more difficult task not only requires more time by the group to reach a solution, but also increases the probability that the solution will be less than acceptable to all members. These findings should not surprise academicians or managers because experience should tell them that the more difficult the task, the more the group must contend with uncertain information and divergent opinions by group members.

Research investigating one of the causes of task difficulty—information-processing demands—revealed that as the amount and complexity of information needed for group decision making increased, the errors in decisions also increased.[18] The more time groups spend on transmitting pertinent information, the greater the emphasis placed on group interaction and the greater the probability that errors will occur.

What strategy for the division of work is best when groups face either easy or difficult tasks? Stated differently, when encountering easy or difficult tasks, which strategy is most effective—dividing the work into independent units, or sharing the work responsibilities between group members? A number of research efforts in this area suggest that when the task is relatively easy and requires little coordination, a division-of-labor strategy may be most efficient. When the task becomes more difficult, coordination requirements increase; thus, shared labor may become more appropriate.[19] For example, a group of laboratory technicians in a hospital may be given the responsibility of providing a complete blood analysis on a patient. To accomplish this task, the group leader will divide up a blood sample and have one technician do a white-cell/red-cell blood count, another an analysis of cholesterols, a third do a microscopic analysis, and so on. After each has completed his or her task, the results are combined and reported back to the physician.

Consider a more difficult task, such as that of the mission-control group at NASA who are responsible for monitoring the communication and operations of a space mission. Although each individual is responsible for a specific task, such as verbal communications or the monitoring of life systems, all systems must be coordinated at all times, which requires group members to share responsibilities and be in constant interaction with each other. Task difficulty, therefore, seems to be a major determinant of the necessity of task-related interaction among group members for good group performance. The greater the difficulty of the task, the more essential it becomes that members interact effectively in order to attain a high level of performance.

Group Composition

Research on group behavior suggests that the kinds of individuals who make up a group create a set of powerful determinants of group behavior and performance. In fact, the term *assembly effect* has been developed to refer to the variations in group behavior that are a consequence of the particular combination of people in the group.

Many of the studies that have investigated the relationship between group composition and group performance have attempted to categorize group composition on the basis of homogeneous or heterogeneous characteristics. This breakdown classifies groups according to the extent to which the members' individual characteristics (e.g., needs, motives, orientation, and personalities) are similar or different. Each of these categories presents a different set of attributes that can lead to group performance. For example, in homogeneous groups the compatibility with respect to needs, motives, and personalities has been found to be conducive to group effectiveness because it facilitates group cooperation and communication.[20] Although the homogeneity tends to reduce the potential for conflict, it also can create an overabundance of conformity, resulting in unproductive group activity. In heterogeneous groups, the variations in individual characteristics help produce high performance levels and a high quality of problem solving because members stimulate the intellectual abilities of one another. The heterogeneity of individual characteristics in such groups can, however, create situations in which the potential for conflict is great.

A discussion of the relationship between group composition and performance would be incomplete without considering the nature of the group task. Studies concerning group composition have pointed out that the performance of groups depends to a large degree on the requirements of the task of the group, where such task requirements are defined in terms of routine versus complex decisions and problem-solving approaches. Groups composed of individuals with similar and compatible characteristics (homogeneous) may be expected to behave in similar ways and will perform more effectively on tasks that are routine, and less effectively on tasks that are complex and require a diversity of problem-solving approaches.[21]

An example of such an arrangement could be a group of tellers in a savings and loan association. The tellers' task is relatively routine and one that requires a high degree of cooperation between other tellers, customers, and members of the association. Given this task, we would expect a group of homogeneous composition (pleasing personalities, friendly and socially oriented, able to closely conform to the standards and norms) to be most effective.

Heterogeneous groups, conversely, can be expected to perform more effectively on tasks that are complex and require creative or innovative approaches to the problem, but less effectively on tasks that are routine and require a high level of individual conformity and coordination.[22] For example, consider a group of research chemists attempting to develop new uses and applications for a product. The nature and complexity of the task requires a diversity of talents, knowledge, and creative approaches, which is provided more effectively by a heterogeneously composed group.

Summary

Situational factors influencing intragroup behavior can be reviewed in terms of group size, social density, task, and group composition. Research has shown under certain conditions that each of these factors can affect group performance. The most important aspect for managers to understand about this discussion is that type of task is a key determinant of the extent to which the other factors influence group performance. Stated simply, the effects of group size and social density on performance and the success of group development depend to a large extent on the type of task performed by the group.

Group-Development Stages

Formal groups in organizations develop their internal characteristics and productive capabilities over a period of time.[23] Because these stages overlap and different groups require different lengths of time for development, it is difficult to accurately pinpoint the particular stage that a group is in. Nevertheless, it is crucial for the manager to understand the developmental nature of groups because performance is heavily influenced by where the group is in its development. The model of group development presented in this chapter focuses primarily on task or project groups and assumes that such groups follow four stages of development: (1) orientation; (2) internal problem solving; (3) growth and productivity; and (4) evaluation and control.[24]

Orientation occurs when individuals are brought together for the first time. This stage is characterized by such behaviors as: (1) beginning of communication patterns; (2) development and knowledge of interdependencies among members; (3) acquaintance with the structure and goals of the group; (4) expression of expectations; and (5) mutual acceptance among members of each of the others as a group. For example, when members of a newly formed project group are initially brought together, the first interactions generally involve a preliminary discussion of group objectives, becoming acquainted with each other's knowledge and abilities, and developing a plan for future interactions and activities.

Internal problem solving is the second stage. At this point, problems arising from the orientation stage are confronted, and attempts at solving these problems are made. This stage is characterized by the increased potential for interpersonal conflict because individuals bring to the group unresolved problems relating to different feelings toward authority, power, dependencies, and leadership structure. Unless these problems or conflicts are confronted and solved to the satisfaction of each member, the performance of the group will be adversely affected and the group may never advance beyond this particular stage.

The *growth and productivity* stage is characterized by group activity directed almost totally to the accomplishment of the group's goals. The interpersonal relations within the group are marked by increasing cohesion, sharing of ideas, providing and getting feedback, and exploring actions and sharing ideas related to the task to be done. This period is also characterized by individuals feeling good about being part of the group, emerging openness, and satisfactory performance toward goal accomplishment.

The final stage, *evaluation and control,* focuses on the evaluation of individual and group performance. This is accomplished through the adherence to group norms, strengthening group interdependencies and structure, and various feedback mechanisms. A summary of the four stages of group development is presented in exhibit 7–4.

Changes in the structure and processes may force groups to revert to earlier stages during their existence. For example, changes in leadership, member composition, physical location, or a major revision of tasks can force a group to revert to the *orientation stage* from the *evaluation and control* stage, just as unresolved interpersonal conflict can cause a group at the *growth and productivity stage* to revert to the *internal problem-solving stage*.

Knowing which stage of development a group is in is an important factor for managers in determining which style of leadership would be most effective for moving the group toward goal accomplishment. For example, if a group of project engineers is experiencing interpersonal conflict during the internal problem-solving stage, the manager or group leader should attempt to resolve the major internal problems before sending the group on a construction site to accomplish a particular task. Unresolved internal problems may create more serious problems, which will adversely affect group performance. For the project engineers, conflict arising from questions of interdependencies (e.g., "Who is supposed to do what and when?") may result in not completing the project on time. A further discussion relating group development to leadership style is presented in chapter 9.

Exhibit 7–4 Stages of Group Development

Stage	Group Activity
Orientation	1. Establishment of structure, rules, and communications networks. 2. Clarifying relations and interdependencies among group members. 3. Identification of leadership roles and clarification of authority and responsibility relationships. 4. Developing a plan for goal accomplishment.
Internal Problem Solving	1. Identification and resolution of interpersonal conflict. 2. Further clarification of rules, goals, and structural relationships. 3. Development of a participative climate among group members.
Growth and Productivity	1. Group activity directed toward goal accomplishment. 2. Development of data-flow and feedback systems for task performance. 3. Growing cohesion among members of the group.
Evaluation and Control	1. Leadership role emphasizes facilitation, feedback, and evaluation. 2. Roles and group interdependencies are renewed, revised, and strengthened. 3. Group exhibits strong motivation toward goal accomplishment.

Structural Dimensions

Within any group in an organization, some form of *structure* for group activity develops over a period of time. Group structure can be viewed as the framework or pattern of relationships among members that assists the group in working toward its goal. As shown earlier in exhibit 7–1, group structure is influenced by individual characteristics of group members, situational factors, group development, and previous performance. Our discussion of group structure will be twofold. First, a brief theoretical introduction to group structure is presented. Second, the structural dimensions of norms, status, roles, and group cohesion will be discussed.

Group Structure and Achievement Theory

A theoretical framework that focused on group structure was developed by Stogdill.[25] The theory is concerned with the individuals who make up group membership, the emergent group structure, the joint action of the group members, and the result of their interactions. The theory is presented in exhibit 7–5.

The theory focuses on member inputs, mediating variables, and group output. Performances, interactions, and expectations are shown as *behavioral inputs,* which are attributes of individual group members. The effects of these behavioral inputs are exhibited in the form of group structure and group operations. The result of member inputs, mediated through group structure and operations, is group achievement. Group achievement is defined in terms of productivity, morale, and integration.

Interaction, a member input, is defined as an interpersonal situation in which the reaction of any member is a response to the action of some other member of the group. Interaction includes two or more persons, and consists of actions and reactions, or performances. *Performances* are responses that are part of an interaction, such as decision making, communication, planning, and cooperative work. *Expectation* is the readiness for reinforcement that assists in determining group purpose, role differentiation, and group stability.

The three member inputs are not independent of one another. For example: performances and interaction combine to determine structure and group identity;

Exhibit 7–5 Stogdill's Theory of Group Structure and Achievement

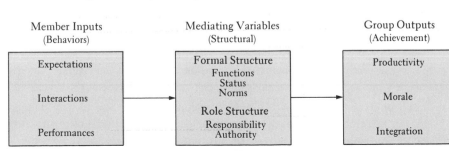

Member Inputs (Behaviors)	Mediating Variables (Structural)	Group Outputs (Achievement)
Expectations	Formal Structure Functions Status Norms	Productivity
Interactions		Morale
Performances	Role Structure Responsibility Authority	Integration

performances provide the means by which an individual's expectations are reinforced; and interaction and expectation combine to produce purpose and the mutual
reinforcement of norms.

Mediating variables are the result of member inputs and include both formal
structure and role structure. *Formal structure* is the result of the patterns of behavior and interaction of group members, which in time develops differentiated positions in the group, such as status and functions. Status is the hierarchical relationship between two or more members, which determines the degree to which the
individual members can initiate and maintain the goal-directed behavior of the
group. Functions specify the nature and extent of the contribution that each group
member is expected to make toward the accomplishment of the group goals. *Role
structure,* consisting of responsibility and authority, concerns the pattern of the
group structure and focuses on the individual group member. Responsibility is the
pattern or established set of performances that an individual group member is
expected to exhibit during the course of his or her employment. Closely related
to responsibility is the concept of authority, which concerns the latitude or limits of performances to be exhibited by the person. In linking *formal structure*
with *role structure,* Stogdill stated that the higher a person's status, the greater
the authority and the nature of the person's functions are related to the degree of
responsibility.

Group achievement, defined in terms of productivity, morale, and integration, is
the result of the interaction of *member inputs* (performances, interactions, and
expectations) and the *mediating variables* (formal structure and role structure).
Productivity represents the value (positive or negative) of the change created in the
inputs on which the group performs its functions (i.e., task). Morale concerns the
effects of restraints on behavior to group goal accomplishment in the attitudes of the
members. Finally, integration involves the degree or extent to which the group can
maintain its structure and interactions under stress. Stogdill implies that group
integration is similar to the concept of group cohesiveness (to be discussed later in
the chapter), which is determined by such aspects as mutual respect, trust, and
member satisfaction with group behavior.

Stogdill's theory of group achievement has been subject to certain criticisms
because of the complex nature of the theory. It does, however, provide a useful
framework that not only is internally consistent with existing studies but can also
provide the practicing manager with insight into the factors affecting or influencing
group performance. For example:

1. Groups place a great emphasis on goal achievement. Outstanding achievement
   serves to increase the status and prestige of the group relative to other groups.

2. Success in group activities acts to reinforce the expectation that further success
   may be attainable. Group morale is thus seen to be related to group productivity.

3. Group productivity is enhanced when function and status are clearly defined
   and when members in high status positions (leaders) maintain group structure
   and goal direction. Productivity is, therefore, related to leadership.

4. Because structure is determined to a high degree by the leadership of a group,

and because morale is a function of structure, morale is therefore closely related to leadership.

5. Integration is facilitated when there is common agreement among the members of the group on the goals of the group.

6. The level of group motivation consists of setting attainable goals, reinforcing goal attainment, providing freedom of action, and providing sufficient structure for concerted action for goal accomplishment.

Many of the terms discussed by Stogdill—status, roles, norms, productivity, integration (cohesiveness)—are important concepts for the study of groups. These concepts will be examined in depth in the remainder of this chapter.

Norms

Norms are defined as standards or rules of behavior that are established by group members in order to provide some order to group activities. If each individual in the group were permitted to act, interact, and perform his or her function as he or she saw fit, the result would be increased frustration, anxiety, stress, and conflict and decreased morale and group performance.

Although some have criticized the use of norms as being detrimental to individual creativity, they do provide a basis for understanding the behavior of group members and why they initiate their particular action. The primary purpose for the formation of group norms is to place some boundaries on the behavior of group members in order to insure that group performance will be maintained.[26] In other words, norms insure that individual action will be oriented towards group performance.

Norms do differ among group members. First, norms may apply to every member or they may apply only to some members. Each member is expected to comply with the production norm; only the group leader may change the production norm. Second, norms may be accepted differently by group members. All group members may agree to produce at the norm of twenty-eight units per day, but certain members may resist the suggestion of limiting overtime work because they have family financial problems. Third, different types of norms apply to different positions in the group. Everyone in a group of maintenance workers is expected to be ready for work at 7:30 a.m.; only the group leader may be permitted to occasionally start somewhat later if he or she decides to stop in at the safety department to discuss a problem.

Norm conformity.   An important issue facing all managers of groups is the degree to which employees conform to group norms. Two aspects of norm conformity are particularly crucial for the manager: (1) what factors influence conformity to group norms; and, (2) the degree of socialization exhibited by the individual in group activities. Four general classes of variables have been identified that can influence conformity to group norms:[27]

1. *Personality* research has shown that more intelligent individuals are less likely

to conform than are less intelligent individuals and that the more authoritarian an individual is, the less likely it is that he or she will conform to group norms.

2. *Situational factors* are such variables as group size, structure of the group, and the social context of group interaction. For example, research has shown a slight tendency for norm conformity to increase with the size of the group up to some point (possibly four to six individuals). This is because listening to more people agreeing with a particular point (or performing at a specific level) weakens the individual's confidence in his or her own judgment while strengthening the group norm.

3. *Stimulus factors* concern the clarity of the aspects that the individual faces each day. The more ambiguous the stimulus, the greater will be the conformity to the group norms. For example, if a group of accounting consultants who have worked only with industrial firms is given the task of consulting with a hospital, the group will conform to previous norms they had established while working with industrial firms until the experience of working with a hospital clarifies new standards and establishes new norms.

4. The last factor, *intragroup relationships*, refers to the relationships among the members of the group. It encompasses such variables as the kind and extent of group pressure exerted, how successful the group has been in achieving group goals, and the degree to which a member identifies with the group. For example, suppose a newly hired machine operator soon realizes that by concentrated effort he can produce a total of forty-eight units each day. After a few days at this level of production, the new operator is confronted by other members of the work group who inform him that the established production level for the group is thirty-six units per day, a standard that has been decided over a long period of time. The group informs the new operator that they do not believe he can continually maintain the higher level of performance and would like to see conformity to the established production norm. The new operator faces a dilemma: should he continue at his pace, or should he adhere to the wishes and norms of the group?

This example points out the potential negative aspects of conforming to group norms. Research on this topic has shown that conformity is often a requirement for continued group membership. The member who does not adhere to established norms is first pressured by the group to conform, and, if that fails, the individual may be punished. One form of punishment is to reject or isolate the individual from the group's activities. For example, no other group member will sit with the individual at the lunch table. Some group theorists believe that conformity results in the establishment of only moderate levels of performance norms, and hence, lower productivity could be the result. This points up the importance of the manager being able to influence the establishment of group norms and being aware of group performance levels at all times.

Socialization. A second issue important in understanding the impact of group norms on group performance is closely related to norm conformity—group socialization. Group socialization is a pivotal element for determining the contribution of individual members, the extent of interaction and participation in the group, and subsequent group performance.

Research has identified three individual reactions to socialization:[28]

1. *Rebellion,* which is an extreme situation, in which the individual rejects and rebels from the norms, values, and procedures of the group. Such behavior will result in the termination or exclusion of the individual from the group, disruption and decreased group performance, or a concerted effort by the group to alter the person to adhere to established group norms and procedures.

2. *Conformity,* at the other extreme, is exemplified by the individual who totally accepts all the norms, values, and procedures of the group. Although this may be the classic "organization man," he may be less than an optimum member for the group because this attitude may diminish the individual's creative activity.[29]

3. *Creative individualism,* which is between rebellion and conformity, is shown by an individual who accepts the basic or most important norms, values, and procedures of the group, but allows some leeway for creative or innovative activity. This type of socialization may be the most successful individual posture for group performance, but it is difficult for the individual to remain in this state due to constant group pressure to conform to group practices.

It has been pointed out that an organization may be more likely to be a healthy organization when the majority of individuals exhibit creative tendencies and fewer individuals are at the extremes (rebellion or conformity). This, however, may be only an ideal state because the pressures for conformity are usually present and it is hard for the group to identify with an individual operating in a creative fashion or trying to tear down the established patterns and behavior of the group.

Status Systems

Status is defined as a social ranking within a group and is assigned to an individual on the basis of position in the group or individual characteristics. Status can be a function of the title of the individual, wage or salary level, work schedule, mobility to interact with others within or outside the group, or seniority. By far, the most influential factor is the job title of the individual. The plant manager is more important and has greater status and authority than the first-level supervisor. The supervisor, on the other hand, has greater status than the machine operator. In some cases, particularly in groups of individuals who have the same or similar titles, a person is given status because of some personal characteristics, such as age, skill, sex, or education. The oldest nurse in a group of ward nurses may enjoy higher status because of her age, tenure, and expertise on the job.

The existence of status systems in organizations can have both positive and negative consequences for the manager. For example, status systems can clarify the relationships between group members by providing for clear definitions of authority and responsibility. However, an overemphasis on status tends to reduce both the interactions between group members and the frequency of communications.

Status systems can have a direct influence on group performance through *status congruence,* which is defined as the agreement between group members on the level of status of individual group members. When there is full agreement on member status levels (status congruence), the major activity of the group is directed toward goal accomplishment. However, when there is disagreement on status levels within the group (status incongruence) some group activity is diverted from goal accomplishment and directed toward resolving this conflict.

For example, the administrative committee of a college consists of the dean, associate dean, assistant dean, and five department chairpersons. Immediately prior to the committee's weekly meeting, the dean is called to attend an emergency meeting with the university president. The dean leaves word that he wants the administrative committee to hold their meeting to handle some important business. At the meeting, however, the assistant dean rather than the associate dean attempts to act as temporary leader of the group and begins the meeting by making some unilateral decisions without consulting the rest of the group. By previously defined lines of authority and status level, the associate dean should have been delegated the temporary leadership role. The meeting degenerates into a number of arguments between individual members and the assistant dean resulting in three of the department chairpersons leaving the meeting before any firm decisions can be made.

Roles

Superiors, subordinates, and peers expect each individual in a group to behave in certain ways. This behavior or "expected role" of the individual in the group can be specified by a number of means, including job description, position title, or by other directions from the organization. The administrator of a hospital is expected to organize and manage the overall operations of the hospital. The director of nursing is expected to organize and manage the department of nursing. The pediatrics head nurse is expected to organize and manage the activities of the children's ward. Each of these expected behaviors is not only agreed upon by the administrator, director of nursing, and head nurse, but also by other members of the hospital community.

Besides expected roles, there are also perceived and enacted roles (see exhibit 7–6). The *perceived role* concerns the set of activities or behaviors in the group that an individual believes he or she should do. The perceived role in most cases corresponds to the expected role; however, as discussed earlier, many factors may be present in a situation that can distort the individual's perception and thus make the perceived role inaccurate. The *enacted role* is the way that the individual group member actually behaves. The enacted role is generally dependent on the perceived role, and hence, the expected role.

To the extent that there are differences among the *expected, perceived,* and *enacted* roles, the probability of role stress, conflict, and negative effects on group performance increases. Two terms have been developed that reflect the differences among the three role activities: role ambiguity and role conflict.[30]

Role ambiguity is the lack of clarity regarding job duties, authority, and responsibility that the individual perceives in his or her role. Role ambiguity can be caused by a number of different factors. First, it can be influenced by a lack of a clear job

Exhibit 7–6 Role Relationships

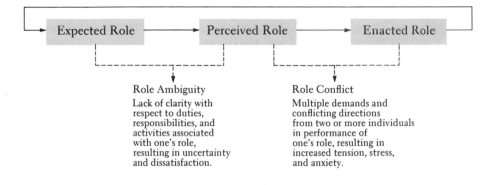

Role Ambiguity	Role Conflict
Lack of clarity with respect to duties, responsibilities, and activities associated with one's role, resulting in uncertainty and dissatisfaction.	Multiple demands and conflicting directions from two or more individuals in performance of one's role, resulting in increased tension, stress, and anxiety.

description assigned to a particular position. The individual must "sink or swim" on his or her own or attempt to find his or her own way. Second, occupational level has an impact on the development of role ambiguity. Research studies have shown that as the individual's task becomes more complex, or oriented toward managerial duties, the probability for role ambiguity increases. A study of different nursing levels found significantly greater role ambiguity at the associate director of nursing level than at the next-lower occupation level, the head nurse.[31] Further investigation revealed that the twenty associate directors were recently promoted from the head nurse group, where they had patient responsibility and their duties were clearly specified by standard practices and rules, to a new administrative level, where they no longer had patient responsibility. This, coupled with lack of training, experience, and clear job responsibilities resulted in confusion, conflict, and lower performance. Third, certain individual characteristics may help to create role ambiguity. Studies indicate that individuals who can be classified as "self-confident" perceive less role ambiguity and act to clarify job duties faster than do less self-confident individuals.[32]

Role conflict occurs when multiple demands and directions from one or more individuals creates uncertainty in the worker's mind concerning what should be done, when, or for whom. In our discussion of roles, we have implied that the individual receives directions or expectations over time and only from one source. This, of course, is far from reality because in most cases employees have multiple roles and, therefore, can receive multiple directions.[33] Two different types of role conflict can exist: (1) *intrarole conflict*, created by many different directives sent simultaneously to someone occupying one role, making it impossible for the individual to satisfy all directives at the same time; and (2) *interrole conflict*, created by many simultaneous roles presenting conflicting expectations.

The type of position and level in the organization occupied by the individual has been shown to influence the development of both intrarole and inter-role conflict.[34] The classic example of a position with potential *intrarole conflict* is the first-level supervisor. At least four sources of conflicting demands can be made on the first-line production supervisor; for example: (1) the production superintendent demanding greater emphasis on steady production levels and attention to cost control; (2) the sales manager asking not only for a greater variety of products, but also differing qualities of products for select customers; (3) the maintenance superintendent desiring a shutdown of the production line to complete repairs; and (4) the supervisor's subordinates wanting more overtime, better working conditions, and less interference in their work from supervisors. The supervisor can accurately be classified as the person in the middle.

Interrole conflict can also be influenced by the position occupied by the individual. For example, consider the assistant director of development in a plastics company. In addition to direct supervision of two separate laboratory development projects, in the next ten days the assistant director must also: (1) prepare a summary of development activities for top management; (2) meet with a new product-planning task force to develop the introduction of a new product line; (3) put together a program for a meeting of a professional society; and (4) give a speech to the local chamber of commerce on the impact of the company's new product lines on the local economic situation. The principal component of inter-role conflict here revolves around the assistant director's reaching decisions on which project should get the most attention and how much time to devote to each.

It is clear from studies of role behavior in organizations that continuing high levels of role ambiguity and/or role conflict can result in decreased group performance. The response of the group member to these role problems can be twofold. First, the individual can maintain a status quo position and attempt to live with the situation. Unless the situation can be controlled, however, the individual may succumb to the stress of the role and resign or selectively withdraw from certain activities or interactions by not giving them any attention. The result can only be lower performance and further problems for the group because the situation has not been corrected. Second, attempts may be made to modify the demands on the individual. For example, the supervisor could ask his or her immediate superior to act not only as a "buffering agent" for these conflicting directions but also to establish clearly defined expectations and criteria on how the supervisor's performance will be evaluated. For the assistant director of development, a possible alternative (beyond elimination of certain activities) could be to assign certain duties, such as direct supervision of projects, to select subordinates. The assistant's time could then be devoted to other topics; however, such an alternative may result in a lack of control over some important activities, which may adversely affect certain performance areas.

Cohesiveness

Some groups seem to possess a certain atmosphere of closeness, or common attitudes, behavior, and performance, that is lacking in other groups. This closeness, called *group cohesiveness*, is generally regarded as characteristic of the group in which the factors acting on the group members to remain and participate in the group are greater than those acting on members to leave it.

There are many factors that operate internal or external to a group that can serve to increase or decrease cohesiveness (see exhibit 7–7).

Exhibit 7–7 Factors Affecting Cohesiveness

Factors Increasing Cohesiveness	Factors Decreasing Cohesiveness
Agreement of group goals	Disagreement on group goals
Frequency of interaction	Group size
Personal attractiveness	Unpleasant experiences with the group
Intergroup competition	Intragroup competition
Favorable evaluation	Domination by one individual

Factors increasing cohesiveness

1. *Agreement on group goals.* If the group agrees on the purpose and direction of its activities, this will serve to bind the group together and structure interaction patterns towards successful goal accomplishment.

2. *Frequency of interaction.* When group members have the opportunity to interact frequently with each other, the probability for closeness to develop will increase. Managers can provide opportunities for increased group interaction by calling frequent formal and informal meetings, providing a common meeting place (such as a conference room or lounge), or physically designing the facilities so that group members are within sight of one another or are within close walking distance.

3. *Personal attractiveness.* Cohesiveness is enhanced when members are attractive to one another if mutual trust and support already exists. Personal attraction also helps group members overcome obstacles to goal accomplishment and personal growth and development. The group members may have similar or different individual characteristics and traits; the key factor, however, is that they enjoy working with each other.[35]

4. *Intergroup competition.* Competition with other groups, both within and external to the organization, is a mechanism that acts to bring group members closer together for attaining a common purpose. In organizations, the implementation of decentralized management techniques has served to bring large-sized groups together in competition with other groups.

5. *Favorable evaluation.* If a group has performed in an outstanding manner, some recognition for its performance by management serves to elevate the "prestige" of the group in the eyes of the group members and other members of the organization. Favorable evaluation helps make group members feel proud about being members of the group. During the Mercury, Gemini, and Apollo programs, the National Aeronautics and Space Administration (NASA) began a very comprehensive program of achievement awards for project groups who attained outstanding performance ratings. Such awards were shown to develop group cohesiveness and to support continued outstanding performance.

Factors decreasing cohesiveness

Generally speaking, the opposite relationships act to decrease cohesiveness. These include:

1. *Disagreement on goals.* Just as agreement on group purpose and direction acts to bring groups together, disagreement serves to provide conflict and infighting, thus decreasing cohesiveness.

2. *Group size.* As the size of the group increases, the frequency of interaction each member has with other group members decreases, thus decreasing the probability that cohesiveness will develop. Past studies have shown that groups of four to six members provide the best opportunity for interaction.

3. *Unpleasant experiences with the group.* When group members are not attracted to each other or there is a lack of trust or a coercive environment, interaction may become a painful or unpleasant experience, resulting in a lack of closeness in the group.

4. *Intragroup competition.* Although intergroup competition acts to bring groups together, intragroup competition causes conflict, infighting, and development of forces to break the group apart. Such practices by managers as showing favoritism to individual members (or providing awards not based on performance) create intragroup competition and should be avoided.

5. *Domination.* When one or more of the group members dominate the group, or because of certain personality traits prefer not to interact with other group members, cohesiveness cannot adequately develop. Such behavior can create smaller "cliques" within the group or identify individual members as isolates or deviates.[36]

Because cohesive groups are composed of individuals who are attracted to the goals of the group and to each other, we would expect to find a strong relationship between cohesiveness and group performance. Studies in this area have pointed out that the greater the cohesion, the greater the influence the group will have over the behavior of members and, subsequently, group performance.[37]

Because individual group members value highly the membership in a cohesive group, we would expect that the individual would be more responsive to the demands and norms of the cohesive group. If this assumption were correct, we would expect to find that: (1) the major difference between highly cohesive and low-cohesion groups would be how closely members conformed to the group norms; and (2) group performance would be influenced not only by cohesion, but by the level of group norms. For example, consider two separate but highly cohesive groups of machine operators. The first work group has established a high performance norm (thirty-four units per day), and we would predict that all group members would tend to conform closely to that high performance norm. The second work group had established a performance norm markedly lower than the first group (twenty-six units per day), and we would expect that the group members would be equally faithful in conforming to the low performance norm.

The findings concerning norms, cohesiveness, and performance are summarized in exhibit 7–8. This figure shows that highly cohesive groups can perform at high *or* low levels, depending on the level of performance norms established by the group.

It might appear from the foregoing discussion that the factors that make up a highly cohesive group may be dysfunctional for group or individual performance. As some researchers have pointed out, however, such a conclusion would be very pessimistic. Striving to develop low cohesion in groups would indeed lower the probability of obtaining the negative consequences of high cohesion, such as conformity to low performance norms, but would also preclude the positive consequences of high cohesion.

The problem for the manager is finding how to direct the activities of highly cohesive groups toward the successful attainment of organizational goals. Although the research in this area has been sparse, at least some guidelines for the manager can be given.

Task-accomplishment emphasis

One approach involves redirecting the activities of the group from interpersonal issues to the emphasis on task accomplishment. If management could increase the group's commitment toward goals that are more compatible with organizational goals, the level of group performance could be positively influenced. This could be done in some cases by instituting group incentive pay plans or by expanding or changing jobs to be more challenging to the individual. However, as we have discussed in earlier chapters, not all individuals are motivated in similar ways, which makes it imperative that managers clearly understand the motivational profiles of group members.

Exhibit 7–8 Relationship Between Group Cohesiveness, Performance Norms, and Performance

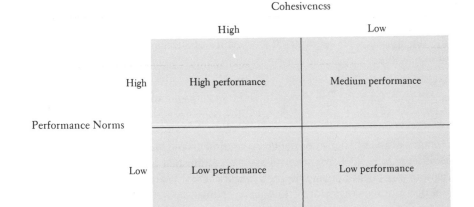

	Cohesiveness	
	High	Low
High (Performance Norms)	High performance	Medium performance
Low (Performance Norms)	Low performance	Low performance

2) Participative management

Another possible approach, closely related to task accomplishment emphasis, is to incorporate participative management in the group. Participation in establishing goals and norms creates a commitment by those participating. If the established goals and norms are challenging, the group may concentrate more on task accomplishment than on interpersonal issues. Some groups, however, may perceive this process as another act by management to manipulate employees, thus creating more resistance than acceptance of management directives.

3) Intergroup competition

If managers can get their group members to engage in competition with other groups in the organization, a "team spirit" can develop that results not only in higher cohesion but also greater group commitment to the accomplishment of the task. Intergroup competition, however, has the potential for some long-run negative consequences for the organization. The all-out emphasis on "winning" by groups could result in resources, personnel, or information purposely being withheld from a competing group or distorted, resulting in adverse effects for the total organization. One common strategy for managers to use to overcome this negative consequence of intergroup competition is to introduce an overall superordinate goal that all groups can adopt. For example, the establishment of a total organizational productivity goal could be developed, and comparisons not only between actual and predicted productivity levels but also between the organization and its competitor could be reviewed.

4) Disband the group

One final strategy is for management to partially or totally disband selected cohesive groups by transferring members to other departments. This can provide the manager the opportunity to begin working with a relatively new group and exerting influence on the entire group formation and development process. This strategy, however, should be considered as a last resort and may be impossible if the unionization of group members does not permit such managerial action.

Each of these approaches may have potential advantages and disadvantages that must be weighed carefully. The significant advantages of cohesiveness in groups should be considered and evaluated with great care. Patience, understanding, and careful diagnosis are all necessary if any chance of success is to become a reality in the organization.

Summary

A summary of the relationships between the dimensions of groups and performance is shown in exhibit 7–9. Managers should be aware that each of these dimensions can have a significant impact on group performance. When faced with groups that are not performing satisfactorily, the manager must be able to effectively diagnose the situation in order to determine which factor, or combination of factors, may be causing the low performance.

Exhibit 7–9 Dimensions of Groups and Performance

Dimensions	Relationship with Group Performance
Individual Characteristics	1. Little or no direct relationship between individual characteristics has been found. 2. Performance is influenced by: individual characteristics → group composition → performance.
Situational Factors Group Size	Increasing group size tends to decrease satisfaction, but does not influence performance.
Social Density	For interrelated jobs, increasing social density tends to improve satisfaction. Performance impact has not been totally investigated.
Task	1. The greater the difficulty of the group task, the more information is transmitted, resulting in the possibility for more errors. 2. The type of task generally affects the degree to which group size and social density influence performance.
Composition	1. Homogeneous groups perform well on tasks that are uniform and routine. Homogeneity, while reducing the potential for dysfunctional conflict to arise, may be detrimental to performance if there is an overemphasis on conformity. 2. Heterogeneous groups perform well on tasks that are complex and nonroutine and that require a diversity of talents and viewpoints. Heterogeneity, however, can create conflict.
Group Development	Groups tend to perform better during the latter stages of development.
Structure Norms	1. Norms act as standards of behavior and performance. Groups attempt to perform at a level equal to their established performance norms. 2. The degree of socialization will affect not only the level of performance of individual group members but whether the individual will remain a group member.
Status	Groups characterized by high status congruence tend to perform better than do groups in which there is status incongruence.
Roles	Group performance is adversely affected when members experience high levels of role ambiguity and/or role conflict.
Cohesion	Group performance is a function of the levels of performance norms and the degree of cohesion. The highest levels of group performance are found with highly cohesive groups who have established high performance norms.

Applications and Implications for the Manager

Intragroup behavior

1. Groups and the management of groups are important factors for the success of any organization. Managers must be aware of why groups are formed, their development stages, the important dimensions of groups, and the process of influencing group behavior.

2. The determinants of group performance consist of four major dimensions— individual, situational, group development, and structural. The structural dimensions tend to have the greatest impact on group behavior and also are the dimensions that the manager influences the most.

3. Various types of groups exist within the framework of organizations, from the formal functional and task or project groups to the generally more informal interest and friendship groups. Whatever the classification of the group—formal or informal—it is important for the effective functioning of the organization that the goals of such groups be congruent with the overall goals of the organization. Groups with incongruent goals create a situation of conflict, interpersonal problems, and reduced effectiveness.

4. Group members bring with them certain individual characteristics that may have an effect on subsequent group behavior. The manager should be aware that these characteristics—biographical, physical, abilities, intelligence, personality, and expectations—have an effect on the individual's ability to interact with fellow group members, the degree to which he or she conforms to norms and accepts rules, and the member's level of performance. Although these individual characteristics have been found to be only minor influences on group performance, they can provide the manager with either a workable or unworkable climate for the influence of group activity.

5. The impact of social density on group performance appears to be a function of the type of task. Increasing social density for group members with highly interrelated tasks tends to improve performance by making interaction easier.

6. Tasks may also be classified as emphasizing production, discussion, or problem-solving requirements. The manager's role in each of these tasks is somewhat different, which in effect requires a change in managerial style. Groups working on production tasks place great emphasis on getting the task done on time and with a minimum of error. In discussion tasks, a more participative orientation is needed because a major amount of time and effort is expended by members in the process of clarifying, explaining, and presenting different positions. Groups working on problem-solving tasks place an emphasis on getting the task done on time and also require enough time for group members to present, clarify, and explain their positions. The manager of this type of group must be effective in task orientation and in providing time for clarification and explanation.

7. The influences of group composition on group performance are affected by the complexity and difficulty of the group task and the interpersonal needs of the individual group members. Groups composed of individuals with homogeneous, or similar, characteristics tend to perform better on simple, routine tasks but may develop unproductive modes of behavior that overemphasize conformity to group norms. Heterogeneously composed groups tend to perform more effectively on complex and varied tasks, but this dissimilarity of characteristics provides an environment of possible conflict.

8. Although different types of groups develop at different rates, they all tend to follow a similar four-stage pattern—orientation, internal problem solving, growth and productivity, and evaluation and control. Each of these stages is characterized by different types of behavior required of individual members and of the organization. Changes in the composition of the group, its task, or leadership can result in the group reverting to any earlier stage.

9. Research studies have shown that conformity to group norms is a function of four factors: personality of the group member; situational factors; stimulus factors; and intragroup relations. Individuals conform to group norms generally in one of three ways: conformity, rebellion, or creative individualism. The manager should be concerned not only with the degree of norm conformity, but to which norms individuals are conforming—norms that are congruent with the goals of the organization, or norms that are incongruent with the organization goals, resulting in less than satisfactory performance.

10. Status in groups is a structural aspect present in most groups. The manager's knowledge of status systems should be oriented to making clear to all members the accepted status levels of all other members (status congruence) such that internal conflict arising from unclear status distinctions (status incongruence) can be minimized.

11. Roles are the structure of activity required of each individual group member for group performance. Roles consist of three aspects: the expected role; the perceived role; and the enacted role. Individual role problems occur when there are differences between either the expected role and the perceived role (role ambiguity) or between the perceived role and the enacted role (role conflict). The manager can assist in eliminating role ambiguity by structuring the task and clarifying the expectations of the individual. Role conflict can be reduced by eliminating conflicting sources of directions and reducing the work demands imposed on the individual by other members of the organization.

12. Every group possesses a certain degree of cohesiveness. This closeness or attractiveness can be a powerful influence on group performance. The manager can influence such factors as frequency of interaction, favorable evaluation, and intergroup competition in order to increase the cohesiveness and subsequent performance of the group.

13. Studies of group cohesiveness have shown that cohesive groups can formulate performance goals and norms that exceed, meet, or are below management expectations. Because conformity to group norms is a key characteristic of cohesive groups, groups performing at lower than organizationally accepted norms require some form of managerial intervention.

14. Management can direct the activities of cohesive groups and have successful goal attainment through three possible strategies: task accomplishment emphasis; participative management; or intergroup competition. If these fail, management can resort to the strategy of disbanding the group.

Review of Theories, Research, and Applications

1. Think of a group with which you have been involved on a regular basis. What type of group was it, according to the discussion in the chapter? Can you identify the development stages that this group may have followed?

2. Describe the possible conditions that would cause a group in the evaluation and control stage to revert to the internal problem-solving stage.

3. Can you identify particular jobs, occupations, or organizations in which group behavior is not important?

4. Discuss the development of trade unions in terms of type of group, and stages of development.

5. How would you present Stogdill's model to a group of practicing managers?

6. Four reasons "why groups form" were discussed. Identify groups of which you have been a part recently that represent each of the four reasons for group formation.

7. When a manager believes his or her group has set performance norms well below what they are capable of attaining, what can be done and by what means can the manager raise the performance norms to a higher level?

8. Under what managerial conditions can status incongruence develop? What can the manager do to eliminate this situation?

9. How do group members learn the status hierarchy and norms of the group? What means can the group use to reveal to individual members these group aspects?

10. Can the manager control the composition of the group that he or she manages?

11. Describe some sources of intra-role and inter-role conflict. How can these sources be controlled by the manager?

12. Is cohesiveness a more important aspect to group performance for functional groups than for task or project groups? Explain.

13. How may the manager increase the frequency of group interaction to increase cohesiveness? Explain.

14. Would it be a sound managerial policy to break up highly cohesive groups?

Notes

1. See A. Paul Hare, *Handbook of Small Group Research* (Glencoe, N.Y.: Free Press, 1962); and D. Cartwright and A. Zander, eds., *Group Dynamics: Research and Theory* (New York: Harper & Row, 1968).

2. See Marvin E. Shaw, *Group Dynamics: The Psychology of Small Group Behavior* (New York: McGraw-Hill, 1971).

3. Ibid., p. 37.

4. See Ralph M. Stogdill, "Personnel Factors Associated with Leadership: A Survey of the Literature," *Journal of Psychology*, January 1948, pp. 35–71; P. R. Costanzo and Marvin E. Shaw, "Conformity as a Function of Age," *Child Development*, 1966, pp. 967–75.

5. See R. S. Crutchfield, "Conformity and Character," *American Psychologist*, 1955, pp. 191–98.

6. Shaw, *Group Dynamics*, pp. 169–80.

7. Lyman W. Porter, Edward E. Lawler III, and J. Richard Hackman, *Behavior in Organizations* (New York: McGraw-Hill, 1975), pp. 172–78.

8. J. Weitz, "Job Expectancy and Survival," *Journal of Applied Psychology*, 1956, pp. 245–47.

9. Robert F. Bales, *Interaction Process Analysis: A Method for the Study of Small Groups* (Cambridge, Mass.: Addison-Wesley, 1950), p. 33.

10. P. E. Slater, "Contrasting Correlates of Group Size," *Sociometry*, 1958, pp. 129–39.

11. A. Baum and S. Valina, *Architecture and Social Behavior* (New York: Wiley, 1977).

12. Ernest J. McCormick, *Human Factors in Engineering and Design* (New York: McGraw-Hill, 1976).

13. T. J. Allen and D. I. Cohen, "Information Flow in R&D Laboratories," *Administrative Science Quarterly*, 1969, pp. 12–25.

14. Robert H. Miles, "Role-Set Configuration as a Predictor of Role Conflict and Ambiguity in Complex Organizations," *Sociometry*, 1977, pp. 21–34.

15. Andrew D. Szilagyi and W. E. Holland, "Changes in Social Density: Relationships with Perceptions of Job Characteristics, Role Stress, and Work Satisfaction" *Journal of Applied Psychology*, in press.

16. J. Richard Hackman and L. E. Jones, "Development of a Set of Dimensions for Analyzing Verbal Group Products," *Technical Report No. 23, ONR Contract*

NR 177–472 (University of Illinois, 1965).

17. J. Richard Hackman, "Effects of Task Characteristics on Group Products," *Journal of Experimental Social Psychology,* 1968, pp. 162–87; C. G. Morris, "Effects of Task Characteristics on Group Process," *Technical Report No. 2, APOSR Contract AF 49 (638)–1291* (University of Illinois, 1965).

18. J. T. Lanzetta and T. B. Roby, "Effects of Work Group Structure and Certain Task Variables in Group Performance," *Journal of Abnormal and Social Psychology,* 1956, pp. 307–14.

19. S. C. Shilflett, "Group Performance as a Function of Task Difficulty and Organizational Interdependence," *Organizational Behavior and Human Performance,* 1972, pp. 442–56.

20. J. H. Davis, *Group Performance* (Reading Mass.: Addison-Wesley, 1969).

21. Hare, *Handbook of Small Group Research,* p. 201.

22. C. G. Smith, "Scientific Performance and the Composition of Research Teams," *Administrative Science Quarterly,* December 1971, pp. 486–95.

23. Warren G. Bennis and Herbert A. Shepard, "A Theory of Group Development," *Human Relations,* Summer 1963, pp. 415–57.

24. Bernard Bass, *Organizational Psychology* (Boston: Allyn & Bacon, 1965), pp. 197–98.

25. Ralph M. Stogdill, *Individual Behavior and Group Achievement* (New York: Oxford, 1959), p. 18.

26. Solomon E. Asch, "Effects of Group Pressure upon the Modification and Distribution of Judgements," in *Group Leadership and Men,* ed. H. A. Guetzkow (Pittsburgh: Carnegie Press, 1951), pp. 177–90.

27. H. T. Reitan and Marvin E. Shaw, "Group Membership, Six Compositions of the Group, and Conformity Behavior," *Journal of Social Psychology,* October 1969, pp. 45–51.

28. Edgar H. Schein, "Organizational Socialization and the Profession of Management," *Industrial Management Review,* 1968, pp. 1–16.

29. W. H. Whyte, Jr., *The Organization Man* (Garden City, N.Y.: Doubleday-Anchor, 1956).

30. Robert L. Kahn et al., *Organizational Stress: Studies in Role Conflict and Ambiguity* (New York: Wiley, 1964).

31. Henry P. Sims and Andrew D. Szilagyi, "Leader Structure and Satisfaction of Nurses: A Path Analysis Approach," *Journal of Applied Psychology,* April 1975, pp. 194–97.

32. Charles N. Green and D. W. Organ, "Role Ambiguity, Locus of Control, Role Dynamics and Job," *Journal of Applied Psychology,* December 1973, pp. 101–2.

33. Andrew D. Szilagyi, "An Empirical Test of Causal Influences Between Role Perceptions, Job Satisfaction, Performance, and Organizational Level," *Personnel Psychology,* 1977, pp. 375–88.

34. Andrew D. Szilagyi, Henry P. Sims, and Robert T. Keller, "Locus of Control, Role Dynamics and Job Behavior," *Academy of Management Journal,* June 1976, pp. 259–70.

35. A. J. Lott and B. E. Lott, "Group Cohesiveness as Interpersonal Attraction: A Review of Relationships with Antecedent and Consequent Variables," *Psychological Bulletin,* October 1965, pp. 259–309.

36. N. M. Tichy, "An Analysis of Clique Formation and Structure in Organizations," *Administrative Science Quarterly,* June 1973, pp. 194–208.

37. Stanley E. Seashore, *Group Cohesiveness in the Industrial Work Group* (Ann Arbor: University of Michigan, Institute for Social Research, 1954).

Additional References

BANDURA, A. *Social Learning Theory.* New York: General Learning Press, 1971.

BION, W. R. *Experiences in Groups.* New York: Basic Books, 1959.

COLLINS B. E., and GUETZKOW, H. A. *Social Psychology of Group Processes for Decision Making.* New York: Wiley, 1964.

GIBBARD, G. S.; HARTMAN, J. J.; and MANN, R. D. *Analysis of Groups* (San Francisco: Jossey-Bass, 1974).

HACKMAN, J. "Group Influences on Individuals." In *Handbook of Industrial and Organizational Psychology,* edited by M. D. Dunnette. Chicago: Rand McNally, 1976.

HINTON, B. L., and REITZ, H. J., eds. *Groups and Organizations.* Belmont, Calif.: Wadsworth, 1971.

HOLLANDER, E. P. *Leaders, Groups and Influence.* New York: Oxford University Press, 1964.

HOMANS, G. C. *The Human Group.* New York: Harcourt, Brace & World, 1950.

KATZ, D., and KAHN, R. L. *The Social Psychology of Organizations.* 2nd ed. New York: Wiley, 1978.

KEMPER, T. D., and McGRATH, J. E. "Reference Groups, Socialization, and Achievement." *American Sociological Review,* 1968, pp. 31–45.

KENT, R. N., and McGRATH, J. E. "Task and Group Characteristics as Factors Influencing Group Performance." *Journal of Experimental Social Psychology,* 1969, pp. 429–40.

KLEIN, S. M. *Workers Under Stress: The Impact of Work Pressure on Group Cohesion.* Lexington, University of Kentucky, 1971.

LEWIN, K. *Field Science in Social Sciences.* New York: Harper & Row, 1951.

McGRATH, J. E., and ALTMAN, J. E. *Small Group Research.* New York: Holt, Rinehart & Winston, 1966.

MILLER, J. "Living Systems: The Group." *Behavioral Science,* 1971, pp. 302–98.

MILLS, T. M. *The Sociology of Small Groups.* Englewood Cliffs, N.J.: Prentice-Hall, 1967.

SCHUTZ, W. C. *FIRO: A Three-Dimensional Theory of Interpersonal Relations.* New York: Holt, Rinehart & Winston, 1958.

SHEPHARD, C. R. *Small Groups: Some Sociological Perspectives.* San Francisco: Chandler, 1964.

SMITH, P. B. *Groups Within Organizations.* New York: Harper & Row, 1973.

STEINER, I. D. *Group Process and Productivity.* New York: Academic Press, 1972.

THIBAUT, J. W. and KELLEY, H. H. *The Social Psychology of Groups.* New York: Wiley, 1959.

ZANDER, A. *Motives and Goals in Groups.* New York: Academic Press, 1971.

A Case of Groups

The United Chemical Company

The United Chemical Company is a large producer and distributor of commodity chemicals with five chemical production plants in the United States. The operations at the main plant in Baytown, Texas, include not only production equipment but also is the site of the company's research and engineering center.

The process design group consists of eight male engineers and the supervisor, Max Kane. The group has worked together steadily for a number of years, and good relationships had developed among all members. When the workload began to increase, Max hired a new design engineer, Sue Davis, a recent masters degree graduate from one of the foremost engineering schools in the country. Sue was assigned to a project involving expansion of one of the existing plant facility's capacity. Three other design engineers were assigned to the project along with Sue: Jack Keller (age thirty-eight, fifteen years with the company); Sam Sims (age forty, ten years with the company); and Lance Madison (age thirty-two, eight years with the company).

As a new employee, Sue was very enthusiastic about the opportunity to work at United. She liked her work very much because it was challenging and it offered her a chance to apply much of the knowledge she had gained in her university studies. On the job, Sue kept fairly much to herself and her design work. Her relations with her fellow project members were friendly, but she did not go out of her way to have informal conversations during or after working hours.

Sue was a diligent employee who took her work quite seriously. On occasions when a difficult problem arose, she would stay after hours in order to come up with a solution. Because of her persistence, coupled with her more current education, Sue completed her portion of the various project stages usually a number of days before her colleagues. This was somewhat irritating to her because on these occasions she went to Max to ask for additional work to keep her busy until her fellow workers caught up to her. Initially, she had offered to help Jack, Sam, and Lance with their part of the project, but each time she was turned down very tersely.

About five months after Sue had joined the design group, Jack asked to see Max about a problem the group was having. The conversation between Max and Jack was as follows:

Max: Jack, I understand you wanted to discuss a problem with me.

Jack: Yes, Max. I didn't want to waste your time, but some of the other design engineers wanted me to discuss Sue with you. She is irritating everyone with her know-it-all, pompous attitude. She just is not the kind of person that we want to work with.

Max: I can't understand that, Jack. She's an excellent worker whose design work is always well done and usually flawless. She's doing everything the company wants her to do.

Jack: The company never asked her to disturb the morale of the group or to tell us how to do our work. The animosity of the group can eventually result in lower quality work for the whole unit.

Max: I'll tell you what I'll do. Sue has a meeting with me next week to discuss her six-month performance. I'll keep your thoughts in mind, but I can't promise an improvement in what you and the others believe is a pompous attitude.

Jack: Immediate improvement in her behavior is not the problem, it's her coaching others when she has no right to engage in publicly showing others what to do. You'd think she was lecturing an advance class in design with all her high-power, useless equations and formulas. She'd better back off soon, or some of us will quit or transfer.

During the next week, Max thought carefully about his meeting with Jack. He knew that Jack was the informal leader of the design engineers and generally spoke for the other group members. On Thursday of the following week, Max called Sue into his office for her midyear review. Certain excerpts of the conversation were as follows:

Max: There is one other aspect I'd like to discuss with you about your performance. As I just related to you, your technical performance has been excellent; however, there are some questions about your relationships with the other workers.

Sue: I don't understand—what questions are you talking about?

Max: Well, to be specific, certain members of the design group have complained about your apparent "know-it-all attitude" and the manner in which you try to tell them how to do their job. You're going to have to be patient with them and not publicly call them out about their performance. This is a good group of engineers, and their work over the years has been more than acceptable. I don't want any problems that will cause the group to produce less effectively.

Sue: Let me make a few comments. First of all, I have never publicly criticized their performance to them or to you. Initially, when I was finished ahead of them, I offered to help them with their work, but was bluntly told to mind my own business. I took the hint and concentrated only on my part of the work.

Max: Okay, I understand that.

Sue: What you don't understand is that after five months of working in this group I have come to the conclusion that what is going on is a "rip-off" of the company. The other engineers are "goldbricking" and setting a work pace much less than they're capable of. They're more interested in the music from Sam's radio, the local football team, and the bar they're going to go to for TGIF. I'm sorry, but this is just not the way I was raised or trained. And finally, they've never looked on me as a qualified engineer, but as a woman who has broken their professional barrier.

Max: The assessment and motivation of the engineers is a managerial job. Your job is to do your work as well as you can without interfering with the work of others.

As for the male-female comment, this company hired you because of your qualifications, not your sex. Your future at United is quite promising if you do the engineering and leave the management to me.

Sue left the meeting very depressed. She knew that she was performing well and that the other design engineers were not working up to their capacity. This knowledge frustrated her more and more as the weeks passed.

Case Primer Questions

1. Does Sue value her membership in the group? Explain.

2. What is Sue seeking from membership in the design group? What are the other members seeking from membership in the group?

3. How do you rate the way Max handled his meeting with Sue?

4. Discuss this situation in terms of the stages of group development.

5. Discuss this situation in terms of structural dimensions of groups.

6. What should Sue do next? What should Max do next?

Experiential Exercise

The Young Rehabilitation Hospital

Purpose

1. To study the difficulties in diagnosing problems in group behavior.

2. To consider the criteria used to evaluate group performance.

Required understanding

The student should be acquainted with the basic dimensions of group behavior.

How to set up the exercise

Groups of four to eight students should be established for this forty-five to sixty minute exercise. The groups should be separated from each other and requested to talk only with members of their own group. They should then be asked to read the following:

The Young Rehabilitation Hospital is one of the foremost rehabilitation centers in the world. The hospital, named after its founder and director, Dr. Sydney Young, specializes in the rehabilitation of spinal cord injury patients. Because of its staff and reputation, this 100-bed hospital received patients from all over the United States.

During Dr. Young's frequent travels, he heard a new organizational arrangement for patient treatment being discussed by other hospitals that was based upon the geographic team concept. The traditional organizational structure used by the Young Hospital was based on functional arrangements: separate departments for nursing, physical therapy, occupational therapy, social work, physicians, and other medical services (i.e., finance, food preparation, and personnel).

Dr. Young was known for trying new and innovative techniques, and he decided to try the geographic treatment approach on a small scale in his hospital. He selected twenty employees (one M.D., two social workers, two occupational therapists, two physical therapists, six nurses, and seven nurses' aides) to be part of the team. Each

233

of the members was drawn from the main functional groups and were told that they would now report to the M.D. in charge of the team, not to their respective department heads. The treatment team would care for only one ward of ten patients. Dr. Young hoped that the new team arrangement would result in better performance and job satisfaction of the employees and that the process of patient rehabilitation would be improved.

After the treatment team approach had been in operation for one year, Dr. Young requested that a preliminary evaluation of its effectiveness be conducted. He asked the head physician to review the data on the ten patients in the team's ward and also asked the personnel director to conduct interviews with each of the team members regarding their opinions of the team arrangement. The results of each of their investigations is shown in exhibit 7–10.

Exhibit 7–10 Summary of Results on Geographic Treatment Team After One Year

Patients	Team Members
1. Patients responded significantly faster to therapeutic treatment.	1. Team members reported greater satisfaction with their fellow team members.
2. Patients put forth more effort during exercise periods.	2. There was no "true supervisor" present to give directions or orders on a regular basis.
3. Patients exhibited some resistance to employees not on the team who occasionally filled in for ill team members.	3. Significantly lower satisfaction with promotional opportunities was reported.
4. Patients were discharged 10 percent earlier than the average (sixty days).	4. Overtime hours for team members was 28 percent lower than for the rest of the hospital.
5. Closer relationships were developed between patients and team members.	5. Problems developed concerning the extent of an employee's authority and responsibility over patient care.
6. Patient treatment costs increased 22 percent over nonteam approaches.	6. Team members preferred to treat a patient throughout his or her rehabilitation, rather than intermittently as previously done.
	7. There was a lack of cooperation from other hospital units or functions.
	8. Absenteeism of team members was 42 percent lower than the rest of the hospital.
	9. Ten of the twenty members have requested transfers back to their functional units.
	10. Pressure from the administration to have the team approach "look good" was felt.

Instructions for the exercise

1. *Individually*, group members should do the following:

(a) Develop a set of criteria to evaluate the effectiveness of the team approach.

(b) Evaluate the team approach from the basis of: (1) patients; and (2) team members.

(c) What should Dr. Young do next:
(1) Disband the team and return to the functional approach? or
(2) Establish teams throughout the hospital? or
(3) Other alternatives?

2. As a *group*, repeat points (a) to (c) above. Report your group decision to the instructor.

CHAPTER 8

Intergroup Behavior

In the previous chapter, we examined the foundations and structural elements of individuals performing within a group, or *intragroup behavior*. In this chapter, our focus will be concerned with the interactions, activities, and behavior between two or more groups, or *intergroup behavior*. For our purposes, the study of intergroup behavior is important for two reasons. First, it is through the interaction and performance of various groups that the goals and objectives of the organization can be accomplished. It is therefore important for managers to develop an understanding of the major influences on intergroup behavior and to improve their skills in diagnosing and evaluating intergroup processes. Second, the discussion of intergroup behavior will serve as a foundation for our discussion of the larger structure or design of the total organization.[1]

This chapter is divided into four major sections. First, we will develop a basic framework for the study of intergroup behavior and performance. We will identify key intergroup concepts and examine how they influence intergroup performance. In the second section, a number of strategies for managing intergroup relations will be discussed. In the last two sections, we will examine two important elements of intergroup behavior—power and conflict—and how they relate to intergroup performance.

A Framework for Intergroup Performance

The processes that occur between two or more interacting groups are called intergroup behavior. The interacting groups may be two groups within a large department, such as market research and sales, or groups that are in separate departments or within the same organization, such as personnel and maintenance departments.

Intergroup performance, just as intragroup performance, depends on a number of different factors. These characteristics, shown in exhibit 8–1, include: (1) interdependence; (2) task uncertainty; and (3) time and goal orientation. Consistent with exhibit 2–2, we will define intergroup performance in terms of three levels of analysis: (1) individual level (e.g., satisfaction, goal achievement); (2) group level (e.g., morale, productivity); and (3) organization level (e.g., profitability, efficiency, turnover).

Exhibit 8–1   A Framework for Intergroup Performance

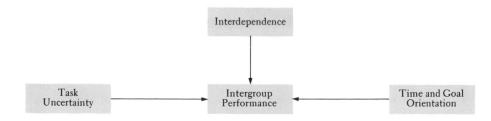

In order to illustrate the three intergroup characteristics, assume there is a division in a large manufacturing company whose basic structure is shown in exhibit 8–2. The division is headed by a divisional vice president, who has a general manager of manufacturing, general manager of marketing, director of research and development, and director of administrative services reporting to him or her. Each of the subordinate managers in turn have other managers reporting to them (e.g., managers of manufacturing and shipping reporting to the general manager of manufacturing, and so on). Exhibit 8–2 will serve as an ongoing example of intergroup behavior throughout this chapter.

Interdependence

Interdependence between two or more groups is the degree to which the interactions between the groups must be coordinated to attain a desired level of performance.

Exhibit 8–2   Intergroup Behavior Example Division

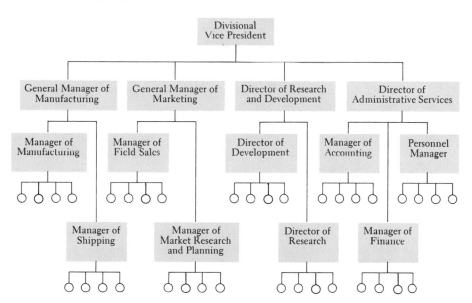

Three types of interdependence have been most frequently discussed: (1) pooled; (2) sequential; and (3) reciprocal.[2]

Pooled interdependence.   *Pooled interdependence* describes the situation in which groups are relatively independent of each other, but each renders a discrete contribution to the larger organization and is supported by the organization. The Chevrolet Vega plant in Ohio may be considered independent of the Cadillac plant in Michigan on most automobile assembly matters. They are, however, interdependent in a pooled fashion because each contributes to the overall profit of General Motors.

In our example company division (exhibit 8–2), we may consider the manager of shipping and the director of research as being interdependent in a pooled manner. That is, the two departments do not interact on a frequent basis nor are they dependent on each other. Each department, however, contributes separately to the performance of the division.

Sequential interdependence.   When the outputs of one group are the inputs to another group, *sequential interdependence* exists. In our example, sequential interdependence exists between the departments of manufacturing and shipping. The outputs of the manufacturing department, finished products, are the inputs to the shipping department.

With sequential interdependence, there is an element of uncertainty to be considered. The input function, shipping in the above example, is dependent on the output function (manufacturing) for finished products in order to perform its work. Readjustments must be made when an output function performs improperly or fails to meet the expectations of the input function. If a piece of equipment malfunctions in the manufacturing process, the flow of product will be disrupted, resulting in a lack of work, or idle time, for the shipping and loading crew.

Reciprocal interdependence.   The third form of interdependence exists when certain outputs of each group become inputs for other groups. There is reciprocal interdependence between the development engineering and marketing functions. The output of the development process—test quantities of the new product—serve as inputs to the marketing function to be used to test initial consumer acceptance. However, a less than satisfactory level of consumer acceptance—a potential output of the marketing function—serves as an input to the development engineering function for further refinement and testing.

Reciprocal interdependence also occurs between the manufacturing and marketing functions. The output of the manufacturing area—large quantities of a new product—serve as the inputs for the marketing function for the purpose of generating consumer sales. Problems of product quality or requests by consumers for different packaging forms—the output of the marketing function—serve as inputs to the manufacturing function for additional work or investigation.

In test marketing, the marketing function must be aware of the quality and quantity limitations of the development engineering plant. The development function should be prepared to act quickly on the initial consumer reaction provided by the marketing function. Also, in full-scale manufacturing, marketing should be cognizant of the difficulties associated with the start-up of the production of a new product, but manufacturing should be prepared to adapt or adjust to different consumer demands as forwarded by the marketing function. In each case, the quality and accuracy of the interaction between the interdependent elements has a strong influence on the level of intergroup performance. The three types of interdependence are summarized in exhibit 8–3.

For intergroup performance, it is important for managers to understand that as one progresses from pooled to reciprocal, the three types of interdependence require greater interaction, and it also becomes increasingly difficult to coordinate toward task accomplishment. That is, when advancing from pooled interdependence to sequential interdependence, and finally to reciprocal interdependence, there must be an increased awareness by everyone involved that the activities of one group are dependent on the actions and behavior of the other groups. Intergroup performance is a direct result of how this interdependence is successfully controlled and coordinated.

Task Uncertainty

Managers in various positions in organizations have jobs that may be the same from day to day or may involve new and different problems each day. For example, the processing of financial data by accounting managers may be structured such that the only major variation in their work from day to day may be the size of the workload.

Exhibit 8–3 Summary of Interdependence Types

Type	Degree of Dependence	Description	Example
Reciprocal	High	Certain outputs of each group become inputs for other groups, or to each other	1. Relationship between development and market research departments. 2. The interaction between operations and maintenance in a domestic airline company.
Sequential	Moderate	Outputs of one group become inputs of other groups	1. Relationship between manufacturing and shipping departments. 2. Automobile assembly-line activities.
Pooled	Low	Groups or units are relatively independent of each other, but contribute to the overall goals of the organization.	1. Relationship between research and shipping departments. 2. Separate manufacturing plants of a single organization that interact only infrequently.

On the other hand, the manager of customer technical service may face different problems each day depending on the volume and nature of customer requests or inquiries.

The basic concept illustrated by this example is that many jobs vary in the degree of *task uncertainty* that can be encountered during each work period. The degree of task uncertainty varies with two factors: (1) task clarity; and (2) the task environment.

Task clarity is the degree to which the requirements and responsibilities in the group are clearly stated and understood.[3] Generally, task clarity refers to the extent that rules, procedures, and policies are used by groups to direct the everyday activities of members. In our previous example, the task clarity for the manufacturing managers is relatively high. Whenever changes in product quality, quantity, or equipment maintenance are required, procedures have generally been established that let the managers know what must be done when a particular situation or problem arises. In the manufacturing of many food products, a key quality-control variable is the percentage of water contained in the product. If the percentage is too high, the manufacturing manager can increase the temperature in the drying stage; if the percentage is too low, the drying temperature may be lowered.

In contrast, consider the research scientist. The process of developing a new product usually involves a theoretical foundation coupled with a high degree of creativity and innovation in developing and evaluating different product formulas and types. Rules and procedures are generally not available, but are usually developed as the development progresses. In these two examples, the manufacturing manager's task would involve a low degree of task uncertainty; a high degree of task uncertainty would characterize the research scientist's job.

Task environment are those factors or elements, internal or external to the organization, that are relevant or can affect the level of performance of a unit or group.[4] That is, included within the primary functions of all organizational units is the requirement to interact with other units, some internal, some external to the organization. Manufacturing managers interact primarily with other units within the organization, such as accounting and personnel. However, they may also interact with elements external to the parent organization, such as raw-material suppliers and transportation companies. The marketing manager's primary interaction patterns are with units or groups external to the organization, principally customers. Yet, there can be considerable interaction with units or groups internal to the organization, such as manufacturing and the research labs.

The important aspect to consider is that the task uncertainty varies with two elements of the task environment: (1) the number of different elements, units, or groups; and (2) the stable-dynamic nature of the environment. For example, the research scientists in our product-development example are faced with high task uncertainty. Not only do they deal with a number of different groups or units external to the organization in search of new knowledge, but the scientific environment is constantly changing, with information on new developments being frequently transmitted. At the other extreme are the manufacturing managers who face a relatively low degree of task uncertainty. The number of potential interactions, mostly internal to the organization, are relatively few, and the nature of the task environment is fairly stable from day to day.

Time and Goal Orientation

Managers who spend a number of years in a particular type of job tend to become accustomed to organizing their work in a predictable fashion, orienting themselves to organizational goals, time deadlines, and to other individuals in a manner that helps them perform that job effectively.[5] As we pointed out in the sections on interdependence and task uncertainty, different types of tasks require the management of different levels of predictability or uncertainty. These various types of tasks and levels of uncertainty require different work orientations. Two particular work orientations can influence intergroup performance: (1) time orientation; and (2) goal orientation.[6]

Time orientation is the time span required to obtain information or results relating to the performance of a task. For example, in our previous illustration, manufacturing and marketing managers deal with situations or problems that provide rapid feedback about results. The manufacturing manager is concerned with hourly quality-control and productivity data; the marketing manager may focus his or her attention on weekly or bimonthly reports of sales volume.

On the other hand, the research scientists and development engineers in our example tend to have longer-range concerns because tangible results of their performance can be evaluated only after they have solved the technical problems associated with the new product. In many organizations, the acquisition and presentation of results on scientific projects is typically limited to monthly, quarterly, or yearly progress reports. Exhibit 8–4 depicts the predicted time orientation for the different managers in our example company division (see exhibit 8–2).

Goal orientation focuses on the particular set of task objectives or goals that are of major concern to individuals in organizations. To be effective, managers should focus their attention clearly on goals and objectives that are directly related to their work.[7] In our example, manufacturing managers could focus on such goals as raw-material costs, processing and storage costs, production volume, and the quality of the finished product. The task goals of marketing managers are oriented toward goals that include sales volume and revenue, market share and penetration, and customer satisfaction. The research scientists, on the other hand, often concentrate on task goals involving the development of scientific knowledge and translating that knowledge into potential market applications. Finally, development engineers are often oriented toward goals of translating scientific discovery into new

Exhibit 8–4 Differences in Time and Goal Orientation

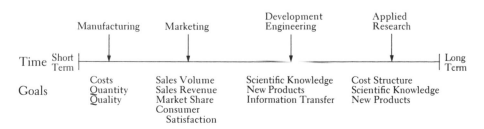

products, but also insuring that the new product can be produced within a cost structure that will result in economic gains in large-scale manufacturing.

These examples of different goals deal with three orientations: (1) techno-economic (i.e., manufacturing and accounting departments), dealing with cost control and the implementation of manufacturing technology; (2) market (i.e., marketing function), concerning the consumer response to the organization's products; and (3) science (i.e., research and development engineering functions), concerning contributions to scientific knowledge.[8]

The different goal orientations provide a basis for establishing criteria for evaluating the performance of the particular group or unit. We would expect that the primary criteria of performance for manufacturing would focus on quality, quantity, and cost considerations (techno-economic), sales volume and market share for marketing (market), and number of new products and contributions to scientific knowledge for research and development engineering (science).

For intergroup behavior, the importance of time and goal orientation is that they establish a state of differentiation.[9] *Differentiation* is defined as the degree to which groups differ from one another in time (short term to long term) and goal orientation (techno-economic, market, or science). As shown in exhibit 8–4, manufacturing and research departments would be highly differentiated from each other. On the other hand, research and development would have a lesser degree of differentiation.

A summary of intergroup characteristics for a sample of the group, or departments, in exhibit 8–2 is presented in exhibit 8–5.

Intergroup Performance

The three intergroup characteristics of interdependence, task uncertainty, and differentiation (time and goal orientation) establish three intergroup *managerial requirements* that influence the quality of intergroup performance. First, the type of interdependence between groups influences the nature of *interaction requirements*. Interaction requirements refer not only to the frequency and quality of interaction required for task accomplishment but also to the number of levels or individuals in each group that are required to interact with counterparts in other groups. Interaction requirements increase as interdependence moves from pooled, to sequential, to reciprocal interdependence. When companies test market new products, the development and sales departments are reciprocally interdependent. In this situation, we would expect interaction to be quite frequent and involve many representatives in each group.

Second, the degree of task uncertainty inherent in one or more of the interacting groups influences the degree of *information-flow requirements* between the groups.[10] Information-flow requirements refer to the amount and quality of information and communication that must be processed between interacting groups. Toward the end of the fiscal year, we would expect to find a great deal of information flowing from the accounting department to all other operating departments (e.g., manufacturing).

Finally, time and goal orientation (i.e. differentiation) introduces the concept of

Exhibit 8–5 Summary of Intergroup Characteristics

Group	Interdependence Examples	Task Uncertainty	Time and Goal Orientation
Research	*Reciprocal* with development *Sequential* with market research *Pooled* with shipping	High	*Time:* Long term *Goal:* Science
Development	*Reciprocal* with market research *Sequential* with manufacturing *Pooled* with shipping	Moderate to High	*Time:* Long term *Goal:* Science and Techno-economic
Sales	*Reciprocal* with market research *Sequential* with manufacturing *Pooled* with personnel	Moderate	*Time:* Moderate terms *Goal:* Market
Manufacturing	*Reciprocal* with accounting *Sequential* with shipping *Pooled* with research	Low	*Time:* Short term *Goal:* Techno-economic
Accounting	*Reciprocal* with manufacturing *Sequential* with finance *Pooled* with shipping	Low	*Time:* Short term *Goal:* Techno-economic and Market

integration requirements. Integration deals with the degree of collaboration, co-operation, or structural relationships required and achieved between the various interacting organization groups. In the early stages of the product-development process, there is a high degree of differentiation between the research unit and the marketing unit because of differences in time orientation (long term versus short term) and goal orientation (science versus market). In order to attain a high level of intergroup performance between these two units during this early product-development stage, there must be a commensurably high degree of integration. The relationship between intergroup characteristics, intergroup requirements, and performance is shown in exhibit 8–6.

The three intergroup requirements combine to determine the level of difficulty managers face in achieving high levels of intergroup performance. For example, interacting groups with low interaction requirements (pooled interdependence), low information-flow requirements (low task uncertainty), and lower-level needs for integration (minimal differences in time and goal orientation) would encounter the least difficulty in achieving a high level of intergroup performance. Conversely, interacting groups with high interaction requirements (reciprocal interdependence), high information requirements (high task uncertainty), and high required levels for integration (large differences in time and goal orientation) would experience the greatest difficulty in achieving a high level of intergroup performance. In the next section, we will examine various managerial strategies for improving intergroup performance.

Exhibit 8–6 Intergroup Characteristics, Requirements, and Performance

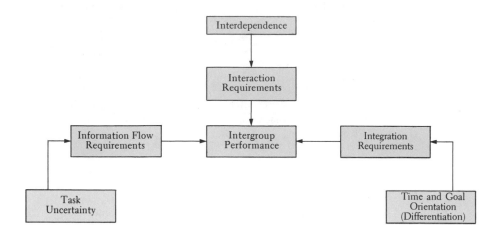

Strategies for Managing Intergroup Performance

There are a number of different methods or mechanisms available to managers to insure a high level of intergroup performance. Exhibit 8–7 identifies seven possible methods for managing intergroup performance.[11] This list of intergroup management strategies is by no means an exhaustive list of possible or potential means for insuring intergroup performance. The seven have been chosen on the basis of their frequency of use in various types of organizations.

The intergroup management strategies are ordered on a single continuum that reflects increasing intergroup requirements (i.e., interaction requirements + information flow requirements + integration requirements).

A more realistic interpretation would be that the continuum represents the degree or level of commitment and resource requirements given by the organization to effectively manage intergroup performance. A particular strategy or strategies appropriate for the various levels of interaction, information-flow, and integration requirements are noted on the continuum. Finally, in advancing from the low end of the continuum (i.e., rules) to the high end (i.e., integrating departments), a strategy previously used will probably still be used along with the new strategy for managing intergroup performance. That is, if a manager depends on planning techniques for managing intergroup relations, it is likely that he or she also depends on the use of hierarchy and rules. Consistent with our previous discussion, we will continue to use exhibit 8–2 to illustrate the various intergroup management strategies.

Rules and Procedures

The most basic or simplistic method for managing intergroup performance is to specify in advance, through *rules and procedures,* the required activities and behavior of group members.[12] Interacting employees learn that when certain situations

Exhibit 8–7 Intergroup Management Strategies

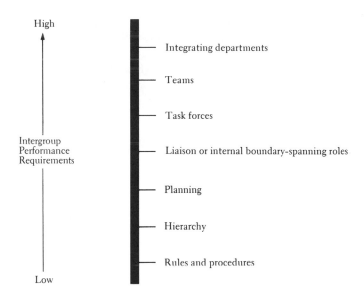

arise there is a particular set of actions that should be used. For example, the packaging and shipping department knows that when the manufacturing department changes the manufacturing process from producing the medium-grade product to the higher-grade product at 10:00 a.m. each day, that they must use a different packaging container and labeling process. Little, if any, interaction between the two groups is necessary because the procedures have spelled out in advance the required behaviors.

The principal benefit of rules and procedures is that they eliminate the need for extensive interaction and information flow between groups or units. Rules and procedures also provide a means of stability to the organization. Employees may come and go, but the procedures remain for future interactions.[13]

Rules and procedures, however, are limited methods for managing intergroup performance. They are most applicable when intergroup activities can be anticipated in advance and when the responses or required behaviors can be developed. When there is a high degree of task uncertainty and therefore increased information-flow requirements, rules and procedures may prove to be inadequate as an intergroup management strategy.

Hierarchy

When the use of rules and procedures proves inadequate for effective intergroup performance, the use of the *hierarchy,* or common supervisor, becomes the primary intergroup managerial strategy. For example, when there are intergroup problems between manufacturing and shipping, such as inadequate inventory to load a box-car, the problem is brought to the attention of the manufacturing general manager for solution.

The basic assumption for using the hierarchy or common supervisor as an intergroup managerial strategy is that higher-level managers have the power and authority to make these decisions. However, as in the case of rules and procedures, this method has its limitations. Whenever interaction, information-flow, and integration requirements increase, the manager's time may be totally taken up resolving these exceptions or problems of intergroup relations. Less time can be devoted to more pressing issues, such as planning the construction of a new plant. Additional difficulties are encountered when problems between two separated units, such as shipping and sales, arise. The common supervisor is the divisional vice president, who becomes the sole arbitrator of day-to-day problems.

Planning

As the problems between interacting units or groups develop beyond the control of rules, procedures, or hierarchy, organizations increasingly use *planning* activities to improve intergroup performance. Planning activities involve setting goals or targets that can lead to task accomplishment.[14]

For example, consider the construction of a new manufacturing plant. Various interdependent and interacting groups are involved in such aspects as erecting the frame of the building, installing the electrical and utility requirements, installing the manufacturing equipment, and connecting all raw-material and finished-product processing lines. Rather than having constant interaction between these groups, plans have been made so that each group or unit can perform its task over a specific period of time. Each group has a set of goals or targets for required hours of construction, delivery of construction materials, and completion dates.

The task of constructing a building can be effectively accomplished through the use of plans because the complexities can be controlled and the majority of the future interactions (excluding, of course, unforeseen environmental events) can be programmed. On the other hand, the intergroup processes involved in developing a new product from the laboratory to full-scale market introduction cannot be totally planned. As we noted earlier, this process involves a high level of interaction because of the many varied groups that are involved and because such events as scientific knowledge generation and the pattern of consumer reaction cannot be fully spelled out in advance. Certain intergroup relations are well adapted to the use of plans; other intergroup activities, however, can use plans to manage only selected interactions between units or groups. These intergroup activities must, therefore, develop and use other strategies to manage their interactions.

Liaison or Internal Boundary-Spanning Roles

When the number of interactions and volume of information between two or more units or groups grows, it may become necessary to establish a specialized role to handle these requirements. Such a role has been variously termed a *liaison,* or more formally, an *internal boundary spanner.*[15]

In the example shown in exhibit 8–2, a liaison or internal boundary-spanning role could be established between the applied research and market research functions.

This is shown in exhibit 8–8. Individuals who operate in this role provide lateral communications and facilitate interaction between the two functions in a number of areas. One important area is the coordination of activity directed toward ascertaining the potential of a new product developed by the applied research unit. The effective interaction provided by the liaison role may enable the product to progress to the development stage more quickly or may force the applied research scientists to revise their work in light of a negative evaluation from the market research unit. In each case, decisions related to the new product may be made earlier than if a liaison role had not been established.

These liaison or boundary-spanning roles in organizations serve a number of purposes. First, they can facilitate the flow of information between two or more interacting units. The normal flow of information between units usually is based on formal, time-consuming mechanisms, such as memos and formal meetings. The liaison role provides a more informal mechanism that can reduce the time necessary for accurate information flow. Second, because of frequent interactions, the liaison person is generally well acquainted with the nature of the work of each of the interacting groups. This knowledge can provide such benefits as: (1) ability to assist in the coordination of various complex activities; (2) ability to provide the interacting units with a better understanding of each other's functions and responsibilities; and (3) providing a continuous way of keeping each interacting unit aware of the current progress of intergroup relationships and day-to-day decision making.

A number of negative consequences can develop when organizations use a liaison role strategy to manage intergroup performance. First, performing in liaison or

Exhibit 8–8 Liaison Role

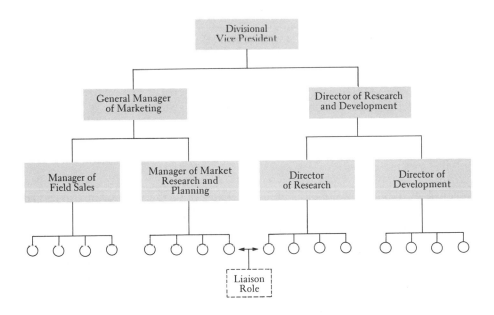

boundary-spanning roles may have negative effects for the individuals who hold these positions. A number of research studies have found incumbents of boundary-spanning roles to experience such dysfunctions as lower job satisfaction, higher role conflict, and higher role ambiguity.[16]

The basic explanation for these negative characteristics is that those in boundary-spanning roles must face conflicting expectations for performance from the different groups with which they interact. In contrast, a nonboundary spanner, dealing only with the expectations for performance from his or her group, would face less conflicting and ambiguous expectations.

Second, the effectiveness of intergroup relations is limited by the ability of the liaison person to handle the complexities and information flow between the interacting groups. In addition, as these aspects increase, more and more individuals begin functioning in liaison roles, which acts to remove them from performing their primary functions. When this situation arises, organizations seek other methods to manage intergroup performance.

Task Forces

When the complexities of interaction increase, such as when the number of interacting units grows in size beyond two or three groups, the coordinating or decision-making capacity of the liaison role becomes overloaded. One mechanism to overcome these problems is to establish a "temporary" *task force* consisting of one or more representatives from each of the interacting units. Task forces exist only so long as the problem of interaction remains. When a solution is reached, each member returns to his or her normal duties.[17]

For example, suppose a problem has arisen with the customers of a division concerned with product quality. Because this is a problem that has not been encountered before, the divisional vice president appoints a task force to investigate the problem and suggest possible solutions. The task force consists of one member from each of the following units: manufacturing, shipping, sales, research, and development. This task force, shown in exhibit 8–9, is charged with identifying the source of the quality problem, developing and selecting alternative solutions, and implementing whatever solution is chosen. When the problem has been remedied, the task force disbands, and each member returns to his or her respective group.

Teams

Similar to task forces, *teams* are a collection of individual members used to manage intergroup activities where there are more than two or three interacting units. The distinguishing aspect of the team concept is that the problem to be solved usually is long term in nature, requiring a relatively permanent formal assignment to the team. Team members maintain a dual responsibility: one to their primary functional unit, and the second to the team. When the team has accomplished its task, each member returns full-time to the functional assignment.

Exhibit 8–9   Product-Development Task Force

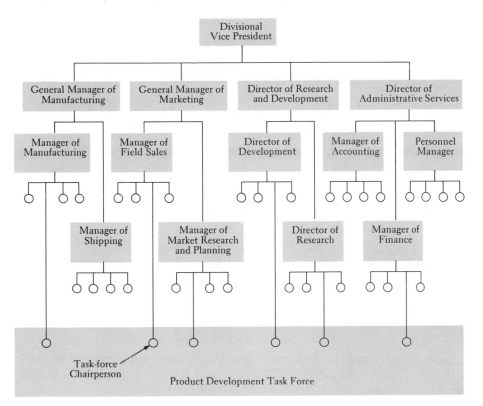

Product Development Task Force

Integrating Departments

As the degree of interaction, information-flow, and integration requirements increase, the frequency and magnitude of intergroup relations may grow beyond the capacity of plans, task forces, or teams. In response to this situation, organizations may seek more permanent, formal, and authority-based mechanisms that represent the general manager's perspective.[18] Such mechanisms are known as *integrating departments*.

In its basic form, an integrating department consists of a single person who carries a title, such as product manager, project manager, brand manager, or group manager. These managers rarely supervise any of the actual work required in intergroup interactions. They are, however, generally held responsible for the effective integration of intergroup activities. Their decision-making authority is acquired through a direct reporting relationship to a higher management position.

When the complexities of intergroup relations increase even more, such as situations in which intergroup decisions are multiple and may have significant impact on the total organization, the organization may seek to increase the importance of the integrating department. This is done by increasing the authority of the department in two ways. First, the department head may be given a number of subordinates or staff specialists who report directly to him or her. Collectively, they form a true integrating department. These subordinates may be specialists in particular areas, such as market research or financial analysis, or in the case of the product-development team, may include one or more members from each of the interacting units. These specialists may report directly to the product manager, and only secondarily to the manager of their functional area.

A second way to increase the authority of the integrating department is to give it a major influence in decision making for the intergroup activities. This can be done by including the integrating department in any decision made by a functional unit or by giving it a major voice in the budgetary process. For example, in the product-development process, the manager of the integrating department would have to approve the change in the development engineering budget related to his or her product line. In extreme cases, the entire budgetary process, from budget planning to allocation and review, may be within the authority of the integrating department.[19]

The integrating department represents the organization's most sophisticated and formal mechanism for managing intergroup relations. The next level of sophistication requires a major rearrangement of the structure of the organization. The topic of organizational structure and design will be discussed in chapters 10 and 11.

Summary

A summary of the various mechanisms or strategies for managing intergroup performance is shown in exhibit 8–10. This table indicates that as the complexities of interaction, information-flow, and integration requirements increase, the organization focuses on two responses: (1) increase in the number of personnel involved in managing intergroup relations; and (2) move from informal to more formal managerial involvement. The effectiveness of achieving a high level of intergroup performance depends not only on the choice of a management strategy but also on the commitment that the organization gives to the improvement of intergroup relations. The choice of such mechanisms as teams and integrating departments may require a significant departure from the management philosophy of the organization. Such departures from traditional norms may have repercussions in other parts of the organization, upsetting the degree of participation and the balance of power and causing the development of dysfunctional conflicts between organizational units. Two of these aspects—power and conflict—will be discussed in the next two sections.

Intergroup Power Relationships

In the discussion of intergroup power, we will examine three related topic areas: (1) the different *dimensions* of power in intergroup relations; (2) the various *determinants* of power; and (3) how different organizational groups or units *acquire* power over other units.

Exhibit 8–10 Strategies for Managing Intergroup Performance

Strategy	Description
1. Rules and Procedures	The required activities and behavior between interacting groups are spelled out in advance. Employees learn that when certain situations arise, a particular behavior set should be used. Rules are a limited strategy; they cannot specify all behaviors in advance.
2. Hierarchy	When rules and procedures prove inadequate as an intergroup management strategy, the emphasis switches to the use of the hierarchy, or common superior. This is a limited strategy in that the higher-level manager's time may be totally devoted to resolving intergroup plans.
3. Planning	Goals and targets are set for group interaction. The effectiveness of the strategy is limited by the complexities of interaction and how precisely future interaction patterns can be detailed in advance.
4. Liaison or Internal Boundary-Spanning Roles	A specialized, generally informal role is created to transmit vital information and coordinate intergroup activities. Certain dysfunctions, such as role conflict, may affect the behavior of the liaison person.
5. Task Forces	Selected members of interacting groups are brought together to form a task force. Task forces generally coordinate intergroup activities for a specific period of time, and thus are temporary in nature. They are also limited to an advisory role, leaving the final decision making to higher-level managers.
6. Teams	Similar to task forces, teams are more permanent and may be given certain decision-making authority.
7. Integrating Departments	These provide the most formal strategies for managing intergroup performance. The department manager generally reports to the highest management level and may be given great decision-making authority, consisting of a large staff and budgetary responsibility.

Power relationships involving intergroup relations can be thought of as focusing on the elements of *influence* and *dependency*. First, *power* may be defined as one group's ability to influence another group or groups to carry out certain directives or orders.[20] For example, we can say that the board of directors of a corporation has power over the top management team if the latter responds to the directives (e.g., changes in the company's dividend policies) of the board of directors.

The influence of one group on another group's behavior, however, also involves the element of *dependence*. For example, in a hospital the x-ray technicians are dependent on the physicians in proportion to the technicians' need for patients, which the physicians can provide, and in inverse proportion to the availability of these patients from sources other than the group of physicians.[21] In intergroup relations, the physicians will have power over other groups, such as the technicians, to the extent that the physicians have the capacity to fulfill the requirements of other groups and to the degree to which the physicians monopolize this ability.

As another example, consider two separate chemical-processing plants, plant A and plant B, within a large chemical-manufacturing complex. Each plant produces a separate product line; however, one of the raw-material inputs for plant B is a byproduct of the process of plant A. Under these conditions, we would say that plant A has a form of power over plant B because the byproduct of A is required for the continued operation of B and there are no other sources of this raw material available to plant B. The power of plant A over B, however, would be diminished if substitute raw materials could be used in B's process or if other sources of this raw material could be located.

Dimensions of Intergroup Power

There are two major dimensions of power that relate to intergroup behavior: (1) scope or weight; and (2) domain.[22] The *scope* or *weight* of power is the range of activities and the extent or degree to which the behavior of one group can influence the behavior of another group. For example, consider the Fisher Body Division of General Motors, which is responsible for the manufacture of the majority of automobile frames for this company. In relationship to the Buick Division, Fisher Body has a great deal of power, from a scope or weight perspective, because without frames from its only source, the assembly of Buicks would cease after inventory has run out. Similarly, integrating departments with budgetary responsibility have significant power over, for example, the manufacturing department when it comes to allocating financial resources.

The *domain* of power relates to the number of other groups a given group influences by its behavior. In the General Motors example, Fisher Body has significant power because its domain of power includes all the company divisions (i.e., Chevrolet, Pontiac, Oldsmobile, Buick, Cadillac, GMC, and so on). An integrating department can have domain power over all other interacting groups (i.e., manufacturing, marketing, engineering, and so on). The power of one group over other groups is greatest when scope or weight and domain are large. A decrease in either of these dimensions will result in a lower level of power.

Determinants of Intergroup Power

Earlier in this chapter, we pointed out that certain intergroup characteristics—interdependence, task uncertainty, and time and goal orientations—were related to the major requirements for intergroup performance—namely, interaction, information-flow, and integration requirements. The determinants of intergroup power are also related to the intergroup characteristics and performance requirements. This relationship is shown in exhibit 8–11.

This exhibit indicates that there are potentially three determinants of intergroup power: (1) the degree of success that an interacting group has in *coping with uncertainty;* (2) the degree to which one group can obtain, or *substitute,* the ac-

Exhibit 8–11 Determinants of Intergroup Power

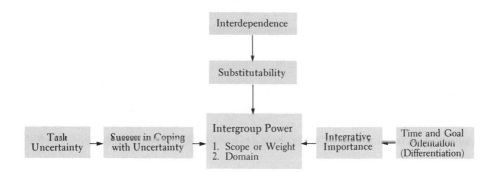

tivities, services, or resources provided by another group from alternative sources; and (3) the *importance* of a group as an *integrating mechanism* with other interacting groups.[23]

Coping with uncertainty.   Uncertainty, as we discussed previously, is inherent in many organizational tasks and concerns the lack of information about future events such that alternative actions and their outcomes are unpredictable. Uncertainty itself is not a determinant of power; the ability to *cope* with and *control uncertainty* in intergroup relations is. The lifeblood of any organization involves the effectiveness or certainty with which inputs can be transformed into goods and services. Therefore, those groups or units that cope with or control the most uncertainty should be accorded the greater intergroup power because this "uncertainty absorption" reduces the impact of uncertainty on other groups in the organization.[24] This coping with uncertainty confers power through the dependencies that are created.[25]

For example, consider the relationship between a manufacturing plant and the marketing group. Because of its time and goal orientation toward the control of costs, quantity, and quality, the management of the manufacturing plant seeks to obtain a smooth and continuous production flow. Customer orders from the marketing groups may entail a number of differing order quantities and product quality levels, so that the stability of the production process could be interrupted. In order to control this uncertainty, a production scheduling and control group may be formed. The purpose of this group would be to take customer orders and aggregate them so that the manufacturing managers can produce long, similar production runs that also satisfy marketing's needs by providing the customer with delivery within an acceptable period of time. The performance of the production scheduling and control group acts to control the uncertainty for both the manufacturing and marketing groups. Therefore, this group is accorded a certain level of power over the other groups.

Substitutability.   Another determinant of intergroup power is the degree to which a group can obtain the resources and services required for its performance from one or more different sources. There is an inverse relationship between substitutability and power; that is, the less the needed resources and services of a group can be substituted, the greater will be its power over the groups it supplies.[26] As shown in exhibit 8–11, substitutability is related to the interdependence between two or more groups. That is, as the interdependence between two or more groups increases from pooled to sequential to reciprocal, there is less substitutability between groups, and thus, greater centralization of power in one or more of the groups.

Consider, for example, the relationship between the aircraft operations and aircraft maintenance functions of a large domestic airline corporation. These two functions can be considered to be reciprocally interdependent. The output of the maintenance function (a fully operational airliner) is an input for the operations function. In addition, the output (or byproduct) of operations (an airliner needing maintenance) is an input for the maintenance function. Power, as determined by substitutability, can be accorded each of these functions over the other by different mechanisms. The maintenance function can have power over the operations function if it has only one major maintenance shop (e.g., Houston, Texas), which requires operations to schedule all aircraft needing maintenance through this central shop. A significant rearrangement of aircraft scheduling to get the airliner to the maintenance area may be necessary. If the maintenance function opens other regional maintenance shops, this substitutability reduces its power over operations. Conversely, if the maintenance function depends solely upon the aircraft from its own company for its work, operations is accorded power over the maintenance function. On the other hand, if, during idle times, maintenance can repair other aircraft not belonging to its parent company, this substitutability reduces the power of operations over the maintenance function.

Integrative importance.   The third determinant of intergroup power concerns the *degree of integrative importance* a group has to the overall success and performance of intergroup behavior.[27] This integrative importance is a function of two elements: (1) the degree to which the resources provided by one group are connected to the activities of other groups (resource requirements); and (2) the impact on the organization's performance if the integrative group would be eliminated (performance impact). The greater the resource requirements and performance impact of a group, the greater its power over other groups.

In a hospital, the accounting department provides resources and interacts with many other hospital functions. If it were eliminated, however, the hospital's performance would be impeded, but not to the point at which the survival of the hospital would be in question. On the other hand, the department of nursing not only provides resources and interacts with many other units, but its elimination would create severe problems to the hospital's performance in providing quality patient care. Therefore, the accounting department would have a moderate level of power over other hospital units, but the department of nursing's power would be much greater due to its integrative importance to the performance of the hospital.

A similar point can be made with the different strategies used to manage intergroup behavior and performance. Liaison managers may interact with only two units, and could be eliminated without a great deal of disruption to intergroup performance, at least in the short run. However, integrating departments interact with many different organizational units. The elimination of this integrating department before its task is accomplished could have a significant impact on the organization's performance because the major decisions and coordinative responsibilities may reside within this department. The power of the intergroup management strategy increases as the organization proceeds along the continuum, shown in exhibit 8–7, from rules to integrating departments.

Cooperative Strategies for Power Acquisition

Even when power relationships are established through uncertainty coping, substitutability, and integrative importance, there exist other organizational strategies that groups can use to acquire intergroup power. These strategies are called *cooperative strategies* because they involve an agreement between two or more groups for the adjustment of intergroup relations.[28]

Power-acquisition strategies are a conscious agreement between two or more groups to reduce the uncertainty one group's activities have on each of the other interacting groups. That is, the effective achievement of power for the group of x-ray technicians rests on its ability to negotiate a work agreement with the physicians group, whereby the uncertainty of each group about the other is controlled. There are three basic cooperative strategies for acquiring intergroup power: (1) contracting; (2) co-opting; and (3) coalescing.

Contracting.   The negotiation of an agreement between two or more groups for the controlled exchange or guaranteed interactions for the future is called *contracting*. Collective bargaining agreements between management and labor are an example. Each group poses a degree of uncertainty to the other group; management requires a stable, productive work force in order to attain corporate economic goals; labor desires adequate wage scales, benefits, and job security. Through a successful collective bargaining agreement, these uncertainties posed by each group on the other are removed for a period generally of one to three years. The result is that both management and labor acquire a certain level of power through the control of uncertainty and the stability of the dependency relationship.

Co-opting.   The second cooperative power acquisition strategy, *co-opting,* is defined as the process of absorbing new elements or groups into the leadership or policy-making structure of an organization as a means of averting threats to its stability or survival.[29] By absorbing, or co-opting, other interacting groups, the uncertainty of the effects of one group on the other can be controlled.

For example, in order to maintain stable relationships with financial lending institutions, corporations may add to their board of directors representatives of prominent banks with which they interact for financial support. In order to maintain a stable supply of crude oil, a medium-sized oil company specializing in refining and marketing oil-related products may absorb, through a purchase or merger, another company that specializes in crude-oil exploration and transportation. Also, within an organization, rather than have separate and autonomous units for manufacturing and shipping, a new arrangement may be developed so that the particular shipping area is absorbed, or co-opted, into the manufacturing unit.

Although each of these examples of co-opting results in a decrease in the uncertainty that one group poses for another group, it is a more constraining form of cooperation than contracting because certain negative consequences can develop. For example, when co-optation is effective, it adds to the co-opting group an element that is in a position to raise questions and exert influence on other aspects of the group's activity. It would be naive to think that the financial institution representatives on a board of directors of an organization would limit their influence and interactions to financial procurement or allocation issues alone. By the nature of their position on the board, they have the right to impact on such decisions as management succession, new product development, dividend policies, and so on.

Coalescing.   A combination or joint venture by one organizational group with another group for the purpose of reducing uncertainty is called *coalescing.* A coalition is formed between two or more groups when contracting and co-opting either are impossible to obtain or are ineffective in reducing the dependency of one group on another group, resulting in a high level of uncertainty in intergroup interactions.

In politics, particularly in the international realm, coalitions are frequently used mechanisms for gaining power. This is particularly true where a multi-party political system exists when the main political party receives less than a majority of the vote. In order to gain control and to remove the uncertainty of the interactions of other political entities, the main political party may form a coalition with one of the minority groups. The result is a coalition that may act as a unified group with respect to certain goals. Such political coalitions can be unstable, however, particularly when there is disagreement among coalition members. If a disagreement becomes uncontrollable, the minority party may remove their support, resulting in high uncertainty, and most probably, a call for a new election.

In other organizations, the *dominant coalition,* or more specifically, the executive team, plays a prominent role in the decision making of the organization.[30] Due to growing size and complexity of many organizations, there is generally a wide distribution of power. Few organizations can function effectively without a consolidation of power in the form of a central figure with his or her select group. In a broad discussion of power in organizations, Zaleznik states:

> The failure to establish a coalition within the executive structure of an organization can result in severe consequences, such as paralysis in the form of inability to make decisions and to evaluate performance, and in-fighting and overt rivalry within the executive group.[31]

Without a dominant coalition to centralize and control the wide distribution of power in organizations, uncertainty will pervade, resulting in a lack of direction, absence of common goals, conflict, and lower organizational performance.

Examples of dominant coalitions are found in all types of organizations, such as church or parish councils in religious organizations, executive committees in corporations, management groups in hospitals, and administrative committees in colleges of business. If the coalition and coalition members represent and promote the main goals, objectives, and purposes of the organization, they will be retained. If they do not, the coalition will be disbanded, and a new one will be formed.

The Consequences and Outcomes of Power

The elements relating to the discussion of intergroup power are summarized in exhibit 8–12. Power is seen as being determined and acquired through two mechanisms: (1) positional determinants (uncertainty coping, substitutability, and integrative importance); and (2) organizational strategies (contracting, co-opting, and coalescing). The results of intergroup power are shown to involve both *consequences* and outcomes.

The consequences of intergroup power concern the important behavioral processes of compliance and involvement.[32] *Compliance* describes the behavior of a group or individual that yields to a powerful other either to get an expected reward or to avoid being punished. There are three forms of establishing compliance with which we are most familiar: *remunerative, coercive,* and *normative.* The most common form in organizations is remunerative, which relates to power through the allocation of pay, fringe benefits, job assignments, and the like. The coercive basis of compliance, the threat or application of some form of punishment, is most readily seen in prisons; prisoners adhere to the stated rules in order to avoid punitive actions from the guards. Finally, normative rewards for compliance relate to control through the

Exhibit 8–12   Summary of Intergroup Power Relations

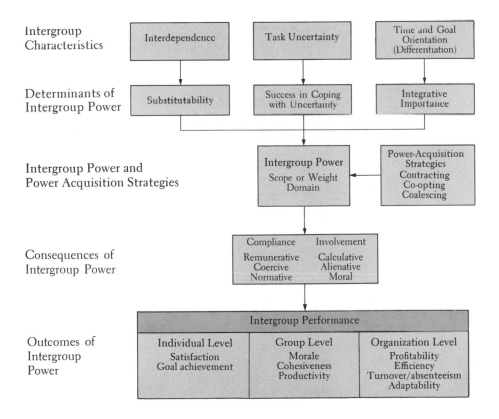

257

manipulation of symbolic rewards, such as prestige or esteem, or through moral persuasion. An example would be compliant behavior to the teachings of various religious institutions.

Three types of *involvement* of people in organizations are usually associated with the form used to demand compliance: *calculative* for remunerative (compliance as a means to an end, or the attainment of a self-goal), *alienative* for coercive (compliance, but an intensely negative orientation), and *moral* for normative (internalization of norms and identification with those in authority).

The important factor for managers to understand is that the effectiveness of the organization is related strongly to the proper use of power; in other words, there must be congruence between the basis used to achieve compliance and the form of involvement. For example, a bank will be more effective if it relies on a good wage and salary program than if it attempts to get compliance and involvement through the use of moral persuasion or the promise of prestige factors. Similarly, a church will be more effective if it bases its desired compliance and involvement on moral teachings than on threats of punishment or physical sanctions. In essence, if power is properly used, the end result is a set of positive *outcomes* for the organization. When power is improperly used—when incorrect bases of compliance and involvement are forced on the organization's participants—dysfunctional behavior and lower levels of effectiveness generally result.

Because organizations are complex and dynamic entities, intergroup relations cannot always be effectively maintained by management strategies or through the exercise of power. This disruption in intergroup behavior is termed *intergroup conflict* and is the subject of the next section.

Intergroup Conflict

The various subunits that make up an organization develop different and highly specialized ways of viewing their work and the work of other groups. When these different groups interact during the course of everyday activities, there is also the potential for intergroup conflict.

The manner in which organizations view and treat intergroup conflict has changed measurably during the last fifty years. These different approaches to intergroup conflict, traditional and contemporary, are shown in exhibit 8–13.

The old-line, traditional approach views intergroup conflict as something to be avoided, caused by personality conflicts or a failure of leadership, and resolved only by physically separating the conflicting parties or by a superior's intervention. The contemporary approach, however, views intergroup conflict as an inevitable consequence of organizational interactions, caused primarily by the complexities of our organizational systems. Through such mechanisms as problem-solving approaches, the solution of conflict may help to bring about positive organizational change. In our examination of intergroup conflict, we will focus on two topics: (1) sources of intergroup conflict; and (2) possible conflict-resolution strategies.

Exhibit 8–13 Traditional and Contemporary Views of Intergroup Conflict

Traditional View	Intergroup Conflict	Contemporary View
Conflict is dysfunctional to the organization and should be avoided.	Philosophy	Conflict is an inevitable consequence of organizational interactions, and can be resolved by identifying the sources of conflict.
Conflict is caused by personality differences and a failure of leadership.	Cause	Conflict is generally the result of the complexities of organizational systems.
Conflict is resolved by physical separation or the intervention by higher management levels.	Resolution	Conflict is resolved through identifying the causes and problem solving. Conflict can be a force for positive change in organizations.

Sources of Intergroup Conflict

There are three basic sources of intergroup conflict: (1) goal incompatibility; (2) decision-making requirements; and (3) performance expectations. These sources of intergroup conflict are shown in exhibit 8–14. The three characteristics of intergroup behavior—interdependence, task uncertainty, and time and goal orientation—discussed earlier in this chapter also serve as preconditions for intergroup conflict.

Goal incompatibility. *Goal incompatibility,* which is defined as the lack of agreement concerning the direction of group activity and the criteria for evaluating task

Exhibit 8–14 Sources of Intergroup Conflict

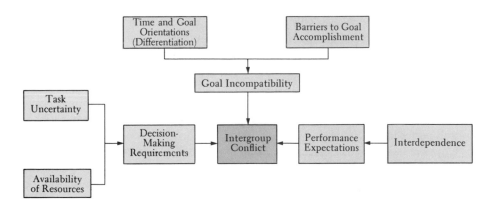

accomplishment, is the most frequently identified source for intergroup conflict.[33] Two elements contribute to goal incompatibility: (1) time and goal orientation; and (2) barriers to goal accomplishment.

Different time (short versus long term) and goal (techno-economic, market, and scientific) orientations create a state of differentiation between two or more interacting groups. When two widely differing groups, such as manufacturing (short-term and techno-economic orientation) and research (long-term and scientific orientation) interact, this state of *time and goal orientation* differentiation can act as a source of conflict.

If goal attainment by one group is seen as preventing other groups from achieving their goals, *barriers to goal accomplishment* arise. For example, one of the large automobile manufacturers may be contemplating the introduction of a radically new engine for its small-sized cars. Because this new venture requires considerable capital investment, top management has decided to introduce the new engine in only one of its many automobile divisions (e.g., Chevrolet, Pontiac, Oldsmobile, Buick, or Cadillac). Because the new engine may create a competitive advantage in the marketplace, each of the divisions may desire the new engine, but only one will receive it in the short term. Those divisions not receiving the new engine face a significant barrier to their goal accomplishments.

Decision-making requirements.   The second potential source of intergroup conflict concerns the particular requirements for decision making used by each of the interacting groups. Two aspects are related to decision-making requirements: (1) degree of task uncertainty; and (2) the availability of resources.

Degree of task uncertainty refers to one of the basic characteristics of intergroup behavior. As we noted earlier, the nature of the particular task being performed by each of the interacting groups may require different amounts of information flow before a decision can be reached. The greater the task uncertainty inherent in each task, the greater the need for additional information. Thus, conflict can arise between two interacting groups when one of the groups desires additional information before they believe a decision can be reached.

Availability of resources causes conflict when there is a struggle between interacting groups for limited resources needed to accomplish their goals. An organization must divide limited financial, equipment, and manpower resources among different groups in what they believe is the most efficient and equitable manner. However, what is perceived by one group as efficient and equitable may not be perceived in a similar manner by other groups. A group that believes it is not receiving a fair share of the organizational resources relative to other groups often becomes upset and antagonistic toward the organization and other groups. This conflict situation can result in such negative consequences as withholding information, disruptive behavior, and similar dysfunctional activities that can adversely affect the organization's overall performance.

Consider the applied research and development division of a large manufacturing company. During the budgeting process, the director of research may ask to be allocated additional money in order to hire ten additional scientists. The director of development may also ask for approval to hire ten development engineers. The organization, faced with limited sources of funds, may approve the hiring of eight engineers, but only three new scientists. Unless there has been a mutual agreement between top management and each of the two divisions, this situation may serve to promote ill will and future conflict situations between the two groups.

Performance expectations.   The third source of intergroup conflict concerns the situation in which the activities or performance of one group affects the subsequent performance of other groups. For example, in hospitals, surgeons perform their function after the anesthesiologists have successfully performed their role; on assembly lines, tires are placed on automobiles after workers have installed the brakes; and carpenters construct the frame of a house after the concrete slab has been poured.

Performance expectations in intergroup behavior are directly related to the type of interdependence existing between groups. The nature of the three types of interdependence presented earlier in this chapter—pooled, sequential, and reciprocal—pose a respectively increasing potential for conflict between interacting groups. That is, as intergroup relations progress from pooled to reciprocal interdependence, there is an increasing dependence of one group on another to perform their particular task. When one group acts improperly or fails to meet the performance expectations of the other group, a potential conflict situation can arise. This potential for conflict is greatest with reciprocal interdependence due to the intensity of the interactions between groups.

Effects of Intergroup Conflict

As an example of intergroup conflict, consider two political candidates and their respective organizations who are associated with the same political party, but are vigorously fighting each other during a primary runoff for a U.S. Senate position. Conflict, in this case, has its origins in goal incompatability and decision-making requirements; they stand in the way of each other (i.e., barriers to goal accomplishment) in order to obtain the single position (i.e., availability of resources). When conflict exists, we can expect to see changes in two areas: (1) changes within each group; and (2) changes between each group.

Changes within each group

At least four behaviors can be observed within conflicting groups:

1. *Cohesiveness increases between members.* Similar to our discussion in chapter 7, an external threat causes a group to pull together as a unit. In our example above, behavior in each campaign organization would stress unity of purpose, the group becomes more attractive and important to individual members, and loyalty and conformity are accepted, while individual differences of opinion are set aside. Personal sacrifice, such as putting in long hours or going without lunch or dinner, are the norm.

2. *The group becomes more task oriented.* There is less idle time or "goofing off"; all efforts are directed to meeting the challenge of the other group. Political workers become more serious and concerned with the importance of their task.

3. *There is an increased emphasis on organization.* In order to assure successful task accomplishment, an increased focus is placed on rules, procedures, and centralization of responsibilities. New rules are created and enforced.

4. *Leadership becomes more autocratically based.* Consistent with points 2 and 3 above, there is less tolerance for participative behaviors; there is a demand for strong, definitive leadership. Most political campaign chairpersons become "no nonsense" leaders; they become adept at issuing orders and making quick, almost unilateral decisions. The crisis nature of political activities place a high value on the ability to control peoples' behaviors.

Changes between conflicting groups

Four behaviors also characterize the changes in activities between conflicting groups:

1. *Hostility and negative attitudes increase.* The rival group is seen as the "enemy" and are viewed with hostility. The other political campaign workers, and even the candidate himself or herself, are frequently viewed and discussed on the basis of their weaknesses.

2. *Negative stereotypes become dominant.* In political activities, we frequently see attempts by one party to "label" the other candidates in negative tones: for example, they are characterized as for big business and against the little person, minorities, and a strong defensive posture toward international foes. One candidate is "good," and the other is "bad."

3. *Communication between groups decreases.* As conflict grows, the level of interaction and communications between groups diminishes. The other group has nothing good or of value to say. In addition, interacting with the other group is contrary to the group's new cohesion; fraternizing with the enemy is viewed as nonconformist or deviant behavior and is not tolerated. In other words, not speaking to the other group members is viewed as a norm. We frequently see in political campaigns candidates who refuse to talk to each other or even shake hands.

4. *The other group's activities are closely monitored.* There is an increased emphasis on surveillance activities on the other group. The observed behaviors are not only used to evaluate their performance but also to check for illegal activities that may serve to verify the negative stereotypes.

The behavior of conflicting parties in most organizations rarely degenerates into open hostility, although some union-management conflicts may be considered exceptions. Negative stereotypes, decreased communications, and surveillance activities are typical reactions to intergroup conflict in most organizations.

Strategies for Resolving Intergroup Conflict

Because intergroup conflict is inherent in the nature of today's complex organizations, it is necessary that management be capable of resolving this conflict before the dysfunctional consequences affect organizational performance. The ability to minimize and resolve conflict successfully is an important skill that managers must develop. The various strategies for minimizing and resolving intergroup conflict can be classified into three categories: (1) avoidance; (2) defusion; and (3) confrontation.[34]

Avoidance

The avoidance strategy involves a general disregard for the causes of the conflict by enabling the conflict to continue only under certain controlled conditions. Three separate methods prevail under an avoidance philosophy: (1) nonattention; (2) physical separation; and (3) limited interaction.

Nonattention involves the manager totally avoiding or ignoring the dysfunctional situation. Individuals tend to "look the other way" or disregard hostile actions in hopes that the situation will resolve itself in time. Because the sources of conflict are not identified by this method, it is likely that the situation will continue or worsen with time.

Physical separation involves actually moving conflicting groups physically apart from each other. The rationale for this strategy is that if the groups cannot interact, conflict will diminish. The disadvantages of this strategy are that not only have the sources of the conflict not been identified, but if the groups are highly interdependent, physical separation will adversely affect the overall effectiveness of the organization. It is at best only a stopgap measure and may eventually require more organizational resources for continuous surveillance to keep the groups separate.

Limited interaction is not an all-inclusive strategy, as is physical separation, because conflicting parties are permitted to interact on a limited basis. Interactions are permitted generally under only formal situations, such as a meeting at which a strict agenda is followed. The same disadvantages caused by physical separation (i.e., sources of conflict still prevail, problems of high interdependency, and future dysfunctional consequences) can result from a limited interaction strategy.

Defusion

Defusion strategy attempts to buy time until the conflict between two groups become less emotional or less crucial. It involves solving minor points of disagreement, but allows the major points to linger or diminish in importance with time. Two particular methods are classified as defusion strategies: (1) smoothing; and (2) compromise.

Smoothing involves a process of playing down the differences between two groups while accentuating their similarities and common interests. Identifying and stressing similarities and common interests between conflicting parties can eventually lead to the groups realizing that they are not as far apart (e.g., goal incompatibility) as they initially believed. Although building on a common viewpoint is preferable to an avoidance philosophy, the sources of conflict have not been fully confronted and remain under the surface. Sooner or later, the central conflict issues will surface, possibly creating a more severe situation in the future.

Compromise is a "give and take" exchange, resulting in neither a clear winner nor loser. Compromise can be utilized when the object, goal, or resource in conflict can be divided up in some way between the competing groups. In other cases, one group may yield on one point if it can gain something in exchange from the other group. Some types of management-labor negotiations can be viewed as compromise. For example, management will agree to a cost-of-living pay increase if labor will guarantee productivity level increases. Compromise is generally effective when the conflicting groups are relatively equal in strength. However, in situations where one of the groups is significantly stronger or in a better position than the second group, a compromise strategy would probably not work because the stronger group would hold out for a one-sided solution.

The important point to remember about using a compromise strategy is that because each group gives up some position, neither group may be totally satisfied with the outcome. Because of this, a compromise solution is usually only temporary, and the sources of conflict that initiated the situation may occur again in the future.

Confrontation

This final conflict-resolution strategy, confrontation, differs from avoidance and diffusion approaches in that the sources of conflict are generally identified and discussed, which emphasizes the attainment of the common interests of the conflicting groups. Three techniques are categorized as confrontation methods: (1) mutual personnel exchange; (2) emphasis on a superordinate goal; and (3) problem-solving or confrontation meetings.

Mutual personnel exchange involves increasing the communication and understanding between groups by exchanging personnel for a period of time. The basic assumption underlying this strategy is that the exchanged personnel can learn about the other group and communicate their impressions back to their original group. For example, a common practice among manufacturing firms is to have shipping supervisors and sales representatives exchange roles. During the short exchange period (usually three to six weeks), it is hoped that each will gain an appreciation for the other's job. This approach is limited because it is only a temporary solution mechanism. In addition, on their return to their permanent group, the exchanged personnel may be treated as outsiders, which may result in their knowledge and opinions not being fully utilized.

Superordinate goals are common, more important goals on which the conflicting parties can focus their attention.[35] Such goals are unattainable by one group alone and generally supersede all other goals of each group. A common superordinate goal could be the survival of the organization. Petty differences are considered unimportant when the survival of the overall organization is in question.

A number of preconditions are required for this technique to be a successful conflict-resolution mechanism. First, mutual dependency of the groups is required. Second, the superordinate goal must be desired by each group and have a high degree of value attached to it. Finally, there must be some form of reward for accomplishing the goal. By identifying and working toward a common interest, superordinate goals provide a realistic strategy for resolving intergroup conflict.

Problem-solving involves bringing together conflicting groups in order to conduct a formal confrontation meeting. The objective of this approach is to have the groups present their views and opinions to each other and work through the differences in attitudes and perceptions. Issues regarding who is right or wrong are not allowed; only the discussion of the identification of problems and possible solution alternatives is permitted. This technique is most effective when a thorough analysis of the problem and identification of points of mutual interest can be made and alternatives can be suggested. A problem-solving approach, however, requires a great deal of time and commitment and usually is ineffective when the source of conflict originates from value-laden issues.

Applications and Implications for the Manager

Intergroup Behavior

1. Managers must be aware that three basic characteristics pervade all intergroup interactions: interdependencies, task uncertainty, and time and goal orientations.
   (a) *Interdependence,* which can be pooled, sequential, or reciprocal, involves increasing degrees of dependency between groups.
   (b) *Task uncertainty* concerns the relative predictability workers experience with respect to the results of their work. It is a function of the degree of task clarity and the complexities of the task environment.
   (c) *Time and goal orientation* refers to the differences in time (short term versus long term) and goal orientations (science, market, and techno-economic) that exist between interaction groups.

2. The three intergroup characteristics create three distinct determinants of intergroup performance: interaction requirements, information-flow requirements, and integration requirements. The ability to manage intergroup behavior becomes increasingly difficult as these three requirements increase.

3. A number of different intergroup management strategies are available to managers. Rules and procedures, hierarchy, planning, and the use of liaison roles are usually adequate mechanisms to handle many intergroup interactions. However, when the interaction, information-flow, and integration requirements increase, organizations must adopt more formal strategies, such as task forces, teams, or integrating departments. The use of such mechanisms requires a greater amount of resources and a higher level of commitment to manage intergroup performance.

4. Power is seen as an influence-dependency process, and varies in terms of domain and scope or weight.

5. Power is accorded groups by two mechanisms: (1) by acquisition mechanisms, such as uncertainty coping, substitutability, and integrative importance; and (2) by cooperative strategies, such as contracting, co-opting, and coalescing.

6. Coalition management is an important power-acquisition strategy used by many organizations. Dominant coalitions generally represent the top-management team and are responsible for the major policy-making decisions in organizations. If the dominant coalition does not adequately promote the goals, objectives, and purposes of the organization, the overall performance of the organization may suffer or the coalition will be replaced.

7. Intergroup conflict is inevitable. The manager should not view conflict as a failure of leadership, but as a consequence of the complexities of modern organizations. In some cases, conflict can be a focus for positive change.

8. The major sources of conflict—goal incompatibility, decision-making requirements, and performance expectations—are related (as in intergroup power) to the three main intergroup characteristics of interdependence, task uncertainty, and time and goal orientation.

9. Intergroup conflict in organizations cannot be totally eliminated; it can, however, be minimized or resolved. The strategies for conflict resolution include avoidance, defusion, and confrontation. Avoidance and defusion are questionable tactics because the sources of conflict are rarely identified and discussed. The

dysfunctional consequences of conflict may occur again.

10. A confrontation strategy is more appropriate for today's organizations because it focuses on both the causes and possible resolution mechanisms. Three potential confrontation approaches were discussed: mutual personnel exchange, superordinate goals, and problem solving. Each requires the manager to develop both diagnostic skills and the knowledge and ability to work through a conflict-resolution strategy.

Review of Theories, Research, and Applications

1. Why is diagnosis an important managerial skill for improving intergroup performance?

2. Discuss how interdependence, task uncertainty, and time and goal orientation are related to: (1) intergroup performance; (2) power; and (3) conflict.

3. Why does reciprocal interdependence pose greater problems for the management of intergroup behavior than pooled or sequential interdependence?

4. Under what conditions would a task force or team approach be more appropriate for intergroup management than liaison roles?

5. Discuss the advantages and disadvantages of contracting, co-opting, and coalescing as power acquisition mechanisms.

6. Why is goal incompatibility usually identified as the major cause of intergroup conflict?

7. Explain why some intergroup conflict may be a desirable force in organizations.

8. Discuss the importance of the dominant coalition in organizations.

9. Why are superordinate goals difficult to formulate and implement as a conflict-resolution strategy?

10. Why is an avoidance approach to conflict resolution typically viewed as a short-term strategy?

Notes

1. Jay W. Lorsch and Paul R. Lawrence, "Organization for Product Innovation," *Harvard Business Review,* May–June 1965, pp. 109–22.

2. James D. Thompson, *Organizations in Action* (New York: McGraw-Hill, 1967), pp. 54–55.

3. Jay W. Lorsch and J. J. Morse, *Organizations and Their Members: A Contingency Approach* (New York: Harper & Row, 1974),

4. William R. Dill, "Environment as an Influence on Managerial Autonomy," *Administrative Science Quarterly* (March 1958), pp. 409–43.

5. E. H. Neilsen, "Understanding and Managing Intergroup Conflict," in *Managing Group and Intergroup Relations,* ed. Jay W. Lorsch and Paul R. Lawrence (Homewood, Ill.: Irwin, 1972), pp. 34–39.

6. Paul R. Lawrence and Jay W. Lorsch, *Organization and Environment* (Homewood, Ill.: Irwin, 1969), pp. 34–39.

7. Ibid., p. 37.

8. Ibid., p. 39.

9. Jay W. Galbraith, *Designing Complex Organizations* (Reading, Mass.: Addison-Wesley, 1973), p. 4.

10. Lawrence and Lorsch, *Organization and Environment,* p. 11.

11. Galbraith, *Designing Complex Organizations,* p. 15.

12. James G. March and Herbert A. Simon, *Organizations* (New York: Wiley, 1958), p. 44.

13. Max Weber, *The Theory of Social and Economic Organization,* trans. A. M. Henderson and Talcott Parsons (New York: Oxford, 1947).

14. Galbraith, *Designing Complex Organizations,* p. 12.

15. Robert L. Kahn et al., *Organizational Stress: Studies in Role Conflict and Ambiguity* (New York: Wiley, 1964), p. 101.

16. Robert T. Keller and W. E. Holland, "Boundary Spanning Activity and Research and Development Management: A Comparative Study," *IEEE Transactions on Engineering Management,* November 1975, pp. 130–33.

17. Galbraith, *Designing Complex Organizations,* p. 80.

18. Ibid., p. 89.

19. A more complex management strategy, termed *matrix organizational design,* will be presented in chapter 11.

20. Talcott Parsons, *The Social System* (Glencoe, N.Y.: Free Press, 1951), p. 121.

21. R. M. Emerson, "Power Dependence Relations," *American Sociological Review,* February 1962, pp. 20–32.

22. A. Kaplan, "Power in Perspective," in *Power and Conflict in Organizations,* ed. Robert L. Kahn and Kenneth E. Boulding (London: Tavistock, 1964), pp. 11–32.

23. D. J. Hickson et al., "A Strategic Contingencies Theory of Interorganizational Power," *Administrative Science Quarterly,* March 1971, pp. 216–29.

24. Thompson, *Organizations in Action,* p. 13.

25. Hickson et al., "A Strategic Contingencies Theory," p. 220.

26. Robert Dubin, "Power and Union-Management Relations," *Administrative Science Quarterly,* January 1957, pp. 60–81.

27. Hickson et al., "A Strategic Contingencies Theory," p. 221.

28. Thompson, *Organizations in Action,* pp. 34–35.

29. P. Selznick, *TVA and the Grass Roots* (Berkeley: University of California, 1949).

30. Thompson, *Organizations in Action,* p. 130.

31. Abraham Zaleznik, "Power and Politics in Organizational Life," *Harvard Business Review,* May–June 1970, p. 51.

32. Amitai Etzioni, *A Comparative Analysis of Complex Organizations* (Glencoe, N.Y.: Free Press, 1961).

33. S. M. Schmidt and T. A. Kochan, "Conflict: Towards Conceptual Clarity," *Administrative Quarterly Review,* July 1972, pp. 359–70.

34. Robert R. Blake and Jane S. Mouton, *Managing Intergroup Conflict in Industry* (Houston: Gulf Publishing, 1964).

35. M. Sherif and C. W. Sherif, *Social Psychology* (New York: Harper & Row, 1969), pp. 228–62.

Additional References

BLAU, P. M. *Exchange and Power in Social Life.* New York: Wiley, 1967.

CYERT, R. M., and MARCH, J. G. *A Behavioral Theory of the Firm.* Englewood Cliffs, N.J.: Prentice-Hall, 1963.

DRUCKER, P. F. *Management: Tasks, Responsibilities, Practices.* New York: Harper & Row, 1973.

DUTTON, J. M., and WALTON, R. E. "Interdepartmental Conflict and Cooperation: Two Contrasting Studies." *Human Organizations,* Fall 1966, pp. 207–20.

FILLEY, A. C. *Interpersonal Conflict Resolution.* Glenview, Ill.: Scott, Foresman, 1975.

LAWRENCE, P. R., and LORSCH, J. W. "New

Management Job: The Integrator."
Harvard Business Review,
September–October 1967, pp. 142–51.

LITTERER, J. A. "Conflict in Organizations:
A Re-examination." *Academy of
Management Journal,* September 1966,
pp. 178–86.

McCLELLAND, D. C. *Power: The Inner
Experience.* New York: Wiley, 1975.

ORGAN, D. W. "Some Variables Affecting
Boundary Role Behavior." *Sociometry,*
1971, pp. 524–37.

PONDY, L. "Varieties of Organizational
Conflict." *Administrative Science
Quarterly,* May 1969, pp. 499–507.

ROBBINS, S. P. *Managing Organizational
Conflict: A Non-Traditional Approach.*
Englewood Cliffs, N.J.: Prentice-Hall,
1974.

TEDESCHI, J. T. *Perspectives on Social
Power.* Chicago: Aldine, 1974.

WALL, J. A., and ADAMS, J. S. "Some
Variables Affecting a Constituent's
Evaluation of Behavior Toward a
Boundary Role Occupant."
*Organizational Behavior and Human
Performance,* June 1974, pp. 390–408.

WAYS, M. "More Power to Everybody."
Fortune, May 1970, pp. 110–18.

WILKINSON, I., and KIPNIS, D. "Interform
Use of Power." *Journal of Applied
Psychology,* June 1978, pp. 315–20.

WOOD, M. T. "Power Relationships and
Group Decision-Making in
Organizations." *Psychological Bulletin,*
1973, pp. 280–93.

ZALD, M. N. *Power in Organizations.*
Nashville: Vanderbilt University, 1970.

A Case of Intergroup Behavior

The James Engineering Company

The James Engineering Company is a medium-size engineering design and construction company located in Indianapolis, Indiana. The company, founded by its
President, Mr. Tom James, in 1962, specializes in the design and construction of
small manufacturing and processing plants. Since the company was founded, sales
have increased steadily at approximately 18 percent per year. In 1978, the company
recorded sales and after-tax profits of $8 million and $950,000, respectively. The
vast majority of the company's projects have been located in a five-state area,
including Indiana, Kentucky, Ohio, Michigan, and Illinois. An increasing number
of construction projects, however, were being contracted each year in the states of
Georgia, Tennessee, and Arkansas.

Initially, the president, Mr. James, had four department managers reporting
directly to him: (1) manager of engineering design; (2) manager of construction; (3)
manager of contract sales; and (4) manager of administrative services. This arrangement proved to be successful during the early years of James' growth when
only one or two construction projects were in progress. During the last two years,
however, an average of four to six projects were in various stages of completion at
any one time.

With the increasing business, Mr. James was concerned that the present departmental arrangement was not adequate for handling the numerous coordination
problems that had developed. Of particular concern to Mr. James were problems

that had arisen with current projects related to increased costs and the inability to meet schedule deadlines.

In order to overcome these problems, early in 1975 Mr. James created the project manager position and promoted three of the company's best engineers—Jim Thomas, Charlie Holt, and Kathy Williams—into these positions. The project managers, who reported directly to Mr. James, were given full responsibility for coordinating one or two projects from the design stage through construction. To accomplish their job, the project managers would have to depend upon the expertise, resources, and cooperation of the other four departments. Only a secretary and a planning and cost analyst were under direct supervision of each of the project managers. The new organizational arrangement is shown in exhibit 8–15.

After the project manager arrangement had been in effect for approximately one year, Mr. James had the following conversation with project manager Charlie Holt:

James: Charlie, I called you in today to get your informal evaluation of the way the project manager concept has worked out for you. As you know, I created your position in the belief that our growing number of projects could be better coordinated. I must say, however, that I really haven't seen any major improvement in our ability to meet time or cost schedules.

Holt: Let me say that I really enjoy my job. It's exciting, and I truly like the autonomy I have and the opportunity to work with all areas of the company and with a variety of customers. On the other hand, I feel totally frustrated and powerless in trying to get the projects done.

James: What do you mean, Charlie?

Holt: Well, it basically boils down to a job that's all "responsibility" but no "authority." We're supposed to coordinate our different projects from beginning to end, but we don't have the power or authority over resources to get the job done.

Exhibit 8–15   T. W. James Engineering Company: Organizational Structure

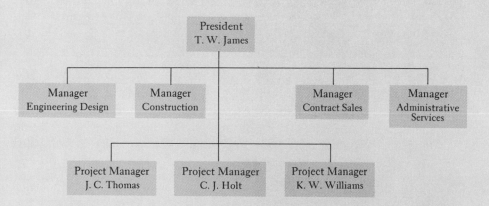

James: I don't understand. You report directly to me—isn't that authority enough?

Holt: Not really, Tom. I can come to you with big problems, but for everyday work I have to depend on the design and construction departments for assistance. Getting help out of them is like pulling teeth. I have to "beg, borrow, and steal" just to keep a project moving forward. This is the major reason why Jim Thomas quit two months ago. He plainly got frustrated with the lack of cooperation from the other departments.

James: When I set up this new arrangement, I thought I made it clear to everyone that the project managers were the key people in our organization. I hoped that the total organization would cooperate and support you people.

Holt: There's cooperation, but only to a point. The problem is that over time, the different department managers have developed particular routines and procedures for doing their work. When we come in with requests that are different from what has been done before—like asking for more design engineers to be put on a project than we have done before—all we get is the big "put-off" or comments like, "We just don't operate that way in this department." It's just frustrating!

James: I'll see what I can do for you, Charlie.

Later that week, Mr. James called Frank Miller, manager of engineering design, into his office for a conference. Excerpts from their conversation are as follows:

James: Frank, another point I'd like to discuss with you relates to some coordination problems I've heard about concerning the project managers.

Miller: I was wondering when you'd be asking questions about that group. They *were* good engineers, but as project managers, they're more trouble than they're worth.

James: Explain yourself, Frank.

Miller: Well, if you want to get down to gut issues, the project managers are more concerned with power grabbing than getting the job done. They always overstep their bounds as managers.

James: For example?

Miller: For example, they continually run into my office demanding more people on this job, quicker turnaround on that job, special consideration given to certain customers, more resources given to a project, and so on. We've developed a good design department at James—if I went along with all their demands, they would have all the decision-making power and the people reporting to them, which would leave me and the other department managers without jobs. They're supposed to coordinate projects, not give orders that disrupt our well-established and effective procedures.

Case Primer Questions

1. Evaluate the project manager arrangement as an intergroup management strategy.

2. Evaluate Frank Miller's comment concerning the power-acquisition behavior by the project managers.

3. What is the source(s) of conflict between the department managers and the project managers?

4. What should Mr. James do to solve this problem?

Experiential Exercise

Intergroup Conflict

Purpose

To study the causes and possible resolution strategies for intergroup conflict.

Required understanding

The reader should be familiar with the issues and concepts relating to intergroup conflict.

How to set up the exercise

Set up groups of four to eight students for the forty-five to sixty minute exercise. The groups should be separated from each other and asked to converse only with their group members. Before forming the groups, each person is asked to complete the exercise by themselves and then to join the group and reach a decision. They should read the following:

Assume that you are employed by a medium-sized corporation specializing in the manufacture and marketing of commodity and specialty chemicals. Your particular position is Manufacturing Manager: Plastics. You report to the vice president of manufacturing, who, in turn, reports to the divisional vice president.

Currently, your firm is experiencing a relatively high growth rate in sales and profits due to the recent introduction of new product lines, of which your products

represent a major portion of this high growth rate. In order to provide better coordination of new product development and marketing efforts, the president of your firm decided to establish *product-planning teams* for each new product or product lines. Each team is responsible for the effective planning and coordination of efforts necessary to bring the new product through the pilot plant, plant construction, and initial marketing phases.

Last year, a product-planning team was established in order to coordinate the introduction of a new, extremely durable, but expensive plastic to be used in the electronics industry. The team consists of yourself, and representatives from engineering, research, and marketing departments. The representative from engineering has been appointed as chairperson of the planning team. Pilot plant studies have been concluded, and the team will be meeting shortly to discuss the various aspects of construction of the new plant.

This morning, the planning team conducted a meeting at which you presented a plan for the construction of the new plant. The plan contained material, equipment, and capacity details and a proposed construction time schedule. Incorporated in your plan was the use of new processing equipment that will provide considerable manufacturing cost savings over existing equipment. The delivery time of this newer equipment, however, is estimated to be twelve months longer than equipment that is currently available.

During the team meeting, the marketing representative voiced strong opposition to your plan, indicating that the primary emphasis should be on placing this new product on the market as soon as possible. You, however, pointed out that the *long-term* benefits of your plan, in terms of manufacturing cost savings, outweigh *short-term* marketing considerations. The discussion becomes increasingly heated and tense as each of you becomes further entrenched in your positions. In addition, the engineering representative believes that you have the most valid point, and decides to go along with the original plan. The research representative, however, agrees with the marketing representative, which results in a stalemated meeting with no decision being made.

After the meeting as you reflect on what has happened, you are clearly upset and disturbed. You are aware that the views expressed by you and the marketing team

member represent not only your personal views, but the positions of the total manufacturing and marketing departments.

Because you believe that this is a serious problem between the two departments, you decide that something must be done quickly to insure the success of the project. You see the alternatives as follows:

1. You can rework your plan to go along with the objections of the marketing representative, and do the best you can with the long-term manufacturing cost considerations of the plan.

2. You can have a meeting with the marketing representative at which time you can stress the positive aspects of the project and point out that the new equipment will make the company the foremost producer of the product in the world.

3. You can send a letter to the president resigning your position on the team.

4. You can tell the marketing representative that if he or she goes along with your

Exhibit 8–16 Intergroup Conflict Exercise

Conflict-Resolution Alternative	Individual		Group	
	Type of Resolution	Rank	Type of Resolution	Rank
1.				
2.				
3.				
4.				
5.				
6.				
7.				
8.				
9.				
10.				

position now, you will give full support to his or her new marketing plan that is to be presented to the team in the near future.

5. You can go to the divisional vice president and request that he or she intercede for your position.

6. You can ask the marketing representative to meet with you for a full day next week in order to work out your differences and come up with an alternative solution.

7. You can ask a member of the divisional vice president's staff to sit in on all team meetings and act as the new chairperson and arbitrator of all problems.

8. You can send the marketing representative a letter (with copies to all team members, the divisional vice president, and president) indicating that his or her opposition to your plan is holding up a potentially profitable project.

9. You can ask the divisional vice president to attend the next team meeting in order to

stress the importance of this project to the continued growth of the company.

10. You can immediately walk into the marketing representative's office and ask him or her to justify his or her position to you.

Instructions for the exercise

1. *Individually,* group members should:
   a. Identify the cause(s) of the present conflict situation.
   b. On exhibit 8–16, identify the type of conflict resolution and rank order each of the ten possible alternatives from 1 (the most desirable) to 10 (the least desirable).

2. Form into the preassigned groups and answer question 1 as a group. Fill in the group responses on exhibit 8–16.

3. A spokesperson from each group should give the instructor the group's decision and a rationale for that decision.

CHAPTER 9

Leadership

Leadership has been considered one of the most important elements affecting organizational performance. For the manager, leadership is the focus of activity through which the goals and objectives of the organization are accomplished. Leadership has also been the focus of attention of behavioral scientists because the leader may have a significant effect on the behavior, attitudes, and performance of employees.

Leadership has been studied and researched for a number of years, resulting in numerous theories and models.[1] Like motivation, no universally accepted theoretical framework of leadership has been developed. This chapter will examine the development of leadership theory from early studies to current situational approaches. We will first examine the concept of influence as one of the foundations of leadership, and then provide a discussion of the three main theoretical approaches of leadership—trait, behavioral, and situational theories. Finally, we will present some contemporary issues in leadership and combine the presented material into an integrative model that stresses the importance of managers developing the skills and ability to *diagnose* the situation and alter his or her approach of leadership in the most effective manner.

Leadership as an Influence Process

"Who is the leader?" is a question that some individuals may respond to in different ways. For example, consider a group of postal workers responsible for sorting mail in a local post office. A typical response to this question from one of the workers might be, "Who is my leader? Well, my direct supervisor is Roger, but Jerry is really the leader of my group. Roger gives the directions and orders, and generally tells us what to do. He is the 'organization's man,' and we go to him with problems concerning rules, procedures, or policies. Jerry, on the other hand, has the same mail-sorting job as we do, but he has worked here longer than any of us. You might say he 'knows the ropes.' Jerry helps us out with our work by showing us the best methods for doing the job in the most efficient manner. Everyone feels good that Jerry is around—he helps us build confidence in our work and is a real morale booster."

Formal and Informal Leaders

This simple example draws attention to two important leader roles in organizations.[2] Roger is the *formal* leader of the group of mail sorters. As the formal leader, Roger can exercise *formal influence,* which is prescribed or given to an individual because of the position or office he or she has been given by the organization. A leader in this sense is responsible and entrusted to perform such leadership functions as planning, organizing, and controlling the work. A formal leader who exercises these functions does so because of the *authority* given to him or her by the organization.

Leadership, however, can be of an *informal* nature, such as the type Jerry exerts in our example. This type of leader is referred to as the *informal, emergent,* or *peer* leader. Peer leaders exert *informal* influence, which is not prescribed by the organization in terms of position or authority, but nonetheless can affect the behavior of group members. Informal influence originates not from the position held but from some special quality of the particular individual that is desirable for the group. In Jerry's case, this influence is based on his work experience and willingness to help his fellow employees.

Two further points should be brought out with respect to formal and informal leaders. First, in some situations only a formal leader may exist. In the example, if Roger performed his formal leadership role and *also* provided the support and had the necessary qualities, he would also be the informal leader. Jerry held his informal leadership role because of some group *needs* that were not satisfied by Roger's behavior.

Second, informal leaders can serve a very valuable role in organizations *if* their behavior and influence is congruent with the goals and objectives of the total organization. If an informal leader influences group-member behavior such that norms are established that are counter to the behavior desired by the organization, then an incongruency of goals between the organization and the group can develop. This situation can result in lower efficiency and performance from the group. In our example, the goals of Roger and Jerry were congruent with the organization's goals, resulting in a positive influence on group performance.

The discussion thus far has focused on one of the foundations of leadership; namely, the aspect of *influence.* As in our discussion of intergroup power, we will define *influence* as the ability of one person to alter the behavior of another person. The example of the postal workers has drawn attention to the position, or *authority,* determinants of influence. A second important factor is the *power* held by the individual to influence another's behavior.

Power as a Dimension of Influence

Power has been defined as the capacity to influence. Power can be based in the group, as we illustrated in the previous chapter, or in the individual. A number of attempts have been made to identify the various ways in which one individual may have the power to influence another individual. It is important to note that *authority* primarily involves position-related influence. *Power,* on the other hand, includes both position and personal attributes. In the example, Roger exerted power that was based on his position; Jerry's personal attributes and his seniority were his power base.

One of the most widely used descriptions of bases of power was proposed by French and Raven.[3] The different forms of power a leader may possess include the following:

Legitimate power is derived from an individual's position in the structure or hierarchy of the organization. The organization usually sanctions this form of power by recognition from higher management or by the use of titles, such as manager, director, or supervisor.

Reward power is based on the ability to control and administer rewards to others (e.g., money, promotions, praise) for compliance with the leader's directives or requests.

Coercive power is derived from the ability to control and administer punishment to others (e.g., reprimand, termination) for noncompliance with the leader's requests or directives.

Expert power is based upon a special ability, skill, expertise, or knowledge base exhibited by an individual. For example, a new production supervisor may have some questions regarding the functioning of a piece of equipment. Rather than ask the production superintendent, the supervisor contacts the individual who previously held the supervisor's position for assistance because of his or her previous knowledge or expertise with the equipment.

Referent power is based on attractiveness or appeal of one person to another. A leader may be admired because of certain characteristics or traits that inspire or attract followers (e.g., charisma). Referent power may also be based on a person's reference or connection with another powerful individual. For example, the title of "assistant to" has been given to people who work closely with others with titles such as general manager or vice president. Although the "assistant to the vice president" may not have legitimate, reward, or coercive power, other individuals may perceive that this person is acting with the consent of the vice president, resulting in his or her power to influence. The assistant to the vice president is acting in reference to the vice president.

In analyzing these five power bases, a further distinction may be made—namely, that power is based on *resources* or *individual characteristics*. Legitimate, reward, and coercive power are defined in terms of the influential *resources* available to the individual. The other sources of power—expert and referent—are not so much described in terms of resources but refer to the *individual characteristics* of the influencer and the *motivations* of the target person, or individual to be influenced. Exhibit 9–1 provides a framework for analyzing influence based on resources and individual characteristics.

A review of exhibit 9–1 reveals at least two main interpretive points.[4] First, the influence process is assumed to involve at least two individuals: a focal person *(A)*, exerting influence; and person(s) *(B)*, the *target* of the influence. The framework draws attention to the relationship between A's characteristics, available resources, and decision role with respect to the target person. For example, the manager with *reward power* occupies an important position in the organization, has control over rewards, and gives directions or orders with a promise of rewards. For the target of influence, the emphasis is on the relationship between B's characteristics, needs, and role in the decision process with respect to focal person A, the source of influence. In addition, the target person B, who is influenced by manager A with reward power, generally occupies a less important position than A, desires the rewards controlled by A, and decides whether or not to accept the directions of A.

Second, the *degree of acceptance and correspondence* between the characteristics, resources, and decision role of focal person A, and the characteristics, needs, and decision role of target person B generally will dictate the *effectiveness* of the influence process. For example, the department chairperson in a university has the power to reward faculty members with monetary increases in salary on the basis of the teaching, research, and community service contributions. The faculty member, being subordinate in the university system to the chairperson, desires a salary increase, and thus directs his or her effort toward excellence in teaching, research, and community service. Compliance with or acceptance of the influence attempts by the chairperson are thus seen as means to a desired reward (i.e., salary increase).

The Study of Leadership

The Definition of Leadership

Given the previous discussion, we will define leadership as follows:

> Leadership is the relationship between two or more people in which one attempts to influence the other toward the accomplishment of some goal or goals.

The key to this definition is that leadership is a function of the *power base* of the leader, the *approach* or *behavior* of the leader, and the *degree of acceptance* of the leader, and the correspondence of these factors with the characteristics, needs, and decision role of the subordinate. This definition is translated into a framework, or basic model for the study of leadership, and presented in exhibit 9–2. At the end of the chapter, we will attempt to revise this basic model in light of current theories and research on leadership.

Theories of Leadership

In the study of leadership, the early theories and the current situational theories have generally focused on the same objective—identifying the elements or factors that result in leader effectiveness. Stated differently, can we identify certain characteristics, behaviors, or situations that make one form of leadership more effective than any other form?

Three major approaches to leadership will be presented: (1) trait theories; (2) behavioral theories; and (3) situational theories. The basic foundation of each approach is summarized in exhibit 9–3. The early trait theories examined leadership by answering the questions—"In terms of individual characteristics differences,

Exhibit 9-1 A Framework for Analyzing Influence Between Two Persons

Person A
Person Exerting Influence

Power Bases	Characteristics	Resources	Decision Role with Respect to Target
1. Legitimate	Occupies legitimate position of authority; secured position by legitimate methods	Symbols of legitimacy; label of others' action as right or wrong	Announces decision; asks for support
2. Reward	Occupies important position in hierarchy	Control over material rewards (money, promotion etc.)	Makes request, coupled with promise of reward for compliance
3. Coercive	Occupies important position in hierarchy	Control over material penalties (fines, demotions, etc.)	Gives order, coupled with threat of punishment for noncompliance
4. Expert	Expertise: special training, special experience, etc.	Knowledge about how to reach certain goals	Investigates, makes tests, gives information to others
5. Referent	Strong; successful; has attractive qualities	Approval	States own opinions, preferences

who are the most effective leaders?" or "Are there a set of finite individual characteristics or *traits* that can distinguish successful from unsuccessful leaders?" Following the early trait theories, researchers switched their attention from the individual characteristics of the leader to a concern for the *style* of leadership exhibited by the leader. The key question asked was, "Is one leadership style more effective than any other leadership style?" In other words, attention shifted from a concern of "who the leader is" to "what the leader does."

Finally, when the trait and behavioral approaches resulted in less than satisfactory understanding of leadership, contemporary theorists developed *situational* approaches to leadership. These approaches considered leadership to be a complex process that involved the leader, subordinates, and the situation. The main approach that directed these behavioral scientists was the belief that "Effective leadership is a function of the *characteristics of the leader,* the *style of leadership,* the *characteristics of the subordinates,* and the *situation* surrounding the leadership environment."

| | Person B Target(s) of Influence | | |
Characteristics	Needs	Decision Role with Respect to Influencer	Effect of Influencer on Target
Occupies position of subordination; accepts legitimacy of other's position	Wishes to fulfill moral obligations	Gets request from authority	Sees conformity to requested action as morally correct
Occupies less important position in hierarchy	Wants rewards controlled by influencer	Decides whether to accede to request of others	Compliance seen as means to rewards
Occupies less important position in hierarchy	Wants to avoid punishment but maintain self-esteem	Decides whether to accede to order	Compliance seen as way of avoiding penalty but may be seen as blow to self-esteem
Unexpert	Wants to find best ways to reach goals	Reviews information presented by experts	Sees new options; sees new favorable or unfavorable consequences following various actions
Less strong, less successful	Wishes to be similar to, or approved by, influencer	Hears opinions, preferences of influencer	See compliance as way of being similar to, approved by, influencer

Adapted from Martin Patchen, "The Locus and Basis of Influence on Organizational Decisions," *Organizational Behavior and Human Performance* 11 (1974): 197.

1) Trait Theories

Many of the early studies of leadership in the 1940s and 1950s focused on the traits of the leader. Researchers attempted to find a set of identifiable individual characteristics or traits that could differentiate successful from unsuccessful leaders. Researchers began an exhaustive (if not endless) search to identify biographical, personality, emotional, physical, intellectual, and other personal characteristics of successful leaders.

In a review of the research since 1948, Stogdill identifies a leadership classification system that is based on six broad categories: (1) physical characteristics; (2) social background; (3) intelligence; (4) personality; (5) task-related characteristics; and (6) social characteristics.[5] A summary of selected traits within each category is presented in exhibit 9–4.

Exhibit 9–2 A Basic Model for the Study of Leadership

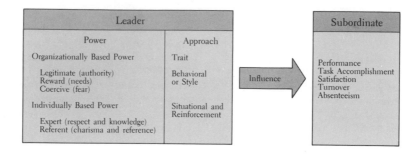

Physical characteristics

Physical characteristics, such as age, appearance, height, and weight, were studied in some of the early leadership research. The findings, however, were somewhat contradictory. Many people visualize the effective supervisor in a steel mill or the marine sergeant in a combat platoon to be a big, burly man who is over 6'2'' tall, weighs in excess of two hundred pounds, possesses a deep voice, and generally has an energy level far exceeding his subordinates. Although some of these factors have been related to effective leadership, it is possible that other situational factors may affect the choice of the leader and the subsequent leader effectiveness.[6] For example, the various military services and many law enforcement agencies place certain restrictions on the height and weight of their members. Although these restrictions may help to dictate who the leader is, there is no guarantee that effective leadership will result. Thus, the assumption that physical characteristics lead to effective leadership is very tenuous.

Social background

A number of studies investigating the socioeconomic background of leaders have focused on such factors as education, social status, and mobility.[7] In general, these studies have concluded that: (1) high socioeconomic status is an advantage in attaining leadership status; (2) more people from lower socioeconomic strata are able to rise to high-level positions in industry today than were able to fifty years ago; and (3) leaders tend to be better educated now than formerly. As with physical characteristics, leadership positions based on social background factors may be a situational phenomena of our maturing society. In addition, no consistent links between leader effectiveness and social background factors have been found.

Intelligence

The numerous studies that have investigated the relationship between intelligence and leadership status indicate that leaders are characterized by superior judgment, decisiveness, knowledge, and fluency of speech. Although somewhat consistent, this relationship was still found to be weak, which suggests that additional factors need to be considered.

Exhibit 9-3 Major Approaches to the Study of Leadership

Approach	Emphasis
Trait (1940s–50s)	There exists a finite set of individual *traits* or characteristics that can be used to distinguish successful from unsuccessful leaders.
Behavioral (1950s–60s)	The most important aspect of leadership is not the traits of the leader but what the leader does in various situations. Successful leaders are distinguished from unsuccessful leaders by their particular *style* of leadership.
Situational (1970s)	The effectiveness of the leader is not only determined by his or her style of behavior but also by the *situation* surrounding the leadership environment. Situational factors include the characteristics of the leader and the subordinate, and nature of the task, the structure of the group, and the type of reinforcement.

Personality

The research investigating personality factors suggests that effective leaders are characterized by such personality traits as alertness, self-confidence, personal integrity, self-assurance, and dominance needs. Although these findings have not been entirely consistent across all groups and industries, they do suggest that individual personality traits must be considered in any approach to leadership. As we discussed in chapter 3, personality is significantly related to such important behavioral factors as perception, attitudes, learning, and motivation. The major problem in this area is finding valid ways to measure personality traits and then apply these results to actual situations.

Task-related characteristics

Research examining task-related characteristics has produced uniformly positive results that suggest that the leader is characterized by a high need for achievement and responsibility, initiative, and a high task orientation. These results suggest that the leader can, in general, be characterized as an individual exhibiting high motivation, drive, and a need for task accomplishment.

Social characteristics

Studies of social characteristics have suggested that leaders are active participants in various activities, interact well with a wide range of people, and are cooperative with others. These interpersonal skills appear to be valued by the group, which tends to provide for harmony, trust, and group cohesiveness.

Summary

Although the results of these trait investigations appear to be helpful in identifying certain salient characteristics of leaders, little has been provided for understanding or predicting leadership effectiveness. The list of important leadership traits is endless and grows with each passing year. It has not yet been shown that a finite set

Exhibit 9–4 Researcheed Leader Traits (Examples)

Physical Characteristics	Social Background	Intelligence
1. Age 2. Appearance 3. Height 4. Weight	1. Education 2. Social status 3. Mobility	1. Intelligence 2. Ability 3. Judgment 4. Knowledge 5. Decisiveness 6. Fluency of Speech

Personality	Task-Related Characteristics	Social Characteristics
1. Aggressiveness 2. Alertness 3. Dominance 4. Enthusiasm 5. Extroversion 6. Independence 7. Creativity 8. Personal integrity 9. Self-confidence	1. Achievement drive 2. Drive for responsibility 3. Initiative 4. Persistence 5. Enterprise 6. Task orientation	1. Administrative ability 2. Attractiveness 3. Cooperativeness 4. Popularity 5. Prestige 6. Sociability 7. Interpersonal skills 8. Tact 9. Diplomacy

of traits can distinguish successful from unsuccessful leaders. Although such aspects as personality appear to be significant factors, they are only a few of the many factors that can contribute to leadership effectiveness.[8]

The significant findings between individual traits and leadership effectiveness may actually be a major contributor to situational factors. That is, self-selection processes may have been operative so that individual traits may have appeared to be more significant than they really were. For example, successful research administrators are usually inquisitive, independent, perceptive, and experts within their field. Successful sales managers are usually high-need achievers, gregarious, enthusiastic, and project a professional stature. What may be important traits for one occupation may not be important for other roles in the same organization. Uniformity of traits across all levels is thus questioned.

In addition, focusing on individual traits does not show what the individual *actually does* in a leadership situation. Traits identify who the leader is, not the behavioral patterns he or she will exhibit in attempting to *influence* subordinate actions. The trait approach has ignored the subordinate and his or her effect on leadership. Influence is the relationship between two or more people; therefore, focusing on one part only of the influence relationship provides an incomplete view of the leadership process.

Finally, the effectiveness of leadership depends to a large extent on the situation or environment surrounding the leadership or influence process. A particular leadership pattern may work effectively for a group of assembly-line workers but may be totally ineffective for a group of rehabilitation nurses. Interactions among the many factors of the situation must be examined before any predictions about leadership effectiveness can be made. This statement will serve as the basis for our discussions concerning the behavioral and situational theories of leadership.

Behavioral Theories

During the 1950s, the dissatisfaction with the trait approach to leadership led behavioral scientists to focus their attention on the actual leader behavior—namely, what the leader does and how he or she does it. The foundation for the "style of leadership" approach was the belief that effective leaders utilized a particular style to lead individuals and groups to achieving certain goals, resulting in high productivity and morale. Unlike trait theories, the behavioral approach focused on *leader effectiveness,* not the *emergence* of an individual as a leader.

A number of definitions of *leadership style* were developed from various behavioral theorists. Although many terms were assigned to the different leadership styles, two factors were stressed in each approach: task orientation and employee orientation. *Task orientation* is the emphasis the leader places on getting the job done by such actions as assigning and organizing the work, making decisions, and evaluating performance. *Employee orientation* is the openness and friendliness exhibited by the leader and his or her concern for the needs of subordinates. Two major research efforts were directed toward investigating the behavioral approach to leadership: the Ohio State University and University of Michigan studies.

Ohio State Studies:
Initiating Structure and Consideration

Among the several large research efforts that developed after World War II, one of the most widely known was that conducted by Ohio State University investigators. The overall objective of the Ohio State studies was to investigate the determinants of leader behavior and to determine the effects of leadership style on work-group performance and satisfaction.[9] Through these studies, two independent leadership dimensions were identified.

1. *Initiating structure,* which concerned the degree to which the leader organized and defined the task, assigned the work to be done, established communications networks, and evaluated work-group performance. In our framework, initiating structure is analogous to a *task-oriented leadership style.*

2. *Consideration,* which was defined as behavior that involves trust, mutual respect, friendship, support, and a concern for the welfare of the employee. Consideration refers to an emphasis on an *employee-oriented leadership style.*

These dimensions were measured through the use of questionnaires. Two separate questionnaires were developed, one to measure the style of leadership *as perceived by the leader* himself or herself (Leadership Opinion Questionnaire),[10] and one to measure the style of leadership *as perceived by the subordinates* of the leader (Leader Behavior Description Questionnaire).[11]

The scores derived from the responses to the questionnaires were used to depict or indicate a manager's style of leadership. The manner in which these scores were reported is shown in exhibit 9–5. This figure shows the scores on five example managers. For example, manager 1 is depicted as exhibiting a high initiating structure and high consideration leadership style, and manager 2 is seen as being high on initiating structure but low on consideration. Manager 5 possesses a leadership style that can be considered as being mid-range on both initiating structure and consideration.

Research on the Ohio State Dimensions

A large number of individual research efforts were conducted to determine the effects of initiating structure and consideration on group performance and morale. Much of the early work was conducted with the belief that the most effective leadership style was high on both initiating structure and consideration. The results revealed, however, that no single style emerged as being best. For example, in some studies the high initiating structure/high consideration style was associated with high performance and worker satisfaction. Other studies revealed that this style produced some dysfunctional effects. In particular, in a study of manufacturing firms consideration was found to be positively related to absences and negatively related to performance ratings of the leader by his superiors, and initiating structure was associated with lower worker satisfaction.[12]

Exhibit 9–5 Initiating Structure and Consideration: Scores for Five Leaders

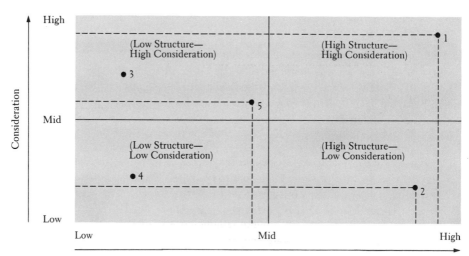

Leader behavior had different effects in studies of research and development and engineering personnel in a petroleum refinery, a business machine manufacturer, and an airframe manufacturer.[13] In each of the studied organizations, a positive relationship was found between initiating structure and satisfaction, although it was weakest in the airframe-manufacturing company, a highly structured organization, and strongest in the business-machines-manufacturing company, which was not as formally or rigidly structured. The formality of the organizational structure, therefore, was an important influence on the effectiveness of a given leadership style. As a result, the major criticism of the initiating-structure/consideration framework concerned the fact that *situational* factors and the influence of these factors on the leadership effectiveness model were not considered.

A second criticism concerns the fact that the measurements of the initiating structure/consideration dimensions by the leader and by his or her subordinates were generally found not to be highly related.[14] The leader viewed his or her style one way, but the subordinates may have viewed it another way. This presents a perplexing problem to researchers: how is leadership style measured—as perceived by the leader or by the subordinates?

Rather than concentrate on criticisms, we should point out the contribution of the Ohio State efforts—namely, a well-designed and detailed effort to define and describe the behaviors exhibited by leaders. The Ohio State studies contributed inmeasurably to the knowledge base of leadership and served as the foundation on which the contemporary approach was built.

University of Michigan Studies: Job Centered and Employee Centered

At approximately the same time the Ohio State research was being conducted, a series of leadership studies was in progress at the University of Michigan. The primary objective of most of the studies emerging from the Institute for Social Research at the University was to identify styles of leader behavior that result in increased work-group performance and satisfaction.[15] Two distinct styles of leadership were developed from their studies:

1. *Job-centered* leadership style, which focused on the use of close supervision, legitimate and coercive power, meeting schedules, and evaluating work performance. Similar to the Ohio State dimension of initiating structure, job-centered behavior refers to the broad factor of *task-oriented* leader behavior.

2. *Employee-centered* leadership style, which is people oriented and emphasizes delegation of responsibility and a concern for employee welfare, needs, advancement, and personal growth. Similar to the Ohio State dimension of consideration, this factor refers to the broad classification of *employee-oriented* leader behavior.

The behavioral scientists at Michigan conducted a number of studies in a wide variety of industries to investigate the relationship between leadership style and effectiveness. One particular study involved 500 clerical employees who worked in four large divisions of a large corporation.[16] The four divisions were assigned to two experimental one-year programs. Each program was randomly assigned one division historically high in production and one division historically low in production. At the start of the experiment, supervisors participated in a six-week training program. Production was measured and computed weekly, and employee attitudes were measured before and after the study.

In two of the four divisions, an attempt was made during the supervisory training program to make supervisors more participative (i.e., more employee centered). In the other two divisions, the supervisory training program emphasized the use of rules, procedures, and close supervision of subordinates (i.e., job-centered behavior).

The results of the study revealed that production increased in both systems: the employee-centered group increased production by 20 percent, and a 25 percent increase was noted in the job-centered group. Different reasons were given for these increases in each group. In the job-centered group, direct pressure and close supervision by the supervisors were assumed to be the reasons for the production increase. In the employee-centered group, however, the clerks themselves reduced the size of the work force and developed more efficient work-flow procedures. These groups were also found to be more cohesive in their interactions, which may also have positively affected productivity.

The results of the attitudinal and behavioral relationships, however, were somewhat different. In the employee-centered group, satisfaction increased; turnover and absenteeism decreased. In the job-centered divisions, however, satisfaction decreased, and turnover and absenteeism increased.

The main conclusion reached from this study was that the effectiveness of a leadership style should not be evaluated solely by productivity measures but should include other employee-related measures, such as satisfaction. In this framework, the supporters of this approach would conclude that employee-centered leader behavior would be the most appropriate and effective.

Generally speaking, critics have made similar comments concerning the Michigan studies as they had about the Ohio State efforts. These criticisms focus on two aspects. First, there is evidence to show that the style or behavior of leaders changes from situation to situation.[17] For example, a leader may exhibit an employee-centered style under normal circumstances, or when group activity is going smoothly. However, under stressful conditions, or when there is pressure to meet important deadlines, the leader may alter his or her behavior to be more job centered. Second, other situational factors, such as the cohesiveness of the group or the nature of the subordinates' personal characteristics or of the task, have not been considered. A leader of a noncohesive group may behave quite differently than would a leader of a cohesive group, even though they may be working on similar tasks.

Summary of Behavioral Theories

A review of the behavioral approach to leadership reveals a number of similarities and conclusions. Some of these points are presented in exhibit 9–6. First, the two

Exhibit 9–6 Summary of Behavioral Approaches to Leadership

Source	Leadership Dimension	How Measured	Summary of Results
Ohio State Studies	*(e. task oriated) leadership style* 1. Initiating structure 2. Consideration *employee onate leadeship style*	Through questionnaires completed by (1) the leader, (2) subordinates, (3) peers, and (4) immediate supervisor	A research-based approach that initially sought to determine the most effective leadership style. The findings indicate that a mix of initiating structure and consideration leader behavior, which achieved the highest effectiveness, depends largely on situational factors.
University of Michigan Studies	1. Job centered 2. Employee centered	Through questionnaire responses completed by subordinates	Employee-centered and job-centered styles result in productivity increases. However, job-centered behavior created tension and pressure that resulted in lower satisfaction and increased turnover and absenteeism. *Employee-centered is the best leadership style. see p. 286*

theories attempted to explain the leadership situation in terms of the *behavioral styles* of the leader; that is, what the leader does, not his or her personal characteristics. Both studies isolated two dimensions of a leader's style that were related to task orientation and employee orientation. The choice of two dimensions of leadership style may be the result not only of statistical analysis but also one of convenience. That is, leadership style is too complex to be viewed as unidimensional, but more than two dimensions may complicate the interpretation of leadership behavior. It should be noted that in later work by both Ohio State and Michigan four to twelve dimensions of leadership style have been studied.[18]

Second, the measurement of leadership style for each of the approaches was accomplished through the use of questionnaires. This method of measurement is both limited and controversial. This is not to say that questionnaires are invalid or of minimal use to researchers. It does mean that measurement is a major problem to behavioral scientists. No measurement methodology—questionnaire, observations, or interviews—has been universally accepted by behavioral researchers.

Finally, in search of the most effective leadership style, the research findings suggested that a universally accepted "best" style was inappropriate for the complexities of modern organizations. For a manager's leadership style to be effective, other situational factors must be considered.

Situational Theories

During the late 1960s, researchers recognized the limitations of the behavioral theories and began to refine and develop new approaches to the study of leadership. This approach focuses on the more complex *situational* theories of leadership. The work of the trait and behavioral style researchers provided a significant foundation for the study of leadership in organizations because the results of these approaches strongly suggested that the most effective way to lead is a dynamic and flexible process that adapts to the particular situation.

One of the most important functions of the manager's job is diagnosing and evaluating the many factors that may impact on the effectiveness of his or her leadership. Diagnosis involves the identification and understanding of the influence of such factors as individual differences, group structure, and organizational policies and practices. A thorough examination of the situation is a crucial process for the leader who is contemplating the application of a particular style. For example, a group of nurses working under conditions of extreme stress to save a patient's life will require a different type of leadership style than would a group of research chemists who routinely analyze the properties of production samples.

The diagnosis of the situation requires an examination by the manager of four important areas: (1) managerial characteristics; (2) subordinate characteristics; (3) group structure and the nature of the task; and (4) organizational factors.[19] These factors are summarized in exhibit 9–7.

1. *Managerial characteristics.* The leader's behavior in any given environment is dependent on the forces or characteristics of the individual. The important factors include:

    (a) Personality characteristics—How much confidence does the leader have in his or her ability to be a leader? Does he or she have the disposition, intelligence, and capabilities to be an effective leader?

    (b) Needs and motives—What particular needs motivate the manager? We normally think of leaders with needs for power and control, but what about other personal needs and motives? In Maslow's framework, a manager with high security needs may believe in imposing tight controls over subordinates. On the other hand, the manager with ego or self-realization needs may tolerate or encourage the use of creative or innovative practices by subordinates.

    (c) Past experience and reinforcement—There are some managers who must work closely with and direct the work of others in order to feel comfortable. Other managers thrive on allowing subordinates the opportunity to become involved and committed to their work. In many cases, leadership tendencies may be a function of the cultural (personal and organizational) background of the manager. Past experience and reinforcement may dictate the manager's current style of leadership. A manager who matures (organizationally) under a task-oriented superior may believe that this style is the only behavior to exhibit to subordinates in all situations.

Exhibit 9–7 Situational Factors Affecting Leader Behavior

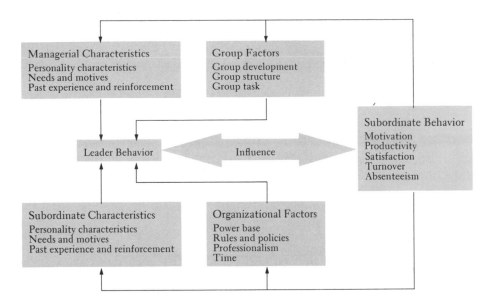

2. *Subordinate factors*. Before a leader decides on a particular behavioral style, he or she should consider the individual characteristics and behavioral patterns of subordinates. The subordinates, like the manager, have internal factors that may affect their behavior. Some of these factors include:

(a) Personality characteristics—Personality may have an effect on how the subordinate will react to influence attempts by the leader. Will a highly self-confident employee accept a leader who is very task oriented? How does the intelligence level of the subordinate affect his or her relationship with their leader?

(b) Needs and motives—Just as needs and motives motivate leaders, subordinate need levels may dictate how the employee will react to a leader's influence attempts. For example, subordinates with dominant lower-level needs may readily accept a task-oriented leader; an employee-oriented leadership style may be more effective with subordinates with dominant higher-order needs.

(c) Past experience and reinforcement—The subordinates' past experience and reinforcement may affect the leadership process. For example, a group of salespersons in a regional office of a large chemical company may have adapted well to the sales manager's participative, employee-oriented style. If, after a number of years, this manager is replaced by a more dogmatic or dictatorial, task-oriented manager, adjustment problems may develop.

3. *Group factors*. As we have discussed in previous chapters, groups are a prominent feature in society and organizations. The particular characteristics of the

group may have a significant impact on the manager's ability to lead the members. Some of the important group factors include:

(a) Group development stage—Where the group is in its development can influence the effectiveness of a particular leadership style. The manager's behavior during the orientation stage may not be appropriate during the internal problem-solving stage, in which conflict resolution is a frequent necessity.

(b) Group structure—How can a manager effectively lead a cohesive group? What style of leadership or managerial behavior can be used to elevate group performance norms? These are important aspects faced by all managers.

(c) Group task—The nature of the task has an important impact on the success of any leader's influence activities. For example, groups working on ambiguous tasks may require a completely different type of leadership than groups involved with routine tasks. Groups performing problem-solving tasks may react negatively to a manager's behavior that was successful for production-type tasks.

4. *Organizational factors*. Among the most crucial, yet least understood, factors in the leadership situation are those that concern the type of organization. Some of the most important considerations are:

(a) Power base—What is the foundation of the leader's power base? Does it consist of legitimate, reward, coercive, expert, and referent power, or some smaller subset? Absence of certain power bases—particularly legitimate, reward, and coercive—may limit the leader's ability to influence subordinates.

(b) Rules and procedures—Organizations vary in the manner in which rules, policies, standards, and procedures are used to guide the work of employees. Many organizations have developed extensive policy systems (such as manuals and standard operating procedures) that may dictate the type of leader behavior required.

(c) Professionalism—Highly trained professionals, such as nurses, scientists, and teachers, may depend more on their educational background or experience to guide their work than on the leader, which may limit the ability of the leader to influence them.

(d) Time—If an immediate decision must be made, or there is a high level of tension and stress, the involvement of other group members may be difficult, if not impossible. In a crisis situation, a participative leadership style may prove to be unsuccessful or impractical.

Two additional factors should be noted from an examination of exhibit 9–7. First, we define *leader behavior* in broad terms to include both *style* and *reinforcement* activities or behavior. This is to recognize that leader behavior includes all facets of the leader's activities, from being directive, participative, or goal oriented (style), to the manner in which he or she rewards (or punishes) subordinate behavior.

Second, we have made the influence arrow represent a two-way process. For too long, we have spoken of leadership as the process of the superior influencing the behavior of the subordinate. This is far too simplistic a notion because in real-life activities we know that the behavior of the *subordinate* can influence the behavior of the *leader*.

This list of important situational factors, although not exhaustive, should help point out that leadership and subsequent managerial behavior is a very complex process. The situational theories to be discussed in the next sections provide at least a partial examination of how these factors impact on leadership.

A Contingency Leadership Model

One of the first situational models of leadership was developed by Fiedler and his associates.[20] The basic foundation of the theory is that the effectiveness of the leader in achieving high group performance is contingent on the need structure of the leader and the degree to which the leader has control and influence in a particular situation. Four factors serve as the framework for Fiedler's model: (1) leadership-style assessment; (2) task structure; (3) group atmosphere; and (4) the leader's position power. The first identifies the *motivational* aspects of the leader; the other three factors describe the *situational favorableness* for the leader. This framework is shown in exhibit 9–8.

Leadership-style Assessment

The principle variable in investigating leader effectiveness in the contingency model is what has been called the least preferred coworker (LPC) score.[21] The twenty-item questionnaire assesses the level of esteem in which the leader holds his or her least preferred coworker. The leader is asked to describe the person with whom he or she has worked least well in accomplishing some task. For example, on the basis of the scores on the four example items below, it would appear that the manager completing this questionnaire has a relatively high evaluation of his or her least preferred coworker.

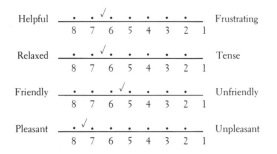

In his original presentation of the contingency model, Fiedler stated:

> . . . we visualize the high-LPC individual (who perceives his least preferred co-worker in a relatively favorable manner) as a person who derives his major satisfac-

Exhibit 9–8   A Contingency Leadership Model: Basic Framework

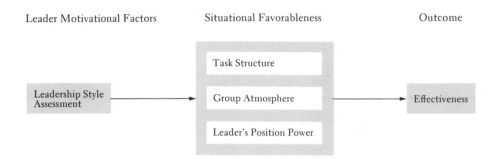

tion from successful interpersonal relationships, while the low-LPC person (who describes his LPC in very unfavorable terms) derives his major satisfaction from task performance.[22]

The model postulates that a low LPC score (unfavorable evaluation) indicates the degree to which a leader is ready to reject those with whom he or she cannot work. Therefore, the lower the LPC score, the greater the tendency for the leader to be *task oriented*. On the other hand, a high LPC score (favorable evaluation) indicates a willingness to perceive even the worst coworker as having some positive attributes. Therefore, the higher the LPC score, the greater the tendency for the leader to be *employee oriented*.

In motivational terms, the high-LPC leader has a basic goal to interact well and be friendly with his or her subordinates. If the leader reaches this goal, he or she will be able to attain such secondary goals as status and esteem. The low-LPC leader, however, has the accomplishment of certain tasks as a goal. Such needs as esteem and status are obtained through task accomplishment, not directly through relationships with subordinates. This is not to imply that a low-LPC leader is not friendly and pleasant toward subordinates, but that, when task accomplishment is threatened, good interpersonal relations assume secondary importance.

Task Structure

The first situational factor, task structure, is the degree to which the group task is routine or complex. The components of task structure include: (1) goal clarity; (2) goal-path multiplicity; (3) decision verifiability; and (4) decision specificity.

If the task of the group is routine, it is likely to have clearly defined goals (goal clarity), involve jobs or problems that can be solved in a few steps or with a limited number of procedures (goal-path multiplicity), have output or performance that can be easily evaluated (decision verifiability), and has only one correct solution (decision specificity). For example, the assembler in a typewriter-manufacturing firm performs a highly routine and structured task. The goals of the job are clearly spelled out, the method of assembling typewriters is detailed and very specific, each of the assembly steps can be checked and verified, and the final product has only one correct solution, namely a properly working unit. In this situation, the leader's ability to influence is constrained because the task has been so clearly defined.

For more complex tasks, the goals may be unclear, the method of accomplishing the task may vary from situation to situation, the task is difficult to check while in process, and there may be a number of acceptable solutions. For example, top-level corporate executives may disagree on whether the goals of the organization should be increased revenues, profits, decreased costs, or just survival. The manner in which these objectives are accomplished are varied and sometimes contradictory, checkpoints are unclear, and the end result of their actions may not be easily identifiable or evaluated.

Group Atmosphere

Group atmosphere is the degree of confidence, trust, and respect subordinates have in the leader. This factor has been called leader-member relations. In the model, the more friendly the relationship between the leader and followers, the easier it is for the leader to obtain group cooperation and effort. Leader-member relations are classified as either being good or poor. When the relationship between the leader and his or her subordinates is poor, the leader may have to resort to special favors to get good performance.

Position Power

The final situational factor concerns the power inherent in the leadership position. It refers to the extent the leader possesses, through legitimate, reward, or coercive power, the ability to *influence* the behavior of other individuals. Key aspects are the degree to which the leader has the power to promote, fire, or direct subordinates to task accomplishment. Fiedler assumes that most managers have high position power, but committee chairpersons, for example, have low position power.

Favorableness of the Leadership Situation

The three situational factors that contribute to the leader's ability to influence subordinates—group atmosphere, task structure, and position power—determine the situation's "degree" of favorableness to the leader. The relationship among favorableness, situational factors, and leadership style is shown in exhibit 9–9. The cells represent combinations of the situational variables and are arranged in order of favorableness to the leader. The model assumes that the leader will have the most influence and control when using a task-oriented style under favorable conditions (cell 1); that is, when he or she is accepted, where the task is structured, and when he or she has strong position power. At the other end of the continuum (cell 8), it is assumed that the leader's control and influence will be minimal because the leader is not accepted, the group's task is relatively complex and unstructured, and the leader has little position power.

Exhibit 9–9   A Summary of Fiedler's Contingency Model

Situational Favorableness	Cell	Leader-Member Relations	Task Structure	Leader Position Power	Suggested Effectual Leadership Styles
Favorable	1	Good	Structured	Strong	Task oriented
	2	Good	Structured	Weak	Task oriented
	3	Good	Unstructured	Strong	Task oriented
Moderately	4	Good	Unstructured	Weak	Employee oriented
Favorable	5	Moderately poor	Structured	Strong	Employee oriented
	6	Moderately poor	Structured	Weak	Employee oriented
Unfavorable	7	Moderately poor	Unstructured	Strong	Employee oriented
	8	Moderately poor	Unstructured	Weak	Task oriented

Adapted from Fred E. Fiedler, *A Theory of Leadership Effectiveness* (New York: McGraw-Hill, 1967), p. 37.

Research on Fiedler's Model

Over a number of years, Fiedler and his associates have studied many military, educational, and industrial leaders. In summarizing the work in sixty-three organizations composed of 454 separate groups, Fiedler suggests which type of leadership is most appropriate for the given situational environment. The results are summarized as the "Suggested Effectual Leadership Styles" in exhibit 9–9.

These findings suggest that each of the leadership styles can be effective in certain situations. Fiedler also suggests that the organization can change the effectiveness of the group's performance by changing the favorableness of the situation or by changing the leader's preferred style through education and training.

A number of research efforts have been reported on Fiedler's contingency model. These studies, conducted in a variety of research settings in order to determine the validity of the model, have identified an increasing number of serious shortcomings.[23]

Although it is beyond the scope of this chapter to evaluate each criticism, certain salient ones persist. First, a longstanding concern is what does LPC really measure? Fiedler's early research assumed LPC was a measure of the leader's personality. His later research, however, revised the measure of LPC to reflect an individual's motivational structure with respect to social need gratification in groups. Whether LPC measures personality or motivational structure, the link with the manager's leadership style remains in an uncertain state. Also, it seems likely that a manager's LPC score may change over time and may vary with experience in different group situations. Engineering the job to fit the manager's style may be a futile effort if the manager's motivational bases are constantly in flux.

Second, there are some researchers who contend that the situational cell predictions are not adequately supported by evidence. That is, the suggestion for task-oriented leader behavior under cell 1 conditions (good leader-member relations, routine task structure, and strong position power) is not always accurate. The predictions are especially inaccurate for cells 3, 4, 7, and 8.

Third, the model does not consider the relationship between the leader and the situational variables. For example, a task-oriented leader style may provide enough structure to make a complex task semiroutine. For another, good leader-member relations over a period of time may help to alter a manager's task-oriented style to a more employee-oriented style. For example, consider cell 5 in exhibit 9–9. There is a strong possibility that a leader with an employee-oriented style may, through his or her activities, improve leader-member relations from moderately poor to good. Such a change, however, could cause a move in cells from 5 to 1, where an employee-oriented style would no longer be appropriate.

Finally, the model suggests that leaders are either task oriented or employee oriented; that is, leadership style is essentially a unidimensional concept. As we discussed in the section on the behavioral approach to leadership, it is possible for managers to be both task oriented and employee oriented, varying from a high to low orientation on each factor. In different situations, a manager may be motivated to alter his or her style from one leadership style to another.

In summary, despite the significant criticisms, Fiedler's contingency model has proven to be a major addition to the study of leadership in organizations for a number of reasons. First, the contingency model was one of the first approaches to leadership that included situational factors within its theoretical framework. The model will probably continue to be an important source of new ideas, propositions, and hypotheses about situational leadership. Second, it provides the subtle but important implication that one should not speak of leadership as being either good or poor. Rather, a more realistic viewpoint would be that a manager's style of leading may be effective in one situation but not in another. Finally, leadership effectiveness is a function of the leader's motivational base and the interaction of situational factors. The organization may improve the effectiveness of a particular work environment by either modifying the situational factors or attempting to change the manager's leadership style. This latter point involves the growing area of organizational change and development, which will be discussed in chapters 15 and 16.

A Path-Goal Theory of Leader Effectiveness

A second situational theory of leadership has been advanced by House and based on the earlier work of Evans.[24] This approach has been called the path-goal theory of leader effectiveness because the foundations of the theory are based on the expectancy theory of motivation.[25] The term *path-goal* refers to the familiar expectancy theory terms of effort-to-performance and performance-to-reward expectancies and valence. As House states in his initial formalization of the theory (which is shown simply in exhibit 9–10):

> . . .the motivational function of the leader consists of increasing personal payoffs to subordinates for work-goal attainment, and making the path to these payoffs easier to travel by clarifying it, reducing roadblocks and pitfalls, and increasing the opportunities for personal satisfaction in route.[26]

The principal function of the leader is thus seen as influencing the valence and expectancy perceptions of subordinates. That is, if the leader can increase valence

Exhibit 9–10 A Framework for Path-Goal Leadership Theory

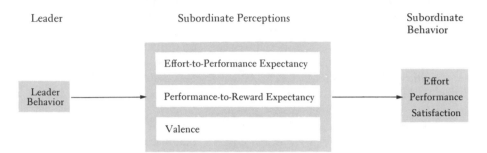

perceptions and clarify and increase expectancy probabilities, greater effort and higher satisfaction and performance will result.

Much of the early path-goal research incorporated *initiating structure* and *consideration* as leader behavior dimensions. Initiating structure provided a mechanism for "path-goal clarification," and consideration was viewed as "making the paths easier to travel." For example, by assigning the work to be done, specifying goals, and providing feedback, a manager's use of initiating structure could serve to clarify the expectancies of engineers working on ambiguous tasks. On the other hand, when expectancies are already clear and employees are working on routine, structured tasks, the use of a high level of consideration by the supervisor could make the job more pleasant to work on. In each of these examples, higher motivation and satisfaction can result.

After the initial research efforts, the theory was revised, expanding the propositions, redefining leader behavior, and including additional situational factors. The revised theory is composed of two basic propositions, the first dealing with the *role of the leader,* and the second concerning the *dynamics of the situation.* These two properties are as follows:[27]

1. The leader's function is a *supplemental* one; that is, leader behavior is acceptable and satisfying to the extent that subordinates perceive such behavior as a source of satisfaction or as instrumental to future satisfaction. Thus, the effect of the leader on the motivation and satisfaction of subordinates depends on how deficient the work environment is in other sources of motivation and support.

2. The *motivational* impact of the leader's behavior is determined by the situation in which the leader functions. Two main factors were suggested as influencing the situational effectiveness of the leader's behavior: (a) the characteristics of the subordinates; and (b) the characteristics of the work environment, including the task, the work group, and other organizational factors.

Styles of Leader Behavior

Although the initial path-goal research utilized the two dimensions of initiating structure and consideration as representative of the leader's behavior, the current framework includes four.[28]

1. *Instrumental behavior* is the planning, organizing, controlling, and coordinating of subordinate activities by the leader. It is similar to the traditional dimension of initiating structure in that the leader's emphasis is on letting the subordinates know what is expected of them.

2. *Supportive behavior* includes giving support consideration to the needs of the subordinates, displaying concern for their well-being and welfare, and creating a friendly and pleasant environment.

3. *Participative behavior* is characterized by the sharing of information and an emphasis on consultation with subordinates and use of their ideas and suggestions in reaching group-related decisions.

4. *Achievement-oriented behavior* is characterized by setting challenging goals, expecting subordinates to perform at the highest level, and continually seeking improvement in performance. The leader wants good performance, but at the same time displays confidence in the abiilty of his or her subordinates to do a good job.

A number of research studies in path-goal theory suggest that these four styles can be exhibited by the same leader in various situations. This set of findings is not consistent with Fiedler's notion concerning the unidimensionality of leader behavior and suggests more flexibility than the contingency model.

Situational Factors

In path-goal theory, two factors are considered situational because they can moderate the relationship between the leader's style and the behavior of the subordinate. The two are the *characteristics of the subordinates* and the *characteristics of the work environment* with which the subordinates must cope in order to accomplish work goals and achieve satisfaction.

The theory proposes that leader behavior will be perceived as acceptable to subordinates to the extent that the subordinates see such behavior as either an immediate source of satisfaction or as needed for future satisfaction. *Subordinate characteristics* are seen to partially determine this perception. For example:

1. *Ability.* An important characteristic is the subordinate's perception of his or her own ability. The greater the perceived ability to effectively accomplish a task, the less the subordinate will accept directive or instrumental behavior because such behavior will be viewed as unnecessary supervision.

2. *Locus of control.* This variable is the degree to which an employee believes that he or she has control of what happens to him or her.[29] People who believe that they control their environment and who believe what happens to them occurs because of their behavior are called *internals.* People who believe what happens to them is not under their control and occurs because of luck or fate are called *externals.* In a sense, locus of control can be thought of as similar to the construct of self-confidence. In path-goal research, it has been suggested that internals are more satisfied with a participative leader, and externals are more satisfied with a more directive leader.[30]

3. *Need and motives*. A subordinate's dominant needs may affect the impact of leader behavior. For example, individuals with high safety and security needs may accept an instrumental leader style, but employees with high affiliation and esteem needs may react more positively to a supportive leader. In addition, dominant needs for autonomy and responsibility in the individual may be more positively influenced by the participative leader than by one with another style.

The *characteristics of the work environment* include three broad aspects: (1) the subordinates' tasks; (2) the primary work group; and (3) the formal authority system.

1. *Subordinates' tasks*. One of the most important work-environment factors concerns the nature of the individual's task. In general, researchers have focused on whether the task is *highly structured* or *highly unstructured* with ambiguous requirements and demands, theorizing that the more unstructured and ambiguous the task, the greater the acceptance by the subordinate of a directive or instrumental leader. Instrumental behavior clarifies and increases the subordinate's perception of expectancies, resulting in increased motivation and satisfaction. For structured, routine tasks, the theory postulates that instrumental behavior would be inappropriate because clear expectancies and perceptions have already been attained. Supportive or participative leader behavior is likely to increase the worker's extrinsic satisfaction on a task that may offer intrinsic satisfaction. For example, in a study of a large hospital, it was found that directive or instrumental behavior resulted in higher satisfaction levels for administrative personnel who work on unstructured, ambiguous tasks.[31] On the other hand, for janitors and aides working on routine tasks, supportive leader behavior resulted in higher levels of satisfaction, and directive or instrumental behavior proved to be dissatisfying.

We can also look at the influence of the task by integrating path-goal theory with the job-design literature (see chapter 6). Exhibit 9–11 presents the relationships between growth need strength, job scope (variety, autonomy, feedback, and identity), and the recommended effective leadership style. The important aspect of this exhibit is the concept of congruence between the individual and job. As we discussed in chapter 6, when individual growth needs and the nature of the job match (e.g., high growth needs and high job scope), there is high congruence. When one of these components does not match (e.g., low growth needs and high job scope), a low level of congruence exists.

To illustrate the relationships, consider situation 1 (i.e., high growth needs and job scope). This could be a young accountant who has been given a complex and challenging project to work on for the next year. Because the job matches the level of growth need, the best leadership style for the supervisor to use is probably one that is facilitative and nondirective (i.e., achievement oriented and participative). In other words, the leader should provide some guidance but let the match between the individual and the job be the key influence factor.

Exhibit 9–11 Leadership Style and Individual and Task Influences

Situation	Growth Need	Job Scope	Congruence Between Individual and Job	Recommended Leadership Style for Effectiveness
1	High	High	High	Achievement oriented and participative.
2	Low	High	Low	Directive
3	High	Low	Low	Supportive
4	Low	Low	High	Directive and Supportive

Adapted from Ricky Griffin, "Task Design Determinants of Effective Leader Behavior," *Academy of Management Review* (April 1979), p. 221.

On the other hand, review situation 2. This could also be a young accountant given a complex project to work on for a year. The high job scope, however, does not match the low growth needs. The supervisor in this situation probably needs to be more involved (i.e., directive style) in order to help the individual through the project.

2. *Work group*. The characteristics of work groups may also influence the acceptance of a particular leader's style. One way of examining the relationship between leadership style and the behavior of the work group is through the framework of group development discussed in chapter 7. The relationship between the stages of group development and leadership style is shown in exhibit 9–12. As the exhibit shows, although one type of leadership style may be more important at a particular stage (e.g., instrumental behavior during the orientation stage), the leader cannot neglect any other components of his or her style. For example, consider a group of tellers in a bank who are in the internal problem-solving stage of development. The branch manager's style of leadership at this stage should not only emphasize conflict resolution through a participative style but should also clarify relationships and expectations through instrumental leadership.

3. *Organizational factors*. The final work-environment factor concerns such aspects as: (a) the degree to which rules, procedures, and policies govern an employee's work; (b) high pressures or stressful situations; and (c) situations of high uncertainty. For example, for key-punch tasks in a data-processing department in which task performance is self-evident due to mechanization, contracts, rules and standards, instrumental behavior will not result in expectancy clarification and may be dissatisfying to subordinates. Also, in the trauma ward of a hospital, where the tasks are stressful and pressure-packed, instrumental behavior may be necessary for task accomplishment (i.e., saving lives), but supportive behavior would result in increased social support and satisfaction with interpersonal relationships. Finally, in a work environment that contains a considerable number of uncertainties, such as the direction of the mission-

Exhibit 9–12   Leadership Style and Group-Development Stages: A Path-Goal Interpretation

| Group-Development Stage | Leadership Style | | | |
	Instrumental	Supportive	Participative	Achievement Oriented
Orientation	Assign tasks; clarify roles, rules, and procedures	Give support and consideration to employee needs and behavior	Consult with subordinates in plans, process, and procedures	Develop plan for task accomplishment; set challenging goals
Internal Problem Solving	Revise and strengthen rules and standards; clarify expectations	Exhibit confidence in subordinates' ability to complete the task	Develop participative climate; resolve conflict	Emphasize completion of tasks
Growth and Productivity	Develop feedback; strengthen information networks	Emphasize personal growth and development of subordinates	Develop cohesion; strengthen or elevate group performance norms	Motivate toward task accomplishment
Evaluation and Control	Develop evaluation mechanisms; strengthen feedback and revise rules and procedures	Support group activities; accentuate group accomplishment; emphasize prestige of group	Consult on evaluation procedures; strengthen cohesion and norms	Motivate toward task accomplishment; revise and evaluate goals and plans

control center of a NASA space flight, the flight director may initially behave in a participative manner with subordinates in order to seek possible solutions to an in-flight problem. However, the director will be very instrumental when the final decision is made.

Exhibit 9–13 summarizes the path-goal theory of leader effectiveness. The figure suggests that leader behavior, modified by the characteristics of the subordinates and the work environment, influences the perceptions of valence and expectancies, which then can result in higher motivation, satisfaction, and performance.

Research on Path-Goal Theory

Even though path-goal theory is a recent development in leadership, a growing number of research efforts have been reported. The reports with respect to instrumental, supportive, participative, and achievement-directed leadership have been

Exhibit 9–13 A Summary of Path-Goal Relationships

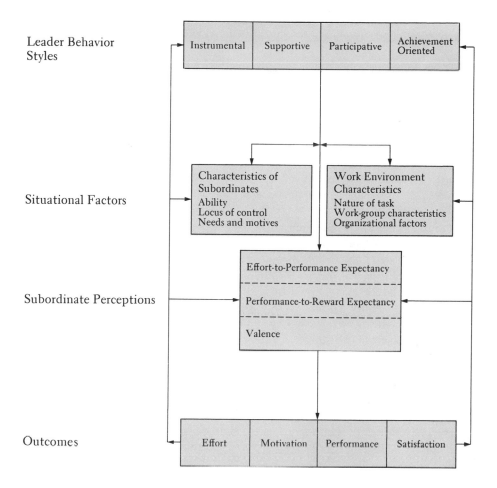

Leader Behavior Styles

Situational Factors

Subordinate Perceptions

Outcomes

encouraging. The majority of the research has focused on the relationship between instrumental and supportive leadership and subordinate behavior for a variety of different tasks. These results tend to support the theory's framework—that instrumental leader behavior is more effective (than supportive behavior) for subordinates working on unstructured tasks, and supportive leader behavior results in high employee satisfaction when subordinates are performing structured, routine tasks.

Not unexpectedly, a number of shortcomings or deficiencies have been reported. First, the measurement of leadership style remains unclear. Initially, initiating structure and consideration scales served as surrogate measures for instrumental and supportive leader behavior dimensions, respectively. It is unclear, however, how participative or achievement-oriented leadership styles can be measured.

Second, the theory's prediction of individual performance remains a cloudy issue. The majority of emphasis has been placed on motivation and satisfaction; however, performance predictions remain unanswered. For example, supervisors of

301

employees who work on routine tasks face somewhat of a paradox. Path-goal theory suggests that a supportive leadership style should be used to increase satisfaction. However, without significant instrumental leadership, the employees may increase their "goofing off," resulting in lower productivity and pressure from top management for increased productivity. Increasing the use of instrumental behavior by the supervisor may increase productivity but create greater dissatisfaction.

Finally, the current formulation of path-goal theory is rapidly developing into an extremely complex framework. As a result, like expectancy theory, a complete test of the theory as well as managers' ability to successfully implement path-goal concepts may be a difficult endeavor.

The theory has not been offered as the final answer to the issue of leadership effectiveness. This important managerial phenomenon is so complex that a universal approach to leadership is not anticipated for years to come, if at all. Overall, however, the path-goal approach to leadership has proven to be a significant contributor to the situational theories because it has identified key leadership styles and situational factors and has shown the relationship between these variables in a complex organizational setting.

The important implication of both Fiedler's contingency model and House's path-goal theory is that the relationship between the leader and his or her subordinates cannot be viewed in a vacuum. A number of different situational factors must be considered before a prediction of leader effectiveness can be made, and the leader's style should vary somewhat with the situation. A summary of these two theories is presented in exhibit 9–14.

Contemporary Issues on Leadership

The study of leadership in organizations has made significant strides during the last thirty years. Much of the progress in the field of leadership can be attributed, in part, to the development of well-formulated theoretical frameworks and the use of well-designed research efforts. As discussed in chapter 2, the integration of theory, research, and application is necessary to the advancement of the field of organizational behavior.

As is the case with most scientific fields of endeavor, there exist a number of contemporary issues that have not been given enough attention. The investigation of these issues may significantly add to the knowledge base on leadership. In this section, we will discuss three such issues: (1) leader reward behavior; (2) the causal relationships between leader behavior and subordinate behavior; and (3) substitutes for leadership.

Leader Reward Behavior

The situational approaches to leadership have generally focused on the impact of the *style* of leadership on subordinate behavior, and *style* has been defined in such terms as task orientation, employee orientation, and instrumental, participative, suppor-

Exhibit 9–14 Summary of Situational Theories

Theory	Leader Behavior Style	Situational Factors	Principal Focus	Research Results
Contingency Model	Task oriented Employee oriented	Leader-member relations Task structure Leader position power	Favorableness of situation for leader (relationship between leader's style and situational factors)	Supportive and nonsupportive findings; major problems concern: (1) how leadership style is measured; (2) unidimensional leadership style; (3) interaction of leadership style and situational factors; and (4) stability of factors and leadership style over time
Path-Goal Theory	Instrumental Supportive Participative Achievement oriented	Individual characteristics: Ability Locus of control Needs and motives Work-environment characteristics: Nature of task Group factors Organizational factors	The leader's function is both supplemental and motivational; leader should exhibit behavior that emphasizes clarification of expectancies and valences	Limited findings, but generally supportive; especially supportive when investigating the interaction with the style of task; major problems concern: (1) measurement of variables; (2) complexity; and (3) lack of predictions with respect to performance

tive, and achievement-oriented behavior. One of the most important aspects of the leadership position—the ability to reward and punish—has recently gained the attention of behavioral scientists and practicing managers.

The framework for the study of the impact of rewards and punishment evolves from the concepts of power and motivation. In particular, both expectancy theory and the operant conditioning approach to motivation stress the importance of rewards based on an employee's behavior and its effect on subsequent attitudes and performance. Positive rewards, such as merit pay increases, recognition, and promotion, that are awarded contingent on the individual's performance serve to strengthen and increase the individual's motivation and performance. The administration of punishment, such as a reprimand from the superior, acts to extinguish undesired behavior on the part of the individual. The anticipated result is that the individual will behave in a manner that is acceptable to the organization.

The studies to date examining the effect of leader reward behavior have been sparse. The findings that have been reported, however, have consistently pointed out two factors that may have a significant meaning for managers. First, the strength of the relationship between positive leader reward behavior and subordinate satisfaction and performance has been found to be significantly greater than that reported for relationships involving leader style components.[32] This suggests that although a manager's style has an important effect on subordinate behavior, the use of positive rewards may have the strongest influence on the behavior and attitudes of employees. This is not surprising if we view the leader from a functional or task-accomplishment perspective. That is, the leader's style generally focuses on the *process* of task accomplishment; leader reward behavior focuses on the culmination of the process, or the actual *degree of task accomplishment*. A group of engineers building a new shopping center may be influenced to perform and are satisfied with the project manager's task-oriented or employee-oriented leadership style during the project's construction phase. However, the subsequent rewards from the manager (e.g., merit pay increases, bonuses, or praise) may have the greatest or most permanent impact on their activities and behavior.

Second, the use of negative rewards, or punishment, by the leader has been found to have different effects on subordinates depending on the individual's organizational level. In particular, research suggests that at the lower organizational levels (e.g., janitors and assembly-line workers), negative rewards have been consistently found to be negatively related to employee satisfaction and performance. On the other hand, at the higher organizational levels (e.g., administrators and managers), negative rewards have been found to be positively related to employee satisfaction and performance. From a situational theoretical framework, it has been suggested that leader-administered punishment may have different effects on the employee, depending on the nature of the individual's task. For example, those in lower organizational levels may view punishment as an indication of their poor job performance. Employees in higher organization levels, such as middle-level managers, may accept punishment or reprimand as a positive factor for their behavior. That is, the nature of the tasks of these higher level employees may be so vague and unclear that punishment is seen as *instrumental* in clearing up ambiguities of their job. In other words, it may be the vagueness of their job that is disruptive to their behavior, not the negative rewards administered by the leader.

Leader Behavior: Cause or Outcome of Subordinate Behavior?

The vast majority of the research efforts examining the area of leadership have been "static" studies; the results, collected at only one point in time, have generally stated that some aspect of leader behavior is "related" to subordinate satisfaction, motivation, or performance.

The major problem with this methodology is that *causality* cannot be investigated. That is, when it is stated that the participative leadership style of a manager is positively *related* to the performance of his or her subordinate, two important questions cannot be answered: (1) Does a participative leadership style cause subordinate performance? or (2) Does subordinate performance cause a participative leadership style? Stated another way, the manager may feel that, "If I am more participative with my subordinates and allow them more freedom and autonomy in their work, they will perform at a higher level." On the other hand, it could be that, "Since my subordinates have performed at such a high level, I will increase their freedom and autonomy by being more participative." To find out which variable comes first, a *longitudinal* study is needed.

The limited number of studies that have investigated the causal relationships between leader behavior and subordinate satisfaction and performance have suggested that certain leader behaviors cause subordinate behavior, and other leader behaviors are a result of certain subordinate actions. The results of some of the research studies to date are shown in exhibit 9–15.[33] At least three possible conclusions can be drawn from this exhibit:

1. Leadership style and reward behavior both lead to job satisfaction (or dissatisfaction).

2. Low-performing subordinates tend to cause leaders to use more task-oriented and punitive award behavior (i.e., punishment).

Exhibit 9–15 Causal Relationships Between Leader Behavior and Subordinate Behavior

Cause	Outcome	Direction	Example
Style			
1. Leader Employee Orientation	Subordinate Job Satisfaction	+	High employee orientation leads to high job satisfaction.
2. Leader Task Orientation	Subordinate Job Satisfaction	–	High task orientation leads to low job satisfaction.
3. Subordinate Performance	Leader Task Orientation	–	Low subordinate performance leads to high task orientation.
Reward Behavior			
4. Leader Positive Rewards	Subordinate Performance	+	High positive rewards (positive reinforcement) lead to high performance.
5. Leader Positive Rewards	Subordinate Job Satisfaction	+	High positive rewards (positive reinforcement) lead to high job satisfaction.
6. Subordinate Performance	Leader Punitive Rewards	–	Low performance leads to high punitive rewards (punishment)

3. For managers, possibly the most important finding is situation 4. Of all the results, this is the only one that shows that leader behavior can lead to, or influence, subordinate performance. This underlines the previous discussion on leader reward behavior, and the material in chapter 5 concerning the importance of reinforcement.

These findings further emphasize the importance to managers of developing the ability to diagnose the various elements of the leadership situation. The effectiveness of a manager's leadership behavior depends to a significant extent on how accurately he or she can diagnose, evaluate, and adapt to the situation. Research efforts examining the causal relationships in leadership style will continue to be of interest to managers and behavioral scientists and to accentuate the dynamic nature of leadership in organizations.

Substitutes for Leadership

In most of our discussion concerning leadership, we have assumed that the leader-subordinate interaction is a formal relationship. This implies that the subordinates are quite dependent upon the leader for direction, support, influence, and rewards.

There are, however, many instances in which "substitutes" for leadership exist that act to reduce the subordinate dependency on the leader.[34] Some of these substitutes for leadership include the following:

Experience and job expertise.   Frequently, an individual employee has worked on a particular job for such a long period that he or she has more knowledge about the job requirements than anyone else, including the supervisor. For example, in many older chemical-manufacturing plants, workers have held their particular job for fifteen years or more, even though there may be frequent changes in supervisors, plant engineers, and plant managers. This senior employee may receive information from the supervisor on the quantity to be produced that day, but the actual manner in which this individual conducts the work may be totally up to him or her. Dependency upon the supervisor is thus minimal.

Professional education, training, and ethics.   Many professional employees— nurses, engineers, and teachers—have gained knowledge of the requirements of their job through pre-employment training and education. Working in various situations, the professional employee may look to professional standards to guide their work, rather than to directions from the leader.

Coworkers and peers.   A third substitute for leadership is the influence that coworkers and peers may have on the individual employee. For example, such factors as group norms, informal leaders, or other managers whom the individual may wish to emulate may have a significant impact on the person's behavior.

Rules, policies, and procedures.   The work of the employee may be so structured and clearly defined that leadership may be considered superfluous. This can occur at all levels in the organization. A rules manual, job descriptions, or contract requirements all may have a significant effect on how the individual performs.

Task satisfaction.   Finally, the employee may derive such satisfaction from working on his or her task that influence attempts by the leader may be viewed as unnecessary. This is particularly the case when considering the leadership styles involving employee-oriented, supportive, or participative behavior. To the extent that satisfaction is provided the subordinate by the task itself, dependency upon the leader for such satisfaction is significantly reduced. This does not mean that in these situations the leader should not be supportive or participative. It does suggest, however, that a mid-range emphasis in such leader behavior may be all that is needed.

The substitutes do not imply that leadership is an unnecessary managerial function. They do suggest, however, that individual employees may be influenced in their work by factors other than the leader's behavior. Leaders are an important part of organizational life. However, management in all types of organizations must be aware that it is too simplistic to consider the subordinate as being guided to goal accomplishment solely by the behavior of the leader.

An Integrative Model of Leadership

In reviewing the three different theoretical approaches of leadership—trait, behavioral, and situational—it should become evident that there is no universally accepted approach to the study and practice of leadership in organizations. It is difficult, if not impossible, for the leader to know and understand all the factors that surround him or her and then to choose the most effective behavior. The study of organizational behavior and performance has not advanced to the point at which accurate predictions of behavioral effects can be made in all situations.

The study of leadership has revealed and identified certain salient factors that are important for the attainment of acceptable levels of performance. An integrative model, presented in exhibit 9–16, attempts to identify these important characteristics or factors.

The model, although not an exhaustive approach, does identify certain important factors that should be considered and evaluated by behavioral scientists and practicing managers, including:

1. *The leader.* Using the leader as the focal point, three factors are identified:
   (a) *Individual characteristics,* including personality characteristics, needs and motives, and previous experience and reinforcement.
   (b) *Leadership style dimension,* including emphasis on instrumental, supportive, participative, achievement-oriented behavior.
   (c) The *reinforcing power* of the leader, particularly the ability to reward and punish.
2. *The subordinate.* The impact of the subordinate on the leadership environment generally originates from the following aspects:
   (a) *Individual characteristics* of the subordinate include such aspects as

Exhibit 9–16 An Integrative Model of Leadership

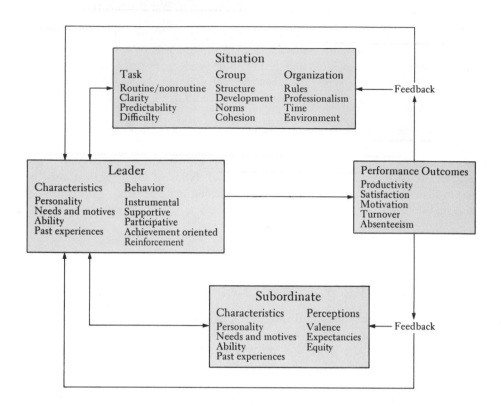

personality, ability, needs and motives, and past experience and reinforcement.

(b) *Perceptions* of expectancies, valence, and equity.

3. *The situation.* Three major aspects should be considered when evaluating the impact of situational factors:

(a) *The nature of the task,* with particular emphasis on such factors as the structure, clarity, predictability, complexity, and difficulty of the task.

(b) *The nature of the group,* particularly the stage of group development, group structure and norms, the group task, and the degree of leader-member relations.

(c) *Organizational factors,* including the emphasis on rules, procedures, and on understanding of professionalism, and environmental uncertainty.

(d) *Nonleader sources of influence,* which may reduce the subordinates' dependency on the leader.

4. *Outcomes.* The result of the leadership process involves the outcomes of the interaction between the leader and his or her subordinates. The *criteria* for

evaluating the outcome include such aspects as productivity, degree of task accomplishment, satisfaction, motivation, turnover, and absenteeism.

5. *Feedback*. The final aspect concerns the dynamic issues of leadership. Consideration must be given to the fact that leader behavior causes certain outcomes, but that certain outcomes may cause or alter the level of leader behavior and have an effect on the other situational variables.

The integrative model attempts to synthesize some of the most important bits of information and knowledge regarding leadership. It does not capture all the variables, but some of the more important ones have been identified and presented. Perhaps the most significant issue for practicing managers is the development of the skill and ability to *diagnose* and *evaluate* the many factors that impact on the leadership process. It is only through this ability to diagnose and evaluate that a manager can alter his or her behavior for maximum effectiveness.

Applications and Implications for the Manager

Leadership

1. Leadership is an attempt at interpersonal influence, which involves the use of power and authority. Authority and the basis of legitimate, reward, and coercive power refer to *organizationally* sanctioned influence. Expert and referent power concern influence based on *individual* characteristics. In analyzing the influence process, attention should be given to the characteristics, resources, and decision role of the person exerting influence in comparison with the characteristics, needs, and decision role of the target person.

2. Three main approaches pertaining to the development of leadership research have been examined: trait, behavioral, and situational theories. The development of leadership research has advanced from a study of individual characteristics of the leader to an examination of the effects of the style of leader behavior, and finally, to considering the impact of situational factors surrounding the leadership environment.

3. The trait approach to leadership emphasized an attempt to identify a finite set of traits or characteristics that would distinguish successful from unsuccessful leaders. The search for these traits included consideration of such factors as physical characteristics, social background, intelligence, and personality. The results proved to be inconsistent across different samples when examining leader effectiveness, but were more promising when the findings were viewed in terms of leader emergence.

4. Dissatisfaction with the trait approach led researchers to examine the actual behavior of the leader in various settings. From these studies, there developed a great deal of confusion and overlap regarding the definition and measurement of leader behavior. Two basic leadership styles, however, are inherent in most behavioral approaches: task orientation and employee orientation.

5. The vast number of studies that have investigated the effects of leadership style from the Ohio State (initiating structure and consideration) and Michigan State (job centered and employee centered) frameworks have generally resulted in inconclusive findings. The evidence suggested that in some cases a task-oriented style was the most effective; in others, an employee-oriented style was best; and in

still others, a style that was high in both task orientation and employee orientation was most effective in relationship with performance and employee satisfaction.

6. Behavioral scientists generally conclude that the findings of the trait and behavioral approaches to leadership suggest that situational variables should be considered in any analysis of the leadership environment. Situational variables include such aspects as the characteristics of the leader and subordinates, nature of the task, group-development stage, group structure, and various organizational factors. The manager's effectiveness as a leader becomes more a function of his or her ability to diagnose the situation and then to determine an appropriate leadership style or to change the various situational factors.

7. Fiedler's contingency model was one of the first approaches to leadership that included situational factors in its framework. His basic proposal was that the effectiveness of groups was dependent on the interaction between leadership style and situational favorableness for the leader. The situational favorableness was determined by an analysis of leader-member relations, task structure, and leader's position power. The criticisms of the contingency model have focused on its validity, theoretical base, and methodology. For practicing managers, the model has great value in identifying some of the important situational variables that must be considered. As an analysis or predictive model, the leader and situational variables affect each other or interact to yield group effectiveness.

8. House's path-goal theory is another situational approach to leadership that is based on the interactions of leadership style and the situational variables of subordinate characteristics and the characteristics of the work environment. The value of this model to practicing managers is twofold. First, the leader's style is identified in terms of four dimensions, rather than one dimension as proposed by Fiedler. This multi-dimensional view of leadership style is more representative of the nature of the manager's job. Second, the path-goal model details the specific interactions between leader behavior and the situational factors. This provides the manager with some knowledge of how his or her behavior may be adjusted to different situations. Major criticisms focused on the growing complexity of the theory and the limitation of the theory to adequately discuss the aspect of performance.

9. Beyond the basic theoretical frameworks, certain contemporary issues are important for practicing managers. It is suggested that: (a) the power of leader reward behavior should not be overlooked as an important influence mechanism; (b) not only can leader behavior cause subordinate behavior, but the reverse can also occur; and (c) in many organizations, significant substitutes for leadership exist, so that dependency of the subordinates on the leader is diminished.

Review of Theories, Research, and Applications

1. Discuss the relationship between authority and power.

2. Under what conditions can the behavior of an informal leader be dysfunctional to the organization?

3. Why has the trait approach to leadership been relatively unsuccessful in predicting leader effectiveness?

4. Discuss the similarities and differences between the Ohio State and Michigan studies.

5. In Fiedler's contingency model, how can the organization engineer the job to fit the manager?

6. Is leadership style flexible or rigid?

7. Discuss the similarities and differences between Fiedler's "situational favorableness" and House's "situational factors."

8. What is the relationship between organizational factors and leadership style?

9. How do House's leadership dimensions and the dimensions of leader reward behavior differ?

10. Why is it important for the manager to develop the ability to diagnose and evaluate the situation?

Notes

1. For a thorough review of leadership theory and research, see Ralph M. Stogdill, *Handbook of Leadership* (New York: Free Press, 1974).

2. James L. Gibson, John M. Ivancevich, and James H. Donnelly, Jr. *Organizations* (Dallas: Business Publications, 1976), p. 160

3. J. R. P. French, Jr. and B. Raven, "The Bases of Social Power," in *Group Dynamics*, 2nd ed., ed. D. Cartwright and A. F. Zander (Evanston, Ill.: Row, Peterson, 1960), pp. 607–23.

4. Martin Patchen, "The Focus and Basis of Influence in Organizational Decisions," *Organizational Behavior and Human Performance*, 1974, p. 197.

5. Stogdill, *Handbook of Leadership*, pp. 74–75.

6. Ralph M. Stogdill, "Personal Factors Associated with Leadership: A Survey of the Literature," *Journal of Applied Psychology* (January 1948), pp. 35–71.

7. R. M. Powell, *Race, Religion, and the Promotion of the American Executive* (Columbus: Bureau of Business Research, College of Administrative Science, Ohio State University, 1969).

8. E. P. Hollander and J. W. Julian, "Contemporary Trends in the Analysis of Leadership Processes," *Psychological Bulletin*, 1969, pp. 387–97.

9. Edwin A. Fleishman, "The Leadership Opinion Questionnaire," in *Leader Behavior and Its Description and Measurement*, ed. Ralph M. Stogdill and A. E. Coons (Columbus: Bureau of Business Research, Ohio State University, 1957).

10. Ibid.

11. J. K. Hemphill and A. E. Coons, "Development of the Leader Behavior Description Questionnaire," in *Leader Behavior: Its Description and Measurement*, ed. Ralph M. Stogdill and A. E. Coons (Columbus: Bureau of Business Research, Ohio State University, 1957).

12. Edwin A. Fleishman, "Twenty Years of Consideration and Structure," in *Current Developments in the Study of Leadership*, ed. E. A. Fleishman and J. G. Hunt (Carbondale: Southern Illinois University, 1973) pp. 1–37.

13. Robert J. House, Alan C. Filley, and Steven Kerr, "Relation of Leader Consideration and Initiating Structure to R and D Subordinates' Satisfaction," *Administrative Science Quarterly*, March 1971, pp. 19–30.

14. A. K. Korman, "Consideration, Initiating Structure, and Organizational Criteria—A Review," *Personnel Psychology*, Winter 1966, pp. 349–61.

15. Rensis Likert, *The Human Organization* (New York: McGraw-Hill, 1967).

16. N. C. Morse and E. Reimer, "The Experimental Change of a Major Organizational Variable," *Journal of Abnormal and Social Psychology,* January 1956, pp. 120–29.

17. Walter Hill, "Leadership Style: Rigid or Flexible," *Organizational Behavior and Human Performance,* 1973, pp. 35–47.

18. David G. Bowers and Stanley E. Seashore, "Predicting Organizational Effectiveness with a Four-Factor Theory of Leadership," *Administrative Science Quarterly,* September 1966, pp. 238–63; Ralph M. Stogdill, *Manual for the Leader Behavior Description Questionnaire—Form XII* (Columbus: Bureau of Business Research, Ohio State University, 1965).

19. Robert Tannenbaum and Warren H. Schmidt, *Harvard Business Review,* May–June 1973, pp. 162–80.

20. Fred E. Fiedler, *A Theory of Leadership Effectiveness* (New York: McGraw-Hill, 1967).

21. Ibid., p. 41.

22. Ibid., p. 45.

23. For example, see G. Graen, J. B. Orris, and K. M. Alvares, "Contingency Model of Leadership Effectiveness: Some Experimental Results," *Journal of Applied Psychology,* June 1971, pp. 196–201; J. T. McMahon, "The Contingency Theory: Logic and Method Revisited," *Personnel Psychology,* December 1972, pp. 697–710; Lars L. Larson and K. Rowland, "Leadership Style and Cognitive Complexity," *Academy of Management Journal,* 1974, pp. 36–45; J. Stinson and L. Tracy, "Some Disturbing Characteristics of the LPC Score," *Personnel Psychology,* 1974, pp. 477–85; R. Vecchio, "An Empirical Examination of the Validity of Fiedler's Model," *Organizational Behavior and Human Performance* (June 1977), pp. 180–206.

24. Robert J. House, "A Path-Goal Theory of Leader Effectiveness," *Administrative*

Science Quarterly, 1971, pp. 321–32; Martin G. Evans, "The Effects of Supervisory Behavior on the Path-Goal Relationship," *Organizational Behavior in Human Performance,* May 1970, pp. 277–98.

25. Victor H. Vroom, *Work and Motivation* (New York: Wiley, 1964).

26. House, "A Path-Goal Theory," p. 323.

27. Robert J. House and Terence R. Mitchell, "Path-Goal Theory of Leadership," *Journal of Contemporary Business,* Autumn 1974, pp. 81–98.

28. Ibid., p. 84.

29. J. B. Rotter, "Generalized Expectancies for Internal vs. External Control of Reinforcement," *Psychological Monographs* 80, no. 609 (1966).

30. Terence R. Mitchell, "Motivation and Participation: An Integration," *Academy of Management Journal,* 1973, pp. 160–79.

31. Andrew D. Szilagyi and Henry P. Sims, "An Exploration of the Path-Goal Theory of Leadership in a Health Care Environment," *Academy of Management Journal,* December 1974, pp. 622–34.

32. Henry P. Sims and Andrew D. Szilagyi, "Leader Reward Behavior and Subordinate Satisfaction and Performance," *Organizational Behavior and Human Performance,* 1975, pp. 426–38.

33. A. Lowin and J. Craig, "The Influence of Level of Performance on Managerial Style," *Organizational Behavior and Human Performance,* 1968, pp. 440–58; Charles N. Greene, "The Reciprocal Nature of Influence Between Leader and Subordinate Performance," *Journal of Applied Psychology,* April 1975, pp. 187–93.

34. Steven Kerr et al., "Toward a Contingency Theory of Leadership Based Upon the Consideration and Initiating Structure Literature," *Organizational Behavior and Human Performance,* 1974, pp. 62–82.

Additional References

Fiedler, F. E., and Chemers, M. M. *Leadership and Effective Management.* Glenview, Ill.: Scott, Foresman, 1974.

Fleishman, E. A. "Twenty Years of Consideration and Structure." In *Current Developments in the Study of*

Leadership, edited by E. Fleishman and J. Hunt, pp. 1–38. Carbondale, Ill.: Southern Illinois University, 1973.

GRAEN, G., DANSEREAU, F.; and MINAMI, T. "Dysfunctional Leadership Styles." *Organizational Behavior and Human Performance,* 1972, pp. 216–36.

GREINER, L. E. "What Managers Think of Participative Leadership." *Harvard Business Review,* May–June 1973, pp. 111–18.

HUNT, J. G., and LARSON, L. L. *Leadership: The Cutting Edge.* Carbondale, Ill.: Southern Illinois University, 1977.

HUNT, J. G., and LARSON, L. L., eds. *Contingency Approaches to Leadership.* Carbondale, Ill.: Southern Illinois University, 1974.

LIKERT, R. *The Human Organization.* New York: McGraw-Hill, 1967.

REDDIN, W. J. *Managerial Effectiveness.* New York: McGraw-Hill, 1970.

VROOM, V. H. "Can Leaders Learn to Lead?" *Organizational Dynamics,* Winter 1976, pp. 17–28.

VROOM, V. H., and YETTON, P. W. *Leadership and Decision Making.* Pittsburgh: University of Pittsburgh, 1973.

YUKL, G. A. "Toward a Behavioral Theory of Leadership." *Organizational Behavior and Human Performance,* 1971, pp. 414–40.

A Case of Leadership

The Distribution Center

Dave Griffin is a supervisor in the receiving and marking department of Singer-Maris' distribution center, a large Midwest retail department store. Dave's particular unit of twenty-five people is responsible for unpacking and inspecting goods (women's fashions) from manufacturers, placing price tags on each product, and separating the goods for shipment to the four branch stores.

At almost 6:30 p.m. on a Friday night, over an hour past his usual time to leave for home, Dave was in his office, looking out the window with a very concerned expression on his face, trying to remember and understand what happened over the last two months. His first thoughts recall the three-day supervisory training program he attended some eight weeks ago at a nearby university management-development center. The program covered many topics, from communications to understanding motivation.

The most vivid experience was a session on leadership, at which he completed a questionnaire that was supposed to measure his style of leadership on two dimensions: task orientation and employee orientation. The results, which showed him to be very high on task orientation but very low on employee orientation, were a surprise to him because he always thought of himself as being pretty much people centered on the job. He also recalled the seminar leader suggesting that the most effective leadership style was one that was high on both task orientation and employee orientation.

This leadership session was of particular importance to Dave because of the problems he was having in his department. The busy spring season was just around the corner, which meant a big productivity push by management to get the increased flow of goods to the stores. His subordinates could be divided almost equally into two groups; those that performed at the 100 percent performance standard (regarding the number of units unloaded, inspected, and priced per day), and those that rarely exceeded 85 percent of the standard.

Two subordinates were key examples of these two groups. First, there was Glenn Fields, who worked as an inspector for the last three years. Glenn was dependable, quality conscious, and always performed between 100 percent and 105 percent of standard. On the other hand, there was Roger Gardner, an inspector on a checking line next to Glenn's, who had been employed at the distribution center for almost two years. In Dave's opinion, Roger spent too much time "goofing" around, socializing with other workers, and being the first one out the door at 5:00 p.m. each day. His performance rarely exceeded 80 percent of standard. Several times, Dave had strongly warned Roger about his lack of attention to his work and his performance. These warnings usually had an effect for a few days, but then his old ways returned. Roger was not the only one who received these warnings from Dave.

The supervisory training program convinced Dave that what he needed to do to improve the performance of his subordinates was to increase his employee-oriented behavior and attempt to be high on each style dimension. He made a special point to be more open and friendly to Roger and other low performers, to take more interest in Roger's personal life, and to try to be more sympathetic about the increased emphasis on performance.

As Dave sat looking out the window, he was both dismayed and puzzled. His attempt at being more employee oriented was a flop. Not only had Roger's performance not changed, but many subordinates, including Glenn Fields, were performing under 90 percent of standard. With the spring season just beginning, his supervisor, the department manager, and even the center's superintendent were on his back to improve his units' performance. He sat there wondering what to do next.

Case Primer Questions

1. Evaluate Dave's experience at the supervisory training program.

2. Why was his attempt to be more "employee-oriented" a failure?

3. What change in Dave's leader behavior is needed to improve the performance of his unit?

Experiential Exercise

Leader Behavior Inventory

Purpose

1. To understand the different components that constitute leader behavior.

2. To measure actual and desired behaviors of supervisors.

Required understanding

The student should be familiar with the literature on leadership.

How to set up
the exercise

Each student should complete the Leader Behavior Inventory either prior to or actually in class.

Instructions for the exercise

1. *Option 1:* The students should complete the Leader Behavior Inventory in exhibit 9–17 as it relates to their supervisors. Note that two responses are required: (1) *actual* (column 1); and (2) *desired* (column 2) behaviors. Score the inventory for the four leader behaviors using exhibit 9–18, in which column 1 are the *actual* scores, and column 2 are the *desired* scores.

2. *Option 2:* The students should complete the Leader Behavior Inventory as a self-analysis instrument. That is, they should put themselves in the role of supervisor. Score the inventory as noted in Option 1.

Exhibit 9–17 Leader Behavior Inventory

The following questions concern various leader behaviors. Each of the questions should be evaluated according to the following responses:

Strongly Disagree	Disagree	Neither Agree nor Disagree	Agree	Strongly Agree
1	2	3	4	5

Two separate responses are required. In column 1, please mark your responses according to how you evaluate the *actual* behavior of the supervisor. In column 2, please mark your responses according to how you would *desire* the supervisor to behave.

Question	Column 1 (Actual)	Column 2 (Desired)
1. Your supervisor decides *what* work will be done and *how* it will be done.	_____	_____
2. Your supervisor would personally pay you a compliment if you did outstanding work.	_____	_____
3. Your supervisor is friendly and approachable.	_____	_____
4. Your supervisor would give you a reprimand if your work were below average.	_____	_____
5. Your supervisor maintains high standards of performance for his/her employees.	_____	_____
6. Your supervisor would praise you for your work performance if it were especially good.	_____	_____
7. Your supervisor looks out for the personal welfare of his/her employees.	_____	_____
8. Your supervisor would recommend that you receive little or no pay increase if your work were consistently below average.	_____	_____
9. Your supervisor treats his/her employees without considering their feelings.	_____	_____
10. Your supervisor would recommend a significant pay increase if your work performance were consistently above average.	_____	_____
11. Your supervisor lets his/her employees know what is expected of them.	_____	_____
12. Your supervisor would reprimand you if your work were not as good as the work of others in your department.	_____	_____

Exhibit 9—18 Scoring Instructions

For each of the four leader behaviors (A to D) below, compute a total score by summing the responses to the appropriate questions. Note that question 9 is *reversed* in value, and the responses have to be subtracted from 6 to get a value. Transfer the scores to the *Final Scores*, where column I are the *actual* behaviors and column 2 are the *desired* behaviors.

Behavior	Column 1 Actual			Column 2 Desired			Final Scores 1 2
	Question		*Response*	*Question*		*Response*	
	(#1)	=	+ ____	(#1)	=	+ ____	
A	(#5)	=	+ ____	(#5)	=	+ ____	
	(#11)	=	+ ____	(#11)	=	+ ____	
	(Total ÷ 3) = A_1 = + ____			(Total ÷ 3) = A_2 = + ____			(___) (___) A_1 A_2
	(#3)	=	+ ____	(#3)	=	+ ____	
B	(#7)	=	+ ____	(#7)	=	+ ____	
	(6 − #9)	=	+ ____	(6 − #9)	=	+ ____	
	(Total ÷ 3) = B_1 = + ____			(Total ÷ 3) = B_2 = + ____			(___) (___) B_1 B_2
	(#2)	=	+ ____	(#2)	=	+ ____	
C	(#6)	=	+ ____	(#6)	=	+ ____	
	(#10)	=	+ ____	(#10)	=	+ ____	
	(Total ÷ 3) = C_1 = + ____			(Total ÷ 3) = C_2 = + ____			(___) (___) C_1 C_2
	(#4)	=	+ ____	(#4)	=	+ ____	
D	(#8)	=	+ ____	(#8)	=	+ ____	
	(#12)	=	+ ____	(#12)	=	+	
	(Total ÷ 3) = D_1 = + ____			(Total ÷ 3) = D_2 = + ____			(___) (___) D_1 D_2

A Performance Oriented Framework to Study Organizational Behavior

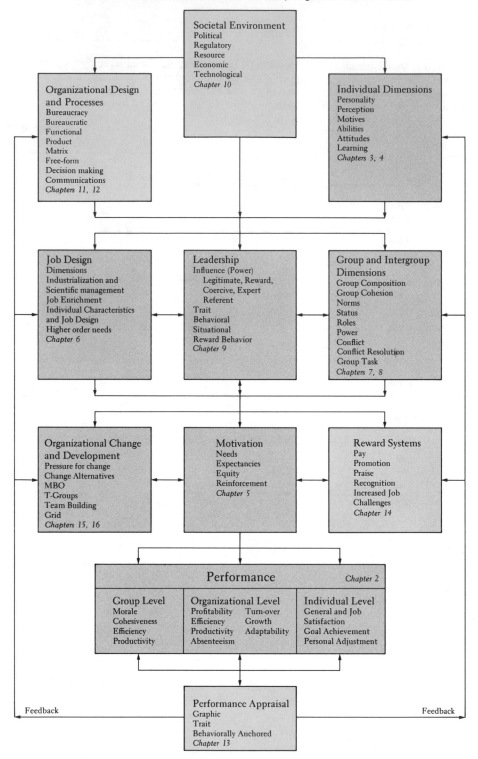

PART FOUR

Organizational Structure and Processes

CHAPTER 10

Organizational Dimensions

Thus far, we have examined the field of organizational behavior, how organizations can be scientifically studied, and both individual and group dimensions. For a comprehensive perspective of the behavior of people at work to emerge, it is necessary to look at another important factor—the organization itself. A close examination of various organizations reveals many similarities and differences, which make them difficult to study, compare, and analyze. It is somewhat tenuous to assume or to propose that the specific properties found in one organization will be found in another. Furthermore, it is bold to suggest that a successful job-design or motivation program in one organization would be as effective in another. In this chapter, we will attempt to review and consider some of the theories and conceptual models of organizations by examining the important organizational characteristics of environmental forces, organizational goals, and technology and the role they play in shaping behavior and performance. The internal design characteristics of organizations will be discussed in the next chapter.

The Organization as a System

Organizations pervade our lives from birth to death. They surround us every minute and certainly have an impact on our experiences. Each of us interacts with a number of organizations at the same time. We receive our mail, work, purchase goods, acquire knowledge, and occasionally suffer and recover from an illness, all within the workings of various organizations. The exact manner in which we view an organization depends to some extent on our particular orientation. The industrial engineer concentrates on the efficiency of operations within an organization. The sociologist is concerned with the structure, processes, and groups within organizations. The operating employee often centers his or her attention on the reward system of the organization.

Often, organizations are described as hierarchies with a superior who delegates authority and in turn passes authority to other subordinates.[1] Because each superior in the system has a number of subordinates, the organization is often conceptualized as a pyramid.[2] This type of arrangement provides basically a top-down approach, which will be discussed in more detail in analyzing organizational design in the next chapter. Another way to view an organization involves an input-transformation-output approach, which is most often referred to as a systems model.

Organizations have various *outputs,* such as number of automobiles produced, banking services provided, patients cured, or students receiving degrees, depending, of course, upon the type of organization. The output at the organizational level of analysis is the result of performing transformations upon various *inputs.* A community hospital's input is sick patients, which it plans to transform into people with good health. In some cases, this transformation is not possible because of the type and state of the illness. The activities of the hospital's personnel and equipment are coordinated so that optimal patient recovery goals are achieved. A simplistic systems view of an organization involves a number of activities, namely receiving inputs; transforming the inputs; controlling, coordinating, and maintaining the transformation activities; and generating outputs. Exhibit 10–1 shows a basic macro-oriented systems model.

Input Factors

Inputs are human, machine, raw-material, informational, and instructional resources. From an organizational perspective, the actions performed within the system depend upon each of these factors, and the transformations that occur require the coordination, control, and maintenance of them.

As indicated in exhibit 10–1, inputs can originate from internal and external sources. *Internal* factors concern, for example, production techniques, technical and managerial knowledge, and internally generated capital. *External* factors generally relate to the *environmental* forces acting on the organization. The source of

Exhibit 10–1 A Basic Systems Model

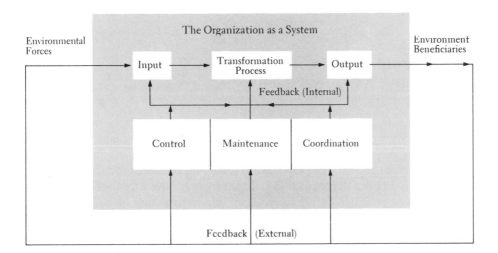

321

these factors can be customers, raw-material suppliers, legislative bodies, the technological community, investors, competitors, a foundation, or other similar societal organizations.

Transformation Process

Organizations perform many different types of transformations upon inputs.[3] The input's form, shape, condition, or attitude can be changed as a result. An oil company takes crude oil and changes it into gasoline for automobiles; a lathe operator works a wooden block into a lamp. The resource input is changed by processes, human skills and judgments, and technological sophistication.

The decisions on how the job tasks are to be grouped and differentiated to transform the inputs into desirable outputs require managerial decision making. The decisions involve the stipulation of how to do the work. Some refer to *technology* as the knowledge of how to do something.[4] It can be defined as the people-machine activities carried out in the organizational system.

It is not uncommon for an organization to be involved in many types of transformations including form, shape, condition, attitude, aggregation, and location. However, one form of transformation will usually predominate. The taxicab driver is primarily engaged in location transformation, and the psychiatrist is concerned primarily with attitude transformation.

Control Subsystem

From an organizational perspective, the system is the organization, which consists of a number of subsystems. One important subsystem involves control. In order to facilitate the flow of inputs, transformation, and outputs, it is necessary to introduce some degree of control. The term *control* has a number of meanings, some of which are:

1. To review.
2. To verify.
3. To compare with standards.
4. To use authority to bring about compliance.
5. To restrain.

The underlying criteria for control are the *goals* of the organization. Goals represent the desired state of affairs for the organization and originate from the decisions of management (internal) and the needs and desires of society (external).[5] For example, a police department in a large city may have a goal of a 10 percent reduction in major crime during the year; an oil company may have a goal of a 12 percent return on investment; a hospital may set a goal of a 15 percent cut in costs with no decrease in service; or a governmental body may set a goal of landing men on the moon by 1970, as did the late President Kennedy. The key points are that goals have internal and external origins and represent performance criteria with time and magnitude components.

Control and goal-setting activities are necessary in every organization. They are used in conjunction with planning, coordinating, and motivating activities to form the foundation of the managerial process. The success of the control activities depends on many factors, such as the measures utilized, the people exercising control and those being controlled, the resources available, and the clarity of organization goals.

Maintenance Subsystem

In order to transform inputs into goods and services that contribute to the goal attainment of the organization, some form or framework must be developed to maintain activities. This maintenance framework is commonly termed the *structure* of the organization, and is the subject of chapter 11. Organizational structure refers to: (1) how jobs are defined and combined into different functions or departments; (2) the distribution of authority, responsibility, and accountability; and (3) the location of major decision-making activities.

The manner in which an organization and resources are structured does not guarantee that employees will comply with assigned role duties and requirements to perform their job. Therefore, subsystems for socializing, rewarding, and sanctioning are needed within an organization. These subsystems primarily function to enhance the interrelationships among people that are so necessary to accomplish goals. They weld people together into an ordered, functioning system and are classified as a *maintenance subsystem*.

The maintenance subsystem results in pressure for institutionalization as a procedure for bringing about an orderly organization. Many specific mechanisms are developed in the interest of maintaining the organization. Selection procedures are used to screen out applicants who do not seem likely to fit the system. Socialization practices are used to help bring people together. Reward systems are used to motivate, retain, and develop personnel. Policies and guidelines are established so that the norms of organizational functioning are understood.

In a general sense, the mechanisms used by most organizations to maintain some semblance of stability seek to formalize organizational behavior. If a standard operating procedure could be legitimitized and established for all human behavior in the system, then the problem of predictability is made easier. Unfortunately, this logical solution for creating a smoothly functioning system has not been discovered, nor is it likely to be.

Coordination Subsystem

The coordination or integration of organizational activities is a function that must be performed continually. *Integration* is defined as the process of achieving unity of effort among the various subsystems in the accomplishment of goals.[6] Organizations typically establish several different mechanisms for coordination. Three primary mechanisms have been suggested: (1) facilitation; (2) voluntary practice; and (3) the administrative system.[7]

Facilitated coordination.   In organizations that face frequent changes in environment, such as electronics or chemical companies, there are often individuals appointed to the task of coordination. In studying how successful firms with a high order of integration operate, researchers have found that liaison positions and departments were used. Some of the required attributes of successful coordinators appear to be the ability to communicate and influence others and knowledge of the environment.[8]

Voluntary coordination.   It is possible for individuals in an organization to be self-starting and self-directing in achieving coordination. In order to voluntarily coordinate, individuals must be aware of the goals of the unit, understand their job role, and be confident in their ability to bring about coordination. This type of knowledge and confidence is really a large requirement. One of the most difficult things for any employee of an organization to grasp involves the goals of the unit. Goal clarity in this era of ever-changing environments and personnel is something that can usually be partially achieved, but to expect 100 percent clarity is somewhat unrealistic. This is especially true for those not involved in the goal-setting process within organizations.

Directive coordination.   Some coordination relies heavily upon the administrative or hierarchical system. Directive coordination involves formal procedural arrangements that are designed to carry out most of the routine coordination work automatically. To the extent that procedures can be made routine, it is not necessary to establish a hierarchy to achieve coordination. For example, the tasks on an assembly line are typically routine and are specified by the supervisor or are dictated by the equipment.

Output Factors

Organizations export some product or service into the environment. The product may be gasoline or automobiles or services such as health care, banking, and electricity. A useful typology to understand the possible outputs of systems is suggested by Blau and Scott.[9] They consider output from the position of the prime recipient of the output. For a business firm, the most obvious beneficiaries of the input-transformation-control-maintenance-coordination processes are the customers, the owners, and the employees. Each of them must receive something from the organization, or they will withdraw their support, which would mean the demise of the company. In this sense, beneficiaries are all considered equal. In reality, some beneficiaries receive more than others.

The recipient of something from an organization undergoes a form of change. If a patient receives an operation to correct a problem, he or she has received the benefit of medical know-how. Stockholders who receive dividend checks increase their bank account or discretionary income. The patient is a beneficiary who has changed because of an intrinsic or personal relationship; the stockholders have changed because of an extrinsic relationship with the company.

Another way of distinguishing the relationship one has with an organization is on the basis of ownership. A tennis club and a prison are set up to change people in them. The tennis club is designed to provide recreational opportunities, and the prison is supposed to provide rehabilitation. The tennis club is owned by the members who pay annual dues and an initiation fee. The members control and influence the direction of the club. In a prison, the inmates do not own the organization, nor do they exercise legitimate control or influence on the system.

Thus, we have identified two broad dimensions that can distinguish among prime beneficiaries of an organization's output: (1) whether the benefits are extrinsic or intrinsic; and (2) whether the ownership is specific or broad. This enables us to establish a two-by-two matrix (see exhibit 10–2) to classify organizational outputs on the basis of the prime beneficiary.

Mutual benefit associations.   In mutual benefit organizations, the members are the prime beneficiaries of the output. The ownership is specified and the benefits are intrinsic. These organizations could be religious orders, professional associations, sororities, fraternities, and so on.

Productive enterprises.   The ownership of a productive enterprise is specific, but the benefit is extrinsic. The typical business organization is the best example of this type of system.

Service organizations.   The prime beneficiary of the output of a service organization is a client. Thus, the benefits are intrinsic, but the ownership is broad. Included in this category would be hospitals, schools, and prisons.

Commonweal organizations.   The general public is the prime beneficiary of commonweal organizations. The benefits are extrinsic, and the ownership general. Police departments, the military, and the Internal Revenue Service are examples.

Now that we have discussed the major features of the basic systems model shown in exhibit 10–1, we can apply it specifically to our discussion of organizational

Exhibit 10–2 A Typology for Classifying Outputs of Organizations on the Basis of Prime Beneficiary

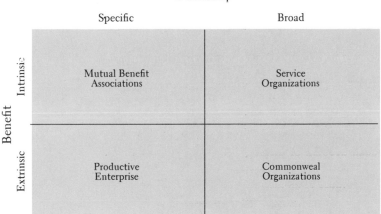

dimensions and use it as the framework for our study (see exhibit 10–3). A number of important points should be noted from exhibit 10–3. First, an organization is in constant interaction with its *environment*. The environment provides not only the input of raw material but also can influence the internal functioning of the organization. For example, governmental concerns over pollution and energy have not only impacted the *goals* of the various automobile manufacturers (e.g., their profits, market shares), but the emissions and gas mileage requirements have forced them to utilize (and sometimes create) new processes and *technologies*.

Second, the environment, organizational goals, and technology are seen as influencing the design or *structure* of the organization (see chapter 11). Third, the *internal environment,* which consists of organizational climate, the important processes of decision making, communication, performance evaluation, rewards, and people as individuals and in groups, is involved in supporting the goals and structure by influencing the outcomes of the organization. The feedback loop brings information from outside and inside the organization, thereby providing information on all facets of goal achievement. This perspective emphasizes that an organization is more than simply a technical or social system. It is more accurate to view it as composed of a number of subsystems attempting to achieve various goals.

Exhibit 10–3 Basic Organizational Dimensions

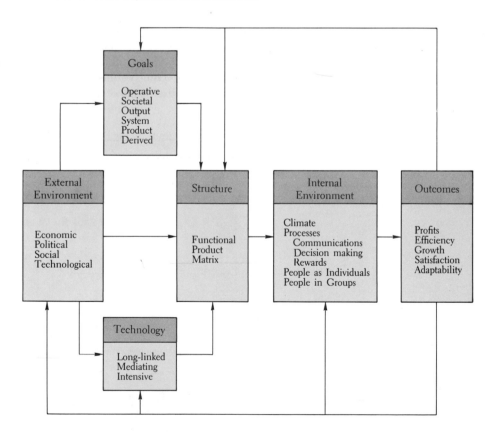

A systems approach to organizations is concerned with the relationship of the subsystems and the environment. It is our intent throughout this book to view the organization as an open system. Traditional management scholars were primarily closed-system advocates. They focused on the internal operations of an organization and studied the organization separately from the environment in which it *~ unrealistic* operated. It is our belief that this view does not provide a realistic or complete picture of organizations and their impact on behavior.

The Organization and
Its External Environment

Organizations must be studied in relation to the interactions they have with the environment. To ignore the internal factors of motivation, group formation, leadership, and organizational structure is to provide only a partial analysis of organizations. The same may be said when the environmental factors impinging upon the organization are not considered. It is therefore essential to consider both the internal factors and the environment when considering organizational behavior and performance. Our discussion of the environment will consider three factors: (1) environmental components; (2) dimensions of the environment; and (3) boundary-spanning activities.

Environmental Components

In the broadest sense, the environment is everything external to the organization's boundaries. However, it is useful to make the distinction between the *general* environment and the specific *task* environment of an organization.[10] Consider, for example, a large company that concentrates on energy-related matters (e.g., Exxon, Gulf, Shell) and a state-supported university. As shown in exhibit 10–4, these institutions operate in a *general* environment with five broad *components:* (1) political; (2) economic; (3) resource; (4) social; and (5) technological. The general environmental factors each affect most organizations.

The individual organization, however, is not influenced *equally* by all general environmental forces. As shown in exhibit 10–4, for example, the specific political environmental component of an energy company is different from that of the state-supported university. The *task* environment is viewed as a more specific set of forces that directly impact the internal functioning of an organization. Although the *general* environment is the same for all organizations, the *task* environment is somewhat or totally different for each organization.

Environmental Dimensions

Beyond the issue of environmental components, the task environment of organizations can be viewed along two *dimensions:* (1) the degree of *change;* and (2) the degree of *complexity.*[11] The degree of *change* refers to the extent to which the components of the task environment remain relatively stable over time, or are in a dynamic state. In essence, can a manager view his or her company's environment as

Exhibit 10–4 General Environment, Task Environment, and Environmental Components

Environmental Component	General Environment	Task Environment	
		State-Supported University	Energy Company
Political	The general political climate of society; public image and attitudes toward product and services.	Funding levels from the state; tenure restrictions; faculty unionization.	Divestiture and regulation; oil embargo; nationalization by foreign countries of company resources.
Economic	The state of the economies of different nations; relationships with customers, suppliers, and competitors.	Increasing education costs; decreased enrollments; relationships with private foundations and other universities.	Increasing production costs; high crude oil prices; varying customer needs.
Resource	The availability of resources and constraints facing organizations.	Constraints on funds from the state, private foundations, and government grant agencies; availability of quality instructors.	Declining raw-material sources (i.e., crude oil); availability of alternative sources (e.g., solar, nuclear, coal).
Social	The general socio-logical and cultural changes in society.	Questions concerning the value of a college degree; continuing education programs.	Attitudes toward price fixing and kickbacks; concerns over pollution and destruction of natural resources.
Technological	The level of techno-logical advancement in society.	Teaching innovations, such as use of computers, video tape, etc.	Movement away from oil to nuclear and solar energy; non-gasoline-powered automobiles.

being fairly stable from year to year with respect, for example, to the political and economic sectors? Or, are situations constantly arising that may take the organization by surprise?

The degree of *complexity,* ranging from simple to complex, refers to whether the components of an organization's task environment are few or many in number. In other words, does the firm interact with several or few customers, suppliers, and competitors? The two dimensions can be combined into a four-quadrant matrix, as shown in exhibit 10–5.

For example, quadrant I in exhibit 10–5 depicts an organization that operates in a fairly stable environment with few external interactions (i.e., with customers,

Exhibit 10–5 Environmental Dimensions

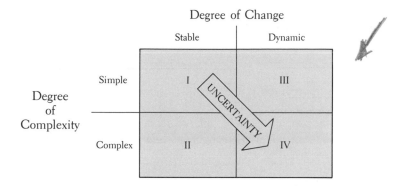

suppliers, and competitors). Such an environment could be that of a container company specializing in corrugated boxes. The task environment has remained relatively unchanged over the years, and the sources of raw material, the number of competitors, and the major customers are easily identified. On the other hand, consider quadrant IV, where a dynamic (i.e., changing) environment is coupled with a complex set of external interactions. This could be a computer software company. The state of the task environment, particularly the technological component, is rapidly changing, and the numbers of users of the product and the competitors grow each month.

The two environmental dimensions contribute to determine what has been termed *environmental uncertainty*.[12] As the task environment of an organization moves from stable and simple to dynamic and complex, the lack of certain information about the environment, and the lack of knowledge about the effects of specific organizational actions, increases to the extent that managerial decision making becomes a highly uncertain process. In our quadrant I example, decisions by managers in a container firm are influenced by few factors or variables. Decisions can therefore be made with some certainty about the end result. On the other hand, in the computer software company in quadrant IV, managers face a quite uncertain state as to the attitudes, behavior, and actions of customers, suppliers, and competitors. Therefore, the decisions are made under conditions of uncertainty.

As we will discuss in subsequent sections of this chapter and in the next chapter, uncertainty affects a number of organizational activities. Not only are goals influenced by the level of uncertainty, but organizations will alter or change certain structural and process components in order to diminish the effects of the uncertainty. An important organizational function that deals with the environment is the *boundary-spanning activity*.

Boundary-spanning Activity

All systems have boundaries that separate them from their environment. Examination of these boundaries aids us in distinguishing clearly between open and closed systems. The closed system has rigid, nonaccessible boundaries, whereas the open system is linked to its environmental components. Boundaries are easier to conceptualize when discussing physical systems than when discussing organizational systems because the organization's "boundary" does not refer to the edge of its property.

In organizational behavior terminology, the *boundaries* are the demarcation lines for the definition of system activities, for admission of members into the system, and for other imports such as resources, technological know-how, and feedback into the system. The boundary can be viewed as somewhat of a barrier between employees and external people. In reality, the boundary serves as a filtering system for the flow of information, material, technology, and energy. Organizations rely largely on the boundary filtration mechanisms because they cannot possibly handle every factor that impacts the system. Without some form of filtration, environmental forces would be uncontrolled and bring about a chaotic condition. If a hospital administrator permitted public sentiment against a group of doctors to dictate the employment decisions concerning these doctors, the professional association to which the physicians belonged would certainly protect its members. Thus, the administrator must listen to complaints received from those outside the system but must resist the temptation to use only the information received from that particular part of the environment.

Although forces from the environment have an impact on the structure and processes of organizations, it is necessary to perform boundary-spanning activities. As the environment becomes more dynamic, the need for boundary spanners increases. This type of activity is described in the following:

> One way to view staff positions is to consider the contact points with the environment—the personnel man recruits, hires, fires, and judges the labor market; the accountant deals with the intake and outflow of money; R and D units survey technical developments; marketing forecasts the demand and product changes.[13]

The boundary-spanning positions in organizations are important, stressful, and affected by both internal and external environmental forces. Changes in health and safety laws, employee attitudes about unionization, competitive advertising programs, and the educational backgrounds of college graduates are just a few of the factors that boundary spanners must consider in reaching decisions. Without astute boundary spanners, organizations are severely limited in how efficiently they react to internal and external environmental changes.[14]

Some boundary roles are performed by sales personnel, purchasing agents, personnel recruiters, legislative representatives, labor contract negotiators, and public relations personnel. There are some potentially unique properties associated with boundary-spanning positions. First, the occupant of such a position is closer to the external environmental forces and is generally more distant psychologically from the organization. Second, the occupant represents the organization to the external environmental audience. Finally, this person is an agent of direct influence on the external environment. He or she attempts to influence the behavior of other persons and organizations. Of course, boundary spanners from other organizations or units are also attempting to influence an organization's boundary spanners. This type of influence is highlighted in exhibit 10–6. The spanners in this model are attempting to influence each other (at point 4), just as they are being influenced by others within their own group or organization (person A_1 ⟷ person A_2 and vice versa). Note that boundary spanning can occur within the same organization (the internal environment) or with individuals in other organizations (the external environment).[15]

As an example, consider the activities involved with NASA's Space Shuttle Program. Although NASA personnel are responsible for the actual operations of the space shuttle, they are assisted by personnel from the various companies involved in the design, development, and manufacture of the program's components (e.g., fuel, engines, ground monitoring equipment, on-board electrical equipment, airframe and wings). These individuals, generally called project managers or directors, must not only act as expert representatives of their companies to NASA, but they must continually provide feedback and information between the two organizations.

As is the case with liaison roles (see chapter 8), there are advantages and disadvantages to performing in a boundary-spanning capacity. Jobs are frequently ill-defined as to responsibility and authority, resulting in the increased potential for role ambiguity and role conflict.[16] Individuals in these jobs are frequently placed in conflict situations, such as when the demands of the customers are incongruent with the goals and objectives of their company, which leaves them torn between the two organizations. On the other hand, such jobs are highly visible to their organizations, their customers, and to other organizations as well. Successes are quickly noted, which could result in fast career advancement within their own organizations or in others.

As one would expect, as the uncertainty of the environment increases, organizations will make more frequent use of individuals in boundary-spanning roles. In this

Exhibit 10–6   The Boundary Spanner

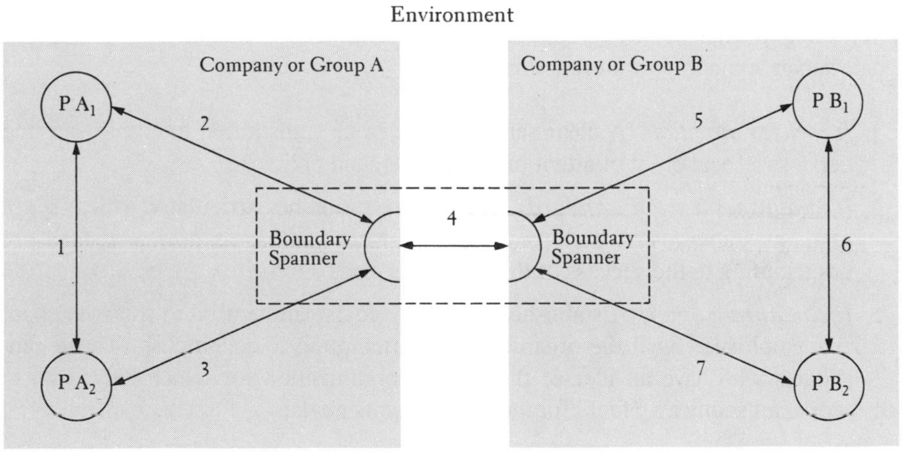

Environment

role, individuals serve as a *buffer* to the uncertainty of the environment, which assists in alleviating some of the problems in decision making.[17] Like a scout for a wagon train, a boundary-spanning job can be exacting, challenging, complex, as well as dangerous.

Organizational Goals

Goals, as many people tend to use the term, are desired states of affairs that organizations attempt to achieve. The specific meaning of the desired state might differ to many people. In an organization, executives at the top view a set of goals that is usually quite different from what the operating employees view as goals. The various interpretations are the result of differences in such factors as background, education, experience, responsibility, authority, power, and knowledge about the internal and external environment.

The goal concept was covered from a micro perspective in chapter 2 when we discussed performance within organizations. Certainly a straightforward and relevant micro goal of all organizations is to achieve optimal performance from the employees. When we move to a macro discussion of organizational goals, the concept becomes more abstract.

Meaning and Importance of Macro Goals

The topic of organizational goals is viewed by some in very broad terms. From one macro view, organizational goals are viewed as an extension of what the society needs for its survival.[18] If we analyze goals at the societal level, the internal functioning of a system is often ignored. Thus, there must be a dual approach to studying goals, one micro and one macro.

Goals by definition are creations of individuals or groups. The goal setting within an organization is influenced by individuals, groups, and environmental forces. There is rarely perfect agreement among those setting goals about what they should be. Despite this lack of consensus, there are distinct advantages in systematically attempting to reach some degree of agreement. The work to establish organizational goals serves some important functions:

1. *It focuses attention.* A clear set of goals can be transmitted to employees and serve as a focal point of attention, programs, and policies.

2. *It establishes a set of standards.* If an organization has articulated a clear set of goals as standards of performance, employees can assess how well they are contributing to the success of the firm.

3. *It can attract others.* Established and clear goals can be used to show prospective employees what the organization is attempting to accomplish. Those candidates who have an idea of the type of organization for which they want to work can acquire a "feel" for the system by its goals.

4. *It directly influences the internal operations.* The goals of a system in many cases can be achieved only through the mutual cooperation of individuals and groups. Thus, the nature, clarity, and importance of goals will have an impact on how people work together.

5. *It reveals the character of the system.* The goals of a system provide insight to employees and outsiders about what the organization is attempting to be. An important factor in unraveling the character of an organization involves the climate.

6. *It provides boundaries on decision making.* Goals that are generally accepted provide constraints on the decision-making practices of a system. In Simon's interpretation, goals provide a framework for decisions to be made. The decision maker continually thinks about the goals of the organization in reaching decisions.[19]

These six features of working on and establishing goals should emphasize their importance. Each individual in an organization is affected by the goals of the system, and it is important to consider how each person views these goals.

Types of Goals

To this point, our discussion has presented in rather broad terms the concept of organizational goals. This general framework can now be supplemented with a discussion of the various *types* of goals.

Organizational level typology

The first distinction among types of organizational goals is that of official, operative, or operational goals.[20] *Official* goals represent the formal statements of purpose made by top management concerning the overall mission of the organization. This type of goal is a broad statement usually presented in official organizational documents, such as annual reports. The public utility is in existence to serve the public, the university is chartered to disseminate knowledge, and the hospital is designed to help improve the health of the patients. Official goals are also typically vague and aspirational in nature (such as, "maximize profits," or "contribute to the welfare of society"), have infinite time horizons, and are only minimally understood by most employees.[21]

The real intentions of organizations are termed *operative* goals. That is, they reflect what an organization is actually trying to do. For example, the officially stated goal of a telephone company may be to serve customers in a particular geographical area in the most effective manner. The operational translation of this goal for the telephone company is to courteously handle all requests for information and to satisfy at least 96 percent, to install equipment for new customers within one week of receiving the orders, and to maximize efficiency in order to increase profits by 15 percent.

An organization's operative goals designate the ends being sought. In part, they are the official goals in more specific terms. They are the standards by which organizational decisions are made. Operative goals also emerge from unofficial sources. Perrow states:

> The personal ambition of a hospital administrator may lead to community alliances and activities which bind the organization without enhancing its goal achievement. On the other hand, while the use of interns and residents as "cheap labor" may subvert the official goal of medical education, it may substantially further the official goal of providing a high quality of patient care.[22]

Operative goals, then, should be interpreted as emerging from both official and unofficial sources. They reflect a more concrete picture of what the organization and its members are attempting to accomplish within the task environment.

Finally, *operational* goals are those that are agreed upon criteria for evaluating the level of goal attainment. In other words, an operative goal is said to be operational to the extent that management can state, in a precise fashion, *how* and *when* the goal will be measured. For example, a farm-equipment manufacturer may state an *official* goal as, "maximize profits through the sale of farm implements." From an *operative* view, the goal could be stated as, "attain a level of 14 percent return on investment from the sale of the company's product line." Finally, as an *operational* goal, the statement would be made as "improve return on investment to a level of 14 percent by December, 1981, by selling 100,000 more units and/or by increasing sales revenues 40 percent over most recent five-year sales figures." The key point of operational goals, therefore, is the emphasis on specificity, quantity, and time.

As shown in exhibit 10–7, another way of viewing official, operative, and operational goals is by the level each affects in the organization. Generally speaking, official and operative goals reflect top management's concerns, and the lower managerial levels are concerned with operational goals.

Exhibit 10–7 Goals and Organizational Level

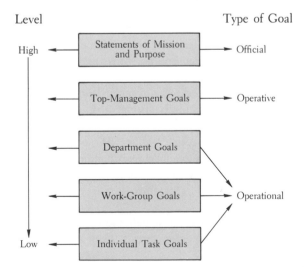

Referent typology

A second way to classify or state goals is by the functions they serve or by referent (i.e., to whom or what the goal is aimed).[23] As shown in exhibit 10–8, this goal typology is broader in nature and is concerned primarily with whose point of view is being recognized.

A Means-Ends View

The operative goals, when translated into objectives, also exist in a hierarchy. The official goals of the organization appear as the *ends*. In analyzing these goals, it is necessary to make decisions on how they will be achieved—the *means*. The means at one level become the subgoals at the next level. A hierarchical flow of means-ends has significant meaning for organizational structural arrangements. The division-of-labor concept within an organization is the consequence of means-ends analyses. An organization attempts to integrate the means-ends chain by structuring the

Exhibit 10–8 Types of Goals and Referents

Type of Goal	Referent	Example
Societal (Official)	Society in general.	Maximize profits; produce goods and services; generate and maintain cultural values.
Output (Operative)	The public in contact with the organization.	Types and level of consumer goods, business and health-care services, and education.
System (Operative)	The state or manner of functioning of the organization.	Emphasis on growth, stability, profits, and internal control functions.
Product (Operational)	The characteristics of the goods or services provided.	Emphasis upon the level of quantity, quality, availability, styling, or innovativeness of the products or services.
Derived (Operational)	The uses to which the organization puts the power it generates in pursuit of other goals.	Employee development; investment and plant location; policies which affect the state of local/regional/national economies; political aims and community services.

relationships between individuals and formal groups. The success of the integration is difficult to predict, but is required if operative goals are to be accomplished.

An example of a means-ends chain for a department of organizational behavior and management is presented in exhibit 10–9. The ends (2) become the means by which the next level achieves its goals, and these goals become the means (3) by which the next level achieves its goals, and so forth. Receiving resources for support services is an objective. It is the end that having new and better trained present faculty serves, but the means by which this new and better qualified faculty achieves its productivity objectives.

A means-ends view is useful to the manager because it helps to sort out the relationships between goals and subgoals. The sorting process forces managers to focus on operative goals and not to spend all their thought on official or more abstract goals. In our example, the goal of national recognition is commendable and important today, but it needs to be operationally articulated before faculty members, legislators, students, and those outside of the department understand what the group is attempting to accomplish.

Need to Understand Goal Changes

A manager would be under less pressure if goals remained static. This is certainly not the case in most organizations, for a number of reasons. First, external pressures brought about by competitive actions, government policies, or community attitudes force a change in goals. Second, internal factors also influence a change in goals. The hiring of new personnel, the establishment of a new department, or a reallocation of funds could bring about a goal change. Etzioni has labeled certain internally

Exhibit 10–9   A Means-Ends Hierarchy

Departmental Goals	
To become a nationally recognized department with regard to research productivity	Ends (4)
	Means
Hire qualified faculty and develop present faculty to level of excellence	Ends (3)
	Means
Receive resources from administration to attract and develop faculty	Ends (2)
	Means
Receive resources to provide faculty with support services— typing, graduate assistants, computer programming	Ends (1)

imparted changes "goal displacement."[24] A familiar type of goal displacement is called *overquantification*. This refers to the tendency for organizations to establish goals that are easily quantified. This overzealous quantification results in playing "numbers roulette." Counting the customers served, the articles published, or the traffic passing a store may be meaningless. The customers may be dissatisfied and never return to a business establishment; the articles may be conceptually and/or methodologically barren; and the cars passing may not even notice the store and its advertisements. A pure numbers game is not sound practice because nonquantifiable goals need to be considered if a complete picture of organizational life is to emerge.

Third, technology changes impact on an organization's goals. The image of technological forces is clearly presented by Lawrence and Lorsch:

> The low performing organizations were both characterized by their top administrators as having serious difficulty in dealing with this environment. They had not been successful in introducing and marketing new products. In fact, their attempts to do so had met with repeated failures. This record, plus other measures of performance available to top management, left them with a feeling of disquiet and a sense of urgency to find ways of improving their performance.[25]

This pressing urgency could result in altering goals because of the technological environment. The organization that responds slowly or not at all could be placed at a competitive disadvantage, which results in losses of revenue, inputs, profits, clients, grants, and so on.

Finally, when goals change as a result of the conscious effort by management to shift the course of the organization's activities, the process is termed *goal succession*. For example, the National Foundation for Infantile Paralysis initially established a goal of funding research to eliminate one specific disease, polio.[26] Through its "March of Dimes" campaign, sufficient research funds were generated to lead to the vaccine that has virtually wiped out polio. Rather than disband, the National Foundation revised its goals to fund research into a new series of congenital diseases.[27]

The discussion of goals is vital when considering organizational dimensions and performance. Goals are guidelines necessary for an organization's set of activities as well as for those of individuals and groups. They provide a foundation for attempting to explain organizational behavior. Without goals, the behavior of people interacting with and within organizations becomes a disoriented exercise in futility. Once we accept the idea of goals, it becomes mandatory to consider goal achievement, which takes us back to the issue of performance at the individual, group, and organizational levels of analysis. We also need to consider the structural designs necessary to achieve goals efficiently.

Technology

Few concepts in the study of organizations are so important, yet so ill-defined or misunderstood, as organizational technology. In recent studies, the concept of *technology* has been viewed in terms of the extent of task interdependence (see chapter 8), degree of equipment automation, uniformity or complexity of materials used, and the degree of routineness of the task.[28] From the varied definitions, it should become evident that when behavioral scientists and managers discuss technology, they are not always focusing on the same concept.

Nature of Technology

There seems to be some convergence on certain important points concerning the technology concept. First, there seems to be some agreement that technology concerns either the mechanical or intellectual processes by which an organization transforms raw materials into final goods or services. In other words, technology refers to the *transformation process* (see exhibit 10–1) whereby mechanical and intellectual efforts are used to change inputs into products.

Second, the diversity of opinions on a definition of *technology* may relate to the level of analysis at which the concept is viewed. Some individuals may study technology as an organization-wide concept, such as an assembly-line process in auto manufacturing. On the other hand, others may view technology at the individual level, relating to the concepts of variety, autonomy, and feedback discussed in chapter 6.

Finally, there seems to be some agreement that technology is influenced by the environment, *and* the structure of the organization is influenced by technology (see exhibit 10–3). An example of environment influencing technology is the development of pocket calculators by the business-machine industry. Only a few years ago, calculators were bulky, slow, expensive, and generally bought for the office as opposed to the home. With the development of microcomputers (technological environment), coupled with a growing consumer demand (economic environment), business-machine companies were forced to develop new manufacturing technologies to produce the new, inexpensive pocket calculators. An example of technology influencing structure is any steel manufacturer. The process for manufacturing steel is well defined, standardized, and expensive (i.e., capital intensive). Because this technology is fairly rigid, effective control and maintenance functions must be provided by the structure of the organization. In other words, structure adapts to technology. We will discuss this situation in more detail in the next chapter.

Types of Technology

If we are to adequately study the relationship between technology, structure, and performance, a scheme for categorizing or identifying different types of technology is needed. One of the best-known approaches to technology classification was presented by Thompson.[29] This classification scheme, based on the overall manner in which units are organized for organizational task accomplishment, identifies three types of technologies: (1) mediating; (2) long-linked; and (3) intensive.

A *mediating technology* is characterized by otherwise independent organizational units joined by the use of standard operating procedures (this concept is parallel to pooled interdependence; see chapter 8). A simple example would be a commercial bank, characterized by low interdependence of the different functions (e.g., savings, investments, loans). Effectiveness is obtained through rules, procedures, and other control mechanisms. Such a technology is moderately adaptable or flexible to changing demands (see exhibit 10–10).

A *long-linked technology* accomplishes its task by sequential interdependence between different units. Characterized by an auto assembly line, this type of technology attains effectiveness through planning and supervisory control coupled with a moderate emphasis on communications. Because of the rigid, sequential nature of interdependence (along with the usual high cost of equipment and materials), this type of technology is not very flexible or adaptable to changing demands.

Finally, an *intensive technology* involves a variety of techniques drawn upon to transform an object from one state to another. The choice of techniques is influenced by feedback from the *object* itself; that is, how the object responds to the application of the different techniques. A good example is that of a hospital. The object being transformed is the patient and his or her health; the techniques involve the various specialties of the hospital (e.g., surgery, pediatrics, x-ray, nursing, physical therapy). The manner in which the patient responds to one of the specialties (e.g., knee surgery) dictates the level of application of other specialties (e.g., physical therapy). As shown in exhibit 10–10, this type of technology is characterized by a great deal of interdependence between units, which is effected through good cooperation and a high level of communication, and is highly flexible.

Although Thompson's scheme was formulated to classify the organization, it should be clear from exhibit 10–10 that this typology has direct bearing on the intergroup relationships—with the accompanying implications for management—that were discussed in chapter 8. Appropriate types of coordination and communication and the degree of flexibility can also be applied to the interactions of individuals within a group.

A second technology classification system was proposed by Hickson, Pugh, and Pheysey.[30] Somewhat broader in scope than the first classification scheme, three categories are suggested: (1) operations technology; (2) materials technology; and (3) knowledge technology.

Operations technology focuses on the types and intensity of work-flow aspects of a transformation process; for example, craftsman (electrician) versus mass production. In addition, a hospital would be characterized as an operations technology, as this is its dominant feature. *Materials technology* involves the types of materials used in the work flow. In addition, an auto manufacturer, which uses and focuses on putting out large amounts of materials, could be said to be predominantly a materials technology. Finally, *knowledge technology* focuses on the level of quality and sophistication of information relevant to decision making in the organization. A research laboratory would be a knowledge technology because knowledge (information) is the focus and prime tool of the organization.

In contrast to the first classification scheme, the categories in this system are not mutually exclusive; that is, an organization cannot only be classified under this scheme, but the levels of all three technology types as used in its transformation process can be described as well. For example, a manufacturer of writing paper uses a highly advanced production process (operations technology), a relatively simple

Exhibit 10-10 Technology Types

Technology Type	Illustration	Interdependence	Characteristics Basis of Coordination	Flexibility	Communication Demands
Mediating	Bank	Low (pooled)	Rules, standard procedures, and supervisory control	Medium	Low
Long-Linked	Auto Assembly Line	Medium (sequential)	Planning and supervisory control	Low	Medium
Intensive	Hospital	High (reciprocal)	Cooperation and mutual adjustment	High	High

materials technology (wood pulp and water), and has a moderate knowledge technology, as its work force is a mix of highly skilled and semi-skilled people.

In summary, technology is important to the organization not only as the focus of the transformation of inputs to products but also as an influence on other organizational factors, such as structure and behavior. It is crucial for managers to understand the nature, requirements, and complexities of the technological process employed by their organization. In fact, it is probably more appropriate to speak of *technologies* in the plural because, in reality, organizations are a composite of many different technologies.

Structure

Because organizations are goal oriented and include various technologies they require some form of structural arrangement to improve the probability of successful performance. Although organizational structure will be discussed in detail in the next chapter, we should identify now the structure that is most often offered as a means of facilitating goal achievement—*differentiation of functions*.[31] Under differentiation, formally specified, different but in most cases interrelated tasks are performed by people in formal groups. For example, the accountant could establish a cost-accounting system that the production function uses and the administrative planning staff carefully monitors. Differentiation should be considered as a means for accomplishing goals more efficiently; in this example, the operative goal is accurate cost accounting, which helps accomplish larger goals in turn.

There are, of course, many ways in which work in an organization can be subdivided. Two broad classifications are *horizontal* and *vertical* differentiation. In most organizations, there are a number of horizontal units of managers and operating employees. The more units, the greater the complexity and the more obvious the need to consider vertical differentiation. One possible model of the two forms of functional differentiation is shown in exhibit 10–11.

Vertical Differentiation

Vertical differentiation deals with the organization's hierarchy—power, influence, status, authority, responsibility, and span of control phenomena. There is a practical need for some to exercise influence over others within an organization, and vertical differentiation can afford the authority to do so. Two forms of vertical differentiation are usually found in organizations: (1) level; and (2) function.

In organizations, there can be many *levels* that create a vertical distance between individuals or groups of individuals. This is sometimes referred to as the scalar chain of command (see chapter 11) or hierarchy. If there are three vertical levels, the distance would be three; if there are four levels, we would discuss a vertical distance of four. Five levels often discussed and found in organizations are the following:

Executive (top) positions—Chief executive in a bank, vice president of operations in a company, or vice president of faculties in a university. Those in executive positions are concerned with policy matters.

Exhibit 10–11   **Vertical and Horizontal Functional Differentiation for an Energy Company**

Product

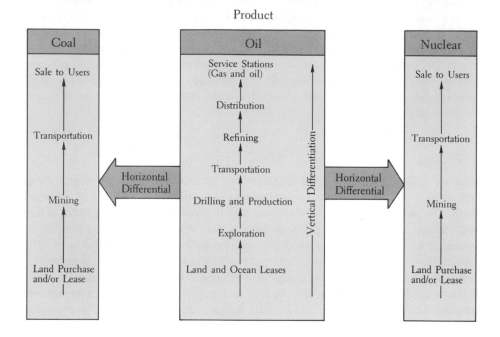

Middle-manager positions—Department manager, plant supervisor, dean of a college. Those in middle-level positions are involved in coordination and control decisions.

Lower-manager positions—First-level supervisor, accounts manager, instructor. Those in lower-level positions carry out decisions and coordinate the work of operating employees.

Skilled operating employees—Technicians, mechanics, nurses, programmers. Skilled employees perform specialized tasks that they are trained to perform.

Unskilled operating employees—Janitors, assembly-line workers. Those in unskilled positions carry out unskilled task duties.

These five broad categories illustrate one possibility of how an organization can use vertical differentiation by level to pursue its goals. The unskilled operating employee views goals differently, possesses different abilities and expectations, and performs different roles than do the middle managers or any of the others in the various layers. It should also be recognized that the requirements for performance at each level are different. Therefore, a middle-level manager may be outstanding at that level, but may be unable to deal with more elusive policy issues that prevail at the top levels of management.

Vertical differentiation by function is illustrated in exhibit 10–11 for an oil company. The functional differentiation involves the involvement, and hence *control,* the organization has over the input-output process. In the case of a fully vertically differentiated oil company, the firm has control over the process from land ownership to sale at the gas pump. The key feature of this arrangement is that by involvement in the total process, the organization has removed or controlled a great deal of the uncertainty of the environment from the operations of the firm. Both types of vertical differentiation involve authority and control (level, of individuals; functional, of specialized groups or units), and both help control environment (level, of internal environment; functional, of external environment). In these ways, goal achievement is forwarded.

Horizontal Differentiation

The horizontal differentiation of groups is basically the division of labor. The marketing group performs work in their specialty, and the research and development laboratory does their specific job. The division of labor is a reality at all levels in organizations. It is a basis for grouping individuals *within levels* of an organization; vertical integration is a way of controlling these groups. Some criteria suggested to establish horizontally differentiated groups were clearly set years ago by Taylor for operating employees and have since been broadened to include managerial personnel. Gulick stated that employees in any organization can be grouped or divided on the basis of: (1) the purpose they are fulfilling; (2) the process they are using; (3) the persons or things on which they are acting; and (4) the place in which they are carrying out their job duties.[32]

Horizontal differentiation can also be viewed as a product-line change or departmentalization. As illustrated in exhibit 10–11, an oil company can horizontally differentiate itself by expanding into similar areas, such as coal and nuclear fuel. This example organization could now be more accurately classified not as an oil company, but as an energy company. Some large organizations, such as holding companies, are horizontally differentiated into many *un*related areas as well (e.g., banks that own land for noninvestment purposes).

Horizontal differentiation has certain inherent dangers, however. In our example, expanding horizontally into coal production may not only involve different and relatively unknown *technologies* to the original organization, but such expansion has drawn the attention of various legislative and regulatory bodies concerned with the growing control of resources exhibited by such organizations.

The degree of horizontal and vertical differentiation within an organization has a significant impact on communication networks, informal-group formation, attitudes of employees, motivation state of employees, leadership effectiveness, and numerous other organizational phenomena. The interrelatedness of differentiation with these factors provides ample reason to carefully consider them when attempting to explain and predict organizational behavior.

The Organization and
Its Internal Environment

The internal environment of an organization is created by the interaction of the external environment, goals, technology, and structure (see exhibit 10–3). For our purposes, the internal environment consists of organizational climate and individuals and groups within the organization.

Organizational Climate

Researchers concerned with the internal functioning of systems have borrowed theories and methodologies from differential psychology and have used the term *organizational climate* in place of *internal environment*.[33] One way to acquire a better understanding of climate is to consider the components of the construct. There are those who believe that climate consists of a set of characteristics that describes an organization, distinguishes it from other organizations, is relatively enduring over time, and influences the behavior of people in it.[34] Others believe that climates emerge within systems as the result of the style of management, the organization's policies, and its general operating procedures.[35]

From the endless interpretations offered by theorists, we define *climate* as:

> A set of properties of the work environment, specific to a particular organization, that may be assessed by the way the organization deals with its employees and its general and task environments.

This definition suggests a set of properties that interact to form a climate. Exactly what this set involves has certainly not been uncovered for an industry or different individuals. For example, Litwin and Stringer identify six crucial properties of climate.[36]

1. *Structure*—The organization's constraints, rules, regulations, and red tape.

2. *Individual responsibility*—The feeling of "being one's own boss."

3. *Rewards*—The feeling of being adequately and equitably rewarded by the organization.

4. *Risk and risk taking*—The degree of challenge and risk in the work situation.

5. *Warmth and support*—The feeling of helpfulness and good fellowship in the job setting.

6. *Tolerance and conflict*—The degree of confidence with which the climate can tolerate differing opinions.

These properties have been used to distinguish between various organizational subunits. They are typically based on the perceptual responses of unit members.

A more scientifically based study of climate properties was performed by Schneider and Bartlett.[37] They studied a group of sales agencies in two different insurance companies. Through factor analysis, they discovered six interpretable climate properties:

1. *Managerial support*—The manager's active interest in the progress and development of subordinates.

2. *Managerial structure*—The manager's practice of requiring agents to comply with procedures.

3. *Concern for new employees*—The concern for the training of new agents.

4. *Intra-agency conflict*—The presence of in-groups within an agency and the undercutting of managerial authority by the agents.

5. *Agent independence*—The degree of autonomy exercised by agents.

6. *General satisfaction*—The agents' satisfaction with various management and agency activities.

It is the contention of Schneider and Bartlett that within these agencies these six climate properties are possible predictors of agent performance. It is our belief that it is too early in the study of climate to attempt a synthesis of the numerous properties identified by theorists, researchers, and practitioners. There appears to be some commonality in most lists of climate properties. Most of the lists include at least five or six properties. Usually, we find structure, reward, warmth, autonomy, and conflict on these lists. There are, however, theoretical and methodological issues as yet unresolved.[38] Thus, we offer only some general opinions about climate:

1. It appears that each work organization creates a number of different types of climate. The type of climate found will depend on the unit of analysis. That is, studying a work group, an occupational group, a functional department, and the total organization could result in four sets of climate properties.

2. There is some sharing of perceptions among employees, no matter what level of analysis is used, about the internal climate.

3. To date, most assessments of climate have not been sufficiently descriptive or valid to offer definitive synthesis work.

4. An understanding of climate will aid a manager in understanding how organizational practices and procedures are reflected in human behavior.

5. There have been too few studies of the connection of external environment and internal organizational climate. The impact of these connections on performance is not known and can only be speculated about at this time.

Perhaps one of the most important comments on the topic of climate is that if managers are to more fully understand the people with whom they work they must think about the properties that have the largest impact on performance.[39] It is of course performance that is the ultimate bench mark of a person's success in an organizational system.

Individuals within Organizations

The core element of all organizations is the employees. The study of organizations is hollow without taking into account the behavior of individuals working alone and as members of groups. Individuals, such as the salesperson on the road, the manager preparing a report in an office, or the lawyer preparing to defend a client, occasionally work alone. These moments of solitude are rare; the salesperson must communicate to sell products, the manager must display the report to others, and the lawyer needs to discuss the case with the client. The fact that an individual rarely works alone within the organizational setting indicates that the system and its subsystems, environment, and other people have a considerable impact on an employee's behavior.

As mentioned in chapters 3 and 4, an individual brings a repertoire of behavior to the organization. The person's motives, personality, and attitude structures have been formulated at home, in communities, in school, and in other organizations. The mix of structures brought to an organization is often not congruent with the goals, procedures, or tasks of the system, so the organization needs to integrate individuals with different attributes and backgrounds. This is certainly no easy task for managers.

In addition, it is generally safe to assume that a person will rarely commit his or her total being to an organization. A person devotes *portions* of time and energy to a particular work organization. Although people spend about one-half of their waking hours in a work organization, there is still other time available to commit to other groups or organizational systems. Thus, it seems that in order to consider the impact of an organization on the behavior of people, managers also need to take into consideration the notion of commitment. It is, of course, easier to discuss commitment than it is to measure it in a scientific manner.

The mix of partially committed employees must interact with each other to complete job duties at all levels in an organization. The quality of interaction depends on such factors as individual behaviors, the goals of the system, the input-transformation-output process, and the environmental properties and how they impact people. There are presently no predictive models that combine these factors together to yield a statement on interaction quality.

Groups within Organizations

In chapters 7 and 8, we discussed the importance and pervasiveness of groups within organizations. There is nothing so apparent in an organization as the numerous groups that are formally established or that informally emerge. As defined, groups consist of a number of individuals who interact and share, to some extent, values, beliefs, and norms. These characteristics are found in both formal and informal groups.

A formal group, such as a marketing department, research and development unit, or credit department, is established by the organization. Jobs are grouped together and a structure is established so that goals are achieved more frequently. The formal group as structured and sanctioned by the organization can exert powerful influences on individuals and other groups. The exact nature of these influences depends to some extent on the structure, process, development, cohesiveness, and goals of the group.

In order to clarify the linkages among formal groups, organizations typically construct charts. These charts are essentially maps of the interactions among groups within the system. In some instances, the chart displays a reasonable degree of accuracy, but in other cases the interactions do not occur as planned or as drawn because of problems or barriers. One possible barrier could be that the formal leaders in two groups dislike each other and consequently they bypass the normal channels of interaction. The press of time to complete a project might force one group to circumvent the normal interaction with another group. Thus, organization charts are normative maps that attempt to illustrate what is *supposed* to occur between two or more groups.

The accuracy of an organization chart is also put in jeopardy by the emergence of informal groups. These units, which form because of common interests, communication patterns, friendships, or tasks, are not clearly identified by the organization.

The presence of informal groups introduces a somewhat blurred factor into a manager's process and practice procedures. Managers know that individuals belong to more than one informal group and that these groups influence behavior. These facts were well documented and analyzed in the famous Hawthorne studies, which revealed that informal groups influence a person's performance, attitude, and interaction patterns.[40] It is indeed a rare individual who can withstand the pressures of an informal group to comply with norms, expectations, and behaviors.

The Organization as a Necessary System

In this chapter, we have attempted to understand some characteristics of organizations. We have discussed them in separate sections, even though we know and understand that each of them is interrelated. The systems approach emphasizes the interrelatedness, and this is why it is considered useful for studying organizations. The organization attempts to hire personnel that can be trained, indoctrinated, and influenced to perform jobs so that organizational goals are achieved. It is not, however, safe to conclude that individuals then have only a minimum impact on the organizational system. It is the individual who gives the organization character, goals, and human skills and abilities, which are needed to survive.

The theme we have attempted to project in this chapter and throughout the book is that behavior in organizations is based on organizational, group, individual, and environmental factors. Each factor plays an important role in how employees will act in various situations. In some situations, organizational factors are predominant; in others, the individual factors are the most significant. No matter which factor is most significant in a particular situation, there is the need to recognize the importance of organizations in our society and in our lives.

The linkages within an organization and between the organization and the environment emphasize the dynamic and complex considerations facing managers. The characteristics that have been stressed can be summarized by saying that organizations are:

1. *Systems* in constant interaction with the external environment.

2. *Goal* oriented.

3. Transformers of inputs with *technologies*.

4. *Structured* to achieve goals.

5. Creators of an *internal environment*.

6. *People* as individuals.

7. *People* as groups.

None of these seven characteristics means anything unless we discuss or consider each of the others. A system without people is not a social organization. People without goals tend to flounder and become frustrated. Social systems without structured arrangements often result in chaos and low morale among members. Therefore, the integrating force in industrialized societies is the organization. Organizations are unwieldly, unpredictable, and occasionally socially irresponsible, but they have provided comforts and jobs that are now a part of the fabric of our society.

The distinguishing characteristics of organizations are presented in the model shown in exhibit 10–12. This system is more complete than the basic model presented in exhibit 10–1. This systems perspective can be subdivided and analyzed in parts. The arrows are used to specify pressures or forces that are directed toward the organization as a system. The manager is encouraged to view organizations in the terms discussed in this chapter and shown in exhibit 10–12.

Applications and Implications for the Manager

Organizational Dimensions

1. Organizations surround us and play a significant role in our everyday lives. Therefore, attempting to understand what their distinguishing features are can provide more meaning to what organizations are about.

2. The open-systems perspective is the most thorough way of viewing organizations. It enables one to consider an organization as a system operating within the general and task environments. The environment is not considered in a closed-system view of organizations, and this failure results in an incomplete picture of the organization-individual interaction.

3. A number of major subsystems exist within organizations. Specifically highlighted are the control, maintenance, and coordination subsystems. In order to facilitate the flow and processing of inputs, control must be used. Maintenance subsystems are needed to enhance the

interaction of people. Coordination brings about a unity of effort within the system.

4. A useful method for considering the outputs of an organization is to classify the people who benefit from them. The Blau and Scott typology concentrates on prime beneficiaries. This enables us to categorize organizations as mutual benefit, productive, service, or commonweal.

5. Our generalized model of organizations suggested the significant impact of the environment. That is, the task environment influences not only the goals and technology of the organization but the resulting structure as well.

6. The general environment impacting organizations includes political, social, resource, economic, and technological factors. In addition to these forces, each organization is influenced by its own unique task environment, which includes its customers, suppliers, competitors, regulation for the industry, and pertinent

Exhibit 10–12 The Organization as a Necessary System

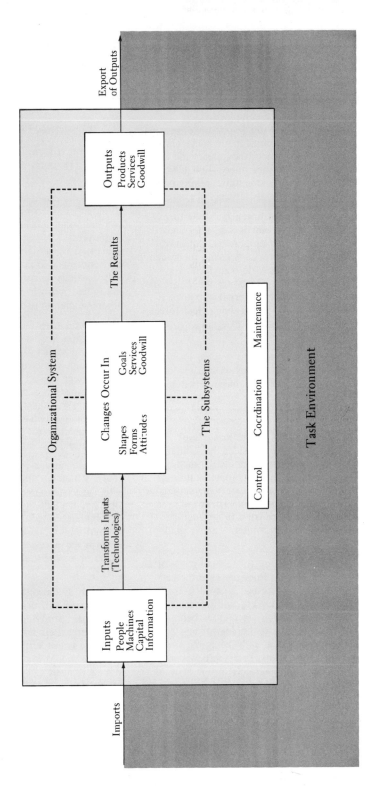

General Environment

Organizational System

Inputs
People
Machines
Capital
Information

Transforms Inputs
(Technologies)

Changes Occur In

Shapes   Goals
Forms   Services
Attitudes   Goodwill

The Results

Outputs
Products
Services
Goodwill

The Subsystems

Control   Coordination   Maintenance

Task Environment

Imports

Export
of Outputs

technological issues—all factors that directly impact the internal functioning of the organization as a unique subset of the general environment.

7. The degree of change (stable/dynamic) and the degree of complexity (simple/complex) are important dimensions of the task environment for managers to consider. Combined, they create the degree of environment uncertainty—an input that affects the goals, structure, and behavior of individuals in organizations.

8. Goals help an organization to focus attention on relevant issues, set standards, attract and retain employees, influence internal operations, understand the system's character, and provide boundaries for decision making. Goals are not static; they change because of external pressures, internal factors, and technological forces, which are a subset of external environmental forces.

9. Goals are needed to provide insights on the organization's direction and character for members and outsiders interacting with the organization. Official goals, originating at the top of organizations, need to be translated into operative and then operational goals at the lower levels. It is also important to consider the similarities and differences in individual, group, organizational, and environmental goals. It is unrealistic to assume that the subsets of goals will be congruent. This cannot be accomplished because different people are involved in formulating these goal mixes.

10. The technology (or technologies) of an organization constitute the core of the transformation process. Viewed from a mediating, long-linked, and intensive typology, technology is seen as being influenced by the technological task environment *and* as influencing the structure of the organization. In essence, technology places certain constraints on the style of structure that evolves.

11. Because organizations are goal oriented, they need structure to improve efficiency and performance. Horizontal differentiation, or division of labor, and vertical differentiation, or establishing a hierarchy, are used to create efficient structures. Each organization contains a degree of both, and the astute manager must be aware that there is a point of diminishing returns. The point depends upon the other dimensions of the organization.

12. There is an internal environment or climate that emerges within the organization and has some influence on behavior of employees. The internal climate is also influenced by the general and task environments. To date, this connection is only partially understood and needs to be considered more in future studies of organizations as open systems.

13. The features that distinguish each organization are its unique system, interacting with its own task environment, and developing its own internal environment, called a climate. The core of the organization is the people as individuals and group members interacting with each other. These members create and attempt to achieve meaningful goals for their particular organization.

14. Organizations are open systems with goals, structure, and people, that interact with their environments and transform inputs. The challenge ahead for managers is to stimulate employees in creating the most optimal system, goals, and structure to perform the necessary transformations on inputs to export the outputs to the real world.

15. Each of the distinguishing characteristics of organizations interact with each other. Studying them separately or considering their influence on behavior one at a time is not sufficient to capture what a manager should know about organizations. Managers need to be aware of the interrelatedness of these characteristics.

Review of Theories, Research, and Applications

1. What is the main difference in studying organizations as open systems as opposed to closed systems?

2. Provide some examples of location and form transformation processes.

3. What is meant by the concept of *prime beneficiary* of outputs?

4. Why are operative and official organizational goals different?

5. How can the authority system in an organization influence what is called the "climate"?

6. Why is the boundary-spanning role internally and externally important to an organization?

7. Is there only one perspective of analyzing organizations? Why?

8. How can the reduction in potential inputs into an organization influence the behavior of employees?

9. How can environmental uncertainty affect the internal operations and behavior of an organization?

10. How does technology affect an organization's structure?

Notes

1. Max Weber, *The Theory of Social and Economic Organization* (New York: Free Press, 1947), pp. 145–46.

2. Chester I. Barnard, *The Functions of the Executive* (Cambridge, Mass.: Harvard University, 1938), p. 73.

3. Material for this discussion draws heavily from Eric J. Miller and A. K. Rice, *Systems of Organizations* (London: Tavistock, 1967).

4. This view is well presented by Joseph A. Litterer, *The Analysis of Organizations,* 2nd ed. (New York: Wiley, 1973), p. 27.

5. James D. Thompson, *Organizations in Action* (New York: McGraw-Hill, 1967), p. 9.

6. Paul R. Lawrence and Jay W. Lorsch, "Differentiation and Integration in Complex Organizations," *Administrative Science Quarterly,* June 1967, pp. 3–4.

7. Litterer, *Analysis of Organizations,* pp. 454–66.

8. Lawrence and Lorsch, "Differentiation and Integration in Complex Organizations," p. 5.

9. Peter M. Blau and W. Richard Scott, *Formal Organizations* (San Francisco: Chandler, 1962).

10. William R. Dill, "Environment as an Influence on Managerial Autonomy," *Administrative Science Quarterly,* March 1958, pp. 409–43.

11. Robert B. Duncan, "Characteristics of Organizational Environments and Perceived Environmental Uncertainty," *Administrative Science Quarterly,* September 1972, p. 315.

12. Ibid., p. 316.

13. Charles Perrow, *Organizational Analysis: A Sociological View* (Belmont, Calif.: Wadsworth, 1970)

14. For research studies of boundary spanners in organizational settings, see Robert T. Keller and W. E. Holland, "Boundary-Spanning Roles in Research and Development Organization: An Empirical Examination," *Academy Of Management Journal,* June 1975, pp. 388–93; James A. Wall and J. Stacy Adams, "Some Variables Affecting a Constituent's Evaluation of and Behavior Toward a Boundary Role Occupant," *Organizational Behavior and Human Performance,* June 1974, pp. 390–408.

15. For an excellent and thorough discussion of boundary roles, see J. Stacy Adams, "The Structure and Dynamics of Behavior in Organizational Boundary Roles," in *Handbook of Industrial and Organizational Psychology,* ed. Marvin D. Dunnette (Chicago, Rand McNally, 1976), pp. 1175–99.

16. Robert T. Keller, Andrew D. Szilagyi, and W. E. Holland, "Boundary Spanning, Job Characteristics and Job Satisfaction," *Human Relations,* 1976, pp. 699–716.

17. Thompson, *Organizations in Action,* p. 20.

18. Talcott Parsons, *Structure and Process in Modern Societies* (Glencoe, N.Y.: Free Press, 1960), p. 17.

19. Herbert A. Simon, "On the Concept of Organizational Goal," *Administrative Science Quarterly,* June 1964, p. 2.

20. Charles Perrow, "The Analysis of Goals in Complex Organizations," *American Sociological Review,* December 1961, p. 855.

21. Richard M. Steers, *Organizational Effectiveness* (Santa Monica, Calif.: Goodyear, 1977), p. 24.

22. Perrow, "The Analysis of Goals," p. 856.

23. Ibid., p. 857.

24. Amitai Etzioni, *Modern Organizations* (Englewood Cliffs, N.J.: Prentice-Hall, 1964), p. 40.

25. Paul R. Lawrence and Jay W. Lorsch, *Organization and Environment: Managing Differentiation and Integration* (Cambridge, Mass.: Harvard Graduate School of Business Administration, 1967), p. 42.

26. D. Sills, *The Volunteers: Means and Ends in a National Organization* (New York: Free Press, 1957).

27. Steers, *Organizational Effectiveness,* p. 32.

28. Ibid., p. 70.

29. Thompson, *Organizations in Action,* pp. 15–18.

30. D. J. Hickson, D. S. Pugh, and D. C. Pheysey, "Operations Technology and Organizational Structure: As Reappraisal," *Administrative Science Quarterly,* 1969, pp. 378–97.

31. The differentiation of function section was stimulated by the discussion provided by Lyman W. Porter, Edward E. Lawler III, and J. Richard Hackman, *Behavior in Organizations* (New York: McGraw-Hill, 1975), pp. 87–93.

32. Luther Gulick, "Notes on the Theory of Organization," in *Papers on the Science of Administration,* ed. Luther Gulick and Lyndall F. Urwick (New York: Institute of Public Administration, 1937).

33. Benjamin Schneider, "Organizational Climates: An Essay," *Personnel Psychology,* Winter 1975, pp. 447–80.

34. G. A. Forehand and B. V. H. Gilmer, "Environmental Variation in Studies of Organizational Behavior," *Psychological Bulletin,* 1964, pp. 361–82.

35. H. H. Meyer, "Differences in Organizational Climate in Outstanding and Average Sales Offices: A Summary Report," General Electric, Behavioral Research Service and Public Relations, Personnel Services, 1967.

36. G. H. Litwin and R. Stringer, "The Influence of Organizational Climate on Human Motivation," Paper presented at conference on organizational climates, Foundation for Research on Human Behavior, March 1966, Ann Arbor, Mich.).

37. Benjamin Schneider and C. J. Bartlett, "Individual Differences and Organizational Climate in the Research Plan and Questionnaire Development," *Personnel Psychology,* 1968, pp. 323–34.

38. Robert M. Guion, "A Note on Organizational Climate," *Organizational Behavior and Human Performance,* February 1972, pp. 120–25; R. E. Johanesson, "Some Problems in the Measurement of Organizational Climate," *Organizational Behavior and Human Performance,* August 1973, pp. 118–44.

39. For a psychological perspective of climate impact on performance, see James F. Gavin and John G. Howe, "Psychological Climate: Some Theoretical and Empirical Considerations," *Behavioral Science,* June 1975, pp. 228–40.

40. The specific source for these studies is Fritz J. Roethlisberger and W. J. Dickson, *Management and the Worker* (Cambridge, Mass.: Harvard University, 1939).

Additional References

BLAU P. M. "A Formal Theory of Differentiation in Organizations." *American Sociological Review,* 1970, pp. 62–72.

GABARRE, J. J. "Organizational Adaptation to Environmental Change." In *Organizational Systems.* Homewood, Ill.: Irwin, 1973.

GEORGOPOULOS, B. S. "An Open-System Theory Model for Organizational Research." In *Modern Organizational Theory,* edited by A. R. Negandhi. Kent, Ohio: Kent University, 1973.

GIGLLONI, G. B., and BEDEIAN, A. G. "A Conspectus of Management Control Theory: 1900–1972." *Academy of Management Journal,* 1974, pp. 292–305.

GOODMAN, P. S.; PENNINGS, J. M.; and ASSOCIATES. *New Perspectives on Organizational Effectiveness,* San Francisco: Jossey-Bass, 1977.

HALL, R. H. *Organizations: Structure and Process.* 2nd ed. Englewood Cliffs, N.J.: Prentice-Hall, 1977.

JACKSON, J. H., and MORGAN, C. P. *Organization Theory.* Englewood Cliffs, N.J.: Prentice-Hall, 1978.

JAMES, L. R., and JONES, A. P. "Organizational Climate: A Review of Theory and Research." *Psychological Bulletin,* 1974, pp. 1046–112.

KATZ, D., and KAHN, R. L. *The Social Psychology of Organizations.* 2nd ed. New York: Wiley, 1978.

McMAHON, J. T., and PERRITT, G. W. "The Control Structure of Organizations: An Empirical Examination," *Academy of Management Journal,* 1971, pp. 327–40.

MAGER, R. F. *Goal Analysis.* Belmont, Calif.: Fearon, 1972.

MILES, R. E., and SNOW, C. C. *Organizational Strategy, Structure, and Process.* New York: McGraw-Hill, 1978.

PFEFFER, J., and SALANCIK, G. R. *The External Control of Organizations.* New York: Harper & Row, 1978.

ROGERS, R. E. *Organizational Theory.* Boston: Allyn & Bacon, 1975.

SLEVIN, D. P. "The Innovation Boundary: A Specific Model and Some Empirical Results." *Administration Science Quarterly,* 1971, pp. 471–87.

THOMPSON, J. D. *Organizational Design and Research.* Pittsburgh: University of Pittsburgh, 1971.

TOFFLER, A. *Future Shock.* New York: Random House, 1970.

A Case of Organizations
and Their Environment

The Josef Pratz Company

The Josef Pratz Company, located in Athens, Washington, was the ultimate fast-track brewery company of the 1970s. Its only product, Pratz Premium beer, was the "cult" beer of everyone from college sophomores to U.S. senators. On return trips from the West Coast, Air Force One was known to have a few cases of Pratz Premium stored along with the luggage of the plane's main passenger.

With all headquarters and manufacturing operations centralized at the Athens, Washington, location (claimed to be the world's largest single-location brewery), the company amassed a phenomenal financial record. Although its distribution was only regional (to fifteen Western states), by 1975 Pratz became the third largest brewer—based on barrels sold—in the United States. Because of its distinct taste and high quality, coupled with Pratz Premium's scarcity east of the Rockies, a tremendous marketing mystique was created for consumers all over the country. As a result, Pratz was able to sell every drop of beer it made for eighteen years straight. Pratz's profitability was highest in the brewing industry, and its stock sold for $97 per share as recently as 1976.

The company had been managed by the Pratz family since it was founded over 100 years ago. By owning nearly 65 percent of the stock, the family kept a tight grip on the operations of the company. The company's top three management positions were held by family members: George Pratz, chairman; Andrew Pratz (brother of George), president; and Jeffrey Pratz (George's eldest son), executive vice president. All had literally grown up in the brewery and were well respected in the brewing industry for the quality of their product and the level of efficiency of the manufacturing function. George Pratz was well-known to West Coast residents not only for his brewery but for his extensive charitable work and ownership of major pro football and soccer teams.

By late 1978, however, Pratz Brewery was facing a number of internal and external problems. For the first time in nearly two decades, sales in 1977 and 1978 were lower than full capacity of the brewery. As a result, earnings (after taxes) declined by 15 percent, and the price of the company's stock fell below $60 per share for the first time since 1968. An executive committee meeting, attended by George, Andrew, and Jeffrey Pratz, illustrates some of the problems facing the company.

George (chairman): Did you see the Titans on T.V. Sunday? They beat the Rams by two touchdowns and they did it in L.A.! I smell the Super Bowl coming!

Andrew (president): What you should be smelling is trouble for the brewery. We're about to register our second straight year of declining sales and earnings. You know what that means—the stock price goes down and *we* lose money! In two years, we've lost over 35 percent in the price of Pratz stock. Unless we start worrying more about beer and less about quarterbacks, we'll all be bench warmers for the Titans.

George: Oh Andy, don't give me that junk again. You forget that forty-three day strike we had earlier this year. We can't sell beer if we can't make it!

Jeffrey (executive vice president): Agreed, the strike hurt us plenty. But Dad, there are internal problems that are short term. It's the external and marketing problems that potentially have the biggest impact on us.

George: Namely?

Jeffrey: Namely, we're a one-product company—Pratz Premium. Our competitors have come out with not only low-calorie "light" beers for the diet-conscious, but also super-premium "dark" beers for consumers who want that stout European taste. In addition, the eight-ounce bottle has really taken hold in certain areas of the country. It's no longer a brewer's industry! You can't ignore the marketing revolution in beer, Dad! Look at the facts—we were number three in 1975, now we're number six in barrels sold. Andy is right—we've got to change our focus quickly! People are no longer mystified by the Pratz name—we need new products.

Andrew: I tend to agree with Jeff, but let's not forget the manufacturing problems with low-cal and dark beers. My process-engineering department tells me that we need to spend over $2,800,000 on new equipment to make these products. We'll also need new packing machines for the small bottles.

George: I'm not living in a vacuum—I know about these problems. I also know what I want to do. My planning group's latest report predicts a sharp *decline* in beer consumption over the next ten years. Wine and other specialty spirits will significantly grow in volume.

Jeffrey: If that's so, shouldn't we strengthen our efforts into new product development?

George: No! What I want to do is diversify beyond the beer business. In particular, I want to buy out Milsom Sporting Goods Company, the world's largest. The leisure industry is getting bigger and bigger, and I want to be in the middle of it. We can acquire Milson with a simple exchange of stock.

Jeffrey: A simple stock exchange? Come on, Dad, you know what that means? Our 65 percent hold on Pratz will decrease to less than 40 percent—we'll lose our majority vote! You also forget that our 65 percent of the stock is distributed throughout the entire Pratz family. Over eighteen people are involved. I don't think they'll support your venture outside the beer industry.

(The meeting is interrupted with a long-distance phone call for George Pratz).

George: I think the family will support me. Now, you'll have to excuse me for a while. Pete Rozelle is on the phone to discuss playoff procedures.

Case Primer Questions

1. Discuss the changing external environment of Pratz in terms of environmental components and dimensions.

2. How will the goals of the company change if they decide to stay in the beer industry and produce low-cal and dark beers? How will the goals change if they acquire the sporting-goods company?

3. What is the influence of the environment on the company's technology?

4. How do the personal values of the executive team affect company goals?

Experiential Exercise

Organizational Goals

Purpose

To study how goals influence managerial decision-making.

Required understanding

The reader should be familiar with the issues and concepts associated with organizational goals.

How to set up the exercise

Set up groups of from four to eight persons for the thirty to forty-five minute exercise. The groups should be separated from each other and asked to converse only with their group's members. Before forming the groups, each person is asked to complete the exercise by themselves and then to join the group and reach a consensus decision. Each person should read the following:

Assume you are the top-management team of the Davis Industrial Gas Products Company, a large industrial gas supplier located in St. Louis, Missouri. The firm specializes in packaging and distribution of gas cylinders to industries within a 200-mile radius of St. Louis. The firm's main products are oxygen, hydrogen, helium, acetylene, and other gas mixtures, which are used, for example, in hospitals (oxygen) and manufacturing firms (acetylene for metal cutting). The company purchases the various gases from chemical plants located nearby, processes the gases to improve the level of purity, and then packages the products in different-size cylinders. The firm's financial statement at the end of 1979 is shown in exhibit 10–13.

Your top-management team will meet shortly to discuss four problems or issues currently facing the company. Decisions on each of the four problems *must be made at this meeting*. The four problems are as follows (remember, the problems are *occurring at the same time*):

Problem 1. The local civic club has frequently complained to your company and to the city council about the air pollution originating from your plant. Although the pollution's source has not been proven, the age of your equipment suggests a number of leaks could exist. Your legal advisors have told you that to prove that air pollution exists and that Davis is the source would take a minimum of two to three years. Your options are to repair the possible pipe leaks, costing approximately $100,000 (option 1), or to do nothing (option 2).

Problem 2. Your company is pleased with the success in sales of oxygen cylinders to the area hospitals. Your management believes that there is good growth potential not only in selling other products to hospitals but also in selling oxygen in smaller cylinders to doctors' offices and nursing homes. You would, however, face increased competition in each of these markets. The new equipment and

Exhibit 10–13 Income Statement of Davis Industrial Gas Products Company

A. Income Statement: 1979

Revenue		$10,000,000
Expenses		
Raw materials	$5,500,000	
Salaries, wage, and benefits	2,950,000	
Depreciation	1,000,000	
Research and Development	200,000	
Advertisement	50,000	
Training	40,000	
Public Relations	60,000	
Interest Expense	300,000	
Total Expenses		10,100,000
	Net Loss	($ 100,000)

B. Net profit (loss) and revenues for four years

Year	Revenue	Net Profit (loss)
1978	$10,000,000	($100,000)
1977	9,500,000	380,000
1976	8,000,000	300,000
1975	7,800,000	($ 50,000)

increase in sales force will cost $300,000. The options are to spend the money (option 1), or to do nothing (option 2).

Problem 3. The relations with the union representing your hourly workers has been tense for years. The three-year union contract will expire in four months. In your initial bargaining, the union has made known their demands for a significant increase in wages and benefits. The cost over the three-year term of new contract would be $250,000. Finished inventory at the time of the contract's expiration would last six to eight weeks. Your options are to settle with the union on terms similar to their demands (option 1), or to take a chance on a long and bitter strike (option 2).

Problem 4. Your company has experienced a 35 percent turnover in supervisory and management personnel during the past year. Recently, a consultant's report indicated that not only are salaries for managerial personnel below the area average, but the company is in need of extensive revisions in its training and development programs. Your options are to spend $100,000 on personnel selection, training, development, and salary upgrading (option 1), or to do nothing (option 2).

Instructions for the exercise

1. *Individually,* group members should:
   a. Make decisions on each of the four problems discussed above. Remember: (1) decisions on these problems must be made now; (2) the problems are occurring simultaneously; and (3) you only have two options on each problem.
   b. *Rank order* the underlying goals or objectives that were important in your overall decisions. Mark your responses on exhibit 10–14.

2. As a *group,* repeat the above decisions. Mark group choices, distribution of individual choices, and group ranks on exhibit 10–14.

Exhibit 10–14 Goals in Decision Making

A. Decisions on the Four Problems

Problems	Individual Decisions Option 1	Option 2	Distribution of Individual Decisions Option 1	Option 2	Group Decision Option 1	Option 2
	(circle your choice)				(circle group choice)	
1. Air pollution	1	2			1	2
2. Improved product line	1	2			1	2
3. Labor relations	1	2			1	2
4. Management development	1	2			1	2

B. Rank order the underlying goals in individual and group decisions (1 = most important, 6 = least important)

Goal	Individual Rank	Group Rank
1. Company survival		
2. Improved competitive position.		
3. Community image.		
4. Stability.		
5. Employee relations and development.		
6. Internal cost control.		

CHAPTER 11

Organizational Design

In the previous chapter, we alluded to the importance of organization structure or design in influencing the behavior and performance of individuals. The *design* of an organization is the formal system of specialization, hierarchy, authority, responsibility, formalization, and departmentalization. During this century, there have been many design theories and models suggested as the "one best way," or universal approach to designing an effective organization. As we will discuss, there is *no such thing* as a best way to design an organization. Highly effective hospitals are usually quite different in their design from effective airline companies; the same can be said for insurance firms, social-service agencies, and manufacturing companies. In fact, research and development teams, sales groups, personnel departments, and production units in the same organization are often organized differently. Thus, in reality there are different designs *within* and *between* organizations.

In this chapter, we will examine the evolution of organizational design. It is our intent to examine the history of design strategies, review some of the different approaches to design now being utilized in organizations, and consider the differences in behavior and performance in organizational systems employing different design strategies. We will not offer a particular design as the answer to organizational problems, but will propose some steps that managers should consider before designing their organizations.

The Basic Concepts of Organizational Design

In the study of organizational design, there are a number of concepts that pervade most theories, models, and strategies. They are the foundation of the design strategy and are viewed differently by each person. Initially, it is important to understand that designing an organization involves the process of creating a structure of job tasks and authority within the system. The process requires creativity, evaluation, and testing. The costs and benefits of various design strategies need to be considered. Before establishing a cost-benefit analysis of the particular design, the evaluators need to agree on the core concepts generally considered in most strategies. Some of these concepts are discussed to provide the background for a more in-depth analysis of various design strategies. These concepts were selected for inclusion because they have been used by classicists, behaviorists, and contingency theorists alike.

Job Specialization

Organizations generally divide the work to be accomplished into specialized tasks and place them into specific units. For example, the personnel department may have a training specialist, a wage and salary specialist, and a labor contract negotiation specialist. The division into specialized tasks provides an identity for the job and those performing it. The identity is called the *job definition,* and theoretically it is an indicator of the degree of job specialization. The more limited the variety of tasks required to complete the job, the more obvious is the degree of specialization.

Departmentalization

Combining jobs of various degrees of specialization into a unit is called *departmentalization.* The pediatric nursing department in a hospital contains professional nurses performing nursing jobs that vary in degree of specialization. One nurse may work caring for premature babies, another provides care to babies requiring special attention because of respiratory problems, and yet a third nurse may care for babies with congenital heart problems. They are grouped together because of common backgrounds and similar goals.

Scalar Chain of Command

The existence of superior-subordinate relationships and interactions, found in most organizations, is basically characterized as a chain from a superior to subordinates. Organization charts depict the chain as a connecting line. The chain is scalar and formally spells out the division of authority, responsibility, and accountability among the superior-subordinate combinations, or the vertical differentiation.

Authority, Responsibility, and Accountability

Once job tasks are divided, grouped into departments or units, and a scalar chain is created, formal managerial positions are established. These positions are referred to by titles, such as department manager, and involve managing the work of others. The managers must plan, organize, control, and direct the activities of those working with them. To accomplish their tasks, managers exercise authority, hold subordinates responsible, and require accountability. The term *authority* means the right to require compliance from subordinates on the basis of position in the scalar chain. The superior is in the predominant authority position in the chain. The subordinate, like the manager, is *responsible* for accomplishing the assigned job tasks. The term *accountability* designates the obligation of the subordinate to carry out responsibilities and be accountable for decisions and activities.

Authority, responsibility, and accountability are imbedded in all design strategies in slightly different ways, from the orthodox classical bureaucracy to the unorthodox free form. These three concepts form a basis for discussion of centralization-decentralization, line-staff roles, and span of control.

Centralization-Decentralization

Although it is often thought that organizations can centralize authority to reach decisions in an elite or prestigious unit, *or* they can decentralize it to lower levels in the organizational hierarchy, decision making is anything but an either/or proposition in dynamic organizations. Some organizations encourage centralized authority for a number of decisions and decentralization for other decisions. The degree of centralization-decentralization encouraged varies among organizations.

Line-Staff Roles

As organizations increase in size and complexity, it is necessary to introduce personnel with specialized knowledge and skill, resulting in the establishment of line and staff positions. Individuals in these positions perform roles that require the use of authority. A relationship in which the occupant of one position can exercise legitimate, direct command over the occupant of another position is called *line authority*. A relationship in which the occupant of one position can advise or counsel but not command the occupant of another position is called *staff authority*. An individual can have line authority in his or her department or group and staff authority with a counterpart in the same group or with another department.

Span of Control

Superior-subordinate teams are created whenever tasks are specialized; departments or units are formed; and authority, responsibility, and accountability are established. The *span of control* is the number of subordinates who report directly to a supervisor. Note that the term is used to describe the number of subordinates, *not* the effectiveness of a supervisor.

Formalization

The degree to which the work is detailed and specified relates to the concept of *formalization*. The more detailed and clearly specified are the individual roles and tasks, the greater the formality of the structure. High formalization requires both high specificity and high compliance enforcement. With reference to our discussion in chapter 8, formalization can be thought of as the extent to which the organization uses rules, policies, and procedures to govern behavior and performance.

The level of formalization can vary within the organization. The lathe operator's work may be strictly governed by such standards as quality (e.g., .001 inch tolerances) and quantity (e.g., 400 units per week). On the other hand, the research chemist may operate in a more relaxed, self-determined set of activities directed toward a development or new discovery. The reader should note that the different degrees of formalization in these two examples are essential to the effective performance of these quite different tasks.

Complexity

Complexity generally refers to its degree of *structural differentiation,* or the number of different components within an organization. *Vertical* complexity refers to the number of distinct management levels; *horizontal* complexity concerns the number of different occupational groups or specialized subunits within an organization. In essence, structural complexity can be thought of in terms of the length of the *scalar chain of command* (vertical) and breadth of *job specialization* or the division of labor (horizontal). The greater the complexity, the more elaborate and costly the coordination and control function of the organizational design must be.

Form

Finally, the form or configuration of an organization relates to the criteria used to determine the extent of departmentalization and complexity. As shown in exhibits 11–1 and 11–2, the two most popular design configurations are the *functional* and *product* forms.

Exhibit 11–1 A Functional Organizational Design

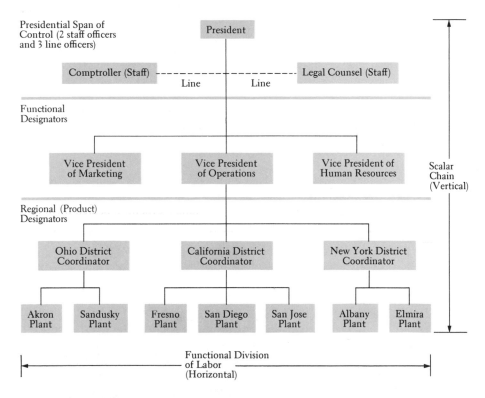

362

Exhibit 11–2   A Product Organizational Design

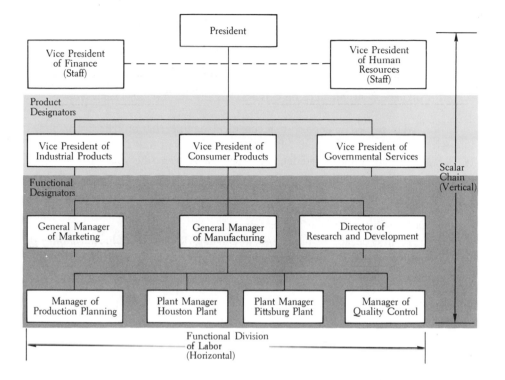

In the *functional* structure, the first operating level under the chief executive is structured along classic functional business lines (i.e., marketing, operations, personnel, and so on). The different product lines generally make up the level following the particular function. For the *product* structure, the sequence is reversed. That is, the product-line differentiation constitutes the first level under the chief executive, followed by the functional components. The product structure can reflect product line, project, or regional differences. For example, most national merchandising firms are organized along regional differences. Federated Department Stores, headquartered in Cincinnati, is structured by regional stores: Atlanta (Rich's), Miami (Burdines), and Houston (Foley's).

The reasons why firms choose a functional or product structural design form the basis of the contingency approach. As we will note later in this chapter, the nature of the organization's environment and technology play important roles in this decision.

Classical Design Perspective

There are various theoretical perspectives in the literature about how to design organizations. One approach is referred to as the *classical design theory*. There are two main streams of thought to this theory of design: (1) scientific management; and (2) ideal bureaucracy.

1) Scientific Management

The last few years of the nineteenth century resulted in the accumulation of resources and developing technology in American industry. Labor in manufacturing plants was highly specialized, and there was a heavy reliance on the expertise of industrial engineers to help design organizations to optimize efficiency. Engineers designed the equipment, supervised its installation, and provided suggestions on how to manage the work force.[1] One engineer who stands out as a major force in the scientific management influence on classical organization theory was Frederick W. Taylor.[2]

Taylor, who earned a degree in mechanical engineering in 1883, concluded through observation, working, and investigation, that poor managerial-worker relations, working conditions, and incentive pay plans were the rule in most work organizations. These conditions motivated him to determine *scientifically* what the workers ought to be able to do with their equipment, tools, and activities. The use of scientific fact finding to determine empirically, instead of intuitively, how to perform job tasks is the core of the Taylor approach.

During the first decade of the twentieth century, Taylor wrote his *Principles of Scientific Management.*[3] The objectives of his work to improve efficiency were stated as:

> First. To point out, through a series of simple illustrations, the great loss which the whole country is suffering through inefficiency in almost all of our daily acts.
>
> Second. To try to convince the reader that the remedy for this lies in systematic management, rather than in searching for some unusual or extraordinary man.
>
> Third. To prove that the best management is a true science, resting upon clearly defined laws, rules, and principles, as a foundation. And further to show that the fundamental principles of scientific management are applicable to all kinds of human activities, from our simplest individual acts to the work of our great corporations, which call for the most elaborate cooperation.[4]

In *Principles,* Taylor espoused a philosophical position on how to manage workers that he believed was applicable at all levels in organizations and even in different societies. His philosophical stance attempted to move scientific management away from a purely "efficiency expert" connotation, which he disliked. The essence of his philosophy and its relationship to organizational design are found in Taylor's four basic principles of managing. These are:

> *First.* Develop a science for each element of a man's work that replaces the old rule-of-thumb method.
>
> *Second.* Scientifically select and then train, teach, and develop the workman. In the past he chose his own work and trained himself as best he could.
>
> *Third.* Heartily cooperate with the men in order to insure all of the work being done in accordance with the principles of the science that has been developed.
>
> *Fourth.* There is almost an equal division of work and responsibility between the management and the workmen. The management takes over all work for

which they are better fitted than the workmen; in the past, almost all the work and the greater part of the responsibility were thrown upon the men.

These four principles present the operational thrust of Taylor's scientific management. Notice that he advocated scientific analysis, rather than pure common sense and intuition, and scientific selection, training, and development of workers to achieve effectiveness in an organization. Taylor emphasized cooperation and offered the scientific principles to achieve this in organizations. Finally, he recommended clear job definition through specialization so that those best suited to perform managerial tasks and operating tasks are able to clearly understand their roles.

As we have discussed in chapters 5 and 6, critics have stated that Taylor and other scientific management advocates have not included the human being in their principles, methodologies, or strategies for improving organizational effectiveness. Admittedly, his main focus was on job tasks rather than individuals in managing work, but he did despise efficiency experts because of their promise to solve problems quickly, and his writings do show concern for human relations. For example, he states that:

> No system of management, however good, should be applied in a wooden way. The employer who goes through his works with kid gloves on, and is never known to dirty his hands or clothes, and who either talks to his men in a condescending or patronizing way, or else not at all, has no chance whatever of ascertaining their real thoughts or feelings. . . . The opportunity which each man should have of airing his mind freely, and having it out with employers, is a safety-valve; and if the superintendents are reasonable men, and listen to and treat with respect what their men have to say, there is absolutely no reason for labor unions and strikes.[5]

The Taylor philosophy did not exclude human beings. He supported human development through scientific selection, training, fatigue reduction, incentive systems, and cooperation. Taylor's focus was on the individual and not on groups of employees. The lack of group emphasis may be the reason critics incorrectly claim that Taylor paid no attention to the human being in the workplace.

The scientific management approach has certainly left its mark on organizational design.[6] It has significantly influenced most strategies of design since its inception. The logic of efficiency is still powerful in organization, but the strategies to achieve it have been modified by different theorists, researchers, and practicing managers.

'Ideal' Bureaucracy

Bureaucratic design, as conceptualized by Max Weber, a sociologist, would enable organizations to most efficiently accomplish their goals. The Weberian model was certainly more rigid than the classical principles. He firmly believed that bureaucracy was superior to any other form of organizational design. Thus, he specifically formulated a plan to achieve the bureaucratic design.

The Weber plan recommended that organizations adhere to a number of strategies.[7] These were:

1. All tasks necessary to accomplish organization goals must be divided into

highly specialized jobs. A worker needs to master his trade, and this expertise can be more readily achieved by concentrating on a limited number of tasks.

2. Each task must be performed according to a "consistent system of abstract rules." This practice allows the manager to eliminate uncertainty due to individual differences in task performance.

3. Offices or roles must be organized into a hierarchical structure in which the scope of authority of superordinates over subordinates is defined. This system offers the subordinates the possibility of appealing a decision to a higher level of authority.

4. Superiors must assume an impersonal attitude in dealing with each other and subordinates. This psychological and social distance will enable the superior to make decisions without being influenced by prejudices and preferences.

5. Employment in a bureaucracy must be based on qualifications, and promotion is to be decided on the basis of merit. Because of this careful and firm system of employment and promotion, it is assumed that employment will involve a lifelong career and loyalty from employees.

Strict adherence to these strategies was assumed by Weber to be the best way to accomplish organizational goals. A close examination of the five strategies reveals that the way goals are attained is through an emphasis on *control* and *stability*. By controlling behavior and stabilizing operations and interrelationships, performance is hopefully enhanced.

Despite the name, rarely do we find an "ideal" bureaucracy, for it is difficult to strictly adhere to these basic principles. Problems with a bureaucratic design are numerous.[8] For example, the concept of "environment" is given little, if any, consideration. In addition, criticism can be directed toward the supposed "universiality" of the approach, the overemphasis on rules and procedures (see chapter 8), and the lack of reality in demanding and achieving impersonal dealings with others. These are serious aspects that need to be considered when the Weberian model is applied. As we will discuss later, however, there are some organizations that perform quite effectively under a bureaucratic design.

Integration of Scientific Management and Bureaucratic Concepts

The integration of scientific management and bureaucratic strategies yields what we call the classical design perspective. This perspective is controversial and often disregarded by some scholars and practitioners. It is controversial because of its rigidity and overemphasis on the structural components of organization and its lack of emphasis on the human factor. It is also criticized because of its over-reliance on principles that evolve from nonempirically based ideas and thoughts.[9] Despite these and other criticisms, which will be discussed as we cover other organizational design perspectives, there are a number of major structural dimensions and operational features that evolve from classical design theory.

The scientific management and ideal bureaucracy provide what some call *anatomical,*[10] or structural, dimensions and operational features. Some of these are presented in exhibit 11-3. The arrow between the dimensions and features shows that they are interrelated. The dimensions and features are also connected to the context factors, such as the environment and technology, and to behavioral consequences, such as performance and satisfaction. A full explanation of our view of these relationships and interactions will be presented later in the chapter.

Behavioral Analysis Perspective

There is no question that classical design approaches do not analyze in any systematic way the interaction of individual personalities, attitudes, learning capacities and motives, informal groups, and interorganizational conflicts. The human relations school of thought, beginning with the Hawthorne research, and the more recent findings reported by researchers such as Likert, have offered modifications to the classical approach. The modifications are more scientifically derived than the prescriptions offered by classicists, which were based on personal experiences.

Modification to Classical Approach:

Likert's System 4 Suggestion

Likert's field research led him to propose that effective organizations differ markedly from ineffective organizations along a number of identifiable structural properties.[11] It is Likert's position that an effective organization is one that encourages supervisors to focus their attention on endeavoring to build effective work groups with high and challenging performance goals. In contrast, less effective organizations encourage supervisors to:

5 features of

1. Introduce a high degree of job specialization.
2. Hire people with the skills and aptitudes to perform specialized job tasks.
3. Train these employees to do their jobs in the best and most efficient manner.

Classical Design

Exhibit 11-3 Structural Dimensions and Operational Features Related to Structure

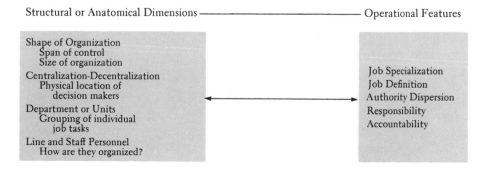

Structural or Anatomical Dimensions ———————————— Operational Features

Shape of Organization
  Span of control
  Size of organization
Centralization-Decentralization
  Physical location of
    decision makers
Department or Units
  Grouping of individual
    job tasks
Line and Staff Personnel
  How are they organized?

Job Specialization
Job Definition
Authority Dispersion
Responsibility
Accountability

4. Closely supervise the performance of these job specialists.

5. Where feasible, use incentives in the form of individual or group piece-rates.[12]

These five points are associated with the core features of classical design. By examining organizations with such tendencies, Likert concluded that a more behaviorally or people-oriented design that encourages groups working together is more effective. He describes this more effective, people-oriented organization in terms of eight dimensions and calls it a System 4 organization. The classical design is designated as System 1. Likert believes that System 1 organizations are ineffective because they no longer respond or cope with changes in their environments. Environmental changes naturally create pressures for change, and, to react to them, the organizational design needs to be more flexible. The System 4 and System 1 dimensions described by Likert are compared in exhibit 11–4.

The System 4 organization contains the features required to cope with changing environments, according to Likert. Communication flows freely, and this process is required to reach decisions, exercise control, and lend emphasis. Likert, like Weber with his ideal bureaucracy, assumes that there is a "one best way" organizational design. In Weber's case, it was the bureaucracy; in Likert's, it is System 4. Perhaps Likert, although he has some research evidence to support his superiority claim, is too enthusiastic in presenting one organizational approach as the best. It should be noted that it was not only the classicists who offered the "best way," but also behavioralists such as Likert.

Bennis: A Philosopher with a Behavioral Prescription

Bennis, like some of the classical organizational theorists, has forecasted the demise of bureaucracy.[13] He assumes that bureaucracy will wither and become less prevalent in organizations because managers will be unable to manage the tension, frustration, and conflict between individual and organization goals. In addition, bureaucracy will fade because of the scientific and technological revolution in industrialized nations. The revolutionary changes require adaptability to the environment, and bureaucracies are assumed to have difficulty doing this.

Based on experience and no empirical foundation, Bennis outlines organizational life into the 1990s.

1. The *environment* will show rapid technological change with a large degree of instability or turbulence.

2. Because of a greater educational background, people in jobs will want more involvement, participation, and autonomy in their work.

3. The *tasks* of organizations will be more technical, complicated, and unprogrammed. There will be a need to group specialists together in a project design arrangement.

4. Organizational structures will be more temporary, adaptive, and organic. These adaptive organizational structures will gradually replace bureaucracy as described by the classicists.

Exhibit 11–4   Classical Design and System 4 Organization

Classical Design Organization	System 4 Organization
1. *Leadership process* includes no perceived confidence and trust. Subordinates do not feel free to discuss job problems with their superiors, who in turn do not solicit their ideas and opinions.	1. *Leadership process* includes perceived confidence and trust between superiors and subordinates in all matters. Subordinates feel free to discuss job problems with their superiors, who in turn solicit their ideas and opinions.
2. *Motivational process* taps only physical, security, and economic motives through the use of fear and sanctions. Unfavorable attitudes toward the organization prevail among employees.	2. *Motivational process* taps a full range of motives through participatory methods. Attitudes are favorable toward the organization and its goals.
3. *Communication process* is such that information flows downward and tends to be distorted, inaccurate, and viewed with suspicion by subordinates.	3. *Communication process* is such that information flows freely throughout the organization—upward, downward, and laterally. The information is accurate and undistorted.
4. *Interaction process* is closed and restricted; subordinates have little effect on departmental goals, methods, and activities.	4. *Interaction process* is open and extensive; both superiors and subordinates are able to affect departmental goals, methods, and activities.
5. *Decision process* occurs only at the top of the organization; it is relatively centralized.	5. *Decision process* occurs at all levels through group processes; it is relatively decentralized.
6. *Goal-setting process,* located at the top of the organization, discourages group participation.	6. *Goal-setting process* encourages group participation in setting high, realistic objectives.
7. *Control process* is centralized and emphasizes fixing of blame for mistakes.	7. *Control process* is dispersed throughout the organization and emphasizes self-control and problem solving.
8. *Performance goals* are low and passively sought by managers who make no commitment to developing the human resources of the organization.	8. *Performance goals* are high and actively sought by superiors, who recognize the necessity for making a full commitment to developing, through training, the human resources of the organization.

Source: Adapted from Rensis Likert, *The Human Organization* (New York: McGraw-Hill, 1967), pp. 197–211.

As we have shown, the classical design approach sought to solve the problems of efficiency by emphasizing vertical, or top-down, functional structure by relying on the hierarchical power of managers. Likert and Bennis, on the other hand, elevate the individual and groups to a status of prominence in design decisions. Both approaches, classical and behavioral, are "one best way" recommendations that do not consider enough of the complexities of organizational design. They are simplis-

in view of

tic in that they are either/or choices. Organizational design decisions are anything but simple today. Consequently, it has been necessary to consider contingency design strategies.

=)

The Contingency Approach

In chapter 10, the systems orientation provided a macro paradigm for the study of formal organizations. This model emphasizes the complexities of organizations and seriously questions a purely classical or behavioral approach to design that is universally presented. Although Weber's ideal bureaucratic presumptions are macro, they are rather simplistic in that they exclude consideration of the environment, technology, and individual preference differences concerning organizational design. What has emerged in the organizational design literature and in practice is what is referred to as a *contingency approach*. It seems more reasonable to discuss *approaches* because no one model has been adopted as the final answer to design problems.

Using the theories and research of classical and behavioral scholars enables one to offer a broad definition of the contingency view of organizational design.

> A *contingency* approach attempts to understand the interrelationships within and among organizational subsystems as well as between the organizational system as an entity and its environments. It emphasizes the multivariate nature of organizations and attempts to interpret and understand how they operate under varying conditions and in specific situations. The approach strives to aid managers by suggesting organizational design strategies which have the highest probability of succeeding in a specific situation. The success criteria revolve around the accomplishment of organizational goals.[14]

The contingency approach to organizational design has appeal for practicing managers for a number of reasons. First, advocates of "one best way" approaches enthusiastically offer them as answers to managerial decisions about design. Often, after implementing a "best" approach, managers find little improvement in goal achievement. The manager's mix of circumstances just does not always fit perfectly with the specific approach. The contingency approach supports no one particular design; it encourages searching through the many variables that are important and selecting a design decision for the organization that is appropriate for a given moment in time and in the existing environment.

Second, the contingency approach, although empirically based, incorporates personal opinions about the situation facing an organization. It encourages the use of different models, systems, scientific management, bureaucracy, and/or System 4, if they properly fit the situation. This openness and willingness to use what fits best is refreshing and realistic if one considers the dynamic nature of organizations and their environments.

Finally, the contingency approach clearly points out that various departments of a single organization may require different organizational designs to accomplish goals. Thus, the same organization may have multiple designs as opposed to a strictly bureaucratic or System 4 structure. The exact designs used by an organization's departments are based on the situational mix of variables affecting their goal progress and achievement.

The exact nature of the factors upon which an organization's design is contingent is open to question. If space allowed, we would devote more comment to these factors, but, because it does not, we have selected environmental, technological, and sociotechnological factors as the most important contingencies in the design of organizations. To better understand the nature of these contingencies, we need to explore the theory by reviewing the more important attempts to clarify and study them.

Burns and Stalker: Environment

Burns and Stalker examined approximately twenty industrial organizations in the United Kingdom.[15] They were interested in determining how the pattern of managerial activities in planning, organizing, and controlling was related to the external environments. They gathered their data by performing field interviews. It was their intent to analyze the interview responses and reach some useful conclusions about how the environment and organization interact.

Early in the course of their work, Burns and Stalker discovered that management processes were different in various industries and environments. They reached the conclusion that each firm in their study sample could be viewed as an information-processing network:

> The information received may be anything from the visible presence of bits of material at the side of an operator's bench . . . to a managing director's remark to the effect that we ought to start thinking seriously about color television.[16]

The Burns and Stalker study on information processing treated the predictability of environmental demands facing organizations. They rated environments on a five-interval scale, from "stable" to "least predictable." Each of the five environments was then discussed with regard to the different management processes.

They studied a rayon manufacturer, an engineering company, and an electronics firm. The rayon company operated in the most stable or predictable environment. This stability was related to the organization, which was run on the basis of clearly defined roles, specialized tasks, limited information flowing downward, the concentration of decision-making authority at the upper managerial levels, and a distinct scalar chain of command.

The engineering company operated in a rapidly changing commercial environment. The environmental fluctuations required internal organizational design changes. Thus, the structure was more flexible or fluid. Tasks were not as clearly defined as in the rayon firm, and lines of authority and responsibility were not emphasized.

The organization operating in the least predictable environment was a newly created electronics-development organization. Job tasks were not defined well; the specific task assignments were made on an individual basis between superiors, peers, and subordinates. This type of interactive and dynamic task decision making was the result of the organization's rapidly changing situation. The structural dimensions of this firm were matched with the unpredictability of the environment.

The interview responses and their interpretations led Burns and Stalker to conceptualize organizational design and management processes as being primarily related to environmental uncertainty. The environment was considered an extrinsic factor by these researchers.

> These extrinsic factors are all, in our view, identifiable as different rates of technical or market change. By change, we mean the appearance of novelties: i.e., new scientific discoveries or technical inventions and requirements for products of a kind not previously available or demanded.[17]

The perspective acquired from their analysis of the twenty companies resulted in the identification of two management systems, the *mechanistic* and the *organic*. These systems are related as dependent variables to the rate of environmental change. Burns and Stalker adopt the position that environmental change refers to the technological bases of production and to the market situation.

The characteristics of mechanistic and organic organizations are presented in exhibit 11–5. A number of important points need to be emphasized. First, structure in the organic organization is based on expertise in handling current problems. In this type of organization, there is a less rigid hierarchy, but there is a structure that is used to avoid confusion and chaos. Second, in the organic organization the indi-

Exhibit 11–5 Some of the Burns and Stalker Identified Characteristics: Mechanistic and Organic Organizations

Mechanistic		Organic
Highly specialized job tasks	Specialization	Low specialization of job tasks
In a select group at top of the system	Locus of Authority	At whatever level skill or competence exists
By superior	Conflict Resolution	By interaction
Direction and orders	Basis of Communication	Advice, counsel, information
To the organizational system	Loyalty	To project and group
Based on position in system	Prestige	Based on personal competence
Stable	Environment	Dynamic, unstable

vidual's loyalty is developed around the work unit to which he or she belongs. The group has a special value to satisfying needs of employees in the organic system. Finally, organic systems are more associated with unstable environmental conditions. This type of system is more flexible and able to cope with and adjust to changes in the technological and the market situations. Rigidity of structure in the mechanistic organization hinders its ability to adapt to change. Thus, it is most appropriate to implement it in a more stable environment.

Lawrence and Lorsch: Environment

If the environment of an organization is complex and varied, it may be necessary to develop specialized subunits to deal with the parts of the environment. Organizations must match their subsystems to the environment. Lawrence and Lorsch conducted field studies to determine what kind of organizational design was able to best cope with various economic and market environments.[18]

They studied six firms in the plastics industry to sharpen their analytical procedures and theoretical propositions. After this phase of their study, they examined a highly effective organization and a less effective one in the plastics, food, and container industries. These three industries were included because they were assumed to be operating in environments that contained varying amounts of uncertainty. To assess environmental certainty, they asked executives in the organizations about clarity of market information, the rapidity of technological change in the industry, and the length of time required to determine how successful a product is in the marketplace.

In their research, Lawrence and Lorsch wanted to analyze the relationship between the environmental uncertainty facing an organization and its internal organizational design. They concentrated on three main subsystems—marketing, economic-technical, and scientific—and hypothesized that the structural arrangement of each subsystem or department would vary with how predictable its own environment was. They proposed that the greater the degree of environmental certainty, the more formalized or rigid would be the structure.

These contingency researchers also were concerned about what they called the *differentiation* and *integration* within the system. They assumed that by separating or grouping job tasks into departments the behavior of members of the unit would be influenced. The unit members would become specialists in dealing with their tasks and would develop particular work styles. Thus, *differentiation* is defined as the state of segmentation of the organization's subsystems, each of which contains members who form attitudes and behavior and tend to become specialized experts.

Lawrence and Lorsch took their research even further by calling attention to the differences that could exist among personnel in differentiated units. They studied the extent to which managers in different subsystems differ in their orientation toward goals; they studied the time orientation (short versus long run) of employees in different subsystems; and they studied the differences in the way managers deal with their colleagues or their interpersonal orientation.

A potential consequence of differentiation is a problem with bringing these individuals together to accomplish organizational goals. Because the members of each subsystem develop different attitudes, interests, and goals, they often find it difficult to reach agreement. These built-in organizational conflicts illustrate the importance of *integration*. Lawrence and Lorsch define *integration* as the quality of the state of collaboration that exists among departments and is required to achieve unity of effort.

The researchers' questionnaires and interviews revealed that subsystems within each organization tend to develop a structure that was related to the certainty of their relevant environment. For example, production subsystems tended to be faced with a relatively stable or certain environment. They had the most formal and structured design of the subsystems studied. On the other hand, research subsystems operated in a less predictable environment and had the least formal and rigid structure. Sales operated in what Lawrence and Lorsch refer to as a moderately predictable environment and had a moderate degree of structure when compared to production and research. Exhibit 11–6 displays how the Lawrence and Lorsch differentiation dimensions fit together for a high performing plastics organization, and exhibit 11–7 illustrates this firm's integration dimensions along with those of high performing container and food organizations.

The Lawrence and Lorsch findings point out that successful firms in different industries achieve a high level of integration. The amount of managerial time and effort required to achieve successful integration seems to be dependent upon two factors: diversity and interdependence. The more diverse the tasks of the firm's main units, the more differentiated those units will be in an effective organization. Differentiation, by creating and encouraging different viewpoints, generates conflict.

Exhibit 11–6 Differentiation Dimensions of a High Performing Plastics Organization

		Production Tasks	Sales Tasks	Research Tasks
Dimensions describing the diversity of the firm's subsystem task	Major variables	Costs, quality, quantity	Sales, volume, customer needs	Quality and volume of new ideas
	Uncertainty of information	Low	Moderate	High
	Time span of feedback	Short	Medium	Long
Fit				
	Pattern of goal orientation	Focused on costs, quantity	Focused on customer service	Focused on discovery of new knowledge
Dimensions of differentiation	Pattern of time orientation	Short	Medium	Long
	Pattern of interpersonal organization	Task	Social	Task

Adapted from Paul R. Lawrence and Jay W. Lorsch, *Organization and Environment* (Homewood, Ill.: Irwin, 1969), p. 36. Originally published by Division of Research, Graduate School of Business Administration, © 1967 by the President and Fellows of Harvard College. By permission of Harvard University Press.

Exhibit 11–7 Integration Dimensions of High Performing Organizations in Three Industries

		Container Organizations	Food Organizations	Plastic Organizations
Dimensions describing the organization's main subsystems	Diversity	Low	Moderate	High
	Amount of interdependence	Low	Moderate	High
	Key inter-dependencies	Sales-Production	Sales-Research Research-Production	Sales-Research Research-Production
	Key subtask to goal achievement	Sales	Sales-Research	Integrating unit's task
Dimensions of integration in the organization	Unit in which high integration is achieved	Especially in sales and production	Especially in sales-research and re-search-production	Especially between integrating unit and all others
	Managerial time & effort devoted to achieving integration	Low	Moderate	High
	How influence flows	Pyramidal, sales having the most	Fairly evenly distin-guished, sales & research the most	Fairly evenly dis-tinguished, integrating unit with the most
	How conflict is resolved	Confrontation	Confrontation	Confrontation
	Type of structure	Mechanistic	Mechanistic (with use of teams and task forces)	Organic

Fit (Dimensions describing the organization's main subsystems ↕ Dimensions of integration in the organization)

Thus, the greater the state of differentiation, the larger the potential conflict and the more effort and time it takes the manager to resolve these conflicts to benefit the firm. Furthermore, the more interdependent the tasks of the major subsystems, the more information processing is required for effective integration.

Interestingly, Lawrence and Lorsch found one behavior pattern related to integra-tion that was common in all successful organizations and did not seem to be contingent upon the firm's task. The conflicts among the firm's subsystems tended to be resolved primarily by confronting the issues at hand and looking for the most optimum solution, rather than smoothing over problems, forcing a solution on another unit, or bargaining for a resolution. The exact set of integrative relationships for successful firms in these different industries are shown in exhibit 11–7.

To summarize the major work of Lawrence and Lorsch briefly, whenever an organization's design does not fit its mission, environments, and resources, the effectiveness of the organization will suffer. If an organization's environments, resources, and mission never changed, managers would find the best design and keep it to achieve high levels of effectiveness. Of course, in the real world of administration and managing, each of these elements changes often. It is not un-common for an organization to operate for years in a fairly stable, calm, and certain set of environments and not even recognize when they begin to change in basic, subtle ways. Because organizational changes are difficult and energy consuming to cope with, managers often cling to the organizational form of design that has proved successful for years until the organization forces a change or until the firm is destroyed. Lawrence and Lorsch contend that whenever a mismatch exists between the organization's task and degree of differentiation, it loses relevant information and will become less effective over time unless modifications are made.

The state of differentiation, shifts in mission, environments, and resources each can create integration problems. Unless some reasonable degree of integration is achieved, an organization will lose information, face dysfunctional conflict, or make poor decisions.

Lawrence and Lorsch have focused on the viewpoint that there is no one best way to design organizations. They also show that a number of organizational designs can exist within the same firm. Their research is certainly a pioneering effort in the area of contingency organizational design. It has some critics, who contend that the measurement of environmental uncertainty is tenuous at best.[19] This criticism is indeed serious because the accurate measurement of environmental uncertainty is crucial in determining the appropriate degree of differentiation and integration for an organization. Until more accurate scales are developed for assessing the dimensions discussed in the Lawrence and Lorsch research, the claims that they make need to be treated with caution by practicing managers.[20]

Woodward: Technology

The studies of Joan Woodward and her associates are as important to the contingency organizational design literature as those of Lawrence and Lorsch. She and her team secured a sample of one hundred firms that employed at least one hundred people, in South Essex, England. The researchers spent from a half a day to a week collecting relevant data on the organizations and management. Through reviewing company records, interviews, and observation, they developed a profile of specific dimensions for each organization in the sample.[21] They profiled the following points:

1. The mission, historical background, and important events over the years.
2. The manufacturing processes and methods being used.
3. The organizational and task design of the firms.
4. The organization's success in the marketplace, including fluctuations of stock prices, changes in share of the market, and the growth or stagnation of the industry in which the firm belonged.
5. The understanding by employees of the organizational design being used. The researchers also used a mechanistic and organic classification system and found that the employees in mechanistic firms were more conscious of the organizational design being used.

These and other profile facts and figures were used to clarify the differences in structure and managerial processes among the organizations. The researchers found that the number of managerial levels varied from two to twelve, with a median of four, and the span of control of chief executives varied from two to eighteen, with a median of six. The first-line supervisory spans of control varied from twenty to ninety, with a median of thirty-eight, and the ratio of industrial line employees to staff personnel varied from less than one-to-one to more than ten-to-one.

The analysis of the profiles and figures resulted in a number of disconcerting discoveries. First, the researchers found that the organizational data did not relate, as they hypothesized, to the size of the organization or to its general industry affiliation. For example, job specialization did not seem to be more intense in larger companies than in smaller ones. Second, the twenty organizations that were classified as effective had little in common with regard to organizational properties. This was also the case among the twenty least effective organizations. These two findings implied that the classical design principles were not significantly related to organizational effectiveness. Approximately one-half of the successful organizations utilized an organic management system, which, of course, is contrary to the prescriptions of Weber.

In seeking answers to the issues they discovered, the Woodward team found that by classifying firms on the basis of technology a better interpretation of the data emerged. Technology is a very controversial factor.[22] The Woodward system of classification seems to interpret technology as "who does what with whom, when, where, and how often."[23] The three categories of technology were:

1. Unit and small batch.
2. Large batch and mass production.
3. Long-run process production.

The Woodward sample of organizations is shown in exhibit 11–8. This three-category system and the subgroups comprising it provided Woodward's team with a rough scale of predictability of results and the degree of control over the production process. In unit and small-batch manufacturing, each unit of production is made to order for a customer, and operations performed on each unit are nonrepetitive. Mass-produced products, such as automobiles or bottles for a soft drink, are usually more or less standardized, and the production steps are predictable.

The results of classifying organizations on the basis of technology among effective firms in the sample are summarized in exhibit 11–9. The number of managerial levels varied among the three technological group categories, with process-production firms having the longest chain of command. Similarly, the chief executive's span of control varied with technology, with managers in process manufacturing having the widest span. The first-level supervisors' span of control also varied with type of technology, but in this case the relationship was curvilinear. Unit, small-batch, and process first-level supervisors tended to have smaller spans of control, with those in mass-production facilities having the highest. Furthermore, the more advanced technologies, subgroups VII to X in exhibit 11–8, utilized proportionately more administrative and staff personnel.

 re, process production

Exhibit 11–8 Woodward Classification of Ninety-Two Firms on Basis of Technology

	Number of firms		Total number of firms
A. Unit and Small Batch	5	I. Production of units to task requirements	17
	10	II. Production of prototypes	
	2	III. Fabrication of large equipment in stages	
B. Large-Batch and Mass Production	7	IV. Production of small batches to customer's order	41
	3	V. Production of large batches: assembled diversity	
	25	VI. Production of large batches on assembly lines	
	6	VII. Mass production	
C. Process Production	9	VIII. Process production combined with the preparation of a product for sale by large-batch or mass-production methods	34
	13	IX. Process production of chemicals in batches	
	12	X. Continuous flow production of liquids, gases, and solid shapes	

*Note that 8 of the 100 firms are not classified because it was difficult to place them in a particular category according to Woodward.

Woodward's research team also found that there were differences in operational procedures in the different technology categories. At what she calls the "top and bottom of the technical scale," (i.e., unit and process firms) there was a tendency for fewer rules, controls, definitions of job tasks, and more flexibility in interpersonal relations and delegation of authority compared to the middle-range mass-production firms. Furthermore, organizations in the technological category that deviated from this general pattern were most often less effective. The most effective mass-production firms were those that emphasized job specialization, tight controls, rigid chain-of-command adherence, and that in general followed classical design principles. A mass-production firm that was more flexible or organic tended to be less effective. On the other hand, organic and flexible process-production firms were more effective than more rigid and bureaucratically inclined process firms.

Woodward aptly summarized the thrust of her contingency-oriented research by using the Burns and Stalker concepts: "Successful firms inside the large-batch production range tended to have mechanistic management systems. On the other hand, successful firms outside this range tended to have organic systems."[24]

The Woodward-inspired research on organizational design is limited to manufacturing facilities, but it has significant import for contingency-based analyses being

Exhibit 11–9 Summary of Woodward's Research Findings on the Design Features of Effective Organizations

Levels of Organization and Characteristics	Technologies		
	Unit and Small-Batch Production	Large-Batch and Mass Production	Process Production
Lower levels	Informally organized	Organized by formal structural arrangements	Organized by task and technological specifications; wide spans of control
Upper levels	Informally organized; no clear distinction between line and staff	Organized hierarchically with clear line and staff distinction	Informally organized; no line-staff distinction; narrow spans of control
Overall characteristics	Few levels; broad span of control; no clear hierarchy; low ratio of administrators to operating employees	Employees conscious of design; clear job specialization; clear chain of command	Many hierarchical levels; moderate consciousness of design dimensions
Most effective structure	Organic	Mechanistic	Organic

conducted by a manager. Those organizations engaged in small-batch operations face the largest number of contingencies. These firms, however, have a production technology that can adapt to these contingencies. At the other extreme are the process firms, which are faced with a minimal number of contingencies. Because process firms have continuous-flow facilities, they rely upon systematic and orderly work flows. A breakdown or disruption of these work flows can be very serious because effectiveness suffers. In order to respond to the dangers of disruption, these firms require an organic structure so that emergencies can be properly handled.

Sociotechnical Systems

The sociotechnical-systems approach to organizational design is based on the framework that any organizational system requires both a technology and a social system linking the employees with the technology and to each other.[25] The purpose of the sociotechnical-systems approach is to design organizations to perform in the most effective manner possible.

Individual and organizational effectiveness are related to the *joint* operation of the technical and social subsystem. Stated differently, the findings from the classical design approaches (scientific management and bureaucracy) have shown that if the technical subsystem is optimized (i.e., Theory X) at the expense of the social system, the results are less than optimal (see chapter 6). Likewise, optimizing the social subsystem (i.e., Theory Y) would fall short by failing to capitalize on the most efficient technical or production system.[26] The implications for *technical* specialists (e.g., industrial engineers, plant-design engineers, and architects) and *social* specialists (e.g., industrial psychologists, behavioral scientists, and human relations experts) are quite clear—organizational effectiveness comes from *working together* to achieve the joint integration and optimization of the technical and social subsystems. The key components of the sociotechnical-systems approach to organizational design are shown in exhibit 11–10.

External environment. The sociotechnical approach clearly recognizes the role of the external environment not only in determining technical and human requirements but also in influencing the need for internal change in the organization.

Technical system.   The general requirements for an effective production system are included within the technical-system component. Concern is given to the type of process (i.e., technology), the needed tools and equipment, and the standards of efficiency and effectiveness.

Social system.   As discussed in chapters 3 through 9, emphasis is given to the importance of the individual and the group—their performance and satisfaction—in the operations of the organization.[27]

Sociotechnical system.   The integration of the technical and social system leads to the sociotechnical design components. The components include:

1. *Organizational factors.* Emphasis is placed on controlling the *variance* of the work cycles and a recognition of the important work-related interdependencies.

2. *Group factors.* Autonomous work groups are established to assume the responsibility for task accomplishment and the allocation of members to various

Exhibit 11–10 Sociotechnical-Systems Approach to Organizational Design

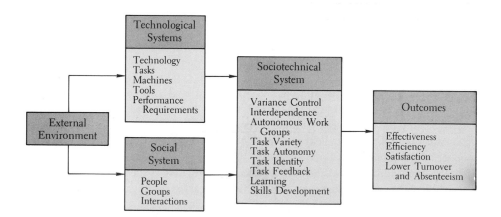

functions.[28] The cohesiveness of these groups hopefully would influence work-group performance.

3. *Individual factors.* These factors are clearly related to job design principles. The emphasis is placed on providing some meaningful work (variety), with inherent responsibility (autonomy), knowledge of the task and results (identity and feedback), and opportunities for growth (learning and skills development).

In applying the sociotechnical approach to organization design, the manager should recognize certain important points. First, the emphasis is placed on flexibility and adaptability rather than the rigid components suggested in the classical approaches. The manager looking for a way to develop an organization chart would be somewhat perplexed with this approach. In essence, the focus is on *choice* of design, as opposed to the *one best way.* Second, the importance of the group and the interrelationships between groups is brought to the forefront. The astute reader will note the similarities between sociotechnical systems and the experiences of Volvo and General Foods discussed in chapter 6.

Finally, sociotechnical systems can be viewed as an approach to job design. In chapter 6, the approach to contemporary job redesign was distinctly *micro,* or psychological in orientation. The sociotechnical-systems approach is founded on a *macro* framework (i.e., environment, technology, and so on). However, the end result of both approaches to job design is an emphasis on the components of variety, autonomy, feedback, and skills development.

Contemporary Design Strategies

In this chapter, and the previous chapter, we have criticized past approaches to organizational design for implying that there is "one best way" to structure an organization. There are too many factors—environment, technology, and goals, for example—that vary from organization to organization and influence the effectiveness of any design (see exhibit 10–3). A recognition of the importance of these factors to organizational design serves as the foundation for the contingency approaches.

If there is a single, unifying thread that characterizes the contingency approaches, it would be the concern for the impact of the *environment* on designs. From Burns and Stalker to sociotechnical systems, the dominant role of the organization's environment on design was stressed. Given the importance of the environment, what are some of the various design strategies used by organizations? The relationships between the environment, design characteristics, and design strategies are shown in exhibit 11–11. These strategies are not offered as the only contingency strategies available. Instead, they are provided as a sample of contingency approaches to cope with certain design problems.

The exhibit is based on exhibit 10–5, which pointed out how the environmental dimensions of degree of change (stable/dynamic) and *degree of complexity* (simple/

Exhibit 11–11 Environment and Organization Design Characteristics

Environment			Design Characteristics				Design Strategy
Degree of Change	**Degree of Complexity**	**Quadrant***	**Decentralization**	**Span of Control**	**Formalization**	**Complexity**	
Stable	Simple	I	Low	Few	High	Low	Functional or mechanistic design. (exhibit 11–1)
	Complex	II	Low	Many	High	High	Functional or mechanistic design with use of teams or task forces. (exhibit 8–9)
Dynamic	Simple	III	High	Few	Low	Low	Product or organic design. (exhibit 11–2)
	Complex	IV	High	Many	Low	High	Matrix designs—combination of functional and product designs. (exhibit 11–12)

*See exhibit 10–5.

complex) influenced the concept of *environmental uncertainty.* The four quadrants—stable/simple, stable/complex, dynamic/simple, and dynamic/ complex—are repeated in exhibit 11–11 and consist of the following:

Quadrant I. The environment for an organization in this quadrant is characterized by a relative lack of rapid change (stable) and a minimum of complexity (simple) with respect to external interactions. An example could be a city government. Internally, there is a high degree of centralization of authority and responsibility, low complexity (division of labor and chain of command), limited span of control, and an emphasis on rules and procedures (formalization). Because effectiveness is based on internal control (i.e., costs), the most effective design strategy under these conditions would be a *functional* (exhibit 11–1) or *mechanistic* design. In other words, a bureaucratic-type structure would apply to organizations in quadrant I.

Quadrant II. In this quadrant, the environment remains stable, but the degree of complexity increases because of an expansion in the number of external interactions (e.g., with customers, suppliers, and competitors). Manufacturers of home appliances (e.g., washing machines, dryers, and refrigerators) are an example of companies that sell a variety of products across different markets (e.g., direct to consumers, commercial establishments, or national retail stores under a brand name) that all exhibit a fairly stable demand or environment. Internally, centralization and formalization remain high. However, because of the different markets served, the complexity and span of control increase over firms in quadrant I. The prominent design strategy is a *functional* or *mechanistic* structure with the addition of the use of task forces or teams (see exhibit 8–9). The task forces are usually temporal in nature and generally concern issues of product development or market testing.

Quadrant III. A dynamically changing but noncomplex environment characterizes organizations in this quadrant. Specialty producers, such as clothing manufacturers, are an example. Such organizations generally specialize in only a few products that are made to order (or fashion) in a rapidly changing environment. The high degree of decentralization particularly stresses the use of a *product* design strategy (see exhibit 11–2) that has an emphasis on flexibility, adaptive behavior, and low formalization.

Quadrant IV. Finally, organizations in quadrant IV are faced with a highly complex and rapidly changing environment. Energy companies, engineering firms, and computer manufacturers in this type of environment are internally highly complex, emphasize decentralization of authority and responsibility, low formalization of rules, and require a wide span of control for managers. The design strategy for effectiveness requires the *control* elements of a functional structure *and* the *flexibility/adaptive* elements of a product structure. A design that combines the best of both these structures is a *matrix* organization design.[29]

The Matrix Design

The term *matrix* has been used to describe organizations that include a number of projects, programs, or task forces. Decentralization was and still is a typical response to growth in organizational size, markets, and competition. Decentralization is feasible because it is possible to break the organization up into fairly autonomous units. However, rapid changes in technology, the environment, and preferences of the work force have posed problems for decentralized organizational design. These changes have made it necessary for organizations to have large numbers of specialists to handle research and development, marketing research, and human resources development. Thus, the increased interest in the matrix or program-management approach is a consequence of problems inherent in the decentralization of decision-making authority.

When a matrix design is developed, the easiest description is that of a product structure *superimposed* on a functional structure. As an example, consider exhibit 11–12, which depicts the structure of a hypothetical medical school, the Hoffman College of Medicine, that is located in a multi-hospital medical center in a large city. The typical educational activities (teaching and research) are conducted within a functional design with the use of department chairpersons. However, because patient care and service are also functions for which the college is responsible, certain clinics are established in each of the nearby hospitals. The responsibility for the operations of the clinics are under the authority of a clinic director (i.e., product manager or project director within a product design). The end result is that the *control* features of a functional design (department chairpersons) and the *adaptive* aspects of a product design (clinic directors) are obtained in one design.

For effective functioning, a matrix design requires recognition of certain important factors. First, the classical *scalar chain of command* principle (i.e., each subordinate has only one supervisor) is thrown out. In our example, the typical resident M.D. reports to the chairperson on teaching and research matters but to the clinic director on patient issues. Second, the key managers in this design (chairpersons and clinic directors) must agree on a balance or *sharing of power* over resources. Decisions on financial, physical, and human resources must be made *jointly* and with a knowledge that power will be shifting between the two units over time. Third, because conflict will inevitably occur, there must be an open and frequent use of *confrontation* as a resolution mechanism. Conflict over financial resources, for example, will create service problems if attacked with an avoidance or defusion philosophy (see chapter 8).

As one might expect, the key to the effectiveness of a matrix design rests with the individual subordinates. Consider an M.D. assistant professor, represented by *A* in exhibit 11–12. This individual is responsible for teaching and research in the department of pediatrics, and treats patients through the St. Marks Hospital Clinic. This boundary-spanning position can create anxiety, stress, and frustration because there is both a lack of clarity of responsibilities (i.e., there is role ambiguity) and a possible conflict in directions (i.e., role conflict). For example, how is this individual's time divided? Is it 60 percent/40 percent—teaching to patients—or is it 80 percent/20 percent, 50 percent/50 percent, or what? In addition, who evaluates *A*'s performance at merit review time? Is it the clinic director, the chairperson, or both?

Exhibit 11–12 Hoffman College of Medicine—A Matrix Design

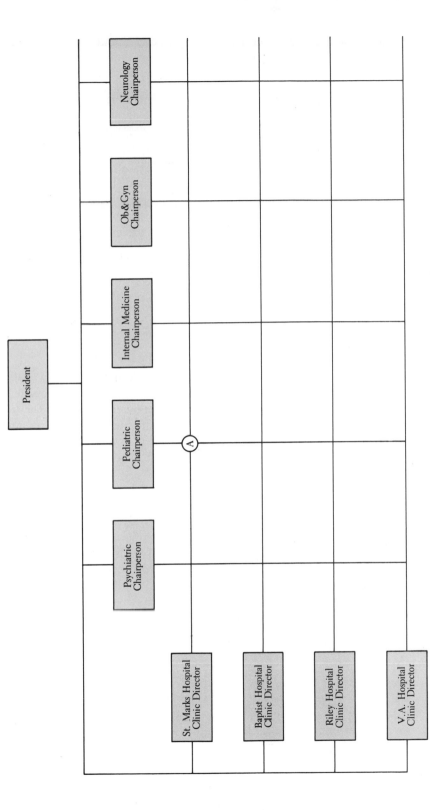

Naturally, these are questions that are answered differently by various organizations. Generally speaking, organizations tend to stay away from hard time allocations (e.g., 70/30) in favor of a flexible time schedule. Such a scheme, however, requires frequent monitoring and audit. Performance evaluations are generally conducted by the functional manager (chairperson), with major input from the product manager (clinic director), though this can vary in different organizations.

Despite the relative youth of the matrix design, companies such as Honeywell, Texas Instruments, and General Electric have used it for some time. When General Electric decided to quit the computer business, Honeywell acquired the pieces. It set up twenty managerial task forces, made up of approximately 200 people from both its own staff and General Electric's, to integrate manufacturing, marketing, engineering, field sciences, personnel, software, and the inventory of actual product lines. Honeywell's top executive claims that this design approach resulted in a smooth and effective merger of two large oganizations.[30]

Before the matrix design is even considered as effective as bureaucracy or System 4 in various settings, it needs to be more thoroughly studied. It is different and appealing for some situations. Determining the proper situations is necessary and important.

Free-Form or Conglomerate Designs

A second type of design that is found in quadrant IV organizations is called the *free-form* or *conglomerate structure*.[31] The free-form design can be depicted as an amoeba, constantly changing shape as necessary in order to survive. The focus of free-form designs is change. Managers in organizations using this approach need to be flexible and creative to cope with change.

Free-form designs reduce the emphasis on hierarchy, rigid authority roles, chain of command, and superior-subordinate formalization. A *profit-center* arrangement instead of the classically recommended functional departments is used. The profit centers are results oriented and are managed as a total team striving to accomplish goals. There is an emphasis on effectiveness through participation, teamwork, self-control, and autonomy. In other words, each profit center is probably designed in a different manner. Thus, the behavioral emphasis is definitely present in the free-form approach. However, the bottom-line results recommended by classicists are also crucial in this design strategy.

Free-form designs seem to be more compatible to some industries than to others. Organizations that require adaptability to shifting market demands or interests are attracted to this approach. These forms require centralized control (bottom-line efficiency) and decentralized operations, and this means that computerized information systems are almost imperative. Examples of firms using the free-form design to various degrees are Litton Industries, Xerox, Textron, and Polaroid.[32]

Large, diversified *conglomerates* often employ the free-form design. The conglomerates, by growing through mergers and acquisitions, require much more flexibility than that offered by the classical theorists' suggestions and those programs recommended by behavioralists. What degree of freedom in form any organization can tolerate is still an unanswered question. Only by researching this type of design and its impact on processes within an organization can we offer this unorthodox design as a solution for some managers. To date, little empirical research is available to support or reject the design in different settings. This design has some of the ingredients of being a contingency approach to design, which is currently the most publicized strategy.

The Impact of Design Variables on Behavior

There is a relationship between the major dimensions presented in exhibit 10–3 and behavioral consequences. The research on how these dimensions are linked to behavioral consequences such as those listed in our model could fill this volume. Therefore, we have selected three of the most researched variables to give some indication of the findings. We have selected size, shape (span of control), and formalization as examples of how design variables can influence behavior.

Size

The relationship of size to individuals' attitudes and behavior has been studied for years. The majority of this research has made comparisons across different-size subunits of a particular organization.[33] A review of this research results in some generally cautious implications. Larger units seem to be related negatively to job satisfaction and to the employee's tendency to stay on the job rather than leave the organization.

The majority of evidence suggests that large-sized units may have a negative impact on behavior. This evidence is in no way perfect for a number of reasons. First, there are studies that indicate that size has no relationship to productivity. Two researchers found that there was no relationship between size of the organization and scientific productivity as measured by publications.[34] They also found that there is a curvilinear relationship between size and job satisfaction. Satisfaction is greater in medium-sized (twelve to fifty employees) rather than in either large or small organizations. These researchers further conclude that variables other than size are probably more important in accounting for morale and satisfaction.

Second, the majority of research on size has focused on male rank-and-file or operating employees. Consequently, it is not clear how size of an organization affects managerial or female behavior. Third, the concept of size is interpreted differently by various researchers. The lack of agreement on how to operationally measure size provides limited comparability across studies.

At present, it seems safe to state that size has a variable impact on behavior. It does not seem to be as important as other organizational properties in predicting behavior. Size is a static condition, and more dynamic indicators appear to be better predictors. The size variable has been minimally studied in various segments of the work force. Thus, it should not be embraced as the best predictor of behavioral consequences.

Shape

Organizational shape is a popular topic in the discussion of structural properties. Such terms as *tall, flat,* and *pyramidal* are used to discuss shape. There are few empirically based studies available that examine such variables as shape, employee attitudes, and performance.

Worthy studied approximately 100,000 employees of Sears, Roebuck over a twelve-year period. He compared the attitudes and performance of Sears' employees working in flat-structured units with their counterparts working in tall-structured groups. His research led him to conclude that the employees in tall units reported lower morale and had lower individual output. Worthy concluded that the tall pyramidal structure, which indicates a proliferation of levels of management, encouraged centralization of authority and increased job specialization.[35]

There have been some studies that indicate that the flat versus tall dichotomy does not really account for differences in attitudes and performance. Porter and Siegel studied approximately 3,000 middle and top-level managers in a wide variety of sizes and types of organizations in thirteen countries. They found that in organizations of less than 5,000 employees, flat structures were correlated with greater satisfaction; in organizations of 5,000 employees and over, there was no difference between manager satisfaction and the shape of the organizational structures.[36]

The shape property is interesting, but, like the size factor, it does not appear to be as important as some of the contextual variables. We are not stating that shape has no importance in predicting behavioral consequences, but rather that it is one of the numerous features and dimensions that is interrelated. There appear to be some employees who have little concern about shape and its ramifications on their behavior. On the other hand, some people prefer a shorter administrative distance between themselves and the decision-making authority in the organization. The difficult issue involves the specification of what constitutes "shorter." To some, two levels of management or structure is too long a distance to traverse to communicate a key point or complaint. In summary, shape has been studied and is generally influenced by span of control, and it appears that some people are affected by different arrays of hierarchy. The manager needs to diagnose how his subordinates are influenced by shape, if at all, before reaching a conclusion on how the organization or unit should be shaped.

Formalization

The rules and procedures designed to handle organizational problems, occurrences, and emergencies are part of the operational feature of *formalization.* These rules and procedures can vary from highly stringent to extremely lax. Procedures can also vary along a continuum from routine to nonroutine. An example of highly formalized procedure is the mass-production assembly line. The item being worked on passes through specific procedural steps the same way every time. Those working on the item perform the same task every time. The formal procedures are learned by employees, and they follow them to complete the work. At the other end of the formalization continuum would be research and development employees who develop their own procedures to test a new idea or develop a new technique.

Hage and Aiken capture the essence of formalization when they state:

> Formalization represents the use of rules in an organization. Job codification is a measure of how many rules define what the occupants of positions are to do, while rule observation is a measure of whether or not the rules are employed.[37]

A similar orientation is revealed by Pugh et al., who state that formalization is "the extent to which rules, procedures, instructions, and communications are written."[38] The concepts in these interpretations of formalization are operationalized by asking the members of organizations to respond to a series of questions about the points raised. Of course, perceptual scale scores may not yield an accurate picture of formalization because respondents may not provide accurate information.

Despite the problems of operationalizing formalization, there are a number of important points for managers to consider. The personal dysfunctions of highly stringent formalization were pointed out years ago when the "bureaucratic personality" was identified.[39] The personnel who value individual freedom cannot function effectively when they are less free to act, decide, and communicate in the formalized organization. Thompson describes "bureaucratic behavior" as a culprit in organizations. He believes that formal organizational hierarchy fosters self-perpetuating, rigid behavior. Superiors want to follow specific rules and procedures rigidly because this protects them from making erroneous decisions and actions on their own. This adherence results in a "drift" toward more rules and procedures because insecurity thrives on rigidity.[40]

In studies of professionals, a number of interesting points have been made. Professionals, such as engineers, accountants, and physicists, bring to organizations norms and standards that are externally inclined. That is, their professional affiliations external to the organization guide their behavior. Formalization appears to be a duplication of standards and is perceived as less valid than professional norms. It has been found that the greater the degree of formalization, the greater the alienation from work.

These empirical results in no way detract from the importance of formalization. Some formalization is necessary in most organizations. The important point is attempting to determine what the proper amount should be. The manager should keep under careful scrutiny the employee impressions and attitudes about rules and procedures. There are some subsystems and personnel who want formalization to be high; others require less formalization.

The three factors reviewed point out a number of important issues to managers. First, there is no single structural dimension or operational feature that will determine the best or most appropriate design. In addition to these dimensions and features, we need to also consider the contextual dimensions and their interrelationships. Second, there is no ideal size, shape, or degree of formalization. In fact, different preferences are found within the same department. Third, managers need to continually investigate the preferences of employees concerning dimensions and features. Preferences, like environments, change, and this often necessitates some type of managerial response.

A Concluding Note

The historical background of organizational design theory, research, and application provides us with an overview of structural phenomena. We cannot offer a set of definitive conclusions about design. We can, however, offer some tentative conclusions and suggestions. First, it seems clear that the classicist, behaviorist, and contemporary design strategies are each interesting and for some situations probably the most effective approach. None of these approaches is universally the best, nor should they be accepted as such. They are the foundation for the contingency approaches, which seem better suited for our changing society and its organizations.

Second, organizational designs require that managers study and diagnose environments, technologies, and sociotechnical systems. Managers need to search for answers to a number of complex questions, which include:

1. Is my current organizational design significantly under, over, or properly differentiated?

2. Is my current organizational design enabling my firm to under, over, or properly integrate the differentiated subsystems?

3. What are the cost and benefits of the present and needed states of differentiation and integration?

4. How can my organization achieve the most appropriate mix of behavioral consequences through organizational design?

These questions represent a challenge to the skill and creativity of managers to design what is best for them at that particular time in their career and the organization's history. It is not an easy job to master, but it certainly is challenging.

Third, people respond differently to structural dimensions and operational features. What is good for one person is frustrating and debilitating to another. Again, managers have to probe the behavioral responses of subordinates to learn how they respond to size, formalization, authority, control, and other structurally related phenomena.

Fourth, there appears to be evidence that supports the contention that multiple designs need to exist in organizations. The single, pervasive design is too static and universal to be implemented if we can accept the Lawrence and Lorsch and Woodward research as even having some validity. Sales-unit designs are different from research-and-development-unit designs in effective organizations, and this is an important bit of evidence to justify considering multiple designs.

Finally, for any organization to properly match individual employee needs, skills, and attitudes with organizational design is virtually an impossible task. We should talk instead about the best match for a particular organization and employees. It is our belief that we need to talk about matching designs so that individual, group, and organizational goals are generally achieved. To claim or support total achievement is reverting back to classical principles and behaviorally recommended universal models. Organizational design needs to be considered perhaps as an effort to achieve multiple goals instead of just to satisfy employees or to earn additional profit and satisfy the board of directors.

Applications and Implications for the Manager

Organizational Design

1. It is important to understand that designing an organization initially involves consideration of a number of basic design concepts. These include: job specialization (division of labor); departmentalization; scalar chair of command; authority, responsibility, and accountability; centralization-decentralization; line-staff roles; span of control; formalization; complexity; and form.

2. The most visible basic concept is form, which is usually depicted by the organization chart. Two forms are the most popular: functional and product or project. Functional design, most commonly known as bureaucratic structure, features an emphasis on control. Adaptability and quick reaction time to environmental changes appear to be salient points for product designs.

3. The classical design approach incorporates an engineering and practitioner base to recommend principles and structural arrangements. It emphasizes organizational effectiveness through compliance with the principles of specialization, departmentalization, chain of command, and so on.

4. Many of the classical design prescriptions have met the test of time and continue to be used by many organizations. For some organizations, they are undoubtedly what is needed to achieve desired goals.

5. Behavioralists, such as Likert and Bennis, criticize the principles of the classical design approach and dislike its less than first-class treatment of individuals and groups and the consequences resulting from strict adherence to the principles.

6. Likert offers his System 4 organization as an ideal and tested approach to design. It is our contention that his strategy is good for some situations but must be treated cautiously or not implemented at all in others.

7. The contingency approaches to organizational design seem to us to make more sense than the more universal or static approaches. The contingency thrust emphasizes understanding the interrelationships within and among organizational subsystems as well as between the organization as an entity and its environments. It is a multivariate approach to organizational design.

8. Three main variables in the contingency approaches are environment, technology, and sociotechnical systems. They are considered contextual variables that are related to behavioral consequences. The research of Burns and Stalker, Lawrence and Lorsch, and Woodward are seminal works that capture the theme of contingency organizational design. These researchers have found that indeed different designs are appropriate for various environments, subsystems, people, technologies, and organizational missions. As in all research work, there are critics of the conceptualization, operational measurement, and conclusions reached by the contingency theorists. We believe that the complexity of contingencies has been especially well handled by these pioneers, and their work needs to be examined by all managers faced with design problems.

9. Some modern design strategies have emerged and serve as hybrid designs in that they incorporate the theory, models, and suggestions of both the classical scholars

and behavioralists. Two such strategies are the matrix and free-form designs.

10. Managers who are involved in design decisions need to be diagnosticians. They must review the present degree of differentiation and integration and the cost and benefits of designs with which they are now faced. These factors must be weighed against the desired behavioral consequences of performance and morale. Failure to diagnose will often result in an inability to cope with changes, which are continually occurring in organizations, environments, and among employees.

11. There is no one best organizational design, and it is inconceivable that one will ever emerge. What is best for an organization, its departments, and its employees changes over time. Thus, be open to new arrangements and different suggestions. To do otherwise is not advisable especially when the best organizational design research clearly indicates that adaptability in the form of organic design strategies is effective in some settings, and the mechanistic strategy is better in other settings. There are also strategies between these two that need to be considered and are by the most astute, up-to-date, and successful managers.

Review of Theories, Research, and Applications

1. What are the positive and negative features of functional and product designs?

2. How can the formalization feature of organizations be changed by management?

3. What are the differences between an "ideal" and a "real" bureaucracy?

4. Why have behavioral scientists harshly criticized the principles and prescriptions about organizational design offered by classicists?

5. Why is it reasonable to assume that some units in an organization may have a mechanistic structure, while other units have an organic structure?

6. Why is it difficult to operationally measure the environments of an organization?

7. How are the contextual factors interrelated with the structural dimensions, operational features, and behavioral consequences?

8. What are the positive and negative features of the matrix design?

9. Why would some people consider a free-form design a contingency approach?

10. How can undesirable behavioral consequences result from improper use of a particular organizational design?

Notes

1. Daniel A. Wren, *The Evolution of Management Thought* (New York: Ronald Press, 1972), p. 112.

2. An interesting perspective on Taylor can be found in Sudin Kakar, *Frederick Taylor: A Study in Personality and Innovation* (Cambridge, Mass.: MIT, 1970).

3. Frederick W. Taylor, *Principles of Scientific Management* (New York: Harper and Brothers, 1911).

4. Ibid., p. 7.

5. Frederick W. Taylor, *Shop Management* (New York: Harper & Row, 1903). Reissued as part of Frederick W. Taylor, *Scientific Management* (New York:

Harper & Row, 1947), pp. 284–85.

6. Harrington Emerson, *Efficiency as a Basis for Operations and Wages* (New York: Engineering Magazine, 1911). For an interesting biographical sketch of Taylor, see "High Priest of Efficiency, Milestones of Management," *Business Week,* 21 October, 1964, pp. 8–9.

7. Max Weber, *Essays in Sociology,* trans. H. H. Gerth and C. W. Mills (New York: Oxford, 1946), p. 214; Max Weber, *The Theory of Social and Economic Organization,* trans. A. M. Henderson and Talcott Parsons (New York: Oxford, 1947), p. 330.

8. R. Levy, "Tales from the Bureaucratic Woods," *Dun's Review,* March 1978, pp. 94–96.

9. Herbert A. Simon, *Administrative Behavior* (New York: Macmillan, 1957), p. 58.

10. For a well-presented design model that has relevance to any perspective on organizational design, see Lyman W. Porter, Edward E. Lawler III, and J. Richard Hackman, *Behavior in Organizations* (New York: McGraw-Hill, 1975), p. 223.

11. See Rensis Likert, *New Patterns of Management* (New York: McGraw-Hill, 1961); Likert, *The Human Organization* (New York: McGraw-Hill, 1967).

12. Ibid., p. 6.

13. Warren G. Bennis, *Changing Organizations* (New York: McGraw-Hill, 1966).

14. This definition is modified from that offered by Fremont S. Kast and James E. Rosenzweig, *Contingency Views of Organization and Management* (Chicago: Science Research Associates, 1973), p. 313.

15. Tom Burns and G. M. Stalker, *The Management of Innovation* (London: Tavistock, 1961). A brief review of twelve recent books on management or organizational behavior reveals that the Burns and Stalker work is cited to introduce the concept of contingency approaches to management.

16. Ibid., p. 78.

17. Ibid., p. 83.

18. Paul R. Lawrence and Jay W. Lorsch, *Organization and Environment* (Homewood, Ill.: Irwin, 1969).

19. Henry L. Tosi, Ramon Aldag, and Ronald Storey, "On the Measurement of the Environment An Assessment of the Lawrence and Lorsch Environmental Uncertainty Scale," *Administrative Science Quarterly,* January 1973, pp. 27–36.

20. H. Kirk Downey, Don H. Hellriegel, and John M. Slocum, Jr., "Environmental Uncertainty: The Construct and Its Application," *Administrative Science Quarterly,* December 1975, pp. 613–29.

21. Joan Woodward, *Industrial Organization: Theory and Practice* (London: Oxford, 1965).

22. For discussion of technology, see E. D. Chapple and Leonard R. Sayles, *The Measures of Management* (New York: Macmillan, 1961); Charles Perrow, "A Framework for the Comparative Analysis of Organizations," *American Sociological Review,* 1967, pp. 194–208; D. S. Pugh et al., "Dimensions of Organizations Structure," *Administrative Science Quarterly,* 1968, pp. 65–105; James D. Thompson, *Organizations in Action* (New York: McGraw-Hill, 1967).

23. E. D. Chapple and Leonard R. Sayles, *The Management of Management* (New York: Macmillan 1961), p. 34.

24. Woodward, *Industrial Organization,* p. 71.

25. D. N. Rousseau, "Technological Differences in Job Characteristics, Employee Satisfaction, and Motivation," *Organizational Behavior and Human Performance,* June 1977, pp. 18–42.

26. R. Cooper and M. Fosta, "Sociotechnical Systems," *American Psychological Review,* 1971, pp. 467–74.

27. L. E. Davis, "Job Satisfaction—A Sociotechnical View," *Report 575-1-69* (Los Angeles: University of California, 1969), p. 8.

28. E. L. Trist and L. W. Bamforth, "Some Social and Psychological Consequences of Long-Wall Method of Coal-Getting," *Human Relations,* 1951, pp. 3–38.

29. S. M. Davis and Paul R. Lawrence, *Matrix* (Reading, Mass.: Addison-Wesley, 1977).

30. Joel E. Ross and Robert G. Murdick,

"People, Productivity, and Organizational Structure," *Personnel,* September–October 1973, pp. 8–18.

31. For a look at free-form designs, see John J. Pascucci, "The Emergence of Free-Form Management," *Personnel Administration,* September–October 1968, pp. 33–41; Thomas O'Hanlon, "The Odd News About Conglomerates," *Fortune,* June 1967, pp. 175–77.

32. Dalton E. McFarland, *Management* (London: Macmillan, 1970), p. 286.

33. Frederick T. Evers, Joe M. Bohlen, and Richard D. Warren, "The Relationship of Selected Size and Structure Indicators in Economic Organizations," *Administrative Science Quarterly,* June 1976, pp. 326–42.

34. Leo Meltzer and James Salter, "Organizational Structure and the Performance and Job Satisfaction of Physiologists," *American Sociological Review,* June 1962, pp. 351–62.

35. James C. Worthy, "Organizational Structure and Employee Morale," *American Sociological Review,* June 1950, pp. 169–79.

36. Lyman W. Porter and Jacob Siegel, "Relationships of Tall and Flat Organizational Structure to the Satisfaction of Foreign Managers," *Personnel Psychology,* Fall 1965, pp. 379–92.

37. Jerald Hage and Michael Aiken, "Relationships of Centralization to Other Structural Properties," *Administrative Science Quarterly,* June 1967, p. 79.

38. D. S. Pugh et al., "Dimensions of Organizational Structure," p. 75.

39. Robert K. Merton, "Bureaucratic Structure and Personality," in Merton, *Social Theory and Social Structure* (New York: Free Press, 1957), pp. 200–201.

40. Victor Thompson, *Modern Organizations* (New York: Knopf, 1961), p. 154.

Additional References

BLAU, P. M., and SCHOENHERR, R. A. *The Structure of Organizations.* New York: Basic Books, 1971.

CHILD, J. "Managerial and Organizational Factors Associated with Company Performance, Part I. A Contingency Analysis." *Journal of Management Studies,* 1975, pp. 175–89.

———. "Managerial and Organizational Factors Associated with Company Performance, Part II: A Contingency Analysis." *Journal of Management Studies,* 1975, pp. 12–27.

CHILD, J., and MANSFIELD, R. "Technology, Size, and Organization Structure." *Sociology,* 1972, pp. 369–93.

DU BICK, M. "The Organizational Structure of Newspapers in Relation to their Metropolitan Environment." *Administrative Science Quarterly,* September 1978, pp. 418–34.

DUNCAN, R. B. "Characteristics of Organizational Environments and Perceived Environmental Uncertainty." *Administrative Science Quarterly,* September 1972, pp. 313–27.

GALBRAITH, J. W. *Organization Design.* Reading, Mass.: Addison-Wesley, 1977.

HALL, R. H. "Interorganizational Structural Variation." *Administrative Science Quarterly,* 1962, pp. 295–308.

———. *Organizations: Structure and Process.* 2nd ed. Englewood Cliffs, N.J.: Prentice-Hall, 1977.

HARVEY, E. "Technology and the Structure of Organizations." *American Sociological Review,* 1968, pp. 249–58.

JACKSON, J. H., and MORGAN, C. P. *Organizations Theory.* Englewood Cliffs, N.J.: Prentice-Hall, 1978.

KATZ, D., and KAHN, R. L. *The Social Psychology of Organizations.* 2nd ed. New York: Wiley, 1978.

KELLER, R. T.; SLOCUM, J. W., JR.; and SUSMAN, G. I. "Uncertainty and Type of Management System in Continuous Process Organizations." *Academy of Management Journal,* 1974, pp. 56–68.

LORSCH, J. W., and LAWRENCE, P. R. *Studies in Organization Design.* Homewood, Ill.: Irwin, 1970.

MELCHER, A. J. *Structure and Process of Organizations.* Englewood Cliffs, N.J.: Prentice Hall, 1976.

MILES, R. E.; SNOW, C. C.; and PFEFFER, J. "Organization and Environment:

Concepts and Issues." *Industrial Relations,* 1974, pp. 244–64.

MILES, R. E., and SNOW, C. C. *Organizational Strategy, Structure, and Process.* New York: McGraw-Hill, 1978.

MOBERG, D. J., and KOCH, J. L. "A Critical Appraisal of Integrated Treatments of Contingency Findings." *Academy of Management Journal,* 1975, pp. 109–24.

MOHR, L. B. "Organization Technology and Organizational Structure." *Administrative Science Quarterly,* 1971, pp. 444–59.

OSBORN, R. N., and HUNT, J. G. "Environment and Organization Effectiveness." *Administrative Science Quarterly,* 1974, pp. 231–346.

PFEFFER, J. "Size and Composition of Corporate Boards of Directors: The Organization and Its Environment." *Administrative Science Quarterly,* 1972, pp. 219–28.

ROGERS, R. E. *Organizational Theory* Boston: Allyn & Bacon, 1975.

SCOTT, W. G., and Mitchell, T. R. *Organization Theory: A Structural and Behavioral Analysis.* Homewood, Ill.: Irwin, 1972.

TOSI, H. L. *Theories of Organization,* Chicago: St. Clair Press, 1975.

WIELAND, G. F., and ULRICH, R. A. *Organizations: Behavior, Design, and Change.* Homewood, Ill.: Irwin, 1976.

A Case of Organizational Design

The McGraw-Edison Company

Edward J. Williams, chairman of McGraw-Edison Co., strolled to the altar two weeks ago at his daughter's wedding, a ceremony that Williams jokingly refers to as a "divestiture." It will likely be his last one for a long while.

Williams has spent six years at the Elgin (Ill.) company—which manufactures electrical products ranging from toasters to huge transformers—selling off ailing businesses and inefficient plants, slashing thousands of jobs from the payroll, and recasting the management setup. But now, Williams believes his laborious chore is complete. McGraw-Edison earned $57 million last year on sales of $1 billion for a return on shareholders' equity of 13.6 percent, up sharply from the 8.7 percent return that occurred before Williams came to the company from GAF Corp. in 1972.

Even competitors are generally impressed with the change at McGraw-Edison. They add, however, that some of the company's new vitality is attributable to the lift in demand for the equipment used by utilities, as the electric companies move ahead now with upgrading programs that have been delayed by the recession. Such products contributed 36 percent of McGraw-Edison's operating income last year on 27 percent of sales. Noting this, one competitor remarked that "there's nothing like orders to make management look good."

The Investments

Moreover, the company's recent performance is still well below Williams' current goal of a 21 percent return on equity. And despite the improvement, McGraw-

"McGraw-Edison: Expanding Again Now That the Pieces Are Together," *Business Week,* 10 July, 1978. Used with permission.

Edison lags far behind such industry leaders as General Electric, Emerson Electric, and Square D, all of which posted return-on-equity figures of more than 20 percent last year.

To reach Williams' target, McGraw-Edison is embarking on a program that calls for developing new products, increasing its presence abroad, and pursuing acquisitions again after a long hiatus. "Because we had so many problems to solve internally, we had to put a hold on acquisitions," says Williams. "But now, we are in shape to go after both large and small opportunities outside the company." Earlier this month, for example, McGraw-Edison acquired Specified Products Inc., a small producer of energy-saving light fixtures with about $1 million in sales.

The gains that Williams wants so badly may prove elusive unless the company can markedly increase the profitability of its consumer products division. Once the company's leading business, this group has contributed little to McGraw-Edison's earnings in recent years—its Speed Queen washers and dryers and Toastmaster small appliances have lost market share. Consumer products accounted for 27 percent of the company's sales last year, but only 8 percent of operating profits.

'Obsolescence'

Its main problem in the consumer field, company executives and outsiders agree, is that needed investments were put off until recently. Thus, plants that were starved of capital became inefficient, existing products were not remodeled, and few new products were developed. "Our problems in the consumer area were building for years," says Williams. "But they were masked by a healthy market that continued through the early 1970s."

Then, in the 1974–75 period, when materials costs for the company's consumer products rose by 45 percent, McGraw-Edison was unable to produce the compact, less expensive models made by competitors. This shortcoming was particularly apparent in its large appliances. As Williams observes: "The big leap in materials costs speeded up obsolescence."

Trying to remedy this situation, Williams has taken a number of steps. First, more capital spending has gone for the consumer group in the last few years than for any of the other three divisions: the industrial, commercial, and utility equipment groups. Speed Queen, for instance, is spending more than $10 million to retool its plants to make space-saving models that nonetheless handle larger loads of clothes—the first major design change in fifteen years.

Independent divisions

Meanwhile, three plants, accounting for more than 30 percent of the division's capacity, have been shut down. Such lackluster products as barber clippers and so-called weight-reducing machines were dumped, while new entries such as a food processor, a doughnut maker, and others were added. And McGraw-Edison executives point to this year's first quarter, when the consumer unit's operating profits almost doubled to $3.8 million, as evidence that the investment campaign is paying off. Still, the division's profitability does not yet approach the level of the company's other businesses. Says one skeptical analyst: "Williams did some of the basic things that were needed, but it's still pretty much the same old McGraw."

Yet, as the recent strength in McGraw-Edison's other businesses implies, the company has changed considerably under the Williams regime. When he came aboard, Williams found a confederation of thirty-nine fiercely independent divisions, largely the byproduct of some fifty mergers engineered by founder Max McGraw and his successor Alfred Bersted. The separate divisions, Williams recalls, "didn't even know where Elgin was, and the corporate management consisted of only a half-dozen staff members."

Williams set to work dismantling and reorganizing these independent fiefdoms, establishing seventeen divisions that report to four group executives. He also assembled a corporate staff of more than two hundred members to give headquarters the control over most financial, planning, legal, and purchasing decisions. Williams then called for a painstaking review of all products and operations. Based on that analysis, thirty-one plants were closed, products that accounted for $100 million in sales were eliminated, and the work force was cut by about two thousand.

Larger deals ahead

Until recently, McGraw-Edison's problems at home prevented it from moving aggressively into foreign markets. As one competitor notes: "Outside the U.S. and Canada, we just don't bump into McGraw." But Williams wants to change that. He has quadrupled the international marketing staff to 250 and streamlined its distribution operations. He also plans to invest heavily abroad, hoping to boost foreign business to 25 percent of company sales by the early 1980s, up from 16 percent today.

Acquisitions, too, should play a significant role in McGraw-Edison's growth plans. While the Specified Products acquisition was tiny, the company apparently is now ready to make much larger deals, especially ones that would add to its industrial or commercial product lines. But this month's acquisition also suggests that while Williams has altered the management approach at McGraw-Edison, the freewheeling go-it-alone philosophy has not been altogether forgotten. According to one exasperated corporate executive, the company's lighting subsidiary decided to announce the Specified Products acquisition without even bothering to ask for the required go-ahead from headquarters.

Case Primer Questions

1. Identify the key design concepts that are involved in this case.

2. What are the forms of organizational design *before* and *after* the change?

3. Identify the goals of the company and how they relate to organizational design.

4. Discuss how the environment and technology influenced the choice of a new organizational design at McGraw-Edison.

A Case of Organizational Design

Houston Memorial Hospital

As hospitals grow, they become more specialized and in most instances more complex. The proliferation of services at Houston Memorial Hospital has, according to its administrator Nora Rogers, a number of organizational drawbacks. She believes that the ability of the hospital to coordinate the components necessary for the delivery of effective care to patients has diminished since the hospital has doubled in size in the past three years.

Since this rapid growth pattern, Houston Memorial has considered converting to a more functionally oriented organizational design, that is, grouping activities according to major tasks, such as institutional, financial, patient care, and professional. This arrangement would not entirely be followed by such units as nursing services. The nursing services are currently a mixture of process, territorial, and product organizational design. Three nursing activities have strong elements of process departmentalization: surgery, delivery, and emergency care. The nursing stations, where patients receive their twenty-four hour care, are grouped primarily along territorial lines (i.e., third floor, Fondren Wing, Eller Wing). The product specialization is based on obstetric, surgical, or medical patient categories.

A reorganization plan

Nora believed that a reorganization of the entire hospital away from the mixed process, territorial, and product arrangement such as that found in nursing services to what she calls unitary departmentalization is appropriate. This would be accomplished by transforming activities currently organized along functional and process lines to activities grouped by product or territory. It is assumed that such a change in design will increase the decentralization of hospital operations and the delegation of authority to subunits. The key advantage, according to Nora, of the suggested reorganization is that it would place the level of integration at a lower point in the organization, thus improving the opportunity to coordinate activities closer to the point of action. Unless some "pushing downward" of the point of integration is instituted, she believes that reduced efficiency and decreased morale will become significant problems in the growing hospital.

An example of the results of reorganization

Nora used nursing services to provide examples of the anticipated results of the change. She believed that there would be a greater delegation of authority to head nurses, two or three of which would be responsible for each 100 beds. There would be a chief clinical nurse to serve each 100-bed "minihospital." The chief clinical nurse and head nurses would be specialized in the branches of medicine most appropriate for the patients hospitalized in their units.

The hospital's director of nurses would hold no line authority over the nurses in the 100-bed units. The director would instead concentrate on the recruitment and training of qualified nursing personnel, the evaluation of patient care in the unit, and the development of communication links between various units.

The major change in medical staff organization would be the creation of a "medical coordinator and advisor" for each 100-bed unit. This person would perform the following duties:

1. Provide advice to the nursing staff on specialty-related clinical matters.

2. Coordinate between the unit and physicians admitting patients to the unit.

3. Participate in the management of the unit, working with the chief clinical nurse and assistant administrator.

The coordinator and advisor would be a young physician who had recently completed residency training and who could on a part-time basis fill this important new integrative role.

Functional authority

Nora assumed that functional authority was essential in the reorganization plan. Line authority, of course, represents the use of the "chain of command." Line supervisors are responsible for the operations of the hospital. Staff personnel exercise staff authority, which is based on knowledge and is used only in an advisory capacity. Because of the difficulty in maintaining a clear distinction between line and staff and because of open conflicts between line and staff supervisors, "functional authority," which constitutes a blending of line and staff, seemed appropriate. When a supervisor delegates functional authority, he or she identifies that portion of authority and grants it to a staff specialist. The staff specialist acquires line authority in the area delegated, rather than mere advisory power.

A subordinate in the functional arrangement has two supervisors: one concerned with general matters and one concerned with specialized matters. The nurse in a hospital has dual responsibility: to a nursing superior for general matters and to a physician for specialized medical matters.

The proposed organizational design

The concept of functional authority is highlighted in exhibit 11–13, which provides a summary of Nora's reorganization plan. This plan possesses both advantages and disadvantages that Nora had to identify and present to the hospital board at the next meeting.

Case Primer Questions

1. What is meant by the concept of integration discussed in this case?

2. Is Nora utilizing a contingency approach in this reorganization decision? Explain.

3. What are the advantages and disadvantages of Nora's reorganization plan?

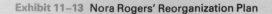

Exhibit 11–13 Nora Rogers' Reorganization Plan

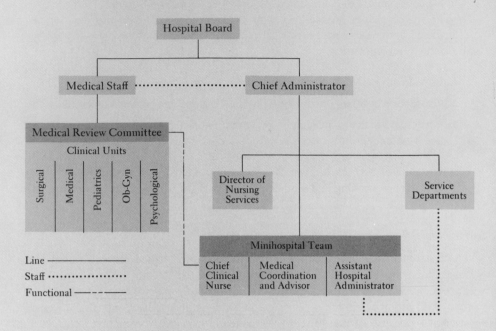

CHAPTER 12

Decision Making
and Communication

So far, we have examined the nature of individual members of organizations, the influence of group membership and processes on their behavior and performance within organizations, and the formal organizational structure within which group and individual behavior occurs. The two most frequent kinds of activities that managers engage in while carrying out job responsibilities are decision making and communication.

The topics of this chapter, decision making and communication, constitute the major processes involved in carrying out the work of the organization. In a very real sense, they constitute the "life processes" of the organization, just as respiration and electrochemical impulses of the nervous system are life processes of the human body. Indeed, the organizational processes we will discuss in succeeding chapters (performance evaluation, rewarding performance, and organizational change and development) require that decisions be made and the results communicated to various members and groups within the organization.

Three major factors—individuals, group, and the formal organization—influence work performance. The major process by which performance occurs is through decision making. That is, performance results because a decision or choice has been made. Decisions can be made at three levels. Individuals may decide on a given level of performance, as when sales representatives set their own sales goals. We have already seen the ways in which groups can informally arrive at a group consensus of decisions regarding norms or production quotas. Finally, organizations engage in formal decision processes when establishing corporate goals and choosing strategies to achieve those goals.

In this chapter, we will point out that the single most critical ingredient in a decision is information. We all have had the experience of making a choice when we had very little information or information we knew was inaccurate. For most of us, it was an uncomfortable and somewhat frightening experience, depending upon the seriousness of the results. A great deal of evidence as well as common sense suggests that the more and better quality information one has, the better will be the quality of the decision. The major avenues by which information is gathered and exchanged among parties is through communication. Hence, the process of communication among individuals, informal groups, and formal units is necessary to decision making.

The purpose of this chapter is to study the processes of decision making and communication in detail. Our focus will take three directions on both topics. First, we will define decision making and communication conceptually. Second, we will present major models of these processes and review empirical research relevant to them. Finally, we will discuss implications of these results for practicing managers.

Decision Making

Nature of Individual Decision

The fundamental activity influencing performance is making decisions. We all have become accustomed to facing and making decisions in all aspects of our lives. The student trying to settle on a career, the job applicant trying to select from among three job openings, a worker trying to figure out how much to produce under a new incentive system, and the hospital administrator trying to decide between allocating a $1 million bequest to new surgical rooms or a vocational rehabilitation center are all faced with a decision.

Elements in decision process

Although the substance and circumstances of these decisions vary greatly, they all have a number of critical factors in common. First, the decision maker faces a number of alternative choices regarding actions to be taken. Second, various outcomes or results are possible depending on which action is chosen. Third, each outcome has some probability or chance of occurring, and the probabilities may not be equal for each outcome. Fourth, the decision maker must determine the value, utility, or importance to be attached to each action-outcome combination. If a given action is chosen and a given outcome occurs, for example, what is the importance or value of this outcome to the decision maker? These four elements in the decision process have been identified as the major dimensions in a decision situation and are shown in exhibit 12–1.[1]

Exhibit 12–1 Elements in a Decision Situation

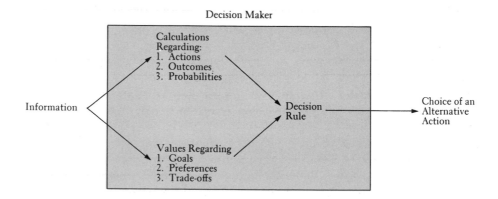

Decision Maker

Calculations
Regarding:
1. Actions
2. Outcomes
3. Probabilities

Information

Values Regarding
1. Goals
2. Preferences
3. Trade-offs

Decision
Rule

Choice of an
Alternative
Action

Classical Decision Theory

The earliest approach to decision models focuses on the individual decision maker and has become known as classical decision theory. Our discussion of classical decision theory will involve four topics: (1) information; (2) decision rules; (3) risk; and (4) decision aids.

Information

The classical decision theory approach to the decision situation in exhibit 12–1 can be illustrated by the case of a private medical clinic's decision regarding the possibility of adding a new wing and expanding its staff to treat an expected increase in patient demand. The first need of the person responsible for making the decision is for information. Exhibit 12–1 suggests that several types of information will be required. First, calculations need to be made regarding the options open to the clinic. In this case, information sources show that two choices exist: (1) remain the same size and do not open a new wing (referring additional patients to other clinics); or (2) open the new wing and take on additional patients. Second, the possible outcomes that can result under the two options must be determined. In this case, information suggests that either: (1) no significant increase in patient load will occur; or (2) a predicted doubling in patient load will occur.

A third information requirement is a knowledge of the probability or likelihood that each of the two possible outcomes will occur. In this case, let us suppose that the probability of the patient load remaining at current levels is 40 percent and that the probability of the expected increase in patient load occurring is 60 percent. The decision maker in this case has so far considered three pieces of information: (1) alternatives open; (2) outcomes that would occur once a decision is made; and (3) the probability of the outcome occurring. This information is summarized for this example in exhibit 12–2.

In addition to knowledge of outcomes, actions, and probabilities, the manager has to have some basis for placing values on each action-outcome combination. Exhibit 12–1 suggests that decision makers must have information regarding the goals, preferences, and trade offs desired by the organization before such values can be specified. Assume in this case that the major objective of the clinic is to maximize the profit or net revenue (given that adequate standards of clinical care are maintained). Such a goal would indicate that the decision should be evaluated in terms of the financial outcomes associated with each action.

The information in exhibit 12–2 allows us to calculate the profit the clinic would earn under each possible action-outcome combination. If the clinic does not expand (cells 1 and 2), it will earn $200,000 per year, no matter what the level of patient demand. If the clinic opens a new wing, on the other hand, two profit levels are possible depending upon patient demand. If patient demand does not increase, profit will drop to nothing (cell 3) because of increased cost of operating the new wing. If patient demand does increase as expected (cell 4), however, profit will increase to $500,000 per year. The profit figures in the cells of the decision matrix in exhibit 12–2 are formally called *conditional values*. They express the value or meaning of events to the decision makers in terms of their goals and objectives.

Exhibit 12–2 Decision Situation Facing Medical Clinic

Options	Outcome A No Increase in Patient Load P = .40	Outcome B Expected Increase in Patient Load Occurs P = .60	Expected Annual Profit
Do Not Open New Wing	$200,000[1]	$200,000[2]	$200,000
Open Wing	$0[3]	$500,000[4]	$300,000

Analysis of Conditional Costs

	Case 1 Do not open wing and patient load increase does not occur	Case 2 Do not open wing and patient load increases	Case 3 Open wing and patient load does not increase	Case 4 Open wing and patient load increases
Revenues	$2,000,000	$2,400,000	$2,000,000	$2,700,000
Less operating costs	1,800,000	$2,200,000	2,000,000	$2,200,000
Net Profit	$ 200,000	$ 200,000	$ 0	$ 500,000

Decision rules

Finally, the hospital needs a decision rule to combine calculations regarding outcomes, actions, and probabilities, with conditional values attached to action-outcome combinations. Decision rules are based on the objectives of the organization and tell the decision maker what choice to make once he or she has knowledge of actions, outcomes, probabilities, and conditional values. Decision rules fall into two major classes:

1. *Nonprobabilistic decision rules* ignore the probabilities of various outcomes occurring. Decision makers act *as if* they have perfect information. A *pessimistic* decision maker, for example, would examine the decision matrix in exhibit 12–2 and look for the worst possible outcome (in this case, opening a wing and having no increase in patient load). The effect of the rule is to presume that the probability of no increase in patient load occurring is 100 percent. Classical decision theorists call such a rule a "mini-max" rule, that is, "minimize the maximum loss." In this case, the pessimistic decision maker would recommend not opening the wing.

   An *optimistic* decision maker, on the other hand, would focus on the greatest profit possible ($500,000 when the clinic opens the wing and patient load doubles). In effect, he or she is presuming that the probability of patient load doubling is 100 percent. Classical decision theorists call such a rule a "maximax" rule, that is, "maximize the maximum payoff." In this case, the optimist would recommend that the clinic build and open the new wing.

2. *Probabilistic decision rules* deal directly with the probabilities associated with various outcomes. In the case of the clinic, the decision makers would combine information about probabilities and conditional profits and evaluate the two alternatives in terms of expected long-run annual profits. The data in exhibit 12–2 indicate, for example, that if the clinic does not expand, they can expect to average $200,000 per year in profit. If they expand, they can expect to average $300,000 per year in profit. Under a probabilistic decision rule, the decision makers evaluate the decision in terms of statistical expectations. The decision rule in this case would be "maximize *expected* profit." Thus, they would choose to open the new wing.

The difference between types of decision rules reflects the different circumstances under which decisions are made. Whether nonprobabilistic or probabilistic decision rules are appropriate depends upon: (1) whether the decision is an individual or institutional decision; and (2) the state of the decision maker's knowledge about the situation. Exhibit 12–3 illustrates the differences between individual decisions and perfect certainty on one hand and institutional decisions made under risk on the other. In addition, the exhibit demonstrates a continuum of knowledge about events ranging from perfect certainty to complete uncertainty.

At one extreme of the continuum, individual decisions differ from institutional decisions because they are made infrequently. In addition, the decision maker may not be able to afford a short-run loss or error. An individual's choice of an occupation, an organization, or a marital partner are examples of an individual decision. In these cases, the decision makers may choose to ignore risk and act as if they have perfect information about decision outcomes, choosing the alternative that maximizes the payoff or minimizes the cost to them. In cases such as these, nonprobabilistic decision rules are used.

Exhibit 12–3 Type of Decision and Type of Knowledge

State of Knowledge		
Perfect Certainty	**Risk**	**Perfect Uncertainty**
Under perfect certainty, individual decisions are made: Infrequently Short-run loss cannot be afforded	Under risk, institutional decisions are made: Frequently Short-run loss can be afforded	No decision possible

At the opposite end of the knowledge continuum in the exhibit, the decision makers are operating under perfect uncertainty; that is, they have no knowledge whatsoever about outcomes, alternatives, and likelihoods and, therefore, cannot make a decision. Most behavioral scientists believe that such a situation is rare in actual organizational settings.[2] Any decisions attempted under such circumstances would be irrational according to classical decision theory.

Risk

Most organizational decisions are made under varying degrees of risk rather than certainty or uncertainty. These decisions are institutional in nature in that they are made frequently and in most cases the organization can afford short-run losses or errors. Behavioral scientists point out that such decisions are made under risk because the decision maker does not have perfect information. Instead, he or she must deal with probabilities or likelihoods of various events occurring, and there are several ways of estimating such probabilities. Close to the perfect-uncertainty end of the knowledge continuum are guesses or hunches the decision maker has about the situation. The manager who stocks a new fad toy because he or she "feels that it's going to take off" or the nurse who checks on a critical patient just in time to ward off a crisis will report that they had no special information, just a feeling or hunch upon which they acted. In technical terms, behavioral scientists say that such decisions are made on the basis of *subjective* or *personal* probabilities. They are neither derived from empirical data nor formalized. They are based on the informal experience of the decision maker.

Moving away from the perfect-uncertainty end toward the perfect-certainty end of the continuum, the organization can formalize its previous experiences with similar decisions into *objective* probability estimates or relative frequencies. These are estimates of the relative number of times in the past each of several events has occurred under similar circumstances. Thus, when an organization is making production plans for a given month, it will rely on previous demand data for the same month in determining how many units to produce.

Decision aids

The advent of electronic data processing (EDP) and growth in the field of management science have led many organizations to formalize various principles of classical decision theory through the use of mathematically powerful and sophisticated decision models.[3] These models are intended to allow the decision maker to optimize the goals of the organization in a variety of different decision settings. The Program Evaluation and Review Technique (PERT) and the Critical Path Method (CPM) are models that allow the decision maker to plan projects in a way that will maximize efficiency by explicitly identifying critical task accomplishments, sequences, and completion times.[4]

In addition, goal programming is a recent adaptation of linear programming that allows decision makers to identify several goals simultaneously, establish priorities or relative values for their achievement, and select courses of action subject to a variety of constraints that maximize each.[5] Highly sophisticated mathematical models, such as queueing theory and Markov chains, have been adapted to maximize allocation decisions about employees in organizations.[6]

The purpose of this chapter is not to review these mathematical techniques in any detail, but rather to identify them as applications of classical decision theory to ongoing managerial decision aids. They are all normative decision models in the sense that they tell managers *how* to make the best decision. They do not focus on the process by which actual decisions are made, and are not, therefore, descriptive or process models of human decision making. In order to understand the process by which humans make decisions, we must turn to more recent theoretical developments.

Elements of classical decision theory

Many managers have often felt uncomfortable when trying to use the models derived from classical decision theory. A major source of concern among practicing managers is that these are "ideal" models and make some very demanding assumptions about human nature and organizational behavior:

> The decision maker is a rational person who will always choose an alternative that optimizes the organization's goals.

> The decision maker has ready access to perfect information concerning all aspects of the decision situation.

> Multiple goals can be cast in a linear fashion and combined mathematically into a single simplifying equation.

> All people will handle information in the same manner when faced with the same decision situation.

> Communication, perception, personality, and motives do not influence the actions or choices of the decision maker.

Very often, the actual choices individuals operating alone or in groups make are not predictable from a "rational" decision theory standpoint because one or more of these assumptions are violated in actual organizational settings. Three major bodies of theory have developed during the past fifteen years that have taken a behavioral rather than a normative approach toward decision making. The emphasis of these models is on predicting decisions from a description and understanding of the psychological, group, and organizational processes leading up to the decision.

We will examine three major behavioral decision models in this chapter: (1) the work of March and Simon and Cyert and March who were among the first to suggest that an understanding of the processes of decision making is central to an understanding of the behavior of organizations (work for which Simon was awarded the Nobel prize in economics in 1978);[7] (2) human information-processing models, which suggest that an understanding of the way in which people attend to and process information will lead to a knowledge of the implicit or explicit policies that guide their choices and decisions; and (3) recent models that view decision making as a social process and examine the process of decision making as events that occur between people.

Behavioral Decision Theory

The first major integration of decision theory and organizational behavior was introduced by Barnard, March, Simon, and Cyert in a series of theoretical statements about the decision-making behavior of individuals, groups, and organizations.[8] The major premise of their theory is that decision making is the fundamental process of behavior and performance within organizations. Indeed, these authors define an *organization* as a structure of decision makers acting at times as individuals and at other times as groups.

A behavioral view of decision making within organizations argues that the assumptions of classical decision theory about human nature cannot be accepted without question. These assumptions must be investigated empirically before a descriptive model of organizational decision making can be developed. Thus, the Barnard, March, Simon, and Cyert view of organizational behavior is to examine the *motivational, cognitive,* and *computational* limitations under which actual decisions are made.

Bounded rationality

In contrast to the ideal decision maker in classical decision theory, March and Simon indicate that actual decisions are made under conditions of *bounded rationality:* unlike ideal decision maker in classical decision theory

> This, then, is the general picture of the human organism that we will use to analyze organization behavior. It is a picture of a choosing, decision-making, problem-solving organism that can do only one or a few things at a time, and that can attend to only a small part of the information recorded in its memory and presented by the environment.[9]

The definition of bounded rationality implies that employees make decisions under a number of external and psychological constraints. The manager, for example, who must decide how many units of various items to stock does not, in fact, have perfect information. Indeed, he or she often makes the decision without seeking out all the information available.

A number of important implications about decision making arises from the concept of bounded rationality. First, decision makers tend to make decisions in sequence; that is, if the individual (or organization) is satisfied with present conditions, no search is made for more alternatives or better strategies. Decision makers, therefore, search for new alternatives only if they are dissatisfied with present outcomes. This phenomenon is illustrated in exhibit 12–4. The model indicates the sequence of events prompting a decision maker's search for information regarding alternatives. The following conclusions can be drawn from the model in this figure:

> The lower the decision maker's satisfaction with present outcomes, the greater the search for better alternative actions (indicated by the minus sign in the figure).

> The greater the expected value of the decision's outcome, the higher the level of satisfaction (indicated by the plus sign in the figure). + level of aspiration

Exhibit 12–4 General Model of Adaptive Motivated Behavior

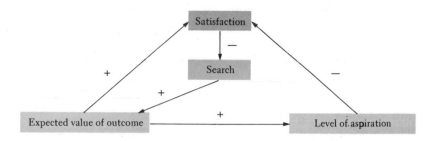

The higher the expected value of the decision's outcome, the higher the level of aspiration (indicated by the plus sign).

The higher the level of aspiration, the lower the level of satisfaction (indicated by the minus sign).

The case of the health-care clinic provides a good illustration of this process. So long as the decision makers are satisfied with amount and quality of health services rendered, there will be no motivation or force to search for new alternatives to their present set of operations. (This fact fits in with the motivation and performance model presented in chapters 2 and 5). Should the clinic decision makers become dissatisfied with their current performance, however, a search process is motivated. The higher the degree of search, the greater will be the expected value of its outcomes. In this example, the greater the amount of effort put into exploring ways to improve its performance, the greater will be the clinic's expectation of improved performance. In addition, the decision maker's satisfaction will increase.

The greater the expected value of the outcome, the greater will be the level of aspiration (in this case, the goals that are set for the clinic). The higher the level of aspiration, other things being equal, the lower will be the level of satisfaction. The net effect on satisfaction will depend on which is rising faster, the expected value of decision outcomes or the clinic's level of aspiration.

Implications of bounded rationality

The major conclusion to be drawn from the model in exhibit 12–4 is that decision making and the search for alternatives is not a spontaneous, ongoing activity such as breathing. It takes work and effort to make decisions, and such behavior must be motivated. Exhibit 12–4 suggests that level of aspiration (or goal setting) keeps the organization dynamic and assures that periodically a search for alternatives will be motivated. It is also important to note that the phenomenon of motivated search applies to all levels of decision making. In this case, we used an example of formal organizational decision making. The model works equally well when analyzing the decisions of informal groups and individuals.

A second important implication of the concept of bounded rationality is that decision makers use the most convenient and least expensive information, not necessarily the information that will result in the maximum amount of knowledge about the outcomes, alternatives, values, and probabilities involved in the decision. In pricing decisions, for example, the store manager may simply set the manufacturer's suggested retail price, rather than carrying out an intensive survey of retail prices on the item in the store's marketing area, even though the local survey may result in more accurate price information. The published price list is also less costly. The point is that information is not a free good and not readily available in usable form to the decision maker. Hence, there is very great motivation to use the most convenient and least costly information available.

A third critical implication of bounded rationality is that the direction of the decision maker's search for alternative actions is often influenced by personal perceptions, values, beliefs, experiences, and training. A manager with an accounting background, for example, may limit a search for alternative solutions to a problem by searching for financial and auditing solutions, but a manager with heavy training in the field of organizational behavior may search for solutions to a problem and limit the search to group conflict-resolution techniques.

These three implications of the bounded rationality concept suggest that individuals, groups, and organizations rarely maximize goal attainment in their decisions. Rather, they *satisfice;* that is, they tend to evaluate decision alternatives against standards that set minimally acceptable levels of attainment on each objective rather than maximum standards. If a decision alternative is found to be minimally acceptable with respect to standards, it is chosen, and a search for additional alternatives or strategies is discontinued. The notion of satisficing has received a great deal of empirical support in the study of corporate profits. A number of investigators have found that large, private organizations in the United States tend to return a steady rate of profit annually, which meets satisfactory levels of the owner's expectations, rather than maximizing profits each year.[10]

Decision Programming

We have said that institutional decisions are routine; that is, they are made over and over again, and the organization can accumulate very accurate information regarding alternative outcomes, actions, and values. Examples of such decisions would be the number of valves to order for a production plant's normal weekly assembly schedule, the number of units of children's jeans to be kept in inventory for a given store, or the selection of a job applicant for a job that requires routine clerical skills.

Behavioral scientists have noted that these routine decisions are amenable to *programming* within the organization.[11] Management attempts to reduce the cost of a decision and exercise control over performance through the development of standard operating procedures; that is, the establishment and implementation of policy that directs the choices made by individual employees. Thus, for example, when deciding on the number of valves to be ordered for a week's production, a plant manager may simply consult a chart that indicates the number to be ordered, given a knowledge of production demanded.

Organizations routinize decisions for three major reasons:

1. *Economy*—Savings in time, money, and other resources.

2. *Uncertainty reduction*—By developing routines, organizations protect their most critical activities. The likelihood of costly errors in a hospital's operating room, for example, can be reduced through standardizing decisions and procedures.

3. *Coordination and control*—Implementation of standard policies will coordinate decisions among people and make their choices more consistent. This will result in a greater degree of predictability and control over the organization's operations.

Information Processing

An area of concern among behavioral scientists in recent years has been the question of how individuals and groups utilize information in making decisions and arriving at evaluative judgments.[12] Research in this area treats decision making as an information-processing activity and attempts to predict the decisions made by people from a knowledge of the way they handle information. An information-processing approach to decision making asks three basic questions:

1. What information does a decision maker use in making a decision?

2. What are the relative weights or importance placed on various pieces of information?

3. In what ways does the decision maker combine information from various sources in arriving at a choice?

The first question involves the kinds of information a decision maker uses and involves much of the same considerations we raised earlier when discussing the phenomenon of bounded rationality. Behavioral scientists have answered this question empirically by trying to predict the decisions people would make from the several pieces of information available. If the information empirically does not predict the decision, the researcher concludes that it was not important in forming the decision maker's judgments. If, on the other hand, the information does predict the decision, there is strong evidence that it was important to the decision maker. One study, for example, studied the graduate-admissions decisions of a formal committee of faculty members over a five-year period.[13] Information available to the committee included applicant's sex, age, citizenship, undergraduate grade point average (GPA), verbal scores on the Graduate Record Examination (VGRE), quantitative scores on the Graduate Record Examination (GRE), the quality of the candidate's undergraduate institution (rated in a study carried out by the American Council on Higher Education), a written statement of the candidate's career interests and objectives, and letters of recommendation. Of all this information, only three pieces of information consistently predicted the committee's acceptance decisions: undergraduate grade point average and the two Graduate Record Examination scores. In several other cases, quality of the candidate's undergraduate institution and letters of recommendation also influenced decisions.

The second question outlined above concerns the relative importance the decision maker places on different pieces of information. It is possible that a person will treat all pieces of information as equally important in making a judgment. For example, in making a merit evaluation judgment, a supervisor might consider an employee's rate of absenteeism, quality of performance, and quantity produced as equally important. Another supervisor might not be worried at all about absenteeism and focus almost solely on quality of performance. Researchers can make an empirical determination of the relative importance placed on various kinds of information in making decisions by comparing the strength or importance of each in predicting the actual decision. In the study cited above, for example, it was found that undergraduate grade point average explained more than twice the variation in committee decisions than undergraduate school quality, indicating that the former was treated as far more important than the latter in admitting students to the graduate program.

A final issue in the study of information processing and decisions concerns the way in which people combine information in making a decision. Several alternative models have been proposed as representative of human decision processes and are summarized in exhibit 12–5. The case of a supervisor making a promotion decision from among five candidates is a good illustration of each model. Suppose that the supervisor has four pieces of information at his or her disposal: tenure in the firm, supervisory evaluation of performance during the past two years, previous supervisory experience, and test scores measuring supervisory capability.

First, the supervisor could treat the information in a *compensatory* fashion in arriving at an overall judgment about each candidate, whereby a low score on one decision criterion can be offset or compensated for by a high score on another criterion. One employee, for example, may have almost no previous supervisory experience but scores high on the supervisory capability test. Because the high test

Exhibit 12–5   Alternative Decision Processes

Decision Rule	Basis	Example
Compensatory	High value on one criterion can offset low value on another criterion	Test score offsets experience
Conjunctive	Minimally acceptable levels must be achieved on all criteria	Must meet experience, performance, and test-score requirements
Disjunctive	High value on any one of the criteria is acceptable	High test score alone sufficient for promotion

score can offset the lack of experience, this candidate will be evaluated at the same level as a candidate who has an average amount of supervisory experience and who achieves an average score on the supervisory capability test.

As an alternative approach, the supervisor may deal with the information in *conjunctive* or "multiple hurdles" fashion. In this case, the decision maker establishes minimally acceptable levels that must be attained on *each* criterion independently. If a candidate falls below the cutoff or minimally acceptable level on any one criterion, he or she will no longer be considered for the promotion. The supervisor in this case, for example, might establish minimal cutoffs as follows: (1) a minimum of five-years experience with the company; (2) a minimum of three years of previous experience; (3) supervisory performance evaluations that are high enough to place the candidate in the upper 25 percent of his or her fellow employees; and (4) test scores that place the candidate in the top 25 percent of those who take the test. Note that in contrast to the compensatory model, under a conjunctive model high scores on one variable cannot offset a score below the minimum cutoff on some other variables.

Finally, the supervisor might adopt a strategy that is *disjunctive* in nature. Under this strategy, the supervisor merely scans the information about a candidate looking only for some outstanding characteristic. If it is found, the candidate is promoted on the basis of this characteristic alone, ignoring other pieces of information. The supervisor in this case, for example, might determine that one of the candidates has scored extremely high on the supervisory capacity test and that the high score alone warrants promoting the individual.

It is important to note that these strategies are fundamentally different from each other, and often lead to completely different decisions. A great deal of controversy exists today among behavioral scientists about which of these models best represents actual decision making within organizations. Some argue that the compensatory model is simpler mathematically and present empirical evidence suggesting that compensatory models predict actual decisions as well as the conjunctive and disjunctive models.[14] Others argue that compensatory models presume a great capacity to balance many pieces of information simultaneously and weigh them in arriving at a decision. They counter that conjunctive and disjunctive models are far simpler psychologically and better represent actual human decision-making processes. They present evidence in support of their position.[15]

With few exceptions in the empirical research on this question, simple linear and other mathematically unsophisticated models have been at least as effective as more mathematically sophisticated models in predicting decisions. The criterion of parsimony in science (keeping models as simple as possible) would argue for accepting the simpler models as the best representation of a decision maker's policy for the present.

So far, relatively simple decision situations have been studied by those examining information processing in decision making. Some limited evidence suggests that individuals may treat information in a noncompensatory (that is, nonlinear) fashion when the decision task becomes more complex. Decision tasks become more complex, for example, when the decision maker must deal with greater amounts of information, or with objectives that compete with each other, or several constraints regarding possible actions. In addition, the conditions surrounding the decision (whether the decision maker is acting as an individual or as a member of a group) influences the person's use of information. In these cases, it may well be that a more complex, nonlinear model will be a more accurate representation of the decision maker's use of information.[16]

Policy Capturing

Suppose that an organizational analyst examines the decisions of an organization the way we have just described, focusing on (1) the information actually used; (2) the relative importance placed on each piece of information; and (3) the fashion in which the information is combined. What use is such an analysis to the decision maker? To the analyst? An important area is developing in the fields of organizational behavior and management science that engages in *policy capturing;* that is, determining the strategy a decision maker has followed with respect to the three issues just mentioned.

The purpose of policy capturing is to diagnose the strategy implicit in one's decisions and improve the quality of such decisions by making the strategy explicit and uniformly following it. Very often, people go about making decisions in a haphazard fashion, with no conscious policy. Analysis of a series of their decisions will shed light on the way they are using information. Any one of several improvements might result from a policy-capturing analysis. First, the decision maker might find that he or she has not been using the correct information or has not been weighting such information correctly. Thus, he or she adopts a more accurate strategy for using information in future decisions. Second, the analysis might indicate that although the proper information is being used, it is being combined in an erroneous fashion. Thus, the decision maker learns more powerful ways for combining information.

A third possibility is even more intriguing, a phenomenon that decision theorists have labeled "bootstrapping."[17] In a classic study, Dawes captured the policy of a decision maker and found that the information was appropriate, weighted correctly, and combined in a most effective manner. Yet, he was *still* able to improve the accuracy and effectiveness of the decisions by making what had been an implicit policy explicit. If the information is already being used optimally, how could the policy-capturing analysis improve the decision? Dawes explains that simply making the policy explicit forced the decision maker to follow his own policy more strictly in each decision. When the policy was implicit, the decision maker varied slightly from one decision to the next, following the policy closely in some decisions and ignoring it in others. The very act of discovering one's decision policy, making it explicit, and following it (bootstrapping) improves decision making.[18]

The research we have reviewed so far deals with individuals making decisions. Frequently, however, decisions in organizations are made by groups. Chapters 7 and 8 should make clear that when groups make decisions, intra- and intergroup processes add complexity to decision making. Although systematic research on group decision making is very sketchy at this time, several researchers are now beginning to turn their attention to this phenomenon. The next section of this chapter turns to this research and its implications for managers.

Groups and Decisions

Our discussion of decision making so far has presumed that a decision is being made by an individual. Most of the research on information processing and policy capturing, for example, has treated the individual as the unit of analysis and has not explicitly considered the nature of decision making when a group of decision makers are involved. In this section, we will consider three questions related to group decision making:

1. How does group decision making differ from individual decisions?

2. What are the relative advantages and disadvantages of the two kinds of decision processes?

3. What techniques exist for an organization to improve the decisions of group?

Many of the intragroup processes presented in chapter 7 apply in this discussion. Specifically, we are concerned with the impact of group processes on decision making within organizations.

Individual versus Group Decisions

What are the major differences between an individual employee making a decision and a group of employees making a decision? One authority correctly points out that the distinction is not a simple either/or dichotomy between the two conditions.[19] Consider a simple work group consisting of six subordinates and a leader. Suppose a decision has to be made regarding what production objectives the group will take on and what each of the members will do.

Two factors or variables will determine how complex the decision process will be: (1) the level of group involvement in the decision; and (2) degree of conflict over objectives to be achieved in the decision. These factors are illustrated in exhibit 12–6. Consider first the level of group involvement.

At one extreme, the supervisor makes all decisions influencing the group unilaterally, simply setting group objectives and assigning tasks. Less extreme, and involving the group more, would be a process in which the supervisor consults group members concerning alternatives and objectives, yet still makes the final decision. At a higher level of group involvement, the group may consider alternatives and objectives and make a recommendation for action to the supervisor. Finally, at the highest level of group involvement, the group makes the decision and implements the chosen alternative. With each level of group involvement, the decision process becomes more complex.

Conflict over objectives is a second factor influencing the complexity of group

Exhibit 12–6 Complexity of Group Decisions

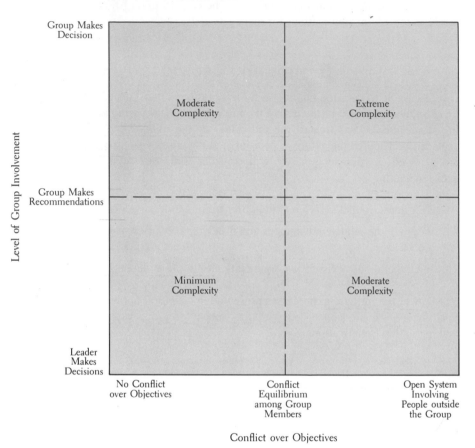

decision making. Two recent reviews of the decision-making literature note that at least three kinds or types of goal conflict can arise in a group decision.[20] At a low level of complexity is a group decision for which no conflict exists concerning the goals group members seek to accomplish. It is a situation very similar to the March and Simon model of bounded rationality. In this case, however, a group of people satisfice on objectives they have established as a group. Thus, for example, three partners in a business enterprise seek to achieve satisfactory levels of profit, not seeking any changes in their operation until they become sufficiently dissatisfied with their current performance.

At a higher level of complexity is a decision situation in which one or more objectives or alternatives is unacceptable to one or more members or subgroup of members within the overall group. According to this model, called *conflict equilibrium,* individuals and subgroups come into conflict over several alternatives, so the decision making requires a resolution of such conflicts. Depending upon the level of group involvement in the decision, a number of processes may be used to resolve the conflicts, ranging from the supervisor making such choices, to persuasion, coalition formation among members, politicking, or other consensus-seeking tactics.

At an extreme level of conflict over objectives is a situation called the *open-system* model. In this case, people outside the immediate group and the organization are involved in the decision (for example, clients of a hospital, the constituency of an elected official, or the students of a university). In this situation, many of the goals or objectives are not even known, and it is therefore impossible to predict or plan for the possible conflicts of interest among group members and people outside the group. Decision making in such situations may well require step or incremental responses to problems as they arise. It is further characterized by bargaining and politicking, which are used to resolve differences between group members and third parties to the decision. The major distinction between this decision situation and the two discussed above is the degree of environmental uncertainty surrounding the decision. The decision makers must not only resolve their own conflicts but must react to resolve ill-defined pressures from people outside the group. An illustration of the open-system decision model would be the deliberations of the power structure in a political party deciding on a slate of candidates for public office that would satisfy the demands of a widely varied political constituency.

Examination of exhibit 12–6 should indicate that levels of group involvement and conflict over objectives jointly contribute to the complexity of a group decision. At an extreme level of complexity would be the political party just described. A group of people rather than a single leader is making the decision, and the party is an open system, influenced by people and constituencies outside the immediate group.

Exhibit 12–6 also illustrates the fact that, as a decision situation moves towards the upper right quadrant, differences between an individual decision and a group decision become more extreme, characterized by:

Less certain information about objectives to be satisfied.

A greater potential variance or conflict among objectives to be satisfied.

A need to engage in conflict-resolution activities in addition to the normal decision-making steps.

Group Decision Strategies

The strengths and weaknesses of group versus individual decision making have been well documented. A number of theorists have assumed that an interacting group would make more effective decisions than an individual for the following reasons:

Several people can gather more information than a single person can.

Several people will be more likely to represent the complete range of values at stake in the decision than would a single person.

Several people can provide a variety of perspectives on the problem and provide a more creative approach to finding solutions.

People are more likely to be committed to the decision if each has participated in making the choice.

These reasons can be more explicitly shown as follows:

| Group Decision-Making Effectiveness | = | Sum of Independent Individual Effort | + | Assembly Effect | − | Process Losses |

Where:

Sum of independent individual effort is a positive feature, reflecting that the more individuals involved, the better the information. In other words, two heads are better than one.

Assembly effect is a sound, positive feature, representative of what has been termed a "synergy" effect. In essence, the interaction of individuals, with views being stated and refined, results in a group decision that is better than the single best individual decision.

Process losses is a negative factor consisting of two components. First, groups take more *time* to make a decision than does a single individual. If time is an important factor for an organization, groups score less effectively than do single individuals. The second component concerns *motivation efforts*. In essence, certain individuals can choose to be "hidden" in the group and not be fully committed to the decision—a "let George do it" philosophy.[21]

Despite these potential advantages of group over individual decision making, a number of people have pointed out some clear disadvantages to group decision processes. Perhaps the most dangerous of these is the phenomenon of "groupthink" discussed by Janis.[22] In studying several major fiascos involving high-level decisions (the Bay of Pigs incident of the Kennedy Administration, the Johnson administration decision to escalate the Vietnam War, the failure to be prepared for the Japanese attack on Pearl Harbor, and the stalemate of the Korean War), Janis concluded that group processes involving advisors to the presidents actually prevented an effective decision.

His analysis contends that a pressure for consensus among group members led to eight major symptoms of a problem he labels "groupthink":

1. *Invulnerability*—Most or all the group members develop an *illusion* of invulnerability that leads them to ignore obvious dangers or important constituencies. This leads them to become overly optimistic and to take enormous risks.

2. *Rationale*—Just as group members believe themselves to be invulnerable, they collectively construct rationalizations to discount warnings or any other sources of information that run contrary to their thinking. Thus, sources of any negative information are discredited in group deliberation.

3. *Morality*—Members of the group begin to believe unquestioningly in the inherent morality of the group's position. This belief inclines the group to cast their position in absolute moralistic language. Opposing views simultaneously are

thought of as inherently evil. In addition, Janis points out, such thinking leads group members to ignore the ethical or moral consequences of their actions.

4. *Stereotypes*—groupthink leads group members to engage in stereotyped perceptions of other people and groups (a perceptual error explained in chapter 4). Opposing leaders, for example, are cast as evil, satanic types, or dunces who could not possibly understand reasonable positions. Such stereotyping effectively blocks any reasonable negotiations between differing groups.

5. *Pressure*—Members suffering from groupthink apply pressure to any members who express opinions that threaten group concensus. They are branded as obstructionist. If any member doubts the group's illusion of invulnerability, rationale, morality, or stereotypes, he or she will be branded as subverting the welfare of the group and may even be banished from the group. Thus, there is great pressure to conform and avoid rocking the boat.

6. *Self-censorship*—Janis cites several examples of parties to high-level deliberations ruefully regretting, after a debacle, not having spoken up and expressed doubts or positions. His observation is that most group members suffering from groupthink err on the side of keeping quiet in group deliberations and avoiding issues that are likely to upset the group. This is seen as a response to the perceived pressure to conform.

7. *Unanimity*—Self-censorship leads to the illusion of unanimity of opinion within the group. The false assumption is that anyone who remains silent in the discussion is in full agreement with the group's decision. The illusion of unanimity leads members to be complacent in the group's decision and to fail to properly consider all alternatives.

8. *Mindguards*—Finally, members affected by groupthink appoint themselves as what Janis calls 'mindguards'—people who have the self-appointed duty to protect the leader and other key group members from adverse information that might shake the complacency of the group. As an example, Janis cites the instance of Attorney General Robert Kennedy warning Arthur Schlesinger not to share his doubts about the Bay of Pigs invasion with the president, because the president's mind was already made up.

Thus, a simple interacting group can be very ineffective in decision making because of the nature of group processes. Three approaches to group decision making have recently been introduced that attempt to avoid these problems: (1) the Nominal Group Technique;[23] (2) the Delphi Technique;[24] and (3) the Vroom-Yetten-Jago model.[25] The Nominal Group and Delphi techniques are specifically designed to overcome the groupthink problems inherent in group decisions. The Nominal Group is a formal meeting of individual members that proceeds as follows:

1. Each member silently expresses his or her ideas about the problem and alternative solutions in writing without any consultation with other members.

2. At the end of the time period (about ten to fifteen minutes), each member shares his or her views with the other members in a highly structured round-

robin fashion. When a member's turn comes up, he or she may share only one idea per round.

3. As each member expresses an idea, a recorder writes down the idea on a flip chart or board. This process continues until all ideas are listed, with no reference to which idea is whose.

4. All ideas on the board are then discussed with respect to their merits, feasibility, and all other qualities.

5. The group then votes silently on the ideas (usually rank ordering the ideas in terms of their preference). The pooled outcome of the individual ranking or rating determines the group's choice.

The Delphi technique is very similar to the Nominal Group technique, except that members in the Delphi technique are physically dispersed and do not meet face to face for group decisions. Instead, a carefully structured sequence of questionnaires is followed. With each subsequent round of questionnaires, feedback of opinion from previous questionnaires is provided to each member. Finally, in a last round of questionnaires, each member is asked to vote on the issues, and the aggregation of individual votes determines the group's choice. A comparison of interacting groups, the Nominal Group, and the Delphi group is presented in exhibit 12–7.

The Nominal and Delphi techniques both presume that the nature of the decision facing a group is truly a group rather than an individual problem. The techniques do not explicitly provide a decision maker(s) with a method for making such a determination. Recently, Vroom and his associates have presented a model that deals directly with this issue. Specifically, their model focuses on the social interaction between the leader and subordinates in a group faced with a decision.[26] Their model has both descriptive and normative properties.

The model begins by making a distinction between two major types of decision problems: individual and group. *Individual problems* are those whose solutions affect only one of the leader's subordinates. Problems that affect several of the subordinates are defined as *group problems*. Research on the model has led to the identification of a number of different decision processes that can be followed to reach a solution. A model of these is presented in exhibit 12–8.

The letters A, C, G, and D represent decision processes that increasingly involve subordinate participation in the decision. A processes are very autocratic, not involving the subordinate at all. The Roman numerals denote variants of the same process. C processes are consultative; they involve the group in the actual decision process. G processes are group processes involving members as actual participants in the decision to be made. D processes constitute delegation of the entire decision to individual subordinates or groups of subordinates. Thus, exhibit 12–8 contains five decision strategies each for individual and group problems that are commonly used by managers in actual situations. In this sense, the model is descriptive of actual decision making.

The investigators have also asked, in a normative fashion, under what conditions will each of these alternative decision processes result in an optimal solution? They

Exhibit 12-7 Comparison of Qualitative Differences Between Three Decision Processes Based upon Evaluations of Leaders and Group Participants

Dimension	Interacting Groups	Nominal Groups	Delphi Technique
Overall Methodology	Unstructured face-to-face group meeting High flexibility High variability in behavior of groups	Structured face-to-face group meeting Low flexibility Low variability in behavior of groups	Structured series of questionnaires and feedback reports Low variability in respondent behavior
Role Orientation of Groups	Socio-emotional Group maintenance focus	Balanced focus on social maintenance and task role	Task-instrumental focus
Relative Quantity of Ideas	Low; focused "rut" effect	Higher; independent writing and hitch-hiking round robin	High; isolated writing of ideas
Search Behavior	Reactive search Short problem focus Task-avoidance tendency New social knowledge	Proactive search Extended problem focus High task centeredness New social and task knowledge	Proactive search Controlled problem focus High task centeredness New task knowledge
Normative Behavior	Conformity pressures inherent in face-to-face discussions	Tolerance for nonconformity through independent search and choice activity	Freedom not to conform through isolated anonymity
Equality of Participation	Member dominance in search, evaluation, and choice phases	Member equality in search and choice phases	Respondent equality in pooling of independent judgments
Method of Problem Solving	Person-centered Smoothing over and withdrawal	Problem centered Confrontation and problem solving	Problem-centered Majority rule of pooled independent judgments
Closure Decision Process	High lack of closure Low-felt accomplishment	Lower lack of closure High-felt accomplishment	Low lack of closure Medium-felt accomplishment
Resources Utilized	Low administrative time and cost High participant time and cost	Medium administrative time, cost, preparation High participant time and cost	High administrative
Time to Obtain Group Ideas	1½ hours	1½ hours	5 calendar months

Used with permission from Andrew Van de Ven and Andre Delbecq, "The Effectiveness of Nominal, Delphi, and Interacting Group Decision-Making Processes," *Academy of Management Journal*, 1974, pp. 605–21.

Exhibit 12–8 Decision-Making Processes

For Individual Problems	For Group Problems
AI. You solve the problem or make the decision yourself, using information available to you at that time.	AI. You solve the problem or make the decision yourself, using information available to you at that time.
AII. You obtain any necessary information from the subordinate, then decide on the solution to the problem yourself. You may or may not tell the subordinate what the problem is in getting the information from him. The role played by your subordinate in making the decision is clearly one of providing specific information that you request, rather than generating or evaluating alternative solutions.	AII. You obtain any necessary information from subordinates, then decide on the solution to the problem yourself. You may or may not tell subordinates what the problem is in getting the information from them. The role played by your subordinates in making the decision is clearly one of providing specific information that you request, rather than generating or evaluating solutions.
CI. You share the problem with the relevant subordinate, getting ideas and suggestions. Then *you* make the decision. This decision may or may not reflect your subordinate's influence.	CI. You share the problem with the relevant subordinates individually, getting their ideas and suggestions without bringing them together as a group. Then *you* make the decision. This decision may or may not reflect your subordinates' influence.
GI. You share the problem with one of your subordinates, and together you analyze the problem and arrive at a mutually satisfactory solution in an atmosphere of free and open exchange of information and ideas. You both contribute to the resolution of the problem with the relative contribution of each being dependent on knowledge rather than formal authority.	CII. You share the problem with your subordinates in a group meeting. In this meeting, you obtain their ideas and suggestions. Then, *you* make the decision, which may or may not reflect your subordinates' influence.
DI. You delegate the problem to one of your subordinates, providing him or her with any relevant information that you possess, but giving him or her responsibility for solving the problem alone. Any solution that the person reaches will receive your support.	GII. You share the problem with your subordinates as a group. Together, you generate and evaluate alternatives and attempt to reach agreement (consensus) on a solution. Your role is much like that of chairman, coordinating the discussion, keeping it focused on the problem, and making sure that the critical issues are discussed. You do not try to influence the group to adopt "your" solution and are willing to accept and implement any solution that has the support of the entire group.

have identified three basic criteria for evaluating the success of a social decision: (1) the quality or rationality of the decision; (2) the acceptance or commitment on the part of the subordinates to execute decisions effectively; and (3) the amount of time required to make the decision.   *see p. 423*

These three criteria have been combined into a series of questions to be asked about the decision situation confronting the leader. Once these questions are answered, the model indicates the optimal decision process to use under the given circumstances. Vroom and his associates arranged these questions in sequential fashion and designed a decision tree, reproduced in exhibit 12–9, for managers to use in selecting an appropriate decision process.

The first step in using the model is to state the problem and examine it. Questions *A* through *H*, arrayed in sequential fashion across the top of the decision tree, are a series of questions representing the criteria for effective decisions. They can be answered with a yes or no answer. The decision maker should work through the tree

Exhibit 12–9 Decision-Process Flow Chart for Both Individual and Group Problems

A. Is there a quality requirement such that one solution is likely to be more rational than another?
B. Do I have sufficient information to make a high quality decision?
C. Is the problem structured?
D. Is acceptance of decision by subordinates critical to effective implementation?
E. If I were to make the decision by myself, is it reasonably certain that it would be accepted by my subordinates?
F. Do subordinates share the organizational goals to be attained in solving this problem?
G. Is conflict among subordinates likely in preferred solutions? (This question is irrelevant to individual problems.)
H. Do subordinates have sufficient information to make a high quality decision?

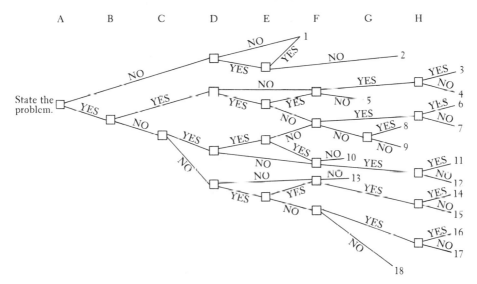

The recommended strategy for each problem type (1–18) for group (G) and individual (I) are as follows:

	Group	Individual		Group	Individual		Group	Individual
1	AI	AI	7	GII	GI	13	CII	CI
2	GII	DI	8	CII	CI	14	CII	DI
3	AI	AI	9	CI	CI	15	CII	CI
4	AI	AI	10	AII	AII	16	GII	DI
5	AI	AI	11	AII	DI	17	GII	GI
6	GII	DI	12	AII	AII	18	CII	CI

Source: Victor H. Vroom and Arthur Jago, "Decision Making As A Social Process: Normative and Descriptive Models of Leader Behavior," *Decision Sciences,* 1974, p. 748.

423

in sequential fashion until an optimal decision process is indicated. For example, according to the tree, if decision process 1 is reached after analysis, AI is the best decision strategy for both group and individual problems. If the result is 2, GII is the best for group problems, and DI is the best for individual problems. The reader is urged to examine the decision tree and work through several hypothetical problems using it. An experiential exercise employing the decision model is presented at the end of this chapter.

Exhibit 12–10 summarizes the normative decision rules underlying the Vroom-Yetton-Jago model. This exhibit indicates the best choice for the leader, given decision quality, subordinate acceptance, and amount of time.

Exhibit 12–10   Vroom-Yetton-Jago Rules Underlying the Normative Model

1. *The Leader Information Rule:*
   If the quality of the decision is important and the leader does not possess enough information or expertise to solve the problem by himself, then AI is eliminated from the feasible set.

2. *The Subordinate Information Rule:*
   (applicable to individual problems only) If the quality of the decision is important and the subordinate does not possess enough information or expertise to solve the problem himself, then DI is eliminated from the feasible set.

3a. *The Goal Congruence Rule:*
   If the quality of the decision is important and the subordinates are not likely to pursue organization goals in their efforts to solve this problem, then GII and DI are eliminated from the feasible set.

3b. *The Augmented Goal Congruence Rule:*
   (applicable to individual problems only) Under the conditions specified in the previous rule (i.e., quality of decision is important, and the subordinate does not share the organizational goals to be attained in solving the problem), GI may also constitute a risk to the quality of the decision taken in response to an individual problem. Such a risk is a reasonable one to take only if the nature of the problem is such that the acceptance of the subordinate is critical to the

effective implementation and prior probability of acceptance of an autocratic solution is low.

4a. *The Unstructured Problem Rule (Group):*
   In decisions in which the quality of the decision is important, if the leader lacks the necessary information or expertise to solve the problem by himself and if the problem is unstructured, the method of solving the problem should provide for interaction among subordinates. Accordingly, AI, AII, and CI are eliminated from the feasible set.

4b. *The Unstructured Problem Rule (Individual):*
   In decisions in which the quality of the decision is important, if the leader lacks the necessary information to solve the problem by himself and if the problem is unstructured, the method of solving the problem should permit the subordinate to generate solutions to the problem. Accordingly, AI and AII are eliminated from the feasible set.

5. *The Acceptance Rule:*
   If the acceptance of the decision by subordinates is critical to effective implementation and if it is not certain that an autocratic decision will be accepted, AI and AII are eliminated from the feasible set.

Source: Vroom and Jago, "Decision Making as a Social Process," p. 748.

The Vroom-Yetton-Jago model represents an important improvement over classical decision theory with rather immediate implications for decision making as a social process. They have identified major decision strategies that are commonly used socially in making decisions, and they have established criteria for evaluating the success of the various strategies under a variety of conditions. In addition, they have developed an applied model for leaders to use in selecting social decision strategies, which improve the quality of decisions, acceptance of the decisions by subordinates, and minimize the time consumed in decision making.

Finally, work has begun on empirically validating the model in actual settings. One test of the Vroom-Yetton-Jago model among managers, for example, demon-

---

Exhibit 12–10 (continued)

6. *The Conflict Rule:*
   (applicable to group problems only)
   If the acceptance of the decision is critical, an autocratic decision is not certain to be accepted and disagreement among subordinates in methods of attaining the organizational goal is likely, the methods used in solving the problem should enable those in disagreement to resolve their differences with full knowledge of the problem. Accordingly, AI, AII, and CI, which permit no interaction among subordinates, are eliminated from the feasible set.

7. *The Fairness Rule:*
   If the quality of the decision is unimportant, but acceptance of the decision is critical and not certain to result from an autocratic decision, the decision process used should permit the subordinates to interact with one another and negotiate over the fair method of resolving any differences with full responsibility on them for determining what is equitable. Accordingly, AI, AII, CI, and CII are eliminated from the feasible set.

8. *The Acceptance Priority Rule:*
   If acceptance is critical, not certain to result from an autocratic decision and if (the) subordinate(s) is (are) motivated to pursue the organizational goals represented in the problem, then

methods which provide equal partnership in the decision-making process can provide greater acceptance without risking decision quality. Accordingly, AI, AII, CI, and CII are eliminated from the feasible set.

9. *The Group Problem Rule:*
   If a problem has approximately equal effects on each of a number of subordinates (i.e., is a group problem) the decision process used should provide them with equal opportunities to influence that decision. Use of a decision process such as GI or DI which provides opportunities for only one of the affected subordinates to influence that decision may in the short run produce feelings of inequity reflected in lessened commitment to the decision on the part of those "left out" of the decision process and, in the long run, be a source of conflict and divisiveness.

10. *The Individual Problem Rule:*
    If a problem affects only one subordinate, decision processes which *unilaterally* introduce other (unaffected) subordinate, decision processes which constitute an unnecessary use of time of the unaffected subordinates and can reduce the amount of commitment of the affected subordinate to the decision by reducing the amount of his opportunity to influence the decision. Thus, CII and GII are eliminated from the feasible set.

strated that it predicted the technical quality, subordinate acceptance, and overall effectiveness of final solutions chosen better than did alternative decision models.[27]

In each of the decision models we have examined, from classical decision theory to group decision making, an underlying assumption is that information has been sought relevant to all aspects of the decision. Further, we should note that as the nature of the decision becomes more complex (i.e., as the level of group involvement increases or conflict over objectives increases—see exhibit 12–6) information needs become increasingly critical. The success of a decision, then, rests squarely upon the accuracy and quality of information generated. It is important, therefore, to turn our attention to the process by which information is generated and exchanged among parties to a decision—communication.

Communication

We have already said that communication is necessary for effective decision making. First, communication is the vehicle by which information relevant to decisions is transferred. Second, communication is fundamental to the implementation of decisions. Communication, whether written, oral, formal, or informal, is goal directed in organizations. It is broadly intended to secure performance at all levels that results in the implementation of decisions and the achievement of organizational goals. *furchetal to*

Probably more has been written about communication over the past fifty years than about any other topic in organizational behavior. Our purpose here is to summarize some of the most important conclusions about communication that have resulted from research in the field of organizational behavior. We will first examine the major purposes served by communication. Second, we will present and examine a model of communication that treats the process as a social interaction among individual organizational members. Finally, we will examine some of the common problems associated with communication; problems that interfere with the achievement of objectives and efficiency of organizations.

Functions of Communication

Scott and Mitchell have identified and described the major functions communications processes serve within organizations.[28] They identify four major purposes served by communication and classify the process further by identifying: (1) the orientation of the communication; (2) the objectives served by the communication; and (3) theoretical and research issues emphasized by those who study that particular aspect of communication. A basic communications model is shown in exhibit 12–11.

Emotive.   Communication networks are made up of people, and much of what people communicate to each other has emotional content. Our discussion of employee motivation in chapters 3 and 5 identifies the need to interact with others socially as a major motive of employees. Communication, formal and informal, is a major means for satisfying these needs. Through communication, employees can
social

Exhibit 12–11 Purposes of Communication

Function	Orientation	Objectives	Theoretical and Research Focus
1. Emotive	Feeling	Increasing acceptance of organizational roles	Satisfaction; resolution of conflict; tension reduction, role definition
2. Motivation	Influence	Commitment to organizational objectives	Power, authority, compliance; reinforcement and expectancy theory; behavior modification; learning
3. Information	Technological	Providing data necessary for decisions	Decision making; information processing; decision theory
4. Control	Structure	Clarifying duties, authority, accountability	Organizational design

Reproduced with permission from *Organization Theory: A Structural and Behavioral Analysis* by William G. Scott and Terence R. Mitchell (Homewood, Ill.: Irwin, 1976ⓒ), p. 193.

express their frustrations and satisfactions to each other and to management. In addition, communication provides a mechanism by which individuals can compare attitudes and resolve ambiguities about their jobs, their roles, and areas of conflict between groups and individuals. If an employee, for example, is dissatisfied with his or her pay, he or she will often communicate with others informally, to determine whether the feelings are justified or not.

Motivation.   A second major function of communication is to motivate, direct, control, and evaluate the performance of organizational members. Our treatment of leadership in chapter 9, for example, stresses the fact that leadership is an influence process by which supervisors attempt to control the behavior and performance of subordinates. Communication is the major vehicle of such control available to leaders. Hence, leadership activities, such as issuing orders, rewarding behavior and performance, reviewing and evaluating performance, making job and task assignments, and training and developing subordinates, all involve communication. Indeed, the principles of reinforcement theory, presented in chapter 5, are enhanced by the fact that humans are capable of receiving and incorporating information relevant to desired behaviors and reward contingencies that makes behavior and the change in behavior more efficient.

3\ *Information.*   In addition to emotive and motivational functions, we have already seen in this chapter that communication serves a vital information function for decision making. Unlike feelings and influence, communication in this case has primarily a technological orientation. Empirical research in this area of communication has focused on information-processing activities and ways to improve the accuracy with which communication channels carry information going into individual, group, and organizational decisions.

4\ *Control.*   Finally, communication and organizational design are closely linked. Indeed, organizations attempt to control the activities of individuals through the design and use of formal communication channels. Organization charts, for example, represent formal channels of communication in an organization. We mentioned earlier in the chapter that March and Simon proposed that organizations tend to routinize decision making through the use of *programs*. Most types of programs or standard operating procedures have a large communication component to them. That is, they demand that routine decisions and activities be initiated through formal communication and that results and performance be reported back through formal channels. Hence, formal communication channels represent a major structural means of control within organizations.

A Communication Model

Of the many models of communication that have been proposed, one of the more useful for understanding communication as a process is one derived from the field of social psychology. The model is called *symbolic interaction* and is illustrated in exhibit 12–12.

Symbolic interaction defines *communication* as the process by which one individual or group transmits meaning to others. Another way of defining *communication* is to view it as the process by which understanding is transmitted. As indicated in exhibit 12–12, when one person (the transmitter) wishes to communicate with another person(s) (the receiver), that individual has some *intended meaning* in mind. Short of telepathic communication, however, he or she cannot place the message directly in the mind of the receiver. Instead, the transmitter must rely on the manipulation of something that exists outside of himself or herself, namely a sym-

Exhibit 12–12 Symbolic Interaction

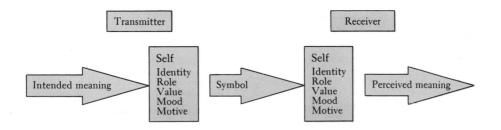

bol, to transmit meaning. A *symbol* is something that exists between people and can be manipulated to exchange messages. Symbols have been called the objective or tangible side of subjective (or internal) ideas and meaning. Symbols take a wide variety of forms:

Language—Written and oral, constitutes a major vehicle for transmitting ideas.

Facial and body expression—Can be symbolic of messages a person is trying to convey.

Clothing—For example, a police officer's uniform that is used as a symbol of authority.

Voice modulation—Can be used to express surprise, anger, frustration, or fear, quite apart from what is actually being said.

Religious signs—Such as a cross, carry messages regarding one's religious faith.

Virtually any object or action can be used as a symbol in an attempt to communicate among people, groups, and organizations.

If communication were completely successful, there would be a total overlap between the intended meaning and the perceived meaning; that is, the receiver would interpret the manipulation of symbols in a way identical to that intended by the transmitter. In reality, we know that communication within organizations is rarely flawless. In fact, two communication processes intervene between two or more people and often result in imperfect communication: (1) symbolic manipulation (encoding) by the transmitter; and (2) symbolic interpretation (or decoding) by the receiver result in a *filtering* of the transmission and determine the *message* actually received.

Symbolic manipulation is the activity by which the transmitter translates his or her ideas into a set of symbols to be conveyed to the receiver. The activity is not simple. It involves not only the manipulation of symbols that transmit the message, but also the manipulation of symbols that establish the *context* within which the message is transmitted. Social psychologists call this context a *Self*. It represents the transmitter and establishes his or her *identity*, the *role* in which he or she is communicating, his or her *values*, the *mood* in which the message is being transmitted, and the *motive* or reason for communicating. The Self then provides the context within which communication takes place. The same symbol can be interpreted in entirely different ways depending upon the context within which it is manipulated.

Symbolic interpretation is the process by which the receiver translates the symbol into his or her own interpretation or received message. Again, not only is the symbol itself interpreted but also the context within which the symbol is transmitted. The Self of the receiver is the context within which the message is interpreted. As in the case of the transmitter, the receiver's identity, role, values, mood, and motives influence the decoding and interpretation of the transmitted symbol. Symbolic interpretation, therefore, is a second filtering of the transmitted message.

A number of important conclusions can be drawn from viewing communication as a symbolic-interaction process. First, the two-way process of filtering can lead to distortions and noise in communication. Second, the context within which communication takes place must be established and accepted by both parties before they can communicate. Before employees can respond to communication, they must evaluate the source of the communication. Prior to this, they will neither receive nor be influenced by the communication. Researchers have found, for example, that the same message will be interpreted in entirely different ways depending upon the source of the message.[29] Finally, symbolic-interaction theory suggests that to maximize effectiveness in communication, the transmitter must take the receiver into account very carefully. The transmitter should become as familiar as possible with the identity, values, mood, role, and motives of the receiver and should establish a Self or context that is compatible with that of the receiver.

Barriers to Effective Communication

A supervisor sent a memo to a subordinate congratulating him on the timely completion of a task and expressing the hope that such performance would be typical in the future. The supervisor *intended* the message to be purely congratulatory. The employee received the memo and complained, "Isn't that just like the supervisor! You work hard to get one thing done on time in this place, and they turn around and tell you that they expect that kind of action all the time!"

Conventional wisdom would say in reaction to this example, that "What we have here is a failure to communicate." Although communication breakdowns might appear to have simple causes, they actually stem from a multitude of rather complex causes. Examination of the symbolic-interaction model in exhibit 12–12 suggests a number of factors leading to communication breakdowns. These problems fall into two major categories: (1) distortion in communication; and (2) information overload. We will examine each of these problems in turn.

Distortion in communication

The symbolic-interaction model suggests that communication is a complex manipulation of symbols involving, on one hand, the manipulation or encoding of symbols to carry a message as well as to establish the context of the message and, on the other, the interpretation or decoding of symbols to form a received message. At each stage of this interaction, slippage or noise is possible, creating unintended and misinterpreted meanings. Such barriers include at least the following:

1. *Attributes of the receiver.* Different people may react in radically different ways to the same message for a variety of personal reasons. As we pointed out in chapter 4, previous learning or experiences in the same situation may lead to habits of interpretation. Thus, for example, two people raised in different cultures may react quite differently to the same political message. An individual raised in an environment that places a great value on the pronouncement of respected political figures may take an elected official's pronouncement very seriously. However, a person encouraged to be critical of politicians and to have little faith in their word may cynically discount the same pronouncement.

In addition to previous learning, the material in chapter 3 indicates that motives and personality can also influence the decoding or symbolic-interpretation process (which is a form of perception as described in chapter 4). An employee who has a highly felt need for advancement in an organization and whose personality tends to be quite optimistic might read a smile and casual comment from a supervisor as an indication that he or she is a "favorite child" being groomed for a promotion. A person with a low need for advancement and a pessimistic disposition may read nothing more than a casual comment unrelated to anything else into the supervisor's comment.

2. *Selective perception*. Receiving a message is a form of perceptual behavior discussed in chapter 4. People have a tendency to listen to only part of a message and "block out" other information for a variety of reasons. One of the most important of these is a need to avoid or reduce cognitive dissonance. Thus, people have a tendency to ignore new information that conflicts with or denies already established beliefs, values, and expectations. Selective perception occurs when the receiver evaluates the context of the communication including the role, identity, values, mood, and motives of the sender.

   Indeed, a strict interpretation of symbolic-interaction theory would suggest that a message cannot be decoded until these contextual factors are interpreted by the receiver. One aspect of the sender's identity and role would be his or her formal position in the formal organization. Status symbols used by the organization to enhance a formal position may include the size and appointments of an office, titles, special equipment, and secretaries. Such symbols can often distort the intended meaning of a communication from a person in that position. A routine request for information coming from a dean's office, for example, may be met with apprehension on the part of a faculty member simply because the dean and not somebody lower in the administrative hierarchy is requesting the information.

3. *Semantic problems*. We have already said that communication consists of the manipulation and interpretation of symbols. A major set of symbols so employed is language. The problem is that many words commonly used in communication carry quite different meanings for different people. Two general kinds of semantic problems present barriers to communication. First, some words and phrases are so general or abstract that they invite varying interpretation. Thus, a newly appointed board chairman in addressing the management group of the firm may say very earnestly, "A major item on my agenda is to involve each of you in reorienting the firm in new directions. We need new goals and must consider our options." Three different managers may very well read three different messages into the same words. Abstract words, such as *involve, reorienting, directions, goals,* and *options,* invite varying interpretations. A suspicious manager, for example, may interpret involvement in reorienting the firm as a strategy of close supervision that may indeed limit and narrow the discretion he or she already has. An optimistic manager, in contrast, may interpret the phrase to mean an expansion of duties to include areas of discretion he or she does not presently have.

   A second semantic problem arises when different groups develop their own technical language or argot. Patients, for example, have been perplexed to see a smiling physician report back that the test results (e.g., a pap smear for detecting cancer) were "negative." In this rare case, the technical meaning of the word *negative* refers to the fact that the test showed the *absence* of cancer, not its presence (which would certainly be a negative outcome from the patient's point of view). As another illustration, the lay person may be confused by the title, "Initial instrumentation of a behaviorally specific battery for assessing risk propensities," until someone explains that it refers to designing a questionnaire intended to measure the degree to which a person takes chances.

4. *Time pressures*. Managers often reflect that their scarcest valuable commodity is time. Time is always short, and this fact often leads to distortion in communications. A major temptation when pressed for time is to short-circuit formal communication channels. A doctor treating a patient in a clinic, for example, may decide that a patient should be administered a given drug. He is running an hour late, however, and instead of writing up a formal order, he informally instructs the nurse to administer the injection. The immediate demands of the situation are met, but a number of unintended consequences may result. First, nobody but the doctor, nurse, and patient know for sure the specific drug was administered. The billing office never gets the information, and fails to bill the patient for the service (driving up the operating costs of the clinic). Of even more potential danger is the fact that the dose never appears on the patient's record and does not become a part of his medical history. To the extent that this drug in combination with others taken concurrently can be hazardous, or to the extent that it can have serious side effects, the patient's health is placed in jeopardy.

Information overload

A second major barrier to communication is information overload. A common complaint among managers within modern organizations is that they are literally drowned in communications; if all communications were attended to, the actual work of the organization would never take place. One manager of a metal-fabricating division of a larger firm reported to one of the authors that he received six hundred pages of a computer printout each day detailing the output of each production line, the location of various materials, and other indexes of the operation. He said that it would take him approximately three full days to simplify the information into usable form. Instead, he found an empty storage room, stacked the printouts there, and subcontracted with a trash removal firm to remove the printouts, untouched, once a month.

Improving Organizational Communications

The symbolic-interaction model suggests a number of ways managers can minimize a number of communication barriers. In general, communications can be improved in two ways. First, the manager must sharpen his or her skills in manipulating symbols, the process of encoding. This implies taking as much care as possible in choosing symbols and in establishing the context within which the message is transmitted. In addition, the model prescribes that the transmitter take his or her audience into account when encoding a message. A manager, therefore, should place himself or herself in the shoes of the receiver and attempt to anticipate personal and situational factors that will influence the symbolic interpretation or decoding of the message. One commentary on communication concludes, "They [managers] must strive not only to be understood but also to understand."[30] A number of techniques are commonly employed by managers to accomplish these ends.

Followup and feedback.   The principle involved in followup and feedback is to establish either an informal or formal mechanism by which the sender can check on how the message was actually interpreted. In effect, the process of feedback makes communication a two-way process. In a face-to-face situation, the sender should try to become sensitive to facial expressions and other signs that indicate how the message is being received. It is often important to solicit questions of clarification from the receiver. Where more formal, written communication is involved, the writer may specify specific forms and times for responding to insure feedback.

Parallel channels and repetition.   A major principle in communication technology is to provide parallel channels of communication that reinforce each other. Thus, a verbal request may be followed up with a memo. In this way, the sender has insured getting the attention of the receiver (through a face-to-face verbal exchange) and has also insured that the sender will have a record for reference (the memo) in case he or she forgets any details in the order.

Scientists who study language effectiveness report that redundancy is a critical element in assuring communication accuracy. In fact, the English language has been estimated to be 40 percent redundant. Redundancy (especially involving parallel forms) insures that if a part of the message is lost in one form, it will be received elsewhere. Thus, in a training course, a great deal of material in the books used will duplicate or overlap the lectures presented in class.

Timing.   We have already said that people will react and filter messages as a matter of timing. A manager may ignore a memo or request simply because other problems are pressing in at the same time. Two kinds of actions can be taken by management to insure the accurate reception of communication through timing. First, it may want to *standardize* the timing of specific messages. Thus, if the second Tuesday of the month is established as the time for distribution of a particularly important report, the attention of people is assured because they expect to receive it at that time. Second, many organizations establish "retreats" or time away from normal job pressures to transmit material, ideas, and instructions to employees. This action insures the undivided attention of the receivers.

Attention to language.   Many times, a person will not take the time to choose the appropriate style and level of language in writing to another person. Students have often wrestled through lecture note-taking trying to understand the language of the professor. Similarly, some pompous language employed by governmental officials has been met with confusion by the public. The important consideration, again, is taking one's audience into account when choosing a style of language. Effective use of language consists of tailoring one's message for the context of the receivers in order to maximize overlap between the intended and received messages.

Information communication and information centers.   Running parallel to formal communication channels in an organization are informal networks commonly called *grapevines*. They tend to be a universal fact of life in all organizations. They have been shown to serve not only informational functions but motivational functions as well. A number of employee needs are served by this powerful reinforcer.

The grapevine can be a large source of communication between management and employees in an organization. First of all, grapevines tend to be more rapid means of exchanging information than formal channels. Second, the grapevine is more flexible, reaching more people on a face-to-face basis. Thus, grapevines provide excellent sources for feedback. Effective communicators often combine formal and informal (grapevine) channels of communication. Thus, a manager may reinforce information received through formal channels with an off-the-record talk with key subordinates. In a reverse direction, he or she might reinforce and clarify a formal written order with an informal chat session among employees.

Although the grapevine can be remarkably accurate in conveying information (one source estimates as much as 75 percent of the information in a grapevine is accurate), misinformation and unfounded rumors transferred through grapevines can disrupt the effective flow of communication in organizations.[31] In order to correct such distortions, a number of organizations have instituted organizational audit groups or information centers.[32] The purpose of such groups is to provide instant and, hopefully, unbiased information about performance in critical areas of the organization's operations. To facilitate this objective, such groups can bypass formal channels of command and audit an operation directly.

Exception principle and need to know.   In order to deal effectively with the information overload problem, many organizations try to establish certain principles for actually limiting the extent of communication. Many firms, for example, implement an "exception principle" in communication channels. This principle orders that only communications regarding exceptional deviations from orders, plans, and policies be communicated upward on a routine basis. Hence, upper levels of management will receive only that information which truly demands their attention.

A closely related principle involves downward communication. Here, managers should be selective and transmit information on a "need to know" basis. In this way, lower-level personnel receive only communication that is immediately critical to carrying out their tasks. The success of these two principles depends at least in part on the type of organization within which jobs are carried out. They will be most effective in highly structured organizations where tasks are relatively simple and routine. In less formal organizations, in which the work is rather complex and not highly structured, communication needs to be as open and unrestricted as possible. The exception principle and the need-to-know principle may actually reduce the effectiveness of such organizations.

In summary, decision making and communication are central processes within organizations. Indeed, virtually all activities of managers consist very heavily of communicating and making decisions both as individuals and in groups. It follows logically that, to a great extent, managerial effectiveness can be measured by how effectively managers communicate and make decisions.

Applications and Implications for the Manager

Decision Making and Communication

1. Decision making and communication are linked processes that constitute the major activities of organizations. Most organizational activities that influence performance of individuals, groups, and units require that decisions be made and results communicated.

2. Three major perspectives on decisions are examined. The first, classical decision theory, is normative in nature and prescribes the optimal choices to be made among decision alternatives. More recent developments in the study of decision making emphasize the behavioral and social properties of decisions and tend to be more descriptive and process oriented. The March, Simon, and Cyert notion of bounded rationality is presented as a more realistic model of the decision-making processes of actual individuals. In addition, several perspectives on group decision making were examined. The Nominal Group and Delphi techniques attempt to overcome some of the problems inherent in group decisions, and the work of Vroom and his associates assists leaders and group members in deciding whether or not a decision is an individual or a group problem.

3. Communication is considered as an interpersonal process that results in the exchange of information. As such, the process serves a number of organizational functions, including: (1) the expression of emotions; (2) the motivation of behavior and performance; (3) the transmittal of technical information required for decision making; and (4) the control of the organization's activities. A symbolic-interaction model of communication emphasizes the role of symbolic manipulation and symbolic interpretation in the exchange of ideas.

4. A series of barriers commonly exists, leading to problems of distortion in communication and information overload. Attributes of the receiver, including attitudes, personality, motives, and previous learning, lead to a filtering process that can distort a message. In addition, people typically selectively perceive messages, ignoring information that runs counter to their beliefs and expectations. In other cases, semantic problems lead to communication barriers. Some words and phrases are so general, for example, that they invite varying interpretations by different individuals. In addition, technical and in-group language can lead to misunderstandings. Time pressures also play a role in preventing effective communication. Finally, too much information may overload the receiver and lead him or her to ignore critical communications.

5. A number of techniques are available for overcoming communication barriers. They include the activities of followup and feedback in communicating with others, making communication a two-way process. In addition, the use of parallel channels and redundancy will assure the correct interpretation of messages. The timing of communication is a third aid. Standardizing the time at which critical messages are transmitted can assure attention to them. In addition, setting aside "retreats" that block out distracting sources of communication assures clarity. We emphasize that a transmitter must carefully take the listener into account as an audience in choosing the level and style of language to be used in communication. The use of informal

communication channels or grapevines can clarify and reinforce messages. In some cases, the implementation of a "need to know" and "exception principle" in reducing the volume of information in vertical communication channels can be effective in counteracting the problem of information overload.

Review of Theories, Research, and Applications

1. What is the difference between decision making and communication, on one hand, and other characteristics of organizations, including motives of individuals, group behavior, leadership, and organizational structure, on the other?

2. Briefly describe the role of decision making and communication in organizational behavior.

3. What is the difference between classical decision theory as defined in this chapter and behavioral decision theory?

4. Discuss the concept of bounded rationality. In your discussion, point to at least three implications of the concept for understanding organizational behavior, and give an illustration.

5. What is the difference between a probabilistic and nonprobabilistic decision rule? Under what conditions is each type of rule appropriate?

6. What is the implication of March and Simon's model of motivated search for understanding the decision processes of managers?

7. What is the role of information in decisions? Are there any ways to capture decision policies by studying the use of information in decisions?

8. What distinguishes Nominal Group processes or the Delphi technique from interacting groups when making decisions?

9. Define *groupthink*. How is this a problem in group decisions?

10. What is the nature of the Vroom-Yetton-Jago decision model? What distinguishes this model from March and Simon's? From classical decision theory?

11. What are the major functions of communication within organizations? Give a concrete illustration for at least two of these functions.

12. Symbolic-interaction theory suggests a number of ways distortion can develop when communicating. Give three illustrations of such communication problems.

13. Discuss the problem of distortion in communication. Consider and present two ways in which organizations can reduce distortion problems.

Notes

1. For more detail on this topic, see Irwin Bross, *Design for Decision* (New York: Macmillan, 1953); Clifford Springer, Robert Herlihy, and Robert Beggs, *Advanced Methods and Models* (Homewood, Ill.: Irwin, 1965).

2. R. L. Ackoff, *Scientific Method: Optimizing Applied Research Decisions* (New York: Wiley, 1962); Victor H. Vroom and P. W. Yetton, *Leadership and Decision Making* (Pittsburgh: University of Pittsburgh, 1973).

3. M. Sovereign and H. Zimmerman, *Quantitative Models for Production Management* (Englewood Cliffs, N.J.: Prentice-Hall, 1974).

4. Harry F. Evarts, *Introduction to PERT* (Boston: Allyn & Bacon, 1974); Martin Starr, *The Structure of Human Decisions* (Englewood Cliffs, N.J.: Prentice-Hall, 1967); and R. Levin and R. Lamone, *Quantitative Disciplines in Management Decisions* (Homewood, Ill.: Irwin, 1969).

5. J. L. Cochrane and M. Zeleny, eds., *Multiple Criteria Decision Making* (Columbia: University of South Carolina, 1973); David Goodman, "A Goal Programming Approach to Aggregate Planning of Production and Work Force," *Management Science,* 1974, pp. 1569–75.

6. D. J. Bartholomew and A. R. Smith, eds., *Manpower and Management Science* (Lexington, Mass.: D. C. Heath, 1971).

7. James G. March and Herbert A. Simon, *Organizations* (New York: Wiley, 1958); R. M. Cyert and James G. March, *A Behavioral Theory of the Firm* (Englewood Cliffs, N.J.: Prentice-Hall, 1963).

8. Chester I. Barnard, *The Functions of the Executive* (Cambridge, Mass.: Harvard University, 1938); Herbert A. Simon, *Administrative Behavior* (New York: Macmillan, 1957); March and Simon, *Organizations;* Cyert and March, *Behavioral Theory of the Firm.*

9. March and Simon, *Organizations,* p. 11.

10. W. Baumol, *Business Behavior, Value, and Growth* (New York: Harcourt Brace Jovanovich, 1967); R. Monsen and A. Downs, "A Theory of Larger Managerial Firms," *Journal of Political Economy,* 1965, pp. 221–36; K. Boudreaux, "Managerialism and Risk Return Performance," *Southern Journal of Economics,* 1973, pp. 366–72.

11. James D. Thompson, *Organizations in Action* (New York: McGraw-Hill, 1967); March and Simon, *Organizations,* chap. 6.

12. N. H. Anderson and J. C. Shanteau, "Information Integration in Risky Decision Making," *Journal of Experimental Psychology,* 1970, pp. 441–51; Rene M. Dawis and B. Corrigan, "Linear Models in Decision Making," *Psychological Bulletin,* 1974, pp. 95–106; H. Einhorn, "The Use of Non-Linear, Non-Compensatory Models as a Function of Task and Amount of Information," *Organizational Behavior and Human Performance,* 1971, pp. 1–27; L. R. Goldberg, "Five Models of Clinical Judgment: An Empirical Comparison Between Linear and Non-Linear Representations of the Human Inference Process," *Organizational Behavior and Human Performance,* 1971, pp. 458–79; H. Einhorn and R. M. Hogarth, "Unit Weighting Schemes for Decision Making," *Organizational Behavior and Human Performance,* 1975, pp. 171–92.

13. Marc J. Wallace, Jr., and Donald P. Schwab, "A Cross-Validated Comparison of Five Models Used to Predict Graduate Admission Committee Decisions," *Journal of Applied Psychology,* October 1976, pp. 559–63.

14. Dawis and Corrigan, "Linear Models in Decision Making."

15. Einhorn, "Use of Non-Linear, Non-Compensatory Models."

16. R. M. Dawis, "A Case Study of Graduate Admissions: Application of Three Principles of Human Decision Making," *American Psychologist,* 1971, pp. 180–88.

17. Ibid.

18. Ibid.

19. D. Hellriegel and John W. Slocum, Jr., *Organizational Behavior: Contingency Views* (St. Paul: West Publishing, 1979).

20. P. Nutt, "Models For Decision Making In Organizations and Some Contextual Variables That Stipulate Optimal Use," *Academy of Management Review,* 1976, pp. 84–98; D. Hambrick and C. C. Snow, "A Contextual Model of Strategic Decision Making in Organizations," *Proceedings of the 37th Annual Meeting*

of the *Academy of Management,* 1977, pp. 109–12.

21. Marvin E. Shaw, *Group Dynamics,* 2nd ed. (New York: McGraw-Hill, 1978), p. 35.

22. Irving L. Janis, "Groupthink," *Psychology Today,* November 1971. Janis, *Victims of Groupthink* (Boston: Houghton Mifflin, 1972).

23. A. Van de Ven and A. Delbecq, "The Effectiveness of Nominal, Delphi, and Interacting Group Decision Making Processes," *Academy of Management Journal,* 1974, pp. 605–21; A. Delbecq, A. Van de Ven, and D. Gustafson, *Group Techniques: A Guide to Nominal and Delphi Processes* (Glenview, Ill.: Scott, Foresman, 1975).

24. N. Dalkey, *The Delphi Method: An Experimental Study of Group Opinions* (Santa Monica, Calif.: Rand Corp., 1969).

25. Victor H. Vroom and Arthur Jago, "Decision Making as a Social Process: Normative and Descriptive Models of Leader Behavior," *Decision Sciences,* 1974, pp. 743–69.

26. Ibid.

27. Victor H. Vroom and Arthur Jago, "On the Validity of the Vroom-Yetton Model," *Journal of Applied Psychology,* 1978, pp. 151–62.

28. William G. Scott and Terence R. Mitchell, *Organization Theory: A Structural and Behavioral Analysis* (Homewood, Ill.: Irwin, 1976), chap. 9.

29. Charles A. O'Reilly and Karlene Roberts, "Information Filtration in Organizations," *Organizational Behavior and Human Performance,* 1974, pp. 253–65.

30. James L. Gibson, John M. Ivancevich, and James H. Donnelly, Jr., *Organizations* (Dallas: Business Publications, 1979).

31. Keith H. Davis, *Human Behavior at Work* (New York: McGraw-Hill, 1972).

32. Leonard R. Sayles, *Managerial Behavior at Work* (New York: McGraw-Hill, 1972).

Additional References

Dewherst, H. D. "Influence of Perceived Information-Sharing Utilization." *Academy of Management Journal,* 1971, pp. 305–15.

Ebert, R. J., and Mitchell, T. R. *Organizational Decision Processes.* New York: Crane, Russak, 1975.

Greenbaum, H. H. "The Audit of Organizational Communication." *Academy of Management Journal,* 1970, pp. 139–54.

Level, Dale A., Jr. "Communication Effectiveness: Method and Situation." *Journal of Business Communication,* Fall 1972, pp. 19–25.

Lewis, G. H. "Organization in Communication Networks." *Comparative Group Studies,* 1971, pp. 149–60.

Mears, P. "Structuring Communication in a Working Group." *Journal of Communication,* 1974, pp. 71–79.

O'Reilly, C. A., and Roberts, K. "Task Group Structure, Communication, and Effectiveness in Three Organizations." *Journal of Applied Psychology,* 1977, pp. 674–81.

Porter, L. W.; Lawler, E. E., III; and Hackman, J. R. *Behavior in Organizations.* New York: McGraw-Hill, 1975.

Porters, G. "Non Verbal Communications." *Training and Development Journal,* June 1969, pp. 3–8.

Roberts, K. and O'Reilly, C. A. "Failures in Upward Communication in Organizations: Three Possible Culprits." *Academy of Management Journal,* 1974, pp. 205–15.

Sayles, L., and Strauss, G. *Human Behavior in Organizations.* Englewood Cliffs, N.J.: Prentice-Hall, 1966.

Vardaman, G. T., and Halterman, C. C. *Managerial Control Through Communication.* New York: Wiley, 1968.

Vesper, K. H., and Sayeki, Y. "A Quantitative Approach for Policy Analysis." *California Management Review,* 1973, vol. 15, no. 3, pp. 119–26.

Vroom, Victor, and Jago, Arthur. "On the Validity of the Vroom-Yetton Model."

Journal of Applied Psychology, 1978, pp. 151–62.

Wood, M. T. "Participation, Influence, and Satisfaction in Group Decision Making." *Journal of Vocational Behavior,* 1972, vol. 2, pp. 389–99.

A Case of Communication Filtering

The Management Luncheon Meeting at Field International

Field International is a relatively large production company operating three divisions: Field Records, Field Productions, and Field Advertising. Field Records produces and distributes several lines of stereo records and tapes in the popular music and classical music lines. Field Productions independently produces and markets television game shows and several variety programs that are purchased by approximately 250 local network affiliates and independent stations throughout the United States and Canada. Field Advertising is a new venture for the parent corporation. Field's objective is to enter the business of producing, filming, and distributing television promotions developed by large advertising companies. In effect, the division will depend upon such firms subcontracting the actual production of various advertisements to Field.

Lawrence Field, the president and chairman of the board, began the business fifteen years ago and has directed the growth and diversification of the business. Each division is directed by a vice president selected by Field and operates in a highly independent fashion. Field has emphasized the fact that he views each division as a critical profit center and evaluates each on that basis.

Recently, Mr. Field became aware of the fact that the new advertising division was running into some short-term budgeting, staffing, and production problems. He had received phone calls from two highly valued clients (two of the major advertising companies in New York), who complained that their productions were running two to three weeks behind schedule and that they were being pressured by their clients to get the promotions under way.

Field called his executive assistant, Ron Durkey, on the morning after the phone conversations and said, "We've got some problems with the advertising division. Apparently, they've fallen behind schedule on two critical projects. Be careful with this one. You know my belief that each division should run autonomously, and that they will sink or swim under their own efforts. Yet, I don't want to lose those clients. I'm thinking that the new division could benefit from the experience of the other two divisions. What do you think of establishing a weekly luncheon where I could sit down with each of the division vice presidents and brainstorm solutions to operating problems within each division? Put out a memo to each of the VP's and let's set the first lunch here at corporate headquarters for next Wednesday at noon."

Durkey's office sent out the following memo later that same afternoon:

MEMORANDUM
TO: Vice Presidents, Field Divisions
FROM: Ron Durkey
RE: President's Luncheon

President Field today directed that I establish a weekly luncheon to be attended by each of you and Mr. Field. The topic of discussion will be problems each of you is having in your divisions. The first of these is scheduled for next Wednesday, June 16, in the executive dining room of corporate headquarters at 12 noon. Please call me if you have any questions.

The luncheon meeting was almost a total disaster. Each of the vice presidents arrived and sat down with Field. The atmosphere was sullen, defensive, and uncomfortable for all. Mr. Field tried to be genial and encouraged open discussion of mutual problems. He started the conversation by asking the newly appointed vice president of the advertising division if he were having any problems and if any of the others there could give him any help.

The vice president replied that there were really no serious problems and that he could take care of everything himself. He expressed anger at the two clients who went over his head and bothered Field and proceeded to attack the clients for unrealistic expectations and misunderstanding of the division's original commitment to them.

At this point, the vice president of the records division said that he was concerned about the idea of Mr. Field radically changing the nature of Field International's structure and developing a style of such close supervision over division operations. He said, in effect, that if Field didn't like the operations of the records division, he would be happy to resign his position.

Field was dumbfounded by all of this. He expressed dismay at their reactions and tried to reemphasize the fact that these lunches were intended only as a friendly device for sharing ideas and solutions to problems. After two subsequent lunches which followed the same pattern, Field quietly dropped the whole idea.

Case Primer Questions

1. What do you think provoked the reactions of the vice presidents to Mr. Durkey's memo?

2. Do you think the source of the memo had anything to do with the problem?

3. What kinds of characteristics (personal attributes of each individual and the setting as a whole) contributed to the filtering problem in this case?

4. Can you suggest an alternative way of communicating the meeting that might have alleviated the problem?

Experiential Exercise

Executive Decision

Purpose

This exercise applies the principles of the Vroom decision model presented earlier in this chapter. The objectives of this exercise are to:

1. Give you experience in making an actual series of decisions.

2. Allow you to analyze the various aspects and contingencies in a complex decision.

3. Emphasize the central role of decision making in the exercise of leadership.

Required understanding

To complete the exercise, you will need to refer to exhibit 12–8 and exhibit 12–9 in the text.

How to set up the exercise

1. Each student will work on his or her own.

2. Have all participants read the following statement:

You are the administrative director of a large health maintenance organization (HMO) operating with sixteen local clinics in three neighboring states. The HMO provides a full spectrum of medical and dental services to members and has experienced rapid growth during your five years as director (when you started in your position, there were four clinics operating).

The tremendous growth of the HMO has been due, in part, to some timely decisions of your own, but you also believe that the time was right for HMO's, that you have virtually no competitors in this area, and that circumstances apart from your decisions have heavily contributed to the success of your operation.

An unfortunate byproduct of this success is that you have developed a reputation as a brilliant decision maker among your subordinates. It has caused them to look to you for leadership and guidance in decision

making beyond what you consider appropriate. You would prefer them to make more decisions on their own.

The board of directors has recently allocated funds to your office to build and staff a seventeenth clinic. The problem is to select a suitable location. You know that there are no "clear" solutions to the decision, and a number of alternative locations will have to be evaluated on a set of complex criteria. You have asked your clinic directors to keep their eyes open for promising locations, and believe that their intimate knowledge of specific local areas will be extremely helpful in making the final site selection.

Their support for the new operation will be extremely important because the success of the new clinic will depend upon their willingness to supply staff and technical assistance to the new operation during its initial weeks of operation.

The success of the new operation will influence everyone directly because they will benefit from the increased base of operations. Indirectly, they will also benefit because they are part of a growing and successful enterprise.

Instructions for the exercise

1. Each participant will play the role of administrative director and analyze the decision problem according to the formula presented in exhibit 12–9. Specifically, the decision maker must analyze the problem with respect to the eight yes/no criteria presented in the decision tree:

A. Quality: Yes or No?
B. Leader's information: Yes or No?
C. Structured: Yes or No?
D. Acceptance: Yes or No?
E. Prior probability of acceptance: Yes or No?
F. Goal congruence: Yes or No?
G. Conflict: Yes or No?
H. Sufficient subordinate information: Yes or No?

2. Based upon an individual analysis of the decision problem, develop a synthesis of the

problem and recommend a decision strategy from those presented in exhibit 12–8:

Problem Type (determine from the decision tree analysis in exhibit 12–9):
Feasible Decision Strategy Set:
Recommended Strategy:

3. The class should regroup and each student should present his or her choice. Class members should analyze and develop class discussion around points as they arise.

CHAPTER 13

Performance
Evaluation

The framework for studying organizational behavior presented in chapter 2 characterizes performance as an outcome of the organizational system (macro and micro) and processes. Performance is a dependent variable of interest in the study of organizational behavior because the goals and objectives of the organization are measured in terms of performance achievement. In the organization, performance might translate into measures of group task completion, quality, and efficiency. At the individual level, performance might translate into behaviors and actions as rated by superiors and peers.

An examination and review of the framework in chapter 2 emphasizes that organizations obtain feedback from reviewing and evaluating performance, which allows for adjustments to be made with respect to structures, individuals, groups, and processes (including decision making and communication). The intention of such adjustments is to improve performance through the techniques of organizational change (to be discussed in chapters 15 and 16). *Performance evaluation,* then, should be defined as the process by which an organization obtains feedback about the effectiveness of its employees. In general, the process serves an auditing and control function, generating information upon which many organizational decisions are made. In practice, however, performance evaluation is very difficult for several reasons. First, performance evaluation must serve many purposes, from evaluating the success of selection decisions, to assessing the effectiveness of a leader, to evaluating training efforts, to making reward decisions. Second, the assessment of performance itself is a difficult measurement task because so many factors influence performance, including environmental, organizational, and individual factors. Finally, a great number of ethical and emotionally charged issues arise when performance is evaluated. The results of the process can have profound influences on employees' jobs and careers.

A Performance Dilemma

The following example illustrates many of the major issues that arise in the process of performance evaluation. Suppose a vice president of sales for a corporation must select one of two regional sales managers for promotion to the position of general sales manager. He has decided to promote Jack Arnold over Ted Bessemer, and

Bessemer has contested the decision to the personnel manager, claiming that he has been unfairly treated. In his argument to the personnel manager, Bessemer makes the following points. First, he questions the adequacy of the performance review form used to make six-month performance reviews. He argues that how well one scores on the form depends upon who is doing the evaluation. In addition, he believes that the form does not assess the truly appropriate aspects of his job. Second, he charges that the vice president of sales is blatantly biased against him because he is Jewish, and the sales manager who got the promotion is a Roman Catholic (like the sales vice president). Third, he charges that the sales vice president made the decision based on only one aspect of performance (sales revenue for the manager's region) and ignored other important aspects of performance, such as the company's product image in the region, the satisfaction of salespeople reporting to the regional manager, the number of returned items from dissatisfied customers, and the cost of sales in the region. Fourth, he argues that although sales generated may be appropriate as a criterion for making a pay decision, some other criterion such as ability to supervise the work of others is far more relevant for making a promotion decision of this kind.

In addition to these complaints, Bessemer raises several other questions. For example, why did the vice president always review him during the worst six-month period for sales (June to December) rather than the best six-month period? Finally, Bessemer claims that extenuating circumstances could explain the fact that his regional sales were always below those of the manager who was promoted. He charges that his region was faced with far more competition in the product market than Jack Arnold's region was.

Performance Review Issues

This illustration raises a number of issues in performance evaluation that will be examined in more detail in this chapter. First, employee performance is not usually unidimensional; that is, there are many aspects of performance that must be assessed. Second, the group of dimensions or aspects of job performance a manager considers depends upon the purpose of the performance review. Where training needs are being assessed, for example, the manager should focus on specific acts or behaviors in order to determine skill deficiencies. When a compensation decision is being made, in contrast, the manager should focus on more outcome-oriented performance criteria, such as sales or market shares achieved by the employee's division. Third, the same type of act or behavior will not always result in the same level of performance outcomes. What might be very successful behavior in one setting, for example, may result in failure in some different setting. Fourth, factors beyond the control of the employee being evaluated can also influence performance assessments, particularly when outcome-oriented criteria, such as sales, productivity, and profit, are being used.

Finally, Bessemer's complaint raises questions about two major qualities of performance assessment: reliability and validity. In order for performance assessment to be reliable, it must be free of error. Errors influencing *reliability* of performance assessment include disagreement between two different observers evaluating the performance of the same employee, or obtaining two different ratings with the same form at different times, when, in fact, the employee's performance has not changed. *Validity* concerns the relevance of performance assessment. To what extent is the assessment technique actually measuring what it is intended to measure? Are the characteristics being assessed relevant to the promotion decision?

A good example of an error source affecting reliability and validity is time. The timing of a performance appraisal can influence results quite apart from the employee's actual performance. The same employee evaluated at 8:30 A.M., when the supervisor is fresh, may get a completely different evaluation than if he or she were evaluated at 4:30 P.M., when the supervisor is fatigued and has formed opinions based on earlier appraisal sessions.

The issues raised in this case can be categorized into four major topics: (1) the purposes of performance appraisal; (2) the use of job analysis in the development of problem-free performance appraisal methods; (3) the choice of appropriate performance appraisal techniques; and (4) procedural and administrative matters in carrying out performance appraisal.

Purposes of Performance Evaluation

Performance evaluation is the most important single device available to an organization for setting and obtaining goals. Typically, goal setting (as discussed earlier in this book) is a process that involves many parties at all levels within the organization. Top management and the board of directors usually formulate goals in terms of broad, global outcomes to be achieved by the organization. These may include, for example, statements regarding optimal growth in the market value of the firm's stocks, optimal growth in the overall scale of the company's operations, and some target return in terms of profit per share of the firm's common stock.

Each of the organization's units, in turn, must translate such overall goals into specific objectives that can be expected to contribute to overall goals. A marketing division, for example, may decide that, to achieve an overall goal of growth, sales will have to increase by 20 percent. This objective, in turn, may translate into specific sales quotas for each of the firm's sales representatives.

A production division, on the other hand, may recognize that it can increase profit rates by making its operations more efficient. They may choose, therefore, to introduce new capital equipment that will increase each operator's efficiency by 30 percent. With some thought, the reader can imagine the many ways in which global goals must be translated into specific performance objectives for each division and, indeed, every individual employee.

The process we have been describing is, in fact, a four-step cycle, as illustrated in exhibit 13–1: (1) establishing standards; (2) recording actual performance; (3) reviewing performance in light of standards; and (4) determining corrective action.

These four steps taken together constitute a control function. Performance evaluation plays an important role in control because it serves as an audit facilitating control. Performance evaluation, then, is an auditing procedure that generates the information necessary to control and direct the process of an organization. Typi-

Exhibit 13–1 Performance Review Cycle

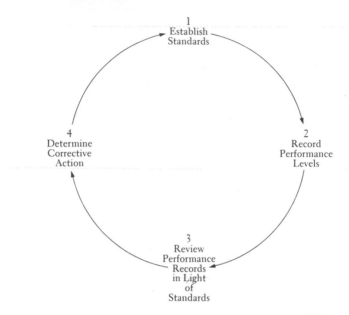

cally, the review procedure would start at the first level of operations—each employee's performance is reviewed by immediate supervisors in each department. Entire departmental performance would be reviewed at the next level of analysis. Finally, the board of directors or trustees would evaluate the global performance of the entire organization.

Control itself can take many forms, all involving management decisions. One way of controlling performance is through selection, job placement, and promotion. The kind of person selected for employment and the type of job in which he or she is placed have a direct influence on level of job performance. Another set of decisions intended to control performance involves job and organizational design. Performance results may be used to suggest ways of redistributing tasks and responsibilities in the organization. In addition, when management wants to tie rewards and performance together, performance evaluation is critical as a basis for making differential reward decisions. Finally, any decisions the organization makes with regard to improving performance through training and other forms of organizational change and development must be based on appraisals of skill deficiencies made during performance review.

Performance appraisal or evaluation serves at least the following purposes:

1. Promotion, separation, and transfer decisions.

2. Feedback for the employee regarding how the organization views his or her performance.

3. Evaluations of relative contributions made by individuals and entire departments in achieving higher-level organizational goals.

4. Reward decisions, including merit increases, promotions, and other rewards.

5. Criteria for evaluating the effectiveness of selection and placement decisions, including the relevance of the information used in those decisions.

6. Ascertaining and diagnosing training and development needs for individual employees and entire divisions within the organization.

7. Criteria for evaluating the success of training and development decisions.

8. Information upon which work-scheduling plans, budgeting, and human resources planning can be based.

The remainder of this chapter examines some specific issues and problems that must be addressed by managers in developing and applying performance appraisal.

(2) Developing Performance Measures through Job Analysis

If performance appraisal is to serve its purposes, the measures of performance used in appraisal must be both reliable and valid, two issues that we address in the next section. Insuring the reliability and validity of performance appraisal methods is not only a logical requirement for managers but has recently become a legal one as well.[1] In order to insure corporate compliance with federal equal employment opportunity legislation, organizations will now have to demonstrate the reliability and validity of their performance appraisal procedures.[2] The first step toward this goal is knowing exactly what performance is expected.

Defining Performance through Job Analysis

So far, we have said that performance is a complex outcome consisting of many dimensions. Furthermore, measures of performance must be reliable and valid. *Job analysis* is the major method available to managers to insure the development of performance measures satisfying these two requirements. We examined the larger issues of job design in chapter 6. Now, we narrow our focus to analyzing jobs in order to design explicit measures of performance effectiveness.

An important definition of a *job* and *job analysis* is as follows: "A job is a relatively homogeneous cluster of work tasks carried out to achieve some essential and enduring purpose in an organization. . . . Job analysis consists of defining the job and discovering what the job calls for in employee behaviors.[3] Job analysis, then, is a procedure for gathering the judgment of people who are knowledgeable about the organization, the positions within it, and the specific content of a job. Furthermore, the *content* of the job is defined to be specific work activities or tasks. In effect, *job analysis* is a broad term describing an entire series of judgments that are made in the design of an organization. Exhibit 13–2 illustrates the purposes served in job analysis.

The first task in job analysis, once a structure of jobs has been established through job design, is to specify the primary duties or tasks to be carried out by

Exhibit 13–2 Purposes of Job Analysis

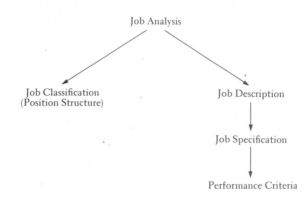

people assigned to each job. The result of this part of job analysis is a *job descrip-tion* that specifies responsibilities and reporting relationships. In addition, job analysis should also yield a *job specification*. This is a statement of the employee characteristics and qualifications that are required in order to perform the job adequately: skills, knowledge, capacities, attitudes, education. Exhibit 13–3 illustrates the job description for a dentist and the job description for an assistant carrying out expanded functions in a dental health team. Finally, the job description and the job specification provide the information necessary for developing and establishing measures of performance effectiveness.

Defining Job Content

A major problem that develops in job analysis is deciding upon the appropriate mix of tasks for a job. For example, where does the work of a carpenter stop and a cement mason begin if a wooden form must be taken down after the concrete has been poured and set? Where does the work of a surgeon stop and an operating room nurse begin at the completion of a surgical procedure? In each case, the job analyst is searching for a set of homogeneous work tasks that logically define the content of a job. These are not easy questions to resolve in job analysis, and a number of bases are commonly employed for making such determinations in practice:

Common skills and qualifications required by the job.

Work tasks that occur at the same place and time—that is, those linked by the nature or technology of the process.

External demands that the tasks be clustered; for example, professional definitions, union demands, or legal and licensing requirements.

Tradition.

In organized labor, lines of task responsibility are strictly drawn to avoid jurisdictional disputes—arguments over who does specific tasks. One of the most difficult

Exhibit 13–3   Job Descriptions for Dentist and Expanded-Function Auxiliary in a Dental Health Team

Dentist's Responsibilities	Expanded Duty Dental Auxiliary Responsibilities
1. Direct patient contact	1. Materials preparation and cleanup
2. Diagnosis and treatment planning	2. Assisting dentist in clinical procedures
3. Administrative functions	3. Performing intra-oral clinical procedures (e.g., placing a filling after the dentist has prepared the cavity)
4. Assisting auxiliaries	
5. Reviewing and evaluating work of subordinates	4. Assisting and instructing patients
	5. Record keeping
6. Training	6. Assisting other auxiliaries
7. Consulting with other dentists	7. Consulting with nonclinical personnel
8. Review daily records	8. Consulting with dentist
9. Consulting with nonclinical personnel	9. Supervision of others
10. Consulting with clinical personnel	
11. Directing staff meetings	

barriers in introducing paramedics and expanded-duty dental auxiliaries are laws and licensing restrictions that strictly reserve a variety of clinical procedures to the licensed doctor or dentist. Where laws and union agreements do not exist, a common technology and skill base together with temporal and physical proximity of tasks provide the most common bases for defining jobs or positions.

Once the tasks have been defined for a job, measures of performance effectiveness for each task must be developed. The considerations involved, shown in exhibit 13–4, make accomplishing this objective difficult. First of all, no single, universal dimension of job performance exists. At the very least, management must consider immediate, intermediate, and ultimate criteria of effectiveness. Second, within each level of performance criteria there are many independent dimensions. Very rarely, for example, does a job consist only of a single task (an exception might be the work of an automated assembly-line worker). Nor are task performance outcomes and overall organizational effectiveness outcomes unidimensional. The challenge in job analysis is to select the specific subset of task dimensions that properly represents effective performance.

Problems to Be Addressed
by Designing Performance Measures

All the problems to which managers and employees point in performance evaluation can be summarized by two terms: *reliability* and *validity*. Both are qualities of the entire evaluation process and refer to the adequacy of the information that is generated and employed in subsequent decisions about employees. Hence, when a man-

Exhibit 13–4 Considerations in Choosing an Appropriate Performance Appraisal Method

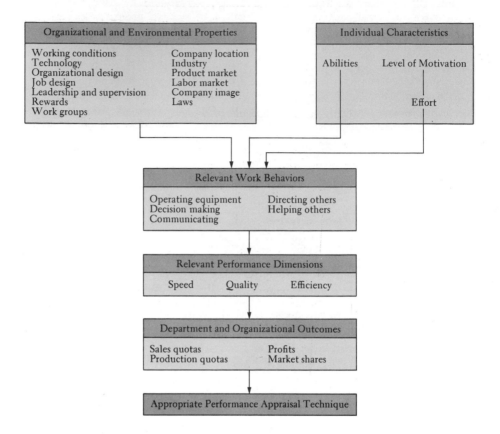

ager says that he or she made a mistake when promoting someone because the information was bad, he or she is referring to the reliability and validity with which such information was gathered.

Reliability

The first demand that must be made of a performance appraisal procedure is that it be reliable. Reliability actually refers to two major characteristics of the method by which performance information is collected: consistency and stability. *Consistency* demands that two alternative ways of gathering the same data should agree substantially in their results. When two items are used on the same rating form to measure the same aspect of job performance, for example, the supervisor's responses to them should agree with each other when evaluating the same subordinate. Similarly, two interviewers who evaluate the same employee should agree substantially in their findings. *Stability* demands that the same measuring device give the same results several times in a row if the characteristic it is supposed to be assessing has not changed. Thus, if the way in which a nurse treats patients has not changed between Monday and Tuesday, we would expect a rating form to yield the same information about this aspect of performance on both days. ⟶ contrast effects, supervisor's mood, deficiency

General sources of Error In actual practice, a variety of situational and personal factors can lead to either form of unreliability (inconsistency and instability) when employees are evaluated. The most common error sources are illustrated in exhibit 13–5. Suppose a supervisor must write up a report evaluating the job performance of a brick mason. There are three basic aspects or qualities of the job one would assess: (1) speed or rate of work; (2) accuracy of work; and (3) amount of wasted materials (bricks, mortar, etc.). If there were some perfect method for evaluating the brick mason's work, we could adequately measure performance, and we would generate information represented by circle A in the figure. Unfortunately, many sources of error creep in when performance is assessed, and we end up with information represented by circle B. In other words, although we would always like to have perfectly accurate information, human weaknesses of the observer yield information that is always subject to some degree of error.

The first problem might crop up when the supervisor, who is in a hurry, ignores the accuracy of the mason's work, and rates only speed and waste. In this case, the assessment would ignore one of three dimensions of performance completely, and the assessed performance would be deficient. The dimensions of performance ig-

Exhibit 13–5 Sources of Error in Performance Appraisal

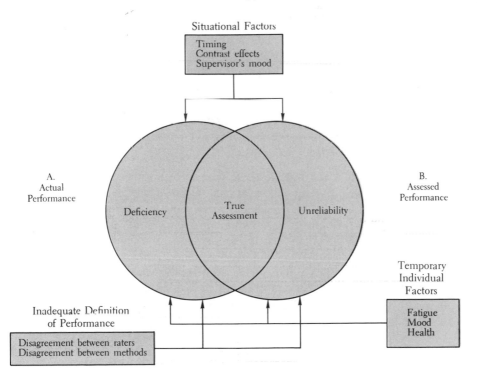

451

nored by the supervisor is represented by the nonoverlapping section of circle A. In this sense, the method employed by the supervisor is deficient.

In addition to deficiency, three other general situational factors can lead to inconsistency and instability in performance appraisals: the timing of the assessment, contrast effects, and characteristics of managers doing the appraisal, such as their mood. Suppose, for example, that the mason gets a consistently higher rating if the supervisor evaluates his or her work at the end of the day, after extraneous debris has been cleared away. In this case, the timing of the evaluation influences the results, when, in fact, it should have no effect. Contrast effects are phenomena involving relative comparisons that intrude upon and distort the evaluator's judgments. The rating received by the brick mason, for example, may vary depending upon whom the supervisor has just previously evaluated. His or her work may appear better than normal if it is evaluated following an extremely poor performance by another brick mason. Conversely, the work may appear worse if he or she is evaluated following an excellent brick mason. Finally, several temporary characteristics of supervisors personally may influence their appraisals, including their mood and how fatigued they are.

Inadequate definition of job performance can also lead to unreliable appraisals. In addition to the problem of ignoring some major dimension of performance when carrying out an evaluation of an employee's work, two other kinds of errors can develop. First, two supervisors can disagree on what constitutes job performance. In this case, it is very likely that their ratings of the same employee at the same point in time would disagree. Second, the kind of evaluation form or method used can cause unwanted variation in appraisals. In research and practice, for example, it has been found that performance appraisals carried out using the interview as a method often disagree with more patterned methods, such as formal ratings.

A third general source of error in performance ratings has to do with temporary changes in the employee that will influence the evaluation and give an incorrect picture of his or her actual performance. The most common forms of such error are fatigue, sickness, and mood of the employee. If, for example, the performance review takes place when the employee is extremely tired (at the end of a hard week), or ill, or depressed, performance as measured by the supervisor may appear far below levels that are, in fact, more typical.

Improving reliability.   The three general sources of error or unreliability in performance appraisals just outlined (situational factors, inadequate definition of performance, and temporary individual changes) limit the stability and consistency with which managers evaluate the work of employees. In practice, managers have a number of ways to determine just how reliable a given appraisal system is and several techniques for maximizing its reliability. The most commonly used technique involves multiple observations of job performance. For example, if managers define one major dimension of the brick mason's job to be accuracy, several alternative questions should be designed for the rating form to assess this same aspect of performance. Agreement among these items would show consistency in assessment.

It is important to have performance evaluated by more than one observer when possible. Disagreement among appraisers indicates that there is inconsistency among observers in the appraisal process. The raters' agreement can be maximized by educating observers about the qualities of performance for which they should look and standardizing the methods they use.

Finally, management should attempt to get several readings on performance over short periods of time. Agreement between assessments made a week apart (assuming performance actually has not been altered) would indicate stability in the appraisal process. Probably, the single best way to insure against unreliability in performance appraisal is to be vigilant; that is, to search for ways in which inconsistencies and instability may be influencing evaluator's judgments.

The importance of reliability. Why worry about reliability? We have said that reliability has to do with the consistency and stability of measurement, and validity has to do with relevance. Obviously, validity is an extremely important quality of information upon which managerial decisions are based. However, a measurement method can be no more valid than it is reliable as an indicator of performance.

This means that if managers begin performance appraisal with unreliable methods, they are doomed to failure because there is no way in which appraisals can result in information relevant to such control decisions as promotion, separation, transfer, development, rewards, and work scheduling. Hence, it is extremely important for managers to assure themselves that performance appraisal methods are at least reliable. Finally, we must recognize that no specific appraisal forms or methods are universally reliable across industries and firms. Indeed, the burden of reliability rests on the shoulders of those who are going to use the assessment technique in each specific organizational setting. A form or technique that is reliable in one organization may be totally unreliable in a different organization.

Validity

Although reliability is a necessary precondition for validity or relevance, it does not alone insure that a measure will actually be valid. In order for a method of performance appraisal to be relevant or valid, a number of considerations beyond reliability must be taken into account. Research, together with practical managerial experience, over the past twenty years proves that managers must concern themselves with five factors in addition to reliability in the design of performance appraisal measures:[4] (1) the performance dimensions to be assessed (static tasks); (2) level of abstraction; (3) time; (4) employee-determined changes in the job; and (5) situation-determined changes in the job. Taken together, these factors should be thought of as *job dynamics,* which must be adequately represented in order for performance measures to be valid.[5]

Performance dimensions. The validity problem with respect to performance dimensions is to adequately determine the different aspects of work behavior and performance to be evaluated. In our earlier illustration, we suggested three dimensions of a brick mason's job performance: speed, waste, and accuracy. Very rarely is there a job that is unidimensional. The job of a physician, for example, must include at least the accuracy of clinical judgments, quality of direct patient treatment, management of paraprofessionals and nurses, and interaction with patients.

One of the first major steps in performance appraisal research in an organization is to empirically determine how many dimensions of performance must be assessed in order to validly appraise an employee's job performance. Research carried out on the job of a dentist, for example, has determined eight independent dimensions of their performance (regarding personnel) that must be evaluated.[6]

1. Responding to team members' needs for assistance.

2. Demonstrating trust, respect, and appreciation.

3. Keeping team-member relations pleasant.

4. Reviewing and evaluating team-member performance.

5. Assignment of work responsibilities.

6. Organizing and arranging work facilities, instruments, and materials.

7. Training and developing team members.

8. Encouraging and using staff suggestions.

Performance measures that do not define and assess all relevant dimensions of the job will be *deficient,* and therefore not completely valid. On the other hand, measures that include dimensions that are not properly part of the job will also have a validity problem—contamination. The problem of determining which work behaviors are relevant is illustrated in exhibit 13–6, showing examples of performance dimensions to be considered.

Level of abstraction.   In addition to static performance dimensions, the validity of a performance measure depends upon using the proper level of organizational analysis. In chapter 2, we pointed out that there are many models of organizational

Exhibit 13–6 A Model for Dealing with Criterion Problems in Performance Appraisal

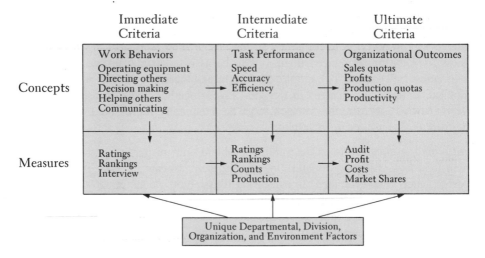

	Immediate Criteria	Intermediate Criteria	Ultimate Criteria
Concepts	**Work Behaviors** Operating equipment Directing others Decision making Helping others Communicating	**Task Performance** Speed Accuracy Efficiency	**Organizational Outcomes** Sales quotas Profits Production quotas Productivity
Measures	Ratings Rankings Interview	Ratings Rankings Counts Production	Audit Profit Costs Market Shares

Unique Departmental, Division, Organization, and Environment Factors

effectiveness. Many of them differ in the level at which they conceptualize effectiveness (organizational, group, or individual). In practice, an evaluation system must incorporate and deal with all three levels of analysis. We have indicated this problem in exhibit 13–6, which also illustrates three possible levels of analysis or abstraction in performance appraisal.

Work behavior may well be considered an immediate criterion of performance; the achievement of group tasks may be considered an intermediate criterion; ultimate criteria of success will probably include measures of organizational outcomes such as profit, market shares, and productivity.

It is important to distinguish among these levels of criteria for at least two reasons. First, they are sequentially related to each other, as indicated by the direction of the arrows in the upper half of exhibit 13–6; in other words, the success of group performance depends upon the work behaviors of individual members, and the achievement of overall organizational goals, in turn, depends upon the task performance of groups, as indicated in the performance model developed in chapter 2.

In addition, immediate criteria are different from ultimate and intermediate criteria in terms of the information they carry and their measurement qualities (reliability and validity).[7] On one hand, a manager wants a performance measure to be as reliable and valid as possible. Immediate performance measures focus on very narrow aspects of performance and tend to be most reliable and valid. On the other hand, managers need information more relevant to the operations of the firm than the immediate behavior of employees. They need information regarding the goal attainments of groups of employees, divisions, and, ultimately, the entire organization. Unfortunately, however, as one moves from immediate to intermediate to ultimate measures of performance effectiveness, assessment becomes more difficult. Thus, as management tries to measure broader and broader effects of performance, measurement reliability and validity decrease.

In practice, the answer to the problem lies in considering all levels of analysis in performance appraisal. In designing such a system, managers should begin by conceptualizing and defining ultimate criteria of organizational effectiveness. They should then move backward through the various conceptual levels of goals indicated in the upper portion of exhibit 13 6. At each stage in this analysis, managers must judge which aspects of group task performance will be most critical for achieving desired organizational outcomes. In turn, they must determine which aspects of individual behavior will be most critical in achieving desired group task outcomes. Indeed, this stage of performance criteria development is deductive in nature. Each lower level of criteria are deduced logically from criteria that have already been chosen at a higher or less immediate level of consideration.

Time. Time is a third critical dimension influencing the validity of performance appraisal. Time operates in three major ways as an influence. First, immediate, intermediate, and ultimate criteria have a short-run/long-run orientation. Specific and immediate criteria, such as job behaviors, are appropriately measured in the short run, at the time the work is being done. Less immediate outcomes, such as group task performance, and organizational outcomes, such as profit, market shares, and efficiency, may require months and perhaps years to become apparent. Assessing various criteria at too early or too late a time may seriously limit the validity of performance appraisal. For example, a firm may use a measure of divisional effectiveness such as profit as a criterion for evaluating the success of hiring a given executive. If the assessment is made prematurely, before the executive's division has had a chance to establish itself in the market, top management might erroneously conclude that they made a poor selection decision.

Second, all jobs have cycles associated with them that job analysis must take into account and establish as a performance dimension to be appraised. For example, the timing and ordering of tasks in constructing a building are as important in the job of a construction engineer as successful completion of each task considered separately. In practical terms, this fact implies that specific aspects of performance may only be validly appraised at certain points in a work cycle. A critical factor in job analysis, therefore, will be to specify such points.

Finally, in addition to cycles, employees change over time. As an employee gains experience with the job and the organization, the mix of behaviors that will be effective in achieving group, departmental, and organizational goals will change. Managers who are new to the job, for example, may be expected to spend a relatively large proportion of their time in learning activities during the first six months of employment. These activities will probably include assisting a number of different senior managers in a series of jobs included in a job-rotation program. Their performance of these tasks will constitute the relevant aspects upon which to make an evaluation during this time. After six months, however, other aspects of behavior, including decision making, supervising the work of others, and introducing new ideas, will become more appropriate as performance criteria.

Employee-determined changes.   Most people have seen a case in which two different people have achieved the same results while behaving in two entirely different fashions. To some degree, all jobs allow some room for employee determination of the specific way in which job tasks are to be carried out. Two carpenters, for example, may develop different kinds of work habits and achieve the same level of performance. Similarly, two professors may consistently achieve the same results with entirely different lecturing styles. To be sure, the degree to which a job allows individual variations in style depends on the kind of tasks involved. A precise, assembly-line job will allow almost no variation, but a job such as general manager, doctor, lawyer, or professor will allow far greater variation. It is extremely critical that job analysis and the resulting performance appraisal method take employee-determined variation into account. Specifically, the performance appraisal method must specify the broad range of behavioral styles that will be acceptable on the job.

Situation-determined changes.   Organizational and environmental properties influence all levels of performance criteria. It is important that a performance evaluation program (and the job analysis that leads to it) take all these factors into account as explicitly as possible. Any number of situational factors will require completely different types of behaviors in order to be successful. A headwaiter in a restaurant, for example, will behave quite differently with subordinate waiters and with customers. Lawyers adjust their courtroom styles to the situation, including the kind of case that is being heard, whether they are prosecuting or defending, and the makeup of the jury. Behavioral scientists have categorized the major situational factors that must be taken into account in performance appraisal:[8]

1. *Physical factors* include hazards, lighting, temperature, architecture.

2. *Technology* includes types of equipment and methods demanded by work tasks.

3. *Information* includes the kinds of information and sources of information with which the employee must deal on the job.

4. *People* includes the kinds of people with whom and circumstances under which the employee must interact.

5. *Group situation* includes the nature of group influence surrounding the employee in carrying out job tasks.

6. *Historical precedents* includes traditions and precedents established by earlier employees on the job.

7. *Organizational climate* includes properties of the work environment, perceived by the employee, that presumably influence his or her work behavior.

Thus, the time at which an evaluation is made, the employee whose performance is being evaluated, and the circumstances under which the evaluation is made all are critical factors in determining the validity or relevance of a performance appraisal.

③ Methods of Performance Appraisal

Choosing an Appraisal Method

Because performance appraisal serves so many purposes, there can be no general method appropriate for all purposes. The problem for management is to determine what kind of performance appraisal method is adequate, given the purpose to be served. It is important to remember that performance criteria consist of many dimensions, only a part of which may be relevant for a specific auditing purpose. In addition, the specific purposes of performance evaluation vary widely between different kinds of organizations. Hospitals, insurance firms, universities, police departments, welfare departments, courts, and architectural firms, for example, vary widely in terms of most environmental, organizational, and individual factors influencing performance. This fact is illustrated in exhibit 13–4, which recasts the performance framework presented in chapter 2 in the performance appraisal focus considered here.

Specifically, the problem for managers is to select a performance appraisal method that is appropriate given the following considerations:

Specific *organizational and environmental properties*, such as technology, the design of the organization, the firm's industry, and other factors indicated in the exhibit.

Unique *individual characteristics* influencing performance, including specific skills and abilities and motivation levels.

The mix of specific *work behaviors* that are appropriate given organizational and individual considerations.

The mix of *relevant performance dimensions,* given a consideration of the organization and individuals involved.

The specific set of *goals* to be achieved at departmental and organizational levels.

Each of these conditions must be specified in turn in order to choose an appropriate system for evaluating performance. It should be apparent after examining exhibit 13–4 that there are no universal methods of evaluation that can be applied in all organizations for all purposes. The central problem in performance appraisal is the design of a system that: (1) suits the purpose for the appraisal; and (2) is tailored to the unique characteristics of each organization.

A number of investigators have recently examined the process of performance appraisal with the objective of making it more reliable and valid.[9] They divide the most frequently employed methods of performance appraisal into two categories: (1) traditional methods; and (2) behaviorally based methods. Behaviorally based methods have a number of well-documented advantages over traditional methods, which we will examine in this section.

Traditional Methods

The most frequently used forms of appraisal today are still based on traditional methods and usually take one of two basic forms: rating or ranking. Both kinds of appraisal methods are based on traditional, descriptive forms of job analysis.[10] In this case, observers make a very brief study of the job, focusing on several major task dimensions. They note these in broad, descriptive language, and in turn use these dimensions as a basis for designing ad hoc rating scales or ranking forms.

A typical rating form

Exhibit 13–7 (pp. 460–61) shows a typical rating scale evolving from the procedure described above. Note that dimensions of performance are only broadly defined for the individual making the evaluation. In addition, for the most part the levels of each performance dimension are not defined in any detail. For example, precisely what is meant by the terms *considerably below standards, acceptable,* and *exceptionally high quality?* Scales of this sort are known as *global rating scales* because they define the qualities to be assessed and levels of such qualities in broad, global terms. As such, they are extremely vulnerable to a variety of errors that reduce their reliability and validity. The most common of these errors can be summarized as follows:

Halo error occurs when the evaluator incorrectly treats two or more dimensions of performance as if they were identical or highly correlated. The evaluator making this error, for example, might believe that if an employee's work performance deserves a high rating on quality, it should also merit a high rating on cooperation. The result is that employees show no variation in ratings across dimensions—they either are rated consistently high, medium, or low on all performance dimensions.

Strictness error occurs when an evaluator rates all employees as very poor performers. The ratings of this evaluator tend to cluster closely towards the low end of the rating scale, as indicated in exhibit 13–8.

Leniency error is the opposite of strictness. In this case, the evaluator mistakenly gives all employees uniformly high ratings. Ratings given by this individual cluster together at the high end of the scale in exhibit 13–8.

Central tendency error is similar to leniency and strictness, except that in this case the ratings made by the evaluator cluster artificially at the middle of the scale in exhibit 13–8.

Strictness, leniency, and central tendency are all errors that involve a misjudgment on the evaluator's part of the true distribution of work performance among a group of employees.

Ranking appraisals

Many companies have tried an alternative method to rating, called *ranking,* to overcome these problems. Although there are many variations of the basic ranking method, all have in common the fact that they *force* the evaluator to distribute scores representing performance effectiveness. In a typical ranking procedure, a single, global dimension of performance would be defined for evaluators. They would then be asked to rank in order several employees in terms of this dimension from highest to lowest.

A number of flaws exist in ranking procedures, however, that cause problems of reliability and validity. First, by design they are forced to be unidimensional in nature. The evaluator is rarely asked to rank employees on more than one dimension. Hence, they fail to reflect the multidimensional aspects of most jobs. Second, they are very cumbersome to use in practice. An evaluator may be able to accurately rank four, five, or six individual employees. It would be virtually an impossible task, however, for a supervisor to rank the performance of twenty or thirty subordinates. A modification of a straight ranking procedure called *paired comparisons* has been introduced to alleviate this problem. Under paired comparisons, evaluators compare only two employees at a time. They carry this out until all two-way comparisons have been made among the employees. Thus, if five employees are to be ranked, 10 paired comparison judgments are required. An employee's final rank in the group is determined by the number of paired comparisons in which he or she was rated first. Even paired comparisons can become unwieldy for the evaluator as the number of employees to be evaluated increases. A ranking of five employees, for example, would require only 10 paired comparisons. A ranking of ten employees, in contrast, would require 45 paired comparisons, and a ranking of twenty employees would require 190 paired comparisons.

A third problem with ranking as an evaluation method is that forcing the supervisors to distribute their evaluations may lead to distortions that are just as bad as

Exhibit 13–7 Traditional Performance Appraisal Form

Non-Supervisory Employee Appraisal

PRIVATE

EMPLOYEE'S NAME: _____ DIVISION: _____

TITLE: _____ DISTRICT: _____

DATE CURRENT TITLE OBTAINED: _____ PRESENT WAGE RATE: _____

SERVICE DATE: _____ FAMILY STATUS: _____

OUTSIDE INTERESTS: _____

Review Carefully and Check One Block as Appropriate

Consider employee's efforts since the last review dated _____ and show by a check (X) any changes in each of the categories

	(A)	(B)	(C)	(D)	(E)	HAS IMPROVED	LITTLE OR NO CHANGE	HAS GONE BACK
1. Safety Performance Consider all facets of safety in connection with his or her present job title, in carrying out company safety policies.	☐ Careless of safety of self and others	☐ Occasionally causes mishaps	☐ Accepts safety as part of job.	☐ Practices good safety habits and is considerate of others.	☐ Exercises great care and foresees hazards to self and fellow employees.	☐	☐	☐
During Past 2 Years No. Disabling Work Injuries ____ No. Medical Treatment Injuries ____ No. Motor Vehicle Accidents ____								
2. Attendance and Punctuality Consider attendance on the job and reporting on time.	☐ Undependable, absent or late without proper notice.	☐ Frequently absent or late.	☐ Some absence with good cause.	☐ Occasionally absent or late. Notifies in advance.	☐ Record is perfect.	☐	☐	☐
During Past Year No. Days Incidental Absence ____ No. Days Benefit Absence ____ No. Times Tardy ____								
3. Quality of Work Considers the completeness, neatness, and acceptability of work done.	☐ Considerably below job requirements.	☐ Has not reached expected level.	☐ Acceptable.	☐ Definitely better than the expected level.	☐ Exceptionally high quality.	☐	☐	☐
4. Quantity of Work Considers amount of work done within a given time compared to expected results.	☐ Considerably below job standards.	☐ Has not reached expected level.	☐ Acceptable	☐ Definitely better than the expected level.	☐ Exceptional productivity.	☐	☐	☐

Factor	(A)	(B)	(C)	(D)	(E)			
5. Sales Effort and Ability Consider the type of work group, the sales instructions given and how results compare with the expected results.	☐ Does not make sales effort. (A)	☐ Tries sales techniques occasionally. (B)	☐ Accepts sales as part of job (C)	☐ Practices good sales techniques on most visits. (D)	☐ Does an outstanding job on sales work. (E)	☐	☐	☐
6. Job Knowledge Consider the completeness of knowledge of job duties.	☐ Has very little knowledge of job duties. (A)	☐ Has fair knowledge of job duties. (B)	☐ Average job knowledge (C)	☐ Knows most all job knowledge well. (D)	☐ Unusually detailed knowledge of job. (E)	☐	☐	☐
7. Cooperation Consider attitude towards work, associates and supervision. Willingness to work with and for others.	☐ Poor team worker. (A)	☐ Fair team worker. (B)	☐ Generally cooperative. Works reasonably well with others. (C)	☐ Good team worker—works and cooperates well. (D)	☐ Excellent team worker—goes out of way to cooperate. (E)	☐	☐	☐
8. Initiative and Application Consider to what extent the employee is a "self starter," also the attention and effort applied to his work.	☐ Wastes time, never looks for work, needs abnormal amount of supervision. (A)	☐ Inclined to take things easy. Requires occasional prodding. (B)	☐ Steady and willing worker. (C)	☐ Energetic, demonstrates initiative. (D)	☐ Exceptionally industrious, resourceful and attentive to all of his or her duties. (E)	☐	☐	☐
9. Dependability Consider the manner in which the employee applies himself or herself to work, and consider other items regarding dependability.	☐ Cannot be relied upon. Has to be closely checked. (A)	☐ Good worker but needs more checking than others on same type of work. (B)	☐ Can be entrusted to do a job with a minimum follow-up. (C)	☐ Applies himself or herself well. Requires only an occasional check. (D)	☐ Justifies utmost confidence. Carries out his or her work in all details. (E)	☐	☐	☐
10. Physical Fitness Consider energy, endurance, physique, and general health in relation to the employee's ability to do work.	☐ Poor health. (A)	☐ Health below normal Flexibility limited. (B)	☐ Good health. Only occasional illness. (C)	☐ Good health and energy. Rarely ill. (D)	☐ Excellent health. Very active, lots of energy and endurance. Never ill. (E)	☐	☐	☐

Exhibit 13–8 Leniency, Central Tendency, and Strictness in Performance Ratings

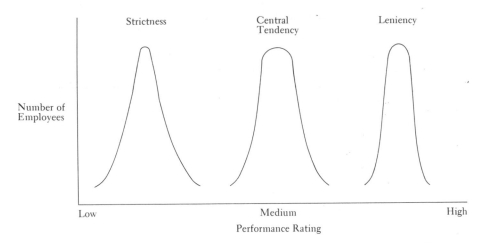

those ranking is supposed to overcome. For example, two employees may actually be so close together in terms of their performance that no reasonable distinction can be made between them. The ranking system would yield an invalid picture of performance differences where no such difference exists.

(2) Behaviorally Based Methods

In recent years, a series of techniques has been developed that show promise of overcoming the problems of reliability and validity. They are called _behaviorally based measures_ of job performance because they focus on detailed evaluation of specific acts or behaviors, rather than on global aspects of performance. By design, they treat job performance as multi-dimensional and use actual instances of behavior as illustrations of effective and ineffective performance on these dimensions. Two most frequently used behaviorally based methods, behaviorally anchored rating scales (BARS) and behaviorally anchored checklists (BACL), have been developed and used in a variety of occupations, including engineering, business management, nursing, police work, and dentistry.[11]

The development of a behaviorally anchored rating scale or checklist depends critically upon the judgment of those employees and supervisors who are closest to the job itself and who will be the ones using the final instrument to make performance evaluations in practice. Development of a behaviorally based measure follows these steps:[12]

1. Expert judges, those closest and most familiar with the job, are interviewed and asked to make two kinds of judgments about the job. First, they are asked to identify the basic task dimensions of the job. Second, they are asked to relate in as much detail as possible specific "critical incidents" illustrating either effective or ineffective behavior with respect to each dimension. The results of these interviews are written up in a series of critical incidents.

2. Several other groups of expert judges are asked to evaluate the critical incidents generated in the initial interviews. They are asked, first, to assign each incident to a particular task dimension. Second, they are asked to rate the behavior in the incident in terms of how effective or ineffective it is in accomplishing the task dimension.

3. Based upon the judgments made in the second step, items (critical incidents) are retained only if there is substantial agreement among the judges as to the dimension of the job to which they refer and its effectiveness in terms of success on that dimension. Items for which there is disagreement on dimension assignment or effectiveness are thrown out.

The result of a job analysis carried out according to these three steps is a pool of very specific items describing effective and ineffective behavior in the language of those closest to the job and those who will actually be making performance evaluations on scales or checklists that use these items. Exhibit 13–9 presents a facsimile of a behaviorally anchored rating scale designed to measure one of nine managerial dimensions of the dentist's job in a health care team, "Responding to team members' needs for assistance." Note that the evaluator does not have to rely on general adjectives such as "extremely effective" in evaluating a dentist's performance on this dimension. Instead, the evaluator can concentrate on specific job behaviors on the right-hand side of the scale in deciding how effective the dentist was.

Although there are still some doubts concerning how much more effective behaviorally based methods are than traditional methods, researchers are impressed, by and large, with the promise such methods hold for improving performance evaluation.[13] A major reference on managerial performance evaluation has summarized the advantages of behaviorally based measures over traditional methods as follows:

> Such scales incorporate all the important bench marks of an effectiveness measure . . . for example, (1) they are derived from experienced observers' reports of actual behavioral episodes regarded as illustrative of . . . actions instrumental to continued organizational functioning; (2) they sample behavior over the long term, as opposed to short-range judgments or impressions; (3) they specify with precision the myriad information-processing activities making up the multiple facets of effective . . . behavior; (4) they imply many possible configurations or patterns of effective . . . [behavior] . . . rather than just one presumed best mode; (5) they force attention on what the [employee] himself does on the job, thereby guarding against defining his level of success in terms of other causal agents; and (6) they take account of [an employee's] membership in several organizational units and of his potential impact on their continued functioning.[14]

Assessment Centers

The traditional methods of performance appraisal as well as behaviorally based methods just discussed make use of a single technology and source of information regarding the performance effectiveness of an employee. When a supervisor, for example, uses a graphic rating scale to evaluate an employee's performance, the organization is using an extremely narrow and restricted form of information. In many cases, jobs are too complex to be reduced to a single index number. In these

Exhibit 13–9 Behaviorally Anchored Performance Rating Scale

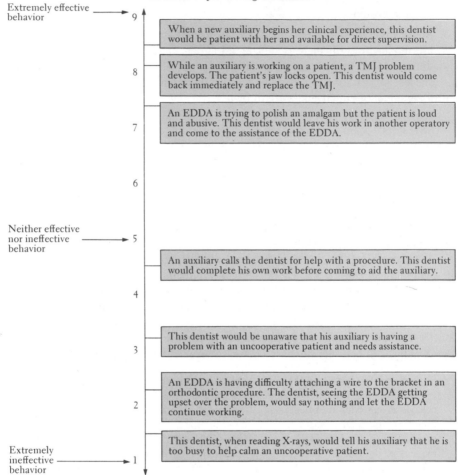

Responds to team members needs for
assistance in performing their tasks.

Extremely effective behavior ⟶ 9

When a new auxiliary begins her clinical experience, this dentist would be patient with her and available for direct supervision.

8

While an auxiliary is working on a patient, a TMJ problem develops. The patient's jaw locks open. This dentist would come back immediately and replace the TMJ.

7

An EDDA is trying to polish an amalgam but the patient is loud and abusive. This dentist would leave his work in another operatory and come to the assistance of the EDDA.

6

Neither effective nor ineffective behavior ⟶ 5

An auxiliary calls the dentist for help with a procedure. This dentist would complete his own work before coming to aid the auxiliary.

4

3

This dentist would be unaware that his auxiliary is having a problem with an uncooperative patient and needs assistance.

2

An EDDA is having difficulty attaching a wire to the bracket in an orthodontic procedure. The dentist, seeing the EDDA getting upset over the problem, would say nothing and let the EDDA continue working.

Extremely ineffective behavior ⟶ 1

This dentist, when reading X-rays, would tell his auxiliary that he is too busy to help calm an uncooperative patient.

cases, the organization must seek multiple sources of information on job performance to adequately represent the employee's full range of performance and potential for being promoted to jobs of increasing importance in the organization.

A number of companies have recognized this problem in the evaluation of upper-level managers and executives, and professionals and have instituted a multi-faceted approach to performance evaluation known as the *assessment center*.[15] Assessment centers have been designed primarily as a device for identifying those in the organization who show potential for promotion to higher levels within the organization (although some firms in recent years have adapted the technique for selecting executives from outside the organization).[16]

The assessment-center method is uniquely designed to assess skills and aptitudes not amenable to simple, unidimensional paper-and-pencil measures. Most frequently, the following kinds of executive skills are assessed in the technique:

Leadership	Resistance to stress
Organizing and planning	Use of delegation
Decision making	Behavior flexibility
Oral and written communication quality	Human relations competence
	Originality
Initiative	Controlling
Energy	Coordinating
Analytical ability	Self-direction

The key to the assessment-center approach is that the employee is assessed using a wide variety of techniques—some, simple paper-and-pencil tests; others, very complex simulations. A typical assessment center might involve a combination of the following assessment methods:

In-Basket Exercise. Typically, the candidate is presented with a full basket of items to be attended to, including memos, phone messages, and so on. The candidate must dispose of these items. In assessing the performance, evaluators look for how the candidate established priorities, separated important from unimportant matters, delegated where appropriate, and set up control mechanisms.

Leaderless Group Discussion. Participants in the discussion are presented with a problem or topic and asked to reach a decision in some limited time. Observers record the social-interaction process, looking for such indicators as (1) who ends up leading the discussion; (2) who asks most questions; (3) to whom are most of the questions directed; (4) who facilitates the work; and similar executive activities.

Individual Presentations. Typically, subjects are given ten to fifteen minutes to prepare a five to ten minute oral presentation to a group. Assessors look for communication skills, poise, ability to cope with stress, and ability to impress others with one's position on a topic or issue.

Psychological Tests. All kinds of psychological tests have been employed to supplement the observational techniques described above. These include personality assessments, tests of specific knowledge, tests of general and specific intelligence, vocational interests, values, and clinical appraisals.

Interviews. Most assessment centers also include interviews. Their content may include questions about values, attitudes, interests, background, and a variety of information.

Other Assessments. Beyond the general techniques outlined above, many firms have adapted specific techniques to their own uses. J.C. Penney Company, for example, uses an "irate customer phone call," in which the subject must use tact and courtesy in handling a customer's unreasonable demands.[17]

Assessment centers have also been employed extensively by companies other than J.C. Penney, such as, AT&T (where the idea was originally developed in its present form), I.B.M., SOHIO, and a variety of public-sector organizations. One of the authors participated in the adaptation of the technique in the selection of a police chief for a major city.

Very little research has been carried out to evaluate the success of assessment centers. The method's very broad-band approach to measurement opens it up to significant problems of unreliability. Most reviews of the technique conclude that it has great potential for clinically identifying skills, capacities, and attitudes that are not amenable to more narrow and accurate measurement techniques. These reviews caution, however, that care must be taken to systematize the way in which interpretations are drawn from assessment-center information.[18] One study, for example, reports that assessment-center predictions were more accurate when the information was standardized and organized mechanically, rather than in nonstandard, clinical fashion.[19]

A final concern in assuring the reliable and valid use of any performance evaluation method is for the organization to assure itself, empirically, that measures of employee performance do, in fact, predict group and organizational outcomes. Reference to the bottom section of exhibit 13–6 indicates a series of arrows linking immediate criterion measures with intermediate and ultimate criterion measures. These arrows indicate observed relationships between these levels of criterion measures. In other words, management should assure itself through empirical research that first-level measures of performance, such as behaviorally anchored ratings, in fact predict and are associated with measures of group effectiveness, such as productivity.

(4) Administering Performance Appraisals: Matters of Procedure

Three critical administrative questions are implicit in exhibit 13–1 and must be resolved before performance review can be successful in an organization:[20]

1. Who should make the appraisal of an employee's performance?
2. How often should the appraisal be made?
3. How should feedback be handled?

Ill-conceived resolutions to these three questions are probably at the heart of most failures in performance appraisal.

Who Administers the Appraisal?

There are at least five possible sources of performance appraisal: (1) supervisors; (2) peers; (3) the employees to be appraised (self-appraisal); (4) subordinates of the person to be appraised; and (5) people outside the immediate organization, such as clients. In some cases, the appraisal may include a combination. Which of these sources is best depends upon (1) the purpose of the evaluation; (2) the kind of criteria being used in the appraisal; and (3) the nature of the employee being evaluated. Several cases should illustrate the propriety of several completely different sources of appraisal information.

The first case involves a skilled employee operating a lathe in a machine shop. The purpose of the appraisal is purely evaluative—to determine the size of the employee's merit increase for the next year. In this situation, most organizations use the immediate supervisor as the primary source of information. He or she is probably most familiar with the quality of the employee's work and is in the best position to make consistent evaluative judgments about the relative quality of several individual employees' performances.

Compare this case to one in which the major purpose of the appraisal is developmental rather than evaluative. For example, the organization uses the appraisal to help an employee pinpoint training and development deficiencies and to choose courses of action to remedy them. Such actions might involve taking off-the-job training in various job-related skills. In such instances, organizations often use both superior and self-evaluations. A typical performance review session will involve the superior and the person to be appraised in a mutual discussion of the individual's previous performance. The focus is not on relative comparisons but rather on the specific needs of the individual employee.

Still different is a third case involving a highly skilled professional, such as a research scientist working for a highly technical research and development company, such as Bell Laboratories, the Batelle Research Institute, the Brookings Institution, or the Rand Corporation. In these situations, it is quite common for a superior not to be familiar enough with an employee's work to make an adequate judgment. Therefore, the organization usually depends upon self-appraisal and peer appraisal for purposes of pay determination and promotions. Research on self-appraisal and peer appraisal indicates that these two methods work best under conditions of high interpersonal trust and high visibility among peers and when development rather than pure evaluation is the primary concern of the appraisal.[21]

A fourth case illustrates a problem that develops when neither management nor peers are in a position to adequately determine a person's performance effectiveness. Consider three situations: (1) a university professor's teaching effectiveness; (2) a clinical physician's effectiveness; and (3) a supervisor's effectiveness in leading a group of subordinates. In the first two instances, the judgments of people who are not even employees of the organization are required. In the third instance, the judgments of people who are not part of management are required.

The judgments of such outsiders are required when evaluating the long-run impacts of an employee's performance. These are the only people who can be expected to provide meaningful information with respect to such performance criteria. In determining a teacher's effectiveness, for example, only the students are likely to be able to accurately make such judgments. Similarly, a physician's patients may be the only source of accurate information with respect to the doctor's counseling effectiveness. This is not to say that such judgments are not without problems. It often happens that clients are impressed by irrelevant dimensions or aspects of a professional's behavior. Thus, students may be unduly impressed in the short run by a particularly entertaining professor and may not be aware of how little knowledge the professor has actually imparted until five or more years after the course. A patient may be unduly impressed with a physician's bedside manner, ignoring the fact that he or she is incompetently missing or confusing critical symptoms in the diagnosis of a disease. The important point is that the organization must critically determine the *best* source of information for each aspect of an employee's performance and use the combination of these sources in the evaluation process.

How Often Should the Appraisal Be Made?

Two issues or choices are involved in deciding how often to make appraisals. First, an organization may decide upon a standard review cycle, such as every twelve months, or, the organization might choose to evaluate an employee at "natural points," such as the completion of a project. Second, an organization may require that superiors initiate the appraisal or have a system in which employees request the appraisal.

The appropriateness of these alternatives depends upon the nature of the work being carried out and the qualities of the employees involved, as illustrated in the following two cases. If tasks are relatively simple and standard, and/or if subordinates have minimal levels of job-related skills, standard review cycles initiated by the superior are perhaps best. If subordinates are highly skilled and specialized, and if tasks do not follow standard cycles, it probably would be better if subordinates requested the review.[22]

How Should Feedback Be Handled?

Two closely related questions are tied together in the issue of how feedback should be handled. (1) Who shall receive the performance appraisal results? (2) What form will the feedback results take? With respect to the first question, for obvious reasons including ethical considerations, the immediate parties to the evaluation (superior and subordinate) should have access to appraisal results. The supervisor needs information for decisions made regarding the subordinate. In addition to ethical demands on appraisal feedback, the person appraised should have rapid and clear feedback in order to correct any performance deficiencies. The principles of reinforcement presented in chapter 5 clearly indicate that such feedback is necessary for instrumental conditioning to have an impact on improving an employee's performance.

In addition to immediate parties, top management and subordinates of the person evaluated may also have access to appraisal results in some circumstances.

Cummings and Schwab suggest that where review results are particularly positive and substantial incremental rewards are directly linked to performance, knowledge of results shared with the employee's subordinates may serve to motivate them to higher levels of performance. In this sense, the employee's meritorious performance serves as a role model for others in the organization.[23] If these two conditions do not exist, however, they recommend a policy of secrecy. How high performance appraisal results should go in the organization is primarily a matter of "need to know." An argument can be made for storing performance review results in a readily retrievable form to be used for reference when personnel decisions, such as compensation, promotion, transfer, and training, are made. Such a policy presumes, however, that the information has been generated and stored in a reliable and valid fashion.

Cummings and Schwab also prescribe that feedback should emphasize positive or constructive information.[24] They warn against the dysfunctional aspects of negative feedback. They report evidence suggesting that if employees feel threatened by the process, they react to the process negatively. Apparently, it is very easy for a subordinate to fall into the stereotype of expecting to hear only what is wrong with him or her and for the superior to fall into the stereotype of trying to "sell" the appraisal system to a reluctant subordinate. When the feedback is based upon a review of objectives already set and agreed upon by subordinate and supervisor (as is the case in management by objectives), it is possible to break these stereotypes and use appraisal results constructively.

Applications and Implications for the Manager

Performance Evaluation

1. The question of performance appraisal or evaluation is essential to a discussion of organizational behavior because it is a major source of information employed in control decisions. In this sense, performance appraisal serves an auditing function to the organization regarding the performance of individuals, groups, and entire divisions.

2. Because performance evaluation serves so many different functions, there are no universally acceptable methods of appraisal. Thus, it is extremely important for managers to establish the purpose of the appraisal system before selecting a given method or technique.

3. Managers should be aware of the many sources of error in appraisal that can reduce the reliability and validity of evaluations. Major sources of such errors include (a) the person making the evaluation; (b) the person being appraised; and (c) the circumstances under which the evaluation is being made.

4. In order to insure reliability and validity, an appraisal system must deal appropriately with three kinds of dimensions. First, the appraisal must take into account the correct aspects of the job. Appraisals can be deficient (when they do not include all relevant aspects of the job) or they can be contaminated (when they include irrelevant aspects of the job). Second, the level of abstraction or analysis is critical in performance appraisal. In each case, managers must determine whether they are dealing with individual behavior, group outcomes, or organizational outcomes in their evaluations. In addition, criteria at each level must be established and evaluated in terms of criteria at the next highest level of analysis in the organization. Third, the manager must also consider the importance of time in choosing relevant performance review criteria.

5. In considering alternative appraisal techniques, the manager faces a choice between traditional methods of global rating and ranking, and more recently developed behaviorally based techniques. The evidence so far suggests that the latter are superior in terms of minimizing such errors as halo, unreliability, central tendency, leniency, and strictness. In addition, it is critical that methods of appraisal be validated in each setting in which they are used because there are no guarantees that a form or technique used in one setting will be accurate in another.

6. Assessment centers are techniques sometimes used for combining several sources of information regarding executive skills and capacities not amenable to simple paper and pencil measures.

7. Finally, we said that managers must resolve a number of procedural matters in administering performance appraisals. Three kinds of issues arise in this regard. First, who makes the appraisal must be determined. Under different circumstances, superiors, subordinates, peers, and outsiders may be the best source of appraisals. Second, the timing of appraisals is critical. Finally, rules must be established and followed regarding the provision of feedback of performance review results.

Review of Theories, Research, and Applications

1. List and explain three reasons why the process of performance appraisal is as difficult and complex as it is. Give a practical illustration for each of your reasons.

2. Identify and describe the purposes served by performance appraisal.

3. Is it possible to develop a universally applicable system for performance appraisal? If so, how would it accomplish all the purposes of performance appraisal?

4. What has control got to do with performance appraisal? What role does performance appraisal play in the control process?

5. Describe the concept of reliability. How does it affect performance appraisal?

6. Describe the concept of validity. How does it influence the performance appraisal process?

7. Discuss how the person carrying out a performance evaluation could be a source of error in the process. What kinds of errors should a person doing a performance evaluation guard against?

8. Of what importance is time in making a performance evaluation? How does time influence the process? Use practical illustrations in your answer.

9. Of what importance is level of analysis in making performance evaluations? Use practical illustrations in your answer.

10. What are the differences between traditional methods of performance appraisal, behaviorally based methods, and assessment centers?

Notes

1. Griggs v. Duke Power, U.S. Sup. Ct. (1971), 3 FEP Cases 175. W. Holley and H. Field, "Equal Employment Opportunity and Its Implications for Personnel Practices," *Labor Law Journal,* 1976, pp. 278–86.

2. N. Fredric Crandall and Jacquelyn Vilet, "Problem Areas For Management With Performance Appraisal" (Southern Methodist University, 1979).

3. Marvin D. Dunnette, *Personnel Selection and Placement* (Belmont, Calif.: Wadsworth, 1966), p. 69.

4. See, for example, Marvin D. Dunnette, *Personnel Selection;* Ernest J. McCormick, Robert P. Mecham, and R. Paul Jeanaret, "A Study of Job Characteristics And Job Dimensions Based on The Position Analysis Questionnaire," *Journal of Applied Psychology Monograph,* 1972, pp. 347–68; Edwin L. Thorndike, *Personnel Selection* (New York: Wiley, 1949); Lee J. Cronbach and Goldine Gleser, *Psychological Tests and Personnel Decisions* (Urbana: University of Illinois, 1965); and Frank Landy and Dan Trumbo, *Psychology of Work Behavior* (Glenview, Ill.: Scott, Foresman, 1976).

5. Dunnette, *Personnel Selection.*

6. Marc J. Wallace, Jr., et al., "Behaviorally Based Measures For Assessing the Non-Clinical Effectiveness of Dentists in Health Care Teams," *Journal of Dental Research,* 1975, 1056–63; Marc J. Wallace, Jr., Philip K. Berger, and John Harris, "Behaviorally Based Measures For Assessing the Effectiveness of Expanded Function Dental Auxiliaries in Health Care Team," *Journal of Dental Research,* forthcoming.

7. Thorndike, *Personnel Selection;* Cronbach and Gleser, Psychological Tests.

8. See, for example, Milton Blum and R. Naylor, *Industrial Psychology* (New York: Harper & Row, 1968); and Landy and Trumbo, *Psychology of Work Behavior.*

9. See, for example, Larry Cummings and Donald P. Schwab, *Performance In Organizations* (Glenview, Ill.: Scott, Foresman, 1973); and John P. Campbell, et al., *Managerial Behavior, Performance, and Effectiveness* (New York: McGraw-Hill, 1970).

10. Cummings and Schwab, *Performance in Organizations,* p. 81.

11. Wallace et al., "Behaviorally Based Measures for Assessing the Non-Clinical Effectiveness;" and Wallace, Berger, and Harris, "Behaviorally Based Measures for Assessing the Effectiveness of Expanded Function."

12. B. A. Barron, J. Hirsch, and M. Glucksman, "The Construction and Calibration of Behavioral Rating Scales," *Behavioral Science,* 1970, pp. 220–26; W. C. Borman and Marvin D. Dunnette, "Behavior-Based Versus Trait-Oriented Performance Ratings: An Empirical Study," *Journal of Applied Psychology,* 1975, pp. 561–65; John P. Campbell, R. D. Arvey, and L. V. Hellervik, "The Development and Evaluation of Behaviorally Based Rating Scales," *Journal of Applied Psychology,* 1971, pp. 3–8; O. Harari and Sheldon Zedeck, "Development of Behaviorally Anchored Scales for Evaluation of Faculty Teaching," *Journal of Applied Psychology,* 1973, pp. 261–65; Wallace et al., "Behaviorally Based Measures," forthcoming; and J. Flanagan, "The Critical Incident Technique," *Psychological Bulletin,* 1954, pp. 327–58; Patricia Smith and Lorne M. Kendall, "Retranslations of Expectations: An Approach to the Construction of Unambiguous Anchors for Rating Scales," *Journal of Applied Psychology,* 1963, pp. 149–55.

13. See, for example, Campbell et al., *Managerial Behavior;* W. C. Borman and Marvin Dunnette, "Behavior-Based Versus Trait-Oriented Performance Ratings: An Empirical Study," *Journal of Applied Psychology,* 1975, pp. 561–65; L. R. James, "Criterion Models and Construct Validity for Criteria," *Psychological Bulletin,* 1973, pp. 75–83; Donald P. Schwab, H. G. Heneman III, and T. DeCotiis, "Behaviorally Anchored Rating Scales: A Review of the Literature," *Personnel Psychology,* 1975, pp. 549–62.

14. Campbell et al., *Managerial Behavior,* pp. 123–83.

15. D. W. Bray and D. L. Grant, "The Assessment Center in the Measurement of Potential for Business Management," *Psychological Monographs,* 1966; W. C. Byham, "Assessment Centers For Spotting Future Managers," *Harvard Business Review,* 1970, pp. 150–70.

16. A. Howard, "An Assessment of

Assessment Centers," *Academy of Management Journal,* 1974, pp. 115–34.

17. Ibid.

18. Ibid.

19. H. B. Wollowick and W. J. McNamara, "Relationship Of The Components of an Assessment Center to Management Success," *Journal of Applied Psychology,* 1969, pp. 348–52.

20. Much of the material on these issues is drawn from Cummings and Schwab, *Performance In Organizations.*

21. Ibid.

22. Ibid.

23. Ibid.

24. Ibid.

Additional References

ANDERSON, H. E.; ROUSH, S. L.; and McCLARY, J. E. "Relationships among Ratings Production Efficiency and the General Aptitude Test Battery Scales in an Industrial Setting." *Journal of Applied Psychology,* 1973, pp. 77–82.

BAIRD, L. S. "Self and Superior Ratings of Performance: As Related To Self-Esteem and Satisfaction With Supervision." *Academy of Management Journal,* 1977, pp. 291–300.

BERNADIN, H. JOHN. "Behavioral Expectation Scales versus Summated Scales: A Fairer Comparison." *Journal of Applied Psychology,* 1977, pp. 422–27.

BLANZ, F., and GHISELLI, E. "The Mixed Standard Scale: A New Rating System." *Personnel Psychology,* 1974, pp. 197–201.

BURMAN, WALTER C. "Exploring Upper Limits of Reliability and Validity in Job Performance Ratings." *Journal of Applied Psychology,* 1978, pp. 135–44.

CASCIO, WAYNE F., and VALENZI, ENZO R. "Behaviorally Anchored Rating Scales: Effects of Education and Job Experience of Raters and Ratees." *Journal of Applied Psychology,* 1977, pp. 278–82.

CUMMINGS, L. L. "A Field Experimental Study of the Effects of Two Performance Appraisal Systems." *Personnel Psychology,* 1973, pp. 489–502.

DUNNETTE, M. D. "Managerial Effectiveness: Its Definition and Measurement." *Studies in Personnel Psychology,* 1970, pp. 6–20.

FEILD, H., and HOLLEY, W. "Subordinates' Characteristics, Supervisors' Ratings and Decisions To Discuss Appraisal Results." *Academy of Management Journal,* 1977, pp. 315–20.

GELLER, M. "Subordinate Participation and Reactions in the Appraisal Interview." *Journal of Applied Psychology,* 1975, pp. 544–49.

GOODALE, J. G., and BURKE, R. "Behaviorally Based Rating Scales Need Not Be Job Specific." *Journal of Applied Psychology,* 1975, pp. 386–88.

GORDON, M. "The Effect of Correctness of the Behavior Observed on the Accuracy of the Ratings." *Organizational Behavior and Human Performance,* 1970, pp. 366–77.

GREY, RONALD J., and KIPNIS, DAVID. "Untangling the Performance Appraisal Dilemma: The Influence of Perceived Organizational Context on Evaluating Processes." *Journal of Applied Psychology,* 1976, pp. 329–35.

GUION, R. M. *Personnel Testing.* New York: McGraw-Hill, 1965.

HINRICHS, JOHN R. "An Eight-Year Follow-up of a Management Assessment Center." *Journal of Applied Psychology,* 1978, pp. 596–601.

HOLZBACH, ROBERT L. "Rater Bias in Performance Ratings." *Journal of Applied Psychology,* 1978, pp. 579–88.

HUMPHREYS, L. G. "Statistical Definitions of Test Validity for Minority Groups." *Journal of Applied Psychology,* 1973, pp. 1–4.

KAVANAGH, M. J.; MacKINNEY, A. C.; and WOLINS, L. "Issues in Managerial Performance: Multitrait-Multimethod Analyses of Ratings." *Psychological Bulletin,* 1971, pp. 34–49.

KEAVENY, T., and McGANN, A. "A Comparison of Behavioral Expectation Scales and Graphic Rating Scales." *Journal of Applied Psychology,* 1975, pp. 695–703.

KEELEY, M. "Subjective Performance Evaluation and Person-Role Conflict Under Conditions of Uncertainty." *Academy of Management Journal,* 1977, pp. 301–14.

KINDALL, A. F., and GATZA, J. "A Positive Program for Performance Appraisal." *Harvard Business Review,* 1963, pp. 153–57.

KRAUT, A. "A Hard Look at Management Assessment Centers." *Personnel Journal,* 1975.

KRAUT, A. and SCOTT, G. "The Validity of an Operational Management Assessment Program." *Journal of Applied Psychology,* 1972, pp. 124–29.

LAWLER, E. E., III, "Control Systems in Organizations." In *Handbook of Industrial and Organizational Psychology,* edited by M. D. Dunnette. Chicago: Rand McNally, 1976.

LOPEZ, F. *Evaluating Employee Performance.* 1968. Washington D.C.: International Personnel Management.

McGREGOR, D. "An Uneasy Look at Performance Appraisal," *Harvard Business Review,* 1957, pp. 89–94.

MEYER, J.; KAY, E.; and FRENCH, J. R. P., JR.

"Split Roles in Performance Appraisal." *Harvard Business Review,* 1965, pp. 123–29.

SCHMITT, NEAL, and HILL, THOMAS E. "Sex and Race Composition of Assessment Center Groups as a Determinant of Peer and Assessor Ratings." *Journal of Applied Psychology,* 1977, pp. 261–64.

SCHNEIER, and BEATTY, R. "The Influence of Role Prescriptions on the Performance Appraisal Process." *Academy of Management Journal,* 1978, pp. 129–34.

SCHWAB, DONALD P., and HENEMAN, HERBERT G. "Age Stereotyping in Performance Appraisal." *Journal of Applied Psychology,* 1978, pp. 573–78.

WHISLER, T. L., and HARPER, S. F., eds. *Performance Appraisal: Research and Practice.* New York: Holt, Rinehart & Winston, 1965.

ZEDECK, S., and BAKER, H. "Nursing Performance as Measured by Behavioral Expectation Scales: A Multitrait-Multirater Analysis." *Organizational Behavior and Human Performance,* 1972, pp. 457–66.

A Case of Alleged Sex Discrimination
in Performance Appraisal

Jayne Burroughs and John Watson are both employed as technicians in the pathology lab of Central Catholic Hospital, a major medical center in the core of a major city. They both hold specialist degrees and are licensed pathologist's assistants. Both have been employed in their jobs for five years.

Last month, Dr. Clarence Cutter, the chief pathologist and supervisor of the lab, decided to reorganize his operation. He decided that supervising the work of both assistants was taking up too much of his time. He reasoned that if he were to promote one of them to a mid-level supervisory position, he could reduce the time he spent in direct supervision. Dr. Cutter presented his argument to Fred Wunderlich, the hospital's director of personnel. Wunderlich agreed and added that Dr. Cutter could probably use even more help in the lab. He suggested that either Burroughs or Watson be promoted to a new job titled Administrative Assistant to the Pathologist and that a new person be hired to fill the vacated lab technician position. Thus, a new structure was developed for the department in which two lab technicians reported to an administrative assistant, who in turn reported to the chief pathologist.

The next task for Dr. Cutter was to decide which of his lab technicians to promote to the new position. In order to make the decision, he pulled the latest six-month performance evaluations he had made on Burroughs and Watson. Exhibit

Exhibit 13–10 Six-Month Performance Reviews for Burroughs and Watson

Employee: _Jayne Burroughs_   Supervisor: _Dr. Cutter_
Department: _Pathology_   Date: _11-28-76_

Work Quantity		Work Quality		Cooperation	
Far below average	☐	Far below average	☐	Far below average	☐
Below average	☒	Below average	☐	Below average	☒
Average	☐	Average	☒	Average	☐
Above average	☐	Above average	☐	Above average	☐
Far above average	☐	Far above average	☐	Far above average	☐

Employee: _John Watson_   Supervisor: _Dr. Cutter_
Department: _Pathology_   Date: _12-24-76_

Work Quantity		Work Quality		Cooperation	
Far below average	☐	Far below average	☐	Far below average	☐
Below average	☐	Below average	☐	Below average	☐
Average	☒	Average	☐	Average	☐
Above average	☐	Above average	☒	Above average	☐
Far above average	☐	Far above average	☐	Far above average	☒

13–10 reproduces their performance review results. On the basis of the performance reviews, he promoted John Watson to the administrative assistant position.

Upon learning of Watson's promotion, Burroughs went to Dr. Cutter and demanded that he justify why he promoted Watson instead of her. He told her that he was not obligated to present a justification to her; that he was perfectly within his rights as chief pathologist to make such a decision and that she should rest assured that his decision was made on grounds that were fair and equitable to her and Watson.

This explanation did not satisfy Burroughs, and she filed a formal complaint alleging sex discrimination in a promotion decision, both with Mr. Wunderlich, the personnel manager, and Robyn Payson, the Hospital's Equal Employment Opportunity officer.

A hearing was scheduled by Wunderlich to resolve the issues. Wunderlich and Payson constituted the review board at the hearing, and Cutter and Burroughs were invited to present their cases. In the hearing, Burroughs opened the case by presenting her formal complaint: Both she and Watson have identical credentials for their jobs and have equal tenure on the job (five years). In addition, it is her belief that she and Watson have performed equivalently during this period of time. Therefore, according to her charge, the only reason Dr. Cutter could possibly have had for promoting Watson over her would be her sex. She noted that a decision of that nature is in clear violation of Title VII of the Civil Rights Act of 1964, which reads in part:

> It shall be an unlawful employment practice for an employer to fail or refuse to hire or to discharge, or otherwise to discriminate against any individual with respect to his compensation terms, conditions, or privileges of employment because of such individual's race, color, religion, sex, or national origin. (Title VII, Sec. 703, Par. a-1 of the Civil Rights Act of 1964, as amended by P.L. 92-261, effective March 24, 1972.)

Dr. Cutter countered by justifying his decision on the basis of actual performance review data. He argued that sex had nothing whatsoever to do with his decision. Rather, he presented to the board the latest six-month performance evaluations, which showed Watson to be performing better than Burroughs on three performance dimensions: (1) work quantity; (2) work quality; and (3) cooperation (see exhibit 13–10).

The performance results served to anger Burroughs further. She requested that the hearing be adjourned and reconvened after she had had a chance to review the results and prepare her case further. Wunderlich and Payson agreed and rescheduled a second hearing two weeks later.

At the second hearing, Burroughs presented the following list of grievances with regard to the promotion decision and the information upon which it was based:

1. The decision is still in violation of Title VII of the Civil Rights Act because the way the performance evaluation was carried out served to discriminate against her on the basis of sex. Her reasoning on this point included the following charges:

(a) Dr. Cutter is biased against females, and this factor caused him to rate males in general above females in general.

(b) Dr. Cutter and Mr. Watson are in an all-male poker group that meets on Friday nights, and she has systematically been excluded. Thus, ties of friendship have developed along sex lines, which created a conflict of interest for Dr. Cutter.

(c) Dr. Cutter has said to her and to others on several occasions that he doubts females can carry out managerial tasks because they must constantly be concerned with duties at home and they get pregnant.

2. The measuring device itself failed to include a number of activities she carries out that are critical to the functioning of the lab. For example, while Dr. Cutter and Watson are talking over coffee, she frequently is cleaning up the lab. She says that, although Mr. Watson's work is good, he tends to concentrate on all visible work outcomes, and leaves much of the "invisible work," like cleaning up, to her.

3. The timing of the performance review was bad. She charged that it was unfair to her to base the decision on only one six-month evaluation. Dr. Cutter has a total of ten performance reviews for each of them. Why didn't he base his decision on all ten, rather than on just the latest review?

4. Also with respect to timing, Ms. Burroughs pointed out that her review had been made a month earlier than Mr. Watson's. She charged that December 24 was Christmas Eve and the day of the lab's office party. She charged that the spirits of the occasion (liquid and other) tended to shade Dr. Cutter's judgment in favor of Watson.

Case Primer Questions

Put yourself in the position of Mr. Wunderlich and Ms. Payson. Decide whether there is any justification to Ms. Burroughs' charges, or if Dr. Cutter is justified in his decision. In making your decision, address yourself to the following questions:

1. Are issues of reliability involved in this case? If so, what sources of error must you consider in making a judgment?

2. Are issues of validity involved in this case? If so, what sources of error must you consider in making a judgment?

3. Is the measuring instrument itself at issue in this case?

4. If your answer to question 3 is yes, what kinds of recommendations would you make for changing the instrument?

5. Are problems of administration an issue in this case?

6. If your answer to question 5 is yes, what changes in administration would you recommend?

7. Do you think the problem would have arisen had Dr. Cutter adopted and followed a policy of open feedback on performance review results?

Experiential Exercise

The Performance Dilemma

Purpose

1. To study the difficult choices a manager faces in using performance-related information in making necessary decisions.

2. To consider the performance criteria used within one organization.

3. To consider how multiple criteria are influenced by less than objective factors.

Required understanding

The reader should understand the issues of multiple criteria versus single criterion and subjectivity versus objectivity in performance considerations.

How to set up the exercise

Set up groups of four to eight students for the forty-five to sixty minute exercise. The groups should be separated from each other and asked to converse only with their group members.

Before forming the groups, each person should complete the exercise alone and then join the group and reach a decision within the time alotted. Each person should read the following:

The Naylor Product Corporation is a medium-size manufacturing company located in the suburbs of Tampa, Florida. The company is nonunionized and has attempted during the past two years to incorporate an objective performance review system that has been designed purposefully to provide feedback to employees. The system is designed to be objective, time oriented, and representative.

The loss of a contract bid to a competitor has forced the Naylor management to consider laying off one, two, or three of the poorest performers next week in the generator-contracting unit. This unit produces generators that are sold to electronics firms. The layoff may only be temporary, but management wants to be sure that they have been fair in presenting an objectively based decision to the employees.

The eight people in the unit that is to be cut back to five are the following:

Max Rogers: white; age forty-two; married; three children; two years of high school; fourteen years with the company.

Tom Banks: black; age thirty-seven; widower; two children; high-school graduate; eight years with the company.

Marsha Beloit: white; age twenty-four; single; high-school graduate; two years with the company.

Ray Lasifier: white; age fifty; single; finished junior college while working; fifteen years with the company.

Nina Palmond: white; age thirty-six; married; four children; high-school graduate; three years with the company.

Steve Castro: hispanic; age forty; married; one child; high-school graduate; four years with the company.

John Sailers: white; age thirty-nine; divorced; two children; two years of college; seven years with the company.

Bob Wilks: white; age forty-two; married; no children; one year of college; nine years with the company.

The company has evaluated these generator-unit employees on a number of factors, listed in exhibit 13–11. The ratings shown in exhibit 13–11 have been averaged over the past eighteen months of performance evaluation.

Instructions for the exercise

1. Each person is to rank the employees from 1 (the first to be laid off) to 8 (the last to be laid off). The individual rankings should be given to the instructor on a sheet of paper before the person joins the assigned group.

2. Each group of four to eight people is to reach a ranking consensus. These rankings are to be placed on a sheet of paper with a brief explanation for the rationale used to arrive at the final order.

Exhibit 13–11 Naylor Management Most Recent Performance Review of Generator Employees

				Factors Evaluated by Immediate Supervisor			
Employee	Average Weekly Output[a]	% of Defective Generators[b]	% Absent[c]	Cooperative Attitude[d]	Loyalty to Company	Potential for Advancement	Initiates Personal Development Attitudes
Max Rogers	19.8	4.9	7.3	good	good	fair	no
Tom Banks	21.7	5.3	8.9	poor	fair	fair	no
Marsha Beloit	17.6	.9	1.4	excellent	good	good	yes
Ray Lasifier	20.2	4.7	14.2	excellent	excellent	fair	no
Nina Palmond	20.1	9.6	10.3	poor	fair	poor	no
Steve Castro	19.8	3.4	7.1	good	fair	poor	no
John Sailers	18.1	4.8	6.0	good	good	fair	no
Bob Wilks	22.6	7.0	4.6	fair	fair	good	yes

[a] Higher score designates more quantity of output.
[b] Lower score designates fewer defective generators.
[c] Lower score designates less absenteeism.
[d] The ratings possible are poor, fair, good, excellent.

CHAPTER 14

Rewards in Organizations

Even a casual acquaintance with people in organizations will demonstrate that they choose careers, join organizations, decide to stay or leave employers, and decide to perform at given levels for a wide variety of reasons. A teacher, for example, might argue that he or she enjoys the opportunity to influence the development of children's minds, and likes the status of the job. Social workers, while not liking the low pay associated with the job, might enjoy the opportunity of providing a very tangible service to those who need it most. A truck driver, on the other hand, may not really like anything about the job, except that it pays extremely well and allows him or her to be free of close supervision. Similarly, an assembly-line worker may reason, "Where else can a person with less than an eighth-grade education earn $20,000 a year with job security?" In contrast, a management trainee just out of business school might be very happy with a relatively low starting salary of $13,000 per year, knowing that his or her job has a career potential for very lucrative and powerful positions within the managerial hierarchy of the organization.

Rewards and Individuals

Several important issues about rewards in organizations arise in these illustrations. First, people work at a particular job for a tremendous variety of reasons. Very few employees have a single overriding reason for working where they do, and each differs from others in his or her several reasons. Second, money is not often the only reward a person seeks through employment. Indeed, in some cases money may even be of secondary importance after several other considerations, as in the case of the management trainee. Third, what employees seek as rewards can vary over time with changes in the individual's life situation, interests, and tastes. For example, fathers or mothers with young children may well prefer the majority of their rewards to take the form of current income to pay for mortgage and educational bills. An older employee may prefer a number of deferred compensations as well as nonsalary benefits to ease his or her current tax burden and prepare for an adequate income during retirement.

Finally, management has varying degrees of control over the amount and distribution of rewards, depending upon the nature of the reward. For example, a company may have direct control over the policy by which monetary rewards are set and administered while having little or no control over facets of the job that the employee finds inherently interesting. In an exhaustive series of interviews with employees about their jobs, one investigator discovered the rather disturbing fact that a surprising number of jobs in America are inherently boring.[1]

Personality and Work-Related Needs

An individual's personality influences the needs he or she seeks to satisfy through work. In other words, a major part of personality is the unique profile of needs that are important to an employee.

Like other aspects of personality, a needs profile is relatively permanent but does not appear all at once. Rather, it develops slowly as a child becomes an adult, experiences work for the first time, and pursues a career. Thus, the specific kinds of educational and employment experiences one has leads to the specific work-related needs a person experiences at any point in time.[2]

This phenomenon is illustrated in exhibit 14–1, which depicts the development and elaboration of needs as a person moves from childhood, through formal education, through the early phases of a career, and finally becomes established in a career. Several implications should be drawn from this exhibit. First, the types and relative strength of needs varies over time. Early in life, a person's needs are relatively small in number and general. As people experience increasingly narrow and sophisticated educational environments (moving, perhaps, from high school studies to majors in college to specific professional training), greater numbers of very specific needs are acquired.

Exhibit 14–1 Developing Work-Related Needs

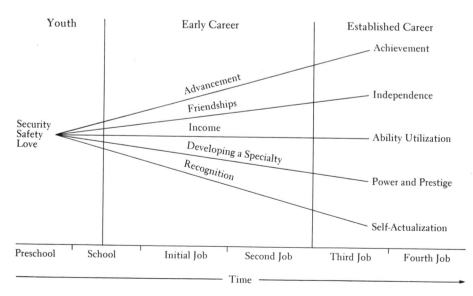

As a person enters the early stages of a career in an organization, he or she is probably concerned with prospects for advancement, developing friendships, earning money, developing valued specialities or skills, and achieving recognition from peers and superiors. Once a person has become well established in a career (perhaps between the ages of forty and fifty-five) a slightly different set of needs are felt. They may include a need for finally achieving long-run career goals, autonomy in one's work, and achieving power and prestige among a wider group of people (often including professional colleagues beyond the immediate organization).[3]

A second important implication of exhibit 14–1 is that needs change throughout a career in organizations primarily through the process of learning. Thus, the kinds of reinforcements or rewards a person experiences in formal education and on various jobs influence the development of subsequent needs. Medical doctors, for example, learn many of the professional needs they seek to satisfy in medical-school training. Similarly, many of the needs for income and status sought by new managers on their first jobs are acquired in business school.

Although behavioral scientists still speculate about specific needs that characterize employees' personalities, the Minnesota Studies in Work Adjustment offer a rather complete profile of work needs that influence level of job performance as well as organizational choice, turnover, and absenteeism.[4] Exhibit 14–2 presents a list of these needs together with short definitions of each. It is important to note in studying the figure that the feeling for each need can vary independently in strength. Thus, an employee's felt need for independence on the job does not influence his or her felt need for compensation.

Exhibit 14–2 Common Work-Related Needs

ABILITY UTILIZATION: The chance to do something that makes use of abilities.
ACHIEVEMENT: The feeling of accomplishment gotten from the job.
ACTIVITY: The chance to keep busy all the time.
ADVANCEMENT: The chances for advancement on this job.
AUTHORITY: The chance to tell other people what to do.
COMPANY POLICIES AND PRACTICES: The way company policies are put into practice.
COMPENSATION: The pay for the amount of work done.
COWORKERS: The way coworkers get along with each other.
CREATIVITY: The chance for an employee to try his or her own methods of doing things.
INDEPENDENCE: The chance to work alone on the job.
MORAL VALUES: The chance to do things that do not go against an individual's conscience.
RECOGNITION: The praise for doing a good job.
RESPONSIBILITY: The freedom to use personal judgment.
SECURITY: The way the job provides for steady employment
SOCIAL SERVICE: The chance to do things for other people.
SOCIAL STATUS: The chance to be "somebody" in the community.
SUPERVISION—HUMAN RELATIONS: The way the boss handles subordinates.
SUPERVISION—TECHNICAL: The competence of the supervisor in making decisions.
VARIETY: The chance to do different things from time to time.
WORKING CONDITIONS: The amount of comfort and safety on the job.

One way behavioral scientists have devised for measuring how important various *rewards* are to employees is to assess how important the fulfillment of various *needs* are to a person. Suppose, for example, a manager designed a series of questions asking how important each of the job characteristics listed in exhibit 14–3 is to an employee. After the employee responded to the questionnaire, an analyst could calculate a score for that person for each outcome (perhaps a 1 to 7 scale, with 1 indicating extremely low and 7 indicating extremely high). Low numbers would indicate the outcome is not very important at all; high numbers would indicate that the outcome is very important to the person. Finally, the analyst could look at the importance attached to the entire set of outcomes by examining a *profile,* that is, a graphical representation of the person's responses to all outcomes. Hypothetical need profiles are displayed in exhibit 14–3 for a physician and an automobile mechanic.

Exhibit 14–3 Hypothetical Need Profiles for Two Kinds of Workers

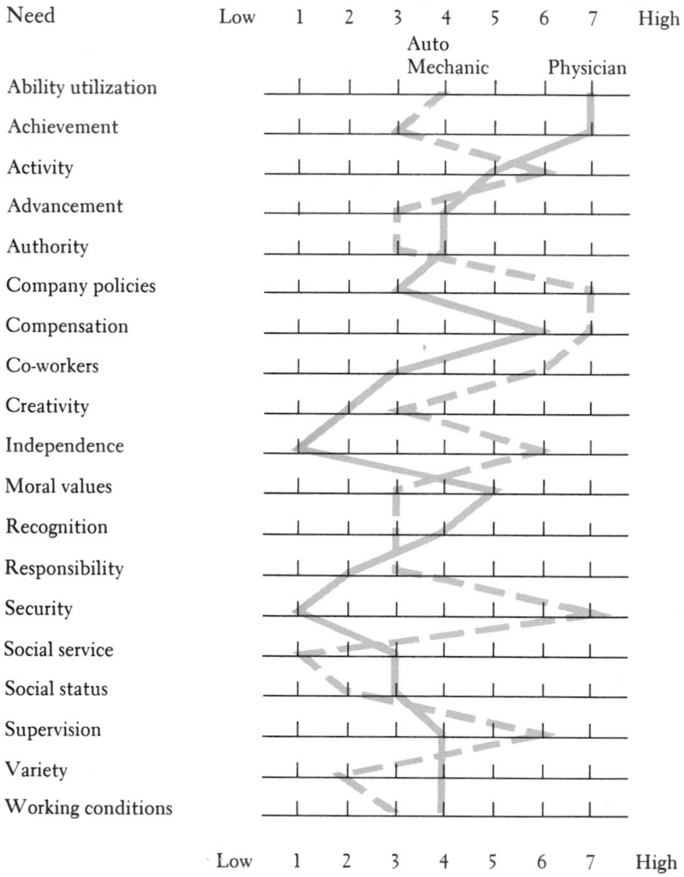

It is important for managers to understand that a variety of rewards offered by an organization are of potential importance in motivating employee behaviors. Very rarely do all employees have a single need profile. Rather, managers must consider the personalities of specific employees. The critical factor in predicting employee behavior and performance is the *match* between an individual's need profile and the mix of rewards offered by the organization.

Influence of Rewards on Behavior and Performance

The belief that rewards will serve to motivate performance, reduce turnover, reduce absenteeism, and attract qualified job applicants presumes that rewards themselves influence employee motivation in predictable ways. In general, we can say that *people will tend to behave in ways that the organization rewards*. Therefore, the anticipation of rewards can operate as a strong incentive motivating a level of behavior and job performance or motivating the choice of an organization as a place to work. In addition, rewards are important to individuals because they serve to fulfill work-related needs.

Placed in the context of the performance model introduced in chapter 2 as well as the integrative motivation model developed in chapter 5, rewards act as reinforcers for a variety of individual behaviors. Rewards serve to satisfy needs (or reduce drives), lead to the learning of new behaviors, and serve to direct a person's choice among behavioral alternatives. According to this model, satisfaction with the job is an individual reaction to the degree to which the rewards on the job have fulfilled work-related needs. Behavior will continue in a given direction, or change direction, or new behaviors will be learned in part on the basis of job satisfaction. If an individual employee, for example, is constantly dissatisfied with pay from an employer, he or she may well be motivated to begin a search for a job that pays better. Under an incentive system that links pay directly with performance, however, the same employee may alter his or her behavior by increasing work output (in order to increase gross income). Hence, an understanding of the rewards available on a job together with a knowledge of how individuals value those rewards is essential to an understanding of work behavior and performance.

Purposes of Rewards

The reward process is a major control or influence mechanism available to organizations. As indicated in the performance model developed in chapter 2 and partially reproduced in exhibit 14–4, the kinds of rewards available through employment and the ways in which rewards are distributed influence the behavior of individual employees.

Organizational rewards influence a variety of behaviors—those that have an internal impact on the organization as well as those that have an external impact on

Exhibit 14-4 **Rewards and Performance**

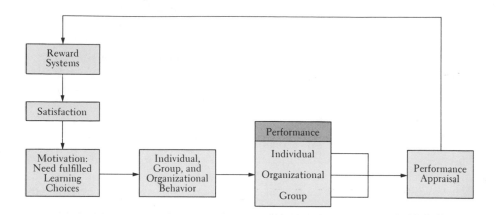

the organization. Specifically, rewards can serve the following internal and external purposes for an organization:

1. Internal—enhancing job performance, reducing absenteeism, and retaining skilled employees.
2. External—attracting a pool of skilled labor. *i.e., wages + salaries, not visible reward*

    The first purpose, that of enhancing job performance, is a major concern of many managers. Numerous organizations have attempted to motivate effective job performance by tying rewards directly to behavior and performance. Payment on a commission basis makes the link between income and sales performance clear. The more a salesperson sells, the greater will be his or her income. In other cases, organizations attempt to tie promotion decisions to performance. Thus, an employee may perform at a higher than normal level in anticipation or hope of a promotion to a higher position. We will examine several kinds of reward policies that attempt to motivate job performance through the selective distribution of rewards to employees.

    Another area of concern to managers is retaining valued employees and making the best use of their time. This problem involves the dual tasks of reducing turnover (the rate at which people leave the organization during a given period of time, such as year) and minimizing the time lost through absenteeism. Rewards can be used to keep the organization and the job itself attractive.

    Finally, the organization's reward policy has external influences on sources of labor supply. All organizations face varying degrees of competition in a variety of labor markets. Supply and demand conditions in these markets require that organizations offer rewards that are competitive enough to attract a sufficient number of competent job applicants. In practice, this requires that an organization offer rewards that are not too low to attract such applicants, but that are not unnecessarily high. Of the variety of rewards a firm offers, research suggests that wages and salaries are the single most visible reward offered by an organization to those who are actively seeking employment.[5] This does not deny the fact, however, that other rewards are also considered by prospective employees.

Whether the purposes served by a rewards system are internal or external, reward policy remains a major control mechanism available to managers to influence the direction of behavior and performance. Such policy is not a simple matter for organizations, however. At the very least, the following issues must be resolved in order to develop and implement a rewards policy:

What kinds of rewards are sought by individuals working within and/or seeking employment by the organization?

What are the rewards over which management has control?

What shall be the basis for distributing rewards within the organization?

In what ways to rewards influence employee decisions and performance?

Answers to each of these questions must be found in order to understand and predict the influence of rewards on individuals.

Intrinsic versus Extrinsic Rewards

The term *reward policy* implies that management can control both the level of rewards and the way in which rewards are distributed. In fact, the degree of control a company has varies with different types of rewards. In addition, a manager can choose among different bases for distributing rewards that, in some instances, conflict with each other. Reward policy, then, consists of the rules governing the types of rewards a company offers its employees and the way in which such rewards are distributed. Policy can be intentional (as when management makes a conscious decision regarding reward distribution), or it can be unintentional (as when management finds that employees are sacrificing quality of output for quantity because of a poorly designed incentive system).

Behavioral scientists have distinguished between intrinsic and extrinsic rewards within organizations for many years. *Intrinsic rewards* are those associated with the job itself. These include (1) the sense of feeling personally responsible for a meaningful part of the work; (2) work outcomes that constitute a highly visible cycle of operations, lead to completion of some process, and allow the individual to use a variety of highly developed and valued skills and abilities; (3) the opportunity to engage in a number of different meaningful activities while carrying out the job; and (4) the provision of information regarding the amount and quality of work from a creditable source. The source may be the employee himself, a valued coworker, or the formal organization. Indeed, as we indicated in our discussion of job design in chapter 6, many programs in job enrichment and job redesign focus on these four intrinsic rewards.

The work of physicians in most cases would offer a high degree of intrinsic rewards according to the formula just outlined. They work, for example, with a great deal of autonomy, making a number of clinical decisions on the basis of their own authority. In addition, their work is highly visible to others, and is intrinsically meaningful. The cure of a patient constitutes a tangible and valued cycle of work activities. Further, in most cases, the work of physicians is varied. They see many different patients in a day, and confront an often confusing array of symptoms and diseases. Finally, physicians have excellent opportunities for feedback regarding the results of their work.

Contrast this with the work of an assembly-line worker in an automobile plant. The assembly-line worker has little autonomy, is not carrying out meaningful tasks or seeing the completion of work cycles, has little variety in the type of tasks carried out, and has very little feedback concerning the results of his or her work.

Extrinsic rewards are those that are not associated with the work itself. They accrue to the individual from other sources in the organization, including coworkers, informal groups, and the formal organization. Extrinsic rewards include the following:

Financial rewards—The wage or salary being paid the individual.

Fringe benefits—Paid vacation time, paid lunches, payment of life insurance premiums, provision of health insurance, company discounts, and any other discretionary payments other than direct wages or salaries. In addition, most employers must also make contributions to the employee's Social Security account, unemployment insurance, and workers' compensation insurance.

Profit sharing and incentive plans—A number of plans have been designed over the years that attempt to encourage participation and performance among employees by having them share in the profits of the enterprise. In some cases, the incentive formula is directly based on work output, such as a piece-rate payment plan that pays $2.00 for each unit completed. A sales person's commission is another illustration of a direct incentive. In other cases, profit-sharing formulas have been developed that create a pool of retained income to be distributed among employees as a bonus. One plan has a formula for sharing part of the money *saved* in an entire division or operation among employees.[6]

Professional and peer recognition—Satisfying a need to be respected for one's achievements by colleagues in the field.

Promotions—Increasingly fewer jobs in American organizations are "dead end," leading to no other positions in the organization. Many employees seek a career path leading to a series of promotions and new positions during employment with a company.

Supervision—Rewards in the form of compliments, friendship, and leadership offered by a superior are important to a number of people.

Friendships—Membership in informal groups is important to many employees as a reward apart from the work itself. Informal group activities provide a number of rewards, including the chance to socialize, the opportunity to informally lead others, the opportunity to share information about work with others, and the common protection provided by the group from management and other individuals outside the group.

Deferred compensation—Many organizations attempt to commit employees for long periods of employment through the use of deferred compensation plans; that is, payments to individuals that will not commence until some specified time in the future (often at the time of one's retirement). A major form of deferred compensation is payment to employee retirement pension accounts. Provision of a pension plan allows employees to have an income during retirement years at a lower rate of income taxation than during employment years. Another form of deferred compensation are stock options. These are options assigned to an individual to purchase shares in the company's stock at a fixed price over some period of time. If the value of shares increases during the time, the individual can exercise the option and purchase shares at a savings.

As we have seen in chapters 5 and 6, several behavioral scientists have proposed that intrinsic rewards are more important than extrinsic rewards in influencing behavior and performance.[7] Although a great deal of controversy still exists over this belief, many behavioral scientists still believe that it is important to distinguish between intrinsic and extrinsic rewards.[8] The basis for this reasoning is that rewards do not have a predictable influence on individual behavior unless the individual's own goals and intentions are taken into account.

Locke's theory of motivation and incentives, presented in chapter 5, underlines the importance of individual goals and intentions as determinants of work performance.[9] According to this theory, individuals are very conscious decision makers with respect to their behavior. Also, according to this model, intrinsic and extrinsic rewards are seen as environmental events. The influence of such events on performance is mediated by at least three intervening processes: (1) the individuals' perceptions or cognitions of the reward; (2) their evaluation of the reward (that is, the incentive value they place on it); and (3) their own goal setting and intentions. Empirical research on this model has investigated a number of managerial efforts at influence, including: (1) work instructions; (2) time limits; (3) knowledge of results; (4) competition; (5) money; (6) praise; (7) reproof; and (8) participation. In each case, empirical results indicate that only if individuals evaluate these incentives and set their own goals accordingly will they have a predictable and desired influence on performance. Thus, for example, a promise of a 10 percent increase in pay as an incentive will not influence an employee's performance unless the employee places high personal value on the increase and sets a corresponding increase in performance as his or her own personal goal.

Locke points out that in actual work situations employees are influenced by a _combination_ of incentives. They receive instructions, they get knowledge of results in the form of feedback, they may compete with others for pay and promotion, they get paid, and sometimes participate in decisions. No combination of these factors influences behavior and performance independent of behavioral intentions set by the individual in response to them.

In light of Locke's theory, the intrinsic-extrinsic distinction may still be of some use in understanding the influence of rewards on performance. Specifically, intrinsic aspects of the job may be the most likely to give rise to recognition, evaluation, and acceptance as rewards for an individual, whereas less direct means of influence, such as praise, reproof, and money, would not provide these rewards. In other words, the greater the degree to which a reward is an integral part of the job itself, the more likely it will be accepted as a goal by employees, and, therefore, the greater will be its influence on performance. Only if this is the case is the intrinsic-extrinsic distinction useful.

A second reason for maintaining a distinction between extrinsic and intrinsic rewards on a job is that management's degree of control over them varies. Management has most direct control over extrinsic reward policy. Where direct pay, fringe benefits, and other forms of direct compensation are concerned, managers can create tangible policy through the practice of compensation administration. Through the procedures of job evaluation, for example, managers establish relative rates of pay for each position in the organization. In addition, the establishment of formulas for awarding fringe benefits is a matter of direct managerial control. Finally, formal classification plans usually specify policy for selecting and promoting individuals to various positions through job descriptions and job specifications.

Management has far less control where intrinsic rewards are considered. Unlike wages, there are no direct means of increasing, decreasing or distributing the sense of personal responsibility over one's job, meaningful work, visible work, and feedback to employees. As we discussed in chapter 6, the only policy tool available to management for controlling intrinsic rewards is job design. In other words, in structuring the work in an organization and in designing jobs, an attempt can be made to cluster tasks into jobs that provide greater levels of intrinsic rewards. Research evidence on attempts at redesigning jobs to heighten intrinsic rewards (including job enlargement and job enrichment) is mixed.[10] In several cases, the redesign of jobs has not led to corresponding increases in employee satisfaction and performance. Mixed evidence of this nature suggests that the provision and control over intrinsic rewards is far more difficult for managers than is providing for extrinsic rewards.

Bases for Reward Distribution

A striking observation that can be made in most organizations is the degree of inequality in the distribution of rewards and, even more striking, the large-scale acceptance of this fact. Although much of what we say here applies to most forms of rewards, wages and salaries provide the clearest illustration of this point. In most large corporations, the range in financial compensation is enormous. The chairman of the board, for example, may receive an annual salary of $800,000 (not including fringe benefits), but a plant guard or maintenance employee may be paid only $9,000 per year. Similarly, sizable differences exist across salaries received by individuals with fairly comparable educations and work-related experience. The average annual salary paid to professors in the engineering school of one university, for example, is

$27,000, but the salary for professors in the arts college of the same university is
$21,000.

If management were beginning from the start to decide how to allocate financial
rewards within an organization, the first and greatest problem would be deciding
upon a policy for making such an allocation. Each of the following rules have
provided a basis for distributing money rewards at one time or another:

> *Equality*—All individuals receive equal shares of rewards. An illustration of
> this policy would be an agreement among business partners that the company's
> profits be divided equally among the members. A policy that specifies that each
> share of stock in a corporation receives equal dividends is another illustration.

> *Power*—Rewards are distributed according to each individual's ability to wrest
> a portion of the total rewards available. According to this rule, the strongest
> take what they want, and the weaker pick up the leftovers. In some ways,
> trade-union activities can be explained by such a rule. Attempts at limiting
> entry to an occupation, requiring work rules that allow only members to per-
> form certain critical tasks, and threatening work stoppages in critical areas are
> ways of using power to increase the share of benefits going to the members of
> the union.

> *Need*—Rewards are distributed to people according to their need. The greater
> one's need for a reward, the larger is one's share. During the Great Depression,
> many employers gave preference to male heads of household over unmarried
> men and women in hiring and layoffs. The rationale for this policy was that
> fathers needed a job to support their families more than other people did.

> *Distributive justice*—Members of an organization should receive a share of the
> rewards equivalent to their inputs. Distributive justice is achieved, according to
> equity theorists, when the ratios of rewards to inputs are equal for all members
> of the organization. For example, according to a merit rule, people will be paid
> according to merit, that is, the effectiveness of their performance either as
> individuals or as groups.

In practice, management is often confronted with the need to satisfy demands
made on the basis of several of these rules at the same time, leading to conflict in
reward policy. The case of administering a wage and salary program provides an
excellent illustration of this problem. Designing and administering a compensation
program consists of three major steps: (1) determining the relative worth of each job
in the organization; (2) pricing each job in the structure to remain reasonably
competitive with prevailing wage rates in the labor market; and (3) establishing
individual pay policies, that is, criteria for making pay distinctions among people
who are on the same job.

The first step is called *job evaluation*. Jobs are clustered into homogeneous
groups for the sake of comparison. The groupings can be based on location in a
common division, sharing the same occupation, serving the same function, or on
some other basis such as tradition. A key job is chosen in each cluster to serve
several purposes. First, the rate of pay established for the key job will serve as the

basis for the rate established for the subordinates in the cluster. Second, key jobs will be used to establish relative rates of pay across clusters within the organization. Finally, key jobs alone will be used to make pay comparisons outside the organization to determine the dollar amounts to be paid to various jobs.

A typical job evaluation formula will rate each job within a cluster on each of several compensable factors. Exhibit 14–5 illustrates the results of such an analysis for the jobs in two divisions of a city government. The factors judged were: (1) responsibility; (2) effort; and (3) education and/or experience required. Note that the absolute points accumulated across factors for each job are used in establishing the relative worth of each job. If the points assigned to a police chief, for example, are 30 as compared to the 40 assigned to the position of commissioner, then the chief's position should be paid 75 percent of the amount paid to the commissioner. The objective of a job evaluation is to establish relative rates of pay for each position in the organization that will be perceived as equitable by members. In order to achieve this objective, the job evaluation system itself must be accepted as fair by the organization's members. The underlying rule in job evaluation is to distribute rewards according to the inputs the job demands; that is, distributive justice.

Conflicts with the principle of distributive justice (or equity) often arise, however, when managers attempt to price each job in the organization according to external market realities. The results of wage surveys often indicate, for example, that supply and demand conditions are such that some jobs must be paid a salary far

Exhibit 14–5 Job Evaluation for Department of Public Safety, North Englebrook Township.

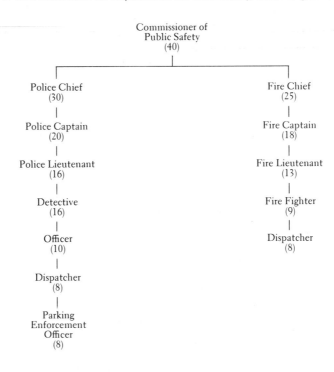

above that indicated by the job evaluation in order to attract qualified employees. In other cases, market conditions may be such that a company can pay a wage far below that indicated by the job evaluation and still attract qualified people. In this instance, a rule of economic power (supply and demand conditions) is in direct conflict with norms of internal equity.

In addition to conflicts between equity and market conditions, conflict has arisen in recent years between a criterion of need (based on cost-of-living demands) and a criterion of equity (based on merit demands). The conflict has arisen in the third step of compensation administration, making individual pay distinctions for people who are on the same job. Consider two accountants working in the same job for a corporation. Any number of criteria may be employed to justify pay differences between the two. One may be paid more because he or she has worked longer on that job (a seniority criterion). One may receive a higher pay increment this year because his or her performance has been rated higher than the other's (a merit criterion). Finally, both may demand pay increases this year, arguing that it is management's responsibility to protect their real income in the face of inflation (a cost-of-living criterion). *Real income* is the employee's income "deflated" by a price index to reflect increases in prices. Thus, if prices increase by 10 percent and salary is increased by 10 percent, real income has not increased at all.

A company faced with reasonable fixed salary budgets faces trade offs among these three criteria. The more allocated to cost-of-living adjustments, the less there is to allocate to merit increments or seniority increments. Up until the mid-1960s, straight cost-of-living adjustments were relatively uncommon outside of those organizations dealing with industrial trade unions. Since that time, however, increasing numbers of firms have adopted cost-of-living adjustments for all their employees. A typical cost-of-living formula adjusts everyone's salary by some percentage amount each year to reflect increases in some index of inflation (most commonly, the Consumer Price Index, or CPI, published by the U.S. Department of Labor).

Recent research on the use of cost-of-living formulas suggest that they have had a devastating effect on most organizations' ability to use rewards to motivate behavior and performance. First of all, cost-of-living adjustments limit an organization's capacity to effectively reward on the basis of merit. Hence, there has been a tendency for merit formulas to become meaningless to employees. This outcome has contributed to a long-term reduction in the relative productivity of American labor. Second, adjusting all salaries to cost-of-living standards has led to a phenomenon known as "salary compression." When all salaries receive similar adjustments, salaries in the middle of the wage structure become compressed, that is, lower-level salaries tend to creep up and crowd salaries higher up in the structure. *Business Week,* for example, reported that taxes and inflation have actually eroded middle-level salaries in many organizations that have been using simple cost-of-living adjustments. Exhibit 14–6 demonstrates graphically how salary compression has negatively influenced middle-level incomes and favorably influenced lower-level salaries.[11]

In response to this problem, both *Business Week* and the *Wall Street Journal* report that increasing numbers of organizations have begun to abandon cost-of-living formulas and are returning to merit as a basis for making individual salary

Exhibit 14–6 How Taxes and Inflation Erode an 8 Percent Raise

Adjusted Gross Income		Aftertax Income		Effective Federal Tax Rate[a]	Aftertax Income Adjusted for 6.5% Inflation	Net Change After Taxes and Inflation
1976	1977	1976	1977	1977	1977	1976–77
$15,000	$16,200	$13,339	$14,421	10.98%	$13,541	$ +202
20,000	21,600	17,454	18,759	13.15	17,614	+160
25,000	27,000	21,335	22,833	15.43	21,439	+104
30,000	32,400	24,990	26,744	17.46	25,112	+122
35,000	37,800	28,636	30,531	19.23	28,668	+ 32
40,000	43,200	32,237	34,252	20.71	32,162	− 75
45,000	48,600	35,850	37,743	22.34	35,439	−411
50,000	54,000	38,880	41,022	24.03	38,518	−362
55,000	59,400	41,981	44,813	24.56	42,078	+ 97
60,000	64,800	45,112	46,973	27.51	44,106	−1,006
65,000	70,200	47,382	50,738	27.72	47,641	+259
70,000	75,600	50,579	54,169	28.35	50,863	+284
75,000	81,000	53,731	57,229	29.35	53,736	+ 5

[a] Average derived from actual returns

Data: Effective tax rates supplied by Joint Committee on Taxation; *Business Week* adjustments.

Source: *Business Week,* 12 September, 1977, p. 83. Used with permission.

adjustments. An attempt is being made to use such standards to more effectively tie pay to performance. Many analysts believe that returning to merit criteria is our best hope for increasing the productivity of American workers at all levels.[12] It is certain that when a company adopts a cost-of-living adjustment policy, they are focusing on the wrong market in pricing their jobs. Most cost-of-living formulas employ the Consumer Price Index, an index of prices in the retail market for goods and services. In pricing its jobs, a company should look more appropriately to the *labor* market from which it draws its employees, rather than retail trade markets. If a firm has priced its jobs competitively with respect to the appropriate labor market, it has no additional obligations to guarantee additional increases based on cost-of-living arguments.

A Model of Organizational Rewards and Individual Needs

No predictions of individual behavior and performance can be made until the match between individual need profiles and organizational rewards is considered. A major objective in the design of reward policy, therefore, should be to maximize this fit. A model of the interaction between needs and rewards as they influence performance, turnover, absenteeism, and the choice of an organization as a place to work is displayed in exhibit 14–7, which is adapted from the integrative motivation model presented and developed in chapter 5 (exhibit 5–13).

An excellent practical illustration of organizational attempts to match extrinsic reward policy with individual need profiles (as displayed in exhibit 14–7) is the advent of the "cafeteria" style compensation program. The typical compensation plan in organizations today is to offer a standard base salary plus fringe benefits to all employees. Thus, a typical company may offer an employee a base salary of $15,000 per year plus an additional $5,000 in standard benefits, for a total compensation of $20,000. Under a cafeteria plan, the employee is free to distribute the total of $20,000 across straight salary and benefits (including vacation time, retirement plan payment, insurance payments, stock options, and other forms of deferred payments) in any way he or she desires. Thus, for example, younger employees with new families may prefer a larger share of their compensation in straight salary to meet current financial obligations; older employees with fewer financial obligations may desire a larger share of the total going into deferred compensation plans.[13]

Although hard empirical evidence is scarce and mixed on the effectiveness of cafeteria plans, proponents of the technique point to the following potential advantages for management and employees:

Employees will experience a closer match between their salary needs and rewards offered by the company.

They will be more satisfied with their compensation.

Exhibit 14–7 Model of Organizational Rewards and Individual Behavior

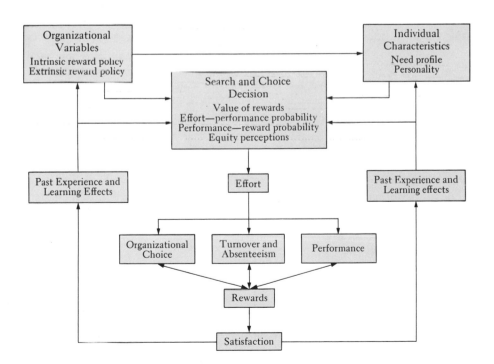

They will be more productive.

They will be less likely to leave.[14]

According to exhibit 14–7, the rewards policy of the organization interacts with such individual characteristics as need profile and personality to influence the motivation behind three kinds of decisions: (1) the decision to perform at a given level; (2) the decision to leave an organization (turnover) or to be absent from work; and (3) the decision to accept an offer of employment from an organization (organizational choice).

The Decision to Perform

Probably the single most critical impact rewards can have is on performance. According to the model, people have a number of outcomes or rewards they would like to achieve from performing their jobs (what we defined as *valences* in presenting expectancy theory). In addition, people also have expectations regarding the likelihood of a given level of effort resulting in a specific level of performance (expectancies) and expectations regarding the likelihood of a given performance level resulting in desired outcomes or rewards (instrumentalities). Valences, expectancy perceptions, and instrumentality perceptions are influenced both by organizational practices and individual characteristics.

Reward policy is an organizational characteristic that consists of the kinds and amount of rewards as well as the way in which they are distributed. Previous experience with a company's reward policy has a direct influence on expectancy and instrumentality perceptions. In addition, individual personality characteristics, especially specific need deficiencies, which influence the felt need or importance attached to various rewards, and personality characteristics, such as internal/external control perceptions, also influence expectancy and instrumentality perceptions.

Given Locke's theory that the employee is a conscious decision maker, and according to expectancy theory and our integrative motivation model, we would expect employees to consider the values and likelihoods of a number of events occurring before choosing a given level of effort in job performance. Once a given level of effort is chosen and a subsequent level of job performance occurs, the employee monitors the results. If reward practices are such that rewards meet the anticipations of employees, satisfaction will result. If expectations are not met following performance, however, some degree of dissatisfaction will result. We have already pointed out that people alter their behavior on the basis of reward contingencies and subsequent satisfaction or dissatisfaction. Thus, an employee's experience with organizational rewards will either confirm beliefs or expectations about the results of a given level of effort and performance, or will lead to a change in behavior.

The Decision to Join and Remain

In addition to performance level, individuals also make at least two other decisions that are influenced by anticipations of rewards. These include the choice of an organization as a place to work and the decision to remain employed by an organization. These decisions are influenced by the same principles that affect the performance decision. According to the model in exhibit 14–7, individuals seek employment with a series of expectations regarding the outcomes or rewards they would like to experience from working. These expectations develop primarily through previous educational and work experience.

In the case of a job seeker faced with three employment offers, for example, the model would predict that the individual would choose the organization in which the likelihoods of valued outcomes or rewards were maximized. The same would hold true in predicting whether an individual employee would choose to remain employed by an organization or seek work elsewhere.

Application of the Reward Model

The reward model is an ideal model; it predicts what choices individuals would make if they were perfectly rational and had access to complete information regarding their decision. In reality, the decision-making theory and research presented in chapter 12 demonstrates that we must temper this model with the knowledge that decisions are rarely made under conditions of perfect information. There will always be some error, therefore, in prediction. Applications of this model should attempt to take such imperfections into account. The case of the job seeker just discussed is a good illustration. In reality, a job seeker has only a limited knowledge of the number of jobs that are actually available.[15] In addition, he or she may not have accurate information about the wages the company is paying or the nonmonetary rewards available on each of several job possibilities. Finally, the job seeker discovers that further information about job opportunities is not a free good. Such information costs time, effort, and money (e.g., the time consumed in looking and the costs of an employment agency). Very rarely do actual decision makers *maximize* the weighted combination of outcomes and likelihood in an objective sense. Rather they *satisfice* by choosing the alternative that appears best in terms of valued outcomes and expectations, *given* the information and time constraints under which the decision is being made.[16] This realization underlines the importance of understanding an individual's perceptions about the decision alternatives he or she faces in predicting employment choices.

Finally, the model explicitly delineates three different and independent individual decisions regarding the organization that can be influenced by reward policy. These decisions occur usually at different times and under different conditions. In addition, they have different results associated with them. The decision to join, for example, is made before the applicant knows a great deal about the organization. Once employed, the individual monitors the employment relationship and compares this with other possible alternatives including employment elsewhere or, in some cases, being absent from work. From the organization's perspective, these decisions result in a given rate of turnover and absenteeism. Finally, the performance decision involves a choice among a number of levels of effort on specific work tasks. The results of this decision are apparent in the variations among employees' performance evaluations.

Rewards and Choice Behavior

The reward model proposed in this chapter indicates that individuals make choices on the basis of anticipated rewards. Even though the individual is in practice making the decision under conditions of imperfect information, he or she will still act to maximize the perceived rewards available. If the model is correct, we would expect rewards to predict a number of work-related choices including (1) performance; (2) turnover; (3) absenteeism; and (4) organizational choice.

Rewards and Performance

A great deal has already been said in this book about the influence of rewards on performance. Theoretically, the connection between them is clear. According to the performance model presented in chapter 2, rewards should serve to motivate performance by satisfying work-related needs. What we often ignore in practice, however, is that people vary in the importance they attach to various rewards, and that no universal reward system is available that will motivate all employees equally.

In fact, the empirical evidence regarding the influence of specific rewards on work performance is mixed. The most studied reward is money. Studies of the influence of pay as a work incentive yield no conclusive picture.[17] In some cases, incentives have been found to be positively associated with performance. In other cases, no association has been found. In still other cases, a negative relationship has been found.

A number of considerations are important in reacting to these results. First, wage incentives are only one of a broad array of rewards important to employees. In cases in which a wage incentive is not valued or in which a wage incentive conflicts with another desired reward (such as equity or friendships within an informal group) the incentive would be expected to have little effect on performance. Extensive research on this question suggests that quite often informal rules develop that place ceilings on output in spite of wage incentives.[18] Group members who violate such norms and work for the wage incentive are labeled "rate busters" and often suffer severe retribution from the rest of the group, including social ostracism and social pressure.

There are a number of reasons for the development of work-restriction rules. First, a group often mistrusts management's intent. The belief of the group (often correct) is that if management finds that members are making too much money under the incentive formula, they will revise the formula so that employees will have to produce more for the same amount of money. A successful incentive formula depends upon a judgment regarding a "reasonable" amount of work for each incentive payment. Time-and-motion study is used to make this determination. What the time-and-motion analysts judge to be "reasonable" and what the group believes to be "reasonable" are often in disagreement.

Another factor in work groups' distrust of incentive formulas is the fear of working oneself literally out of a job. The belief is that if one works too fast and produces too much in a short period of time, management may have no further use for the employee until demand for the work arises again. Groups often like to pace work in order to maintain stable employment. Finally, equity norms can be violated if some members in a group are put on incentive while others remain under an hourly form of payment. In such cases, it is quite possible that an employee who has been earning less than another under an hourly formula can earn more when placed on an incentive plan.

A second consideration with regard to the uncertain effect of incentive wage plans on performance is the finding that although many firms *believe* they have tied pay to performance, in fact their pay policies tie rewards more closely to such factors as age, seniority, job placement, sex, and race.[19] Thus, it is often difficult to assure that pay is actually tied to performance even when this is management's intent.

A third consideration regarding the influence of rewards on performance regards secrecy surrounding pay, which many organizations continue to maintain as a strict policy. The most common justification for such a policy is that public disclosure of salaries would constitute an invasion of individual privacy—that a person's rate of pay and income is a personal matter between employee and employer. A less frequently cited reason for secrecy is that the pay structure itself is inequitable and management fears that publicity concerning it would lead to unrest and dissatisfaction among employees.

Behavioral scientists have pointed out, however, that secrecy policies cripple the effectiveness with which management can link pay and performance. If employees cannot get feedback regarding the relative rewards they have received for their efforts, pay cannot be expected to have any significant effect on behavior.[20] The problem is made even worse by the finding that where secrecy about pay does exist, people consistently *misperceive* the actual pay rates of others in the organization. One study found, for example, that managers tend to overestimate the salaries of other managers in the same organization.[21] Such misperception can lead to dissatisfaction with pay and negate any motivational impact of a reward system. Theoretically, at least, if a company wants to link pay with performance, it must provide information about relative rates of pay. In practice, however, merely making salary information public will not insure that pay will motivate performance. Only if pay is *in fact* linked to performance, and only if employees accept such a policy, can pay be expected to motivate performance.

Role of Money

In considering the impact of money as a reward on performance, we must consider the numerous roles money can have regarding behavior and performance. Money (pay) has been given a number of different roles in influencing the behavior of employees in organizations.[22] First, money could be viewed as an *incentive* or *goal* that is capable of reducing need deficiencies. The need for money serves as an incentive for motivated behavior, and its acquisition reduces the need deficiency. Second, money can be a *hygiene factor*, which, when absent, serves as a potential dissatisfier, but not as a satisfier when present in appropriate amounts.

Third, money can be viewed as an instrument for *gaining desired outcomes*. If money is valued by the individual and he or she perceives a strong path from effort to rewards, then effort toward obtaining this outcome will be exerted. Fourth, money can be used as a point of *comparison* between two individuals. If any inequity exists in this relationship, it would serve as a motivator for action. Finally, money could be a *conditioned reinforcer* if it were awarded to individuals contingent on their level of performance.

In summarizing the research investigating pay as a method to motivate individual performance, Lawler stated the conditions that are necessary for pay to be an effective motivational tool.[23] Three conditions were given for a pay plan to motivate people: (1) a strong belief must exist with employees that good performance will lead to high pay; (2) the perceived negative consequences of performing well (e.g., being perceived as a "rate buster") should be minimized; and (3) an environment should be created such that positive outcomes other than pay (e.g., praise, recognition, and advancement) will be seen to be related to good performance. A classification scheme and the rating of effectiveness of each major type of pay plan is presented in exhibit 14–8.

A number of implications for managers can be drawn from this exhibit. First, of the thirty-six possible combinations of type of plan and performance measures and rewards, only seven are well-known. The blank spaces could be interpreted to mean that a particular plan is not used very often (e.g., salary increases based on individual cost effectiveness), or may indicate the possibility of experimenting with a different approach (e.g., cash bonus based on group cost effectiveness)

Second, individual salary rewards appear to be more effective for employees in developing a strong relationship between good performance and high pay than are group or organization-wide plans. It would appear that the main reason for this is that individuals can clearly perceive the relationship between *their* performance and *their* rewards, but are less clear in their perceptions of their impact on group or organizational plans.

Third, individual salary reward plans are less effective in tying rewards to performance than are individual bonus plans. Bonus plans typically are used to reward *current* performance; salary plans generally reward *past* performance. As reinforcement theory would predict, the shorter the time interval between performance and monetary rewards, the stronger will be the relationship between these two aspects.

Fourth, no one pay plan is effective in minimizing the negative side effects of high performance. Individual bonus plans, however, are the least effective because the individual employee can be singled out by his or her peers. Such consequences as criticism for exceeding established group norms can result if adherence to strong group productivity norms are required by the group.

Finally, group and organization-wide plans (salary and bonus) appear to work well in contributing to the perception that important rewards other than pay result from good performance. With these plans, it is generally to the benefit of every worker to work effectively because good performance is much more likely to result in supervisory recognition, praise, and increased prestige than under individual plans. That is, if an employee believes he or she can benefit from another employee's good performance, he or she is more likely to encourage or help the other employee to perform at a high level.

Exhibit 14–8 Classification and Ratings of Various Pay Plans

Type of Pay Plan	Performance Measure	Type of Rewards		Perceived Pay-Performance Linkage	Minimization of Negative Consequences	Perceived Relationship Between Other Rewards and Performance
		Salary Increase	Cash Bonus			
Salary						
For Individuals	Productivity	—	Piece rate	Good	Neutral	Neutral
	Cost effectiveness	Merit rating	—	Fair	Neutral	Neutral
	Superior's rating	—	—	Fair	Neutral	Fair
For Group	Productivity	Productivity	—	Fair	Neutral	Fair
	Cost effectiveness	—	—	Fair	Neutral	Fair
	Superior's rating	—	—	Fair	Neutral	Fair
For Total Organization	Productivity	Productivity	—	Fair	Neutral	Fair
	Cost effectiveness	Bargaining	—	Fair	Neutral	Fair
	Profits	—	—	Neutral	Neutral	Fair
Bonus						
For Individuals	Productivity	Piece rate	—	Excellent	Poor	Neutral
	Cost effectiveness	—	Sales	Good	Poor	Neutral
	Superior's rating	—	Commission	Good	Poor	Fair
For Group	Productivity	—	Group incentive	Good	Neutral	Fair
	Cost effectiveness	—	—	Good	Neutral	Fair
	Superior's rating	—	—	Good	Neutral	Fair
For Total Organization	Productivity	—	Kaiser,	Good	Neutral	Fair
	Cost effectiveness	—	Scanlon,	Good	Neutral	Fair
	Profits	—	Profit sharing	Fair	Neutral	Fair

Adapted from Edward E. Lawler III, *Pay and Organizational Effectiveness* (New York: McGraw-Hill, 1971), pp. 164–65.

Beyond the crucial and major aspect of linking monetary rewards to performance, there are other issues that the manager must confront if he or she is to use money as an incentive to increase motivation.[24] First, there must be an acceptable level of trust between superiors and subordinates. Lack of trust may lead employees to believe that the awarding of monetary rewards is nothing more than a random or preferential occurrence. Second, more challenging and difficult jobs require greater consideration for monetary rewards than do routine jobs. It may be easier to excel in performance on less difficult jobs, thus creating an inequity with more difficult, and probably more important, jobs if money rewards are distributed equally between both.

Third, individual performance assessment must be made with as much objective data as possible. If individual performance is difficult to measure and only subjective data is available, serious thought should be given to not using pay as an incentive. For example, it is not difficult to link monetary rewards to performance for salespersons when performance is based on sales, profits, or market share. On the other hand, it would be questionable to use monetary incentives for research chemists because their performance is not only difficult to measure but the period of time involved before concrete results are available is usually quite long.

Finally, the amount of monetary rewards given to high performing employees may hinge on whether the organization can afford to give certain employees large raises or bonuses. If large monetary rewards are not tied to excellent performance, then the effect of pay as a motivator is diminished. In addition, large monetary rewards are wasted on those employees who do not feel that pay is an important source of motivation.

Absenteeism and Turnover

Absenteeism and turnover are costly and large-scale problems for many employers.[25] Absenteeism and turnover disrupt schedules, lead to a need to over-staff, and reduce the productivity of the organization. In addition to direct costs of turnover and absenteeism, indirect costs are incurred when money must be spent to recruit replacements and train them. The fact that these problems exist suggest that it cannot be automatically assumed that people will come to work each day or remain in an organization once they are hired. The expected rewards associated with each choice motivate the worker to work on a particular day or to leave the firm and seek employment elsewhere.

If there are few intrinsic rewards associated with the job and there are outcomes associated with absence that are greater than extrinsic rewards offered (pay, promotion), then we would expect an individual to be absent from the job frequently. In most cases, firms use punishment (negatively valued outcomes) to control absenteeism. Although effective in some cases, the technique has questionable value. First, union contracts often make it very difficult for managers to fire somebody. Second, in times of full employment, the threat of firing may have little effect on individuals. They have ample job opportunities elsewhere. Finally, as Skinner has indicated, punishment may serve to disrupt behavior, but it does not lead to any long-term changes in behavior patterns. That is, punishing an employee for being absent one day does not guarantee any significant change in the likelihood of repeated absence.

When positive rewards have been offered for attendance, however, absenteeism has been reduced. In two studies, extrinsic rewards such as pay were tied directly to attendance; those who attended the job regularly received cash bonuses. In both cases, rates of attendance increased dramatically.[26] In addition, it seems reasonable to expect that, if the job offers greater intrinsic rewards, absenteeism would be reduced.

Both intrinsic and extrinsic rewards are also important in motivating people to remain in organizations. Local labor-market research tends to suggest that people leave organizations not because they are attracted by anticipated rewards elsewhere but because they are dissatisfied with their present jobs.[27] This is an important distinction. March and Simon point out that search behavior starts only after a person has become dissatisfied. Thus, the critical determinant of turnover is dissatisfaction with the degree to which needs are being rewarded in one's current job.

Very little is known, empirically, about the effect of intrinsic rewards on the decision to leave an organization. It would seem reasonable to expect, however, that if such intrinsic rewards as autonomy, task identity, variety, and feedback are important to an employee, the lack of such rewards would lead to dissatisfaction and the decision to leave the organization. Indeed, this prediction is made by the theory of work adjustment. According to this model, low levels of satisfaction lead directly to the decision to leave an organization. Where tested, the model's predictions have been confirmed.

Various attempts have been made by organizations to retain superior employees through the use of extrinsic rewards. One common policy is to pay a premium salary to encourage a particularly valued employee to stay. In effect, the firm is willing to play a bidding game with competitors to retain the employee. There are a number of difficulties with this policy, however. The major problem is that such bidding will result in a dislocation of the internal wage structure. Norms of equity are violated, leading to a great deal of resentment and dissatisfaction among other employees. Also, it is possible for management to get so caught up in the bidding that they lose sight of the employee's actual value to the organization. The result of this mistake is retaining a "star" whose work could be done just as well by someone else.

A second strategy for retaining valued employees with extrinsic rewards is to defer rewards and tie them to remaining with the organization. Traditionally, firms required a minimum number of years of employment before a person earned full right to company contribution to pension funds (that is, before pension rights become fully vested). Thus, if an employee left an organization before some specified period of time (in some cases fifteen to twenty years), he or she lost all or at least part of the pension. Such pension rules became a major factor limiting the mobility of middle-aged employees. Since passage of the Employee Retirement Income Security Act in 1974, however, firms must fully vest pension rights after five years. Hence, deferred pension payments are no longer an option for retaining employees for extended periods.

Companies have also used such techniques as stock options and deferred payment contracts to retain key executives. In both cases, income (either from sale of stock or annuities) is <u>promised at some time in the future</u> if the employee stays with the firm. Leaving the firm results in a <u>loss</u> of such income.

Occupational and Organizational Choice

Several investigations suggest that the expectancy model outlined in chapter 5 can predict occupational and organizational preferences of individuals. In several studies, the occupational preferences of students were predicted from the combination of instrumentality perceptions (the likelihood of a given career leading to certain outcomes) and the value or importance of these outcomes to the individual. The same findings have resulted when the individual's choice of an organization is the dependent variable of interest.[28]

Unfortunately, little is known about the psychological processes by which people actually gather information about prospective careers or employers and the processes by which decisions are actually made. Much of the evidence on choice behavior tends to be economic rather than psychological in nature. Research in local labor markets, for example, has shown that: (1) companies that pay higher than average wages have less trouble attracting and retaining high-quality labor; (2) turnover is lower within firms paying higher than average wages; and (3) turnover is lower in times of recession and depression.[29] Although these findings confirm the general hypotheses of the model presented in this chapter, they tell us very little about specific choice processes.

Limited information suggests (in line with March and Simon's proposal) that a majority of people currently employed have very little and very unrealistic information about rewards available from careers and organizations. Similar findings have been reported for students who have not yet entered the labor market.[30] Not until the choice has been made to enter a labor market (either as a new entrant or by leaving an employer) does a search process begin to generate information upon which to base a decision. Further research is needed regarding the perceptual processes that influence the relationship between rewards and occupational and organizational choice.

Careers and Organizational Rewards

A major theme of this chapter regards the nature of work-related needs and ways in which organizations seek to satisfy such needs through reward systems. Increasingly, researchers are turning their attention to the fact that individual careers involve perhaps the most significant set of needs experienced by people. As our knowledge about careers accumulates, organizations are turning their attention to ways to help employees plan their career goals and steps in a way that satisfies the developing and changing needs that have been the subject of this chapter. These attempts constitute a recognition of the increasing importance of career development in people's lives and, therefore, the central importance of career opportunities among the variety of rewards offered by employers. Perhaps the single most important event precipitating this concern has been the large-scale entrance of women into jobs and careers traditionally dominated by men. In the absence of predominant assumptions about what jobs should be held during a given career, or what kinds of things one should be doing at each stage in a career, women are taking a more systematic approach to planning specific life and career steps.[31]

Most behavioral scientists define a *career* as a sequence of jobs that unfolds over time. In addition to moving from one job to the next, an individual moves through identifiable occupational and life stages. These stages may involve periods of formal training and development.[32] Schein, for example, discusses distinct phases of the adult life cycle, each containing a unique set of issues and tasks, many of which involve career concerns. For example, early adulthood (adolescence to early thirties) involves initial career choices, making educational choices, and separating from parents. Later on in one's thirties, issues involve settling into a career and becoming further established, or making radical changes in careers. Additionally, many people experience limitations in their aspirations during this period. During their forties, many people make final career-direction decisions and become more established as individuals in their work. Finally, the fifties and sixties bring about a new range of concerns, including security in retirement, maintaining established friendships and associations, and establishing adult relationships with one's children.[33]

The organizational career involves the period from early adulthood to retirement in one's mid-sixties or at age seventy. It is during these stages that individuals use their skills and abilities to perform certain job-related tasks. As we stressed in our discussion of individual differences in earlier chapters, the goals of an individual strongly influence his or her utilization of the skills and abilities he or she possesses. Exactly how an individual progresses through the establishment and maintenance stages involves the interaction of goals, personal needs, organizational needs, and career choices.

Schein's work describes career movement within an organization.[34] His model focuses on the career as a set of attributes and experiences of the individual who joins, moves through various jobs, and finally leaves the system. The appropriate career pattern is defined by the organization that considers a set of expectations about whom to move, when, how, and how often. The Schein perspective is presented in exhibit 14–9. The *cone model* indicates that career movement can proceed at three levels:

Vertically, which involves increasing or decreasing one's role in the organizational hierarchy.

Radically, which is increasing or decreasing one's importance or centrality in the organization.

Circumferentially, which involves moving from one functional area to another (e.g., from marketing to production) in the organization.

Consider the example of four managers in a retail organization, shown in exhibit 14–10. Individual one (1) may aspire to be a vice president of merchandising. However, the path to this position may start at the assistant buyer position, move

Exhibit 14-9 A Three-Dimensional Model of an Organization

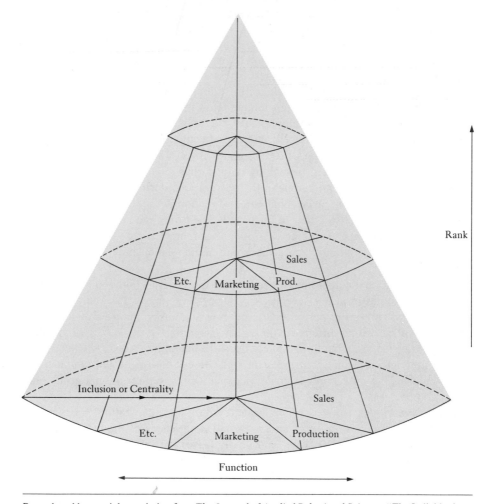

Rank

Sales

Etc.   Marketing   Prod.

Inclusion or Centrality

Sales

Etc.   Marketing   Production

Function

Reproduced by special permission from *The Journal of Applied Behavioral Science,* "The Individual, the Organization, and the Career: A Conceptual Scheme," by Edgar Schein, vol. 7, no. 4, p. 404. Copyright, NTL Institute, 1971.

through the operations function as divisional sales manager and assistant store manager, back to the merchandising area as a buyer, and finally to the vice presidential position. Individual two (2) may desire to be a vice president of personnel. The path to this position will take this person from a program manager in personnel (e.g., compensation, benefits, and so on), to the operations area as divisional sales manager, back to personnel as a group manager, and on to a vice president's position. Individuals three (3) and four (4) each aspire to be the vice president of operations. Their career paths may be quite different. Individual three (3) may start as a department sales manager in a particular store, move to the merchandising function as a buyer, be promoted to store manager, and then on to the vice presidency of operations. Individual four (4), however, may begin as a department sales manager, move on to an assistant buyer position before returning to another department sales manager's job. This is followed by a promotion to a divisional sales manager position in the operations area. A lateral move to the group manager position in the personnel function, followed by a promotion to store manager, may then lead to the position of vice president of operations.

The important feature of this exhibit is that career paths in organizations can be different for each aspiring manager. The manner in which these career paths are developed depends on both the needs of the organization and the needs and required skills of the individual.

Progressing through a career also entails movement that involves different stages. These stages are shown in exhibit 14–11. As the exhibit indicates, each stage of a career involves not only different positions but also a variety of psychological and organizational processes involving transactions between the individual and the organization. Taken together, the aspiring manager must carefully recognize three factors: (1) a career involves distinctly different stages; (2) each stage involves different positions and processes; and (3) the movement from stage to stage can consist of moves across hierarchical *and* functional boundaries.

There is some evidence that major career decisions occur after the individual takes the first job.[35] The fact that individuals have their own career goals and timetables for success makes career planning somewhat difficult because organizations have their own expectations. There is limited research on how organizations

Exhibit 14–10 Example Career Paths in a Retail Organization

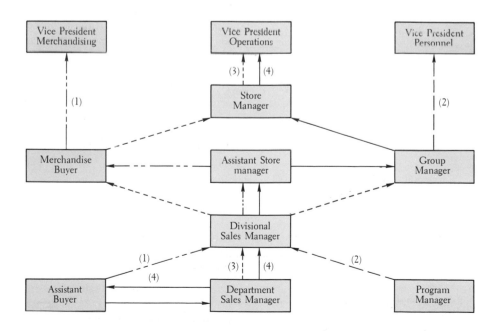

Exhibit 14–11 Basic Stages, Positions, and Processes Involved in a Career

Basic Stages and Transitions	Statuses or Positions	Psychological and Organizational Processes: Transactions between Individual and Organization
1. Preentry	Aspirant, applicant, rushee	Preparation, education, anticipatory socialization
Entry (transition)	Entrant, postulant, recruit	Recruitment, rushing, testing, screening, selection, acceptance ("hiring"); passage through external inclusion boundary; rites of entry; induction and orientation
2. Basic training, novitiate	Trainee, novice, pledge	Training, indoctrination, socialization, testing of the man by the organization, tentative acceptance into group
Initiation, first vows (transition)	Initiate, graduate	Passage through first inner inclusion boundary, acceptance as member and conferring of organizational status, rite of passage and acceptance
3. First regular assignment	New member	First testing by the man of his own capacity to function; granting of real responsibility (playing for keeps); passage through functional boundary with assignment to specific job or department
		Indoctrination and testing of man by immediate work group leading to acceptance or rejection; if accepted, further education and socialization (learning the ropes); preparation for higher status through coaching, seeking visibility, finding sponsors, etc.
Promotion leveling off (transition)		Preparation, testing, passage through hierarchical boundary, rite of passage; may involve passage through functional boundary as well (rotation)
4. Second assignment	Legitimate member (fully accepted)	Processes under no. 3 repeat
5. Granting of tenure	Permanent member	Passage through another inner inclusion boundary
Termination and exit (transition)	Old timer, senior citizen	Preparation for exit, cooling the mark out, rites of exit (testimonial dinners, etc.)
6. Postexit	Alumnus emeritus, retired	Granting of peripheral status

can develop life- and career-planning programs for individuals. To date, few organizations are involved in this seemingly worthwhile endeavor. Recent evidence, however, suggests that such inattention on the part of employers is rapidly ending and that an increasing number of organizations are taking steps to assist their members in life and career planning.

A number of prominent corporations in the United States, including AT&T, Boeing Aircraft, General Motors, I.B.M., Carborundum Corp., Pitney-Bowes, Black and Decker, and Xerox Corporation, have begun formally to address the following corporate issues with respect to career planning:

> A committment to matching organizational needs with career goals of employees.

> Placing responsibility for career counseling at high levels within the management of the company.

> Establishing assessment centers (as discussed in chapter 13) to aid employees in recognizing specific career talents and interests.

> An emphasis on individual initiative in the process in order to avoid paternalism and authoritarian styles of employee relations.[36]

Aplin and Gerster have introduced a model that outlines the most important features in a career counseling program that is reproduced in exhibit 14–12.[37] Their model stresses that career planning involves a sequence of four steps: (1) *inputs*, including individual aspirations and organizational needs and opportunities; (2) *assessment*, a stage in which individual aspirations and organizational needs are matched through two procedures—personal counseling and career-information centers (many organizations have gone to a system of open bidding on jobs to enhance information about job opportunities within the firm); (3) *preparation* and *development*, a period during which individual and formal training programs are undertaken to prepare individuals for the next career stage; and (4) *integration*, in which the individual is placed on the job for which he or she has planned. Finally, the feedback loops in exhibit 14–12 indicate that career planning is a sequential process, occurring in stages. At each stage, both employer and employee should evaluate the success of the previous career-planning effort and adjust the next effort based on this information.[38]

Shepard has developed a number of life- and career-planning exercises that appear to have some merit and that can be empirically evaluated.[39] This exercise involves the following activities:

1. The individual draws a horizontal line from left to right indicating life span. The length represents the totality of the person's experience. This drawing and each of the other steps is first done privately, and then it is shared with a group of between ten and fifteen participants in the exercise.

2. The individual answers the question, "Who am I?" by writing ten short answers on ten cards and ranking them in order of importance.

3. The individual prepares a life inventory of important events, such as:
   (a) Things the person does well.

    (b) Things the person wants to learn.

    (c) Values concerning money, work, and family.

    (d) Things that the person wants to stop doing.

    (e) Things that have resulted in pleasant and rewarding experiences.

4. The first three activities are discussed in subgroups.

5. The individual then develops a hypothetical obituary, including a personal epitaph.

6. Participants are paired off, and the epitaph can be discussed. Then, the partners can write a eulogy for each other and discuss it.

These activities are designed to encourage individuals to plan their careers more carefully. Whether these specific activities can enhance life and career planning is pure speculation at this time. It appears that some type of life and career planning is congruent with the notion that clear and fulfilling career goals can motivate the individual.[40] This idea, of course, needs to be studied before it gains greater acceptance among managers.

Dual Careers

An ever-increasing phenomenon being faced by both individuals and organizations is the problem of managing dual careers. The phrase *dual careers* describes the husband and wife who both have full-time careers, whether in similar or different fields and in the same organization or in different organizations.

One of the major reasons for this situation is the rapid increase in the number of married women who have joined the work force on a full-time basis. According to labor department statistics, more than one-half of all mothers with children under the age of three are in the work force. In addition, nearly 58 percent of all working women are married and living with employed spouses. This statistic indicates that more than 46 million employed men and women—out of 98 million people in the American workforce—are two-career couples.

At least two factors have been discussed as the possible causes for the growth in dual-career families.[41] First, pure economic reasons may be behind the increase in the number of married women seeking full-time employment. The high annual inflation rate has put a significant crunch on many family budgets, forcing major adjustments. As Peter Drucker states:

> The husband is still considered the breadwinner and his income is used for normal household purposes. The wife's income averages 60 percent of the husband's, and is used for extras. Her money provides the margin for a bigger house, the luxury car, the expensive vacation.[42]

Particularly for young married couples, two incomes provide for establishing the "good life" much earlier than their parents could. They have the opportunity to buy large homes, take extended weekend or annual vacations, and purchase luxury items usually *before* children are added to the family. Their parents usually tried to attain this type of life style only *after* the children left the nest.

Exhibit 14–12   Career-Development Process

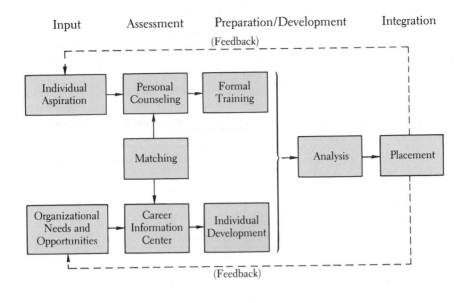

Input   Assessment   Preparation/Development   Integration

J. Aplin and D. Gerster, "Career Development: An Integration of Individual and Organizational Needs," *Personnel* 2 (1978): 25. Reprinted with permission.

The second reason concerns the experience of a need by women for professional growth, development, and recognition. Even the most casual observer will notice that the number of women graduating from colleges and universities has been steadily increasing in both undergraduate and graduate programs. As these women enter the work force, they have the same desires to learn, grow, and advance as their male counterparts do. Whether the dual-career couple is motivated by economic need or professional development, they present unique opportunities *and* adjustment problems for both the organization and the couple.[43]

For the dual-career couple, there are issues that concern whether two careers are a liability or an asset, and what effect it has on career flexibility. For example, if one is offered a significant promotion opportunity in another city that has limited job opportunities for the spouse, how should the couple react? What if the husband and wife work for two different organizations that compete with one another or that present a potential conflict of interests for the couple? There are also issues related to the conflict between career and family needs. A household still must be maintained, and in some cases there are children who must be raised. Some dual-career couples may believe that some of these problems are insurmountable; others look at it as an opportunity for a new start and a chance to give careers an added commitment.

For the organization, there are a number of issues that must be faced. For example, how to manage recruitment if both are desirable employees for the firm; how to handle problems of travel, transfers, or promotions; should the organization get involved in dual career planning?

When dual-career couples first appeared in organizations, neither the couple nor the organization knew how to handle the potential conflicts that invariably developed. Over time, however, a number of *keys* to success have been noted. For the couple, a successful dual career usually results from an emphasis on four factors. First, there must be a *mutual* commitment by the couple to *both* careers. This means that one member does not take precedence over the other on all career matters. Second, there should be an air of *flexibility*—personal *and* job related—by both members. There must be a willingness to change plans, shift gears, try new ways of doing things, and generally be adaptive to many different situations. Third, successful dual-career couples have developed certain *coping* mechanisms to resolve job- and family-related conflicts. Finally, similar to the first two points, an emphasis should be placed on keeping *up to date* in one's career. To be flexible and adaptable, each member of the dual-career family should spend considerable time and effort on self-assessment and continuing education.

Organizations, too, must be able to adapt to dual-career couples because they are becoming more prevalent. Initially, this could involve providing flexible career tracks. Instead of a rigid career path, a more flexible path, possibly involving cross-functional moves, may need to be developed. Second, some internal policies may need to be revised. For example, less rigid transfer policies (so that turning down a transfer does not exclude future promotions), and special recruiting techniques. Third, creation of dual-career support services could prove to be useful. Examples could be helping an unemployed spouse find a new job, locating day-care centers or child-care arrangements, assisting in buying and selling homes, revised fringe-benefit policies, and providing couple career counseling.[44]

In summary, it is important for managers and organizations alike to recognize that the dual-career phenomena is not a short-lived, temporary situation. It is more a reflection of changing societal and cultural norms on one hand, and a recognition that a career is shaped more by the individual than by the organization on the other. Because the individual's career may be redirected from time to time to meet the needs of the person, it is crucial for organizations to develop programs that can utilize these human talents more effectively.

Applications and Implications for the Manager

Rewards in Organizations

1. We can examine the role of rewards in organizations from the perspective of both managers and employees. For management, rewards constitute a major area of policy influencing its success in motivating job performance, retaining qualified employees, reducing absenteeism, and attracting qualified job applicants to the organization.

2. For the individual, rewards are important in the organization because they serve to fulfill work-related needs. Expectations regarding rewards are important in at least three-work-related

decisions: (a) the decision to perform at a given level; (b) the decision to leave an organization or be absent from work; and (c) the decision to join an organization.

3. Individuals typically have a number of different needs they seek to satisfy through employment. The particular profile of needs perceived as important to individuals varies from one person to another and throughout individual life cycles.

4. Career advancement is becoming increasingly important as a reward to individuals. In response, organizations have instituted career-planning aid as a major reward to employees.

5. A major policy issue in reward systems is the distinction between intrinsic and extrinsic rewards. Intrinsic rewards (those associated with the job itself) are the most powerful in terms of motivating employee behavior and performance but are less amenable to direct managerial control. As indicated in chapter 6, about the only tool managers have for manipulating intrinsic rewards is job design. Extrinsic rewards (for example, money compensation, fringe benefits, supervision, promotions, and friendships), although less important to employee motivation, are more amenable to direct managerial control. Compensation policy, job placement policy, and promotion policy are methods for directly

manipulating extrinsic rewards. Finally, no attempts to influence rewards will have an impact on employee behavior unless the employee personally evaluates the reward as important and adopts the desired performance or behavior to achieve a goal.

6. The bases for distributing rewards within organizations are a second area of policy. Equality, power, need, and distributive justice have each provided a basis at one time and in certain organizations for distributing rewards. The major problem facing managers is that demands are made to satisfy more than one of these bases at one time. Thus, for example, an organization may have to reconcile demands for distributive justice with external market power in establishing relative rates of pay. In reality, organizations attempt to reach a compromise among competing demands that is acceptable to a majority of employees.

7. Limited evidence exists from the research regarding the influence of rewards on employee choice behavior, suggesting that anticipation of rewards predicts performance levels, turnover, absenteeism, and organizational choice. The evidence is not all that clear at this point, however, but a number of conditions can be specified under which the effect of reward on behavior and performance would be more predictable.

Review of Theories, Research, and Applications

1. Briefly describe the purposes served by rewards for an organization. Describe how reward policy influences the success of an organization in achieving these purposes.

2. What role do rewards play in employee motivation? What kinds of individual decisions are potentially influenced by rewards?

3. Compare a single young woman, twenty-two years old, who has just graduated with a bachelors degree in business and entered the job market, with a father of four children who is thirty-eight and has been employed as an engineer for sixteen years, with respect to their work-related needs. How might the rewards they seek in their employment differ?

4. How do work-related needs change during a person's lifetime? What kinds of factors influence these changes?

5. What is a career path? How might career planning be rewarding to employees?

6. Describe the difference between extrinsic and intrinsic rewards. Which has the greater potential for influencing behavior? Why?

7. Do managers have more control over extrinsic or intrinsic rewards? Why?

8. Describe the individual processes included in Locke's theory of task performance. What does this model say about the influence of rewards on behavior and performance?

9. Describe the differences between equality, power, need, and distributive justice as bases for distributing rewards in organizations. Which do you think are most commonly employed in business organizations?

10. Is there any evidence to indicate that rewards have an influence on organizational choice?

11. What influence does membership in an informal group have on an individual employee's reaction to a wage incentive program?

Notes

1. Studs Terkel, *Working* (New York: Avon Books, 1972).
2. Douglas T. Hall, *Careers in Organizations* (Santa Monica, Calif.: Goodyear, 1976), chap. 3.
3. Ibid.
4. Lloyd Lofquist and Rene Dawis, *Adjustment to Work: A Psychological View of Man's Problems in a Work-Oriented Society* (Englewood Cliffs, N.J.: Prentice-Hall, 1969).
5. L. Reynolds, *The Structure of Labor Markets* (Westport, Conn.: Greenwood Press, 1971).
6. F. G. Leisieur, ed., *The Scanlon Plan* (Cambridge, Mass.: MIT, 1958).
7. F. Herzberg, *Work and the Nature of Man* (Cleveland: World Publishing, 1966); F. Herzberg, B. Mausner, and B. Snyderman, *The Motivation to Work,* 2nd ed. (New York: Wiley, 1959).
8. Lyman Porter, Edward E. Lawler III, and J. Richard Hackman, *Behavior in Organizations* (New York: McGraw-Hill, 1975); Joseph A. Litterer, *The Analysis of Organizations,* 2nd ed. (New York: John Wiley and Sons, 1973); Edwin A. Locke, "Toward a Theory of Task Motivation and Incentives," *Organizational Behavior and Human Performance,* 1968, pp. 157–89; Peter Frost, "Task Processes

and Individual Performance," *Organizational Behavior and Human Performance*.
9. Locke, "Toward a Theory of Task Motivation," p. 163.
10. J. Richard Hackman and Edward E. Lawler III, "Employee Reactions to Job Characteristics," *Journal of Applied Psychology,* 1971, pp. 259–86; Edward E. Lawler III, J. Richard Hackman, and S. Kaufman, "Effects of Job Redesign: A Field Experiment," *Journal of Applied Social Psychology,* 1973, pp. 49–62; A. P. Brief and Ramon Aldag, "Employee Reactions to Task Characteristics; A Constructive Replication," *Journal of Applied Psychology,* 1975, pp. 182–85.
11. "The Tightening Squeeze on White-Collar Pay," *Business Week,* 12 September 1977, pp. 82–94.
12. Ibid.; and "Merit Money: More Firms Link Pay To Job Performance As Inflation Wanes," *Wall Street Journal,* 7 March 1977.
13. G. T. Milkovich and M. J. Delaney, "A Note On Cafeteria Pay Plans," *Industrial Relations,* 1975, pp. 112–16; S. M. Nealy and J. G. Goodale, "Determining Worker Preferences Among Employee Benefits and Pay," *Journal of Applied Psychology,* 1967,

pp. 357–61; J. Shuster, "Another Look at Compensation Preferences," *Industrial Management Review*, 1969, pp. 1–18; and T. A. Mahoney, "Compensation Preferences of Managers," *Industrial Relations*, 1964, pp. 135–44.

14. Nealy and Goodale, "Determining Worker Preference."

15. Herbert S. Parnes, *Research on Labor Mobility* (New York: Social Science Research Council, 1954).

16. James G. March and Herbert A. Simon, *Organizations* (New York: Wiley, 1958).

17. R. Marriott, *Incentive Payment Systems: A Review of Research and Opinion* (London: Staples Press, 1958).

18. O. Collins, M. Dalton, and D. Roy, "Restrictions of Output and Social Cleavage in Industry," *Applied Anthropology*, 1946, pp. 1–14; M. Dalton, "The Industrial Rate Buster: A Characterization," *Applied Anthropology*, 1948, pp. 5–18; W. F. Whyte, *Money and Motivation* (New York: Harper, 1955).

19. Edward E. Lawler III and Lyman W. Porter, "Predicting Managers' Pay and Their Satisfaction with Their Pay," *Personnel Psychology*, 1966, pp. 3–8; M. Brenner and H. Lockwood, "Salary as a Predictor of Salary: A 20-Year Study," *Journal of Applied Psychology*, 1965, pp. 295–98.

20. Edward E. Lawler III, *Pay and Organizational Effectiveness* (New York: McGraw-Hill, 1971).

21. G. T. Milkovich and P. H. Anderson, "Management Compensation and Secrecy Policies," *Personnel Psychology*, 1972, pp. 293–302.

22. Robert L. Opsahl and Marvin D. Dunnette, "The Role of Financial Compensation in Industrial Motivation," *Psychological Bulletin*, August 1966, pp. 94–113; Marvin D. Dunnette, Edward E. Lawler III, Karl Weick, and Robert L. Opsahl, "The Role of Financial Compensation in Managerial Motivation," *Organizational Behavior and Human Performance*, 1967, pp. 175–217; David C. McClelland, "The Role of Money in Managing Motivation," in Henry L. Tosi, Robert J. House, and Marvin D. Dunnette, eds.,

Managerial Motivation and Compensation (East Lansing: Michigan State University, 1972), pp. 523–39.

23. Lawler, *Pay and Organizational Effectiveness*, p. 102.

24. Ibid., p. 172.

25. Lyman W. Porter and Richard M. Steers, "Organizational, Work, and Personal Factors in Employee Turnover and Absenteeism," *Psychological Bulletin*, 1973, pp. 151–76.

26. Edward E. Lawler III and J. R. Hackman, "The Impact of Employee Participation in the Development of Pay Incentive Plans: A Field Experiment," *Journal of Applied Psychology*, 1969, pp. 467–71; K. C. Scheflen, Edward E. Lawler III, and J. Richard Hackman, "Long-Term Impact of Employee Participation in the Development of Pay Incentive Plans," *Journal of Applied Psychology*, 1971, pp. 182–86.

27. Reynolds, *Structure of Labor Markets*; March and Simon, *Organizations*.

28. Victor H. Vroom, "Organizational Choice: A Study of Pre- and Post-Decision Processes," *Organizational Behavior and Human Performance*, 1966, pp. 212–25; John P. Wanous, "Occupational Preferences: Perceptions of Valence and Instrumentality and Objective Data," *Journal of Applied Psychology*, (1972), pp. 152–61.

29. Dale Yoder, "Organization for Economic Cooperation and Development," *Wages and Labor Mobility*, Paris (1965).

30. L. Reynolds, *The Structure of Labor Markets*; Parnes, *Research on Labor Mobility*; Wanous, "Occupational Preferences."

31. M. Horner, "Toward an Understanding of Achievement-Related Conflicts in Women," *Journal of Social Issues*, 1972, pp. 157–76.

32. D. Super, *The Psychology of Careers* (New York: Harper, 1957).

33. Edgar H. Schein, *Career Dynamics: Matching Individual and Organizational Needs* (Reading, Mass.: Addison-Wesley, 1978).

34. Edgar H. Schein, "The Individual, the Organization, and the Career: A Conceptual Scheme," *Journal of*

Applied Behavioral Science, 1971, pp. 401–26.

35. Super, *Psychology of Careers.*
36. "Who Is Responsible for Employee Career Planning: A Symposium," *Personnel,* 1978, pp. 10–22; P. Benson and G. Thornton, "A Model Career Planning," *Personnel,* 1978, pp. 30–45; and H. Wellbank, et al., "Planning Job Progression for Effective Career Development and Human Resource Management," *Personnel,* 1978, pp. 54–64.
37. J. Aplin and D. Gerster, "Career Development: An Integration of Individual and Organizational Needs, *Personnel,* 1978, pp. 23–29.
38. Ibid.
39. This is reported in Edgar F. Huse, "Organizational Change," *Organizational Development and Change* (St. Paul, Minn.: West, 1975),

p. 267, and modification is reported in Wendell L. French and Cecil H. Bell, Jr., *Organizational Development* (Englewood Cliffs: Prentice Hall, 1973).

40. Wellbank, et al., "Planning Job Progression."
41. Douglas T. Hall, *Careers in Organizations* (Santa Monica, Calif.: Goodyear, 1976).
42. Peter F. Drucker, "The Economics of Contemporary Buyers," *Wall Street Journal,* 1 December 1976.
43. Douglas T. Hall and F. Hall, "What's New in Career Management," *Organizational Dynamics,* Summer 1976, pp. 17–33.
44. F. Hall and Douglas T. Hall, "Dual Careers—How Do Couples and Companies Cope with the Problems?" *Organizational Dynamics,* Spring 1978, pp. 57–77.

Additional References

Annas, J. "Facing Today's Compensation Uncertainties," *Personnel,* 1976, pp. 12–17.

Brewer, J., and Hanson, M. "A New Dimension in Employee Development; A System for Career Planning and Guidance." *Personnel Journal,* 1975, pp. 228–31.

Carlson, H. "G.M.'s Quality of Work Life Efforts." *Personnel,* 1978, pp. 11–23.

Donnelly, J. H., Jr., and Etzel, M. "Retail Store Performance and Job Satisfaction—A Study of Anxiety-Stress and Propensity to Leave Among Retail Employees." *Journal of Retailing,* 1977, pp. 23–28.

Duval, B., and Courtney, R., "Upward Mobility: The GF Way of Opening Employee Advancement Opportunities." *Personnel,* 1978, pp. 43–53.

Gavin, J. F. "Occupational Mental Health—Forces and Trends." *Personnel Journal,* 1977, pp. 198–201.

Gayle, J. "How Job Pressure Affects Rand Productivity." *Research Management,* 1977, pp. 35–37.

Gohfredson, G. D. "Career Stability and Redirection in Adulthood." *Journal of Applied Psychology,* 1977, pp. 436–45.

Gould, S., and Hawkins, B. "Organizational Career Stage as a Moderator of the Satisfaction-Performance Relationship." *Academy of Management Journal,* 1978, pp. 434–50.

Hillebrandt, F., Jr. "Individual Performance-Satisfaction Relationship." *Academy of Management Journal,* 1978, pp. 434–50.

Ivancevich, J. M., and Lyon, H. C. "The Shortened Workweek: A Field Experiment." *Journal of Applied Psychology,* 1977, pp. 34–37.

King, A. "Research: How Rewards Can Be Made More Effective." *Compensation Review,* 1978, pp. 32–40.

Lawler, E. E., III, and Olsen, R. "Designing Reward Systems For New Organizations." *Personnel,* 1977, pp. 48–60.

Lehmann, P. "Job Stress—Hidden Hazard." *Job Safety and Health,* 1974, pp. 4–10.

London, M.; Crandall, R.; and Seals, G. W. "The Contribution of Job and Leisure Satisfaction to Quality of Life." *Journal of Applied Psychology,* 1977, pp. 328–34.

Maitchuk, W. "How To Reconcile the Merit

Principle With Anti-Inflation Regulations," *Canadian Chartered Accountant,* 1976, pp. 41–42.

MORRISON, R. F. "Career Adaptivity: The Effective Adaptation of Managers to Changing Role Demands." *Journal of Applied Psychology,* 1977, pp. 549–58.

PRITCHARD, R. D.; CAMPBELL, K. M.; and CAMPBELL, D. J. "Effects of Extrinsic Financial Rewards on Intrinsic Motivation." *Journal of Applied Psychology,* 1977, pp. 9–15.

TERBORG, J. R., and MILLER, H. E. "Motivation, Behavior, and Performance: A Closer Examination of

Goal Setting and Monetary Incentives." *Journal of Applied Psychology,* 1978, pp. 29–39.

WHITEHILL, A. "Maintenance Factors: The Neglected Side of Worker Motivation." *Personnel Journal,* 1976, pp. 516–19.

WALTER, V. "Self-Motivated Personal Career Planning—A Breakthrough In Human Resource Management—Part I." *Personnel Journal,* 1976, pp. 112–15.

WILLIAMS, D. "Accelerating Pay Raises For Managers Who Switch Employers." *Harvard Business Review,* 1976, pp. 8–12.

A Case of Incentives

The Bonus Policy of Ezell Musical Instrument Company

Ezell Musical Instrument Company (EMI) is located in Frederick, Maryland. It is a medium-sized operation that has grown out of a family-owned company. Like many companies, it has to face tough competition at home and abroad. M. G. Ezell III is now the president of the firm.

Several years ago, when Ezell first took over, he thought about how he might build morale in the company. He felt that the company had good workers and that he would like to reward them for past services to encourage them to be more productive. EMI was not unionized. He hesitated about raising base wages because it might make the firm uncompetitive if foreign competition increased.

EMI was having an exceptionally good year, both for sales and profits. As a result, Ezell thought that the best way to reward the employees was to give them a Christmas-New Year's bonus. As he said to Abe Stick, his personnel manager: "Nothing like the old buck to make a man work harder." His bonus system was as follows:

Wages or Salary	Bonus
< $6,500	$500
$6,501–7,500	$600
$7,501–8,500	$700
$8,501–10,000	$800
> $10,000	8% of salary or wage

The bonuses were well received. Many people thanked the president, and Stick heard lots of good comments from the supervisors in January about how much harder the employees were working.

The next year, more foreign competitors entered the market. Materials were harder to get and more expensive. Sales were down 5 percent, and profits were down 15 percent. Ezell did not feel he could afford the same bonuses as last year. As a result, the bonuses were decreased as follows:

Wages or Salary	Bonus
< $6,500	$250
$6,501–7,500	$300
$7,501–8,500	$350
$8,501–10,000	$400
> $10,000	4% of salary wage

This time, Stick heard little from the supervisors about increased productivity. He asked Harry Bell, one of the supervisors, what the reaction was to the bonuses.

Bell: To tell you the truth, Abe, I have morale problems. My people worked hard this year. It wasn't their fault sales or profits were down. Many expected last year's bonus or better. So they spent most of the old figure for Christmas gifts. When they got that letter from M. G. telling them they were getting only half of last year's on December 27, there was gloom and doom and some mumblings. Some of my people seem to be working less hard than at any time I can remember.

Stick: But that's not fair, Harry. They never received any bonuses before. Now they should be glad they received anything.

Bell: That's not the way they see it!

Stick decided not to discuss the matter with Ezell. Stick figured the problem would blow over. However, this year was even worse. Sales held but were not up to the prior years' levels. Profits were almost nonexistent. The board of directors decided to omit the dividend.

Now, Ezell has come to Stick. Ezell says: "Abe, I don't see how we can pay any bonus this year. Do you think we can get by without causing a big drop in morale?"

Case Primer Questions

1. What does this case illustrate about the motivational impacts of bonuses as incentives?

2. Why should Mr. Bell expect that the employees would react negatively to the reduction in bonuses when they are not guaranteed as part of an employee's compensation?

3. Have rewards been accurately tied to performance by the Ezell compensation policy? If not, how might this failure be the cause of their problem?

4. How might you suggest an alternative formula or policy for disbursing extra income to employees?

Experiential Exercise

Motivation Through Merit Pay Increases

Purpose

1. To examine the application of motivation theories to the problem of merit pay increases.

2. To understand the relationship between motivation and performance.

3. To consider the impact of multiple performance criteria in managerial decision making.

Required understanding

The student should understand the different approaches to motivation in organizations.

How to set up the exercise

Set up groups of four to eight students for the forty-five to sixty minute exercise. The groups should be separated from each other and asked to converse only with members of their own group. The participants should then read the following:

The Gordon Manufacturing Corporation is a small manufacturing company located in San Diego, California. The company is nonunionized and manufactures laboratory analysis equipment for hospitals.

Approximately one year ago, the manager of the Component Assembly Department established three manufacturing goals for the department. The goals were: (1) reduce raw material storage costs by 10 percent; (2) reduce variable labor costs (i.e., overtime) by 12 percent; and (3) decrease the number of quality rejects by 15 percent. The department manager stated to the six unit supervisors that the degree to which each supervisor met, or exceeded, these goals would be one of the major inputs into their merit pay increases for the year. In previous years, merit increases were based on seniority and an informal evaluation by the department manager.

The six department supervisors worked on separate but similar production lines. A profile of each supervisor is as follows:

Freddie McNutt: white; twenty-four; married with no children; one year with the company after graduating from a local college. First full-time job since graduation from college. He is well-liked by all employees and has exhibited a high level of enthusiasm for his work.

Sara Morton: white; twenty-eight; single; three years with the company after receiving her degree from the state university. Has a job offer from another company for a similar job that provides a substantial pay increase over her present salary (15 percent). Gordon does not want to lose Sara because her overall performance has been excellent. The job offer would require her to move to another state, which she views unfavorably; Gordon can keep her if it can come close to matching her salary offer.

Jackson Smith: black; thirty-two; married with three children; three years with the company; high-school education. One of our most stable and steady supervisors. However, he supervises a group of workers who are known to be unfriendly and uncooperative with him and other employees.

Lazlo Nagy: white; thirty-four; married with four children; high-school equivalent learning; one year with the company. Immigrated to this country six years ago and has recently become a U.S. citizen. A steady worker, well-liked by his coworkers, but has had difficulty learning the English language. As a result, certain problems of communication within his group and with other groups have developed in the past.

Karen Doolittle: white; twenty-nine; divorcee with three children; two years with the company; high-school education. Since her divorce one year ago, her performance has begun to improve. Prior to that, her performance was very erratic, with frequent absences. She is the sole support for her three children.

Vinnie Sareno: white; twenty-seven, single; two years with the company; college graduate. One of the best-liked employees at Gordon. However, has shown a lack of initiative and ambition on the job. Appears

Exhibit 14–13 Individual Performance for the Six Supervisors During the Past Year

| Supervisor | Current Salary (000's Omitted) | Goal Attainment[a] | | | | Manager's Evaluation[b] | | | |
		Storage Costs (10%)	Labor Costs (12%)	Quality Rejects (15%)	Effort	Cooperativeness	Ability to Work Independently	Knowledge of Job
Freddie McNutt	$11.5	12%	12%	17%	Excellent	Excellent	Good	Good
Sara Morton	$12.5	12%	13%	16%	Excellent	Excellent	Excellent	Excellent
Jackson Smith	$12.5	6%	2%	3%	Good	Excellent	Good	Good
Lazlo Nagy	$11.5	4%	4%	12%	Excellent	Good	Fair	Fair
Karen Doolittle	$12.0	11%	10%	10%	Fair	Fair	Fair	Good
Vinnie Sareno	$12.0	8%	10%	3%	Fair	Fair	Fair	Fair

[a] Numbers designate actual cost and quality-reject reduction.
[b] The possible ratings are poor, fair, good, and excellent.

to be preoccupied with his social life, particularly around his recently purchased beach home.

Exhibit 14–13 presents summary data on the performance of the six supervisors during the past year. The presented data includes the current annual salary, the performance level on the three goals, and an overall evaluation by the department manager.

The new budget for the upcoming year has allocated a total of $79,200 for supervisory salaries in the Component Assembly Department, a $7,200 increase from last year. Top management has indicated that salary increases should range from 5 percent to 12 percent of the supervisors' current salaries and should be tied as closely as possible to their performance.

In making the merit pay increase decisions, the following points should be considered:

1. The decisions will likely set a precedent for future salary and merit increase considerations.

2. Salary increases should not be excessive, but should be representative of the supervisor's performance during the past year. It is hoped that the supervisors develop a clear perception that performance will lead to monetary rewards and that this will serve to motivate them to even better performance.

3. The decisions should be concerned with equity; that is, they ought to be consistent with each other.

4. The company does not want to lose these experienced supervisors to other firms. Management of this company not only wants the supervisors to be satisfied with their salary increases, but also to further develop the feeling that Gordon Manufacturing is a good company for advancement, growth, and career development.

Instructions for the exercise

1. Each person in the class should *individually* determine the *dollar amount* and *percentage increase* in salary for each of the six supervisors. Individual decisions should be justified by a rationale or decision rule.

2. After each individual has reached a decision, the group will convene and make the same decision as noted in (1) above.

3. After each group has reached a decision, a spokesperson for each group will present the following information to the full class:
    (a) The group's decision concerning merit pay increase for each supervisor (dollar and percentage).
    (b) The high, low, and average individual decisions in the group.
    (c) A rationale for the group's decision.

A Performance-Oriented Framework to Study Organizational Behavior

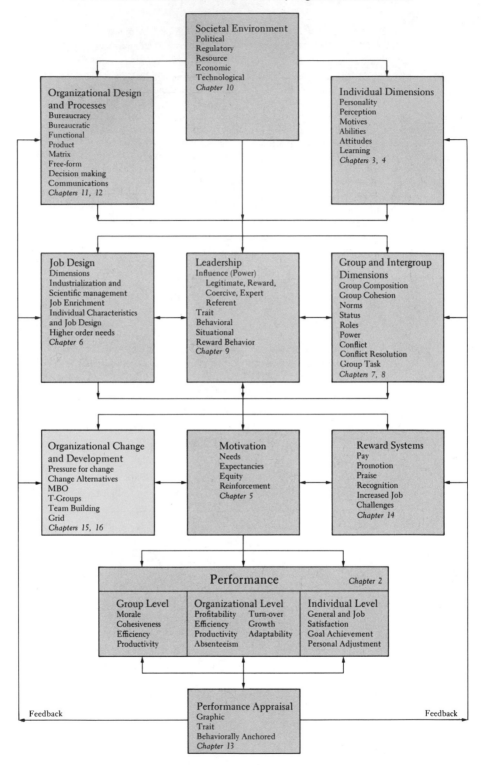

PART FIVE

Organizational Change and Development

CHAPTER 15

Organizational Change and Development: A Framework

We have witnessed remarkable and rapid changes in our life styles, institutions, and values during the latter part of the twentieth century. The advances of modern technology; the tremendous expansion of available scientific, personal, and financial information to reach decisions; and the questioning of social structures, values, and the institutions of industrialized nations have been evident to even the most casual observer. Whether we approve of such changes is now a moot issue. It seems more reasonable to think about how these changes can be efficiently managed.

The modern organization certainly needs to cope with both external and internal changes in the environment and among its employees. The static or totally *reactive* organization will have a difficult time surviving in a changing society. Yesterday's successes mean very little in an environment that wants, needs, and uses products and services that were not available last month or last year. In order to survive, organizations must develop a program that enables them to cope with change. This does not mean that an organization must fear change or that it must completely change or overhaul its organizational design or practices. Instead, organizations need to continually diagnose and be amenable to reworking their plans to adapt to changing conditions. In other words, the key to success—even survival—of many organizations is the degree to which they can become *proactive* organizations.

In this chapter, we will present a basic framework for understanding organizational change and development. Once again, a word of caution is in order for those examining our framework. If a perfect model were available and could be applied to every type of organization, it would be easy to convince managers that change is inevitable and that the application of the model's principles is certain to achieve positive results. Of course, this is not the case. The model is offered as a suggested framework for working through our thoughts and assumptions about organizational change and development. In the next chapter, we will turn our attention to a discussion of individual, group, and organizational change strategies.

The Goals of Organizational Change and Development

Organizational change and development efforts are typically associated with a variety of goals and different terminology. The goals may be and occasionally are written down, but they may be implied by the actions of the management of an organization. Some of the more common goals are increased or higher performance, improved motivation, increased cooperation, clearer communications, reduced absenteeism and turnover, minimization of conflict, and reduced costs.

There is a disagreement among researchers and managers about how organizational change can best be studied. There are those who suggest that the term *organizational development* (OD) describes the process of managing change. These individuals even offer organizational development as a newly emerging discipline directed toward using behavioral science knowledge to assist organizations in adjusting to change.[1] A slightly more thorough interpretation of OD is offered in the following statement:

> Using knowledge and techniques from the behavioral science, organizational development (OD) is a process which attempts to increase organizational effectiveness by integrating individual desires for growth and development with organizational goals. Typically, this process is a planned change effort which involves a total system over a period of time, and these change efforts are related to the organization's mission.[2]

These two interpretations of OD illustrate its relation to organizational change. Those managers engaged in managing change utilize many of the techniques, models, and approaches proposed originally by organizational development experts. Thus, we plan to discuss organizational change in the context of OD. This is not to be interpreted as our acceptance of organization change or development as a discipline or even an emerging discipline. We believe that change and development are a part of the field of organizational behavior. The manager should not be seduced by the term *discipline,* which connotes definitive answers. Managers faced with making decisions concerning organizational change and development know that definitive answers are elusive.

Underlying the specific goals of organizational change and OD are a number of broad goals. Two of these are:

1. Change and development will attempt to focus, when necessary, on an organization's ability to adapt to its environments.

2. Change and development involve, in many cases, the behavior patterns of employees (e.g., managerial and nonmanagerial).

Hospitals, universities, banks, government agencies, and other organizations are in a continual struggle to adapt to their environments. Because the management of any organization cannot completely control its environment, they must continually introduce internal changes in design, reward systems, performance appraisal programs, and so forth, that allow them to cope with new demands for worker dignity and autonomy, of increased competition, and of government legislation. If a plant in a growing community continued to have its skilled technicians check in on a time clock while every competitor eliminated the "punch in" system, there might be a decrease in morale or even an increase in turnover. Management has to *react* to the procedures of competitors. However, there are some changes that are initiated by an organization that set the pace for the competition. These are *proactive* in that the organization has introduced changes internally that may influence the environment.

The second broad goal of change and development involves the modification of behavior patterns. Any change in job design, wage structures, or a goal-setting program is an attempt to modify behavior. The modification attempt may be directed at the individual, a group, the organization, or interacting groups. Modification of employee behavior, like adaptation to the environment, is an extremely difficult and complex task. Therefore, organizational change and development must be implemented with a number of guiding propositions:

1. A planned, systematic program must be initiated by the organization's management.

2. The program must aim at making the organization more adaptable to either the present or anticipated environment.

3. The program must use methods designed to change knowledge, skills, attitudes, processes, behaviors, job design, and organization design.

4. The program must be based on the assumption that organizational effectiveness and individual performance are enhanced to the extent that the process facilitates the optimum integration of individual and organizational goals.

These four propositions suggest a more eclectic view of organizational change and development, which incorporates a number of techniques or strategies. This is opposed to a singular view, which proposes that the answer to a problem can be resolved by sensitivity training or goal setting or by praising good performance.[3] In the area of organizational change and development, as in the areas of organizational design, leadership, and motivation, a best or singular answer is unrealistic because of the contingencies facing managerial decision makers.

Approaches to Organizational Change

Organizational change and development can be introduced into a department, group, or an entire organization through any number of approaches. Some of the approaches emphasize what is to be changed; others stress the process of how change is to be accomplished.

Emphasizing the 'What' of Change

A commonly used conception of what approaches are available to managers is delineated by Leavitt.[4] He identifies structural, technological, task, and people approaches to change. *Structural* approaches introduce change through new formal guidelines, procedures, and policies, such as the organization chart, budgeting methods, and rules and regulations. *Technological* approaches focus on rearrangements in work flow, as achieved through new physical layouts, work methods, and work standards. *Task* approaches focus on the job performed by the individual, emphasizing motivational and job design changes (see chapters 5 and 6). *People* approaches stress modifying attitudes, motivation, and behavioral skills, which is accomplished through such techniques as new training programs, selection procedures, and performance appraisal techniques. A schematic of Leavitt's framework is shown in exhibit 15–1.

It is Leavitt's contention that a change in one of these areas will influence the others. For example, changes in structure to facilitate task accomplishment are not made in a vacuum. People must work within the new structural arrangement using some technological process, procedure, or equipment. On occasion, the people do not fit into the new structure and cannot adapt. The manager needs to carefully understand the interdependencies of these approaches and be willing to examine the economics and behavioral costs and benefits of change.

Emphasizing the 'How' of Change

Another description of approaches to change focuses on the *how* aspects. Based on personal experience and some empirical analyses, Greiner identifies a number of

Exhibit 15–1 Interdependencies in Organizational Change

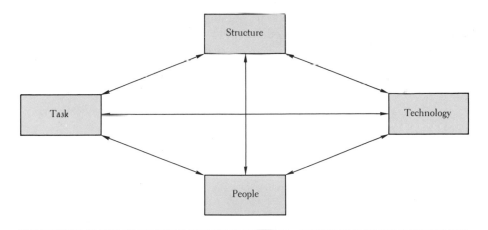

Source: H. Leavitt, "Applied Organizational Changes in Industry: Structural, Technological, and Humanistic Approaches," in *Handbook of Organizations,* ed. James G. March (Chicago: Rand McNally, 1965), p. 1145.

Grener

specific descriptions of change that can be introduced into an organization. He categorizes these under three alternative uses of power.[5] Exhibit 15–2 presents a continuum to highlight these three approaches to change.

Unilateral power

In a unilateral change approach, the subordinate makes little or no contribution. The superior, relying on position power and authority, unilaterally suggests the change. The use of lateral power can be exercised in three distinct forms:

1. *By decree.* This is a "one-way" announcement from the superior that this is the change that will occur and this is what is expected from subordinates. The communication flow is from the superior to subordinates. An example would be an announcement that as of Monday all insurance accident claim forms must be completed within twenty-four hours of the accident. Failure to comply with this change in procedure will be counted against an adjuster in the appraisal system.

2. *By replacement.* Individuals in one or more positions are replaced by other individuals because the superior assumes that by changing people, performance will be improved. Little or no consultation occurs between the superior and subordinates.

3. *By structure.* Instead of decree or replacement of personnel, managers change the required relationships of subordinates working in a situation. They may eliminate a layer of the structure or introduce a new staff advisory group. It is assumed that by changing relationships, behavior and performance will be affected positively.

Shared power

The shared approach is built upon the assumption that authority is present in an organization, but it must be carefully used. If the organization has capable subordinates, there can be a sharing of power in reaching important change decisions. This approach is employed in two slightly different ways:

1. *The group decision.* Group members participate in selecting from several alternate solutions specified in advance by superiors. The group selects what they

Exhibit 15–2 Three Approaches to Change

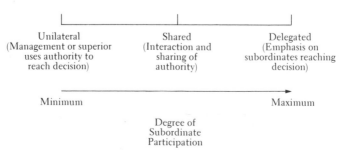

| Unilateral (Management or superior uses authority to reach decision) | Shared (Interaction and sharing of authority) | Delegated (Emphasis on subordinates reaching decision) |

Minimum   Maximum

Degree of
Subordinate
Participation

believe is the best alternative. This approach involves neither problem identification nor problem solving but emphasizes obtaining group agreement. It is assumed that through group decision making there will be a greater commitment to the selected alternative because of the active participation by members.

2. *Group problem solving*. The group solves problems through discussion. The group has wide latitude not only over choosing and diagnosing problems to be discussed but also in developing solutions to these problems.

Delegated power

With delegated power, the subordinates actively participate in the change program from the onset to the implementation. There are two forms:

1. *The case discussion group*. The superior and subordinates meet to openly discuss the case at hand. They diagnose, analyze, and consider alternative solutions. The openness is assumed to motivate the subordinates to offer solutions to problems.

2. *The sensitivity training group*. Individuals are trained in small discussion groups to be more sensitive to the underlying process of individual and group behavior. An emphasis is placed on improving a person's self-awareness. Changes in work patterns and relationships are assumed to follow from changes in interpersonal relationships. The anticipated sequence is to improve self-awareness, which leads to improved interpersonal relationships and eventually improvements in work performance.

In a report that surveyed a number of cases of organizational change, Greiner noted that the shared approach was more successful than either the unilateral or delegated approaches.[6] The unilateral approach seems to disregard any informational inputs of subordinates. In some cases, subordinates know more about the technological and people aspects of the change. On the other hand, the rise of the delegated approach ignores the potential inputs of superiors. Thus, the shared approach is suggested as a "balance between maximized feelings of independence and the need for enforcing policy and authority."[7]

Although both Leavitt's and Greiner's conceptions are useful, they can be viewed as rather prescriptive and somewhat simplistic. One can infer that structural approaches are rather rigid and impersonal, and people-oriented approaches are more humanistic and popular. This does not have to be the case. For example, by changing the structure through increasing the span of control, a manager may not be able to closely follow each step performed by subordinates. This could result in more autonomy for subordinates. On the other hand, a "people approach," such as sensitivity training, can be viewed as degrading and stifling for those who dislike discussing their personal beliefs and values in a group. In addition, more than one approach is typically used in introducing organizational change and development. For example, a leadership-training program to improve diagnostic and awareness skills may prove worthless if modifications are not made in the structural arrangements so that the new skills can be applied.

Common Characteristics Associated with Change

Despite these shortcomings, one can identify some common threads that cut across the Leavitt and Greiner conceptualizations. Managers who are made aware of some of the common characteristics of change can be prepared for unilateral consequences. That is, the manager can systematically analyze change or be overwhelmed by changes. Some common points for managers to be aware of are:[8]

Plan (structured to unstructured). The process of change can be planned in advance or it can be allowed to emerge as issues become clearer. A planned change is structured when timetables for various activities are spelled out in advance. For example, step 1 is to diagnose an assumed problem by a particular date, step 2 is to develop a solution for the problem by another date, and so forth. A planned change is unstructured when the solution is open-ended. An example of such a situation would be implementing a total organizational training program for all managers. The application value of the program would depend on what each manager derived from it. One group of managers may learn that democratic supervision is best for their subordinates, and another group may learn that instituting budgetary controls is needed to improve the performance of their groups. The training program under an unstructured approach stresses individual orientation to the content.

Power (unilateral to delegated). At the heart of this issue is, who is making the change decisions and on what basis? Unilateral decisions are typically based on the position power of the decision maker; delegated decisions depend more on the knowledge and skill of lower-level managers. The manager needs to seriously and honestly consider the ability and skills of subordinates in determining what power distribution should occur. To allow individuals who have no skill or expertise to reach important decisions through participation could set a dangerous precedent in an organization. The issue becomes subjective because superiors are asked to decide if subordinates are skillful enough to participate in change decisions. Some subordinates question the superior's expertise to participate in the same manner.

Relationships (impersonal to personal). Each change approach can take on very personal or impersonal orientations. In some training programs, an effort is made to identify a manager's personal leadership style. This is a very personal thrust. On the other hand, some training programs attempt to display various leadership styles and their potential consequences to managers. This is an impersonal attempt to improve a manager's relationships skills. Just how far one goes in terms of personal considerations is an important issue to consider. A question the manager needs to weigh is whether subordinates can cope with a personal focus. There are many individuals who are not capable of or are uncomfortable with being scrutinized in front of peers, superiors, or subordinates. Knowing what the subordinates' attitudes are about this issue is important information that managers should acquire before plunging into a change program that will be personal in orientation.

Tempo (revolutionary to evolutionary). Any approach to change has a characteristic that is called tempo, which is the speed and depth of the process. A change can begin with many major changes, or it can start out with some minor changes and build into major changes over time. For example, some job descriptions may be changed initially, then there may be some transferring of people among the jobs, and finally a new unit with authority to review budgets may be added. The "micro" change involves descriptions, and the "macro" change is concerned with a total structural orientation.

These four threads are concepts that each manager can weigh when considering change. Rather than state that a particular set or combination of these factors will result in improvement of performance, it seems more plausible to examine the problems, personnel, environment, time constraints, resources, and goals before prescribing a change strategy. The most crucial point, which again needs to be emphasized, is that the critical variables in change are the structure, people, technology, and environments that interact. A change in one will undoubtedly have an influence on the others.

Some Perspectives on Change

Organizational change and development is certainly more complicated than merely deciding which approach should be implemented to modify structure, people, and technology. A variety of forces—individual, group, and organizational—are usually at work before management selects a particular approach. Also, once a particular approach is implemented, many unanticipated problems and consequences are likely to arise. Often, managers are attracted to a neatly packaged or articulated approach to change without understanding or deciding if it is suited to the situation at hand. For example, there are numerous organizations who adopt management by objectives programs without considering the costs, problems, and needs of such a major change.

A suggested way for a manager to get at what is happening is to have a framework in mind that depicts the change process. This can alert the manager to issues that need to be considered if change is to be managed efficiently and serves as an objective reference point that can help to more clearly recognize the pressures of change. It is generally accepted that organizational change and development involves a series of stages. There are obvious phases that set necessary conditions for moving into subsequent phases. Omission of one stage appears to make it rather difficult for the change process to continue forward on an effective basis. When those implementing change overlook early steps, they find themselves perplexed by unanticipated resistance or poor results. A common response to these occurrences is to push the change more intensely and to force people to accept it despite their frustration and disagreement.

Lewin identified three phases of change: *unfreezing, changing, and refreezing.*[9] The *unfreezing* step represents a required first step in stimulating people to feel and recognize the need for change. Management needs to motivate people to search for new ways to relieve some problems, such as poor performance, absenteeism, or apathy. The second step involves *changing* through the application of some technique or program. The change could be structural, technological, or people oriented, or some combination of these categories. Finally, the *refreezing* stage offers the necessary reinforcement to insure that the new attitudes, skills, knowledge, or behavioral patterns are made permanent.

A Micro Perspective

The Lewin model has served as a foundation for empirical inquiries into the change process of *social and personal learning,* by which employees gradually unlearn old patterns of behavior and adopt new ones.[10] This process may involve training in a formal educational setting or on engaging in new behaviors on the job under the scrutiny of a supervisor.

A review of the learning process is presented in exhibit 15–3. This framework highlights four major processes of change and four subprocesses of learning. These processes emerged from a critical review of five studies of what were assumed to be successful organizational change programs.[11]

The Dalton sequential model of induced change emphasizes two antecedent conditions that are present in successful change programs. There is a sense of *tension* experienced within the system. This tension may be experienced by a key individual or group. Guest, in his longitudinal study of leadership and organizational change in an automobile assembly plant, reported that before the arrival of the new production manager, who was successful in "turning the plant around" from the least to the most efficient plant, there was excessive tension. Labor grievances were high, turnover was twice that in other plants, and the plant was openly criticized and closely examined by division headquarters.[12]

In a study of a successful change effort by a consulting-research team from the University of Michigan, it was reported that in the year prior to the interventions of the team, "Banner [the company] dropped to a very marginal profit position. . . . There was a sense of things getting out of control, a feeling shared and expressed by many nonmanagerial people."[13]

This type of tension is also evident in nonindustrial settings. Organizations such as Alcoholics Anonymous, whose central aim is to induce specific behavioral change, refuse to admit anyone unless they are consciously experiencing distress. An applicant must openly admit the failure of previous individual efforts and recognize the need for help.[14] Frank suggests that in psychotherapy the presence of prior emotional distress is closely related to the results of the treatment. He suggests that:

> The importance of emotional distress in the establishment of a fruitful psychotherapeutic relationship is suggested by the facts that the greater the overall degree of expressed distress, as measured by a symptom checklist, the more likely the patient is to remain in treatment, while conversely two of the most difficult categories to treat have nothing in common except the lack of distress.[15]

These examples of tension transcend different situations and settings. This tension, however, is not experienced uniformly throughout the organization. It may be more intense at the top managerial level or at the lower levels in the hierarchy.

Exhibit 15-3 Dalton's Model of Induced Organization Change (Phases of Change)

Processes of Change	Tension Experienced within the System	Intervention of a Prestigious Influencing Agent	Individuals Attempt to Implement the Proposed Changes	New Behavior and Attitudes Reinforced by Achievement, Social Ties, and Internalized Values—Accompanied by Decreasing Dependence on Influencing Agent
Setting objectives		Generalized objectives established	Growing specificity of objectives—establishment of subgoals	Achievement and resetting of specific objectives
Altering social ties	Tension within existing social ties	Prior social ties interrupted or attenuated	Formation of new alliances and relationships centering around new activities	New social ties reinforce altered behavior and attitudes
Building self-esteem	Lowered sense of self-esteem	Esteem building begun on basis of agent's attention and assurance	Esteem building based on task accomplishment	Heightened sense of self-esteem
Internalized motives for change		External motive for change (new scheme provided)	Improvisation and reality testing	Internalized motive for change

Reproduced by special permission from *The Journal of Applied Behavioral Science*, "The Individual, the Organization, and the Career: A Conceptual Scheme," by Edgar Schein, vol. 7, no. 4, pp. 401–26. Copyright, NTL Institute, 1971.

prestige

The forces for change represented by tension must be mobilized and given direction. If the change is to be successful, the model suggests that initiation of it *urge* must come from a respected and *prestigious influence agent*. The employees being influenced need to have confidence that the change is valid, and this confidence can become reality if the perceived change agent is assumed to have the knowledge and power to cope with the change program.

In various organizational studies, successful change attempts were either initiated by the formal head of the unit involved or were given support by this person. In Guest's study, the initiator was the new plant manager, who brought with him a strong reputation for success in his previous position. Furthermore, it quickly became obvious to other employees that he had the support of the district management.[16] The changes at the "Banner Corporation" were initiated by the highest official at the plant.[17]

Thus, the conditions that precede and facilitate change are *tension* and the *prestige* of the change agent. Exhibit 15–3 also distinguishes four major learning subprocesses. Movement along each of them is assumed to follow distinct patterns in successful change programs.[18]

Specific objectives

identifies   *involves*

The first pattern that seems to identify successful change attempts is a movement from generalized goals toward specific and concrete objectives. As the change program progresses, the objectives take on greater immediacy and concreteness. The objectives are then evaluated, modified, and reset if this is necessary. In some programs, these objectives are initiated or assigned by a superior, and sometimes they are jointly set by a superior and subordinates. The consistent element is that one person or groups of people set concrete objectives.

Altering social ties

A second pattern commonly found in successful organizational change programs is the loosening of old social relationships and the establishment of new social ties that support and reinforce the changes in attitude and behavior. Old behavior and attitudes are often deeply embedded in relationships that are based on long periods of interaction, sometimes occurring over a period of years. So long as employees involved in the change maintain these relationships unaltered, changes are unlikely to occur. Not all of an individual's former relationships will hinder an intended change, nor will new relationships always be effective; but any significant changes in structure, technology, or people require some movement from old relationships toward new ones.

Behavioral scientists did not originate the idea that an alteration of old relationships facilitates changes in individuals or groups. A number of institutions in our society purposefully separate the individual whom they wish to influence from his or her regular social and personal contacts. Convents, monasteries, prisons, mental hospitals, and drug rehabilitation centers all attempt to induce total separation.

Breaking down or loosening previous social ties may act to *unfreeze* an individual or group, but this alone provides little assurance that any resulting changes will be in a given direction or that they will be permanent. Establishing new relationships that reward the desired behaviors and support the modified attitudes also seems to be necessary. Otherwise, there will be a continual state of tension to return to the former activities and attitudes and the relationships that reinforced them.

One of the most interesting studies illustrating this phenomenon is the widely publicized International Harvester training program.[19] This program emphasized improving the human relations or "consideration" skills of foremen. Tested before and after the formal two-week training program, the foremen indicated a higher "consideration" score after training. However, over time, the attitudes of trainees were investigated again, and eventually the trainees showed less or lower "consideration" when compared to a control group. Only those foremen whose immediate superiors scored high on consideration continued to score high themselves. The other foremen, whose superiors did not encourage "consideration," returned to a more "initiating structure" approach, which was similar to their boss's approach. Daily interaction minimized the effect of the human relation training program. The foremen's social ties had been interrupted only during the formal training; they returned to a situation that encouraged and supported "initiating structure" behavior. No continuing new relationships had been established that would act to confirm and reinforce any attitude and style changes begun in the training setting.

Building self-esteem

Changes in self-esteem in the individual being influenced appear to be an integral part of a change process. The abandonment of previous patterns of behavior is easier when an individual has an increased awareness and sense of personal worth. The movement reflected in exhibit 15–3 is from a low sense of self-esteem to a heightened sense of self-esteem.

The best-known study demonstrating heightened self-esteem was the Relay Assembly Test Room Experiments in the famous Western Electric Hawthorne plant.[20] This study was originally designed to examine the relation of quality and quantity of illumination to efficiency. The baffled researchers found that efficiency improved in both the experimental and control groups. By carefully examining the study and the participants, the researchers reached the conclusion that the participants were able to see that production was being recorded very carefully by the experimenter. They also felt that they were treated well by their supervisors. The participants seemed to have an increased sense of self-esteem because they were an important part of the experiment. The experimenters made every effort to obtain the participants' cooperation for each change, consulted them about each change in working conditions, and even cancelled some changes that they disapproved. This attention was transformed into heightened self-confidence and esteem.

The experimenters had attempted to hold all factors constant except those that were specifically manipulated. However, they created changes in factors that facilitate change. First, the participants were in a new situation, being observed, and were tense. Second, people with prestige in the company introduced the changes. Third, the objectives of increased productivity were at first vague, but over the course of the study became increasingly clear. Fourth, the participants were separated from their old relationships and routines. Finally, the experimenters created conditions that increased the participants' sense of worth and importance. The combination of these factors facilitated the changes that occurred.

Internalization

The motivating force toward a particular change originates outside the individuals to be influenced. Someone else introduces the idea, the problems, the suggestion, or the model. If the new behavior patterns are to last, individuals being influenced must internalize or accept the motive and rationale for the change. Internalization occurs as an individual finds the ideas and the prescribed behavior intrinsically rewarding in coping with external and internal tension. Individuals adopt new behavior because they believe it to be useful for solving problems or because it is congruent with their own orientation.

Internalization seems to consist of three elements:

1. *A new cognitive structure.* The influencing agent provides a new conceptual framework as a means for recording the information that the person receives from the organization and the environments. For example, a new director of a company may spend considerable time outlining the plan of action that will be followed and how it differs from previous plans.

2. *Application and improvisation.* Introducing a new cognitive structure is not enough for internalization to take place. The individual must apply and modify it when necessary. Thus, an improvisation attempt is often needed because of unanticipated factors or events. For example, after being applied a new organizational structure may have to be modified so that key individuals can use it efficiently. What seems to be very effective in the planning phase often does not work out well when applied in the actual work setting.

3. *Verification.* Testing a new change through personal experience is an important element of internalization. The change in structure, technology, or behavior must be tested against the realities of organizational life.

The Transfer of Learning

A number of the widely used intervention activities, such as sensitivity training, training and education programs, goal-setting training, conflict-minimization workshops, and phases of the managerial grid, are typically conducted away from the job. In some cases, the learning setting for change and development is viewed as a "cultural island." This island is free from the pressures and much of the realism found in the organizational setting to which a participant must return. The norms, structures, relationships, and overall climate in the actual job are often very different from what existed in the learning setting established in a training room or classroom. Thus, when the individual or group returns to the organization and attempts to behave according to the new knowledge, there is no support for such behavior. The old work norms and expectations have not changed, and this often results in confusion for the participant with a newly acquired skill, knowledge base, or personal awareness.

The transfer-of-learning issue emphasizes the importance of understanding whether or not skills, attitudes, and knowledge learned away from the job will transfer to the job. Much of the theoretical discussion of transfer focuses on the question of why transfer takes place.[21] One answer is that transfer occurs to the extent that the elements of the behavior learned away from the job are similar to the elements of behavior required for acceptable on-the-job performance. That is, the off-the-job learning experience must be similar to the on-the-job experience.

Another explanation of why transfer of learning occurs has to do with the application of principles learned in training to actual on-the-job problems. For example, a business game simulation is often used to teach participants an appreciation of the complexity and interrelatedness of decision making in organization settings. It is hoped that by participating in a simulated series of exercises away from the job, the individual, when faced with these issues on the job, will be able to respond effectively.

Before discussing specific intervention activities, it seemed realistic to raise the issue of transfer because it is so vital to successful organizational change and development. The overall goal of any program is to enhance the organization and develop the participants; if there is no transfer from the learning to the actual job setting, there is little value in the effort.

Hilgard offers a number of opinions about learning that make sense when considering the transfer phenomenon.[22] Although there is a lack of unanimous support for these ideas, they seem to have some validity when considering the learning process away from the job. Some of these generalizations are:

A motivated learner acquires what he or she learns more readily than one who is not motivated.

Learning under the control of reward is usually preferable to learning under the control of punishment.

Learning motivated by success is preferable to learning motivated by failure.

Individuals need practice in setting realistic learning goals for themselves, goals neither so low as to elicit little effort nor so high as to preordain failure.

Active participation by a learner is preferable to passive reception when learning.

Information about the nature of good performance and knowledge of successful results and failures aids learning.

Transfer to new tasks will be better if the learner can discover the relationships and if experience is acquired during the process to apply the principles to a variety of tasks.

Each of these guidelines can be incorporated into organizational change and development efforts. There are some critics of such emphasis on the process. Some experts believe that the process and guidelines for learning should be less important in analyzing transfer than the issue of "what is to be learned."[23] A series of questions that managers attempting to bring about a smooth and efficient transfer are asked can focus on the *what* of learning. Some of these questions are:

1. What are the task components of the job?

2. What "mediates" or influences performance on these job tasks; specifically, what needs to be learned to improve performance?

3. How should these mediators be broken down in the change and development program?

4. How should the learning of these elements be arranged to enhance transfer to the job?

Gagne points out that such principles as task analysis, intratask transfer, and sequencing do not negate the importance of traditional principles, such as practice and reinforcement, but rather raise questions about their importance.[24] Perhaps, full consideration of the type of guidelines suggested by Hilgard and the task-oriented or "what is to be learned" approach of Gagne are needed to maximize the effectiveness of learning transfer. They certainly are better than ignoring the issue of transfer or relying solely on trial and error.

A Macro Perspective

A more macro perspective, which cuts across all stages of change, involves the issue of power distribution within the organization. Any change in the decision-making locus or flow usually requires a change in the allocation of power. Research evidence suggests that individuals cannot learn and apply new forms of decision-making behavior unless those with more power are willing to cooperate in the change. This cooperation requirement is exemplified by encouraging subordinates to adopt new forms of behavior and by consistently displaying behavior that emphasizes the importance of subordinate involvement.

There are two important concepts of power that are part of the organizational change literature: power equalization and power expansion. *Power equalization* suggests that power is a fixed quantity that requires that some individuals must gain and some must lose power when organizational change occurs.[25] The concept of *power expansion* proposes that it is possible for all individuals to increase their power over decisions. This can occur when, for example, two managers pool their expertise and knowledge and develop better solutions to problems than they would if they were acting alone. We will now present a model that would encourage *power expansion,* or the pooling of talents within an organization, to systematically correct problems.

A Planned Change and Development Model

The model that we propose in exhibit 15–4 is a sequence of particular phases that managers can follow in any setting to manage change and expand their power. The formulation of the model presumes that forces for change are continually impinging upon the organization, thereby creating noticeable pressures for change. It is the manager's responsibility to recognize these forces and decide whether the magnitude of the problem is significant enough to consider any given structural, technological, task, or people change, or some combination of these approaches. If the problem is of sufficient magnitude, managerial personnel and/or an outside expert must perform a careful diagnosis. When the diagnosis reveals the problem area, change goals are established, change agents are identified, and constraints are discussed. For example, the organization may have only $100,000 available to solve a technological equipment malfunction problem. This and other constraints influence the type of alternatives that are eventually selected to bring about change.

After the limiting conditions are identified, the focus is directed toward considering alternative approaches and techniques available for solving the problem. Then, a decision on which alternative to use must be made. At this phase, planned change requires an evaluation of the alternative selected. The model also identifies two feedback loops from the evaluation stage. The alternative selected may prove to be a poor choice, and only through monitoring and feedback can this problem be rectified. Moreover, feedback to the initial point of pressure and to the program goals must be conducted. The results of change, when combined with changes in the environment, the goals of the organization, and resources available, demand that the sequence of events be considered once again.

The never-ending process of change is aptly labeled by Blau and Scott as the "dialectic processes of change."[26] They propose that a solution to one problem creates new problems that require some changes. For example, by introducing new equipment on an assembly line there may be a sudden increase in output. However, at the same time some workers may dislike being relegated to a lesser role because of the equipment, and a few decide to quit and others stay home as much as possible. Thus, the technological improvement can create behavioral reactions in the

Exhibit 15–4 A Planned Change Model

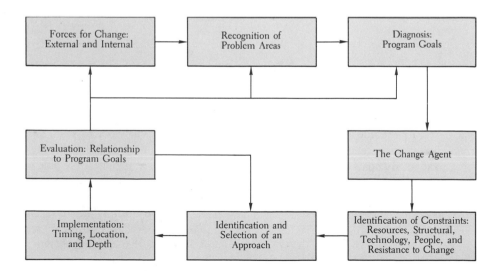

form of lower morale, which manifests itself in increased turnover and absenteeism. The manager must then start at the beginning of our model to analyze the problems that are related to the previous changes.

The Forces

There are both external and internal forces that result in pressure for change. The external forces were discussed in chapters 10 and 11. The general environment forces are political, regulatory, resource, economic, and technological in nature. The task environment forces, which directly impact organizations, are technology, customers, suppliers, competitors, and sociopolitical forces. Changes in these forces have a direct impact on the internal functioning of an organization. When inflation in the economy is skyrocketing, the attitude and morale of some employees suffers and may hinder performance. Furthermore, when a competitor markets a better product that threatens to reduce an organization's market share, there is pressure to get something done immediately to correct this problem. The more uncertain the general and task environmental forces are, the more difficult is the manager's job to systematically utilize the model shown in exhibit 15–4.

Internal forces are structural, process, or behavioral. A structural force would be the inability to transmit important information from the top of the organization to the lower echelons. Because of numerous layers in the hierarchy, information plods slowly from one level to the next. This could be viewed as a process or a behavioral problem involving a failure to communicate effectively. The important point is that there is some type of problem that is hampering the response of the organization.

Process forces could evolve from decision-making breakdowns, communication delays, or leadership ineffectiveness, to name just a few sources. An example of a decision-making breakdown would be the failure of one manager to request expert aid from another manager out of personal jealousy or competition. An optimum decision may be reached in spite of the lack of cooperation, but this is not the most effective procedure for making decisions.

Recognizing when Change is Needed

The flow of accurate information from outside and inside an organization is the basis upon which managers are made aware of problems that require some form of change. Internally, an organization generates reports on resource utilization, human resource development, morale, absenteeism, and other areas of interest. The external data base includes information on competitive actions, customer or client demand, government regulations, and the general public's attitude or impression of the organization. By combining internal and external information, managers are able to detect actual or potential problems. The more accurate the information is, the more knowledge the manager will have available to assess the need for change.

A need for change is obvious when key personnel are quitting in alarming numbers or when market share is rapidly declining or when executives are indicted for price collusion. The less catastrophic problems are those that demand managerial attention in the form of careful monitoring of information systems and the use of diagnostic procedures. In essence, the job of a manager always involves diagnosis, whether the focus is on motivation, job design, leadership, or any other organizational behavior topic.

Diagnosis

In chapter 2, we focused on the use of the scientific method to study organizational properties. This involves diagnosis or study of the properties of interest in a systematic and valid manner. Performing a diagnosis of potential problem areas requires that a manager focus on a number of issues. Some of these are:

1. Determining the specific problems that require correction.

2. Deciding or considering the potential determinants or forces causing these problems.

3. Deciding what needs to be changed and when to change it to resolve the problems.

4. Determining what the goals are for the change and how goal accomplishment will be measured.

Answers to these crucial issues are difficult to generate because managers are typically overextended in their workload or do not have adequate time to perform the necessary diagnostic work.

A variety of diagnostic techniques are employed to determine answers to the four issues cited above. Organizations use committees, reports, consultants, task forces, interviews, questionnaire surveys, informal discussion groups, and other information-generating techniques. The central issue is not which technique or combination of them to utilize, it is the gathering of reasonably valid information. Without good or representative information, a change strategy is virtually worthless because it is blindly based. Thus, a thorough job of diagnosis is vitally important to any hope for success of organizational change and development efforts.

Toward what ends should an organization be changed and developed is also a necessary question that diagnosis can help answer. For example, is the organization interested in high production at any cost, or do they want a happy work force? The amount of performance that will be sacrificed for morale is basically a goal decision. The goals of organizational change and development can be made specific and meaningful through a valid diagnosis program, and they must be specific enough so that a decision can be reached about whether or not they are being achieved. Therefore, specifications that consider operationalization, constraints, costs, and consequences are a desired result of the diagnosis and evaluation steps in our model.

The Change Agent

A change agent may be an internal member of the organization or an outside consultant. The internal member is assumed to have the ability, knowledge, and energy to perform a directive role in the change and development effort. The consultant is a professional who hopefully has been trained in applying each phase of our change model (exhibit 15–4). The important similarity in internal and external change agents is that they are concerned with organizational effectiveness, individual performance improvement, development, and success through change and development.

Although no two change agents, whether internal or external, are similar, it appears that they possess a number of role characteristics:

1. The change agent often must play a variety of roles, among them researcher, trainer, counselor, teacher, and in some cases manager. There are some who argue that the external change agent can more effectively shift from one role to another; some believe that the internal change agent possesses the intimate knowledge needed to shift from role to role. The key issue seems to be that the change agent must be professionally qualified to perform various roles.

2. Change agents intervene at different structural levels in the organization at different times. Thus, they need to understand the political fabric of the intervention point before attempting a particular change.

3. Change agents should have a repertoire of evaluation procedures so that intervention success and failure can be assessed and modified if necessary.

4. Change agents have values that can influence their selection of an alternative technique or how they intervene. These values are a part of the backgrounds that the agent brings to the job.

These characteristics are integrated into a model that was developed after studying and analyzing ninety-one social-change agents.[27] Exhibit 15–5 presents a conceptual example of interaction variables that help shape the role of a change agent. This model shows five key variables interacting with each other. *Background* of the change agent includes personal experience, education, and training. The *value* component designates the agent's personal goals and orientation toward people in general. The *cognitive* component specifies the agent's overall beliefs about change. The fourth component involves the *technology* or the available technique repertoire that a change agent can use. Finally, the actual behavior of this change agent is seen as a result of the four preceding components. If there is a lack of agreement among these variables, there is then the possibility of stress or tension. This model, when combined with our descriptive role characteristics, indicates that the change agent is expected to be a knowledgeable and creative individual who can understand and apply the scientific method to problems. However, this expectation is unrealistic because it is necessary to recognize human frailties, inadequate training background, and organizational constraints as potential barriers to successful intervention activities.

Transfer of learning and the role of change agents are often neglected when progressing through a planned change program. They should not be overlooked because the consequences of change often are greatly influenced by how well managers understand them. An organization can have a sophisticated change program that is forcefully resisted or cannot be transferred from a training room to the

Exhibit 15–5 Selected Components that Shape the Change Agent's Role

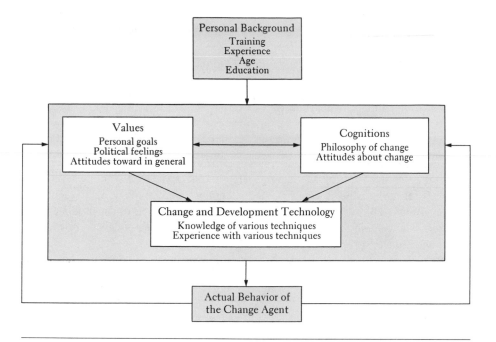

Adapted from N. Tichy, "Agents of Planned Social Change: Consequence of Values, Cognitions, and Actions," *Administrative Science Quarterly* 19 (June 1974): 165, with permission.

organization. Furthermore, if capable change agents are not used to implement and evaluate the program, it serves little purpose for the organization and can have negative consequences. The change agent needs to understand when individual, group, intergroup, or organizational interventions are required.

The Constraints

There are numerous constraints to change and development techniques that need to be considered. The extremely important constraints that impact any type of change—structural, technological, or behavioral—are leadership climate, formal organization, and individual characteristics.[28]

Leadership climate is the atmosphere in the work environment that results from the leadership style and administrative practices of superiors. The climate is set by the leaders, who can influence subordinates to accept or reject changes implemented from the top-executive group in an organization. The leader's values, attitudes, and perceptions are all constraining forces.

The *formal organization design* must have some compatibility with the proposed change. For example, attempting to implement a participative goal-setting program or participative decision-making practices in a rigid and bureaucratically inclined

541

organization is somewhat unrealistic and displays a lack of understanding. There must be some congruence between the program of change and the design of the system if the change is to be effective.

The *individual characteristics* that are important to change and development programs include learning abilities, attitudes, personality, and expectations. If employees do not have the ability to utilize computer information, then it makes little sense to introduce highly sophisticated and expensive computer technology. Managers need to continually consider individual characteristics when analyzing potential constraints of a particular change strategy.

Resistance to Change

Although change is a recurring feature of organizational life, people tend to resist it. Resistance in the form of sabotaging performance standards, staying away from work, filing unfounded grievances, and reducing productivity regularly occur in organizations. The resistance may be overt, such as slowing down production, or implicit, such as feigning illness so that a new machine does not have to be faced on a particular day.[29]

Most changes create a number of potential areas of resistance, such as the manner in which the change is introduced, the magnitude of the change, and the change itself. Employees typically like to have some control over their work environments, the pace of their work, and the manner in which the job is accomplished. When management suddenly announces a change in work design, personnel, equipment, or work flow, there are usually some people who want to have an opportunity to participate in these decisions. In addition, some changes are of such magnitude that they frighten employees because of the uncertainties associated with them. For example, the elimination of an entire layer of the management hierarchy or the closing of a plant and the reassignment of personnel can make the reassigned employees uncertain about their new job, supervisor, and colleagues. To understand why people resist, we need to focus on some of the causes, from individual and group sources.

Fear of economic loss.   Any change that creates the feeling that some positions will be eliminated and employees laid off or terminated is likely to meet with resistance because of the consequential loss of earning power. In a society that requires employment to earn a living, the fear of losing a job is serious. Management would have a difficult time minimizing this fear and would need to make employees believe that job reductions will not follow a change. This involves communication to the work force on why the change is necessary. If employees need to be terminated, the rationale and procedures should be explained. This is not to say that the reduction will be accepted, but a better understanding may result in less disruption in the work process.

Potential social descriptions.   By working with each other, employees develop comfortable patterns of communication and understanding. This comfort makes work more enjoyable and permits friendships to develop. Almost any change in structure, technology, or personnel has the potential to disrupt these comfortable interaction patterns or ties. Changes in the style of the interaction can also threaten these interventions.

Inconvenience.   The introduction of a new procedure for handling a job or a new machine to produce units more efficiently may disrupt the normal routine of performing a job. The normal routine becomes a part of the job ritual. Any change that interferes with the normal patterns of work will generally be resisted.

Fear of uncertainties.   By establishing a normal routine in performing a job, employees learn what their range of responsibilities are and what the supervisor's reaction to their behavior will be in certain situations. Any change creates some potential unknowns. Employees, before and after changes, speculate about what their modified role will be and about how their supervisors will respond to them and the changes. This speculation focuses on uncertainties that did not exist prior to the change and results in some resistance to the change.

Resistance from groups.   Groups establish norms of behavior and performance that are communicated to members. This communication establishes the boundaries of expected behaviors. Failure to comply with such norms can result in ostracism, a lack of respect, or the restriction of desirable rewards, such as praise and recognition. The more attractive or cohesive the group is to its members, the greater the influence that the group can exert on the membership. A group is attractive to the extent to which it satisfies the needs of its members. If management initiates changes that are viewed as threatening to a group's norms, they are likely to meet with resistance. The more cohesive the group is, the greater their resistance to change will be.

How can managers reduce resistance to change? Focusing on the individual, managers can attempt to minimize resistance by forcing or increasing pressure to bring about the change, or they can attempt to improve individuals' attitudes about the change. There are no formulas for reducing individual resistance to every change, but there are some guidelines to be found in the reasons for resistance just discussed. First, the behavior or attitudes of an individual within an organization results from the interaction of such variables as the basic personality structures of employees and their social role in the system. Any change program needs to pay attention to the needs of both the organization and the individual. Thus, the individual must be able to perceive personal benefits to be gained by the change. These benefits and potential problems need to be communicated so that an atmosphere of trust is created.[30] Second, the induced change model shown in exhibit 15–3 recommends having an individual with prestige introduce the change when possible.[31] Third, in some cases individuals or groups want to share in planning, analyzing, and coordinating the change effort. This participation may improve an employee's understanding of the need for change, and this can result in a minimization of resistance. Finally, the knowledge of how the change program is progressing is important to many participants. By receiving knowledge of results, an individual has a better grasp of the problems, responses, and future of the change program. Employees like to have this feedback so that some of their questions can be answered and some of their fears reduced.[32]

From a group viewpoint, the implication of the classic study by Coch and French on overcoming resistance to change is that allowing employees to participate in change programs may be beneficial.[33] These two researchers worked with four different groups of factory workers who were paid on a modified piece-rate system. For each of the groups, a change in the work procedure was installed by a different method, and the consequences were monitored to determine what, if any, problems of resistance occurred. The first group had change introduced through a "no participation" method. Staff people told the group members what changes were to occur. The second group had change introduced by a "participation through representation" method. A representative elected by the group discussed changes with the staff and brought to the group the change idea that the staff suggested.

The third and fourth groups had change introduced by a "total participation" method. All the group members met with the staff personnel and discussed how present work methods could be improved. An agreement was reached, and the workers were trained in the new methods and returned to the job.

The researchers found that the no-participation group output dropped immediately after the change to about two-thirds of its previous level. The lower output existed for thirty days after the change. There were also resignations and open expressions of anger toward management.

In contrast, the total-participation groups showed a small initial drop in output and a rapid output recovery, not to the previous level of production but to an even higher level. In these groups, there were no resignations after the change and no signs of hostility toward management.

The Coch and French study results are sometimes presented as sufficient evidence that participation is the answer to overcoming resistance to change. There are, of course, some employees who do not want to participate or who do not know how to participate. Thus, participation may be effective in some cases but may be a poor method in other situations. Even with participation, there is still a tendency for individuals to resist change.[34]

That individuals and groups resist change is an established fact. When resistance appears, it should be thought of as a signal that something is going wrong.[35] It is in management's best interest to anticipate resistance at the individual and group level and to consider the possible actions to minimize it. It is impossible to eliminate resistance. However, careful diagnosis of individuals and groups can teach managers how best to approach the resistance phenomenon.

Identification of Approach and Techniques

Once managers have identified the goals of the change effort, recognized the constraints, and carefully diagnosed the situation, they must select an approach and techniques to produce the desired end results. The plan may be to improve skills, attitudes, behavior, structure, or knowledge. A useful framework for considering alternative methods of inducing change has been proposed by Lawrence and Lorsch.[36] They stress the importance of carefully diagnosing the organizational terrain and the environment and considering the mismatch, if any, between these two. Then, the manager should consider what type of behaviors need to be changed and the techniques available to bring about changes. The manager must carefully match the behavioral problem with the method of change. Exhibit 15–6 brings together the main points illustrated by Lawrence and Lorsch.

The framework displayed in this exhibit focuses on behavioral change and does not incorporate many of the popular change techniques, such as sensitivity training, goal setting, and the managerial grid. These techniques and others will be covered in more detail later in this chapter and in chapter 16. Some of the structural techniques of change, such as job enrichment and conversion to a System 4 design, were covered earlier when we discussed work and organizational design.

Selection of an Alternative

Eventually, managers must decide what technique or combination of techniques to use, what approach (i.e., unilateral, delegated, or shared) to follow, and when to begin the change program. These considerations involve making the best decisions in light of the goals that need to be accomplished and the constraining conditions present. Unfortunately, a large degree of subjectivity enters this important decision. Managers have favorite techniques, pet ideas, and egos, which are additional per-

Exhibit 15–6 Matching the Degree of Behavioral Change with Some Techniques

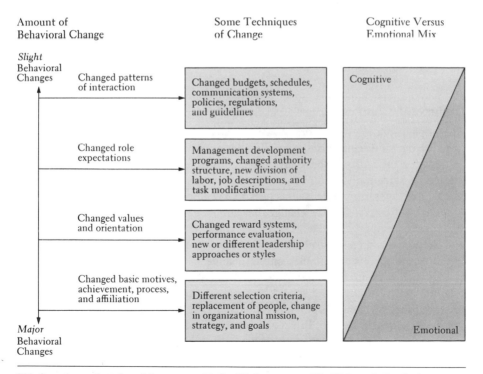

This figure is an adaptation of that presented in Paul R. Lawrence and Jay W. Lorsch, *Developing Organizations: Diagnosis and Actions* (Reading, Mass.: Addison-Wesley, 1969), p. 87.

sonal constraints, that influence the final decision. The degree of subjectivity entering the alternative selection will impact the match between the problems identified through the diagnosis and the appropriateness of the technique.

A study of 117 training directors in the largest U.S. corporations indicates that managers need to know something about what a particular technique can accomplish.[37] The training directors were asked to rate the effectiveness of nine training methods (case, conference, lecture, games, films, programmed instruction, role playing, sensitivity training, and television) in accomplishing four specific objectives. Exhibit 15–7 shows how they ranked three of the training methods. The table shows that the training directors believe that lecturing trainees is a poor technique for accomplishing the objectives. They also believe that role playing can be effective in changing attitudes (ranked second for two objectives). Role playing seems to be effective if trainees in the exercises are asked to act out a role that is the opposite of their own.[38]

The case method was rated the most effective of the nine training methods for improving problem-solving skills. However, only a limited number of studies exist that substantiate this belief. Most of the studies use college students as subjects. One study found that about one-third of the students exposed to case study improved significantly in their ability to handle case problems, about a third showed moderate improvement, and a third made no improvement.[39]

The crucial issue displayed by the findings shown in exhibit 15–7 is that the individuals who are assumed to be the best qualified to make decisions on matching objectives and techniques differ in their choices. Thus, a manager involved in selecting techniques should carefully consider the problem, constraint, and effectiveness potential of each alternative and attempt to choose the optimal technique(s) for a particular situation.

Implementation

The implementation of any organizational change and development technique has three important dimensions: *timing, location,* and *depth.* Timing refers to the *when* of the effort. When is the best time to begin implementation? Two important issues are the organization's operating cycle and the completion of necessary preparation work. If the operating cycle is at its peak and if preparation work, such as informing those to be affected about the change, has not been completed, the timing dimension has not been properly handled. Of course, if an organization is fighting for survival and cannot wait, then survival takes precedence over any timing consideration.

Managers involved in implementing change must decide *where* to initiate the change activities in the organization. Many of the organizational development scholars believe that change should be initiated from the top-management level to the lower-management or operating-employee level. Those advocating this location theory are Argyris, Bennis, Blake and Mouton, and Beckhard.[40] These individuals believe that for change and development efforts to accomplish their goals, top management must display active support for the program. If top management does not show support and commitment, there is a tendency for others in the organization to essentially "go through the motions," but if top management is supporting a

Exhibit 15–7 Rank Order of Three Training Methods in Accomplishing Four Objectives

Method	Objectives			
	Acquisition of Knowledge	Changing Attitudes	Improving Problem-Solving Skills	Improving Interpersonal Skills
Lecture	9	8	9	8
Cases	2	4	1	4
Role Playing	7	2	3	2

Source: Adapted from Stephen J. Carroll, Frank T. Paine, and John M. Ivancevich, "The Relative Effectiveness of Alternative Training Methods for Various Training Objectives," *Personnel Psychology* 25 (Fall 1972): 498.

program and participating in it, there seems to be more enthusiasm and interest among subordinates to follow their example.

There is, however, some support for bottom-up or middle-level initiation of programs. Work design changes through a job enrichment technique are usually initiated lower in the organization. Top management may allow these changes to occur, but they are not necessarily involved in them. Thus, for some change efforts top-management commitment would be displayed through active involvement; in others, it would entail just allowing middle- and lower-level managers and non-managers to work out the details and follow through for change.

The three locations for implementing organizational change are illustrated in exhibit 15–8. The location decision and the popularity of the top-down plan is questioned by Beer and Huse.[41] They believe that full-fledged support or commitment by top management is not always required. Nevertheless, top management must permit the organizational change and development effort to occur, and this seems to be a sound argument for acquiring some form of top management commitment for any plan for change.

The *depth* of the implementation involves the issue of intervention. Should the change program be directed at the total organization, units, groups, or individuals? We will offer a typology of organizational change and development interventions based on target groups in the next chapter.

Evaluation

The final segment of our model in exhibit 15–4 involves evaluation. It is only within recent times that scientifically based studies have been conducted to evaluate the effectiveness or failure of change efforts. Much of the literature on the evaluation of organizational change and development is based on enthusiastic testimonies by advocates of a particular technique, approach, or model. Fads have resulted in extravagant claims of the superiority of a particular program. The reasons for the abundance of testimonial support and the dearth of scientifically based studies of organizational change and development are fairly clear. First, it is difficult to

Exhibit 15–8 Three Potential Locations for Implementing Organizational Change

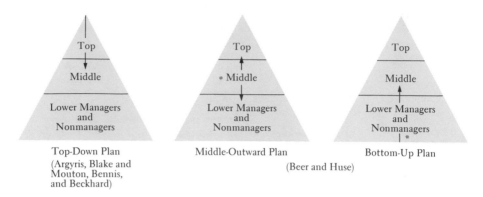

Top-Down Plan
(Argyris, Blake and
Mouton, Bennis,
and Beckhard)

Middle-Outward Plan
(Beer and Huse)

Bottom-Up Plan

*Change initiated in direction of arrowheads.

conduct field studies over a period of time without the occurrence of major, uncontrollable changes, which contaminate the results of the planned change program and discourage many researchers from becoming involved in the necessary longitudinal studies. Second, it is difficult for those with research skills to gain entrée into organizations to perform sound evaluations. Practitioners are concerned, and rightfully so in some cases, about the disruption of normal operations when their organization is intruded upon by researchers, who sometimes refuse to discuss problems in terms that are understandable and application oriented. Finally, many practitioners are not certain about the intent of a particular change or development effort because the objectives of the effort are not clearly stated.

Despite these problems in performing an evaluation, there are signs that more refined and valid research on organizational change and development is occurring. The literature is beginning to indicate that practitioners and researchers are starting to work together more intensely to improve the organizational change and development programs being implemented.[42] Only through evaluation can feedback be provided that can result in needed improvements.

In chapter 2, we discussed some of the techniques for conducting an evaluation of organizational change and development. The evaluation could involve the use of interviews, self-report questionnaires, observation, records, or reports of critical incidents. If at all possible, it seems that a combination of these methods needs to be used to acquire a valid picture of the results of the efforts. The feedback received from the evaluation is returned to the pressure-for-change phase and to the implementation phase in our model. This link between evaluation and the pressure and implementation phases of the model is essential for assessing any changes that have occurred in an organization, group, or individual. It aids the manager in reaching a conclusion about whether the depth of intervention was effective in accomplishing desirable goals.

Applications and Implications for the Manager

Organizational Change and Development

1. Any organizational change and development effort needs to be carefully matched with anticipated goals. Unless the goals are clarified, the selection of the proper approach, techniques, and depth of intervention will be subjectively based.

2. Organizational change and development focus on an organization's ability to adapt to environmental changes and modifications of employee behavior patterns.

3. One conceptual approach to change is to consider the interrelatedness of structural, technological, and people changes. A change in one of these areas is most often accompanied by changes in the other two. Thus, changes in structure will impact technology and people, and managers need to be prepared for these consequences.

4. Power conceptualization to highlight an approach to change considers three approaches—unilateral, shared, and delegated. The originator of this schema, Greiner, offers some empirical evidence to support his claim that the shared approach is the most effective. However, we offer a word of caution that because of time constraints, resource limitations, and individual skill deficiencies, the shared approach may not be practical or wise to implement.

5. Any approach to change requires planning, an understanding of power distribution, consideration of relations, and attention to the tempo. These are four common threads that are found in most discussions of change.

6. A micro perspective of change is offered by Dalton, who stresses a social and personal learning process. Two antecedent conditions for any change are tension and the need for change being initiated by a change agent with prestige. When these conditions are present, the process can proceed through various patterns. The ultimate requirements to create the desired changes are setting specific objectives, altering social ties, building self-esteem, and internalization.

7. In most change and development efforts, some attention must be paid to the transfer-of-learning phenomenon. This is especially important when training or development sessions occur off the job and participants return to the job with the new experience and knowledge. Learning principles and what is to be learned need to be carefully considered. Such issues as motivation, reward systems, practice, and active participation are important principles to consider. In addition, the manager should consider the factors that influence performance on the job—how can they be efficiently learned?

8. A macro perspective of change is offered in our model presented in exhibit 15–4, which emphasizes diagnosis, the establishment of goals, decision making, evaluation, and feedback. Proceeding through each of the eight phases is necessary for accomplishing a match between goals and end results. These phases are each important and need to be systematically followed rather than declaring an organizational change and development effort a success. The model is basically the *scientific method* applied to change and development.

9. Internal and external change agents intervene and play a variety of roles. The change agent has values, personal characteristics, and cognitions that influence the intervention technology that he or she uses and how he or she uses it. An important attribute of a change agent is an ability to establish rapport within the organization among those who will undergo change and development.

10. Resistance to change is pervasive and should be interpreted as a signal of a problem in introducing and preparing for change. Managers need to develop action plans to minimize resistance and should not waste time thinking about the total elimination of such resistance. Some of the key reasons for resistance are the potential

disruption of social interaction patterns, the fear of economic loss, inconvenience, and the fear of uncertainties.

11. The model in exhibit 15–4 stresses the importance of management's understanding of what various techniques can do best. Exhibit 15–6 provides an example of the necessary matching between desired behavioral change and techniques. Major changes require different forms of intervention than minor or slight changes. Thus, management needs to consider how significant the desired changes will be and then what techniques are best suited to bring about this degree of behavioral change. Blind and nonsystematic pursuit of matching often results in not attaining desirable end results.

12. Managers need to embrace the importance of scientific evaluation of organizational change and development efforts. Certainly, evaluation often creates disruption within an organization, but the cost of. weak or no evaluation seems to be too great to omit this most crucial phase in our model. Only through proper evaluation procedures can or should the organizational change and development effort be considered a success. To accept it as a success under any other circumstances is to abdicate the responsibility of control with which managers are entrusted by the owners of an organization.

Review of Theories, Research, and Applications

1. Under what type of circumstances would a unilateral change approach seem to be the most effective?

2. Why is diagnosis such an important part of any organizational change and development effort?

3. Why do managers need to formulate the goals of their organizational change and development programs?

4. Why is top-management commitment necessary in organizational change and development program?

5. What is meant by the phrase "transfer of learning"?

6. Why are change agents important to organizational change programs?

7. Give examples of the different factors that concern resistance to change efforts.

8. Discuss how financial constraints can hinder the potential success of a change and development effort.

9. What is organizational development?

10. Discuss why tension is considered a prerequisite for induced change.

Notes

1. Edgar F. Huse, *Organization Development and Change* (St. Paul, Minn.: West Publishing, 1975), p. 7.
2. W. Warren Burke and Warren H. Schmidt, "Management and

Organizational Development," *Personnel Administration*, March 1971, p. 45.
3. George Strauss, "Organizational Behavior and Personal Relations," *A*

Review of Industrial Relations Research (Madison, Wisc.: Industrial Relations Research Association, 1970), pp. 169–70.

4. Harold J. Leavitt, "Applied Organization Change in Industry: Structural, Technological, and Human Approaches," in *New Perspectives in Organization Research* (New York: Wiley, 1964).

5. Larry E. Greiner, "Patterns of Organization Change," *Harvard Business Review,* May–June 1967, pp. 119–30.

6. Ibid.

7. Paul C. Agnew and Frances L. K. Hus, "Introducing Change in a Mental Hospital," *Human Organization,* Winter 1960, p. 168.

8. These four main threads are carefully documented by Larry E. Greiner and Louis B. Barnes, "Organization Change and Development," in *Organizational Behavior and Administration,* ed. Paul R. Lawrence, Louis B. Barnes, and Jay W. Lorsch (Homewood, Ill.: Irwin, 1976, pp. 625–26.

9. Kurt Lewin, "Group Decision and Social Change," in *Readings in Social Psychology,* ed. T. Newcomb and E. Hartely (New York: Holt, Rinehart & Winston, 1947).

10. Greiner and Barnes, "Organization Change and Development," p. 627.

11. Gene D. Dalton, "Influence and Organizational Change" (Paper read at a conference on Organization Behavior Models, Kent State University, Kent, Ohio, 1969).

12. Robert H. Guest, *Organizational Change: The Effect of Successful Leadership* (Homewood, Ill.: Irwin, 1962).

13. Stanley E. Seashore and David G. Bowers, *Changing the Structure and Functioning of an Organization* (Ann Arbor: University of Michigan, Survey Research Center, Monograph No. 33, 1963), p. 16.

14. O. H. Mowrer, *The New Group Theory* (Princeton, N.J.: Van Nostrand, 1964).

15. Jerome Frank, *Persuasion and Healing* (New York: Schocken, 1963).

16. Guest, *Organizational Change.*

17. Seashore and Bowers, *Changing the Structure and Functioning of an Organization.*

18. Dalton, "Influence and Organizational Change."

19. E. A. Fleishman, E. F. Harris, and H. E. Burtt, *Leadership and Supervision in Industry* (Columbus, Ohio: Bureau of Educational Research, Ohio State University, 1955).

20. Fritz J. Roethlisberger and W. J. Dickson, *Management and the Worker* (Cambridge, Mass.: Harvard University, 1939).

21. Joseph Tiffin and Ernest J. McCormick, *Industrial Psychology* (Englewood Cliffs, N.J.: Prentice Hall, 1965), pp. 280–82.

22. Ernest R. Hilgard, *Theories of Learning* (New York: Appleton-Century-Crofts, 1956).

23. R. M. Gagne, "Military Training and Principles of Learning," *American Psychologist,* June 1962, pp. 83–91.

24. Ibid.

25. A discussion of power equalization versus power expansion is found in Arnold Tannenbaum, *Control in Organizations* (New York: McGraw-Hill, 1968).

26. Peter M. Blau and W. Richard Scott, *Formal Organizations* (San Francisco: Chandler, 1962), pp. 250–53.

27. Alan C. Filley, Robert J. House, and Steven Kerr, *Managerial Process and Organizational Behavior,* 2nd ed. (Glenview, Ill.: Scott, Foresman, 1976).

28. N. M. Tichy, "Agents of Planned Social Change: Congruence of Values, Cognitions, and Actions," *Administrative Science Quarterly,* March 1974, pp. 164–82.

29. Wendell L. French, Cecil H. Bell, Jr., and R. A. Zawacki, *Organizational Development: Theory, Practice and Research* (Dallas: Business Publications, 1978).

30. Huse, *Organization Development and Change,* p. 113.

31. Dalton, "Influence and Organizational Change."

32. Edwin A. Locke, N. Cartledge, and J. Koeppel, "Motivational Effects of Knowledge Results: A Goal-Setting Phenomenon," *Psychological Bulletin,* 1968, pp. 474–85.

33. Lester Coch and John R. P. French, Jr., "Overcoming Resistance to Change," *Human Relations,* Winter 1948, pp. 512–32.
34. For an interesting article on change and resistance, see Paul R. Lawrence, "How to Deal with Resistance to Change," *Harvard Business Review,* May–June 1954, pp. 49–57.
35. Ibid.
36. Paul R. Lawrence and Jay W. Lorsch, *Developing Organizations: Diagnosis and Actions* (Reading, Mass.: Addison-Wesley, 1969).
37. Stephen J. Carroll, Frank T. Paine, and John M. Ivancevich, "The Relative Effectiveness of Alternative Training Methods for Various Training Objectives," *Personnel Psychology,* Fall 1972, pp. 495–509.
38. James Mann, "Effectiveness of Emotional Role-Playing in Modifying Smoking Habits and Attitudes," *Journal of Experimental Research in Personality,* June 1965, pp. 84–90.
39. W. M. Fox, "A Measure of the Effectiveness of the Case Method in Teaching Human Relations," *Personnel Administration,* July–August 1963, pp. 53–57.
40. Chris Argyris, *Intervention Theory and Method: A Behavioral Science View* (Reading Mass.: Addison-Wesley, 1970); Warren G. Bennis, *Organization Development: Its Nature, Origins, and Prospects* (Reading, Mass.: Addison-Wesley, 1969); Robert R. Blake and James S. Mouton, *Building a Dynamic Organization through GRID Development* (Reading, Mass.: Addison-Wesley, 1969); Richard Beckhard, *Organization Development: Strategies and Models* (Reading, Mass.: Addison-Wesley, 1969).
41. Michael Beer and Edgar F. Huse, "A Systems Approach to Organizational Development," *Journal of Applied Behavioral Science,* 1972, pp. 79–101.
42. See recent issues of *Academy of Management Journal, Administrative Science Quarterly, Organizational Dynamics,* and the *Journal of Applied Behavioral Science* for an indication of the increased interest in the evaluation of organizational change and development programs.

Additional References

ARGYRIS, C. and SCHON, D. A. *Organizational Learning: A Theory of Action Perspective.* Reading, Mass.: Addison-Wesley, 1978.

BECKHARD, R. "Strategies for Large System Change." *Sloan Management Review,* Spring 1975, pp. 43–55.

BECKHARD, R., and HARRIS, R. T. *Organizational Transitions: Managing Complex Change.* Reading, Mass.: Addison-Wesley, 1977.

BENNIS, W. G. *Changing Organizations.* New York: McGraw-Hill, 1966.

HARRISON, R. "Choosing the Depth of Organizational Intervention." *Journal of Applied Behavioral Science,* June 1970, pp. 181–202.

LEVINSON, H. *Organizational Diagnosis.* Cambridge, Mass.: Harvard University Press, 1972.

LIPPITT, R., WATSON, J.; and WESTLEY, B. "The Phases of Planned Change." In *Organizational Development: Values, Process, and Technology,* edited by N. Margulies and A. P. Raia. New York: McGraw-Hill, 1972.

MARGULIES, N., and RAIA, A. P. *Conceptual Foundations of Organizational Development.* New York: McGraw-Hill, 1978.

MARGULIES, N., and WALLACE, J. *Organizational Change.* Glenview, Ill.: Scott, Foresman, 1973.

SCHEIN, V. E., and GREINER, L. E. "Can Organizational Development Be Fine Tuned to Bureaucracies?" *Organizational Dynamics,* Winter 1977, pp. 48–61.

TOFFLER, A. *Future Shock.* New York: Random House, 1970.

————. *Learning for Tomorrow.* New York: Random House, 1974.

ZALTMAN, G.; DUNCAN, R.; and HOLBEK, J. *Innovations and Organizations.* New York: Wiley, Interscience, 1973.

A Case of Change

Howard Johnson Company

Howard Johnson—son of an immensely successful father, boss since the age of 26 of a big (1977 revenues: $501 million) food-and-lodging company—was brooding out loud last month. Companies like McDonald's Corp. and Marriott Corp. have long since put Howard Johnson Co. in their shadow and Johnson isn't happy about it. Neither was he happy about takeover rumors which caused a flurry in the otherwise depressed price of his company's stock (which had been selling for just over three times cash flow).

How and why did Howard Johnson Co. lose its dynamism?

"I don't have Dad to talk to anymore," Johnson was saying, "but I do have some fabulous competition. I have to react to a whole new way of eating in the U.S. We face the danger of being thought of as a company that did things so well one way that everyone figures that is the only way we can do it. So we must change not only our business but our image."

The Howard Johnson Co. has scarcely any debt and nearly $4 a share in cash and equivalents; it has preferred to remain liquid rather than expand—in contrast to its faster-stepping competitors. Why? "My [expansion] plans got stalled in the 1974 oil embargo," Johnson went on. "I overreacted. I stopped all expansion, and once you stop, you know how hard it is to get the monster going again. For me the embargo was a shocking thing. Highway travel went way down and we saw some startling internal numbers."

But while Howard Johnson, the man and the company, were standing still, American society wasn't. In many young families now both husband and wife work, and working wives tend to be more interested in entertainment in the evening than in cooking a meal and handing her husband his slippers. The Howard Johnson highway restaurants, mom-pop-&-the-kids-oriented and with unexciting snack counters and decor, have been losing out to "theme" restaurants such as Victoria Station with menus that pass as ethnic or gourmet.

"In a way, this is escape," Johnson says of Middle America's new love affair with flaming desserts, shish kebab and peasant-skirted waitresses. Escape? Johnson explains: "There is a lot of tension in today's fast-paced society. Anything that helps relax that tension will probably succeed."

Worried about the energy crisis, Johnson neglected much else that was changing in American life. Now, however, he is joining the parade. He is quite proud of his new Ground Round restaurants, 103 of them, mostly owned, to date. With a turn-of-the-century atmosphere, these sell nostalgia and nightly musical entertainment along with peanuts in shells and pitchers of beer. Ground Round is everybody's idea of what life was like when grandpa was young.

Johnson's Ground Rounds average $750,000 a year as against only $475,000 for the orange-roofed restaurants.

"We think we have found a hot concept for franchising a potential of maybe 500

Reprinted by permission of *Forbes* magazine from the May 1, 1978 issue. The article was titled, "To Be and What to Be—That Is the Question."

Ground Rounds," says Johnson. "I'm hoping the success of Ground Round will help pay for the changeover of Howard Johnson's Orange Roofs. "A new Howard Johnson's," he goes on, "has just opened up in Scarsdale, N.Y. Its fast-service counters are missing and are replaced by a gazebo-like salad bar, tropical and airy new interior and more service.

"Our biggest job and the one which will be most important long-run will be gradually changing over the Orange Roofs so they will be right for the 1980s but slow enough so they don't lose older people who like them just the way they are. The shift in mood should make them more appropriate for dinner than snacks."

But Johnson worries about changing the Orange Roofs: "Here's the risk. The minute you do get a blurred image you get knocked off."

Johnson's 34 Red Coach Grills are now doing well again since a group of managers walked into his office and urged him: Cut prices, don't shoot for as big a margin. Make the atmosphere more relaxed. "It took a lot of courage to tell the boss he was wrong, so I listened," he says.

His motel-hotel complex, which dropped to break-even during the energy crisis has recovered "and become a gold mine." The occupancy rate rose 15% and room rates went up 25%. Johnson worries, however, about whether new lodging will be a good investment and is holding up expansion there.

What about those takeover rumors? Wouldn't an improving Howard Johnson be an even more tempting target than a sluggish company? "There is no possibility at all of an *unfriendly* merger," he snaps. "If the worst happened, and I don't think it will, we can always be rescued by a white knight. We are such a good company I don't think we'd have any trouble lining one up. Right now it's not necessary."

Probably so. Probably Howard Johnson has a second chance to get Howard Johnson Co. growing again. After all, he's only 45. But he will have to shed the stodginess that is so out of place in a business like food and lodging. Conservatism is one thing. Complacency is something else again.

Case Primer Questions

Using exhibit 15–4 as a model, respond to the following:

1. What are the forces for change influencing Howard Johnsons'?

2. Identify the problem area or areas?

3. What are the goals and constraints that should be developed and evaluated?

4. What should Howard Johnson do (i.e., what are his alternatives and the potential impact)?

A Case of Change

When Bosses Look Back to See Ahead

When former Harvard University Professor Harry Levinson, an acknowledged guru of behavioral science for business, first published his *Organizational Diagnosis* in 1972, it was as though a huge stone had dropped into a pond. The book—which stated that executives must take an extensive, introspective look at their company's history and goals in order to make sound management decisions—created ripples of talk throughout management and academic circles. Then, as suddenly, the whole discussion seemingly died off.

But one of those ripples reached Ebasco Services Inc., an old-line builder of power plants and the first company to try organizational diagnosis. Under the auspices of Andrew O. Manzini, director of manpower planning and development, Ebasco last year put 300 managers through intensive interviews, each lasting 90 minutes or more, to elicit their perceptions of where Ebasco has been, what kind of company it is now, and where it is heading.

The resulting report is a hernia-producing tome—515 pages of data analysis and 130 pages of summary and recommendations—that Ebasco's management is still trying to digest. But the report has already fanned some smoldering ideas for manpower planning within Ebasco, and it is helping the company sharpen its self-image.

Seeking definitions

Although financially sound, Ebasco has some profuse managerial and identity problems—in large part the result of its status as a perennial corporate foster child. Ebasco's original parent, Electric Bond & Share Co., was formed in 1905 as a subsidiary of General Electric Co. In 1925, Ebasco became independent, but was acquired by Boise Cascade Corp. in 1969. When Boise fell on hard times in the early 1970s, it divested itself of Ebasco, which was soon acquired by Halliburton Co. Halliburton was later forced by the Justice Dept. to divest itself of Ebasco, and in August, 1976, the power plant builder found its current home with Enserch Corp., a diversified energy company.

In the midst of all this moving around, Ebasco in 1969 started experimenting with matrix management, a system in which technical people—the mainstay of Ebasco's 4,500-person work force—were responsible for bottom-line results as well as for engineering excellence. But that created new managerial problems. Lines of authority often became blurred. For example, a construction manager, used to choosing equipment only in terms of what works best from an engineering view-point, must now give equal priority to the project manager's budget concerns.

"Suddenly these people are expected not only to fulfill their discipline needs but to look at what they are doing in terms of the entire project on which they are working," explains John A. Scarola, Ebasco's president and chief executive officer.

Source: "When Bosses Look Back to see Ahead," *Business Week,* 15 January, 1979. Used with permission.

"We certainly needed a better definition of how different managers' functions interrelated."

To compound Ebasco's problems, after years of priding itself on being a top-of-the-line power plant builder, the company found its competitors increasingly underbidding it on lucrative projects, in good part because of its reluctance to give practical considerations to costs. "We have always thought of ourselves as the 'Cadillac of the power plant industry,'" notes an Ebasco executive. "But some of our customers want Chevies, not Cadillacs." The organizational diagnosis was necessary, he says, because "we needed to understand our perception of ourselves before we could decide the proper trade-offs between quality and profitability."

Uncertainty

Ebasco's management is convinced that the internal interviews have put the company on the right track toward solving these deep-rooted problems. For Scarola, who moved up to the top job from a position as executive vice-president of operations just in time to receive the report, it meant a quick eye-opener into some of the sensitivities prevalent at Ebasco—sensitivities Scarola admits he ignored as a vice president. "When you get to talk to this many people," he says, "you see that some problems have to be handled."

Among other things, Scarola notes that the study showed widespread concern and uncertainty about staffing plans and about individual futures. This led the company to accelerate the development of its embryonic plans for predicting future manpower needs and for determining where existing personnel fit into that scheme.

Ebasco has also started relating performance appraisals to specific jobs rather than to more general performance standards that might not be important for certain tasks. It also now does "potential appraisals," which outline an employee's projected upward path.

The survey also uncovered considerable confusion about matrix management and strategic planning, and Ebasco has started holding more frequent training and orientation sessions to make employees more comfortable with these techniques. "We've finally accepted that our people must be made to understand more fully how they are expected to interrelate," Scarola explains.

Employee views

Such understanding requires a full knowledge of company goals, and it is Levinson's theory that goals can be set only when a company has a sense of its own history—something he claims few companies have. "If they did," he says, "they wouldn't make the decisions they do." To illustrate, he points to a retailer that has always had a reputation for extreme integrity but whose store managers started indulging in bait-and-switch sales practices. "It wouldn't have happened," he maintains, "if they had recognized the company's long tradition of honest service."

In the introduction to the Ebasco report, Manzini and his manpower planning staff echo Levinson's emphasis on getting employee views of the company. "People's perceptions are reality to them, and their actions will be guided accordingly," it reads. "If enough people 'feel' the same way about certain issues, problems, and circumstances . . . such 'feelings' are generally indicative of what's really happening."

Levinson's recommended questionnaire, which Manzini adopted almost verbatim, is designed to elicit such feelings. The survey asks managers how Ebasco "got to be the way it is today," what "sort of place is this to do your job," what are "the main rules around here that everyone has to follow," and what kinds of things is Ebasco "most interested in keeping up with." Interviewers also told managers to "make believe Ebasco is a person and describe that person." Scarola isolates one question that might easily have opened a Pandora's box: "Suppose Ebasco had to stop doing some of the things it now does—what should not be changed?"

The 'critical mass'

In actuality, both Scarola and other top executives say that while Ebasco got less than overall kudos from its managers, the responses were more often confused than negative. For example, Benjamin E. Tenzer, director of materials engineering and quality assurance, says he was "surprised how ignorant employees were about financial aspects of Ebasco, and how egocentric some people are about their own areas of the company." But he adds: "I was pleasantly surprised at the conviction that the company was better than any of its people. It was akin to someone saying, 'The President stinks, Congress stinks, but America's a great country.' "

Tenzer's enthusiasm is particularly pleasing to Manzini, for Tenzer was one of 23 people he pegged at the outset as crucial to the project's success. To prepare the way for the organizational diagnosis, Manzini conducted a novel power analysis, searching for those people considered the key decision makers within Ebasco. Given the political dynamics inherent in most large companies, such a prelude may have taken more daring than the main study itself. "We simply went around asking employees who they thought had the power around here," says Manzini. "Then we asked those individuals, 'Do you think you have the power?' "

The process turned up 23 people who Manzini calls the "critical mass"—those executives with the power to make or break the diagnosis project. But Manzini went beyond getting their support for the main effort: He gave them a crash course in organizational diagnosis and enlisted their aid as interviewers.

A $74,000 tab

Despite its scope and longevity, the project was relatively inexpensive. Manzini estimates the total cost—including the management time involved—at $74,000. But the drudgery of the project almost led to its being scuttled halfway through. The data gleaned from the interview tapes filled more than 40,000 index cards. "We were suffering from acute data overload," Manzini recalls. "It took us almost a year from start to finish, and only a small part of that time was spent on the interviewing itself."

Still, nearly all the managers involved concede that the diagnosis not only identified the company's problems but also changed their own management styles and concepts. "I pay more attention to trying to communicate information," notes John L. Leporati, vice president of Ebasco's Envirosphere Co. Adds Joe R. Crespo, president of Ebasco's Business Consulting Co.: "It's keeping us focused on some of the main problems—the conflicts between emphasizing quality and keeping costs down, for example." And Tenzer notes: "I learned what a diversity of points of view people can have about subjective questions—a shock for me, since I've always tended to be literal-minded."

For Manzini, though, the project's biggest contribution is in breaking down communications barriers between engineer-managers and their employees. "It's now easier to get company management to address issues not normally pursued," he concludes, "because we've gotten people with engineering backgrounds to work comfortably with psychological processes."

Case Primer Questions:

Using exhibit 15–4 as a model, respond to the following:

1. What are the forces for change influencing Ebasco?

2. What are some of the organization's strengths and problem areas?

3. What are the benefits and shortcomings of Ebasco's approach to organizational diagnosis?

4. What should the company do next? Outline some goals and plans for future action.

CHAPTER 16

Organizational Change and Development: Selected Applications

As we discussed in chapter 15, the success of a particular approach to change in an organization depends on a multitude of variables, including how the change is implemented, how prepared the target group is for the approach, how committed the participants are to the approach, how accurate the diagnosis and the matching of problems and approach are, and how prepared management is to cope constructively with the predicted and unintended consequences of the change and development approach. In other words, success of any organizational change program depends to a large extent on the time, planning, and effort given to change factors *before* implementation.

In this chapter, we will discuss some of the important issues and decisions facing management when they implement change and development approaches. Initially, we will discuss the issue of the depth of intervention. Next, we have selected for discussion a number of the most theoretically developed and empirically studied change approaches that have been applied in numerous organizational settings. Finally, we offer some suggestions for future study and application in organizations.

The Depth of Intervention

In our discussion in chapter 15 of the implementation phase of our change model (see exhibit 15–4), three critical dimensions were identified—timing, location, and depth. Each of these are important, but perhaps the most significant one is depth. The term *intervention depth* is used here to refer to the range of planned and structured activities engaged in by the personnel and/or external change agent associated with the organization.[1]

Discussions of intervention depth generally refers to two aspects: *category* and *target group*. First, a number of broad categories or "families" of intervention are available to managers.[2] Some of the major categories include:

> *Diagnostic activities,* which are fact-finding activities that attempt to determine what is occurring within a unit or organization. An attitude survey or informal meeting to brainstorm about what is occurring may be used to gather information.

Team-building activities, which are designed to improve the effectiveness of units or teams. They may relate to task issues, such as how a job is to be completed, the skills needed to do a job, or the quality of relationships between team members and the leader.

Intergroup activities, which are designed to improve effectiveness of interdependent groups.

Survey-feedback activities, which focus on collecting survey data and designing a plan of action based on the interpretation of the data.

Training-education activities, which are designed to improve knowledge, skills, and abilities of individuals. The specific program may be directed toward improving technical skills for enhancing performance or toward improving interpersonal competence.

Sociotechnical systems, which are focused on improving the effectiveness of the technical or structural contextual variables as they impact individuals and/or groups. This may involve experimenting with new work or organizational design arrangements.

Process-consultation activities, which are practiced by a consultant who attempts to help a client understand and respond to problems in the client's organization and environment. Emphasis in this relationship is on diagnostic-skill improvement for identification of problems in communication, problem solving, and decision making.

Organizational grid activities, which comprise a total organizational program implemented in six phases to upgrade managers' skills and leadership abilities, teamwork, planning, goal setting, and monitoring of events within an organization.

Life- and career-planning activities, which are designed to enable individuals to focus on their life and career objectives and the development of plans to achieve them. The focus is on diagnosing personal strengths, weaknesses, and objectives and on determining what is needed to strengthen deficiencies.

Goal-setting activities, which are designed to help members of an organization understand and cope with conflict.

Conflict-minimization activities, which are designed to help members of an organization understand and cope with conflict.

Second, most of these activities are based on a conceptual foundation and are directed toward specific targets, problems, or processes. For example, the team-building activities are directed toward a group, but the managerial grid activities are generally directed toward the total organization. Because targets each have unique problems and processes, we view intervention as an attempt to improve the effectiveness of a given organizational unit.[3] Exhibit 16–1 is a typology that emphasizes which organizational change and development activities are typically associated with a particular target. Certain factors should be noted. First, the intervener may be an employee in the organization or an outside change agent. Second, interven-

Exhibit 16–1 A Typology of Intervention Activities Based on Target Groups

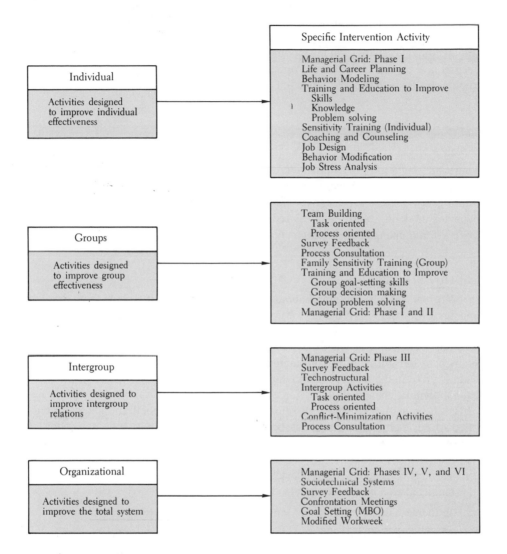

tions are assumed to be planned and structured activities that are directed toward a specific target group. Third, intervention activities can be applied successfully to more than one target group.

To determine if interventions are successful, managers need to scientifically evaluate their impact. There is no certainty that any of the intervention activities will work exactly as predicted. The ultimate answer requires assessment of outcomes, such as organizational effectiveness, personal and group conflict, leadership competence, knowledge, and individual motivation.

In the following sections, we will discuss selected intervention approaches as they apply to the four target groups shown in exhibit 16–1. The approaches we discuss have been chosen because they capture the current emphasis and essence of organizational change and development. The reader should note that certain approaches shown in exhibit 16–1—such as job design, behavior modification, sociotechnical systems, and the modified workweek—have been discussed in earlier chapters. We have treated these approaches separately because of their singular importance to the topics of motivation and job and organizational design.

Individual Intervention Activities

There are numerous individually oriented intervention techniques and activities available to managers. Among these are life- and career-planning programs, various training activities, and sensitivity training. We have selected sensitivity training, behavior modeling, and job-stress reduction as representative programs that focus on *individual* change and development.

Sensitivity or Laboratory Training

In 1946, the National Training Laboratories asked Kurt Lewin to help them develop and present a training program for community leaders. The leaders were brought together to discuss various social problems. Observers of these first laboratory sessions then fed back what they had observed to the participants. The feedback seemed to be well received and increased the participants' awareness about what had occurred in the sessions. From this beginning, training has emerged as a widely used individual change effort.[4]

Based on a detailed review of sensitivity training, Campbell and Dunnette outlined six basic objectives that are associated with most sensitivity training sessions.[5] These are:

1. To increase understanding, insight, and self-awareness about one's behavior and its impact on others.
2. To increase understanding and sensitivity about the behavior of others.
3. To improve understanding and awareness of group and intergroup processes.
4. To improve diagnostic skills in interpersonal and intergroup situations.
5. To increase ability to transform learning into action.
6. To improve an individual's ability to analyze his or her own interpersonal behavior.

These objectives are certainly worthy and, if accomplished, would result in individual improvements. Whether they can be accomplished by sensitivity training is subject to debate among proponents and opponents of sensitivity training.

Training process.   There are three types of sensitivity groups, which include between ten and fifteen members in most situations: stranger, cousin, and family. The *stranger* group would include members who do not know each other. The *cousin* group consists of members of the same organization who do not work together. The *family* group includes members who belong to the same work unit. These groups meet with a trainer. The trainer may structure the content and discussion or may decide to follow an informal or nonstructured format, allowing the group to proceed as they desire.

Sensitivity training stresses "the process rather than the content of training and focuses upon *emotional* rather than conceptual training."[6] The group meets away from the job and engages in an intense exchange of ideas, opinions, beliefs, and philosophy. The trainer may ask the members to discuss their particular leadership philosophies and styles. As each member engages in the exchange of ideas, he or she is expected to learn more about personal inclinations, prejudices, and feelings. As Marrow points out, "It [sensitivity training] says 'Open your eyes. Look at yourself. See how you look to others. Then decide what changes, if any, you want to make and in what direction you want to go.' "[7]

The trainer is the change agent who attempts to facilitate the learning process. The artistry and style of the trainer are critical variables in determining whether sensitivity training objectives are being accomplished. The trainer must interpret the role of participants and encourage them to analyze their contributions without being seen as a disruptive threat to the group. The trainer is described as performing the role of a permissive, nonauthoritarian, sometimes almost a nonparticipative, influencer of trainees.

Because sensitivity training is conducted away from the job, the issue of transfer of learning is of primary importance. Increasing self-awareness in a laboratory is not the same as attempting to influence subordinates to work harder back on the job. The crucial test of sensitivity training, like any intervention activity, is the consequences back on the job.

Evaluations of sensitivity training.   There have been a number of thorough reviews of the evaluation of sensitivity training effectiveness.[8] These suggest mixed results and point out that to date most evaluations are of rather low scientific rigor. Dunnette and Campbell believe that proper scientific standards are necessary for properly evaluating sensitivity training. They suggest that there is an overwhelming amount of anecdotal evidence on its presumed effects. Most reported studies involve introspection, free association, or testimonies collected in an uncontrolled and unsystematic manner.[9] The debate between those requesting the need for more rigor and those asking for some type of evaluation will undoubtedly continue. It is our conclusion that to date sensitivity-training-induced changes in individuals seem to be in the direction of more openness, better self- and interpersonal understanding, and improved communication skills. Because these conclusions are based on some questionable research designs, they must be treated with caution.

An important need in evaluating sensitivity training is to determine if any transfer of learning is sustained on the job. The available research indicates that some positive effects in self-awareness are carried over to the job.[10] In addition to the evaluation of "carry over" or transfer of learning, a number of other issues seem to warrant investigation. Some of these are:

What impact does the trainer's style have on the effectiveness and transfer of learning back on the job?

Is there a difference in impact on voluntary and nonvoluntary participants in sensitivity training?

What are the qualities of an effective sensitivity trainer?

Where and how should sensitivity training be implemented in an organization?

What is a proper procedure for screening the training participants, who will undergo induced anxiety, interpersonal feedback, introspection, and self-evaluation? This question involves the ethical right of managers to direct or subtly recommend that individuals participate in sensitivity training.

These and other research questions need to be investigated to improve our understanding of sensitivity training, which is not a fad that will fade away with time. Thus, more refined attempts to evaluate the impact of sensitivity training should continue to appear in the ever-growing literature on this popular, individual-oriented approach.

Behavior Modeling in Training

The issue of how to effectively develop work-related skills is one that has occupied a great deal of time for both behavioral scientists and practicing managers. Generally thought of as the training and development function, organizations spend millions of dollars annually in this effort. Yet, there is some question on the part of involved individuals as to the true value of the such massive training efforts.[11]

As shown in exhibit 16–2, traditional learning approaches aimed at improved work-related skills have primarily focused on classroom learning sessions to change employee attitudes and values. Example sessions include developing supervisory skills, learning how to communicate and motivate subordinates, and acquiring skills in new planning and budgeting techniques. The main problem associated with traditional training approaches is that there is little *control* over the changes in behavior. In essence, trainers *hope* that the newly learned skills are applied and reinforced back on the job; there is no assurance, however, that such will be the case. In many situations, employees return not only to their jobs but to their old habits and behaviors as well—or, learning has been extinguished (see discussions on extinction in chapter 5).

In *behavior modeling,* the emphasis is placed not so much on classroom-type lectures, but on acquiring (or learning) new skills through experience.[12] As shown in exhibits 16–2 and 16–3, the use of films and video tapes enable the participant to view *and* experience the desired changes in behavior. By focusing on the *behavior* (as opposed to attitudes in the traditional approach), behavior modeling attempts to overcome the main problems associated with traditional training approaches.

Exhibit 16–2 Traditional and Behavior-Modeling Training Approaches

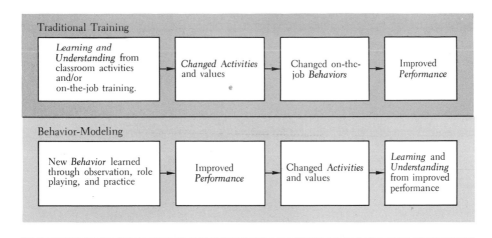

Adapted from: A. I. Kraut, "Developing Managerial Skills via Modeling Techniques," *Personnel Psychology* 29 (1976): 325–28.

To illustrate the components and activities associated with behavior modeling, consider a training program that has been designed to improve supervisors' skills in conducting performance evaluation sessions with subordinates. After a brief presentation of the basic concepts, the participants view various films and/or video tapes of actual performance evaluation sessions. This is termed the *modeling* component or stage. The films or tapes generally use selected organizational employees and show both acceptable and unacceptable example sessions. In the *role-playing* component, the participants are each asked to perform a number of simulated performance evaluation sessions, which are video taped. Later, the tapes are replayed and reviewed by the trainer and other participants. The critiques and feedback received involve the *social-reinforcement* component. Finally, *transfer of learning* is obtained through continued practice and involvement in experiencing the newly learned desired behavior.

Because this organizational change technique has only recently been introduced, the jury is still out concerning its effectiveness over traditional training approaches. Two signs, however, point to its possible value and effectiveness. First, selected evaluations have been published that have stressed the success of the approach in such activities as improving employee safety skills.[13] Second, the list of user companies grows steadily. Such organizations as Federated Department Stores, Xerox, G.E., Union Carbide, SOHIO, AT&T, and Gulf Oil are actively involved in applying behavior-modeling approaches to skills acquisition.

Whether or not behavior modeling will prove to be a better approach to gaining a significant return on the invested training dollar will take more time. Not only are more varied applications in organizations needed; but so also is a greater emphasis on *evaluation*—are the newly acquired skills really utilized on the job, and does this lead to improved performance?

Exhibit 16–3   Behavior-Modeling Components and Activities

Component	Activities	Effective Learning Conditions
Modeling	Employees view films and video tapes of model persons performing desired behaviors.	Acquisition of understanding of desired skills and behaviors.
Role Playing	Employees experience and practice behaviors demonstrated in modeling stage.	Emphasis on participation, practice, and learning of desired skills.
Social Reinforcement	Feedback given to employees by trainers and other participants.	Feedback reinforces newly acquired skills and behavior.
Transfer of Learning	Encouragement to utilize new skills in the job.	Relates new learning experience to behaviors required for good on-the-job performance.

Job-Stress Analysis

It is a well-established fact that most organizations place a high value on the members of their management team. An organization's set of human resources, especially managers, provide the direction, motivation, leadership, and control that leads to profitability, growth, and survival.

Until recently, organizations have stressed the development and retention of management through selection, training, varied job assignments, and an effective reward system. This level of emphasis and resources given to management development, however, can go up in smoke when promising, effective managers are stricken with heart attacks or other physiological disorders.[14] It is because of this situation that many organizations are placing an increased emphasis on understanding and reducing a primary factor in such physiological and health problems—namely, job stress.[15]

Stress, which we will define as an internal experience or position creating a physiological or psychological imbalance within the individual,[16] has been addressed in both the medical[17] and management literatures.[18] It is only recently that the two literatures have been combined into a more comprehensive framework of the relationship between organizational stress and physiological disorders. In general, a review of the two literatures suggests that: (1) a great variety of organizational and environmental conditions are capable of producing stress; (2) different individuals respond to the same conditions in different ways; (3) the intensity and extent of the stress state within the individual are difficult to predict; (4) the outcomes of prolonged stress may be physiological or behavioral, or both; and (5) the consequences of prolonged stress may include chronic diseases, such as coronary heart disease.[19]

In order to more fully understand job stress, a framework for analysis is presented in exhibit 16–4. Five major categories are included in the framework: *stressors; stress moderators;* actual *stress;* the *outcomes* of *stress;* and possible *stress reducers.*

Exhibit 16-4 Job-Stress Analysis Framework

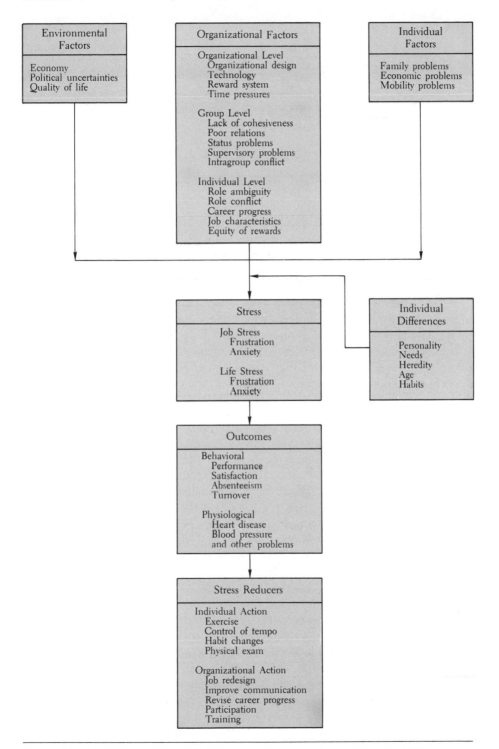

Suggested by John M. Ivancevich and M. T. Matteson, "Managing for a Healthier Heart," *Management Review,* October 1978, p. 17.

Stressors

Exhibit 16–4 identifies three main stressor categories: environmental, organizational, and individual factors. Stressors are essentially the antecedents of stress, or factors that facilitate the development of job stress.

Environmental factors relate to the general environmental situation and its impact on the organization and individuals. Such concerns as the state of the economy (e.g., inflation, recession, unemployment rate, increasing competition), the uncertainties in the political arena (e.g., how will new mayors, senators, governors, and other representatives vote on important issues), and the general quality of life (e.g., pollution, decline of the importance of a family, rising crime) all can create a state of stress and tension.

Many of the aspects of *organizational factors* have been discussed in previous chapters. Looking at the three levels of analysis we have discussed throughout, at the *organizational*-level stress can be induced by an ineffective organizational design (e.g., too much emphasis on rules, procedures, and control systems) or from a less than satisfactory reward system. *Group*-level stressors include problems related to low cohesion, intragroup conflict, or from a coercive supervisor. At the *individual level*, the emphasis is on dysfunctions associated with the role (e.g., role ambiguity and role conflict), jobs that are either too routine and boring or too complex to handle, and from a lack of career progress.[20]

Individual factors concern such stressors as family problems (e.g., illness or divorce), economic difficulties (e.g., rising household and mortgage costs), and issues of mobility (e.g., disruption of family life with a transfer to another state).

Stress moderators

As we pointed out in chapters 3 to 6, individual characteristics by themselves do not consistently determine or cause a person's behavior. Their value in the study of organizational behavior has been as moderators of other relationships (e.g., growth need strength in job design).

Some researchers have suggested that "personality" differences are important stress moderators, involving such concepts as self-esteem, self-confidence, and aggressiveness.[21] The most frequently cited is work of Friedman and his associates, who are responsible for the development of the Type A and Type B personality taxonomy.[22] According to their approach, individuals exhibiting aggressive, hard-driving personality characteristics (Type A) are more susceptible to heart disease than are their more relaxed counterparts (Type B). Other more demographic variables have been shown to relate to stress and physiological disorders. Included are such variables as heredity, age, lack of exercise, diet, and alcohol and tobacco use.[23] As moderators, it is suggested that certain of the variables—singly or in some combination—either accentuate or diminish the impact of the previously discussed *stressors*.

Stress

Consistent with our discussion of the main stressor categories, we have identified stress—perceived and/or actual—as involving two categories. *Job stress* is that stress associated with organizational causes; *life stress* concerns individual and/or family causes. For each stress category, two components of stress are noted. First, *frustration* applies to any obstruction or barrier between behavior and its goal. Frustration can occur from a change, delay, or lack of reinforcement for certain behaviors (e.g., not receiving the promised pay raise for high performance); sheer failure (e.g., a salesperson not receiving a sales contract, even though all preparatory factors were done correctly); or simple obstructions (e.g., rules or procedures that prevent the adoption of a new work technique). Whereas frustration is the blockage or interference with behavior, *anxiety* is the feeling of not having the appropriate response, or feeling a lack of preparation for some activity. Examples could be taking a CPA exam, conducting a performance evaluation, or presenting a marketing plan to the board of directors while not feeling confident in so doing.

Stress outcomes

Outcomes of stress are shown as relating to both physiological and behavioral factors. A number of studies have shown the potential link between stress and such dysfunctional physiological outcomes as heart disease.[24] Similarly, stress and such behavioral outcomes as work dissatisfaction, decreased performance, and increased absenteeism have been reported.[25] There is also some research that suggests that behavioral and physiological outcomes are related; in particular, those that relate job and life satisfaction with heart disease.[26]

Stress reducers

Evidence is growing that suggests that job stress is related to such factors as unclear job discriptions, a nonequitable reward system, unduly strict rules and procedures, time pressures, inability to accomplish challenging goals, and eventually to dysfunctional physiological and behavioral outcomes. Because excessive stress can be related to both organizations and individuals, it is important for managers to both understand the causes and reactions to stress and potential methods of stress reduction.

As shown in exhibit 16–4, one way of presenting stress reducers is from individual and organizational viewpoints or actions.

Individual actions.   First and foremost, a physical exam conducted by a doctor is almost a prerequisite to any stress-reduction program. The knowledge about one's physical condition, smoking and drinking habits, coronary history, and heredity all help in understanding the causes of stress and its potential effects. Other individual actions include increased exercise, changing habits, and the ability to control the tempo of the day's work through relaxation exercises or various forms of meditation.

Organizational factors.   The responsibility for stress reduction also falls on the organization. Because many stressors are related to daily ambiguous or conflicting job activities, the organization may take such steps as improving communications, redesigning jobs to decrease boredom or remove unnecessary demands, revising careers paths to be more realistic, increasing participation in decision making, or training in stress causes and reduction procedures.

Overall, although we have emphasized the negative effects of stress, let us not overlook one very important aspect: stress is and will continue to be a daily fact of working in contemporary complex organizations. Managers must recognize that reducing the dysfunctional consequence of stress is strongly determined by the degree of *understanding* of stressors and the ability to diagnose and be aware of their existence and their causes.

Group and Team Intervention Activities

Team Building

In order to consistently accomplish organizational and individual goals, it is necessary for people to work together. Probably the single most important intervention approach that is concerned with the effective functioning of groups is team-building activities. *Team building* is defined as a planned event with a group of people who have or may have common organization relationships and/or goals that is designed to somehow improve the way in which they get work done. Team-building interventions are typically directed toward four areas: diagnosis, task accomplishment, team relationships, and team and organization processes.[27]

Diagnostic meeting

The purpose of the diagnostic meeting is to conduct an open discussion and critique of the performance of the group. These discussions are supposed to uncover problems that are hindering group performance. Typically, the immediate supervisor of the group and an external consultant will discuss the value of an open group discussion of performance. The supervisor would then put the idea of an open discussion to the group. The group is asked to identify problems that require correction, task accomplishment, and intergroup relationships. If the group, supervisor, and consultant believe that working through problems by discussion would be worthwhile, a formal diagnostic meeting is set.

The group, supervisor, and consultant meet for approximately one day. Everyone is given an opportunity to present his or her own ideas to the entire group. The large group could also break up into small discussion groups. The intent of any diagnostic meeting is to share ideas and information about group performance. The sharing typically results in the identification of major problem areas, such as planning, resource limitations, lack of understanding of the current evaluation system, and inadequate training to cope with problems. These problems can be worked on in an action-planning session. Thus, the diagnostic meeting is assumed to be suited for problem identification and action planning.

A major advantage of the diagnostic meeting is that it enables a group to work through its problems carefully. The use of a professional consultant may or may not be needed. This type of meeting takes little time and can be a mechanism for getting groups to think through problems and methods for correcting them.

Family team-building meeting

Family-group team building is an attempt to help the members of the same work unit become more adept at recognizing the group's problems and solving them. The problems may involve tasks or interpersonal conflict between two or more members.

The consultant may first interview the family members individually, ask the members to complete self-report questionnaires, and also sit in on important group meetings. The data collected would then be carefully analyzed.

At a group meeting, the consultant feeds back the data to the membership. This data is then organized into major categories of interest. The consultant can serve as a resource person, offering expertise on what the data reveal, or as a person facilitating small group discussions of the data. The group would use the data to clarify problem areas and reach some conclusions on courses of action that could possibly minimize the problems.

Significant variations in family team building are available to managers. Some consultants use lectures, role play, and cases to improve learning; others rely primarily on group discussion with inputs made by the expert when appropriate. Family team building is used for both general and specific problems, such as an organizational design change or the introduction of a new supervisor.

A study in a school focused on family team building. A total of fifty-four trainees, employees at the school, engaged in family team-building sessions on three separate occasions.[28] The sessions focused on problems within the school—a lack of role clarity, poor staff involvement and participation at meetings, and poor utilization of resources. The trainees met in a large group, small groups, and dyads in the sessions. The researchers reported a number of significant positive changes after the team building, when participants in this school were compared to employees in other schools who did not participate in team-building meetings.

Role-analysis team building

The role-analysis team intervention is designed to clarify role expectations and responsibilities of team members. In many organizations, individuals lack a clear understanding of what behaviors are expected of them. This lack of role clarity can hinder performance and result in high, dysfunctional levels of anxiety and stress. In a group meeting, each person is asked to define their *focal* role, its place in the group, why it is needed, and how it adds to group performance. These specifications are listed in front of the others and openly discussed. Behaviors are added and deleted by discussion until the role incumbent is satisfied with the defined role.

The next step is to examine the focal-role incumbent's expectations of others. These perceptions are presented, discussed, and modified until some group consensus emerges. The third step is a discussion of what the group expects from the focal-role incumbent. The final product of this give and take is a role profile with which each member is at least somewhat satisfied and that each member is willing to use as a guideline. The profile consists of (1) a set of activities that are classified as to the prescribed and discretionary elements of the role; (2) the obligation of the incumbent to other incumbents in the set; and (3) the expectations of the incumbent by others in the set. It is a comprehensive picture of each group member's role space.[29]

Evaluations of team building

There is a limited amount of empirical research on the effectiveness of team building. Many popular professional journals contain a number of studies evaluating team-building activities. The majority of these studies are of low scientific rigor and rely heavily on questionnaire responses collected immediately after the team-building activities. Of course, the excitement of team building may result in positive responses or socially desirable answers about the process.

The need for sophisticated and carefully controlled evaluations of team building is obvious. Until it can be proven successful through scientific analysis, team building will remain just another organizational change and development intervention activity that seems to have promise. There are, of course, many promising interventions that some practicing managers believe have some potential.

Survey-Feedback Research

In the typology of intervention activities based on target groups shown in exhibit 16–1, survey feedback was placed in three locations. It can be considered, and is used, to improve groups and teams, intergroup relations, and organizational activities. Survey-feedback research involves the process of systematically collecting data about a group or the organization primarily through self-report questionnaires. Occasionally, interviews and other records of the unit being studied are used. The collected data are analyzed and fed back to the group for analysis, interpretation, and corrective action, if needed. The entire process has two major components: the attitude survey and small discussion workshops.

The usual activities involved with survey feedback are as follows:[30]

1. Top-level executives initiate plans for attitude surveys and feeding back information.

2. Data are collected from all organizational employees.

3. Data are fed back to members of the organization in a series of interlocking conferences.

4. Each superior presides at a meeting with subordinates in which the data are discussed and in which they are asked to help interpret the data.

5. Plans are made to implement corrective changes, and plans are made to introduce the data to the next level (the interlocking procedure).

A summary of the main points of the survey-feedback research activity compared to the traditional use of attitude surveys is presented in exhibit 16–5. The active involvement of teams at all levels is a major difference between the traditional and survey-feedback research approaches.

Group discussions and problem-solving sessions that use the feedback are run by the survey research implementors, possibly including an external change agent. The meetings are intended to identify courses of action for correcting some of the problems that were uncovered. The meetings focus on the data analysis and what it means to the group. The change agent can aid the group members in understanding and using the information to better cope with their job situation and the organization.

Because of its relative simplicity and persuasive value, survey feedback has become one of the most widely used interventions in all types of organizations.[31] In

Exhibit 16–5 Traditional Versus Survey-Feedback Characteristics

	Traditional Approach	**Survey-Feedback Research Approach**
Data collection from:	Rank and file, and maybe supervisor	Everyone in the system or subsystem
Data reported to:	Top management, department heads, and perhaps to employees through newsletter	Everyone who participated
Focus	Problem finding	Problem finding, feedback, problem solving
Implications of data are worked on by:	Top management (maybe)	Everyone in work teams, with workshops starting at the top (all superiors with their subordinates)
Third-party intervention strategy:	Design and administration of questionnaire, development of a report	Obtaining concurrence on total strategy, design and administration of questionnaire design of workshops, appropriate interventions in workshops
Action planning done by:	Top management only	Teams at all levels

a sense, however, its real value is not change but *diagnosing* where change is needed. Recalling our planned change model in exhibit 15–4, the basic elements of survey feedback focus on the factors *prior* to implementation—that is, the diagnostics, constraint identification, and selection of intervention technique. Because we have stressed the importance of diagnosis throughout this book, we believe that continued use of survey feedback will result in significant returns to the organization.

There are a number of important issues or questions managers must consider before the survey-feedback method is used.[32] First, *who* should conduct the survey and act as a feedback mechanism? This discussion usually revolves around using an external agent or someone internal to the organization. Both approaches have advantages and disadvantages. For example, external agents may have the survey-feedback skills not available inside the organization, and, because they are divorced from the organization, can obtain and handle highly volatile and critical issues more effectively. On the other hand, external agents may not fully understand the operations or language of the organization, and with large samples they could be quite costly. For internal agents, the opposite may be true; they know the language of the organization and can monitor costs more closely, but may not have the necessary skills. Also, because of their employment in the organization, participants are reluctant to respond in a true, "unbiased" manner.

Second is the issue of which is more important: the data or the feedback process? Some contend that quality data will usually generate constructive feedback and problem-solving sessions. Others, however, believe that the real value of survey feedback is getting organizational members together to discuss important issues. It is our contention that *both* data collection and feedback quality must be emphasized. On this issue, it is important that: (1) highly valid and reliable measures are used; (2) both organizational strengths *and* problem areas are identified; (3) data are presented in a simple and meaningful format that can be understood by all participants; and (4) the feedback session leaders have the necessary skills to stimulate effective identification, classification, and problem solving.

Finally, is survey feedback a one-shot experience, or an ongoing process? If organizations want to be adaptive, proactive entities, clearly the diagnostics and interaction provided by survey feedback justify its ongoing use. The realities of organizational life, however, suggest that many survey feedback programs have suffered from a lack of follow-up work once the feedback sessions have been conducted. After feedback has occurred, the tendency is to greatly diminish further activities, the assumption being that, once begun, problem solving will continue more or less on its own. Experience has shown, however, that the opposite usually occurs because of internal forces. Among these forces are time and resource constraints, resistance in facing difficult and volatile issues, and the lack of top-management support and commitment.

For survey feedback to continue in its importance to managers, at least four factors must be present. First, top-management support and commitment is required throughout the entire process. Without high-level backing and involvement, any change approach will be in vain. Second, the skills of survey-feedback leaders and coordinators as change agents must be stressed. Third, it also would seem advisable to use some "hard" performance criteria to determine whether the survey-feedback research approach has any impact on this important set of factors. Because questionnaires are easy to administer, it should not be concluded that conducting feedback workshops is an easy task for a change agent. It is one of the more difficult tasks because data that are perceived as a threat to workshop participants or that place participants at the bottom of a group are not easy to accept. Managers with groups who look good in the data interpretation are often enthusiastic about feedback; those who look bad are often angry, uncooperative, and cynical about the change agent and the survey-feedback research approach. Finally, survey feedback should be perceived as an ongoing process. In essence, it should become a valuable management tool, not one that is temporarily tacked on to the management system.

Intergroup Intervention Activities

Some degree of conflict is inevitable in organizations that have differentiated departments or work teams. The manager must guard against dysfunctional conflict between interdependent and differentiated groups. For example, when a drafting unit, which furnishes blueprints to project-development engineers, withholds information because of bad feelings and conflict, the organization suffers. Due to limited resources, personal favoritism, and personality differences, among other things, groups reach a point of open conflict that negates goal accomplishment. Of course, there are also reward programs within organizations that encourage group cohesiveness and competitiveness as opposed to a total organizational orientation.

Confronting the reasons for conflict and the ways to minimize it is the basic approach to bring about changes that overcome this problem. One sequence of confrontation techniques has been recommended by Blake, Shepard, and Mouton.[33] Their approach is as follows:

> Step 1: The leaders of the two groups meet with a change agent and discuss the interaction patterns between the two groups. The discussion centers on ways to improve communication, understanding, and respect.
>
> Step 2: The two groups meet in separate rooms and develop two lists. In one, they list their opinions, attitudes, feelings, and perceptions of the other group. In the second list, the group attempts to predict what the other group is saying about them.
>
> Step 3: The two groups come together to share the information on the list. Group 1 reads its list on how it sees Group 2 and what it dislikes about it. The change agent does not permit discussion of the lists. Next, Group 1 reads its list of what it expected Group 2 would say about it, and Group 2 reads its list of what it thought Group 1 would say about it.
>
> Step 4: The two groups return to their separate rooms and are asked to discuss what they learned about themselves and the other group. After a discussion of what was learned, the groups are asked to develop a list of the priority items that need to be resolved between the two groups.
>
> Step 5: The two groups come back together and share their lists with each other. After this discussion, both groups, as a team, make one list containing the issues and problems that need to be resolved to minimize intergroup conflict. Together, they also prepare a list of action steps for how and when the conflict will be minimized.
>
> Step 6: As a follow-up, a time is set for the two groups or their leaders to meet to discuss progress and problems with the action steps.

There are a number of modifications that can be introduced into this sequence. For example, more than two groups can participate, or a change agent may introduce the observed conflict factors and ask the groups to address them and develop action steps. The important point is to confront what is thought to be actual or potential dysfunctional conflict.

In their original study, Blake, Shepard, and Mouton reported improved understanding and relationships between two traditionally antagonistic groups, union and management.[34] However, a more refined and rigorous research design was used by Golembiewski and Blumberg to study the Blake sequence steps. These researchers studied organizational units in the marketing division of a large corporation.[35] An attitude questionnaire was used to make pre- and postintervention comparisons. The results indicated that individuals who were deeply involved in their job had more positive attitudes toward the intervention and the company than did those who were less deeply involved.

Once again, however, the research support is meager. Whether intergroup intervention can have lasting effects on behavior and performance is not known because of the limited, short-term research that is available. We need more studies that investigate the long-run effects of minimizing conflict. Perhaps conflict minimization will have a greater long-run impact, or it should be limited to only some forms of dysfunctional conflict. Identifying the forms of dysfunctional conflict that intergroup intervention activities can alleviate appears to be a worthwhile task for those researchers and practitioners who preach the contingency orientation of managing within organizations.

Organizational Intervention Activities

There are organizational change and development interventions that can have an organization-wide impact. Three of the most publicized and widely used approaches are management by objectives (goal setting), the managerial grid, and the quality of work life philosophy. These interventions have a common-sense appeal to managers and are generally considered worthwhile endeavors for improving behavior and performance. Whether this enthusiasm and support is justified is a much debated topic among academic researchers, but not among those managers using these interventions.

Management by Objectives

When one discusses an organization's management by objectives program (MBO or goal setting), he or she may be referring to a number of practices. Terms used to describe MBO approaches include management by results, work planning and review, performance-planning evaluation, charter of accountability concept, individual goal setting, group goal setting, and participative goal setting. The exact name associated with objective setting has led to some of the confusion about what it involves, where it is implemented, and how it has worked. We will use the terms *management by objectives* and *goal setting* interchangeably in our discussion.

Two of the early proponents of managing by the use of objectives were Drucker and Odiorne. Their interpretations of what this type of program involved were slightly different. Drucker states that:

> . . . the objectives of the district manager's job should be defined by the contribution he and his district sales force have to make to the sales department, the objectives of the project engineer's job by the contribution he, his engineers and draftsmen make to the engineering department. . . . This requires each manager to develop and set the objectives of his unit himself. Higher management must, of course, reserve the power to approve or disapprove these objectives. But their development is part of a manager's responsibility; indeed, it is his first responsibility.[36]

In this passage, Drucker suggests that MBO is a process that encourages manage-rial self-control. The manager is at the core of the process, and he or she controls the progress achieved in accomplishing worthwhile objectives.

Odiorne emphasizes a slightly different set of issues when he states that MBO is:

> . . . a process whereby the superior and subordinate managers of an organization jointly identify its common goals, define each individual's major areas of responsi-bility in terms of the results expected of him, and use these measures as guides for operating the unit and assessing the contribution of each of its members.[37]

The emphasis in this passage is the importance of mutual understanding between a superior and a subordinate. Note that in both the Drucker and Odiorne interpreta-tions of MBO is the implication that through discussions and involvement a subordi-nate will be motivated to work harder and consequently improve performance. In essence, MBO is an intervention approach that is concerned with initiating and stimulating better performance, among other things. It is, as Raia states, a "proac-tive" rather than a "reactive" style of managing.[38]

The philosophical rudiments of MBO provide the bases for a process that in-cludes a series of interrelated and interdependent steps. Exhibit 16–6 presents the major steps and some of the anticipated organizationally based results of the pro-cess. The figure shows that the complete process should include: (1) a diagnosis to assess the needs, job, personnel, and technology; (2) planning via communicating what MBO is, training in the process, establishing objectives, establishing action plans, and establishing criteria to assess whether the goals of the process are being accomplished; (3) objective setting with special attention paid to objective clarity, superior and subordinate participation, establishment of relevant objectives and priorities of the objectives set; (4) intermediate review of objectives originally set, which is a form of feedback and provides an opportunity to modify the original objectives; (5) a final review or discussion and analysis of the results, which are used to initiate the next complete cycle of objective setting; and (6) the accomplish-ment of better planning, control, and organization through motivated involvement that is based on achieved results instead of personality or popularity.

Unfortunately, MBO is often assumed to include only steps 3 (objective setting), 4 (intermediate review), 5 (final review), and 6 (improved results). The transmission of an MBO intervention to individuals, groups, or the total organization certainly requires diagnosis and careful preparation of participants.

By carefully examining exhibit 16–6, and by using the definitions of both Drucker and Odiorne, a number of important principles of action emerge. These are:

Principle I: MBO requires the involvement of superiors and subordinates. The subordinates may be involved in a dyadic relationship, one superior-one subor-dinate, or in a group arrangement of one superior and more than one subordi-nate.

Principle II: MBO relies heavily on feedback, which needs to focus on results and should be as closely connected to behavior and performance as possible.

Exhibit 16–6 An MBO Model for Superior-Subordinate Goal Setting

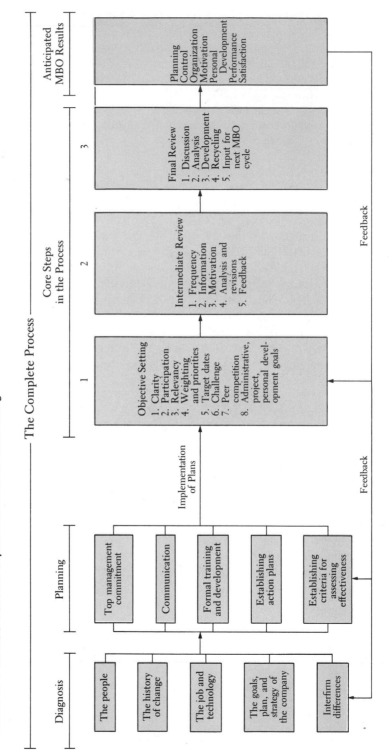

Principle III: The crucial first step in any MBO program should be a thorough diagnosis of the job, the participants, and the needs of the organization.

Principle IV: The superior must be competent in counseling subordinates on the achieved results and the expected or agreed to results for the next cycle. Carroll and Tosi, based on experience in implementing and evaluating MBO programs at Black and Decker Corporation and elsewhere, suggest a number of procedures for providing feedback and counseling.[39] Some of their suggestions are:

The superior should create a trusting atmosphere and not focus on punitive factors.

The superior should listen as much as possible.

The superior should use reflective summaries to minimize misunderstandings.

The superior should encourage the subordinate to vent anger and disagreement.

The superior should encourage the resolution of problems before the end of the counseling or feedback session.

These principles are based on a review of the empirically based MBO literature, which is much too limited considering the worldwide use of this intervention activity. The vast majority of MBO literature that espouses its virtues is based on testimonial claims of consultants, academicians, and convinced practicing managers.

Testimonial support of MBO

The growing popularity of MBO is based primarily on its common-sense appeal, its rather simplistic format, and its articulate supporters.[40] The advocates of MBO propose an attractive list of benefits that will accrue to an organization that implements MBO. Some of these are:

Increased short- and long-range planning.

A procedure for monitoring work progress and results.

Improved commitment to the organization because of increased motivation, loyalty, and participation of employees.

Improved clarity of a manager's job.

Increased communications between superiors and subordinates.

An improved organizational climate in general that encourages improvements in performance.

These and other numerous benefits are certainly attractive to any manager. Unfortunately, some advocates and managers assume that all these benefits flow easily from an MBO effort and in a relatively short period of time. These erroneous assumptions have not been documented and reported in most evaluations of MBO. They also lead to false claims of the superiority of MBO programs over other forms of intervention activities.

Scientific field evaluations of MBO-type interventions

There have been a number of reviews of the literature on goal setting that, for some unexplainable reason, fail to integrate the laboratory goal-setting studies and field MBO efforts.[41] Perhaps, the laboratory purist does not want to be associated with some of the poorly controlled field studies and the extremely complex task of examining MBO efforts in organizational units or systems. We adopt the logic that when the laboratory and field work on objective or goal setting is combined, it offers interesting insights into the effectiveness, or lack thereof, of MBO interventions.

Raia conducted two longitudinal studies of an MBO-type program at the Purex Corporation.[42] In his first study, production records, interview responses, and questionnaire data from 112 managers were analyzed. The data were collected *after* the implementation of the MBO program. He found that productivity, which had been declining at a rate of 4 percent per month, was increasing at the rate of 3 percent per month after the MBO intervention. In addition, managers were more aware of the mission and goals of the organization, were more enthusiastic about evaluating and counseling subordinates, and believed that communications had improved since MBO was introduced.

In the second study at Purex, conducted four years later, Raia again collected data similar to that of the first study from seventy-four of the original participants. Productivity had continued to increase, as did the level of goal attainment. However, a number of complaints surfaced that were not uncovered in the first study. These complaints were:

1. The program was being used as a whip.

2. The program increased the amount of paperwork.

3. The program failed to reach the lower managerial levels.

4. There was an overemphasis on production.

5. The program failed to provide adequate incentives to improve performance.

In essence, these negative attitudes were viewed as indicators that despite some initial production improvements, other problems with the MBO program existed.

As the testimonial support suggests, MBO can improve planning, controlling, and organizing tasks. A study at Black and Decker attempted to determine specifically what MBO can accomplish in an organizational setting over a period of time.[43] The Black and Decker program was designed to:

1. Help the individual improve his job knowledge and skills;
2. Assure two-way communications between the subordinates and supervisors;
3. Convert Black and Decker organizational goals into targets for the individual; and
4. Appraise the individual's performance.[44]

In order to assess exactly what the MBO program at Black and Decker was actually accomplishing, the researchers interviewed participants and used attitude surveys. This analysis focused on the MBO program, and its results provided the basis for a modification of the original program and the implementation of a program based on the survey research results and management consultation.

The original MBO program was initiated by a new personnel vice president. The data analysis revealed that:

Subordinates were more positive toward the program as more difficult goals were set.

Increased goal clarity, relevance, and importance resulted in more positive attitudes toward the program and the interactions between superiors and subordinates.

The more frequent the feedback sessions, the greater the subordinate's satisfaction, goal accomplishment, and relationship with the supervisor.

The second phase of the modified program at Black and Decker involved improving the original program by placing increased emphasis on total organizational involvement in goal setting, increased training of the top managers in goal setting, and the use of a more reliable attitude survey. The second-phase data analysis, in which the interpretation was based on interviews and questionnaire responses, indicated that:

Managers now perceived MBO as a way of developing subordinates.

More managers believed that they had trouble with "personal improvement" goal setting with subordinates.

Satisfaction with MBO increased, and there was an increase in the amount of work effort expended on goal setting.

There was no change in the amount of participation by subordinates in the goal-setting process.

The researchers, after reviewing their findings, suggest that the most important factor in the successful implementation of MBO is top-management support. This same declaration was expressed by Argyris, Blake and Mouton, and Bennis when they recommended the location for implementing organizational change.[45] The one glaring drawback of the Black and Decker research is the lack of a comparison group from the company. Of course, it is not always possible to secure comparison groups in field research, but without them inferences must be cautiously drawn.

At Tenneco, a worldwide conglomerate manufacturing such diverse products as almonds, aircraft carriers, corrugated boxes, tractors, chemicals, oil, and gas products, a slightly different orientation to MBO was used.[46] Five major components made up Tenneco's MBO program, known as Performance Planning and Evaluation (PP&E):

1. *Emphasis on personal development.* As shown in exhibit 16–7, the focus of the program was primarily on personal development of its management group (15,000 worldwide), and only secondarily on wage and salary progression.

Exhibit 16–7 Personal-Development Orientation in MBO

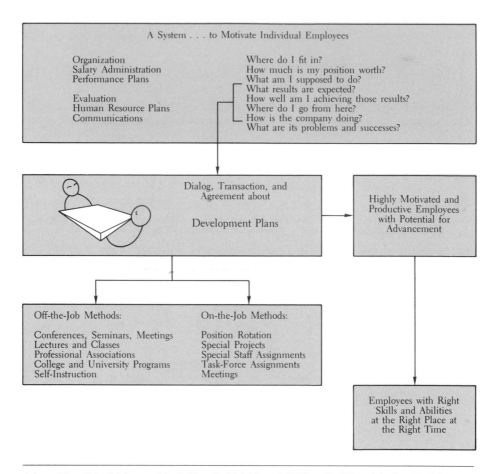

A System . . . to Motivate Individual Employees

Organization
Salary Administration
Performance Plans

Evaluation
Human Resource Plans
Communications

Where do I fit in?
How much is my position worth?
What am I supposed to do?
What results are expected?
How well am I achieving those results?
Where do I go from here?
How is the company doing?
What are its problems and successes?

Dialog, Transaction, and
Agreement about

Development Plans

Highly Motivated and
Productive Employees
with Potential for
Advancement

Off-the-Job Methods:

Conferences, Seminars, Meetings
Lectures and Classes
Professional Associations
College and University Programs
Self-Instruction

On-the-Job Methods:

Position Rotation
Special Projects
Special Staff Assignments
Task-Force Assignments
Meetings

Employees with Right
Skills and Abilities
at the Right Place at
the Right Time

Adapted from John M. Ivancevich, J. Timothy McMahon, J. William Streidl, and Andrew D. Szilagyi, "Goal Setting: The Tenneco Approach to Personal Development and Management Effectiveness," *Organizational Dynamics,* Winter 1978, p. 68.

Tenneco saw MBO as a system to develop and identify high-potential managers.

2. *Top-management commitment.* Top-level managers, including the president and chairman of the board, not only were trained in MBO procedures but were actively involved with it in their own work. This involvement provided needed support and commitment.

3. *Emphasis on diagnosis.* Before any MBO implementation activities, a great deal of emphasis was placed on preliminary analysis and diagnostics of the corporation. A task force of representatives from the various functions met frequently to analyze issues of goals, procedures, learning, communication, and evaluation.

4. *Training.* To ensure proper MBO usage, an extensive training program was developed. The training sessions, which involved participants at all levels of the corporation, focused on developing performance plans and conducting both progress interviews and final performance reviews (i.e., coaching and counseling).

5. *Evaluation.* In order to obtain an accurate and unbiased evaluation of the program, a group of external evaluators were used. Utilizing a modified survey-feedback process, data were collected over a three-year period and fed back to individual companies for more finite feedback to participants.

After a three-year period, the results were impressive. The participants reported greater satisfaction and significantly higher values on various important concepts, such as superior-subordinate relations, group activities, and job characteristics. In addition, a growing cadre of highly promotable managers had been identified. The longitudinal evaluation also revealed that, because of the diversity of the corporation, a "standardized" approach to MBO was not practical. Because the individual units or companies had different customers, technologies, and problems, the MBO efforts in each became more individualized. Internally, the objective was to get the units involved in goal setting to use a common base. However, it was obvious that, as MBO became embedded, each unit would have to make modifications to fit its own specific environment.

The issue and importance of implementation of MBO is pointed out by Odiorne when he notes:

> One of the major reasons for the failure of MBO in many organizations is that those in charge fail to recognize the potential character of the implementation process. MBO is indeed logical and systematic, but it must also deal with a number of factors, including power and authority, the organization form, and the values and expectations of people.[47]

The importance of implementation is sometimes disregarded, and it seems reasonable to pay attention to this component in exhibit 16–6 when considering MBO.

One study of two medium-sized companies focused on implementation of MBO programs.[48] In Company 1, an MBO program was implemented through top management, and in Company 2 the personnel department implemented the program. The power and authority, which Odiorne aptly points to, was not equivalent in the two implementation teams. The personnel unit had significantly less power and authority than did top management. The greatest improvements in job satisfaction in the short-run occurred in Company 1. However, when measurements were taken at the end of thirty months, there was little job satisfaction difference between Company 1 and Company 2. The improvements were not sustained in Company 1. This study suggests that there is a distinct need for reinforcement of MBO procedures, training, and steps if improved performance and/or satisfaction are to be sustained. It also points out that the location of implementation is important, at least during the initial stages of MBO intervention.

This study focused only on attitude information, although it was longitudinal in nature. A thirty-six month study in three plants of the same organization focused on "hard" performance data.[49] Two plants had MBO interventions, and one plant served as a comparison unit. A total of 181 supervisors in production and marketing departments were included in the study. The most significant performance improvements were found in the MBO-influence plant in which a reinforcement program was introduced three months after the introduction of MBO. The reinforcement schedules included the use of letters, memos, counseling on the use of MBO, and discussions between superiors and subordinates about the program. This study suggests that more experimentation with reinforcement programs is needed before the issue of sustained performance improvements is clarified.

Key to success with MBO

MBO and its associate approaches have been used for more than two decades. What have managers learned about its use and results? Although not all inclusive, at least ten keys to success have been identified.

1. *Top-management support, commitment* and *involvement* is mandatory. Without it, MBO will probably decline in usage over time.

2. MBO should be *integrated* into normal, everyday managerial activities. Managers must accept it as part of the management system, not just take it on as a temporal process.

3. MBO should emphasize *objectives* or *goals*, which, when attained, benefit both the organization and the individual manager. In other words, personal development goals must be included in any program.

4. Resources (time and people) should be devoted to preliminary activities concerning *diagnosis* and *training*. A firm foundation of objectives, plans for implementation, and trained personnel make later activities flow smoother.

5. Cognizance of *differences* in units, departments, and functions is essential. Forcing a standardized program on units that contain different methods, processes, and constraints may meet with resistance and possible failure. Slight modifications to a MBO program at the unit level can prove to be quite valuable.

6. Overemphasis on the development of *quantitative* goals (e.g., dollars, time, and so on) will undermine success. Because managerial jobs are inherently ambiguous and difficult to evaluate and measure, qualitative goals are equally useful.

7. An MBO system should not generate too much *paperwork*. An effective program can be run without the massive use of forms, memos, reports, and so on.

8. A great deal of emphasis should be placed on *evaluation*. Specific objectives of the MBO program should be evaluated over time, either with internal or external agents.

9. *Overnight results* should not be expected. Because of its complex nature and time frame, past experience has shown that concrete results probably will not be seen until eighteen to twenty-four months into the program.

10. Finally, a *flexible* and *adaptable* MBO system should be maintained. As the

system is used, new and different factors are learned and evaluated. Be prepared to add or delete components of the system as time progresses.

The work on MBO evaluation and impact is really just beginning, despite over twenty years of reference to managers and subordinates jointly setting objectives. There will undoubtedly be more research on the process of MBO, the impact of MBO upon minority employees, the training requirements of MBO programs, and the differences in results achieved with individual versus group objective setting. This research is needed because managers have been informed that MBO intervention is not a guarantee for improvement but requires careful diagnosis, training, implementation, and reinforcement. These requirements should clearly indicate that although MBO intervention is seductively simple on paper, it is a complex and difficult program to work with at any level—individual, group, or organizational.

The Managerial Grid®

In exhibit 16–1, in which intervention activities were presented, various phases of the managerial grid fit into different target areas. For example, Phase I focuses on the individual, groups, and teams; Phase II is concerned with groups and teams; Phase III involves approaches that are intergroup oriented; and Phases IV, V, and VI are designed to improve the total organizational change and development. It was developed by Blake and Mouton, who have established a corporation, Scientific Methods, Inc., to promote the grid approach around the world.[50] It has been reported that, "The Grid has been adopted in total or in part by thousands of organizations. Almost 20,000 persons have participated in public Grids, while an additional 200,000 have attended in-company Grid learning sessions. In short, the Managerial Grid is the single most popular approach to organization development."[51]

The managerial grid intervention consists of six stages. It is assumed that by progressing through each of the phases, an organization, individuals, and groups will become more effective. Furthermore, it is proposed that progressing through the six grid development phases in a large organization will require from three to five years of effort.

The grid model. The managerial grid model proposes two assumptions about managerial behavior: (1) *concern for production* specifies a manager's concern for accomplishing productive tasks, such as quality, quantity, and efficiency of output; and (2) *concern for people* designates a manager's interest and concern for the personal worth of subordinates, the equity of the reward and evaluation system, and the nurturing of social relationships. In the managerial grid framework, the manager who shows a high concern for both production and people is the most effective manager in an organizational setting. Blake and Mouton display the relationship between the production and people concerns on a 9-by-9 grid, which enables them to plot eighty-one possible combinations of managerial concern (see exhibit 16–8). Managers respond to a managerial style and behavior questionnaire to assess their concerns for production and people. By scoring the questionnaire responses, it is

Exhibit 16–8 The Grid Model

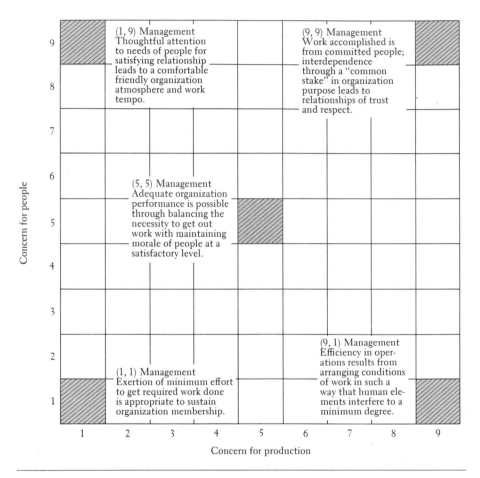

The Managerial Grid figure from the *Managerial Grid,* by Robert R. Blake and Jane S. Mouton. Houston: Gulf Publishing Company, Copyright © 1964, p. 10. Reproduced with permission.

assumed that where a manager fits in the eighty-one cell grid can be determined. The ideal, or the way managers *should* manage, according to Blake and Mouton, is as 9,9 individuals. This indicates a high concern for both production and people. The six-phase development effort is supposed to move managers from the less than ideal plot points, at which most score, to the 9,9 position.

Five basic managerial styles are discussed that provide a concise explanation of what the grid is interpreting. The 1,1 style is called *impoverished* management, which displays little concern for either production or people. The 1,9 style is called *country club* management, which gives people attention while production tasks are overshadowed. The 9,1 style is refered to as *task* management, which emphasizes completing job tasks within time, quality, and budgetary constraints. The 5,5 or *middle of the road* manager attempts to show at least a moderate amount of concern for both production and people. The 9,9, or ideal style, is referred to as *team management*. The manager using this style attempts to help subordinates satisfy self-actualization, autonomy, and esteem needs; develops an atmosphere of trust and supportiveness; and also emphasizes task accomplishment.

Blake and Mouton believe that if the six phases in the managerial grid program are followed systematically, the ideal style of managing, 9,9, can become the predominant practice. The phases emphasize individual, group, and organizational development. The program stresses self-evaluation, problem solving, diagnosis, goal setting, and long-range planning, among other things.

Phase I: The grid seminar.   First, an organization's top management team attends a grid seminar, and then returns to the organization to train the next level of managers. The seminar begins with the study and review of one's own managerial grid position, a plot somewhere on the eighty-one cell grid. It continues with fifty hours of intrinsic problem solving in groups of five to nine members who work together for one week. The team members also analyze each other's position on the grid. Each team then evaluates its own behavior and problem-solving capabilities.

Phase I is intended to create a readiness to work on both human and production problems. By interacting, discussing, and diagnosing, the processes of people working together are observed firsthand. This firsthand learning provides the basis for future learning in the other phases.

Phase II: Team development.   In the second phase, managers are expected to apply the learning of Phase I with their own superiors and subordinates. This phase attempts to implement a problem-solving culture throughout the organization. Accordingly, team members are encouraged to develop an efficient approach to problem solving. The five to nine person teams are asked to establish objectives for team performance and to explore ways to attain higher levels of performance. Individuals are also encouraged to establish performance objectives that mesh with the team's objectives.

Phase III: Intergroup development.   This third phase involves group-to-group working relationships and focuses on building 9,9 ground rules and norms beyond the single work groups. Operating tensions that exist between groups are identified and explored by group members and/or their representatives. The intent here is to move the group from the typical "win-lose" pattern to a joint problem-solving orientation.

A second type of intergroup development involves linking managers who are at the same level but belong to different units, such as first-line supervisors. district sales managers, labor contract negotiators, who may be competing for resources, resulting in competitiveness and the sacrifice of organizational goal achievement. Problem solving through intergroup development is stressed to overcome these dysfunctions.

Phase IV: Developing an ideal model.   The top managers work on developing an ideal model for achieving organizational and individual goals in the fourth phase. The model typically involves a presentation of objectives, structure, decision-making mechanisms, reward systems, and constraints facing the organization. In essence, the model could suggest interventions that result in changes in structure, technology, and people. The model developed by the top managers is then evaluated, criticized, and reviewed by other lower-level managers.

Phase V: Implementing the model.   Blake and Mouton suggest that if the grid's first few phases are systematically conducted, many of the problems of implementation will be minimized. Managers will already be committed to changes that are needed to improve their organizations. In the implementation phase, planning teams are formed for each autonomous unit. These teams are responsible for preparing the unit for the changes necessary to comply with the ideal model. A corporate planning coordinator integrates the teams toward a unified change effort.

Phase VI: Monitoring the ideal model.   The final phase emphasizes evaluation of the grid development intervention. Formal measurement should be taken during and after each phase of the program. The basic instrument used to monitor the program is a 100-item questionnaire that examines individual behavior, teamwork, intergroup relations, problem-solving, corporate strategy, and organizational climate. Respondents are asked to recall the pregrid organization and to state perceptions of the present situation.

The entire managerial grid intervention relies on the use of self-report questionnaires, small group problem-solving exercises, discussion, and attention to the organization's environment, structure, technology, and personnel. The development sessions are generally run by personnel from the organization. In addition, top management is actively involved in the entire program. The involvement of top managers and line managers is an important feature of this intervention. It is assumed that top management and line managers both have the responsibility and are in the best position to bring about the organizational change and development.

Evaluations of the managerial grid.   As is the case for MBO, there is a large amount of testimonial support for the effectiveness of the managerial grid. The grid offers an ideal model of managing—the 9,9 style. Throughout this book, we have warned against such definitive suggestions or claims. The contingency nature of the organizational behavior field precludes making universal or "cure-all" assumptions. Because of individual, group, organizational, and environmental differences, the managerial grid, despite its worldwide popularity, must be scientifically scrutinized.

Research was done in a 4,000 employee Sigma plant of the Piedmont Corporation, which had been experiencing strained relations between the operating and engineering departments.[52] Specifically, accusations of "empire building" were commonly leveled at the various departments. A new plant manager had taken over, and a year later the organization was merged with another company. The six-phase managerial grid program was initiated, with 40 managers taking part in a one-week grid seminar. Over a seven-month period, 800 managers had been through Phase I.

Productivity and profits increased during 1963, as shown in exhibit 16–9. The program was initiated in November 1962, and by the end of 1963 there were fewer employees, but profits had more than doubled. The study reported that 44 percent of the increase in profitability was due to a reduction in controllable costs related to the manpower reduction. Another 13 percent of the decrease in controllable costs could

Exhibit 16–9 Sigma Operating Results (in Percentages)

	1960*	1961	1962	1963
Gross revenue	100	101.6	98.2	106.6
Raw material costs	100	98.8	97.2	103.2
Noncontrollable operating costs	100	97.5	101.8	104.6
Controllable operating costs	100	95.0	94.1	86.2
Net profit before taxes	100	229.0	118.0	266.0
Number of employees	100	95.5	94.1	79.5
Total production units	100	98.5	98.2	102.2

* 1960 is used as a base year because it was the first year that Sigma's records could be compared with postmerger years.

Adapted from Robert R. Blake, Jane S. Mouton, Louis B. Barnes, and Larry E. Greiner, "Breakthrough in Organization Development," *Harvard Business Review* 42 (November-December 1964): 142. Copyright © 1964 by the President and Fellows of Harvard College; all rights reserved.

be attributed to better operating procedures and higher productivity, which the authors of the study suggest resulted in an increase of several million dollars profit.

Behavioral changes were also measured by the researchers but, as is true in most behaviorally based research, it was difficult to develop an accurate set of indices. The primary difficulty in accurately evaluating what, if anything, the grid program was accomplishing was that scientific monitoring of the program began after the intervention was initiated. However, some of the indicators used to assess change included:

The frequency of meetings among managers.

The changes in promotion criteria for management appraisals.

The number of transfers within the plant.

A representative sample of thirty Sigma managers indicated that there had been a 31 percent increase in formal meetings. They also reported that an average of 12.4 percent more time was being spent in "team problem-solving" meetings. Promotion criteria also appeared to change after the grid program began. Young people in line positions (largely held by administrative managers) appear to be better predictors of success than higher age, company seniority, and position in the staff organization. There was also an increase in transfers of 52 percent after the grid program began. The researchers concluded that this increased internal mobility suggests greater flexibility, and the increase in transfers to outside units indicates stronger ties with headquarters.

In a well-designed field study, two other researchers reported mixed results of a managerial grid intervention.[53] A laboratory form of the grid was given to 230 salaried employees of an entire division over a one-year period. Changes were measured by using pre- and post-training questionnaire responses and interviews. The questionnaire measured such dimensions as job satisfaction, group process, intergroup process, and communication. The most significant improvements were found in the plant that was closest to the headquarters unit and in which the division manager actively supported the laboratory seminars focusing on the grid philosophy and practice. When nonparticipating subordinates of the grid training participants were asked questions, both groups, in Plant 1 and Plant 2, indicated positive changes in their superior's leadership style.

Strauss concisely sums up the state of the findings about the managerial grid as follows:

> . . . there is at least some evidence that organizations that have gone through the Grid program become more efficient. But, I am unaware of any study that uses the Grid as a research tool to determine whether 9,9 companies are in fact more efficient.[54]

Quality of Working Life

For hundreds of years, people have been concerned about work as a means for earning a living, as an outlet for creativity, as a framework for social interaction, as a means of attaining profits, and as a contribution to a viable society. These broad factors encompass the many facets of the needs, ambitions, and goals of people, organizations, and different cultures and societies.

Because people spend a high proportion of their waking hours on activities associated with their work, it is not surprising that behavioral scientists and practicing managers have become increasingly interested in the conditions of the workplace and its environment. Given the broad title of *the quality of working life,* the focus of study has largely centered on such questions as:[55]

1. What are the major elements and causes of employee dissatisfaction?

2. What are an individual's needs? How do they change with increased material well-being and with personal development? How are they affected by changes in the work environment and changes in the external environment?

3. To what extent are conditions at work determined by the prevailing technology and organizational structure? Under what conditions do changes in technology and structure culminate in a desired work environment?

4. How can the quality of the work environment affect organizational effectiveness and societal benefits?

5. Is there a conflict between economic performance of an organization and the quality of working life of the individual employee?

Although this is not intended to be an exhaustive or comprehensive list of questions related to the issues of the quality of working life, it does capture its essence. In a sense, it is a composite view of the entire realm of organizational behavior (see exhibit 2–2). It also gives an indication of what the subject matter is and why it has been so difficult to measure.

Measuring quality of working life

The importance of quality of working life seems to be accepted by most people.[56] The manner in which it is conceptualized and measured, however, remains an unresolved issue. At least three ways of addressing the issue have been proposed. Shown in exhibit 16–10, the approaches concern *criteria, level,* and *motive.* The *criteria* approach is distinctly micro in nature, and therefore the focus is primarily on the individual worker.[57] The *level* approach differs from the criteria approach in that the individual, employer, and society are all considered beneficiaries of the quality of working life.[58] Finally, the *motive* approach is again distinctly individual in orientation.[59]

A possible fourth way of conceptualizing the quality of working life issue is by some form of combination of the previous approaches.[60] Shown in exhibit 16–11, this combination approach consists of three major categories: individual change components, change processes, and outcomes.

Individual change components.   The astute reader will note that the six components shown in exhibit 16–11 represent an integration of many of the subjects discussed earlier in this book. *Personal and career development* concerns the issues of learning new skills, satisfaction of growth needs, and satisfactory career ad-

Exhibit 16–10 Different Measures of Quality of Working Life

Criteria (Walton)	Level (Seashore)	Motive (Herrick and Maccoby)
Fair compensation	Worker: Job satisfaction Personal development Self-esteem Physiological states: reduced stress and health disorders	Principle of security Relieve worker from anxiety about safety, security, and future employment
Safe and healthy working conditions		
Opportunity to develop human capacities		Principle of equity Compensate worker according to his/her performance
Growth and security		
Social integration	Employee Productivity Adaptability Loyalty Reduced turnover, absenteeism, tardiness	
Worker rights: privacy, speech, equity, true process.		Principle of individuation Encourage workers to develop themselves, their ability to learn, and their craftsmanship.
Balanced role of worker and personal life		
Social responsibility	Society GNP Increased value of manpower pool Consumer attitudes Life satisfaction	Principle of democracy Allow worker to participate in decisions on what is produced, how money is invested, and for social consequences of production.

Exhibit 16–11   Quality of Working Life Components

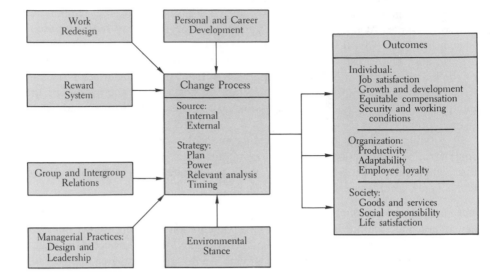

vancement and progression. *Work redesign* relates to the techniques of job rotation, enlargement, enrichment, and redesigned job characteristics. A concern for equitable and motivational compensation and benefits is a focus of the *reward system* component. *Group and intergroup relations* primarily concerns building and motivating effective teams. Appropriate organizational design and effective leadership approaches are the concerns of the *managerial practices* component. Finally, the *environmental stance* concerns issues of consumer goods and services, development of an effective work force, social responsibility, and contributions to the good of society.

Change process.   Two issues constitute this component. First is the recognition of the source or sources for change: internal (employees) or external (customers, suppliers, competitors, or other environmental bodies). The second issue concerns the micro perspective discussed in chapter 15: how will the change be planned, will power for change be centralized or decentralized, how will relationships and interrelationships between people be handled, and what time frame and schedule will be followed?

Outcome components.   This component recognizes that the beneficiaries of a quality of working life program will be the individual worker, the organization, and the general society.

Issues in quality of working life programs

To date, a number of case studies of quality of working life programs have been published.[61] Organizations such as General Motors, Shell, Xerox, and Cummins Engine have been involved with various facets of a quality of working life program for a number of years.

The quality of working life, with its diverse components, is rapidly gaining avid supporters: in an *ideal* sense, to be against its purpose is akin to being against motherhood and the flag! Even so, a number of important issues are being faced by quality of working life proponents. First, as exhibit 16–11 vividly indicates, the rather broad and complex nature of the concept has tempted investigators to use a segmented approach; that is, few programs encompass all components (e.g., work design, reward system, group and intergroup relations, and so on). What occurs is that one organization intervenes with work design and reward system changes, but another focuses on personal development and leadership issues, and so on. What results is a segmented, nonintegrated approach that is difficult to generalize to other organizations.

Second, because of the above, it may be difficult (if not impossible) to develop a single "Quality of Working Life Index"—a criterion that measures, or scores, an organization on each of the components in exhibit 16–11. Third, there is still the unanswered question of whether or not quality of working life concepts and productivity are in conflict. Most organizations believe that improved morale, turnover, and absenteeism, for example, will *eventually* lead to higher productivity. This remains an untested proposition.

Fourth is the recurring issue we have made throughout this book—what is the effect of individual differences? An intervention that may increase the "quality of working life" for one employee may have a detrimental effect on another. Finally, most of the research on quality of working life programs has been reported as case studies. As we noted in chapter 2, such a methodology presents a number of significant problems in interpretations and generalizability.

Over all, quality of working life efforts will continue to expand in all types of organizations. Even though problems will be faced, the broad, pervasive value of the approach will continue to keep at, or near, the forefront of organizational change interventions.

Organizational Change and Development: A Summary View

The activities within and among organizations are filled with many "what ifs," "whys," and other contingencies that need to be identified and evaluated by managers. To cope with the endless stream of forces for change, we suggest that managers should think of organizational change and development as a *continuing* process, not just a series of one-shot interventions. Two of the most important qualities that are needed to face this steady set of change forces are an ability to *diagnose* the environment, groups, individuals, and the total organization, and *proactive* and *reactive stances* to make or anticipate changes in plans when the diagnosis suggests that they are needed.

The need to diagnose and develop a proactive-reactive stance toward organizational change and development clearly calls attention to a number of important points. Some of these points are the following:

1. Organizational change and development should not be viewed as a separate "island" away from the structure, processes, and behaviors that exist within an

organization. The structure of any organization consists of a pattern of interdependent events and activities. Thus, to talk about bringing about change and development in a behaviorally oriented training program or one that focuses on processes seems to be wishful thinking or erroneous deduction. To change and develop an organization means changing behavior, processes, structure, and other core elements, such as work flows and job design. The either/or philosophy or practice of discussing process change without discussing structural change, or micro job-design change without considering behavioral responses, has become outmoded, and rightfully so, with the growing volumes of empirically based research findings.

2. The time has arrived for organizational change and development scholars and practitioners to rely more on theory and research-based findings. For example, MBO or goal setting was accepted as an intervention activity for approximately fifteen years primarily on faith. Today, well-designed studies have provided evidence that some of the claims of advocates were accurate, but other claims were nonsense. Conducting research requires cooperation between practicing managers and evaluators who can design sound studies without causing major disruptions within an organization. This means that the researcher must show managers the value of performing evaluations. The dialogue between these parties needs to be clear, honest, and open so that both parties can benefit from this needed relationship. If planned change is to progress, this type of dialogue is needed so that individuals, groups, organizations, and society will reap the benefits.

3. There is no specific intervention or style of managing that will be successful in every situation. Participative management has been at the core of the organizational development (OD) tool kit. Many behavioral scientists have attempted to convince managers that less autocratic, more participative management of employees would improve organizational performance.[62] Managers have come to realize that one intervention or style is not best for all situations. Thus, the contingency approach is more suitable as a model for reference when considering change and development.

4. After examining the numerous intervention activities, it must be asked, who can be an expert in all of them? We think the answer is obvious—no one person. If, as is true in many situations, a combination of activities are needed to bring about change and development, it is best to consider a team of experts. It is rather easy to declare oneself an organizational change and development expert, but another thing to actually accomplish positive and lasting changes. The team of experts may have to include line managers as change agents to create the type of durable change and development that results in improved performance.

5. The field of organizational change and development has progressed past the parochial view that sensitivity training is the core intervention activity. Sensitivity training in some situations would be a disastrous mistake and should never even be mentioned as a potential change and development activity. The reper-

toire available to managers includes sensitivity training, but it is only one small segment of what is available.

6. The majority of reported organizational change and development efforts were conducted in business settings. Today, nonprofit organizations, such as schools, health-delivery systems, government agencies, and religious institutions, have conducted change and development efforts that provide valuable insights into the process, models, and individual reactions. Thus, there is much to be gained by exchanging and comparing the findings in profit and nonprofit organizations.

7. Finally, as we began our discussion of organizational change in chapter 15, the manager must recognize early that an organizational change effort rarely can be limited in impact to the particular chosen target group. Changes in structure can cause changes in the task, changes in the task can change people's attitudes, and so on. The end result is that those individuals involved in change efforts must carefully *diagnose* the influence of the side effects of a program. It is only after the total picture of the intervention has been evaluated that we can facilitate the potential positive features of organizational change and development programs.

The points we have raised are not predictions, but appear to be present trends or themes. The organization, like individuals and groups, needs to change and develop. These changes and development can be made somewhat easier by considering the seven points raised above. This is not an exhaustive list, but it attempts to focus on some of the main dilemmas that face managers, theorists, and researchers today.[63] Will managers actually plan and manage change, or will change manage the manager, are the questions that each of us must consider.

Applications and Implications for the Manager

Organizational Change and Development

1. The *depth of intervention* refers to the range of planned and structured activities associated with organizational change efforts. Although usually conceptualized as particular interventions applied to specific target groups, the manager must recognize that an intervention in one target group (e.g., intergroup relations) can have side effects on other target groups (e.g., individuals).

2. Sensitivity training is a widely used, individually oriented strategy that stresses the process rather than the content of training and focuses upon emotional rather than conceptual learning. Managers need to consider the ethics of asking someone to undergo emotional confrontation and to judge the effectiveness of transfer of learning. Can emotionally oriented training away from the job influence the job behavior and performance?

3. Behavior modeling involves a different and possibly more effective method for training and development. The use of role playing and video-tape feedback, coupled with on-the-job experience, may help in alleviating the problem of learning extinction.

4. Stress on the job is a fact of life—so is, however, the link between job stress and physiological and behavioral disorders. Organizations are becoming more aware of

the causes of stress (stressors) and the moderating effects of individual differences on stress. Stress-reduction methods are slowly being developed with the focus being placed on diagnosis (physical and job content), improved communications, job redesign, training, and revised habits and exercise programs.

5. Team building is a planned event with a group of people who have or may have common organizational relationships and/or goals that is designed to improve the way in which work gets done. Team building can involve diagnosis, task accomplishment, team relationships, and team and organizational processes. The research on team building is sketchy and is not at a high level of scientific rigor.

6. Survey-feedback research intervention involves the process of systematically collecting data about a group or the organization, primarily through self-report questionnaires. This data is analyzed and fed back in workshop sessions to managers and, in some instances, nonmanagers. Do not underestimate the complexity and difficulty of conducting workshops. Some managers may have groups who do not show well once the data is interpreted.

7. Intergroup intervention activities involve confronting the reasons for conflict by use of team or group analysis and discussions. The value, if any, of confronting conflict through group discussions has been studied by some researchers but needs much more study.

8. The two most widely used organizational strategies are management by objectives and managerial grid. Both activities are used in various forms throughout the world.

Their popularity is based primarily on testimonial support.

9. The MBO activity requires some participation in goal setting, diagnosis, the use of feedback, and a general climate of cooperation, among other things. The simple appearance of MBO on paper becomes a complex reality in an organization. People's resistance to change, the need to transfer learning, and deciding who the change agent will be are issues that need to be covered in implementing or even planning an MBO program.

10. There are an increasing, yet still small, number of rigorous evaluations of MBO in organizations and goal setting in laboratory settings that should be consulted by managers currently using or contemplating the use of this intervention strategy. The importance of goal clarity, challenge, feedback, and acceptance has been found in field and laboratory research.

11. The managerial grid development program is a comprehensive, six-phase, three to five year effort that is targeted to significantly change an organization. The phases involve seminar work, problem solving, team building, organizational planning, and goal setting. A unique feature of the grid activities is that the management of the organization is responsible for each of the phases.

12. The quality of working life concept is an interdisciplinary approach to organizational change. Managers should be cognizant of its benefits but should be made aware of significant issues (e.g., segmentation, productivity versus quality of working life conflict, individual differences, and the emphasis on case-study evaluation.)

Review of Theories, Research, and Applications

1. Why can survey feedback be applied to a variety of target groups?

2. What is the difference between a family sensitivity group and a family team-building intervention?

3. Which of the discussed training approaches—traditional or behavioral modeling—would fit closer to reinforcement theory? Why?

4. Why is there a major weakness in the majority of research that has been conducted of the survey-feedback research intervention activity?

5. How can the personal characteristics of a change agent influence the selection of an intervention activity by the change agent?

6. Why would some managers consider job stress to have a positive influence on performance?

7. Would an advocate of a contingency approach to change and development support the managerial grid ideal style of 9,9? Why?

8. Why is it difficult to conduct longitudinal research of any form of organizational change and development intervention?

9. What are some of the key principles to remember when considering MBO as a possible intervention activity?

10. Why is "the quality of working life" so important, yet so illusive a concept?

Notes

1. Edgar F. Huse, *Organizational Development and Change* (St. Paul, Minn.: West Publishing, 1975), chapter 3.

2. Wendell L. French and Cecil H. Bell, Jr., *Organizational Development* (Englewood Cliffs, N.J.: Prentice-Hall, 1973), pp. 102–3.

3. N. Margulics and Anthony P. Raia, *Conceptual Foundations of Organizational Development* (New York: McGraw-Hill, 1978), pp. 116–17.

4. Huse, *Organizational Development and Change*, p. 25.

5. John P. Campbell and Marvin D. Dunnette, "Effectiveness of T-Group Experiences in Managerial Training and Development," *Psychological Bulletin,* August 1968, pp. 73–104.

6. Henry C. Smith, *Sensitivity to People* (New York: McGraw-Hill, 1966), p. 197.

7. Alfred J. Marrow, *Behind the Executive Mask* (New York: American Management Association, 1964), p. 51.

8. Robert J. House, "T-Group Training Good or Bad?" *Business Horizons,* Spring 1969, pp. 69–77. P. C. Buchanan, "Laboratory Training and Organizational Development," *Administrative Science Quarterly,* December 1969, pp. 466–80; Campbell and Dunnette, "Effectiveness of T-Group;" R. K. Mosvick, "Human Relations Training for Scientists, Technicians, and Engineers: A Review of Relevant Experimental Evaluation of Human Relations Training," *Personnel Psychology,* Summer 1971, pp. 275–92.

9. Marvin D. Dunnette and John P. Campbell, "Laboratory Education: Impact on People and Organizations," *Industrial Relations,* January 1968, pp. 1–27.

10. House, "T-Group Training."

11. *Business Week,* "Imitating Models: A New Management Tool," 8 May 1978, p. 119.

12. A. I. Kraut, "Behavior Modeling Symposium," *Personnel Psychology,* 1976, pp. 325–69.

13. J. Komaki, K. D. Barwick, and L. R. Scatt, "A Behavioral Approach to Occupational Safety," *Journal of Applied Psychology,* 1978, pp. 434–45.

14. American Heart Association, *Heart Facts* (Dallas, Texas: 1977).

15. J. House, "Occupational Stress and Coronary Heart Disease: A Review and Theoretical Integration," *Journal of Health and Social Behavior,* 1974, pp. 12–27; and S. Sales, "Organizational Role as a Risk Factor in Coronary Disease," *Administrative Science Quarterly,* 1969, pp. 325–46.

16. M. T. Matteson and John M. Ivancevich, "Organizational Stressors, Physiological and Behavioral Outcomes

and Coronary Heart Disease: A Research Model," *Academy of Management Review*, July 1979, pp. 347–58.

17. L. Cathcart, "A Four Year Study of Executive Health Risks," *Journal of Occupational Medicine,* 1977, pp. 354–57.

18. A. McLean, "Job Stress and the Psychological Pressures of Change," *Personnel,* 1976, pp. 40–49.

19. C. G. Weiman, "A Study of Occupational Stressors and the Incidence of Disease/Risk," *Journal of Occupational Medicine,* 1977, pp. 119–22.

20. Douglas T. Hall, *Careers in Organizations* (Santa Monica, Calif.: Goodyear, 1976).

21. C. Jenkins, "Psychological and Social Precursors of Coronary Disease, Part I and II," *New England Journal of Medicine,* 1971, pp. 244–55, 307–17.

22. M. Friedman, R. Roseman, and V. Carrol, "Changes in the Serum Cholesterol and Blood Clotting Time in Men Subject to Aychi Variation of Occupational Stress," *Circulation,* 1978, pp. 858–61.

23. R. Marks, "Factors Involving Social and Demographic Characteristics: A Review of Empirical Findings in Social Stress and Cardiovascular Disease," *Melbank Memorial Fund Quarterly,* 1967, pp. 1–192.

24. D. Simbory, "The Statics of Risk Factors and Coronary Heart Disease," *Journal of Chronic Disease,* 1970, pp. 515–52.

25. Joseph E. McGrath, "Stress and Behavior in Organizations," in *Handbook of Industrial and Organizational Psychology,* ed. Marvin D. Dunnette (Chicago: Rand McNally, 1976), pp. 1351–96.

26. S. Sales and J. House, "Job Description as a Possible Risk Factor in Coronary Heart Disease," *Journal of Chronic Diseases,* 1971, pp. 861–73.

27. W. G. Dyer, *Team Building: Issues and Alternatives* (Reading, Mass.: Addison-Wesley, 1977).

28. R. Schmuck, Philip J. Runkel, and D. Langemeyer, "Improving Organizational Problem Solving in a School Faculty,"

Journal of Applied Behavioral Science, October–November 1969, pp. 455–82.

29. I. Dayal and J. M. Thomas, "Operation KPA: Developing a New Organization," *Journal of Applied Behavioral Science,* 1968, pp. 473–506.

30. Floyd C. Mann, "Studying and Creating Change," in *The Planning of Change,* Warren G. Bennis, K. D. Benne, and R. Chin (New York: Holt, Rinehart & Winston, 1961), pp. 605–13.

31. E. C. Miller, "Attitude Surveys, A Diagnostic Tool," *Personnel,* May–June, 1978, pp. 4–10.

32. J. L. Franklin, "Improving the Effectiveness of Survey Feedback," *Personnel,* May–June 1978, pp. 11–17.

33. Robert R. Blake, Herbert A. Shepard, and Jane S. Mouton, *Managing Intergroup Conflict in Industry* (Houston, Texas: Gulf Publishing, 1965).

34. Ibid.

35. Robert T. Golembiewski and A. Blumberg, "Confrontation as a Training Design in Complex Organizations: Attitudinal Changes in a Diversified Population of Managers," *Journal of Applied Behavioral Science,* October 1967, pp. 525–47.

36. Peter Drucker, *The Practice of Management* (New York: Harper & Bros., 1954), pp. 128–29.

37. George S. Odiorne, *Management by Objectives* (New York: Pitman, 1965), p. 26.

38. Anthony P. Raia, *Management by Objectives* (Glenview, Ill.: Scott, Foresman, 1974), p. 8.

39. For perhaps the most comprehensive empirically based evaluation of MBO to date in book form see Stephen J. Carroll and Henry L. Tosi, *Management by Objectives: Applications and Research* (New York: Macmillan, 1973).

40. For an example of these streams of thought, see Rodney H. Brady, "MBO Goes to Work in the Public Sector," *Harvard Business Review,* March–April 1973, pp. 65–74; George F. Carvalho, "Installing Management by Objectives: A New Perspective on Organization Change," *Human Resource Management,* Spring 1972; Dale D. McConkey, *How to Manage by Results* (New York: American Management

Association, 1965); William J. Reddin, *Management by Objectives* (New York: McGraw-Hill, 1971); Edward G. Schleh, *Management by Results* (New York: McGraw-Hill, 1961).

41. Richard M. Steers and Lyman W. Porter, "The Role of Task-Goal Attributes in Employee Performance," *Psychological Bulletin,* 1974, pp. 434–52. For a review that is excellently organized, see Gary P. Latham and Gary A. Yukl, "A Review of Research on the Application of Goal Setting in Organizations," *Academy of Management Journal,* December 1975, pp. 824–45.

42. Anthony P. Raia, "Goal Setting and Self Control," *Journal of Management Studies,* September 1965, pp. 34–53; Raia, "A Second Look at Management Goals and Control," *California Management Review,* Summer 1966, pp. 49–58.

43. Carroll and Tosi, *Management by Objectives.*

44. Ibid., p. 195.

45. See exhibit 15–8.

46. John M. Ivancevich, J. T. McMahon, J. W. Streidl, and Andrew D. Szilagyi, "Goal-Setting: The Tenneco Approach to Personal Development and Management Effectiveness," *Organizational Dynamics,* Winter 1978, pp. 58–80.

47. George S. Odiorne, "The Politics of Implementing MBO," *Business Horizons,* 1974, pp. 13–21.

48. John M. Ivancevich, "A Longitudinal Assessment of Management by Objectives," *Administrative Science Quarterly,* March 1972, pp. 126–38.

49. John M. Ivancevich, "Changes in Performance in a Management by Objectives Program," *Administrative Science Quarterly,* December 1974, pp. 563–74.

50. Robert R. Blake and Jane S. Mouton, *The Managerial Grid* (Houston, Texas: Gulf Publishing, 1964).

51. "Using the Managerial Grid to Insure MBO," *Organizational Dynamics,* Spring 1974, p. 55.

52. Robert R. Blake et al., "Breakthrough in Organization Development," *Harvard Business Review,* November–December 1964, pp. 113–55.

53. Michael Beer and S. Kleisath, "The Effects of the Managerial Grid on Organizational and Leadership Dimensions," in *Research on the Impact of Using Different Laboratory Methods for Interpersonal and Organizational Change,* ed. Sheldon S. Zalkind (symposium presented at the American Psychological Association, Washington, D.C., September 1967).

54. George Strauss, "Organizational Development: Credits and Debits," *Organizational Dynamics,* Winter 1973, p. 14.

55. S. Eilm, "The Quality of Working Life," *Omega,* 1976, pp. 367–73.

56. J. O'Toole, ed., *Work and the Quality of Life* (Cambridge, Mass.: MIT, 1974).

57. R. E. Walton, "Criteria for Quality of Working Life," in *The Quality of Working Life,* vol. 1, ed. L. E. Davis and A. B. Cherns (New York: Free Press, 1975), pp. 91–104.

58. Stanley E. Seashore, "Defining and Measuring the Quality of Working Life," in *The Quality of Working Life,* vol. 1, ed. L. E. Davis and A. B. Cherns (New York: Free Press, 1975), pp. 105–18.

59. N. Q. Herrick and M. Maccoby, "Humanizing Work: A Priority Goal of the 1970's" in *The Quality of Working Life,* vol. 1, ed. L. E. Davis and A. B. Cherns (New York: Free Press, 1975), pp. 63–77.

60. J. Richard Hackman and John L. Suttle, *Improving Life at Work* (Santa Monica, Calif.: Goodyear, 1977).

61. L. E. Davis and A. B. Cherns, eds., *The Quality of Working Life,* vol. 2 (New York: Free Press, 1975).

62. Walter R. Nord and Douglas E. Durand, "Beyond Resistance to Change," *Organizational Dynamics,* Autumn 1975, pp. 2–20.

63. For some excellent discussions of organizational development issues, see Robert L. Kahn, "Organizational Development: Some Problems and Proposals," *Journal of Applied Behavioral Science,* October 1974, pp. 485–502; and W. Warren Burke, "Organization Development in Transition," *Journal of Applied Behavioral Science,* January 1976, pp. 22–43.

Additional References

BERNARDIN, H. J., and ALVARES, K. M. "The Managerial Grid as a Predictor of Conflict Resolutions Method and Managerial Effectiveness." *Administrative Science Quarterly,* March 1976, pp. 84–92.

BLAKE, R. R., and MOUTON, J. S. *Building a Dynamic Organization through Grid Development.* Reading, Mass.: Addison-Wesley, 1969.

BOWERS, D. G. "Organizational Development: Promises, Performances, Possibilities." *Organizational Dynamics,* Spring 1976, pp. 50–62.

FRENCH, W. L., and HOLLMAN, R. W. "Management by Objectives: The Team Approach." *California Management Review,* 1975, pp. 13–22.

GOLEMBIEWSKI, R. T. *Reviewing Organizations: The Laboratory Approach to Planned Change.* Itasca, Ill.: Peacock Publishers, 1972.

LAWLER, E. E., III. "The New Plant Revolution." *Organizational Dynamics,* Winter 1978, pp. 2–12.

LIKERT, R. *New Ways of Managing Conflict.* New York: McGraw-Hill, 1974.

MARGULIES, N., and RAIA, A. P. *Organizational Development: Values, Process, and Technology.* New York: McGraw-Hill, 1972.

PORRAS, J. I. and BUG, P. O. "The Impact of Organizational Development." *Academy of Management Review,* April 1978, pp. 249–66.

RUSH, H. M. *Organization Development: A Reconnaissance.* New York: Conference Board, 1973.

STEELE, F. I. *Physical Settings and Organization Development.* Reading, Mass.: Addison-Wesley, 1973.

WEISBORD, M. R. "The Gap Between OD Practice and Theory—And Publication," *Journal of Applied Behavioral Science.* October 1974, pp. 476–84.

A Case of Change

Can AT&T Become a Marketing Company?

Until very recently, A.T.&T. has been anything but a marketing company. Nurtured in the hothouse of regulated monopoly, it was required to do little more than wait for its customers to call. The imperative for change was forced upon it by an onslaught of competition. Over the last decade, technological advances combined with regulatory and judicial decisions to crack open more and more of Bell's protected markets. Home telephones, complex communications equipment for business, private transmission lines—all of these are monopolies no more.

So Bell's top managers have thrown their weight behind transforming the corporation from a dedicated monopolist, intent on preserving its privileges, into a vigorous marketing company, responsive to customers and capable of thriving on unfettered competition. Chairman John D. deButts has gone on intracompany TV to announce to every employee that "we will become a marketing company." In the past five years, marketing expenditures for the Bell System have more than doubled, to about $2.1 billion. More than 1,500 managers a year from the operating com-

Adapted with permission from "Selling is No Longer Mickey Mouse at AT&T," *Fortune,* 17 July 1978.

panies have passed through special marketing courses arranged by headquarters. And A.T.&T. has recruited over a hundred systems analysts from I.B.M., Litton, Xerox, and elsewhere—an earth-shaking event in an enterprise that has always promoted from within in the belief that nobody can understand the System who hasn't grown up with it.

One of those outsiders is Archie J. McGill, a director of market management and development, who at thirty-three was the youngest vice president in I.B.M.'s history and directed strategic planning for computer systems. McGill calls A.T.&T.'s attempt to become a marketing company "the greatest challenge in American business." He may not be exaggerating. The metamorphosis will require Bell System executives to rethink the fundamental goals of their business, to examine anew their corporate ideology.

The Bell System has historically considered its mission to be providing universal telephone service, tying the nation together in a ubiquitous, reliable, and economical network.

Competition began seeping into residential telephone service back in 1968 with the Supreme Court's famous Carterfone decision, which for the first time allowed Bell customers to attach "foreign" (read non-Bell) devices to the network. For years, A.T.&T. threw up barriers that retarded competitors' progress in this so-called "interconnect" market. But other companies have gradually carved out profitable market niches by selling automatic answering machines and a wide variety of telephone sets that offer styling or special features usually unavailable with standard-issue telephones.

Bell responded four years ago by launching its Design Line of decorator telephones, many of which it buys from outside suppliers. The company also began to open retail Phone Stores for the new line and will have about 1,800 locations by the end of the year. Special kiosks set up during the Christmas shopping season last year moved 80,000 telephones.

The manager of residential market planning sees lots of opportunity for developing innovative services—for example, systems that would enable a customer who is not at home to turn off his stove, air conditioner, or hot-water heater simply by dialing a number. Ten years from now, he says, the total market for residential products and services might come to $55 billion, as opposed to a mere $5 or $6 billion nowadays. But the immediate future is limited. The advent of the "home of the future" will have to wait until A.T.&T.'s nascent consumer research determines what customers really want, and appliance manufacturers and builders tailor their products to the capabilities of the telephone system.

For the short term, A.T.&T.'s ambitions are more modest. It is trying to get more phones into the nation's living rooms, where functional styling has tended to make them taboo. And since in any one month 30 percent of A.T.&T.'s residential customers make no long-distance calls, the company is striving to increase usage by advertising the warmth and family solidarity long-distance calls can create.

Greater opportunities are available for Bell—and for its competitors—in serving the needs of business customers. Here there are essentially two competitive markets, one for interconnect devices, such as switchboards that connect to the Bell System, and another for private transmission lines leased to large users. A.T.&T.

still dominates both the equipment and private-line businesses, but the future looks rather shaky.

The basis of Bell's marketing thrust is a study by McKinsey & Co. commissioned back in 1972, mainly out of concern about the System's ability to respond to growing competition. Essentially, the study found that A.T.&T. lacked internal systems for addressing customer needs, ensuring that new products and services reflected those needs, and delivering individualized solutions to its customers' problems. McKinsey recommended, among other things, that A.T.&T. set up a new marketing department at headquarters under a senior executive, zero in on particular markets where Bell was under strongest attack, and dramatically upgrade the quality of its sales force, which was hardly more than a bunch of order-takers.

Ken Whalen came in from Michigan Bell to take charge of the A.T.&T. marketing staff and set up some functions the company had never had before, including market and product management. "Since I didn't understand market management and nobody else did either," he says, "we had to go outside for the talent we needed." To hire outsiders, Whalen required special dispensation from Chairman deButts.

Archie McGill was one of Whalen's best choices. An independent thinker, he had left I.B.M. to set up a consulting firm that worked with Japanese corporations and the Soviet Union. He brought to A.T.&T. not only a thorough grounding in I.B.M.'s market-planning methods and a number of friends from his alma mater, but a direct personal style guaranteed to fluster Bell managers unused to critical analysis.

McGill's market managers concentrate on anticipating customer needs rather than simply reacting to market developments, as A.T.&T. too often has done in the past. For the first time, A.T.&T. has performed classic analyses à la Armonk, segmenting business customers into more than fifty industry classifications and studying each segment to determine how communications affect profit and loss. The aim of the exercise is to increase the amount of money corporations spend with the Bell System by finding ways they can use communications to fatten their profits— for example, by cutting down on travel.

Based on their studies, the market managers make formal product requests, describing the general characteristics of the products or services they think their industries need. Then a product manager takes over to make sure the market research is translated into new offerings. Under Ed Goldstein, an astute engineer with experience in line operations, the product managers carry out analyses to determine whether there will be enough demand for a new product or service to make money on it; if it proves out, they oversee its development. Once the new entry is in the field, the product manager leads a team of functional specialists in such areas as repair, installation, and accounting who keep track of its costs. All this attention to costs and profits might seem second nature for a Procter & Gamble, but it is a history-making development at Ma Bell.

Goldstein sees the system as an excellent solution to one of A.T.&T.'s historic weaknesses: the tendency of the renowned Bell Labs to come up with products that aren't tailored to a realistic market. "Engineers are notoriously bad at assessing user needs," he says, "and I speak as an engineer. Although we used to have a few marketing gurus who contemplated their navels and said, 'This is what users need,' it was always easier to recommend what the engineers did. But now we have a disciplined approach to understanding market needs and the money to do a thorough job of it."

The cutting edge of the marketing system is the Bell System sales force, which A.T.&T. has decided to reorganize strictly along industry lines. But it is here that the metamorphosis seems most uncertain. The plan is admirably laid out in a document that may be the crowning intellectual achievement of the A.T.&T. staff. Called "Bell Marketing System Business Guidelines," it describes in fifty-two pages the philosophy behind the system and exactly how operating companies must structure their sales organizations.

Account executives are to be assigned to various markets, finely segmented according to the federal government's Standard Industrial Classification, and are to be held responsible for all of the customers in that particular industry. The account exec is supposed to be the single Bell "problem solver" for each of his customers. Problem solver is really a euphemism, however, for the account executive is ordered to build up a customer's trust, penetrate and control his decision making, and even involve himself in the customer's business planning in order to anticipate his needs—and, of course, make sure that his plans include a hefty allocation for all those "systems solutions" Bell will propose.

The kind of "systems selling" A.T.&T. envisions is a far cry from its traditional sales approach. For one thing, the guidelines ask line marketing executives to treat their operating costs not as expenses to be kept down but as investments that will produce revenues and that therefore may have to be increased to get new business. And the marketing manager's performance won't be measured by the host of artificial indices and productivity measures Bell has used in the past—e.g., net service order measurement, which kept track of the number of orders obtained but not the revenue. Now he will be judged only by how much revenue he brings in and how much he has to spend to get it. In short, the new system requires the companies to abandon many of the habits that have grown up around the goal of universal monopoly service—including the emphasis on efficiency for efficiency's sake, and the tendency to wait for a customer to state his needs rather than taking the initiative to serve him.

So, corporate headquarters has had to push very hard to get the system accepted by the operating companies, with McGill acting as chief catalyst and agent provocateur, zeroing in on receptive operating-company managers and trying to infect them with his enthusiasm. His style has apparently disturbed the tranquillity of more than a few of his targets. "Arch's approach," says a former colleague, "is intimidating. He beats people up in debate and can tear apart any plan. But that's what makes him useful to A.T.&T. Once the operating people have encountered him, they're not likely to forget the marketing system or fudge on their homework."

The guidelines were promulgated a year ago, and McGill says that the system is already in place. But there are signs that, for all of McGill's efforts, the system has run into resistance in the operating companies, where such specialists as installers and engineers cling to their old ways of doing business. There has been a tendency for some of the telephone companies, dissatisfied with the plans handed down from A.T.&T., to thoroughly rewrite them, which undermines system-wide coordination and blocks implementation for months. Only about half of the operating companies have assigned salesmen to S.I.C. segments. Most of them still have the salesmen reporting to the vice president of operations, as in the past, rather than to the vice president for marketing, who remains only a staff officer. Some of Bell's largest customers say that they have no single account exec with whom to work but still must deal with a bewildering array of salespeople.

Enormous pressures for change will be building up on the operating companies by the end of this year, when A.T.&T. completes a reorganization of its own. For the first time, the parent company will group all of its "general departments"—the headquarters staffs for customer service, traffic, plant, and so forth—under three executive vice presidents, one for business markets, one for residential markets, and one for the network services that cross market lines. Many of the operating companies plan to follow the parent's lead by breaking up the functional fiefdoms that have existed for decades and specializing along market lines. "The restructuring will force the issue of establishing account executives who are industry specialists," says Thomas Bolger, executive v.p.—business. "We hope that even the large telco's will have switched over by the end of 1979."

Moving the marketing system out of the holding company and into the field will take longer than that, though, for many of A.T.&T.'s salesmen are unqualified to do systems selling, and simply trying to retrain them may not be enough. Charles Schweis, telecommunications manager for Ciba-Geigy and president of the Communications Managers Association, says, "The user's great difficulty is dealing with the inept account man. Some of the people Bell has have been yanked out of mechanical and clerical positions and given a few weeks of training, and they don't even know what a WATS line is. And they're not taking the initiative. When we get a new product, it's because we've asked for it. Sometimes, even when we ask, they 'yes' us to death and nothing happens."

If it is to be successful, the Bell System sales force will have to change the way its customers think. Many corporate communications managers still focus on cost control rather than looking at communications services as a way to improve their own company's profitability. They won't accept higher communications bills unless there is a lot of sophisticated cost/effectiveness analysis to justify them. And they tend to resent account execs who try to do systems selling without enough experience. The director of communications for a $9-billion corporation says, "A.T.&T. salesmen wanted to study our inventory control so they could develop a proposal. But they lack the expertise and sophistication. Why, we have very high-priced inventory-control specialists who've been working on the problem for forty years. The guy who goes to school on the subject for only six weeks has nothing to teach that man. It's *our* guys who end up doing the teaching!"

Developing a force that can do the job, A.T.&T. executives and customers agree, will take at least three more years. By then, Bell will indeed be the "different business" that deButts feared it would become. It will have been driven by competition to adopt a new organizational structure, new management methods, and a new line of products and services. It will have all the outward appearance of a marketing company more than capable of dealing with the likes of I.T.T. and I.B.M. But whether those changes will be more than window dressing—the illusion without the reality—is still uncertain.

Case Primer Questions:

1. Identify the forces for change at AT&T.

2. What are some problems and opportunities that were identified in the analysis of the company and its environment?

3. Who are the change agents and what role and behaviors are they exhibiting?

4. What is AT&T's implementation plan?

5. What are some keys to success, or critical constraints, that AT&T must recognize in order that its change plan work?

Experiential Exercise

Survey Feedback

Purpose

To practice diagnostic skills through survey-feedback results.

Required understanding

The reader should be acquainted with survey feedback and many of the concepts of organizational behavior.

How to set up the exercise

Set up groups of four to eight members for the one-hour exercise. The groups should be separated from each other and asked to converse only with members of their own group. Each person should read the following:

J. P. Hunt Department stores is a large retail merchandising outlet located in Boston. The company sells an entire range of retail goods (e.g., appliances, fashions, furniture, and so on) and has a large downtown store plus six branch stores in various suburban areas.

Similar to most retail stores in the area, employee turnover is high (i.e., 40 to 45 percent annually). In the credit and accounts receivable department, located in the downtown store, turnover is particularly high at both the supervisor and subordinate levels, approaching 75 percent annually. The department employs approximately 150 people, 70 percent of whom are female.

Due to rising hiring and training costs brought on by the high turnover, top department management began a turnover analysis and reduction program. As a first step, a local management-consulting firm was contracted to conduct a survey of department employees. Using primarily questionnaires, the consulting firm collected survey data from over 95 percent of the department's employees. The results are shown in exhibit 16–12, by organizational level, along with industry norms developed by the consulting firm in comparative retail organizations.

Instructions for the exercise

1. Individually, each group member should analyze the data in exhibit 16–12 and attempt to identify and diagnose departmental strengths and problem areas.

2. As a group, the members should repeat point 1 above. In addition, suggestions for resolving the problems and a plan for feedback to the department should be developed.

Exhibit 16–12   Survey Results for J. P. Hunt Department Store: Credit and Accounts Receivable
Department

Variable	Survey Results*			Industry Norms*		
	Managers	Supervisors	Non-supervisors	Managers	Supervisors	Non-supervisors
Satisfaction and Rewards						
Pay	3.30	1.73	2.48	3.31	2.97	2.89
Supervision	3.70	2.42	3.05	3.64	3.58	3.21
Promotion	3.40	2.28	2.76	3.38	3.25	3.23
Coworkers	3.92	3.90	3.72	3.95	3.76	3.43
Work	3.98	2.81	3.15	3.93	3.68	3.52
Performance-to-intrinsic rewards	4.07	3.15	3.20	4.15	3.85	3.81
Performance-to-extrinsic rewards	3.67	2.71	2.70	3.87	3.81	3.76
Supervisory Behavior						
Initiating structure	3.42	3.97	3.90	3.40	3.51	3.48
Consideration	3.63	3.09	3.18	3.77	3.72	3.68
Positive rewards	3.99	2.93	3.02	4.24	3.95	3.91
Punitive rewards	3.01	3.61	3.50	2.81	2.91	3.08
Job Characteristics						
Autonomy	4.13	4.22	3.80	4.20	4.00	3.87
Feedback	3.88	3.81	3.68	3.87	3.70	3.70
Variety	3.67	3.35	2.22	3.62	3.21	2.62
Challenge	4.13	4.03	3.03	4.10	3.64	3.58
Organizational Practices						
Role ambiguity	2.70	2.91	3.34	2.60	2.40	2.20
Role conflict	2.87	3.69	2.94	2.83	3.12	3.02
Job pressure	3.14	4.04	3.23	2.66	2.68	2.72
Performance evaluation process	3.77	3.35	3.19	3.92	3.70	3.62
Worker cooperation	3.67	3.94	3.87	3.65	3.62	3.35
Work-flow planning	3.88	2.62	2.95	4.20	3.80	3.76

*The values are scored from 1, very low, to 5, very high.

CHAPTER 17

Organizational Behavior and Performance: A Synopsis

Throughout this book, we have emphasized a number of important characteristics of the field of organizational behavior. The following points should be noted and reviewed about this field:

Organizational behavior is concerned with behavior and performance at three levels: (1) individual; (2) group; and (3) formal organizational.

In attempting to understand, explain, and predict behavior at each of these three levels, the field of organizational behavior examines a variety of individual, group, and organizational processes: (1) individual motivation, personality, and learning; (2) group and intergroup processes; (3) leadership; (4) communication and decision making; (5) performance appraisal and rewards; and (6) organizational development and change.

In studying these processes, researchers employ the rules of *scientific method.*

Researchers in the field of organizational behavior rely on an *interdisciplinary* set of theories, models, and research findings to interpret and better understand behavior and performance.

The field of organizational behavior relies heavily on principles emerging from the *behavioral sciences:* psychology, sociology, and anthropology.

The breadth of the characteristics just outlined emphasizes the fact that understanding organizational behavior is an extremely complex matter. To help the student in dealing with such complexity, we have broken down our presentation of the field into five major segments originally displayed in exhibit 2–2. These segments constitute the five major parts of the book and are combined in our performance model (illustrated in exhibit 2–2). You should again review the framework presented in this model to integrate the many variables, relationships, and processes that are fundamentally the study of this book.

The Manager: A Diagnostician

Anyone who can read is capable of learning about the field of organizational behavior. Quite another matter, however, is *practicing* organizational behavior. That is, managing an organization and dealing with the many complex processes discussed in this book is far different from an initial understanding of the basic concepts. One can readily learn about any skill by reading, but one can only become proficient through actual practice. We have made a careful effort in this book to emphasize the crucial role of the manager in organizational behavior, that of a *diagnostician.* There are multiple influences, for example, that lead to performance problems in organizations. That one person performs at an exceptionally high level and another seeks to avoid performing is usually not a simple matter. The ability to understand these multiple factors is critical to the manager if he or she is to successfully diagnose the causes of a performance problem and seek to remedy it. A manager whose diagnostic approach is flexible, adaptable, and knowledgeable is the one we believe can best cope with the properties and processes discussed in this book. The importance of the manager's responsibility to probe and diagnose individuals, groups, the total organization, and even the external environment cannot be underestimated. We believe that research has already illustrated that the probing, diagnosing, and flexible manager is able to make significant positive inputs into improving the behavior and performance of employees. The map for understanding the full complexity of what needs to be probed and diagnosed is our performance model. This figure, and our discussion of its parts in the other chapters, is only a starting point and is certainly an incomplete analysis. Despite this, however, we believe that some type of framework is needed to understand individuals, groups, and organizations better.

The manager's ultimate responsibility is to work with others to achieve acceptable end results, or performance. The manager works extensively with special communicative, influential, and diagnostic skills and individual abilities. Often, the results of applying these skills are not readily visible and are difficult to appraise. The results of successful management are often inferred from such indicators as morale, turnover, productivity, grievances, and accidents. Ultimately, the successful manager is judged or appraised, just like the successful nurse, successful gardener, or successful typist.

We have attempted to emphasize that in order to assess whether a manager is successful requires the evaluator to consider not only indicators or criteria, such as turnover and production, but also the *situation,* the *human resources,* and other *organizational factors* that must be dealt with. Consequently, each feature of our model is a part of the manager's work life. Some of these features cannot be controlled by the manager, but there is no reason why he or she should not understand what they are and how they stimulate behavior. The manager of today and tomorrow must stimulate behavior so that accepted levels of performance are achieved.

Some Future Events in the Field of Organizational Behavior

Forecasting the future is extremely risky. It involves logic and a knowledge of present trends and future needs. In this chapter, we will try to take the material we have already presented and, based on some forecasts of future needs, discuss some of the directions we believe the field of organizational behavior will take in the next decade. The needs or demands of individual employees, management, and our society will undoubtedly shape events to come. Although we do not claim to be futurologists, we believe that some consideration of these needs together with what we already know to be true about organizational behavior will point out ways to further improve behavior and performance in organizations.

Individual Dimensions

As evidenced in chapters 3 and 4, individuals vary markedly with respect to a number of critical psychological and behavioral characteristics. Up until just recently, researchers in organizational behavior have often ignored such variation and assumed individual differences away. Increasingly, organizational researchers are taking explicit account of individual differences. Indeed, we will see the field begin to examine more closely the way in which individual characteristics *intervene* and influence the impact of organizational processes (such as rewards) on behavior and performance. The work of Locke presented in chapters 5 and 14 is an example of this type of development. An individual employee's own or self-goal setting behavior has been found to *moderate* the impact of such processes as leadership and rewards on subsequent job performance.

In an effort to deal with individual differences, we will see more intense contingency-based research on individual differences. Research evidence suggests that organizations will have to take several steps in adjusting their programs to individual differences. First, they must determine what kinds of individuals respond best to specific policies and programs and adjust them accordingly. Chapter 6 illustrates the variety of ways individuals can react to the same job-design characteristics.

Second, devising various types of reward packages that comply with personal preferences will be given more attention. Different combinations of fringe benefits, promotion opportunities, and salary and wage increments will undoubtedly be experimented with on a wider basis. Third, different methods of training individuals will be attempted to locate the most efficient procedure for a given individual or group. Fourth, the individuals themselves will probably play a larger role in devising performance appraisal systems. The behaviorally anchored rating system format of employee participation in designing performance appraisal systems should become more popular. Finally, individual goal-setting research and practice should increase significantly. Goal setting is becoming a more popular procedure, and this in itself should stimulate the need for more research to diagnose, interpret, and predict what is occurring in the goal setting process. The interest in personalizing goals should be reflected in the thrust to stimulate goal-setting participants to work harder on developing personal-development goals along with their task goals.

Increasingly, in the next decade, the field of organizational behavior is going to more closely examine the reciprocal nature of the relationship between individuals and organizations. Although such historical approaches as the human relations movement (chapter 5) and the work adjustment studies (chapter 3) emphasized this fact, up until recently the field's major focus has been on ways in which organizations influence individuals. We will continue to turn our attention as well to the individual's impact on the organization. Closely related to this development is a growing interest among managers and researchers to improve the "quality of working life" in organizations. Recognition is being made of individual and societal demands to gain more than simple monetary rewards in the employment relationship. One aspect of the quality of working life concern that is now emerging is the role that job and life stress play in influencing individual satisfaction and effectiveness (chapter 16). In order for the quality of working life to be investigated more fully, however, there will first be a need to conceptually and operationally define this concept. There should be continued debate and discussion among researchers, managers, and employees about what constitutes the important aspects of working life. For example, there is some evidence that in certain work situations, job security is a crucial working life issue. Yet, in the past, this hygiene issue has been discarded as unimportant by some behavioral scientists. A contingency orientation, however, shows the folly of making assumptions about individual differences and ignoring key variables.

Groups and Interpersonal Influence

The study of group behavior and interpersonal influence (i.e., leadership) has been, and will continue to be, one of the major cornerstones of the field of organizational behavior. We anticipate that this dimension of organizational behavior will receive increased attention from behavioral scientists and practicing managers because of one overriding reason—the growing complexities of the internal structuring of the organization coupled with the need to adapt to environmental changes have a direct impact on the manager's ability to insure good individual and group performance.

This internal complexity and need for adaptation will alter many organizational behavioral patterns in the future. We foresee greater attention being directed toward group composition, group structure, decision-making processes, and the use of many temporal groups, such as task forces or teams. We anticipate that further attention will be placed on the effective composition of groups and training programs that will quicken group development and emphasize key group structural components. The growing use of such mechanisms as nominal group development and decision making is a move in this direction.

There also appears to be additional stimulation for organizations to emphasize the development and use of other, possibly more sophisticated intergroup management strategies. The use of task forces and integrating departments is currently widespread in many organizations. Many of these are already beyond their ability to effectively handle intergroup performance. Along with these newer management strategies, we foresee greater attention also being directed toward the use of conflict-resolution methods.

It is a well-known fact that the simple supervisor-subordinate relationship is becoming a rarity today. Many people in organizations already report to more than one supervisor. This situation will create a growing need for the better understanding of the interpersonal influence process. It also draws attention to clearly defining authority and responsibility relationships and to the development of more objective performance evaluation and reward systems.

Finally, we anticipate that greater attention will be directed toward understanding the *causal* direction of organizational behavior dimensions and the impact, or *intervening* influence of certain situational variables. The vast majority of research in organizational behavior has studied simple two-variable relationships (i.e., leadership style → subordinate performance). We believe this approach oversimplifies the complexities of today's organizations.

Organizational Structure

Currently, the bureaucratic organizational design and dimensions dominate the majority of organizations in industrialized nations. We believe that this form of design will continue to be widely utilized, but that some significant changes will occur. Within some bureaucracies, there will emerge less structured units, such as research and development departments, that will act as a part of the total bureaucratic arrangement. Thus, some organizations will have multiple or diverse structures. This diversity will require competent integration and integrators.

The attributes of a successful integrator will become an area of growing interest. Some of the research into the boundary-spanning role (chapter 10) will grow because of the need to know. In conjunction with this growing interest in integrators and boundary spanners will be an increased focus on different styles of integration. Perhaps industry differences will produce particular styles, or situational differences will be the important contingency feature to consider, or some combination of factors will need to be examined. Whatever the factor, there will be a growing list of contingency variables that influence organizational design decisions and performance.

The connection between structure and environment should be given more interest. Shortages of world resources, the expansion of government activities, rising educational levels, increased social awareness, the changing role of women and minorities in society, and the general interest in improved efficiency are environmental forces that must be given more consideration in designing organizations and more research attention. For example, how to attract and integrate more women and minorities into the present organizational structure or some modified structure is already of interest to many administrators. Answers to these questions will require creative ideas and research. Some of the tools for performing this required research are specified in the appendix.

New and different organizational structures will be experimented with on a small scale by more research-oriented organizations. Project arrangements, free-form designs, and other designs will be tried out by more firms. Research should show that these different arrangements will work in some instances and fail in others. Once again, the scientific proof or testing is what we expect to grow in all areas of organizational behavior. The days of nonaccountability for managerial actions are numbered because society is demanding evidence before accepting an approach. These demands transcend the field of organizational behavior.

Organizational Change and Development

An accepted fact is that organizations need to change and develop. There is no dearth of models, techniques, processes, and ideas available for a manager to

611

consider when thinking about change and development. We believe that there will be a "shaking out" of cute OD packages and an increased interest in conducting both laboratory and field research. The interest will grow because managers are being asked for documented proof of the effectiveness of any program they sanction for improving skills, attitudes, or performance. That is, we are asking our managers, in increasing numbers, to display cost-benefit results for their organizational change and development efforts.

The more refined assessments of organizational change and development efforts should stimulate even more interest in performing longitudinal evaluations. The audience for refined research includes researchers and practitioners. As better, more sophisticated research is performed, others should be stimulated to follow suit.

In order for our predictions to come true, it will be necessary to increase the dialogue between researchers and practitioners. They need each other to improve research and to learn more about change and development. The researcher needs the organizational setting to study, and the manager needs answers to questions and suggestions on how to improve performance. Therefore, it seems logical to assume that their interaction will increase.

We also predict that in the area of organizational change and development, as in the field of organizational behavior itself, there will not emerge a unifying theory, model, or framework in the foreseeable future. The search for the unifying approach has been futile. Practitioners and researchers will use many theories, models, and frameworks in attempting to improve performance. The contingency theme will again predominate this segment of our performance model.

There will be a great emphasis among those involved as change agents and implementors of change to do a more thorough job of diagnosis. The diagnosis will be conducted more regularly by many organizations, and the data it collects will be used to consider possible intervention strategies. The diagnosis will involve studying individuals, groups, and the organization. In addition, the environment will also be included. Organizations that devote more attention to diagnosis will become known as leaders in the area of planned change and development. They, in essence, will be able to better cope with change, behavior, and performance.

In Conclusion

We are certainly optimistic about future research and application efforts in organizations. The cornerstone of these efforts will be the field of organizational behavior, which is currently in a state of infancy. The field is now beginning to attract and interest individuals with different skills, needs, and interests. Everything indicates that the field will continue to flourish and work on problems inherent in organizational life. The future suggests challenge, complexity, and change. These ingredients certainly suggest the continued growth of organizational behavior as a field of inquiry. Our future and the future of organizations will be significantly influenced by how managers utilize the knowledge and understanding that emerges from the maturing field of organizational behavior.

Research Approaches to Study Organizational Behavior and Performance

The Collection of Data to Study Organizational Behavior

Through observation of the phenomena to be studied, the scientist and the manager obtain data that are used to test theories, models, and ideas. What makes the scientist's observations different from the manager's is that they are systematically planned to fit the research design strategy being utilized. The scientist works at collecting data that is adequate, representative, and is as precise as feasible. There are numerous data-collection methods used to study organizational behavior, and we have selected for discussion four of the most widely used.

Interviews

Few behavioral scientists fail to use, at one time or another, some sort of interview or conversation with participants in a study. The interview can occur before a change is introduced into an organization, during the course of the experiment being conducted, or to aid in interpreting data collected by other means, such as question-naires. The interview relies on the ability to communicate among people. Asking someone a direct question can save time and effort if the respondent is willing to talk and the answer is honest.

The interview quality depends heavily on mutual trust and the goodwill of respondents. This is also true when collecting data by use of a questionnaire. If trust and goodwill are to be maintained, the interview must cultivate it. The interviewer must assure the respondent of confidentiality before there is a chance of developing trust. In addition, the interviewer must be a good listener to hold a successful interview.

There are a number of different types of interviews used to acquire organiza-tional behavior knowledge. The *structured* interview asks standard questions of all respondents. The response made is somewhat dictated by the questions. For exam-ple, the respondents may be asked whether they have participated in a goal-setting training program. The answer would be either yes or no.

An *open-ended* structured interview is also used to collect data. The questions may be the same for all respondents, but they require a free response. An example of such a question would be: "Could you tell me about your attitude about the new wage plan that was established for your group last month?" The response would be open-ended as opposed to a specific type of answer.

The *non-structured* interview is used to acquire general impressions about the job, organization, or the person. The interviewer talks with the interviewee about various events, ideas, or opinions. From these discussions, the responses are analyzed and inferences are made.

In many data-collection situations, a combination of the three types of interviews are used. Whatever type is used, it should be emphasized that interview responses may not be accurate or valid. For an employee to talk to an outside behavioral scientist and answer job, individual, or organizational questions is a difficult experience because of the trust issue. Thus, the importance of establishing trust should not be underestimated.

Questionnaires

The development of a questionnaire to learn about organizational behavior dimensions such as those presented in exhibit 2–2 is a difficult task. It is more an art than a science. Most behavioral scientists move directly from their theory or model to the development of questions. Perhaps a more feasible procedure would be to interview potential questionnaire respondents before moving directly into questionnaire development. This interview step may prevent preconceived ideas from becoming fixed in the mind of the researcher, which results in an inappropriate set of questions.

After carefully establishing the reasons for using the questionnaire to study a particular theory or model, the researcher then must practice proper procedures of development. The work of Erdos is invaluable in providing starting points in the artful exercise of questionnaire construction.[1] For example:

Is the question necessary?

Is the question repetitious?

Does the question contain more than one idea?

Can the respondent answer the question?

Is an item likely to bias those following it?

Does the sequence maintain respondent motivation?

An example of a questionnaire section used to measure satisfaction attitudes is shown in exhibit A–1. We developed these questions after consultation with executives in a large company, examining other satisfaction questionnaires, and reviewing the empirical data of previous attempts to measure satisfaction attitudes.

The questionnaire can be overused and abused as a data-collection method. To base major organizational changes solely on the results of questionnaire responses is not recommended. We strongly urge managers and readers to refrain from using the questionnaire as the panacea for all organizational ills. It is only one way of collecting data that can be useful if not abused.

Participant Observation

Participant observation is based on the theory that an interpretation of an event can only be approximately correct when it is a composite of two viewpoints, the participant's and an observer's or analyst's. The majority of data collection in the field of organizational behavior is based on interview and questionnaire responses. The

Exhibit A–1 Job Satisfaction Questionnaire

The following questions concern the degree of satisfaction you have with your job, supervisor, pay, coworkers, and promotional opportunities. Please read each statement carefully and circle the response that best represents your opinion.

	Strongly Disagree	Disagree	Neither Disagree nor Agree	Agree	Strongly Agree
1. In general, I am satisfied with my job.	1	2	3	4	5
2. My coworkers are usually uncooperative.	1	2	3	4	5
3. Considering the work that is required, the pay for this job is good.	1	2	3	4	5
4. My supervisor does a good job.	1	2	3	4	5
5. My job offers a good opportunity for promotion and advancement.	1	2	3	4	5
6. I am not satisfied with my supervisor's job performance.	1	2	3	4	5
7. In general, I am satisfied with the relationship I have with my coworkers.	1	2	3	4	5
8. I am satisfied with my pay.	1	2	3	4	5
9. My opportunities for promotion and advancement are limited.	1	2	3	4	5
10. Compared to pay rates of other area companies for similar work, my pay is good.	1	2	3	4	5
11. My job does not challenge me.	1	2	3	4	5
12. I am not paid enough for the level of my performance.	1	2	3	4	5
13. This company promotes people on the basis of good performance.	1	2	3	4	5
14. My pay is poor compared to similar jobs in this area.	1	2	3	4	5
15. My job gives me a sense of accomplishment.	1	2	3	4	5
16. My supervisor is very competent and knows his/her job well.	1	2	3	4	5
17. If I were working in a similar job with another company, I would be making much more money.	1	2	3	4	5
18. My coworkers make my job more pleasant.	1	2	3	4	5

participant-observer source is often ignored. The main reason is that the "scientific community" holds this method in low esteem.

One advantage of the participant-observer method is that it focuses attention on the behavior of individuals rather than simply on a verbal statement or self-report questionnaire response. By looking at behavior, the observer must study all the actions of a person—or the *total* individual—or group. It is the total behavior of people in their work setting that is important to both researchers and managers.

Participant observation can occur in a number of different ways. First, the observer can become a concealed member of a group and study behavior. Second, the observer can ask for permission to study a person or group performing their job tasks. Third, the observer can ask to not only observe but to film or videotape and record the behaviors.

A high level of participation requires time and effort. We are opposed to any form of deception and recommend strongly against the first form of participant observation. Thus, the other two forms of participant observation are what we consider to be viable alternatives or supplements for interviewing and questionnaire administration.

Unobtrusive measures

The major criterion for classifying a data-collection method as unobtrusive is that the data are not contaminated by reactivity. The interview is reactive because the interviewee knows that he or she is being asked questions. The same is true of the questionnaire. Participant observation is a reactive procedure because the observer is a significant source of stimulation that may affect the behavior being emitted by the respondent. However, the lack of reactivity does not necessarily mean that the data generated are accurate.

Webb has suggested four types of unobtrusive measures.[2] They are:

Physical traces.   This involves using information from physical surfaces. For example, determining how long it takes to wear out floor tile in an office could be used to assess the amount of traffic in the office.

Archives.   This involves using documents and records. Subjecting historical company resources or organizational charts to content analysis is a form of archive measure.

Simple observation. Observing where people sit around a conference room table is a form of simple observation. The spatial arrangement can be used to index personal preference, status, and degree of interaction.

Hardware. The use of photoelectric counters on highways is a form of unobtrusive hardware measure. The counter is not visible, but it is used to count the number of vehicles passing.

Despite some obvious advantages of using unobtrusive data collection, there are a number of problems with this method. First, when using archive data researchers are restricted to what exists, and this may not be what is needed to answer crucial questions about organizational behavior. For example, if one is interested in the specific attitudes about an organizational structure that existed two years ago, it is difficult to find this information in archives. Second, unobtrusive measures can run into ethical problems. They can involve invasions of privacy because they are collected without the consent of respondents. Third, the issue of validity is difficult to determine with unobtrusive measures. Whether the wearing of floor tiles or the study of organization charts in a repository are valid measures of phenomena is difficult to assess because single measures can be conceptualized in several different ways. It is best to operationalize something a number of ways so that the construct being studied is validated.

The four methods of data collection—interviews, questionnaires, participant observation, and unobtrusive measures—are currently being used in organizational behavior research studies. There is no single best method for collecting data pertaining to our model in exhibit 2–2. The important point to remember in adopting a data-collection method is to select the most powerful method for answering the questions that are important at a particular time. Methods of data collection are neither good nor bad, but rather are more or less useful in answering particular questions. The scientific study of organizational behavior requires data collection, and which method or combination of methods is used should be selected to test the applicability of knowledge, a theory, or model in a particular setting. The data collected is a part of the research design. Each of the methods we have discussed can be and is used in laboratory and field studies.

Specific Research Designs

In chapter 2, we emphasized the need for the accurate identification of organizational problems, the use of theory and models to help understand the problems, and the establishment of well-developed hypotheses to direct the research effort. Each of these factors is crucial, but without an efficient scheduling and application of an appropriate research design, they are empty. Structure for performing the study of the phenomena in question, whether it involves goal setting, training program effectiveness, motivation, leadership, cohesiveness, selection, or organizational change problems, means design. Research design is needed to provide structure and a step-by-step plan. The researcher, by using a design, attempts to arrive at a scientifically based interpretation of the findings. Thus, it is important to consider a research design as a blueprint that suggests that the researcher do some things and avoid doing other things.

There is no perfect research design. Yet, researchers attempt to satisfy a number of criteria in selecting an appropriate design. Campbell and Stanley have adequately classified design criteria as internal validity and external validity.[3]

Internal validity involves providing answers to three questions:

1. Does the design adequately test the study hypotheses? Many designs are not able to answer the research questions, and this would result in low internal validity.

2. Does the design enable the researcher to control independent variables? A key precept to use is to randomize the selection of subjects and experimental manipulations whenever possible.

3. Does the design control for unwanted sources of variance to influence the subjects and the study in general?

The research design must also have *external validity*. This means that the study results are representative and generalizable. That is, can a particular set of results be generalized to another group of people and situations? A study that can be generalized and is representative is said to contain external validity.

Timing and Research Designs

Research is performed in organizations because someone has a question about some phenomena or is interested in solving a problem, and data must be collected. The clarity of the question or the problem identified can range from complete vagueness to a precise statement. These questions or problems often, but not always, require the use of a research design. Occasionally, the costs of performing the research are not worth the benefits received from the findings, and this results in a manager voting no to a request to perform an organizational study. In this book, we recognize this reality but suggest that managers learn what a research design involves. For example, suppose a manager wants to know whether a new performance appraisal system is better than the present one. The obvious thing to do is to try the new system on a group of employees and see how they react.

Let us assume that we have a number of criteria to measure how good the performance appraisal system is in improving actual performance. The new performance system can be viewed as the independent variable X and the performance observations as O. An observation is any way of acquiring empirical information about the dependent variables being studied. Interview responses, questionnaire answers, participant observations, reviewing company records, and counting the number of completed units are examples of observations made by a researcher. These observations involve the collection of data. The first study design is called a "one shot" design or:

Design 1: One shot: X   O

Time

This design informs us that a given sample of employees worked under the new appraisal system X, and their performance was measured at a later time.

If you do not have accurate records of the employees' performance before the introduction of the new appraisal problem, what could a researcher or manager conclude about the program? Not very much! Perhaps the employees performed better under the old appraisal system or at least they performed as well. This design is certainly a poor one to select because very few answers about the effectiveness of the new program are provided.

Design 2 utilizes a pretest/post-test format. The employees' performance is observed before the new appraisal system is implemented. This design would be symbolically presented as follows:

Design 2: Single group pretest/post-test design O_1 X O_2

Time

Although this design is an improvement over the first, it has some glaring weaknesses. First, other things that have nothing to do with the new appraisal program could have happened to this group of employees between the observation times. For example, the well-respected and inspirational president of the organization could have personally visited the employees. These effects are viewed as a *history* impact on the data. Second, if the time between observations O_1 and O_2 is long, the *maturation* of the employees alone could have produced differences in performance. The employees may have matured and consequently performed more effectively.

A third weakness of Design 2 is called a *testing* effect. The employees may learn at O_1 that their performance is being closely monitored. This increases their alertness and response to the performance appraisal system. A fourth weakness is called *instrument decay*. Perhaps the performance measures at O_1 were taken after a holiday when the employees were not working up to standards, and the second observation occurred in the middle of the week when performance is usually at its highest level in this organization. Thus, instrument changes (i.e., the measurement of performance) or "decay" is present.

Design 2 is a way of obtaining two measures of a dependent variable, performance—one taken before the new appraisal system, and the other after. Another way of obtaining two measures is to use Design 3, or:

Design 3: Static group comparison:　X　　O_1 (Group 1)

　　　　　　　　　　　　　　　　　　O_2 (Group 2)

　　　　　　　　　　　　　　　　Time

Group 1's performance is measured after the performance appraisal system, and Group 2's performance is measured without being exposed to the appraisal system. This design avoids the weaknesses of Designs 1 and 2 but is susceptible to a number of problems. First, the researcher or manager has no assurance that the two groups are well matched or equivalent. This is referred to as a *selection* problem because random assignment to the two study groups was not practiced.

A second potential weakness in Design 3 is that the treatment may affect the *mortality* from the study. This involves subjects dropping out of the study. Those employees receiving the new appraisal approach may covertly drop out by not trying hard or staying away from the organization.

Another potential problem is called the *interactive effects*. This could involve any of the weaknesses of the three designs already discussed and other research designs. For example, pretesting, O_1, may sensitize the subjects if the new appraisal program is implemented immediately after the first observation. Or perhaps the drop-outs from a study may differ in the groups being studied.

These seven weaknesses, which confound experimentally based organizational research results, are summarized in exhibit A–2. These weaknesses suggest that more powerful research designs are required to provide results that enable researchers to improve the knowledge base about organizations. The designs that follow are called *experimentally based designs*.

Design 4 is called a pretest/post-test control group design. It is shown as:

Design 4:　Pretest/post-test control group design　R ——— O_1 X O_2

　　　　　　　　　　　　　　　　　　　　　　　R ——— O_1　O_2

　　　　　　　　　　　　　　　　　　　　　　　　　Time

This design shows that an experimental group's (the top one) performance was measured before and after they were exposed to the new appraisal system X, and the control group's (the bottom one) performance was assessed at the same two times without being exposed to the new performance appraisal system. Notice also the symbol R, to the left of the diagram. The R specifies randomization and indicates that employees in both the experimental and control groups were selected from a

Exhibit A–2 Selected Factors that Are Sources of Research Design Invalidity

Factor	Explanation
History	The performance of the subjects can be affected by events that occur over the course of the study.
Maturation	Changes within the subjects—their feelings, attitudes, learning skills—occur over a period of time. These are independent of any treatment impact.
Testing	Changes can occur in the actions or performance of a subject because observation (measurement) of these factors sensitizes the person that is being investigated.
Instrument decay	A later observation (measurement) can differ from an earlier one because of changes in the instruments (e.g., questionnaire) or conditions, such as fatigue of a researcher observing the work behavior of subjects.
Selection	If subjects are assigned to different groups in any other way than randomly from a pool, systematic differences between groups will result that may have direct effects on performance or that may interact with the manipulation of independent variables and have an effect on dependent variables.
Mortality	If subjects included in the first observation (measurement) drop out of the experiment before the final observation, the distribution of characteristics in the several groups being studies will no longer be the same. These differences may directly affect the dependent variables or may interact with the manipulation of independent variables.
Interactive effects	Any of several of the above factors may interact with the experimental manipulation of variables and produce confounding effects. For example, pretesting may sensitize the subject only when it is closely followed by the manipulation of variables.

common pool of employees and were assigned on a random basis. Random means that the employees were assigned in such a manner that each person in the pool had an equal chance of being in the experimental or control group. Random assignment is a necessary condition for a true experiment. In most cases, organizational constraints often do not permit random choice.

A flaw in Design 4 involves the potential interactive effects of sensitization. The first assessment of performance may sensitize the employees. There are two designs that can minimize the sensitization flaw, one of which is Design 5:

Design 5: Post-test only control
group design: R —— X O_1

R —— O_2

Time

This design minimizes the assessment sensitization problem, but it eliminates a group that receives pretest (O_1) and post-test (O_2) measures of performance. This type of group provides valuable information on history, instrument decay, and other weakness factors.

Finally, by combining Designs 4 and 5, a design known as the Solomon four-group is created. It is shown as follows:

Design 6:   Solomon Four-   R —— $O_1 X O_2$
          group design   R —— O_3 O_4
                          R —— $X O_5$
                          R —— O_6

Time

This design combines the best features of the previous design. It controls for *and* also measures effects of history, maturation, and testing.

The design shown as 4, 5, and 6 are more scientifically rigorous and are recommended over the first three designs. The important differences in the two sets of designs involve randomization of subjects and the use of comparison groups. The importance of these features needs to be clarified by researchers when they are attempting to display the advantages of a particular research design to practicing managers. It is the practicing manager who allows the researcher to perform field studies or experiments. Thus, communication of confounding factors such as those presented in exhibit A–2 is necessary if any type of design is to be used.

The Longitudinal Research Design

Longitudinal or time-series research designs have occasionally been utilized to study the organizational factors shown in exhibit 2–2. This type of design is expensive and disruptive in field research because more than two observations are typically made. Some of the other problems associated with the design involve the mortality factor; subjects are lost due to illnesses, retirement, layoffs, and deaths, and there may be a history effect with the longitudinal design.

A longitudinal or time-series design is presented in the following:

Design 7: Longitudinal time design: O_1 O_2 O_3 X O_4 O_5 O_6

Time

This design indicates that performance would be specifically measured at intervals, perhaps every three months. The new appraisal program would be implemented after three observations were made, and the performance observations would continue for three more time intervals, O_4, O_5, and O_6. If the results are graphed, they might look like exhibit A–3. The graph of the performance data suggests that the introduction of the new performance appraisal system has had an effect that is above the effect of time. Performance appears to be increasing before the new appraisal program—O_1, O_2, and O_3—but a relatively sharp increase occurs after the program—O_4, O_5, and O_6.

Without using control groups, the longitudinal design results must be cautiously reviewed. Even with the addition of control groups and other experimental groups to

Exhibit A–3 Performance Data Plots for the Longitudinal Study Design

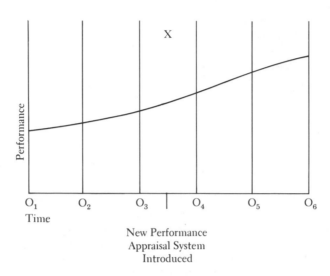

Time

New Performance
Appraisal System
Introduced

the design, it is important to carefully document what has occurred between the observation points. Perhaps around the time of the introduction of the new program, two key supervisors left the organization or a new work area layout was implemented. Keeping a carefully documented diary of changes in structure, technology, environmental conditions, and people is very important in longitudinal research.

The design presented as a longitudinal form can include control groups and other experimental groups. These variants of the approach shown would minimize the mortality and history effects. The problem is to convince managers that long-run assessments with multiple groups will be beneficial to the organization. Remember that managers are held accountable by stockholders, boards of directors, and community action groups that researchers do not have to face. Thus, although longitudinal research has certain scientific attractiveness, it is difficult to perform in real organizational settings.

The Realities of Organizational
Research: Studies and Experiments

The need to conduct careful research of organizational properties and to use systematic research designs is obvious. However, research conducted in organizations, as opposed to contrived laboratory settings, often negates the use of Designs 4 to 7. The researcher, although trained to perform sophisticated research, often must compromise and put together the best design possible under the circumstances.[4]

Some of the typical problems encountered in field research work are the following:

1. Intense resistance from some units that need to be included in a study or an experiment. The organization wants to minimize disruption, so they often will ask a unit to voluntarily cooperate with a researcher. The unit may decide that cooperation would be disruptive or could result in some organizationally imposed policy that is detrimental to the group. Thus, the members of the unit elect to not participate, and this decision is accepted by the organization.

2. The importance of randomization in achieving internal and external validity has been emphasized. It is almost impossible to obtain pure random assignment of subjects or work groups or departmental units in field experiments. The organization often will not permit randomization and in many instances will ask that a unit or group not be partitioned in any particular manner.

3. The rationale for the inclusion of a control group in a research study is difficult to communicate to practicing managers. If they are inclined to allow a researcher to experiment, it is typically their belief that all employees in a unit should receive the experimental treatment. The organization wants the experiment to make or to display positive improvements, and to omit groups called control units is a contradiction of the overall improvement philosophy.

   One quasi-experimental design often used when randomization is not possible is the following:[5]

   Design 8. Quasi-experimental design

   $$O_1 \quad X \quad O_2$$
   $$O_3 \qquad O_4$$
   $$\longrightarrow$$
   Time

   The experimental group would receive the treatment, the new appraisal system, and two measures of performance taken at O_1 and O_2. The control group performance, which is not randomly selected, is assessed at O_3 and O_4, which occur at the same time the O_1 and O_2 measures are taken. The control group is referred to as an *unmatched* or *nonequivalent* group. This design is useful when randomization is not possible.

4. A significant amount of field research must begin after an experimental treatment has occurred. This means that the researcher must do the best job possible to assess the impact, if any, of the variable manipulations. The research purist may state that this type of research is worthless because of the lack of control. We believe that this is too harsh an indictment that must be tempered by the realities of performing organizational research. To advance our knowledge of organizational behavior, improve the quality of work life, and improve our understanding of work, we need to utilize the best research design possible. Thus, patch-up designs, nonequivalent control group designs, and other similar types must be used cautiously.

The realism of field research is often cited as an advantage of this form of research when compared to laboratory-based research. Realism requires creativity and occasional deviation from pure research designs, which are more applicable to laboratory settings. The degree of deviation must be carefully considered by the researcher and any person using the results of a design, which is basically a patch-up approach. The implementation of major changes in structure, process, technology, or job duties based on anything less than sound research designs requires a large degree of common sense and faith. We encourage readers to use common sense, faith, and scientifically based findings in making decisions about organizational behavior and the model shown in exhibit 2–2.

Notes

1. P. L. Erdos, *Professional Mail Surveys* (New York: McGraw-Hill, 1970).

2. E. J. Webb, *Unobtrusive Measures: Nonreactive Research in the Social Sciences* (Chicago: Rand McNally, 1966), pp. 3–8.

3. D. Campbell and J. Stanley, *Experimental Designs and Quasi-Experimental Designs for Research* (Chicago: Rand McNally, 1963), p. 5.

4. Putting a design together is excellently discussed in Martin G. Evans, "Opportunistic Organizational Research: The Role of Patch-Up Designs," *Academy of Management Journal,* March 1974, pp. 98–108.

5. For an excellent discussion of quasi-experiments, see Thomas D. Cook and Donald T. Campbell, "The Design and Control of Quasi-Experiments and Time Experiments in Field Settings," in *Handbook of Industrial and Organizational Psychology,* ed. Marvin D. Dunnette (Chicago: Rand McNally, 1976), pp. 223–326.

List of Key Terms

Abilities Potentials for carrying out specific acts or behaviors. Abilities are necessary but not sufficient conditions for behavior. A combination of ability and effort are necessary for behavior to occur.

Accountability A person's obligation to carry out responsibilities and be accountable for decisions and activities.

Achievement A motive that causes people to prefer tasks that involve only a moderate amount of risk (as opposed to a high degree of risk) and that involve rather immediate and clear feedback on results.

Action standards Internal standards people have regarding the way things should be. In effect, action standards are values.

Affiliation A desire on the part of employees to develop and maintain close friendships.

Assembly effect The variations in group behavior that are a consequence of the particular combination of the people in the group.

Assessment center A multidimensional approach to the measurement of performance and potential that employs many different assessment techniques.

Authoritarianism A personality variable that consists of a set of attitudes characterized by beliefs that there should be power and status differences among people in organizations and that the use of power and authority is proper and important to the successful functioning of the organization.

Authority The right to require compliance from subordinates on the basis of position in the scalar chain.

Avoidance The administration of a reinforcement that prevents the occurrence of an undesired behavior.

Avoidance conflict resolution A strategy that involves general disregard for the causes of conflicts by enabling the conflict to continue only under controlled conditions.

Behavior The tangible acts or decisions of individuals, groups, or organizations.

Behavior modeling A training or skills development technique which emphasizes the use of role playing and video-tape review to afford learning through experience.

Behavioral decision theory Decision models that examine the influence of individual, group, and organization factors in decision making.

Behavioral leadership theories Approaches to leadership that seek to identify leadership styles that are the most effective in various situations.

Behaviorally anchored rating scales (BARS) Performance rating that focus on specific behaviors or acts as indicators of effective and ineffective performance, rather than on broadly stated adjectives such as "average, above average, and below average."

Boundary-spanner role A liaison role that a person or individual performs at the point of contact with environments that exist between groups or the organization and the external environment providing two-way communication and facilitating interaction.

Bounded rationality A term introduced by March, Simon, and Cyert to describe the fact that decision makers do not have access to perfect information when choosing among alternatives. A major implication of this concept is that decision makers *satisfice* rather than maximize objectives.

Career A sequence of jobs that unfold over time, usually involving promotions and occupational progression.

Central tendency An error often associated with traditional rating scales. It consists of a rater incorrectly assigning similar ratings to a group of employees and not accurately representing the true distribution of performance. All ratings tend to cluster at the middle of the scale.

Classical conditioning The learning or acquisition of a habit (stimulus-response connection) through the process of associating an unconditioned stimulus (UCS) with a conditioned stimulus (CS).

Classical decision theory A normative approach to decision making that emphasizes maximizing known objectives by choosing the alternative that maximizes expected returns.

Classical design theory The theoretical approach that is based on scientific management procedures and bureaucratic principles.

Coercive power An influence over others based on fear.

Cohesiveness Closeness and common attitudes, behaviors, and performance of group members.

Communication The process by which information is transmitted and exchanged.

Communication barriers Any number of factors that interfere with messages in the process of communication. They include the distortion of messages due to attributes of the receiver, selective perception, semantic problems, timing, and information overload.

Compensatory decision process In information-processing theory, a rule whereby a decision maker allows a high value on one decision criterion to balance or offset a low value on some other criterion.

Competence The ability to perform well.

Confrontation conflict resolution A strategy that focuses on the sources of conflict and attempts to resolve them through such procedures as mutual personnel exchange, use of superordinate goals, or problem solving.

Conjunctive decision rule In information-processing theory, a rule whereby the decision maker establishes minimally acceptable levels on each of several decision criteria. To decide in favor of an alternative, it must achieve minimally acceptable levels of every criterion.

Consideration The behavior of the leader that emphasizes openness, friendliness, and a concern for the welfare of subordinates.

Consistency One aspect of reliability in performance evaluation that demands that alternative forms or alternative judges employed to rate the performance of the same employee substantially agree in their judgments.

Contaminated appraisals Performance appraisals that include irrelevant dimensions or aspects of job performance.

Content motivation theories Theories that focus on the factors within the person that start, arouse, energize, or stop behavior.

Contingency design approach An attempt to understand the interrelationships within and among organizational subsystems as well as between the organizational system as an entity and its environments. It emphasizes the multivariate nature of organizations and attempts to interpret and understand how they operate under varying conditions and in specific situations.

Critical incident method A job analysis technique that attempts to study the job in terms of specific, identifiable behaviors or actions that are critical to success in carrying out a job. The technique is used to generate critical incidents to be incorporated into behaviorally anchored rating scales.

Cybernetic motive process A motive process in which an individual's comparison of information from the environment to internal standards leads to behavior. The key concept is that discrepancy between the standard and the incoming information serves to motivate behavior.

Data collection The method used to observe phenomena that are important to the behavioral science researcher and manager. The most widely used collection methods are interviews, questionnaires, participant observation, and unobtrusive measures.

Decision making A choice among several mutually exclusive and exhaustive alternative actions. The choice is made after a consideration of all outcomes possible as a result of the decision, the probabilities associated with such outcomes, and the conditional values associated with each alternative-outcome combination.

Decision to perform The choice employees make with regard to performance level.

Decision to stay The choice employees make with regard to leaving or staying employed by organizations. Employees who leave an organization during a given period of time contribute to organizational turnover.

Deficient appraisals Performance appraisals that do not include all relevant dimensions or aspects of job performance.

Defusion conflict resolution A strategy that attempts to buy time to resolve intergroup conflict when it is less emotional or crucial.

Delphi technique A group decision technique closely associated with the nominal group technique, except that members are physically separated from each other. (See *Nominal group technique.*)

Departmentalization The combination of jobs into a specific unit or department.

Diagnostic activities Fact-finding or data-collection activities that attempt to find out what is occurring within a unit or organization.

Differentiation The state of segmentation of the organization's subsystems, each of which contains members who form attitudes and behavior and tend to become specialized experts.

Disjunctive decision rule In information-processing theory, a rule whereby the decision maker scans the decision criteria for one outstanding characteristic. An alternative outstanding on just one decision criteria will be sufficient for a favorable decision.

Drive A need or motive that energizes and maintains an act or series of acts.

Dogmatism A personality dimension characterized by a tendency to be closed instead of open-minded about issues.

Dual careers Describes the husband and wife who both have full-time careers.

Effort The motivated aspect of behavior. When effort is combined with ability, behavior will result. Effort is said to be the amount of energy or force expended by the individual in a given act. Level of effort is influenced by the strength of the individual's motives or needs.

Emergent leader An individual who has emerged from a group to assume a leading role as the informal leader.

Environmental uncertainty The state of the external environment of an organization as defined by the degree of complexity and the degree of change.

Equity theory of motivation A theory that focuses on the discrepancies within a person after the individual has compared his or her output/input ratio to a reference person.

ERG theory of motivation A theory that categorizes needs in terms of existence, relatedness, or growth aspects.

Exception principle A strategy for reducing information overload in vertical communication channels. According to the principle, upward communication is limited to information regarding the most critical aspects of operations truly demanding upper management's attention.

Expectancy The perceived probability that a particular act will be followed by a particular outcome.

Expectancy theory A theory that states that an individual will select an outcome based on how this choice is related to second-order outcomes (rewards). The choice of behavior acts is based upon the strength or value of the outcome and the perceived probability between first and second level outcomes.

Expert power The capacity to influence based upon some skill, expertise, or knowledge.

External validity of a research design This form of validity indicates that the study results are representative and can be generalized.

Extinction The decrease in undesirable behavior because of nonreinforcement.

Extrinsic rewards Rewards that a person receives from sources other than the job itself. They include compensation, supervision, promotions, vacations, friendships, and other outcomes apart from the job.

Fatigue Influence on behavior through inhibition. Its effects are temporary (in contrast to the effect of learning) and are dissipated with rest.

Favorableness The leadership situation, based upon group atmosphere, task structure, and the leader's position power, that contributes to the leader's ability to influence subordinates.

Feedback Knowledge about job performance obtained from the job itself or from other employees.

Field experiment A field study that involves the deliberate maximization of independent variables.

Field study A study that involves the systematic observation of variables or people within real-world settings.

Fringe benefits Rewards given to an employee over and above his or her wage or salary. They include vacation benefits, pension plan contributions, employee discounts, and other nonsalary rewards.

Functional group A group that is created and specified by the structure of the organization.

Functions of communication Emotive (expression of feelings), motivation (providing a vehicle for directing and influencing behavior and performance), information (providing technical information necessary for decisions), and control (providing for the auditing and controlling of operations).

Goal orientation The particular goals (techno-economic, market, or science) with which individuals or groups are primarily concerned.

Goal setting A critical phenomenon identified as having an impact on the success or effectiveness of an incentive plan. In order to motivate performance through incentives, the employee himself or herself must accept the goals established for a task and/or set them themselves.

Goal succession The change in goals as a result of the conscious effort by management to shift the course of the organization's activities.

Goals At the organizational level, desired states that the system is attempting to achieve by planning, organizing, and controlling. They are created by individuals or groups within the organization.

Grapevine A slang term referring to informal communication networks that parallel formal networks within organizations.

Group Two or more individuals who are interdependent and interact for the purpose of performing to achieve a common goal or objective.

Group composition The relative homogeneity or heterogeneity of the group based on the individual characteristics of the members.

Group decision A decision reached jointly by members of a group. One must consider interactions among people in the decision process. In addition, group decision making allows for the possibility of conflict among goals to be considered in the decision.

Group development A series of stages that most groups go through over time (orientation, internal problem solving, growth and productivity, evaluation and control).

Group dimensions Salient dimensions of group activity (individual, situational, and group development) that have an impact on group performance.

Group norms Standards of behavior established by the group that describe the acceptable behavior of members.

Groupthink A group defense reaction that impairs the quality of group decisions.

Habit (See *Stimulus-response.*)

Halo A perceptual error in which a rater fails to evaluate separate dimensions independently.

Incentive A type of motive that focuses on an event or outcome that is attractive to an individual. Incentives are outcomes towards which behavior is directed.

Incentive plan A reward scheme that attempts to tie pay directly to job performance. A piece rate and sales commission are two illustrations.

Individual vs. institutional decisions A distinction drawn between two different circumstances under which decisions are made. Institutional decisions are made repeatedly, allowing for the accumulation of accurate information regarding probabilities of events occurring. In addition, the institution can afford short-run losses, and, therefore, can use a probabilistic decision rule. The opposite is true of individual decisions, which are made very infrequently, without a great deal

of information, and without being able to afford short-run losses. Nonprobabilistic decision rules are used in this type of decision situation.

Inflation The erosion of real income by price increases. Inflation places pressures on organizational reward policies.

Information-flow requirements The amount and quality of information that must be processed between interacting groups in order to ensure intergroup performance.

Information overload A condition in which too much information flows through communication channels. Such a condition leads to ignoring potentially critical pieces of information.

Information processing and policy capturing The study of the ways in which individuals and groups attend to and use information to make decisions.

Information standards Internal standards people have regarding relationships among events.

Initiating structure The behavior of the leader that emphasizes structuring the task, assigning work, and providing feedback.

Instinctive vs. learned behavior A distinction between actions that are instinctive (or inborn) and those that are learned over time.

Instrumental conditioning (See *Operant conditioning.*)

Instrumentality The relationship between first- and second-level outcomes.

Integration The quality of the state of collaboration that exists among departments that are required to achieve unity of effort by the demands of the environment.

Interaction requirements The frequency, quality, and the variety of individuals involved necessarily in intergroup activities.

Interdependence The degree to which two or more groups are dependent on one another for inputs or outputs.

Interest group Informal groups that are created because of some common characteristics or interests. Generally, when the interest declines, the group disbands.

Intergroup conflict Conflict that arises between two or more groups.

Intergroup management strategies In order to manage intergroup activities, organizations adopt various strategies (rules, hierarchy, planning, liaison roles, task forces, teams, or integrating departments), each of which requires a different degree of managerial commitment and resources.

Intergroup power The degree of influence and dependency between two or more groups.

Internal validity of a research design This validity indicates that the design tests the study hypotheses and enables the researcher to control independent variables and unwanted sources of variance.

Interval reinforcement A schedule of rewards that ties reinforcements to time. Such a schedule can be *fixed* or *variable*.

Intervening factor Any variable of characteristics of a person, group, or organization that influences the impact of a management policy or action on performance.

Intervention depth The range of planned and structured activities engaged in by the personnel and/or external change agent associated with the organization.

Intrinsic rewards Rewards that are associated with the job itself, such as the opportunity to perform meaningful work, complete cycles of work, see finished products, experience variety, carry out highly visible cycles of activity, and receive feedback on work results.

Job A homogeneous cluster of work tasks, the completion of which serves some enduring purpose for the organization.

Job analysis The systematic study of jobs that attempts to discover the major task dimensions of a job and what the job calls for in terms of employee behaviors and qualifications.

Job content Factors that define the specific work activities or tasks.

Job dynamics Situational factors surrounding the tasks on a job that must be considered to adequately define the job.

Job enlargement A job design strategy that involves expanding the job range of the individual's job horizontally, giving them more things to do.

Job enrichment A job design strategy, based on the motivator-hygiene theory, that seeks to improve performance and satisfaction by providing more challenge, responsibility, authority, and recognition to jobs.

Job evaluation A method that attempts to determine the relative worth of each job or position to the organization in order to establish a basis for relative wage rates within the organization. It is a major method for establishing reward policy.

Job functions The general requirements of and methods involved in performing a job.

Job rotation A job design strategy that involves moving the worker from task to task over a period of time to reduce boredom on the job.

Job satisfaction An attitude held by a person that reflects an evaluation of a particular component in the work place.

Job specialization Dividing the work or tasks of a job into specialized, standardized, simple tasks, and placing them in specific units. The job occupant would focus on the specific set of tasks associated with the job.

Job stress An individual's internally felt frustration and anxiety with certain job or organizationally related situations.

Laboratory experiments An experiment conducted in a setting that is created specifically to study some variables or behavioral property.

Learning A relatively permanent change in behavior that occurs as a result of experience. Learning is to be distinguished from other factors influencing changes in behavior including fatigue and maturation.

Legitimate power The capacity to influence based upon the leader's position in the organization.

Leniency An error often associated with traditional rating methods. It consists of a rater incorrectly assigning similar ratings to a group of employees without accurately representing the true distribution of performance. All ratings tend to cluster towards the high end of the scale.

Level of abstraction In performance appraisal, refers to the problem of specifying a level of analysis in establishing performance standards. At an immediate level of analysis, one might consider specific work behaviors of individual employees. At an intermediate level of analysis, one might consider the task outcomes of groups of employees. At an ultimate level of analysis, one might consider the achievement of the goals of entire divisions or the organization in its entirety.

Locus of control Personality dimension characterized by beliefs concerning one's influence or control over events occurring in the environment. High internal control types believe that they

629

have a great deal of control over events influencing them. High external control types believe that they have little or no influence over such outcomes.

Macro study of the organization The analysis of organizational design, climate, and processes. It is a focus on the "big picture."

Management by objectives A process in which a superior and a subordinate or a group of subordinates jointly identify and establish common goals.

Managerial grid activities A total organizational program that is implemented in six phases to upgrade individual manager's skills and leadership abilities, teamwork, goal setting, and monitoring of events within an organization.

Matrix design A design that includes the control features of functional organizational design and the adaptive aspects of product design, usually found in organizations that include a number of projects, programs, or task forces. In this arrangement, the special program managers have authority to supervise and divert subordinates from line managers.

Mechanistic organizations Those with highly specialized job tasks, rigid authority systems, top-down flow of communications, and conflict resolution by the superior.

Micro study of the organization An analysis of job tasks and design.

Motivator-hygiene theory The theory that identifies two basic factors: hygiene and motivators. Hygiene factors (e.g., pay, job security, working conditions and so on) act to decrease dissatisfaction, but are not motivational. Motivators (e.g., challenging job, personal growth, recognition and so on) act to increase satisfaction, and hence, affect motivation.

Motives Internal factors that influence observable acts or work behaviors. Motives take many forms. Some are physiological in nature (such as a need for food); others are more psychological in nature (such as a desire for affiliation or wishes and desires). Motives cannot be observed directly, and their presence in the mind must be inferred from observed behavior.

Need development The phenomenon of work needs changing over the course of an employee's working life.

Need hierarchy theory The theory that states

that because people are motivated by needs, when a need is present, it serves as a motivator of behavior.

Need profile The unique configuration of needs experienced by a single employee.

Need to know A principle for reducing information overload in vertical communication channels. According to this principle, downward communications are limited to information lower-level personnel must have in order to carry out their tasks.

Needs The deficiencies that an individual perceives at a particular point in time.

Negative reinforcement The presentation of an escape from an aversive stimulus following a desired behavior.

Nominal group technique A group decision method in which individual member judgements are pooled in a systematic fashion in making decisions. (See *Delphi technique.*)

Operant conditioning A motivation approach that focuses on the relationship between stimulus, response, and reward.

Organic organizations Those with low amounts of job specialization, high degrees of superior-subordinate interaction, some subordinate autonomy, and a climate of superior-subordinate decision making.

Organizational climate A set of properties of the work environment, specific to a particular organization, that may be assessed by the way the organization deals with its employees and its societal and task environments.

Organizational development The use of knowledge and techniques from the behavioral sciences to increase organizational effectiveness by integrating individual desires for growth and development with organizational goals.

Organizations Systems interacting with an environment and developing a climate in which individuals and groups interact. They are also structured to transform inputs with technologies and to achieve goals.

Output The end result of the input-transformation linkage in the organization. It may be products, services, or even goodwill.

Path-goal leadership theory A leadership theory that emphasizes the influence of the leadership on subordinate goals and the paths to these goals.

Pay secrecy A management policy of

maintaining silence or secrecy about individual employee salaries.

People change approaches Modifying attitudes, motivation, and behavioral skills, which are accomplished through such techniques as training programs, selection techniques, and performance appraisal techniques.

Perception A process by which individuals (1) attend to incoming stimuli; and (2) translate such stimuli into a message indicating the appropriate response.

Performance The key dependent or predicted measure in our framework. It serves as the vehicle for judging the effectiveness of individuals, groups, and organizations.

Performance dimensions The basis for making appraisal judgments, consisting of the specific aspects, tasks, and outcomes upon which the performance of individuals and groups are judged.

Performance evaluation The process by which an organization obtains feedback about the effectiveness of individual employees and groups. It serves an auditing and control function in organizations.

Personality The combination of human characteristics or variables that defines, classifies, or types a person. Personality variables include aptitude, interests, values, beliefs, and mental-health variables. Personality classifications are only useful to the extent that they can predict behavior.

Personality measure Any method employed to assess a person on a variety of human characteristics. Frequently employed methods include self-report or paper and pencil measure. The Minnesota Multiphasic Personality Inventory (MMPI), the Strong Vocational Interest Blank (SVIB), the California Personality Inventory (CPI), and the Kuder Preference Record are examples of this kind of measure. A second type of self-report measure is projective technique. The Rorschach ink blot test and the Thematic Apperception Test are examples. A third kind of personality measure is to have another person rate an individual on a series of dimensions. Finally, analysts have tried to assess personality through direct observation of an individual's behavior.

Personality structure The constellation or profile of human characteristics that describes an individual and makes him or her unique.

Plateaus Periods during the learning process during which no new learning is evident.

Positive reinforcement The administration of positive rewards, contingent on good performance, that acts to strengthen desired behavior in the future.

Primary vs. secondary motives A distinction between motives that are instinctive (or inborn) and those that are acquired over time through the process of learning.

Proactive inhibition A process in which previously learned behavior interferes with and obstructs the meaning of a new behavior.

Process motivation theories Theories that describe how behavior is energized, aroused, or stopped.

Punishment The administration of negative rewards, contingent on poor performance, that acts to eliminate undesired behavior in the future.

Quality of working life A series of organizational interventions designed to improve the workplace for employees.

Ranking An alternative method of performance appraisal in which a judge is asked to order a group of employees in terms of their performance from highest to lowest.

Rating A traditional method of performance appraisal that asks a judge to evaluate performance in terms of a value or index that is used in some standard way. Traditionally, rating has involved global rating scales.

Ratio reinforcement A schedule of rewards that ties reinforcements directly to acts or behaviors. Such a schedule can be *fixed* or *variable*.

Referent power The capacity to influence based on some identification with another powerful individual.

Reinforcement schedule The timing or scheduling of rewards.

Reinforcement theory A motivation approach that examines factors that act to energize, direct, and sustain behavior.

Reinforcer or reward An event or stimulus that follows an act and has two effects: (1) reduces the need motivating the act; and (2) strengthens the habit that led to the act in the first place.

Relationships The interpersonal component of the individual's job.

Reliability A measurement quality of any performance evaluation technique that demands that information regarding performance be gathered in a stable and consistent fashion. Reliability is a necessary precondition for validity.

Reward bases The various methods for distributing rewards in organizations. At various times, equity, equality, power and need have served as bases for distributing rewards. A problem arises for management when these bases conflict in the establishment of reward policy.

Reward policy An organizational policy concerning the type, amount, and way in which rewards are distributed in organizations.

Reward power The capacity to influence based on the leader's ability to reward good performance.

Rewards Outcomes or events in the organization that satisfy work-related needs.

Risk The element of uncertainty in making decisions.

Risk propensity A personality characteristic involving a person's like or dislike for taking chances.

Role The expected-perceived-enacted behavior patterns attributed to a particular job or position.

Role ambiguity Lack of clarity regarding job duties, authority, and responsibilities resulting in uncertainty and dissatisfaction.

Role analysis team building Designed to clarify role expectations and responsibilities of team members. This clarification can be brought about by group meeting and discussion.

Role conflict A state of tension created by multiple demands and conflicting directions from two or more individuals in performance of one's role, resulting in anxiety.

Science In a general sense, refers to a method (systematic acquisition and evaluation of information) and a goal (identifying the nature or principles of what is being studied) rather than to any specific phenomena.

Scientific approach A process that involves a number of steps: (1) the recognition of problem, obstacle, idea; (2) the review of theory and model; (3) the development of hypotheses; (4) the selection of a methodology; and (5) the actual observation, test, and experiment.

Scientific management A body of literature that emerged during the period 1890—1930 that reports the ideas and theories of engineers concerned with such aspects as job design, incentive systems, selection, and training.

Sensitivity training A training method designed to increase a trainee's insight, self-awareness, and impact on other people. The focus of sensitivity training is upon the emotional rather than the conceptual aspects of training.

Situational leadership theories Approaches to study of leadership that stress the importance of situational factors (leader and subordinate characteristics, the task, and organizational factors) on leader effectiveness.

Slope A major characteristic of the learning curve, which measures the rate of speed at which behavior is changed by learning.

Social density A physical measure of the number of group members working within a certain walking distance of each other.

Societal environment Forces external to an organization that influence what happens internally. Among these forces are political, regulatory, resources, economic, and technological factors.

Sociotechnical systems design approach An approach to organizational design that attempts to integrate the technological and social subsystems of an organization to create a flexible, organic structure that can deal with environmental variance while affording organizational efficiency and employee satisfaction.

Span of control The number of subordinates who report directly to a supervisor.

Spontaneous recovery The phenomenon in which behavior or job performance makes a spontaneous improvement following a rest period. In effect, the rest has dispersed the inhibiting effects of fatigue.

Stability One aspect of reliability in performance evaluation that demands that a method of appraising performance yields information that remains stable over time as long as the employee has not in fact altered his or her performance.

Status A social ranking within a group assigned on the basis of position in the group or individual characteristics.

Status congruence The agreement of group members about the relative status of members of the group.

Stereotyping A perceptual error in which a person forms a judgement about another person based on ideas or impressions formed about that individual's group. Individual differences within the group are ignored.

Stimulus discrimination The ability to recognize differences between stimuli and change one's behavior accordingly.

Stimulus generalization The ability to recognize similarities between stimuli and thereby transfer behavior from one stimulus to another.

Stimulus-response The basic unit of learning (habit) in both the classical and instrumental conditioning models.

Strictness An error often associated with traditional rating methods. It consists of a rater incorrectly assigning similar ratings to a group of employees without accurately representing the true distribution of performance. All ratings tend to cluster towards the low end of the scale.

Structural change approaches Changes brought about through new formal guidelines, procedures, policies, and organizational rearrangements.

Survey-feedback activities Activities that focus on collecting survey data and designing a plan of action based on the interpretation of the data.

Symbolic interaction A model of communication that stresses the dual processes of symbolic manipulation (encoding messages) and symbolic interpretation (decoding messages). The model implies a number of ways in which distortion can occur in communication.

Task environment Factors internal or external to the organization that can affect the level of performance of a unit or group.

Task group A formal group that is created by the organization to accomplish a specific task.

Task types A classification strategy that categorizes group tasks on the basis of one of three objectives: production, discussion, or problem solving.

Task uncertainty The extent to which internal or external events create a state of uncertainty with respect to job predictability.

Technological change approaches Changes that focus on rearrangements in work flow, new physical layouts, job descriptions, and work standards.

Technology People-machine activities carried out in the organizational system that utilize such technological inputs as capital goods, production techniques, and managerial and nonmanagerial knowledge.

Theory The ordering of relationships among variables in a model of some aspect or portion of the observable world.

Theory of cognitive dissonance A cybernetic model of motives introduced by Leon Festinger. According to his model, most incoming stimuli are informational in nature. If such information denies or diverges from what the individual expects in the situation, cognitive dissonance results. Cognitive dissonance is said to be unpleasant for the individual and serves as a force motivating behavior.

Threshold The level of a stimulus necessary for its perception.

Time orientation The degree to which individuals or groups are oriented toward short-term or long-term results.

Trait leadership theories Approaches to the study of leadership that seek to identify a finite set of characteristics or traits that can distinguish effective from noneffective leaders.

Transformation Process converting the input's form, shape, condition, or attitude with technology.

Unobtrusive measures Collecting data by use of physical traces, archives, simple observation, and hardware.

Valence The strength or value placed by an individual on a particular reward.

Validity A measurement quality of any performance evaluation technique that demands that information regarding performance effectiveness be gathered in a way that insures the relevance of the information to the purpose of the performance review.

Variable A symbol to which numerals or values are assigned.

Work adjustment model A theory of job performance, satisfaction, and turnover, based upon the degree of fit or correspondence between an individual's personality and the demands and rewards available on the job.

NAME INDEX

SUBJECT INDEX